THE COMPETITIVE EFFECTS OF MINORITY SHAREHOLDINGS

The objective of this book is twofold. First, it presents the economics of minority shareholdings, under both merger and antitrust law. In particular, economic analysis provides both an overall assessment of minority shareholdings in the context of concentrations, and Articles 101 and 102 TFEU and the examination of the link between non-controlling minority shareholdings, merger control and antitrust law.

Secondly, the book also provides a legal assessment and an analysis of selected case law. According to settled European case law, minority shareholdings are analysed not only under Regulation 139/2004, but also under Articles 101 and 102 TFEU. Nevertheless, according to current enforcement practice at European and international levels, several national competition authorities have adopted different approaches. The million-dollar question is whether the existing regulatory framework is sufficient to cover all possible cases.

In summary, the book will be a useful tool for students, practitioners, researchers, economic and legal experts, and competition authorities. It provides a comprehensive survey of the subject, which has been missing until now, and answers many questions that have been raised in the literature in the last decades.

Volume 13 in the series Hart Studies in Competition Law

Hart Studies in Competition Law

Intellectual Property, Antitrust and Cumulative Innovation in the EU and the US
Thorsten Käseberg

State Aid and the European Economic Constitution
Francesco de Cecco

The Private Enforcement of Competition Law in Ireland
David McFadden

Cross-Border EU Competition Law Actions
Edited by Mihail Danov, Florian Becker and Paul Beaumont

Competition Laws, Globalization and Legal Pluralism: China's Experience
Qianlan Wu

Joint Ventures and EU Competition Law
Luis Silva Morais

Sanctions in EU Competition Law: Principles and Practice
Michael Frese

Fairness in Antitrust: Protecting the Strong from the Weak
Adi Ayal

European Merger Remedies: Law and Policy
Dorte Hoeg

Media Ownership and Control: Law, Economics and Policy in an Indian and International Context
Suzanne Rab and Alison Sprague

The Interface between Competition and the Internal Market: Market Separation under Article 102 TFEU
Vasiliki Brisimi

Anti-Cartel Enforcement in a Contemporary Age: Leniency Religion
Edited by Caron Beaton-Wells and Christopher Tran

Public Procurement and the EU Competition Rules
Albert Sánchez Graells

The Concept of Abuse in EU Competition Law: Law and Economic Approaches
Pınar Akman

The Competitive Effects of Minority Shareholdings

Legal and Economic Issues

Panagiotis Fotis and Nikolaos Zevgolis

·HART·
PUBLISHING
OXFORD AND PORTLAND, OREGON
2016

Published in the United Kingdom by Hart Publishing Ltd
16C Worcester Place, Oxford, OX1 2JW
Telephone: +44 (0)1865 517530
Fax: +44 (0)1865 510710
E-mail: mail@hartpub.co.uk
Website: http://www.hartpub.co.uk

Published in North America (US and Canada) by
Hart Publishing
c/o International Specialized Book Services
920 NE 58th Avenue, Suite 300
Portland, OR 97213-3786
USA
Tel: +1 503 287 3093 or toll-free: (1) 800 944 6190
Fax: +1 503 280 8832
E-mail: orders@isbs.com
Website: http://www.isbs.com

Hart Publishing is an imprint of Bloomsbury Publishing plc.

British Library Cataloguing in Publication Data
Data Available

Library of Congress Cataloging-in-Publication Data

Names: Fotis, Panagiotis, 1972– author. | Zevgolis, Nikolaos, author.

Title: The competitive effects of minority shareholdings : legal and economic issues / Panagiotis Fotis and Nikolaos Zevgoli.

Description: Oxford ; Portland, OR : Hart Publishing Ltd, 2016. | Series: Hart studies in competition law ; v. 13 | Includes bibliographical references and index.

Identifiers: LCCN 2015050622 (print) | LCCN 2016001583 (ebook) | ISBN 9781849465342 (hardback : alk. paper) | ISBN 9781509900893 (Epub)

Subjects: LCSH: Minority stockholders—Legal status, laws, etc.—European Union countries. | Antitrust law—European Union countries. | Consolidation and merger of corporations—Law and legislation—European Union countries. | Stock ownership—Law and legislation—Economic aspects—European Union countries. | Competition—European Union countries.

Classification: LCC KJE2502.F68 2016 (print) | LCC KJE2502 (ebook) | DDC 346.24/0666—dc23

LC record available at http://lccn.loc.gov/2015050622

ISBN: 978-1-84946-534-2

Typeset by Compuscript Ltd, Shannon
Printed and bound in Great Britain by
CPI Group (UK) Ltd, Croydon CR0 4YY

Panagiotis Fotis would like to thank his wife, Maria Korre for her support throughout the course of writing this book. He also would like to thank his children, Eirini and Nikolaos for their patience and understanding.

Nikolaos Zevgolis, thanking his family not only for the tolerance, but also for the continuous support and inspiration, would like to dedicate this book to his wife, Eleni Gkini, and their children, Katerina-Ariadni and Manolis.

The views expressed herein are strictly and purely those of the authors.

CONTENTS

LIST OF TABLES

LIST OF FIGURES

TABLE OF CASES

European Union

Cases

Commission's Decisions

DOMESTIC

Austria

Brazil

Chile

Germany

Greece

Indonesia

Israel

Japan

Korea

Lithuania

South Africa

Turkey

United Kingdom

United States of America

TABLE OF LEGISLATION

EUROPEAN UNION

Treaties

Regulations

DOMESTIC

Argentina

Republic of Armenia

Australia

Austria

Belgium

Brazil

Bulgaria

Canada

Chile

Chinese Taipei

Croatia

Cyprus

Czech Republic

Denmark

Ecuador

El Salvador

Egypt

Estonia

Finland

Germany

Greece

Hong Kong

Hungary

India

Indonesia

Ireland

Israel

Italy

Japan

Korea

Republic of Latvia

Lithuania

Luxemburg

Malta

Netherlands

Norway

Poland

Portugal

Romania

Russian Federation

Slovakia

Slovenia

South Africa

Spain

Sweden

Taiwan

Turkey

UK

Ukraine

USA

1

The Evolution of Merger Control Regime in EU and Minority Interests

I. Current State of EU Merger Control and Provisions for the Future

Prior to Regulation (EEC) No 4064/89[1] the Commission did not opt to employ crystal-clear borderlines to determine the notion of minority interests within the EU community. The concepts of decisive influence and no influence over the commercial activities of the target firm seem to remain unclear even though the Commission recognized their existence.[2] The Commission appeared increasingly willing to apply Article 85 and especially the *Philip Morris* doctrine. However, after 1990 and the implementation of Regulation (EEC) No 4064/89 the Commission adopted an enhanced interpretation of the decisive influence standard in a number of acquisitions of minority shareholdings that had previously fallen under Article 85(1) of the EC Treaty.

This chapter provides an up-to-date retrospective view of the merger control regime within the Community and a thorough investigation of the concept of minority interests under this regime.

A. Regulation (EEC) 4064/89 as the Starting Point

Regulation (EEC) 4064/1989 is characterized by the Commission as 'the original Merger Regulation'.[3] Its adoption by the Council led to the introduction into European competition law of a comprehensive and systematic approach to ex-ante merger control, based on the relevant cumulative experience of the previous years.

Two main cases are considered to be the precursors for the adoption of Regulation (EEC) No 4064/89: the *Continental Can* case[4] and the *Philip Morris* case.[5] Focusing on the *Philip*

[1] Council Regulation (EEC) No 4064/89 of 21 December 1989 on the control of concentrations between undertakings [1989] OJ L395/1.

[2] [1989] OJ L395, 1, corrected version [1990] OJ L257.

[3] See the Commission Staff Working Document (accompanying the White Paper 'Towards more effective EU merger control') SWD(2014) 221 final, para 5.

[4] Case 6/72 *Europemballage and Continental Can v Commission* [1973] ECR 215, [1973] 8171 CMLR 199.

[5] Cases 142 and 156/84 *BAT and RJ Reynolds v Commission* and *Philip Morris* [1987] ECR 4487, [1988] 4 CMLR 24.

Morris case, it is important to underline the sense and significance of control as it was framed by the European Court of Justice (ECJ):

> That will be true [ie the fact that the acquisition of an equity interest in a competitor does not by itself restrict competition; nevertheless, it might serve as an instrument to this goal] in particular where, by the acquisition of a shareholding or through subsidiary clauses in the agreement, the investing company obtains legal or de facto control of the commercial conduct of the other company or where the agreement provides for commercial co-operation between the companies or creates a structure likely to be used for such co-operation. That may also be the case where the agreement gives the investing company the possibility of reinforcing its position at a later stage and taking effective control of the other company.[6]

Under this pioneering—for the day—system, mergers between undertakings meeting minimum certain turnover thresholds ought to be notified in advance to the Commission, which used—and continues to use—a *competition-based test* in order to decide whether or not they are compatible with the internal market.[7] Since its adoption, merger control has come to constitute one of the main pillars of EU competition law and its basic features are well established.

At the present time EU merger control is making an important contribution to the functioning of the internal market, since on the one hand it establishes a uniform set of rules for corporate restructuring and on the other hand it ensures that competition and consumers are not harmed by concentrations creating excessive market power.[8] As expected in a global economy, EU merger control is increasingly concentrating on cross-border cases and more specifically on cases that have an impact on the European economy.[9] Undisputable confirmation for this is the significant increase in recent years of the percentage of EU merger control cases where non-EU firms have been involved and, conversely, the corresponding decrease in cases where firms from the same Member State are involved; these last cases overall account for only a minor percentage. While both categories of the above-mentioned cases may also have pan-European importance, this trend is consistent with the Commission's intention of focusing on mergers that have a European Economic Area (EEA)-wide or global impact.[10]

[6] Ibid, paras 38 and 39.

[7] This is the reason why, in theory, '[i]t is … important to realize that undertakings may fall within the ECMR on the basis of their turnover even if they have minimal or even no assets within the Community'. See DG Goyder, *EC Competition Law*, 4th edn (Oxford, Oxford University Press) 342. Case IV/M.619 *Gencor/Lonrho* [1996] 4 CMLR 742 (on appeal Case T-102/96 [1999] ECR II-753) and Case IV/M.877 *Boeing/McDonnell Douglas* [1997] OJ L336/16 constitute relevant examples.

[8] Since the application of Regulation (EEC) 4064/89, the essential principle continues to be that 'any concentration with an EU (ex Community) dimension creating or strengthening a position as a result of which effective competition in the internal market (ex Common Market) or a substantial part of it is significantly impeded is to be declared incompatible with the internal market (ex Common Market)'. See Goyder, ibid, 340–41.

[9] However, at least at the beginning (in 1989), 'adoption of the Merger Regulation proved difficult partly because of the concerns of certain Member States, whose power to investigate a merger would be limited by an exclusive competence at the level of the Community'. E Kameoka, *Competition Law and Policy in Japan and the EU* (Cheltenham, Edward Elgar, 2013) 96–97.

[10] Criticism of the 4064/1989 Regulation can be found in: RA Kassamali, 'From Fiction to Fallacy: Reviewing the EC Merger Regulation's Community Dimension Thresholds in the Light of Economics and Experience in Merger Control' (1996) 21 ELRev Checklist No 2 CC/89 and MP Broberg, *The Commission's Jurisdiction to Scrutinise Mergers*, 2nd edn (Dordrecht, Kluwer International, 2003) ch 9.

Simultaneously, national competition authorities (NCAs) are focusing increasingly on mergers within national dimension.[11]

B. Reform Under Regulation 139/2004

The current Merger Regulation is the result of a reassessment of Council Regulation (EEC) No 4064/89; before the publication of Merger Regulation 139/2004, a Commission Green Paper was published in 2001.[12]

The principal aim of Regulation (EEC) No 4064/89 was the 'creation or strengthening of a dominant position' test. However, in 2004, with the implementation of Merger Regulation 139/2004, the 'significant impediment of effective competition' (SIEC) test was introduced (among other things) as the relevant criterion for assessing mergers and the previous 'creation or strengthening of a dominant position' test was replaced.[13]

Merger Regulation 139/2004 continued, like its 'predecessor', to apply only to concentrations, ie those transactions involving acquisitions of control by enterprises over other enterprises or parts of them. Nevertheless, the experience of recent years shows that acquisitions of equity stakes which are below the level of control, and therefore not captured by Regulation 139/2004, may in some cases lead to structural changes in the market. Therefore, the discussion that took place in the Commission Staff Working Document[14] had the intention of examining whether the Merger Regulation should be extended to cover such transactions.

Furthermore, Merger Regulation 139/2004 enables Member States to refer cases to the Commission, and vice versa, before notification; it is also possible for several Member States jointly to refer a case to the Commission after notification. These possibilities create a positive impact as well as some shortcomings that are also analysed in the Commission Staff Working Document.[15]

[11] For instance, Art 7 of the Greek Competition Law (eg law 3959/2011 'Protection of Free Competition' (Gov't Gazette Issue A' 93/20.04.2011)) provides that:

1. Any concentration of undertakings subject to prior notification which *may significantly impede competition in the national market or in a substantial part of it* [emphasis added], in terms of the specific characteristics of goods or services, especially by creating or strengthening a dominant position, shall be prohibited by decision of the Competition Commission.
2. In appraising the potential of a concentration to significantly impede the competition within the meaning of paragraph 1, account shall be taken, in particular, of the structure of all the relevant markets, of the *actual or potential competition from undertakings located inside or outside Greece* [emphasis added], of any legal or other barriers to market entry, of the market position of the undertakings concerned and their economic and financial power, of the alternatives available to suppliers and users, of their access to sources of supply or markets for the goods, of the supply and demand trends for the relevant goods and services, of the interests of the intermediate and ultimate consumers and of the contribution to technical and economic progress and to improving economic efficiency, provided that it is to consumer's advantage and does not form an obstacle to competition.

[12] Green Paper on the Review of Council Regulation (EEC) No 4064/89, COM(2001) 745 final.

[13] See P Fotis, 'Merger Enforcement: Law and Statistical Evidence Worldwide' (2013) 5(3) *International Journal of Economics and Business Research* 272, 273–77.

[14] Above n 3.

[15] Ibid.

C. Substantive Evaluation

i. Assessment Under the SIEC Test

As was mentioned above, the most substantial modification of EU merger control took place in 2004, when the SIEC test was introduced.[16] The new test, based on the Commission's previous practice and the established case law of the Court, maintained that SIECs most prominently arise through the creation or strengthening of a dominant position; however, the new test closed a possible enforcement 'gap' by ensuring that mergers resulting in 'non-coordinated effects' in oligopolistic markets, even if the merged entity would not have become dominant, were 'captured'/covered by the Merger Regulation.

Note, in particular, Recital 25 of the Merger Regulation 139/2004, where it is mentioned that:

> In view of *the consequences that concentrations in oligopolistic market structures may have, it is all the more necessary to maintain effective competition in such markets.* Many oligopolistic markets exhibit a healthy degree of competition. However, under certain circumstances, concentrations involving the elimination of important competitive constraints that the merging parties had exerted upon each other, as well as a reduction of competitive pressure on the remaining competitors, may, even in the absence of a likelihood of coordination between the members of the oligopoly, result in a significant impediment to effective competition. The Community courts have, however, not to date expressly interpreted Regulation (EEC) No 4064/89 as requiring concentrations giving rise to such non-coordinated effects to be declared incompatible with the common market. Therefore, in the interests of legal certainty, it should be made clear that this Regulation permits effective control of all such concentrations by providing that any concentration which would significantly impede effective competition, in the common market or in a substantial part of it, should be declared incompatible with the common market. The notion of 'significant impediment to effective competition' in Article 2(2) and (3) should be interpreted as extending, beyond the concept of dominance, only to the anti-competitive effects of a concentration resulting from the non-coordinated behaviour of undertakings which would not have a dominant position on the market concerned.[17]

Under Regulation (EEC) 4064/1989, the strong possibility that the so-called 'dominance test' would not capture mergers with potentially anticompetitive non-coordinated effects in cases where the merged entity did not become dominant created legal uncertainty. According to economic theory, in an oligopoly where only a few firms[18] are active and none is individually dominant, and where collusion is not possible,[19] merging firms might have the incentive to increase their prices unilaterally, *even if they do not become dominant.* After the merger, the remaining market participants would benefit from the reduction in competitive

[16] See para 3 of Art 2 of the Merger Regulation 139/2004, according to which the Commission ought to assess whether a concentration 'would significantly impede effective competition, in the common market or in a substantial part of it, in particular as a result of the creation or strengthening of a dominant position'. This test replaced the previous substantive test, the so-called '*dominance test*', ie the test demanding 'creation or strengthening of a dominant position', which was enshrined in Art 2 of Council Regulation (EEC) No 4064/89.

[17] Emphasis added.

[18] On this see R Selten, 'A Simple Model of Imperfect Competition where Four Are Few and Six Are Many' (1973) 2 *International Journal of Game Theory* 141–201.

[19] See F Alese, 'The Economic Theory of Non-collusive Oligopoly and the Concept of Concerted Practice under Article 81' (1999) 20 *European Competition Law Review* 379.

pressure and might also increase their prices, leading to an overall price increase in the market. This result is quite possible in markets with differentiated products.[20]

Therefore, the new SIEC test was designed to capture these so-called 'gap' cases, ie mergers that allow firms to raise prices unilaterally even though these mergers do not create or reinforce either a single or a collective dominant position. The *T-Mobile Austria/tele.ring* case constituted the first example,[21] and was followed by many others.[22]

As the Commission intended to increase the transparency and predictability of merger analysis under the new test, it published a set of Guidelines on the assessment of horizontal mergers (the so-called 'Horizontal Merger Guidelines').[23] These were augmented in 2008 by Guidelines on the assessment of non-horizontal mergers (the so-called 'Non-Horizontal Merger Guidelines').[24] The Non-Horizontal Guidelines are highly significant as, with respect to input and customer foreclosure, they define a structured approach based on the SIEC test.[25]

In addition, since Commission decisions in merger cases are frequently subject to demanding judicial review, the EU courts provide relevant guidance. More specifically, the EU courts may examine both the completeness and accuracy of the evidence relied upon by the Commission and whether that evidence is capable of verifying the concluding remarks drawn from it.[26] Nevertheless, since 2004 no Commission decision either approving or prohibiting a merger has been definitively annulled by the EU courts; on the contrary, nearly all decisions in merger cases taken by the Commission over the last decade, despite the fact they were appealed, have been upheld by the EU courts. To be precise, the only Commission decision in a merger procedure taken after 2004 and annulled by an EU court with an irreversible judgment did not concern the compatibility of the merger with the internal market but rather the approval of a proposed purchaser of a business which

[20] See also J Beath and Y Katsoulakos, *Economic Theory of Product Differentiation* (Cambridge, Cambridge University Press, 1990).

[21] See, inter alia, COMP/M.3916 *T-Mobile/Tele.ring*, decision of 26 April 2006.

[22] For example, COMP/M.4141 *Linde/BOC*, decision of 6 June 2006; COMP/M.4187 *Metso/Aker Kvaerner*, decision of 12 December 2006; COMP/M.4844 *Fortis/ABN Amro*, decision of 3 October 2007; COMP/M.5224 *EDF/British Energy*, decision of 22 December 2008; COMP/M.6203 *Western Digital/Hitachi*, decision of 23 November 2011; COMP/M.6497 *Hutchinson/ Orange*, decision of 12 December 2012; and COMP/M.6570 *UPS/ TNT Express*, decision of 30 January 2013.

[23] See the Guidelines on the assessment of horizontal mergers under the Council Regulation on the control of concentrations between undertakings [2004] OJ C31/05.

[24] See the Guidelines on the assessment of non-horizontal mergers under the Council Regulation on the control of concentrations between undertakings [2008] OJ C265/6.

[25] It should be emphasized that the EU courts frequently used both the horizontal and non-horizontal Guidelines as a benchmark for assessing the legality of the Commission's substantial analysis of mergers. According to the settled case law, the Commission is bound by the guidance documents (soft law) it has issued: see eg, Case C-322/88 *Grimaldi/Fonds des maladies professionelles*, 13.12.1989, para 18. See also Von Jurgen Schwarz, 'Soft Law im Recht der Europaischen Union' [2011] *EuR* 3 et seq; C Thibierge, 'Le droit souple' [2003] *RTDCiv* 599 et seq; and KC Wellens and GM Borchardt, 'Soft Law in European Community Law' (1989) 14 *EL Rev* 267 et seq). However, these guidance documents remain subject to scrutiny by the EU courts for their compliance with Treaty provisions and the Merger Regulation (see eg, Case T-282/06 *Sun Chemical ea v Commission* [2007] ECR II-2149, para 55. See also Case 294/83 *Les Verts* [1986] ECR 1339, para 24 and Case 322/88 *Grimaldi v Fonds des Maladies Professionnelles* [1989] ECR 4407, para 18.

[26] See in particular Case T-12/03 P *Commission v TetraLaval* [2005] ECR I-987, paras 39 et seq; Case C-413/06 P *Bertelsmann and Sony v Independent Music Publishers and Labels Association (Impala)* [2008] ECR I-4951, paras 47 et seq; Case T-342/07 *Ryanair v Commission* [2010] ECR II-3457, paras 29 et seq.

had to be divested according to a conditional clearance decision.[27] Besides, the judgment of the General Court in Case T-464/04 *Independent Music Publishers and Labels Association (Impala) v Commission*,[28] which annulled the Commission's unconditional clearance of COMP/M.3333 *Sony/BMG*,[29] was overturned on appeal in Case C-413/06 P *Bertelsmann and Sony v Impala*;[30] hence, the Commission's decision was ultimately upheld.

ii. The Significance of Quantitative and Qualitative Evidence

The introduction of the SIEC test highlighted that, beyond analysing the structural effects of a merger, the Commission also assesses market characteristics (ie product substitutability or differentiation, capacity constraints, elimination of an important competitive force, impediment to competitors' expansion, market contestability, barriers to entry, etc) and whether actual or potential competition is eliminated by the merger.

In certain cases the Commission has found that competition concerns were absent despite the high combined market shares of the parties involved; the existing competitive constraints in these cases constitute the main factor determining that these specific mergers were unlikely to impact negatively on competition and thus on consumers. Nevertheless, there were also certain other cases where the Commission identified non-coordinated effects despite the fact the merged company's market share was similar to, or even lower than, that of its rivals.

In addition, as far as complex mergers are concerned, the Commission now uses a variety of data and empirical techniques to perform more rigorous economic analysis. The techniques used are based on data availability and range from descriptive statistics to merger simulation, taking into account demand estimation or direct evaluations of competitive constraints. It ought to be mentioned that in several recent cases a range of sophisticated economic analyses[31] has been used to assess the existence of a SIEC.[32]

The Commission considers the combination of quantitative and qualitative evidence as a *conditio sine qua non* for a complete and accurate merger analysis. More specifically, on the one hand it considers mainly economic and numerical evidence to be important in assessing merger cases. On the other hand, it considers that this quantitative analysis ought always to be integrated into the context of more qualitative evidence, eg minutes of interviews with horizontal- or vertical-level market participants (suppliers or distributors, etc), replies by customers and competitors to requests for information and internal documents of the parties involved. It is crystal clear that these two types of evidence counterbalance,

[27] See COMP/M.2978 *Lagardère/Natexis/VUP*, decision of 30 July 2004, which was annulled in last resort by judgment of the Court of Justice of 6 November 2012 in Joint Cases C-553/10 P and C-554/10 P *Commission and Lagardère v Editions Odile Jacob* (nyr).

[28] Case T-464/04 *Independent Music Publishers and Labels Association (Impala) v Commission* [2006] ECR II-2289.

[29] Decision of 19 July 2004.

[30] Case C-413/06 P *Bertelsmann and Sony v Independent Music Publishers and Labels Association (Impala)* [2008] ECR I-4951.

[31] A very useful economic analysis regarding the reasons for which firms merge is found in Scherer and Ross, *Industrial Market Structure and Economic Performance*, 3rd edn (Boston, Houghton Mifflin, 1990) 159–67.

[32] See eg, COMP/M.6570 *UPS/TNT Express*, decision of 30 January 2013; COMP/M.6458 *Universal Music Group/EMI Music*, decision of 21 September 2012; COMP/M.6471 *Outokumpu/Inoxum*, decision of 7 November 2012; and COMP/M.6663 *Ryanair/Aer Lingus*, decision of 27 February 2013.

rather than substitute for, each other. The main issue, therefore, is the supplementation and not the substitutability.

iii. *Indicative Example*

In Case COMP/M.6203 *Western Digital/Hitachi*[33] the Commission examined a proposed acquisition in the market for hard disk drives (HDDs). The Commission approved the proposed acquisition of Hitachi Global Storage Technology (HGST)[34] by a US competitor, Western Digital. The approval was conditional on divestment of essential production assets for 3.5-in HDDs, namely a production plant, and certain other measures were also included.

In the specific (oligopolistic) market, the transaction would have reduced the number of active rivals in the HHD sector from four to three and from three to two in the market for 3.5-in HDDs. When assessing the impact of this transaction the Commission took into account two types of data: (a) customer submissions and other qualitative evidence that proved the significance of security of supply for HDD customers; (b) quantitative evidence in the form of commercial data on transactions between the parties involved and their customers, as well as commercial data for the same issues of their main competitors, and bidding data showing the absence of exclusiveness, since most customers multi-source their HDD supplies. Based on analysis of this combined quantitative and qualitative evidence, the Commission established the significance of the presence of a third supplier and that removing Hitachi from the market would harm consumers—hence the Commission's stipulation concerning divestment and accompanying measures.

D. Theories of Harm and Investigation by the Commission in Horizontal, Vertical and Conglomerate Mergers

In recent merger cases, horizontal non-coordinated effects cases have accounted for about 90 per cent of interventions by the Commission. In these cases the Commission intervened either by accepting remedies in Phase I or Phase II, or by prohibiting the merger; there were also cases where the parties abandoned the merger in Phase II. On the contrary, coordinated effects cases have been very rare: the last case was *ABF/GBI* from 2008.[35]

It has to be noted here that a Phase I decision by the Commission is based on Article 6b whereas a Phase II decision by the Commission is based on Article 6c of Merger Regulation 139/2004. Specifically, Article 6b of Merger Regulation 139/2004 states that:

> Where it finds that the concentration notified, although falling within the scope of this Regulation, does not raise serious doubts as to its compatibility with the common market, it shall decide not to oppose it and shall declare that it is compatible with the common market.
>
> A decision declaring a concentration compatible shall be deemed to cover restrictions directly related and necessary to the implementation of the concentration.

[33] Commission's decision of 23 November 2011.

[34] HGST was a subsidiary of Hitachi of Singapore recently renamed Viviti Technologies.

[35] COMP/M.4980 *ABF/GBI Business*, decision of 23 September 2008.

Article 6c of Merger Regulation 139/2004 states that:

> Without prejudice to paragraph 2,[36] where the Commission finds that the concentration notified falls within the scope of this Regulation and raises serious doubts as to its compatibility with the common market, it shall decide to initiate proceedings. Without prejudice to Article 9,[37] such proceedings shall be closed by means of a decision as provided for in Article 8(1) to (4),[38] unless the undertakings concerned have demonstrated to the satisfaction of the Commission that they have abandoned the concentration.[39]

Furthermore, there have been relatively few vertical and conglomerate cases; more precisely, vertical mergers account for just 7.5 per cent and conglomerate mergers, which are much rarer, account for 2.5 per cent of interventions in the period 2011–14. The *TomTom/Tele Atlas*[40] and *Nokia/NAVTEQ*[41] cases constitute challenging cases with vertical concerns. Conglomerate merger cases may also raise interesting competition issues. One relevant example is the *Intel/McAfee* case.[42]

E. Efficiencies (Static and Dynamic) and Innovation

The Commission explains in its Horizontal Merger Guidelines that 'it is possible that efficiencies brought about by a merger counteract the effects on competition and in particular the potential harm to consumers that it might otherwise have'.[43] This is the reason why, during the assessment of a merger's impact on competition, the Commission proceeds to 'an overall competitive assessment', including any likely merger-specific efficiencies to the extent that 'they are likely to enhance the ability and incentive of the merged entity to act pro-competitively for the benefit of consumers'.[44]

In reality the Commission's assessment is a balancing exercise, in which possible anti-competitive concerns are weighed against efficiencies. In fact, it is not an exaggeration to say that it is about a kind of a rule of reason approach.[45]

In particular, the Commission will examine the existence or not of the demanded efficiencies with respect to whether overall (a) the efficiencies are checked and confirmed, (b) the efficiencies are merger specific and (c) the benefits of the efficiencies are likely to be transferred to consumers.[46]

36 According to para 2 of Merger Regulation 139/2004: 'Where the Commission finds that, following modification by the undertakings concerned, a notified concentration no longer raises serious doubts within the meaning of paragraph 1(c), it shall declare the concentration compatible with the common market pursuant to paragraph 1(b).

The Commission may attach to its decision under paragraph 1(b) conditions and obligations intended to ensure that the undertakings concerned comply with the commitments they have entered into vis-à-vis the Commission with a view to rendering the concentration compatible with the common market.'

37 Article 9 of Merger Regulation 139/2004 deals with the procedure under which the Commission referrals a case to the component authorities of the Member States.

38 Article 8(1) to (4) deals with the powers of decision of the Commission.

39 See also the case M.1383 *Exxon/Mobil* in section I.A.iv in ch 5. The Greek Competition Law No 3959/2011 includes corresponding articles for Phase I & II decisions of the Hellenic Competition Commission. See especially Fotis (n 13), 273–75.

40 COMP/M.4854 *Tom Tom/Tele Atlas*, decision of 14 May 2008.

41 COMP/M.4942 *Nokia/NAVTEQ*, decision of 2 July 2008.

42 COMP/M.5984 *Intel/McAfee*, decision of 26 January 2011.

43 Above n 23, para 23.

44 Ibid, para 77.

45 See eg, RH Bork, *The Antitrust Paradox. A Policy at War with Itself* (New York, The Free Press, 1993) 15–22.

46 Above n 44, para 78.

According to the Horizontal Merger Guidelines, the notifying parties must provide, in a timely manner, all the necessary information in order to prove that the efficiencies demanded meet these criteria.

Accordingly, assessment of these efficiencies has become an integral part of merger analysis, and hence inherent to merger control, for at least the past decade.

i. UPS/TNT Express *as an Example for the Significance of Efficiencies*

Case COMP/M.6570 *UPS/TNT Express*[47] constitutes a useful instance of a case where the assessment of efficiencies was extremely important in the competitive evaluation of the proposed merger. In addition, the specific case was considered as a 'gap' case, since it would have probably led to price increases without the creation or strengthening of dominance. DHL would have continued to be a market leader in some countries, but the proposed merger would have led to the removal of a significant competitive player in concentrated markets[48] across the EU.

The efficiencies claimed by the parties were partially recognised by the Commission, which was able to quantify the recognised efficiencies and the expected price rise. More specifically, the Commission noted the economies of scale and scope due to air network synergies resulting mainly from the fact that the merged entity would need fewer, larger aircraft for the combined small parcels volume than the individual parties in the pre-merger stage. By including assessment of the efficiencies in its overall analysis of the effects of the merger, the Commission was capable of excluding anticompetitive effects at least for a number of countries. Nevertheless, the recognised efficiencies were not sufficient to counterbalance the expected negative effects in all countries. In those cases where the parties did not offer sufficient remedies and competition concerns remained, the concentration was prohibited.[49]

It is generally accepted that innovation is a main driver for competitiveness and growth in the global economy.[50] Under European competition rules, merger enforcement can create the necessary conditions for fostering innovation by protecting competition; consequently, it can lead to better market outcomes not only in terms of lower prices and increased output but also in terms of better product quality, variety and innovation. For instance, in the *Intel/McAfee* case concerning central processing units (CPUs)[51] and chipsets,[52]

[47] Commission's decision of 30 January 2013.

[48] For instance, markets with few and strong players/competitors.

[49] However, see R Whish, *Competition Law*, 5th edn (Oxford, Oxford University Press, 2005) 873, who says that '[o]utright prohibitions are rare'.

[50] See J Temple Lang, *European Community Antitrust Law: Innovation Markets and High Technology Industries*, ed B Hawk (Fordham Corporate Law Institute, 1996) ch 23; LB Landman, 'Innovation Markets in Europe' (1998) 19 *European Competition Law Review* 21.

[51] According to the *Microsoft Computer Dictionary* (5th edn, Redmond, WA, 132), the CPU is the device within an electronic device (mostly a computer) that interprets and executes instructions. Therefore, the CPU constitutes the computer's 'brain': it generally comprises millions of transistors that process data and control other devices in a computer system. In addition, the CPU has the ability to fetch, decode and execute instructions and to transfer information to and from other resources over the computer's main data-transfer path.

[52] A chipset refers to a designated group of integrated circuits that is designed to perform more than one related function. Its main task is to connect the CPU to a specified set of other components. The chipset primarily constitutes a 'bridge', which is dedicated to connecting the CPU to the high-speed components, notably the main memory and graphics controllers, and to the lower-speed peripheral devices. Chipsets are generally designed to work with a specific family or generation of CPUs: a CPU and chipset combination needs to be compatible in order to function. See paras 12–13 of the *Intel/McAfee* case.

the remedies/commitments[53] helped to preserve innovation in security software and simultaneously ensured that competitors were not foreclosed.[54]

F. Merger Control During the Financial and Economic Crisis

The experience of the global financial and economic crisis has demonstrated that the EU Merger Regulation can provide all the necessary tools for applying effective merger control even in times of economic distress. The truth is that the Commission has taken due account of the market changes resulting from the economic crisis. However, the Commission stood firm against demands for a more lenient approach to EU merger control. Thus, by maintaining competitive market structures during the economic downturn, the Commission has created the necessary conditions for the foundation of a sustainable subsequent rise.[55]

For example, in the particularly sensitive banking sector, a set of remedies applied to the BNP Paribas–Fortis merger[56] was sufficient to allay competition concerns in the credit card market. In a thoughtful decision, a partial derogation from the suspension obligation was granted in order to ensure that BNP Paribas could give timely and necessary support to the acquired Fortis assets with the intention of keeping them operational.

Similarly, in the *Fortis/ABN Amro* case[57] full implementation was ensured by the Commission of the remedies that it had accepted immediately before the financial crisis aimed at preserving competition in the banking market for small and medium enterprises (SMEs) in the Netherlands after the economic recovery. When circumstances demand, the Commission may use the tools at its disposal to examine the cases, taking also into account the deteriorating economic environment.

In particular, this has been done mainly by thoroughly analysing failing firm arguments (when mergers are notified but not finally accepted)[58] and by developing a refined analysis of the framework for competitive assessment (principally involving analysis of the market, ie contestability, barriers to entry and potential competition).[59] During this assessment, the Commission undertakes a thorough investigation of whether the deterioration of the competitive structure following the merger would have occurred despite the merger.

More specifically, the Horizontal Merger Guidelines declare that:

> [T]he Commission may decide that an otherwise problematic merger is nevertheless compatible with the common market if one of the merging parties constitutes a failing firm. The basic requirement is that the ascertained deterioration of the competitive structure that follows the merger cannot be said to be caused by the merger.[60]

More specifically, it is acceptable[61] for this result to arise in cases where 'the competitive structure of the market would deteriorate to at least the same extent in the absence of

[53] See mainly paras 333–50 and also pp 63 et seq of the *Intel/McAfee* case.
[54] COMP/M.5984 *Intel/McAfee*, decision of 26 January 2011.
[55] Above n 3, para 25.
[56] COMP/M.5384 *BNP Paribas/Fortis*, decision of 3 December 2008.
[57] COMP/M.4844 *Fortis/ABN Amro Assets*, decision of 3 October 2007.
[58] See mainly COMP/M.6796 *Aegean/Olympic II*, decision of 9 October 2013; COMP/M.6360 *Nynas/Harburg*, decision of 2 September 2013.
[59] See eg, COMP/M.6447 *IAG/bmi*, decision of 30 March 2012.
[60] See eg, Joined Cases C-68/94 and C-30/95 *Kali and Salz*, para 110.
[61] Above n 47, paras 89–90.

the merger'.[62] It should be remembered that in order to assess the competitive effects of a merger, the Commission compares the competitive conditions that would result from the notified merger with the conditions that would have prevailed without the merger occurring.[63] In the same context it is useful to note that, accordingly, in the case of a merger that has been implemented without having been notified, the Commission would estimate the merger in the light of the competitive conditions that would have prevailed without the implemented (but not notified) merger. The truth is that in most of the cases the competitive conditions existing at the time of the merger constitute a relevant comparison for evaluating the competitive effects of a merger. Nevertheless, under some circumstances, the Commission may take into account future changes to the market on the assumption that these specific changes can reasonably be predicted.[64] The Commission, when considering what constitutes a relevant comparison, may in particular assess the market's contestability, taking account of the likely entry or exit of firms if (hypothetically) the merger did not take place.[65]

i. COMP/M.6360 Nynas/Harburg *Case as an Example*

Case COMP/M.6360 *Nynas/Harburg*[66] constitutes a useful example. More specifically, the Commission cleared the proposed acquisition by Sweden's Nynas AB of certain Shell Deutschland Oil GmbH refinery assets which were located in Hamburg/Harburg (Germany). The Commission's assessment showed that, in the hypothetical absence of the notified transaction, the Harburg refinery assets would most probably exit the market; this would have been much worse for the competitive structure of the relevant markets in comparison with the reasonably foreseeable effects of the concentration. This case therefore provides a good example of the Commission's approach when it compares the competitive conditions that would prevail in the absence of a merger with the conditions that would result if the same merger is completed.

G. Remedies in Case of Competition Concerns

In the event that the Commission identifies competition concerns when examining a notified merger, the parties involved have the opportunity to offer commitments in order to remedy those concerns. If the Commission considers that the commitments proposed are adequate to minimize the competition concerns and are sufficient to confirm the merger's compatibility with the internal market, it will give permission for the transaction subject to those commitments. As a consequence of this authorization, the commitments are binding on the parties.[67]

[62] Joined Cases C-68/94 and C-30/95 *Kali and Salz*, para 114. See also Commission Decision 2002/365/EC in Case COMP/M.2314 *BASF/Pantochim/Eurodiol* [2002] OJ L132, 45, paras 157–60.

[63] See eg, Whish (n 49), mainly the chapter with the section 'Determining and Applying the Correct Competition Test', 788–90.

[64] See eg, Commission Decision 98/526/EC in Case IV/M.950 *Hoffmann La Roche/Boehringer Mannheim* [1998] OJ L234, 14, para 13; Case IV/M.1846 *Glaxo Wellcome/SmithKline Beecham*, paras 70–72; Case COMP/M.2547 *Bayer/Aventis Crop Science*, paras 324 et seq.

[65] See eg, Case T-102/96 *Gencor v Commission* [1999] ECR II-753, paras 247–63.

[66] Commission's decision of 2 September 2013.

[67] See mainly para 2 of Art 6 and para 2 of Art 8 of Regulation 139/2004.

In reality, commitments are crucial elements of merger control when one considers that the large majority of cases that raise competition concerns are not prohibited, but are cleared with commitments. Indeed, during the last 25 years only 24 transactions have been prohibited. Furthermore, the overall percentage of merger cases where the Commission intervened in order to maintain effective competition in the single market has been stable at around 5–8 per cent of all notified mergers in recent years. It ought to be clarified that these cases include mergers cleared in Phase I or in Phase II with commitments, prohibitions as well as mergers abandoned after the opening of an in-depth investigation. Although this proportion varies depending on the nature of the transactions notified to the Commission, the fact that it generally remains stable at around 5–8 per cent of all notified mergers indicates the maturity of the system.

In addition, the Commission's practice regarding remedies was further revised in its 2008 Remedies Notice.[68] In the revised Remedies Notice it was also explained that a sale of subsidiary commitment is the best way to eliminate competition concerns and, furthermore, constitutes the benchmark against which the suitability of other proposed remedies ought to be measured. The new Remedies Notice promotes a more standardized approach towards remedies, focusing more closely on their effectiveness. In particular, the new Notice clarifies and strengthens the following: (i) the requirements for the scope of a subsidiary's selling, (ii) 'the requirements for appropriate purchasers, (iii) the hold-separate obligations of the parties pending the divestiture, the conditions for so-called carve-out divestitures (in cases where the divestment business is not an existing stand-alone business), and the supervisory role of the monitoring trustee'.[69]

i. The Example of COMP/M.5658 Unilever/Sara Lee

COMP/M.5658 *Unilever/Sara Lee*[70] illustrated the Commission's approach to structural/non-structural remedies. In order to alleviate the Commission's concerns, several non-structural remedies were offered by the merging parties, but the Commission did not consider these measures effective, despite the fact that rebranding in certain Member States was included in the specific measures. Finally, the commitment by the merging parties to sell off Sara Lee's Sanex brand and related business in Europe was accepted by the Commission, since this proposition offered a clear and workable remedy, which was considered sufficient to restore competition conditions in all markets where the Commission had concerns.

H. The Acceptable Risk of Complex Remedies

Simplification often results in efficiency and greater effectiveness. Conversely, complex remedies involve risks that need to be expected a priori. Inappropriate remedies may render official permission impossible, especially in cases where the buyer's identity is crucial, and consequently so-called 'fix-it-first' solutions are necessary. An indicative relevant example

[68] Commission Notice on remedies acceptable under Council Regulation (EC) No 139/2004 and under Commission Regulation (EC) No 802/2004 [2008] OJ C267/1.

[69] Above n 3, para 30.

[70] Commission's decision of 17 November 2010.

is Case COMP/M.6570 *UPS/TNT*:[71] the parties proposed the sale of local subsidiaries in 15 countries and non-permanent access to UPS's air network was included in this proposition. The feasibility of such a remedy depended significantly on the identity of the purchaser, since it would be necessary to connect the sold-off assets to a functioning existing network which the parties involved were unable to suggest within the period required by the Commission's proceedings. Nevertheless, there are also some recent cases showing that the Commission can be flexible in discussing complex remedies: for instance, purchasers paying out at the beginning of the business arrangement or specific buyer requirements under the precondition that they are workable and supported by sufficient protective measures. Recent relevant examples with complex remedies are cases such as COMP/M.6576 *Munksjö/Ahlstrom*,[72] COMP/M.6690 *Syniverse/Mach*[73] and COMP/M.6857 *Crane/MEI*.[74]

I. Forecast: Promoting the Level Playing Field, Cooperation and Convergence

The success of the Merger Regulation 139/2004 is undisputable, since it has truly succeeded both in levelling the playing field and providing a 'one-stop shop' scrutiny for mergers with an EU dimension.[75] Nevertheless, it is also accepted that Member States play significant roles in merger control enforcement in the EU. More specifically, in the seven years between 2001 and 2007 the combined NCAs handled nearly 4,000 merger cases per year on average. The necessity for a truly functional system that will scrutinize mergers throughout the EU demands cooperation, efficient work-sharing, and convergence between the Commission and the 27 Member States exercising merger control (Luxemburg is exempted).

The differentiation of merger rules and practices clearly creates administrative burdens for businesses and inevitably may also adversely affect the internal market. A consultation took place in preparation for a 2009 report from the Commission to the Council on the operation of the Merger Regulation;[76] in this consultation and in subsequent debates, concerns were expressed by stakeholders regarding the administrative burden and risk of differentiating decisions of competition authorities across the EU. More specifically, stakeholders stated that more convergence would be welcomed in this respect. The administrative burden is particularly significant in cases with cross-border effects, since these cases often require clearance from more than one NCA. It is therefore more than obvious that in such cases, differentiating rules may lead to higher costs for businesses and, in exceptional cases, inconsistencies are possible.

[71] Commission's decision of 30 January 2013.
[72] Commission's decision of 24 May 2013.
[73] Commission's decision of 29 May 2013.
[74] Commission's decision of 19 July 2013.
[75] See Whish (n 49) 816 et seq; Hawk and Huser, *European Community Merger Control: A Practitioner's Guide* (Dordrecht, Kluwer Law International 1996) ch IV; Cook and Kerse, *EC Merger Control*, 3rd edn (London, Sweet & Maxwell, 2000) ch 1.9; Levy, *European Merger Control Law: A Guide to the Merger Regulation* (London, LexisNexis, 2003) ch 1.3.
[76] See Communication from the Commission to the Council, Report on the functioning of Regulation No 139/2004, 18 June 2009, COM(2009) 281 final, accompanied by Staff Working Paper SEC(2009) 808 final/2 (the so-called '2009 Staff Working Paper').

Although NCAs usually apply Articles 101 and 102 of the Treaty on the Functioning of the European Union (TFEU) together with their national laws, the EU Merger Regulation itself constitutes a model that is applied to many national merger control regimes. Therefore, a basic *minimum* legislative convergence across national jurisdictions is observed, particularly regarding the substantive test for assessing transactions. One clear example is provided by Germany, which in 2013 replaced the previous dominance test with the SIEC test, thereby following the demands of the Merger Regulation 139/2004.[77]

Furthermore, a level of convergence has already been achieved regarding not only substantive but also jurisdictional issues due to increased cooperation between NCAs and the Commission. In 2010, the Commission and the NCAs established a Merger Working Group, the task of which was to foster further cooperation and convergence among the NCAs of the 27 Member States (with merger control regimes), based on the current institutional and legal framework. One year later (2011), the Merger Working Group adopted a set of best practices for merger cooperation between NCAs.[78] The truly beneficial result is that, in general, a close practical cooperation between the Commission and NCAs (as well as between the NCAs themselves) has now been established.

However, despite the level of convergence achieved to date, harmonisation remains incomplete. More specifically, among the notable points of differentiation are national laws according to which a government may be allowed to prevail over an NCA's negative competition-based merger decision by applying national merger control law, based on other public-interest considerations. Despite the fact such interventions are generally rare, the existence of such regimes has been detected in France, Germany, Italy, Spain and the United Kingdom (Greece was included before the country passed Law 3959/2011).[79]

According to the present data, most of the NCAs apply the SIEC or a similar test in their substantive analysis. Nevertheless, the importance of the way/ways in which such tests are further developed in guidance documents (the Commission's Horizontal and Non-Horizontal Guidelines)[80] and the ways in which they are applied and interpreted not only by competition authorities but also ultimately by reviewing courts should also be underlined. Differentiation in this respect can impact the substantive assessment and result in inconsistencies. Furthermore, Member States do not always follow the same approach regarding remedies.

In addition, the existence of differentiation is possible regarding procedural rules (mainly time frames for review and stand-still rules), leading unavoidably to uncertainty and imposing (at least in some cases) additional costs on the undertakings involved.

For the above-mentioned reasons, the conclusion of the White Paper is that greater convergence, not only between the Commission and NCAs but also among the NCAs, is important for the creation of a truly level playing field and avoidance of undesirable

[77] See Achtes Gesetz zur Änderung des Gesetzes gegen Wettbewerbsbeschränkungen vom 29.6.2013 (BGBl. I, 1738).

[78] More specifically, it is about the EU Merger Working Group, Best Practices on Cooperation between EU National Competition Authorities in Merger Review, 8 November 2011.

[79] See Decision No 40/1996 of the Hellenic Competition Authority, by which the notified merger had been prohibited. Nevertheless, the competent minister approved this merger mainly for social reasons.

[80] Above nn 62 and 33, respectively.

inconsistencies.[81] For these serious reasons, the Commission and the Member States should continue to conform their practices by enhancing cooperation and sharing experience, using all available tools and forums (obviously, the Merger Working Group constitutes the main forum). Furthermore, regarding individual cases, NCAs ought to intensify their cooperation.

Inconsistencies can, in any event, be avoided by the NCAs by reference to the Commission. This is the reason why stakeholders (including NCAs) have proposed that parties should be able to request a referral if there is jurisdiction by only two Member States. According to Article 22 of Regulation 139/2004,[82] if NCAs are of the opinion that the Commission is best placed to achieve consistency, they can refer these cases to the Commission. The reform proposals on Article 22, set out in the White Paper,[83] suggest setting up a system based on an early (a priori) information notice. Such a system could facilitate practical cooperation amongst the NCAs in cross-border and multijurisdictional cases, even if no referral takes place. Hence, the necessity of a proposal that would make practical cooperation easier, and that would improve the exchange of case-related information between the Commission and NCAs is emphasized.

There is thus a necessity at least for a convergent interpretation. However, beyond such a not obligatory, ie voluntary 'soft convergence', Mario Monti[84] has referred to the possibility of extending the use of the substantive EU merger control rules. More specifically, Monti's conclusion was that, on the one hand, there is an interest in achieving greater convergence for the substantive assessment of mergers and the review process at national level and, on the other hand, that the objective of ensuring a level playing field would legally oblige NCAs to apply the substantive EU merger control rules at the national level also in those cases where mergers have cross-border effects. Three years later, the French NCA raised similar proposals in its report.[85]

[81] See recital no 14 of Regulation 139/2004, where the following is stated:

> The Commission and the competent authorities of the Member States should together form a network of public authorities, applying their respective competences in close cooperation, using efficient arrangements for information-sharing and consultation, with a view to ensuring that a case is dealt with by the most appropriate authority, in the light of the principle of subsidiarity and with a view to ensuring that multiple notifications of a given concentration are avoided to the greatest extent possible. Referrals of concentrations from the Commission to Member States and from Member States to the Commission should be made in an efficient manner avoiding, to the greatest extent possible, situations where a concentration is subject to a referral both before and after its notification.

It is observed that the Commission is emphasizing cooperation and deals with referral and competence.

[82] See mainly para 1 of Art 22, where it is stated that:

> One or more Member States may request the Commission to examine any concentration as defined in Article 3 that does not have a Community dimension within the meaning of Article 1 but affects trade between Member States and threatens to significantly affect competition within the territory of the Member State or States making the request. Such a request shall be made at most within 15 working days of the date on which the concentration was notified, or if no notification is required, otherwise made known to the Member State concerned.

[83] Above n 55, ch 4.2 ('The Proposed Measures and Policy Choices in the Area of Case Referrals').

[84] See M Monti, *A New Strategy for the Single Market at the Service of Europe's Economy and Society*, Report to the President of the Commission José Manuel Barroso, 9 May 2010.

[85] Autorité de la concurrence, Rapport au Ministre de l'Économie et des Finances, *Pour un contrôle plus simple, cohérent et stratégique en Europe*, 16 December 2013.

According to this point of view, the current enforcement framework of Articles 101 and 102 TFEU could constitute the appropriate basis for such a change: a move towards a system similar to this framework could be appropriate for transactions in the single market that have cross-border effects, which are increasing in number significantly. Furthermore, it could stop issues arising from the cases where NCAs dealing with the same case reach conflicting/contradictory results and could simplify the administrative burden for parties in multijurisdictional filings. Nevertheless, the undisputable truth is that such a modification, according to which both the Commission and the NCAs would apply the same EU substantive law (the so-called 'EU merger control area'), would inevitably require a more ambitious change of the current merger control system within the EU. So, the million-dollar question is: do we really need such an ambitious change?

II. Minority Interests in the Merger Control Regime: A Retrospective View to the Future

A. Commission's Green Paper

On 11 December 2001 the Commission of the European Communities published a Green Paper on the review of Council Regulation (EEC) No 4064/89.[86] The proposed revision was undertaken in order to ensure that Council Regulation (EEC) No 4064/89 will continue to be an effective tool for the enforcement of mergers and acquisitions within the Community and to enhance cooperation among the Member States. One of the issues under review was the applicability of the concept of concentration on minority shareholdings.

The Commission was particularly interested in transactions among competitors which did not entail acquisition of control, ie acquisitions of non-controlling joint or sole minority shareholdings as well as strategic alliances. The Commission's interest was due to the structural impact of such transactions on the markets involved and the difficulty defining them for the purposes of ex ante notification.[87]

The Commission was also worried about partial-function production joint ventures. As stated in the Green Paper,[88] 'the 1999 White Paper on modernisation of the rules implementing Articles 81 and 82 raised the question of whether partial-function production joint ventures should also be included under the Merger Regulation. However, in its proposal of 27.9.2000, the Commission deferred further examination of this issue to the review of the Merger Regulation.'[89]

Minority shareholdings and interlocking directorships were viewed as vehicles to alter the competitive incentives of the engaged firms in the markets where they were active. In particular, the link between them and joint dominance was an issue that emerged from the

86 See also COM(2001) 745 final.

87 Ibid, para 101.

88 Ibid, para 102.

89 The Commission was also concerned about certain transactions especially in the financial sector (eg venture capital).

relevant case law. However, only a limited number of such transactions raised competitive effects that could not be satisfactorily assessed under Articles 81 and 82 of the Treaty.[90] Therefore, the Commission stated that:

> Under this assumption it would appear disproportionate to subject all acquisitions of minority shareholdings to the ex ante control of the Merger Regulation. At the same time it appears doubtful whether an appropriate definition could be established capable of identifying those instances where minority shareholdings and interlocking directorships would warrant such treatment.[91]

The Commission's proposition regarding partial-function production joint ventures was that they might 'be subjected both to the dominance test and to Article 2(4) of the Merger Regulation'.[92] However, several difficulties that were raised during a subsequent consultation period indicated that this kind of joint venture 'may not be suited to control under a system of mandatory ex ante notifications'.[93] Such difficulties were, for instance, the non-existence of a legal definition for these kind of ventures and the view that they had similar characteristics to other types of joint ventures (R&D or distribution joint ventures) and therefore all of them should be suited to ex ante merger control. It should be mentioned here that partial-function joint production ventures were covered by block exemption regulations under Article 81 subject to a market share threshold of 20 per cent.

B. Commission's Tender Offer COMP/2011/029 on 27 October 2011

On 27 October 2011 the Commission launched a tender offer requiring data on the importance of minority shareholdings in the EU. The purpose of the offer was to promote future policy development regarding the economic importance of minority shareholdings to the EU economy. The Commission's general objective was therefore to acquire a critical database of minority shareholdings.

Prior to the Commission's Tender Offer, 'Commissioner Almunia [Vice President of the Commission responsible for Competition Policy] indicated a concern that EU merger control, in contrast to some national merger control regimes, is unable to investigate minority equity stakes as mergers'.[94] In his speech[95] the Commissioner indicated a potential enforcement gap among Member States and between the EU and the Member States.

C. Commission Staff Working Document 'Towards More Effective EU Merger Control'

On 25 June 2013 the Commission launched a working document concerning two critical issues of merger control within the EU: the ability of the Commission to examine minority

[90] See also COM(2001) 745 final, para 109.
[91] Ibid.
[92] Ibid, para 120.
[93] Ibid, para 121.
[94] See B Ignjatovic and D Ridyard, 'Minority Shareholdings, Material Effects?' (2012) 1(1) *CPI Antitrust Chronicle* 1.
[95] http://europa.eu/rapid/press-release_SPEECH-11-166_en.htm.

interests (or structural links) and the level of cooperation within the Member States through the system of post- and pre-notification referrals to the Commission.[96]

The Commission realized that the number of problematic cases of minority shareholdings was limited. It also noted that the anticompetitive effects of such cases were less pronounced than in full merger cases. However, the Commission also stated that the efficiencies deriving from cases of structural links were likely to be less enhanced than in full merger cases which might lead to a critical restriction of competition and especially to a reduction of effective innovation activity, distortions of demand, and increased prices of products.[97]

At the same time the Commission indicated its restricted ability to deal with cases of structural links. It mentioned that the only way to realize the existence of such links is in the context of a notified merger (pre-existing minority interests/shareholdings).[98] However, even though the Commission had the ability to take these links into account during the analysis of the notified merger, it did not have the competence under the Merger Regulation to analyse their potentially anticompetitive effects if the minority interests had been acquired after the notified merger.

Regarding the link between minority interests and their assessment under Articles 101 and 102 TFEU, the Commission mentioned that its ability to use these articles to intervene against minority shareholdings is limited and therefore does not cover all types of anticompetitive minority interests.[99]

In the light of the above considerations the Commission asked for the opinion of stakeholders 'on whether to extend the scope of application of the Merger Regulation so as to give the Commission the possibility to investigate and, if necessary, intervene against anti-competitive structural links'.[100] Two major options concerning the selection of cases and the procedure were introduced:

a) The first option was a simple extension of the current system of ex ante merger control to minority interests. Under this system all cases of minority interests would have to be notified to the Commission in advance (the notification system).
b) The second option foresaw the discretion of the Commission to select cases of minority interests to investigate. This discretion could be achieved either through a self-assessment system under which the 'obligation to notify a transaction to the Commission in advance would not apply to structural links, but instead the parties would be allowed to proceed with the transaction but the Commission would have the option whether and when to open an investigation'; or through a transparency system under which the parties in a potential problematic case of minority interests are obliged to notify it to the Commission through 'a short information notice (containing for example information on the parties, the type of transaction and possibly limited information on the economic sectors or markets concerned)'.[101]

[96] Commission Staff Working Document, 'Towards More Effective EU Merger Control', SWD(2013) 239 final.

[97] Ibid, 4. The potential anticompetitive effects of minority interests are analysed extensively in chs 4 and 7 below. Also, in ch 5 we provide an exhaustive review of merger cases not only from the EU, but also from the US and nations around the world.

[98] In ch 2 we present in detail the different notions of minority interests.

[99] See also ch 3 for an analysis of the Commission's ability to use antitrust rules in order to deal with minority interests.

[100] Above n 97, 6.

[101] Ibid, 7.

The Commission set out the basic merits of its endeavour which have to be investigated within the framework of minority shareholdings. These can be delineated under the following questions:

- Which acquisitions of minority shareholdings qualify as structural links?
- How can the scope of the Merger Regulation be delineated from the antitrust articles of the TFEU with regard to structural links?
- Will non full joint ventures remain subject to competition scrutiny under the antitrust articles of TFEU?
- Will the Commission continue to have the only power to assess concentrations with a Community dimension?
- Will the engaged firms in cases of minority interests have the option voluntarily to notify the transaction to the Commission?

Most of the answers to these questions were provided in the Commission's White Paper,[102] analysis of which will be presented in chapter 8. Concerning non full joint ventures, the Commission mentioned that these 'could … remain subject to competition scrutiny under Article 101 TFEU, save in exceptional cases where the structural links cannot otherwise be assessed under Article 101 TFEU'.[103] In addition, the Commission stated that the notion of concentrations with an EU dimension will also be applied on cases of minority interests and 'the substantive test foreseen in the Merger Regulation for the examination of "full" mergers, ie whether a transaction "significantly impedes effective competition", … could apply to structural links as well, possibly with some additional clarifications in the relevant Commission guidelines'.[104]

In the next chapter we present the different notions of minority shareholdings, either controlling or non-controlling, and in chapter 3 we investigate their existence under different merger control regimes within the EU, the US and nations across the globe. Chapter 4 introduces the reader to the economics of minority shareholdings, while chapter 5 extensively presents relevant case law. Chapter 6 presents the Greek coastal navigation case and chapter 7, in conjunction with chapter 4, analyses the empirical findings of the economic literature so far.

As we have already mentioned, in chapter 8 we analyse the Commission's White Paper and the proposed targeted system for investigating non-controlling minority shareholdings within the EU. Given the analysis in the previous chapters, in chapter 9 we present our opinion regarding the treatment of non-controlling minority shareholdings and the transparent system proposed by the Commission. Finally, the last chapter of this book presents our conclusions.

[102] White Paper, 'Towards More Effective EU Merger Control' SWD(2014) 449 final.
[103] Ibid, 8.
[104] Ibid, 7.

2

Concepts and Types of Minority Interests

I. Useful Preliminaries Regarding Minority Interests

A. Theoretical Approach

Minority interests consist of various types of non-controlling interests in competitors, such as minority shareholdings and interlocking directorships. Loans and other financial products involving competitors may also play a crucial role in creating mutual interactions among the parties.

Following Meadowcroft and Thompson,[1] there are five different types of minority interests, which may be categorized as follows:

— *Pre-merger holdings*: minority interests purchased as the first step in a takeover (so-called pre-existing minority interests).
— *Blocking holdings*: minority interests purchased to prevent the takeover of the target by a third party (one of the issues facing the Commission in the celebrated Ryanair–Aer Lingus case).[2]
— *Effective control*: minority interests which enable the acquirer to exert control over the policies of the target (so-called active minority interests or interests that materially influence the competitive behaviour of the target firm).
— *Diversification*: minority interests which involve diversification into new markets.
— *Proxy agreements*: holdings which support, or substitute for contractual agreements in continuing trading relationships.

Milanesi and Winterstein[3] argue that there are three main types of minority interests:

— *Proxy agreements* (*Nichtangriffdenken*).[4]
— *Minority holdings in competing undertakings held by an undertaking active on another market*: minority interests which are used by a third party to incite target firms towards

[1] S Meadowcroft and D Thompson, *Minority Share Acquisition: The Impact upon Competition* (Luxembourg, Office for Official Publications of the European Communities, 1986) 1, 8.
[2] See also the analysis provided in ch 5 below.
[3] See EM Milanesi A Winterstein, *Minderheitsbeteiligungen und personelle Verflechtungen zwischen Wettberwerbern—Zur Anwendung von Artikel 81 und 82 EG-Vertrag* (2001), available at http://ec.europa.eu/competition/speeches/text/sp2001_026_de.pdf.
[4] Above n 1.

collusive behaviour. For instance, banks or financial institutions that provide loans or other types of financial tools or hold non-controlling minority interests in other firms may be able to influence the strategic behaviour of these firms towards collusion.[5]

— *Interlocking directorships*: minority interests that result in the anticompetitive exchange of information among competing firms.

Generally speaking, a minority interest is the portion of a consolidated entity that is not owned by the consolidating entity. A consolidated entity may be formed through management/shareholding control and also depends on the prevailing accounting/regulatory environment.

B. Financial Issues

Before we present the concepts regarding minority interests let us first classify some financial concepts which will be very useful in the rest of this chapter. The stock or capital stock of a firm constitutes the equity capital of its owners. It is discharged of all claims such as debt and is separated into shares which represent a fraction of the ownership in a firm.

Shares may be or may be not issued at a par value, the accounting value of the equity in the balance sheet of the firm.[6] They are typically categorized into common and preferred shares. Common shares carry voting rights that can be exercised to affect the decisions made by the firm. Preferred shares typically do not carry voting rights, but holders of these shares are entitled to receive certain dividend payments.[7] When the owner of preferred shares has an option to convert them into a fixed number of common shares in the future, usually after a predetermined period of time, then the shares are called convertible preferred or preference shares.[8,9] In addition, preferred shares may receive fixed returns and voting rights (hybrid preferred shares).[10]

Derivatives (or stock derivatives or derivative securities) are financial products the value of which depends on the underlying securities (stocks or bonds). They are typically divided into futures and options. Futures are contracts between buyers and sellers. Both of these parties are obligated to buy and sell on the contract respectively at a predetermined time in the future, called the maturity date. An option may be either a call option or a put option.

[5] An example of this strategy can be found in D Flath, 'Shareholding Interlocks in the Keiretsu, Japan's Financial Groups' (1993) 75 *Review of Economics and Statistics* 249. In this article the author argues that minority interests are used to resolve agency problems of debt in the target firms. An analysis of this article is provided in ch 7, section I below.

[6] There are three major financial statements describing a firm: the balance sheet, the income statement and the statement of cash flows. A balance sheet or statement of financial position is a review of the financial balances of a firm. A standard balance sheet has three segments: assets, liabilities and ownership equity. Of all the financial statements, the balance sheet is the only statement that applies to a single point in time of a firm's financial year.

[7] A dividend is a payment by a firm to its owners. Usually takes the form of a distribution of firm's profit. If the firm decides to reinvest profit in the business, then this amout is called 'retained earnings'.

[8] See generally Z Bodie, A Kane and AJ Marcus (eds), *Investments*, 9th edn (New York, McGraw-Hill, 2011).

[9] The same argument holds for bonds (debt securities or forms of loans which provide the borrowers with funds to finance investments). See, for instance, the 1981 agreement in the *Philip Morris* case (Report for the Hearing delivered in Joined Cases 142 and 156/84, 4493), where Philip Morris agreed with Rembrandt to acquire half of the convertible Rothmans International bonds. See also n 8, 690–91.

[10] Ibid, where Rothmans Holdings 'held all the cumulative preference shares in Rothmans International, which gave it predominant voting rights with respect to resolutions of exceptional importance'.

The owner of a call option has the right to buy stocks or bonds in the future at a predetermined value and the owner of a put option has the right to sell stocks or bonds in the future at a predetermined value.[11]

A loan is a type of debt provided by firm(s) or individual(s) (lender(s)) to other firm(s) or individual(s) (borrower(s)). It is a reallocation of assets from lender to borrower at an interest rate,[12] which is its cost. A loan is also a note or a contract which entails, inter alia, the amount of the loan, the interest rate and the date of repayment. A debt is an obligation of the debtor to the creditor. It is created when the latter lends a portion of its assets to the debtor. Therefore, the debtor owns the debt and is obligated to repay the original sum of assets plus an interest rate to the creditor.

Even though this book deals with minority interests in terms of competition policy, it is interesting to present here the different types of minority interests in terms of financial economics. In particular, accountants consider an investment in the securities of other firms in the following two categories: (a) a minority passive investment and (b) a minority active investment.

A minority passive investment exists when a shareholder holds less than 20 per cent of the overall ownership of another firm. This type of investment will be held to maturity or will be offered for sale before it. A minority active investment exists when a shareholder holds between 20 and 50 per cent of the overall ownership of another firm. The shareholder of a minority active investment receives dividends.[13]

Minority interests generally show up in the income statement as a non-operating item, and on the balance sheet as a stand-alone liability. In the following sub-sections of this chapter we will try to guide the reader in the field of the minority interests and clarify the different concepts of these interests.

II. Minority Shareholdings

A. The Concept of Minority Shareholdings

The concept of minority shareholdings among firms refers to situations where shareholders hold less than 50 per cent of the voting rights of other firms' equity capital. That is, minority shareholdings are portions of a consolidated entity which do not confer control in the legal sense to their owners and are therefore not notifiable under the worldwide merger notification systems. Minority shareholdings are also called structural links.[14]

[11] See Case M.3696 *E.ON/MOL* (ch 5). In Case M.3101 *Accor/Hilton/Six Continents* (ch 5) where the Commission argued that Hilton, a parent firm of a joint venture which owned only 6.25 per cent of its issued share capital, was able to exercise joint control over it given its option to increase its participation up to 31.25 per cent. See also the German case *Xella Baustoffe* described in ch 5, section I.B.ii.

[12] An interest is the fee charged from lender to borrower. Usually it is calculated over the amount of loan.

[13] Accountants also refer to the term majority active investment. This type of investment exists when a shareholder holds more than 50 per cent of the overall ownership of another firm. A majority active investment between two firms leads to a consolidation of the balance sheets of the two firms. That is, the liabilities and the assets of the two firms are presented as one balance sheet.

[14] See also Commission Staff Working Document, 'Towards More Effective EU Merger Control', Annex 1, 6.

B. The Nature of Minority Shareholdings

i. Active and Passive Minority Shareholdings

Minority shareholdings may be either active or passive in nature.[15] Active minority shareholdings refer to minority interests where their owner, a person or a firm, may exercise some form of control over the 'victim' firm(s).[16] Examples of active minority shareholdings arc thc following:[17]

— A shareholder who holds a minority interest but has the ability to exercise sole control[18] over the 'victim' firm. The minority shareholder effects its strategic behaviour either by appointing the majority of the members of the decision-making bodies, eg the board of directors, or by controlling shareholder meetings due to the fact that the remaining shares of the 'victim' firm are widely dispersed.

— A shareholder who holds a minority interest and has the ability to exercise joint control[19] over the 'victim' firm. The minority shareholder cannot effect its strategic behaviour on its own, but it can block certain decisions by other shareholders and therefore exercises joint control on the 'victim' firm along with these shareholders. A minority shareholder can block certain decisions by other shareholders either by exercising 'veto rights'[20] on critical issues or by jointly influencing with other shareholders the commercial behaviour of the 'victim' firm. The latter may be done through a legal agreement which indicates that the minority shareholders will not act against each other and the majority of the 'victim' firm will behave as a team in order jointly to decide its management.[21]

— Managers of the acquiring firm try to maximize the joint profits of both the victim[22] firm and the acquiring firm. The managers of the [victim][23] firm act similarly. In this way, they make the same decisions that they would if they were actually merged. This is called Coasian joint control.[24]

— A shareholder who holds a minority interest and has the ability to confer negative control over the 'victim' firm. The concept of negative control refers to situations where although the minority shareholder cannot influence the strategic decisions of the 'victim' firm, it may have the ability to block certain other decisions.[25]

[15] In the literature the terms controlling and non-controlling, respectively, are also used. Also, economists used to distinguish between corporate control and partial financial interest. See especially D Brito, R Ribeiro and H Vasconcelos, 'Measuring Unilateral Effects in Partial Horizontal Acquisitions' (2014) 33 *International Journal of Industrial Organization* 22, 22. See also Case COMP/M.2416 *Tetra Laval/Sidel*.

[16] The term 'victim' firm refers to the issuing firm of the asset or claim for which a minority interest is established.

[17] See especially OECD, *Antitrust Issues Involving Minority Shareholdings and Interlocking Directorates* (2009) DAF/COMP(2008)30.

[18] See, eg Commission Consolidated Jurisdictional Notice under Council Regulation (EC) No 139/2004 on the control of concentrations between undertakings [2008] C95/01, para 59.

[19] Ibid, para 62.

[20] Ibid, para 68. See also COMP/JV.55 *Hutchison/RCPM/ECT* (ch 4 below).

[21] Ibid, para 74.

[22] Instead of the word acquired.

[23] Ibid.

[24] See DP O'Brien and SC Salop, 'Competitive Effects of Partial Ownership: Financial Interest and Corporate Control' (2000) 67 *Antitrust Law Journal* 559, 581. See also Table 6 in ch 4.

[25] Above n 18, para 56.

Passive minority shareholdings refer to situations where a minority shareholder cannot be represented in the decision-making bodies of the 'victim' firm. That is, they constitute financial acquisitions/interests or silent financial interest[26] or purely passive financial interests[27] in the 'victim' firm which are related to its profitability. They refer to any asset or claim the return of which is positively related to the 'victim' firm's profitability[28] and their owner(s) cannot have access to crucial information about the 'victim' firm.[29] Therefore, silent financial interests do not confer corporate influence or control in 'victim's' competitive decision-making.[30]

However, there are circumstances where the owner of a passive minority shareholding may receive direct information about a 'victim' firm's main operations. Even though the practical ability of the passive minority shareholder to have access to this kind of information does not provide him with the potential to influence the strategic behaviour of the 'victim' firm, it does provide a sort of control over this firm.[31] This kind of control may alert the competition in the market in which this minority interest operates.

Passive minority shareholdings may be further divided into pre-existing and post-existing minority shareholdings.[32] A pre-existing passive minority shareholding exists in the context of a notified consolidation. That is, a firm holds a minority stake in another firm(s) prior to the notification of a consolidation to the relevant authority.[33] On the contrary, a post-existing passive minority shareholding does not exist in the context of a notified consolidation. That is, a firm acquires the minority interest after the notification of a consolidation to the relevant competition authority.

ii. Horizontal, Vertical and Conglomerate Minority Shareholdings

The distinction between horizontal, vertical and conglomerate minority shareholdings is important due to the fact that the importance of the corresponding mergers on competition is different. It is generally accepted that the effects of a horizontal merger are of greater importance than the equivalent effects of vertical and conglomerate mergers. Therefore, a horizontal minority shareholder may potentially result in greater anticompetitive effects than the other two types of minority interests.[34]

Following the guidelines on the assessment of horizontal mergers[35] a horizontal merger is a merger between companies that are actual or potential competitors in the same relevant

[26] Above n 24.

[27] Ibid, 613.

[28] See RJ Reynolds and BR Snapp, 'The Competitive Effects of Partial Equity Interests and Joint Ventures' (1986) 4 *International Journal of Industrial Organization* 141, fn 1. The analysis of this article is presented in ch 4, section I.A.

[29] The term 'crucial information' refers to commercial or confidential information.

[30] See also O'Brien and Salop (n 24) 559, 577.

[31] See OFT, *Minority Interests in Competitors* (2010), a research report prepared by DotEcon Ltd, OFT1218.

[32] Above n 14, Annex 3, 4–10.

[33] See also the analysis in ch 3, section I.A below.

[34] This is the reason why in this book we are mainly focusing on horizontal rather than other types of minority shareholdings.

[35] See the Guidelines on the assessment of horizontal mergers under the Council Regulation on the control of concentrations between undertakings [2004] OJ C31/05.

market.[36] Thus, horizontal minority shareholdings are minority interests in horizontal competitors.

On the contrary, non-horizontal mergers are mergers among firms that are not actual or potential competitors. Following the guidelines on the assessment of non-horizontal mergers, '[v]ertical mergers involve companies operating at different levels of the supply chain. For example, when a manufacturer of a certain product (the "upstream firm") merges with one of its distributors (the "downstream firm"), this is called a vertical merger.'[37]

Vertical mergers involve a vertical minority shareholder possessing a minority interest in an upstream or a downstream firm, but not in an active or potential competitor.[38]

> Conglomerate mergers are mergers between firms that are in a relationship which is neither horizontal (as competitors in the same relevant market) nor vertical (as suppliers or customers) .... In practice, the focus ... is on mergers between companies that are active in closely related markets (eg mergers involving suppliers of complementary products or products that belong to the same product range).[39]

A conglomerate minority shareholder acquires interests in other firms that are neither purely horizontal nor purely vertical.

iii. Direct and Indirect Minority Shareholdings

Direct minority shareholdings may be either one-way or reciprocal partial ownerships. Suppose that we examine the nature of minority shareholdings between two firms, A and B. A direct, one-way minority shareholding of firm A over firm B is illustrated in Figure 1.

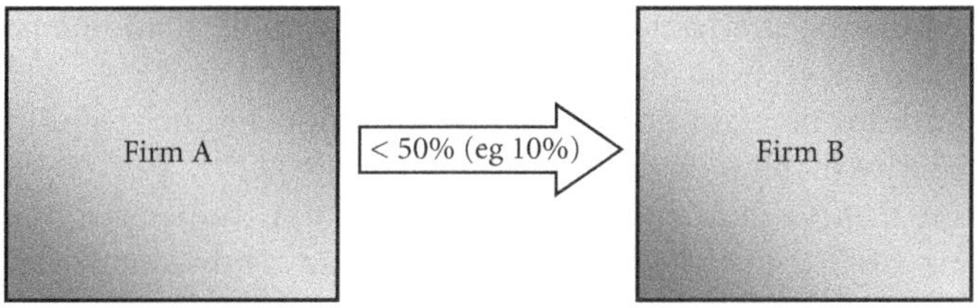

Figure 1: A direct, one-way minority shareholding between two firms

[36] According to the Commission Notice on the definition of a relevant market for the purposes of Community competition law [1997] C372, 0005-0013, 'A relevant product market comprises all those products and/or services which are regarded as interchangeable or substitutable by the consumer, by reason of the products' characteristics, their prices and their intended use.' 'The relevant geographic market comprises the area in which the undertakings concerned are involved in the supply and demand of products or services, in which the conditions of competition are sufficiently homogeneous and which can be distinguished from neighbouring areas because the conditions of competition are appreciably different in those area.'

[37] See the Guidelines on the assessment of non-horizontal mergers under the Council Regulation on the control of concentrations between undertakings [2008] OJ C265/6.

[38] See also D Flath, 'Vertical Integration by Means of Shareholding Interlocks' (1989) 7 *International Journal of Industrial Organization* 369.

[39] Above n 25, para 62.

Firm A's minority shareholding is called direct since firm A holds it directly in firm B without the intervention of a third firm. It is also called a one-way minority shareholding since only firm A holds shares in firm B's equity capital.[40]

Let us now consider Figure 2. Not only does firm A hold shares in firm B's equity capital, but also firm B holds shares in firm A's equity capital. This kind of minority shareholding is called reciprocal.[41]

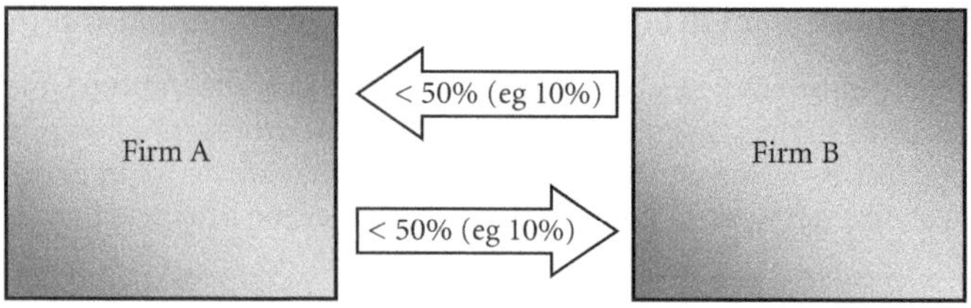

Figure 2: Direct, reciprocal minority shareholdings between two firms

Apart from the example of Figure 2, there exist a variety of different forms of direct, either one-way or reciprocal, minority shareholdings. For example:

— a firm may hold shares in more than one firm in a particular relevant market (multiplied, direct, horizontal, one-way minority shareholdings);
— firms of a particular relevant market hold shares in one another (multiplied, reciprocal minority shareholdings amongst horizontal competitors);
— an upstream firm(s) may hold shares in one or in more than one downstream firm (multiplied, direct, vertical, one-way minority shareholdings);
— upstream and downstream firms hold shares in one another (multiplied, reciprocal, vertical minority shareholdings);
— an upstream firm(s) may hold shares in one or in more than one upstream and downstream firm (multiplied, direct, vertical and horizontal, one-way minority shareholdings);
— upstream and downstream firms hold shares in one another both in horizontal and vertical levels (multiplied, reciprocal, vertical and horizontal minority shareholdings).

Figure 3 illustrates multiplied, reciprocal and one-way, and vertical and horizontal minority shareholdings.

[40] For instance, Ø Foros, JK Hans and S Greg, 'Mergers And Partial Ownership' (2011) 55 *European Economic Review* 916, consider a market with three firms, A, B and C, in which A acquires a minority shareholding in B and C remains independent.

[41] See, inter alia, Case M.3547 *Banco Santander/Abbey National* (ch 5).

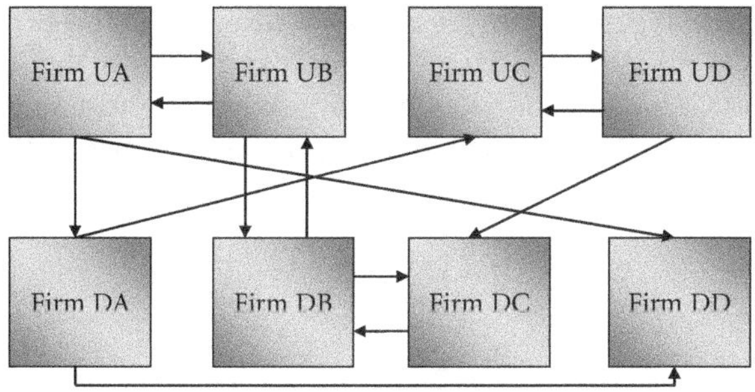

Notes:
U, upstream; D, downstream;
→ Passive minority shareholding (10%).

Figure 3: Direct, reciprocal minority shareholdings among firms in horizontal and vertical markets

In particular, in Figure 3 there exist four horizontal, five vertical, three reciprocal and five one-way direct minority shareholdings. The horizontal minority shareholdings are between UA & UB, UC & UD, DA & DD and DB & DC. Among them there exist three reciprocal shareholdings (between UA & UB, UC & UD and DB & DC) and one one-way direct minority shareholding (between DA & DD).

The horizontal minority shareholdings are between UA & DA, UA & DD, UB & DB, UD & DC and DA & UC. Among them there exist one reciprocal (between UB & DB) and four one-way direct minority shareholdings (between UA & DA, UA & DD, UD & DC, and DA & UC).

As in the case of direct minority shareholdings, indirect minority shareholdings[42] may be either one-way or reciprocal partial ownerships. The simplest form of an indirect one-way minority shareholding is shown in Figure 4.

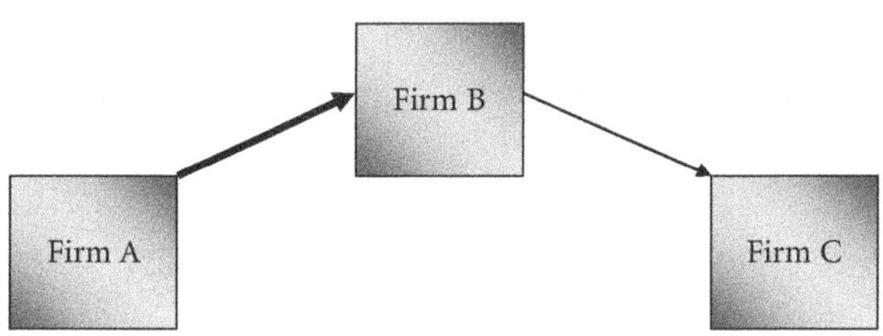

Notes:
➔ Active minority shareholding;
→ Passive minority shareholding.

Figure 4: An indirect, one-way minority shareholding between two firms

We assume that all the firms in Figure 4 are active in the same relevant market. Firm A owns an active one-way minority shareholding in firm B and the latter owns a passive one-way minority shareholding in firm C. Therefore, firm A owns an indirect one-way minority shareholding in firm C. Since all the firms are active in the same relevant market, then this indirect minority shareholding is termed horizontal.

[42] See also D Flath, 'When Is it Rational for Firms to Acquire Silent Interests in Rivals?' (1991) 9 *International Journal of Industrial Organization* 573 and D Flath, 'Horizontal Shareholding—Interlocks' (1992) 13 *Managerial and Decision Economics* 75.

Let us now consider Figure 5. Firm A is the upstream firm and firms B and C are the downstream firms. There exists one reciprocal direct and horizontal minority shareholding between firms B and C, and one indirect one-way vertical minority shareholding of firm A in firm B. Given the active minority shareholding of firm A in firm C, the former indirectly holds a passive minority shareholding in firm B.

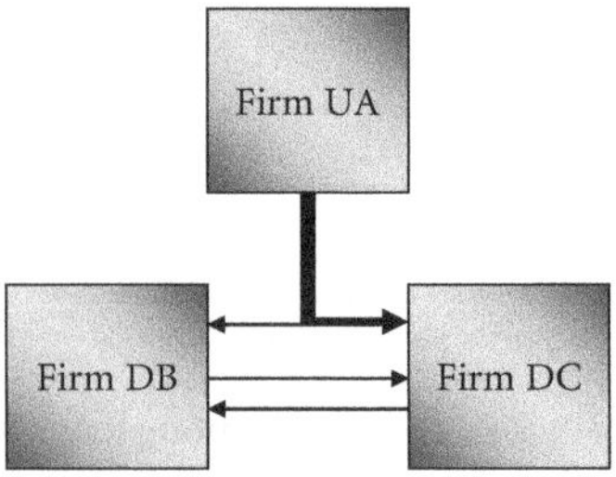

Notes:
U, upstream; D, downstream;
Active minority shareholding;
Passive minority shareholding.

Figure 5: Indirect and direct minority shareholdings between three firms in a vertical market

The striking feature of Figure 6 with respect to Figure 3 is the reduction in the number of independent firms in both the horizontal and vertical markets. The existence of active minority shareholdings of firms UA, UC & DB in firms UB & DA, UD and DC, respectively, has reduced the number of independent firms from eight in Figure 3 to four in Figure 6.

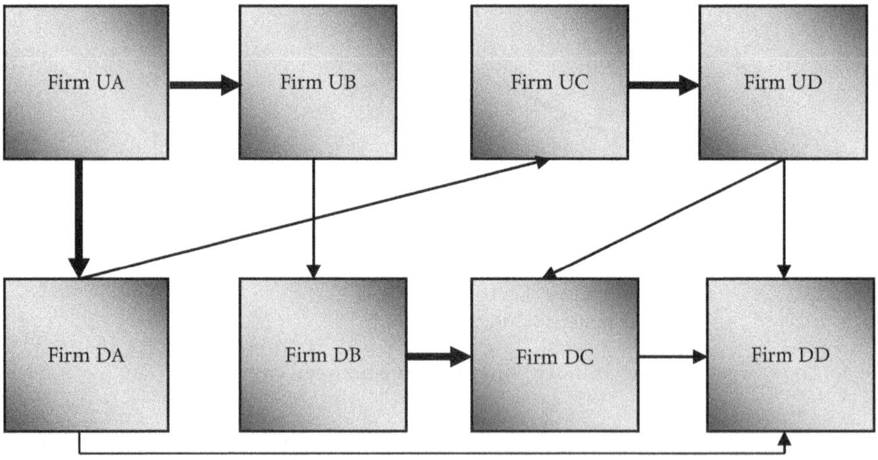

Notes:
U, upstream; D, downstream;
Active minority shareholding;
Passive minority shareholding (10%).

Figure 6: Active and passive minority shareholdings between firms in horizontal and vertical markets

Firm UA owns two indirect minority shareholdings. In particular, it owns a horizontal minority shareholding in firm UC and a vertical minority shareholding in firm DD. In addition, firm UC owns a vertical minority shareholding in firm DC and firm DB owns a horizontal minority shareholding in firm DD.

In addition, Figure 6 reveals the existence of six one-way direct minority shareholdings, both horizontal and vertical. Firm DA owns one horizontal one-way direct minority shareholding in firm DD and one vertical one-way direct minority shareholding in firm UC. Firm UD owns two vertical one-way direct minority shareholdings in firms DC and DD, while firm UB owns one vertical one-way direct minority shareholding in firm DB and firm DC owns one horizontal one-way direct minority shareholding in firm DD.

In some cases an arrangement exists among individuals that is referred to as 'deputization' in which different individuals who represent a single individual or a corporation may be appointed to different competitors' boards on behalf of this single individual/corporation.[43]

C. Other Forms of Minority Interests

i. Interlocking Directorships

Minority shareholdings are not the only forms of minority interests. Interlocking directorships constitute another form of minority interests. Interlocking directorships/directorates refer to situations where competitors either in horizontal or in vertical markets share one or more directors.[44] Common members that serve on boards of directors of competitors can be directors, top executives, non-executives, managers and close relatives, eg spouses and parents, of them (Figure 7).

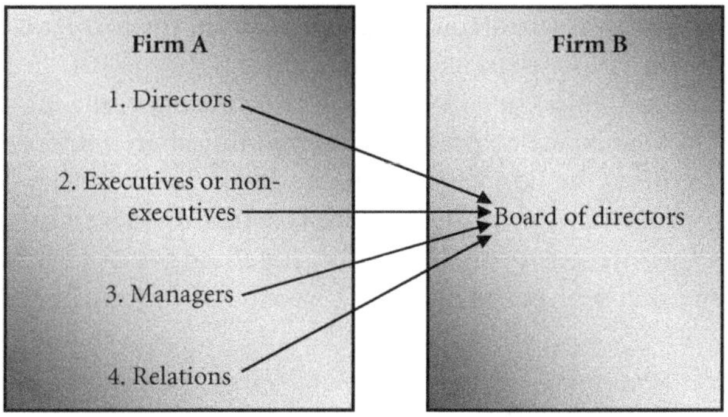

Figure 7: Forms of interlocking directorships

[43] See ME Jacobs, 'Combating Anticompetitive Interlocks: Section 8 of the Clayton Act as a Template for Small and Emerging Economies' (2014) 30 *Fordham International Law Journal* 643, 649.

[44] Above n 17, 23.

As in the case of minority shareholdings there are various forms of interlocking directorships. They can be grouped together in active or passive, horizontal or vertical,[45] direct or indirect, and one-way or reciprocal. In some circumstances officers of firms may hold a seat on the board of directors of competitors. This kind of interlocking directorship is called a management interlock.[46] However, it seems not to raise concerns when competitors share common officers without involving directorships. This kind of interlock is called a 'manager to manager interlock' and will not be discussed further here.[47]

ii. Shareholdings with Access to Crucial Information

In section B.i above we state that there are circumstances where the owner of a passive minority shareholding may receive crucial information[48] about a 'victim' firm's main operations. This statement is reinforced when the owners of minority shareholdings are able to sit on competitors' boards of directors.[49]

The term minority shareholdings with access to crucial information refers to the situation where the owner of the passive minority shareholding has the right to put a member of its firm, eg a director, an executive or non-executive member of the board of directors or a manager, on to the board of directors of its competitors with the right to have access to these competitors' commercial or confidential information. The right is due to the shareholder agreement regarding the acquisition of the passive minority shareholding. This is a mixed form of minority interest, but very important in terms of competition concerns since its owner not only holds a financial interest, but also enjoys the right to draw upon crucial information about it competitors.[50]

The degree of material influence of the 'victim's' competitive strategy stems from the fact that the minority shareholder may have the ability to block certain decisions, eg in circumstances of supermajority (a requirement for a proposal to gain a specified greater level of support than a more than 50 per cent), either on its own or by forming coalitions with the other shareholders. In the latter case the minority shareholder indirectly enjoys more decisive influence over the 'victim's' strategic behaviour than in the former case since the voting rights of the coalition are more than its corresponding rights.

However, the material influence over the strategic behaviour of a 'victim' may be restrained by legal provisions which protect the remaining shareholders of the 'victim' firm. A simple example of this is the fiduciary obligation scenario. 'Fiduciary obligation refers to a scenario in which control by the acquiring firm is constrained by legal rules that create an obligation to serve the interests of the minority shareholders, in particular those with no other holdings.'[51] In other words, the board of directors of the 'victim' firm must behave as

[45] See P Arreda and H Hovenkamp, *Antitrust Law: An Analysis of Antitrust Principles and their Application*, 3rd edn (New York, Aspen, 2010) para 1300, 327.

[46] See also P Arreda and DF Turner (eds), *Antitrust Law* (Boston, Little Brown and Company, 1978).

[47] Above n 44, 23 and BA Hawk and HL Huser, '"Controlling" the Shifting Sands: Minority Shareholdings under EEC Competition Law' (1994) 17 *Fordham International Law Journal* 294, 295.

[48] Above n 29.

[49] See also SF Ennis, 'Competition and Governance: Minority Shareholdings in Small Countries' (2012) 1 *CPI Antitrust Chronicle* 1, 3 and OECD, *Definition of Transaction for the Purpose of Merger Control Review* (2013), DAF/COMP(2013)25, 1, 204. See especially Case IV/34.410 *Olivetti/Digital* (ch 5).

[50] See also Cases M.1673 *VEBA/VIAG*, IV/M.1080 *Thyssen/Krupp* and the Chilean case *Matte Group/Copec SA* (ch 5).

[51] Above n 27, 580.

an independent firm. An example of this is the case where the board appointees of minority shareholders can vote but not in the self-interest of their employers.[52]

Competitive concerns may be stronger in cases where interlocks involve managers rather than directors. Managers who sit on competitors' boards of directors may more easily understand the day-to-day organization of the 'victim' firm than other directors and therefore enjoy more decisive influence over the 'victim's' strategic behaviour. As a result, managers can more easily understand issues that are being considered by the board and act in the interest of their employers.

D. Minority Interests in Mixed Oligopoly Markets

i. The Concept of Mixed Oligopoly Markets

We have so far presented minority interests which are limited to private firms only. However, there are cases of minority interests between private and public or state-owned firms. We call these minority interests in mixed oligopoly markets.[53]

A minority interest in mixed oligopoly markets may be seen as another style of privatization of public or state-owned firms.[54] The state, in the presence of a minority interest, may prefer not to fully privatize a stated-owned firm but rather to choose the optimal level of privatization through a passive minority shareholding. A minority interest in a public firm by a private firm may also signal to the market the profit objectives of state-owned firms.

ii. Public Firms as the Usual 'Victims'

In addition, a partially privatized firm may alter the strategic interactions of the other firms, both private and public, in the market. A private competitor may find it profitable to acquire a passive minority interest in a partially privatized firm since the latter has signalled to its rivals its objectives. This, in turn, may lead to a wave of mergers among the firms in the market.[55] A public firm may also be the victim of a potentially partial acquisition by a private firm. In any case, the presence of state-owned firms in a market offers the opportunity for private firms to enrich their portfolio with passive minority interests in state-owned firms.

In Figures 8 and 9 we depict minority interests in mixed duopoly horizontal and vertical markets, respectively. Since this form of minority interests may exist in markets with more than two firms, the reader should re-examine Figures 3–7 above by replacing one or more private firms with public or state-owned firms.[56]

In Figure 8 we examine the case of mixed horizontal duopoly markets. Figure 8a depicts a direct one-way minority shareholding and Figure 8b shows a direct reciprocal minority shareholding.

[52] Ibid.

[53] See R Jain and Pal R, 'Mixed Duopoly, Cross-Ownership and Partial Privatization' (2012) 147 *Journal of Economics* 45, 46 and footnotes therein. See also ch 5, section I below.

[54] See also F Trivieri, 'Does Cross-Ownership Affect Competition? Evidence from the Italian Banking Industry' (2007) 17 *Journal of International Financial Markets, Institutions and Money* 79.

[55] Above n 53, 81.

[56] For instance, in Figure 4 replace firm C or firm A with a state-owned firm. In which case there exists a partially privatised firm.

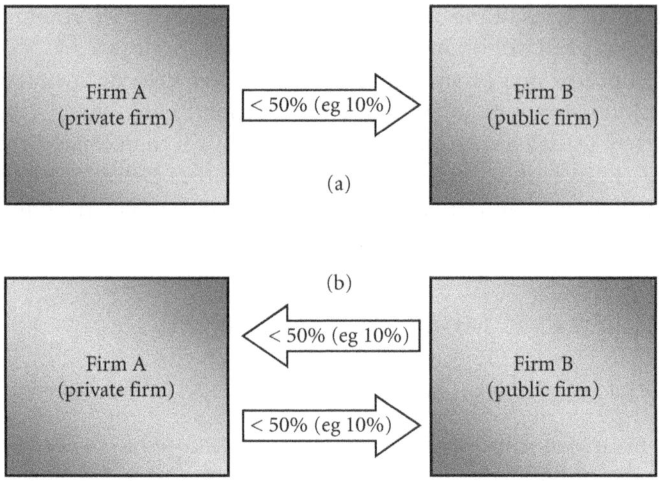

Figure 8: Direct, one-way and reciprocal minority shareholdings between two firms in a mixed horizontal market

In addition, in Figure 9 we examine the case of mixed vertical duopoly markets. Figure 9a depicts a direct one-way minority shareholding and Figure 9b shows a direct reciprocal minority shareholding.

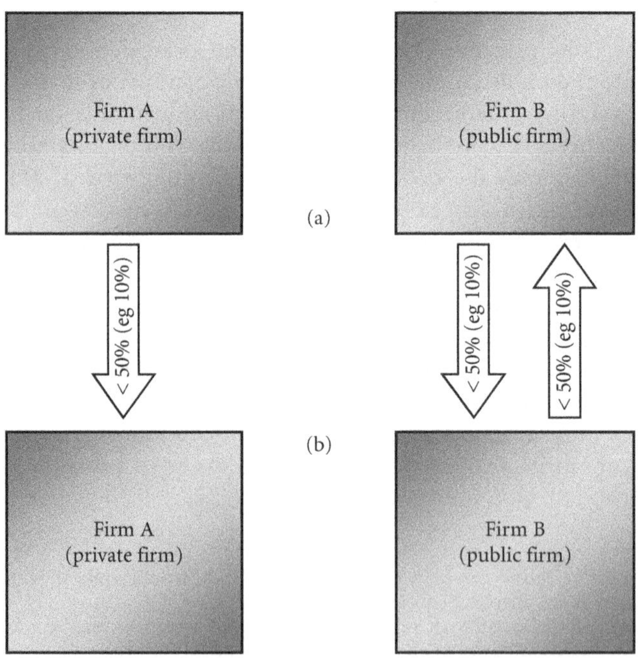

Figure 9: Direct, reciprocal minority shareholdings between two firms in a mixed vertical market

The passive minority interests of Figures 8b and 9b are called reciprocal minority shareholdings in horizontal (Figure 8b) and vertical (Figure 9b) markets. A feature of Figures 8b and 9b is the existence of passive minority shareholdings of which the owners are not private, but public firms. In both cases a state-owned firm acquires part of the equity capital of a private firm.

E. Domestic versus Foreign Minority Interests

i. Useful Definitions and Principles

A domestic minority interest is a minority shareholding in a firm which is based in the locality.[57] That is, suppose that a researcher is interested in analysing minority interests in country X and within the country there are n domestic firms. If a foreign firm, eg a firm that is based outside country X, acquires a minority interest in a domestic firm, then this interest is called a domestic minority interest. In addition, a domestic minority interest exists if $n-1$ domestic firms hold passive minority shareholdings in each other. In this case the 'victim' firms are the domestic firms.

ii. Examples

However, suppose that country X is not the only country in the world, but there exists another country, Y. Within country Y there are p foreign firms. If a domestic firm, ie a firm that is based outside country Y, eg in country X, acquires a minority interest in a foreign firm, then this interest is called a foreign minority interest. In addition, a foreign minority interest exists if $p-1$ foreign firms hold passive minority shareholdings in each other. In this case the 'victim' firms are the foreign firms.

The critical point of a domestic (foreign) minority interest is whether the foreign (domestic) firm is active in the domestic (foreign) country and especially in the domestic (foreign) market in which the minority interest takes place. The existence of a foreign (domestic) firm in the domestic (foreign) market before the minority interest is taken raises horizontal competitive concerns since the foreign firm is a direct competitor of the domestic firms. However, if the foreign (domestic) firm does not exist in the domestic (foreign) market before the minority interest is taken, then the latter consists of an external expansion of the foreign firm in a new country and a new market as well. Following the terminology of section B.ii above, the minority interest is then termed a conglomerate minority interest.

The above-mentioned principles of domestic and foreign minority interests apply both within and outside the EU. Suppose that country X is part of the EU single market, then if a foreign firm, ie a firm based outside the EU, acquires a minority interest in a firm based in X, then this interest is called a domestic minority interest. Conversely, if a domestic firm, ie a firm based eg in the EU, acquires a minority interest in a foreign firm, a firm based outside the EU, then this interest is called a foreign minority interest. Again, the critical point regarding the assessment of a domestic minority interest is whether the firm is active in the EU before the acquisition of the minority interest.

[57] See also H Ono, T Nakazato, C Davis and W Alley, 'Partial Ownership Arrangements in the Japanese Automobile Industry; 1990–2000' (2004) VII(2) *Journal of Applied Economics* 355.

F. Other Financial Forms of Minority Interests

i. General Remarks

Loans, derivatives and other financial instruments, such as bonds and leases,[58] may be used by firms and individuals as other forms of minority interests. In section B above we present some useful financial concepts which enable us here to proceed to an in-depth analysis of how certain financial products constitute minority interests.

ii. Loans

Loans can be either a contract between a lender and a borrower or can take the form of a direct acquisition of a certain amount of a firm's liability, such as debt. The former constitutes a bilateral agreement between two firms or among firms. The latter contains an issuer and a holder of a debt, such as government, local institutions, firms and individuals.

Loans and debt are firms' obligations and they constitute firms' liabilities.[59] Liabilities are divided into current liabilities, such as short-term liabilities that a firm has coming due in the next financial year (accounts payable,[60] short-term loans, short-term part of long-term borrowing,[61] wages, taxes); long-term debt, such as long-term loans or long-term bonds issued to financial markets, in which case the creditors are the investors in the bond; and other long-term liabilities, such as leases, employee benefits (pensions, healthcare programmes, deferred taxes).[62]

Loans among horizontal competitors are of great importance in terms of competition policy. Such loans create a strong link among these competitors since the lender has concerns about the ability of the borrower to pay back the amount of the loan plus interest and the borrower has concerns about its profits. The financial performance of the borrower also affects the lender since a potential inability of the borrower to raise profits will adversely affect the lender's financial position.

In addition, a bilateral agreement among firms or an acquisition of a debt[63] may offer the lender a chance to learn about the way in which the borrower firm capitalizes its assets in order to make profits and to fulfil its day-to-day needs. That is, a firm may acquire critical information about a rival's strategic decisions without any of the obligations of board membership or equity investment.

Bonds are types of loans. Firms lend money to the 'victim' firm when they acquire its bonds.[64] The 'victim' firm must pay interest and repay the principal of the loan. A secured bond is more important in terms of competition concerns than an unsecured bond. A secured bond gives the right to the supplier of the loan to acquire certain assets of the 'victim' firm if the latter cannot repay the loan, while an unsecured bond guarantees the

[58] Above n 8.

[59] See generally A Damodaran (ed), *Investment Valuation: Tools and Techniques for Determining the Value of Any Asset*, 3rd edn (New York, John Wiley, 2012).

[60] Credit received from vendors or other suppliers to firms.

[61] The portion of long-term debt that is coming due in the next financial year.

[62] Taxes that have to be paid in later years are reported in the liabilities as deferred taxes.

[63] Gillette, the leader in the wet-shaving razor blade market, acquired approximately 13.6 per cent of the debt of Wilkinson Sword. See especially *United States v Gillette Co*, 55 FR 28312 (1990) and D Gilo, Y Moshe and Y Spiegel, 'Partial Cross Ownership and Tacit Collusion' (2006) 37(1) *Rand Journal of Economics* 81.

[64] See Case IV/M.754 *Anglo American Corporation/Lonrho* (ch 5).

repayment only by the creditworthiness of the 'victim' firm. Therefore, as in the case of derivative securities, a secured bond may be seen as a future minority interest.

iii. Derivatives

Derivative securities are payoffs the price of which is determined by other financial instruments such as stock or bond prices. One of the primary goals of derivatives is to hedge risks (making an investment to reduce the risk of adverse price movements in an asset) or transfer risks to other firms. A call option gives the opportunity to the holder to reap a payoff when the 'exercise price' is higher than the stock price. The payoff equals the difference between the exercise price and the stock price. An example of derivative securities playing a critical role in determining if a minority shareholding may materially influence the economic/strategic behaviour of the victim is contained in Canada's merger control review process (see chapter 3, section I.C).

In terms of competition policy, derivative securities may be seen as future minority interests. That is, their holders maintain the right to acquire a portion of the equity capital of other firms in the future. This acquisition depends on the financial situation of the 'victim' firm and its ability to increase its value in the short run.

Leases are contractual agreements among lessees and lessors. The contract establishes that the former have the right to use an asset for which it must pay periodic payments to the owners of this asset, the lessors. Capital leases are the most important types of leases in terms of competition concerns.[65] The lessee assumes some of the risks of ownership and enjoys some of the benefits, while the lease is recognized both as an asset and as a liability on the balance sheet. The firm gets to claim depreciation on the asset and also deducts from tax liability the interest expense component of the lease payment each year for the duration of the lease.[66]

Two other special types of leases which may raise competitive concerns are sale and lease-back and leveraged leases. Sale and lease-back occurs when a firm selles an asset to another firm and immediately leases it back. The leveraged lease type is a three-sided agreement among the lessee, the lessor and the lender of the asset. The lessee pays periodic payments to the owner of this asset, the lessor, who puts up no more than the 50 per cent of the purchase price of the asset. The remainder is financed by the lender who receives interest payments from the lessor.

iv. The Commission's Approach

According to the Commission's Consolidated Jurisdictional Notice, 'purely financial agreements, such as sale-and-lease-back transactions with arrangements for a buyback of the assets at the end of the term, do not normally constitute a concentration as they do not change control over the management and the resources'.[67] Also, according to the same Notice, 'franchising agreements as such do not normally confer control over the franchisee's business on the franchisor'.[68]

[65] Common types of leases are operating leases and the financial leases. Both of these types do not assume the risk of ownership since the lessor transfers only the right to use the property to the lessee. In this case the cost of the lease is treated as an operating expense in the income statement and it does not affect the balance sheet of the lessee.

[66] A lease is termed as a capital lease if, inter alia, (a) it exceeds 75 per cent of the life of the asset, (b) there is a transfer of ownership to the lessee at the end of the contract and (c) there is an option to purchase the asset at a 'bargain price' at the end of the contract.

[67] Above n 18, para 19.

[68] Ibid.

III. Final Remarks

The analysis so far has revealed that minority interests are complex and take on various forms in different market structures. The researcher should be aware of this complexity and carefully examine case by case the characteristics that determine the minority interest under scrutiny.

For this reason in Figure 10 we display the different concepts of minority interests mentioned in this chapter so that the reader can easily understand the category in which the minority interest under scrutiny is classified.

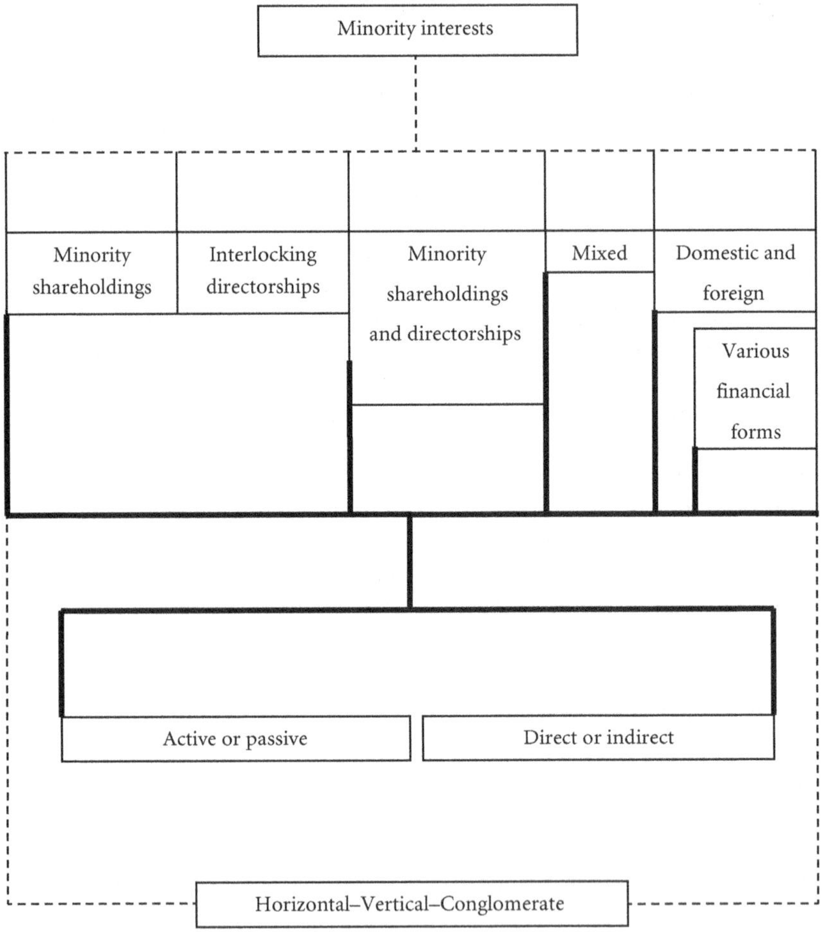

Figure 10: Different concepts of minority interests

3

Minority Interests Under Merger and Antitrust Law

I. Minority Interests Under Merger Law

In this chapter we analyse minority interests under both merger and antitrust law. In section I we will present the treatment of minority interests under merger law. In particular, in section I.A we will focus our analysis in order to present minority interests under the scope of EU Merger Regulation, while in section I.B we will present them in the context of the national laws of the Member States. In section I.C we continue with our analysis by presenting the treatment of minority interests in selected national laws around the world (outside the EU) and in section I.D we will explicitly define them in terms of US merger law. In section II we will analyse minority interests in the context of Articles 101 and 102 TFEU. For simplicity we will use the terms minority interest and minority shareholding interchangeably throughout our analysis in order to capture the mechanisms under which a financial interest falls mainly under the scope of merger law and Articles 101 and 102 TFEU.

Before we proceed in more detail to the treatment of minority shareholdings let us first define the criteria which are used by different jurisdictions in order to delineate the notion of merger transaction. There are, in fact, two major types of criteria, *objective* and the *economic* criteria. However, any combination of the two may be found and as we will see in the following sub-sections there are jurisdictions that use a broad definition of merger transaction which includes any acquisition of shares or assets (see, for example, US law—section 7 of the Clayton Act, 15 USC § 18).

The most prominent example of *objective* criteria is the percentage rule, according to which the acquisition of a specific percentage interest in a 'victim' firm (eg 5–50 per cent) is considered to be a merger transaction and is subject to the merger control system. In Germany and Austria an acquisition of 25 per cent of the capital or the voting rights of another undertaking constitutes, inter alia, a merger transaction under the German merger control regime.[1] In most cases, and especially in merger transactions where the acquired interest in a victim is low (ie under 20 per cent), the percentage rule is accompanied by other specific provisions which may enhance the relationship of the two or more firms involved in the transaction. These provisions include the presence of interlocking directorships or the type of the shareholder that acquires the interest (if it holds the highest interest in the victim or is among the largest shareholders in it).

[1] For more details see sub-section B below.

Economic criteria, on the other hand, aim to define a merger transaction in terms of its competitive harm. Even though they are broadly similar, jurisdictions around the world use different criteria such as *decisive influence* or *material influence*. One prominent example is the notion of decisive influence which falls under the scope of the EU Merger Regulation[2] and has been adopted by many other merger control regimes within or outside the EU. Other regimes have adopted less demanding concepts of influence such as the concept of *material influence* in the UK and the concept of *competitively significant influence* in Germany.[3]

As a general rule, active or controlling minority shareholdings fall under the scope of merger notification systems while passive or non-controlling minority shareholdings are not subject to the majority of control systems found worldwide. Under the EU Merger Regulation[4] the Commission cannot examine minority shareholdings in stand-alone investigations. However, in some national merger laws there are provisions regarding the acquisitions of minority shareholdings in competitors, but the majority of them do not incorporate such provisions in their merger notification systems. In that case, the regulation of passive minority shareholdings falls under the mechanism of antitrust law.

Exceptions to this rule are pre-existing minority shareholdings. This form of minority shareholding exists in the context of a notified consolidation and therefore may be analysed regarding its anti- or pro-competitive effects within the notified transaction. For instance, a national competition authority or the Commission could order the divestiture of the pre-existing minority shareholding if it is found to be anticompetitive. Where a minority shareholding is acquired after the examination of a notified transaction, the competition authority lacks the competence to review this acquisition.

In the subsequent sections we will present the treatment of minority shareholdings under the EU Merger Regulation and around the world. In particular, in section I.A we will review the EU Merger Regulation in order to clarify whether the acquisitions of minority shareholdings fall under its scope or not, and in section I.B we will perform the same exercise regarding existing merger law across Member States. Following this section we will show whether the US has incorporated the control of the acquisition of minority shareholdings into its merger law. In section I.C we will present the legal system in the US regarding mergers and we will try to answer the question whether the US has adopted special provisions in its merger law regarding the acquisitions of minority shareholdings in competitors.

A. The Treatment of Minority Interests Under the Scope of the EU Merger Regulation

In chapter 2, section II.A we presented the definitions of active and passive minority shareholdings, and following on from the previous section of this chapter we note here that active along with pre-existing minority shareholdings are the only forms of minority interests that fall under the scope of the EU Merger Regulation. Active minority shareholdings

[2] For more details see the following sub-section.

[3] Poland had a similar concept in its merger control regime, but it was removed in 2007.

[4] Council Regulation (EC) No 139/2004 of 20 January 2004 on the control of concentrations between undertakings [2004] OJ L24, 1–22.

fall directly and pre-existing minority shareholdings fall indirectly under the scope of this Regulation.

An active minority shareholding exists if it satisfies the major prerequisites of the EU Merger Regulation. In particular, the merger notification system in the EU has three pillars: (a) the notion of concentration, (b) the existence of acquisition of control, and (c) the dimension of the notified transaction. According to the Commission Consolidated Jurisdictional Notice, 'a concentration only covers operations where a change of control in the undertakings concerned occurs on a lasting basis'.[5] That is, 'the concept of concentration is intended to relate to operations which bring about a lasting change in the structure of the market'.[6] The notion of concentrations also applies to joint ventures, which perform 'on a lasting basis all the functions of an autonomous economic entity'.[7]

Article 3(1) of EU Merger Regulation[8] considers two different types of concentrations: 'those arising from a merger between previously independent undertakings' and 'the acquisition, by one or more persons already controlling at least one undertaking, or by one or more undertakings, whether by purchase of securities or assets, by contract or by any other means,[9] of direct or indirect control of the whole or parts of one or more other undertakings'.[10]

Furthermore,

> Control shall be constituted by rights, contracts or any other means which, either separately or in combination and having regard to the considerations of fact or law involved, confer the possibility of exercising decisive influence on an undertaking, in particular by:
>
> (a) ownership or the right to use all or part of the assets of an undertaking;
> (b) rights or contracts which confer decisive influence on the composition, voting or decisions of the organs of an undertaking.[11]

According to the Commission Consolidated Jurisdictional Notice:

> It is ... not necessary to show that the decisive influence is or will be actually exercised. ... the possibility of exercising that influence must be effective.[12] Article 3(2)[13] further provides that the possibility of exercising decisive influence on an undertaking can exist on the basis of rights, contracts or any other means, either separately or in combination, and having regard to the considerations of fact and law involved. A concentration therefore may occur on a legal or a de facto basis, may take the form of sole or joint control, and extend to the whole or parts of one or more undertakings.[14]

[5] Commission Consolidated Jurisdictional Notice under Council Regulation (EC) No 139/2004 on the control of concentrations between undertakings [2008] OJ C95/01, para 7.

[6] Ibid.

[7] Ibid, para 3(4).

[8] Above n 4.

[9] Such as 'situations where the change of control results from the inheritance of a shareholder or where the exit of a shareholder triggers a change of control, in particular a change from joint to sole control'. Above n 5, para 21.

[10] Ibid, para 8.

[11] Ibid, para 3(2).

[12] See the judgment in Case T-282/02 *Cementbouw v Commission* [2006] ECR II-319, para 58.

[13] Of Council Regulation (EC) No 139/2004.

[14] Above n 5, para 16.

The acquisition of control is established in Article 3(3) of the EU Merger Regulation, according to which:

> Control is acquired by persons or undertakings which:
>
> (a) are holders of the rights or entitled to rights under the contracts concerned; or
> (b) while not being holders of such rights or entitled to rights under such contracts, have the power to exercise the rights deriving therefrom'.

The Commission when assessing if an acquisition of control occurred is concerned only with issues that determine the business strategy of the undertaking(s) concerned in the notified transaction and is not concerned with issues regarding their day-to-day management or with veto rights which have the purpose of protecting the minority shareholders. Also, the acquisition of control may be on a contractual basis. According to paragraph 18 of the Commission Consolidated Jurisdictional Notice: 'In order to confer control, the contract must lead to a similar control of the management and the resources of the other undertaking as in the case of acquisition of shares or assets.' Examples of such contracts are lease contracts and rights to use specific assets of the undertaking(s) concerned since they may lead to a structural change in the market if they are very long lasting.[15]

Control may be sole or joint control. 'Sole control is acquired if one undertaking alone can exercise decisive influence on an undertaking.'[16] De jure or on a legal basis sole control is normally established when 'an undertaking acquires a majority of the voting rights of a company'.[17] It 'is normally acquired on a legal basis where an undertaking acquires a majority of the voting rights of a company'.[18] In addition, a 'qualified minority' may be established on a legal basis when specific voting rights, ie preferential shares that enable their shareholder to appoint the majority of the management board, result in their holder determining the strategic behaviour of the undertaking concerned.[19]

De facto sole control or sole control on a de facto basis is normally established when 'the shareholder is highly likely to achieve a majority at the shareholders' meetings, given the level of its shareholding and the evidence resulting from the presence of shareholders in the shareholders' meetings in previous years'.[20] Moreover, a 'qualified minority' may be established on a de facto basis where

> the shareholder is highly likely to achieve a majority at the shareholders' meeting, given that the remaining shares are widely dispersed .... In such a situation it is unlikely that all the smaller shareholders will be present or represented at the shareholders' meeting.[21]

Other transactions that may lead to de facto sole control may be long-term supply agreements with specific structural links among the businesses concerned.

[15] Acquisition of control can be established by national company law and purely economic relationships. For both of these, see ibid, paras 22 and 20, respectively.

[16] Ibid, para 54.

[17] Ibid, para 56.

[18] Commission Notice on the concept of concentration under Council Regulation (EEC) No 4064/89 on the control of concentrations between undertakings [1998] OJ C66, para 13. See also Case M.397 *Ford/Hertz* and Case M.970 *TKS/ITW Signode/Titan* (ch 5).

[19] Commission Notice, ibid, para 14. See also the analysis in Case M.093 *Apollinaris/Schweppes* (ch 5).

[20] See n 14, para 59.

[21] Ibid. See also the analysis in Case M.397 *Ford/Hertz* (ch 5).

Joint control may be established when 'two or more undertakings or persons have the possibility of exercising decisive influence over another undertaking'.[22] In order for joint control to be successful the shareholders of the undertakings involved or the persons 'must reach a common understanding in determining the commercial policy of the joint venture and that they are required to cooperate'.[23] As in the case of sole control, joint control can be either de jure or de facto joint control.

However, a 'deadlock situation' may appear, namely a situation where two or more parent undertakings have the power to block decisions regarding the strategic behaviour of the joint venture, and the main reason for such a situation is the veto rights.[24] The presence of veto rights causes the parent undertakings of the joint venture to be mutually dependent on each other. In order to avoid a 'deadlock situation' the parent undertakings of the joint venture must seek for consensus, which will force them to agree on a common policy in favour of the joint venture.[25]

Joint control can exist when the shareholders of two parent undertakings possess equal or unequal portions of the voting rights of the joint venture or there are more than two parent undertakings. If the parent undertakings own equal shares of votes, then according to paragraph 64 of the Commission Consolidated Jurisdictional Notice they must set up the shareholding agreement in such a way as to be able to deal with any deadlock situations that may arise.

If the parent undertakings own unequal shares of the votes in the joint venture, ie 'minority shareholders have additional rights which allow them to veto decisions which are essential for the strategic commercial behaviour of the joint venture',[26] then these shareholders have to reach a mutual consensus regarding strategic business decisions. In addition, paragraphs 74 and 75 of the Commission Consolidated Jurisdictional Notice stipulate that a joint venture may be established even though a shareholder owns the majority of the voting rights. For example a shareholder who owns 80 per cent of the voting rights of a firm may prefer to act collectively with the shareholder who owns the remaining 20 per cent of the voting rights of the same firm, either by entering a shareholder agreement or by creating a special-purpose vehicle.

Lastly, a joint venture may be established when the parent undertakings exhibit common interests.[27] The burden of proof of a so-called de facto joint venture depends on the undertakings concerned, which must prove that their common interests will have a lasting basis.[28] For example, a 'shifting alliance' or a 'changing coalition', ie a joint venture where it is not possible to determine ex ante which shareholders will form a majority regarding its strategic behaviour, in the absence common interests among shareholders, cannot

[22] Ibid, para 62. Decisive influence in the presence of joint control means the ability of the undertakings concerned to block actions which affect the commercial behaviour of an undertaking.

[23] Ibid.

[24] With the term veto rights we mean veto rights over the budget and the business plan, major investments which indicate control or decisions that alter the management of the joint venture. This type of right is different from veto rights, which are seen as normal minority protections (decisions over the sale, the winding-up or changes to the capital structure of the undertaking concerned). See the analysis of veto rights in ch 2 and the case law presented in ch 5.

[25] See, inter alia, GD Pini, 'Passive–Aggressive Investments: Minority Shareholdings and Competition Law' (2012) 23 *European Business Law Review* 575, 583.

[26] See n 5, 65.

[27] Ibid, paras 76–77.

[28] See, inter alia, Case COMP/M.2066 *Dana/Getrag*.

be treated as a concentration under the EU Merger Regulation, unless the undertakings concerned prove that a de facto joint venture exists.

Regarding the dimensionality of a concentration within the EU, Article 1(2) of the EU Merger Regulation declares that a concentration has a Community dimension if:

> (a) the combined aggregate worldwide turnover of all the undertakings concerned is more than EUR 5000 million;
>
> and
>
> (b) the aggregate Community-wide turnover of each of at least two of the undertakings concerned is more than EUR 250 million,
>
> unless each of the undertakings concerned achieves more than two-thirds of its aggregate Community-wide turnover within one and the same Member State.

However,

> A concentration that does not meet the thresholds laid down in paragraph 2 has a Community dimension where:
>
> (a) the combined aggregate worldwide turnover of all the undertakings concerned is more than EUR 2500 million;
> (b) in each of at least three Member States, the combined aggregate turnover of all the undertakings concerned is more than EUR 100 million;
> (c) in each of at least three Member States included for the purpose of point (b), the aggregate turnover of each of at least two of the undertakings concerned is more than EUR 25 million; and
> (d) the aggregate Community-wide turnover of each of at least two of the undertakings concerned is more than EUR 100 million,
>
> unless each of the undertakings concerned achieves more than two-thirds of its aggregate Community-wide turnover within one and the same Member State.

Even though pre-existing minority shareholdings exist in the context of a notified consolidation and therefore are not initially subject to the EU Merger Regulation, their assessment follows the same pillars as the assessment of active minority shareholdings. The Commission has dealt with a great number of pre-existing minority shareholdings, which will be discussed in chapter 4.

In conclusion, the EU Merger Regulation deals only with active and pre-existing minority shareholdings that satisfy the three above-mentioned pillars of merger notification system in the EU, namely (a) the notion of concentration, (b) the existence of acquisition of control, and (c) the dimension of the notified transaction. That is,

(a) they may confer 'decisive influence' in terms of the EU Merger Regulation, and so give rise to a concentration;
(b) they may confer a share in joint control, once more giving rise to a concentration;
(c) they can feature in substantive analysis of a concentration without themselves being the basis for jurisdiction (pre-existing minority shareholdings).[29]

[29] See AJ Burnside, 'Minority Shareholdings: An Overview of EU and National Case Law' (2013) 13 *Bulletin e-Competitions Minority Shareholdings* Art No 56676, 1, 1–2.

Apart from these, all the other types of minority shareholdings which constitute so-called passive minority shareholdings are not captured under the current regulation, but are examined under the mechanism of Articles 101 and 102 TFEU. That is,

(a) they are applicable under Article 101 TFEU as an agreement by which a minority shareholding is acquired;
(b) they are applicable under Article 102 TFEU as long as the firm which acquires a minority shareholding possesses a dominant position.

B. The Treatment of Minority Interests across Member States

Only a minority of Member States has adopted rules that control the acquisitions of minority interests. Germany, the UK, Austria and Lithuania have already adopted national merger control rules that give them the competence to review minority shareholdings.

i. Germany

The merger control regime in Germany is contained in sections 3–47 of the Act against Restraints of Competition (ARC).[30] The competent authority for the application of this regime is the Federal Cartel Office (FCO). According to Article 37 ARC, German merger control applies if a concentration exists. Establishing the existence of a concentration is based on consideration of the following conditions:

1. acquisition of all or of a substantial part of the assets of another undertaking (Section 37(1) No 1 ARC);
2. acquisition of direct or indirect control by one or several undertakings of the whole or parts of one or more other undertakings. Control shall be constituted by rights, contracts or any other means which, either separately or in combination and having regard to the considerations of fact or law involved, confer the possibility of exercising decisive influence on an undertaking, in particular through
   a) *ownership or the rights to use all or part of the assets of the undertaking (Section 37(1) No 2(a) ARC),*
   b) *rights or contracts which confer decisive influence on the composition, voting or decisions of the organs of the undertaking (Section 37 (1) No 2(b) ARC);*
3. acquisition of shares in another undertaking if the shares, either separately or together with other shares already held by the undertaking, reach
   a) ***50 percent*** (Section 37(1) No 3(a) ARC) or
   b) ***25 percent*** (Section 37(1) No 3(b) ARC)[31]

   of the capital or the voting rights of the other undertaking. The shares held by the undertaking shall include also the shares held by another for the account of this undertaking and, if the owner

[30] Gesetz gegen Wettbewerbsbeschränkungen in der Fassung der Bekanntmachung vom 15.7.2005 (BGBl. I S. 2114; 2009 I S. 3850), zuletzt geändert durch Artikel 1 u. Artikel 4 Absatz 2 des Gesetzes vom 5. Dezember 2012 (BGBl. I S. 2403).

[31] Emphasis added.

of the undertaking is a sole proprietor, also any other shares held by him. If several undertakings simultaneously or successively acquire shares in another undertaking within the parameters mentioned above, this shall be deemed to also constitute a concentration among the acquiring undertakings with respect to those markets on which the other undertaking operates;

4. *any other combination of undertakings enabling one or several undertakings to directly or indirectly exercise a* ***competitively significant influence*** *on another undertaking* (Section 37(1) No 4 ARC).

From section 37 ARC it follows that minority shareholdings are captured when an acquisition of shares reaches 25 per cent of the target's capital (section 37(1) no 3(b) ARC) or any other combination of undertakings are found to exercise a *competitively significant influence* on another undertaking (section 37(1) no 4 ARC).

Section 37(1) no 3(b) ARC has no relevance as to whether or not the acquirer confers decisive influence on the target of the acquisition.

Regarding Section 37(1) no 4 ARC, the threshold for *competitively significant influence* is assumed to catch any other transaction which involves share acquisitions below 25 per cent. That is,

> A competitively significant influence on another undertaking may exist due to any kind of link between two or more undertakings that allows the acquiring party to influence the competitive behaviour of the target in such a way that it is likely to reduce competition between the undertakings, to the degree that they will no longer act independently on the market.[32]

A minority shareholding of less than 20 per cent of the target's capital is generally not assumed to influence the competitive behaviour of the target in an anticompetitive manner,[33] and assessment of the influence must be based not only on economic evidence through supply or financial agreements, but also on corporate law.[34]

Furthermore, section 37(1) no 4 ARC applies to any other form of concentration regulated in the ARC and came into force in order to control acquisitions close to or below the threshold laid down in section 37(1) no 3(b) ARC. A minority shareholding is assumed to exert a competitively significant influence on the target's ordinary business because 'the majority shareholder will take into account the minority shareholder's view' and 'the minority shareholder must be in a position to exert its own business interests'.[35]

Interlocking directorships may also suffice for the creation of a concentration. In the *Xella Baustoffe* case[36] the German competition authority considered that a call option of 50 per cent of the shares of the target firm in association with a right of the acquired firm to

[32] See OECD *Antitrust Issues Involving Minority Shareholdings and Interlocking Directorates* (2008), DAF/COMP(2008)30, 1, 113.

[33] See A Toth, 'TEU Competition Law Aspects of Minority Shareholdings' (2012) 35(4) *World Competition* 599, 604.

[34] See JP Schmidt, 'Germany: Merger Control Analysis of Minority Shareholdings—A Model for the EU?' (2013) 2 *Concurrences* 207, 208.

[35] Ibid.

[36] See Activity Report 2007/2008 of the German competition authority.

appoint a member to its management board might suffice to create a competitively significant influence.[37]

A transaction constitutes a concentration within the meaning of the ARC if the worldwide consolidated turnover of all participating undertakings exceeds €500 million. Additionally, at least one participating undertaking must have a domestic turnover in Germany of more than €25 million and at least one other participating undertaking must have a domestic turnover in Germany of more than €5 million.

There is an exemption from the notification system relating to the size, in terms of turnover, of the participating undertakings. The exemption applies if one undertaking, including any subsidiaries, which is not controlled by another undertaking, has a worldwide turnover of less than €10 million in the last financial year. The FCO 'accepts the application of this exemption in case of the acquisition where the aggregate worldwide turnover of the seller's group remains below €10 million'.[38] The purpose of this acceptance is to protect the sale of the companies in favour of their owners.[39]

ii. UK

In the UK the merger control system is contained in the Enterprise Act 2002 (EA). In contrast to the EU Merger Regulation, in the UK there is no system of mandatory notification of consolidations. Consolidations are notified on a voluntary basis to the Office of Fair Trading (OFT), which either accepts the notified transaction or refers it to the Competition Authority (CC) for an in-depth investigation.[40] Hence, the UK system is completely different not only to the EU law system but also to most other national systems.[41]

Under sections 23 and 33 EA merger control applies if 'two or more enterprises[42] have ceased to be distinct enterprises' (section 23(1) EA) and 'arrangements are in progress or in contemplation which, if carried into effect, will result in a creation of a relevant merger situation' (section 33(1)(a) EA). Under section 26(1) EA enterprises cease to be distinct enterprises if they are brought under common ownership or control. There are three types of control: de jure control, de facto control and material influence control (section 26(2)–(4) EA).[43]

[37] See also cases OLG Düsseldorf, decision of November 12, 2008, VI-Kart 5/08, *A-TEC/Norddeutsche Affinerie*, WuW/E DE-R 2462.

[38] See M Dietrich, P von Hülsen and T Wessing, 'Germany: Merger Control' [2014] *European Antritrust Review* s 3: country chapters.

[39] Ibid.

[40] This does not apply for mergers in the water industry where either the acquirer or the victim of the merger each has a turnover exceeding £10 million. This exception is under s 32 Water Industry Act, which came into force in 1991. Water mergers are subject to mandatory notification to the CC.

[41] The OFT and the CC were responsible for protecting consumer interests throughout the UK until the end of March 2014. Both of them closed on 1 April 2014 with their responsibilities passing to Competition and Market Authority (CMA). Throughout this book and for reasons of convenience we will use the terms OFT, CC and CMA interchangeably.

[42] Activities or part of activities of a business (s 129 EA).

[43] See para 11 of the OFT's decision regarding Case ME/4694/10 *Ryanair/Aer Lingus* and the analysis presented in ch 5, section I.B.

In particular, section 26(4) of the EA states that,

> For the purposes of subsection (1),[44] in so far as it relates to bringing two or more enterprises under common control, a person or group of persons may be treated as bringing an enterprise under his or their control if
>
> (a) being already able to control or materially to influence the policy of the person carrying on the enterprise, that person or group of persons acquires a controlling interest in the enterprise or, in the case of an enterprise carried on by a body corporate, acquires a controlling interest in that body corporate; or
> (b) being already able materially to influence the policy of the person carrying on the enterprise, that person or group of persons becomes able to control that policy.

Material influence of control is the lowest degree of an acquisition that can cause enterprises affected to cease to be distinct. What constitutes material influence is based on a case-by-case analysis by reference to the facts. The OFT has declared that a minority shareholding of 25 per cent or more will trigger the merger control mechanism, even though there are cases where a minority shareholding of less than 25 per cent may be subject to scrutiny if there exist facts that confer material influence.

Other factors that play a substantive role in deciding if a minority shareholding may confer material influence are the degree of dispersion of the shares, special rights and restriction on voting rights, the representation of the acquirer on the target's board of directors, the existence of any agreement between acquirer and victim, etc.

Any transaction is subject to review under the EA if the turnover and the share of supply test are met. That is, the turnover in the UK of the victim must exceed £70 million (the turnover test) and a 25 per cent share of supply of goods or services are created due to merger in the UK or a substantial part of it (the share of supply test).

In particular, section 23(1)–(4) states that:

1. For the purposes of this Part, a relevant merger situation has been created if
   a) two or more enterprises have ceased to be distinct enterprises at a time or in circumstances falling within section 24; and
   b) the value of the turnover in the United Kingdom of the enterprise being taken over exceeds £70 million.
2. For the purposes of this Part, a relevant merger situation has also been created if
   a) two or more enterprises have ceased to be distinct enterprises at a time or in circumstances falling within section 24; and
   b) as a result, one or both of the conditions mentioned in subsections (3) and (4) below prevails or prevails to a greater extent.
3. The condition mentioned in this subsection is that, in relation to the supply of goods of any description, at least one-quarter of all the goods of that description which are supplied in the United Kingdom, or in a substantial part of the United Kingdom
   a) are supplied by one and the same person or are supplied to one and the same person; or
   b) are supplied by the persons by whom the enterprises concerned are carried on, or are supplied to those persons.
4. The condition mentioned in this subsection is that, in relation to the supply of services of any description, the supply of services of that description in the United Kingdom, or in a substantial part of the United Kingdom, is to the extent of at least one-quarter

[44] S 26(1) EA.

a) supply by one and the same person, or supply for one and the same person; or
b) supply by the persons by whom the enterprises concerned are carried on, or supply for those persons.

If the OFT believes that the concentration under consideration may be expected to result in a substantial lessening of competition within the market or the markets concerned in UK, then the merger is referred to the CC under section 22(1) EA. The latter states that:

1. The OFT shall, subject to subsections (2)[45] and (3),[46] make a reference to the Commission if the OFT believes that it is or may be the case that
   a) a relevant merger situation has been created; and
   b) the creation of that situation has resulted, or may be expected to result, in a substantial lessening of competition within any market or markets in the United Kingdom for goods or services.

iii. Austria

In Austria the relevant merger control legislation is the Cartel Act (CA),[47] which came into force in 2005. As a complement to the CA, the Competition Act (Wettbewerbsgesetz) contains some procedural rules.

A concentration is defined in section 7 CA. In particular, a concentration is defined as

the acquisition of an undertaking or a major part thereof, especially by merger or transformation;

the acquisition of rights in the business of another undertaking by management or lease agreement;

the (direct or indirect) acquisition of shares, if thereby a shareholding of 25 per cent or 50 per cent is attained or exceeded;

the establishment of interlocking directorships whereby at least half of the management or members of the supervisory boards of two or more undertakings are identical;[48]

any other concentration by which a *controlling influence*[49] over another undertaking may be exercised; and

the establishment of a full-function joint venture.

It is evident from the above-mentioned definitions of concentrations that the acquisition of a minority shareholding of 25 per cent or more constitutes a legal concentration.

45 The OFT may decide not to make a reference under this section if it believes that (a) the market concerned is not, or the markets concerned are not, of sufficient importance to justify the making of a reference to the Commission; or (b) any relevant customer benefits in relation to the creation of the relevant merger situation concerned outweigh the substantial lessening of competition concerned and any adverse effects of the substantial lessening of competition concerned.

46 Subsection (3) provides that the OFT is prevented from making a reference to the CC if (a) the merger involves a newspaper transfer; (b) the OFT has accepted (or is considering accepting) undertakings in lieu of a reference in relation to the same transaction; (c) the deadline for reference has passed; (d) the merger was referred to the CC before it was completed; (e) the merger raises a public interest consideration(s) and either an intervention notice is in force, or the case has been determined; and (f) the merger is the subject of a request by the UK under Art 22(3) Merger Regulation to the Commission, and the Commission is either considering the request, proceeding with a case in pursuance of the request, or has dealt with the matter in response to the request.

47 Especially ch 3 of part I of the CA (Kartellgesetz).

48 Emphasis added.

49 Ibid.

A concentration within the meaning of section 7 CA has to be notified to the competition authority if

> the combined aggregate worldwide turnover of the undertakings concerned exceeded €300 million,
> the combined aggregate turnover on the Austrian market of the undertakings concerned exceeded €30 million,
> the worldwide turnover of at least two of the undertakings concerned was at least €5 million each.

There are three specific exemptions from the above-mentioned pre-merger notification system, which cover transactions that have not material influence based on the following criteria: (a) only one undertaking involved achieved turnover in Austria of more than €5 million and (b) the other undertaking(s) involved achieved an aggregate turnover of not more than €30 million worldwide.

iv. Lithuania

In Lithuania the relevant merger control legislation is the Law on Competition, as amended in 2004 (Articles 10–15) and Resolution No 45 of 27 April 2000 on the approval of the procedure for submission and examination of notification on the concentration and of the calculation of aggregate turnover (the Merger Regulation). According to Article 3(15) of the Law on Competition:

> 'Control' means any rights arising from laws or contracts that entitle a legal or natural person to exert a decisive influence on the activity of the undertaking, including:
>
> 1. ownership or the right to use all or part of the assets of the undertaking,
> 2. other rights which confer decisive influence on the decisions or the composition of the undertaking's managing bodies.

Article 3(12) states that:

> 12. 'Group of associated undertakings' means two or more undertakings which, due to their mutual control or interdependence and possible concerted actions are considered as one undertaking when calculating joint income and market share. Unless proved otherwise, a group of associated undertakings shall be deemed to be comprised of every undertaking concerned and:
>
> 1. of undertakings in which, as in the undertaking concerned, the shareholding of one and the same natural person or the same natural persons accounts for more than 1/4 of the authorised capital or carries more than 1/4 of all the voting rights;
> 2. undertakings which are subject to joint management or have a joint administrative subdivision with the undertaking concerned or a half or more of whose supervisory board, administrative board or other management body members are also members of the management bodies of the undertaking concerned;
> 3. undertakings in which the shareholding of the undertaking concerned accounts for more than 1/4 of the authorised capital or more than 1/4 of all the voting rights or which have a commitment to co-ordinate decisions relating to their economic activity with the undertaking concerned, or those undertakings the responsibility for the meeting of whose obligations to third parties has been assumed by the undertaking concerned, or those undertakings which have undertaken to transfer all or part of their profit or have transferred the right to dispose of more than 1/4 of their assets to the undertaking concerned;
> 4. undertakings whose shareholding in the undertaking concerned accounts for more than 1/4 of the authorised capital or more than 1/4 all the voting rights, or with which the undertaking concerned has committed itself to co-ordinate decisions relating to its economic activity, or

which have assumed the responsibility for meeting the obligations of the undertaking concerned to third parties, or those to which the undertaking concerned has undertaken to transfer all or part of its profit or has granted the right to dispose of more than 1/4 of its assets,

5. undertakings connected directly or indirectly through other undertakings with the undertakings referred to in subparagraphs 1, 2, 3 and 4 of paragraph 12 hereof in any way specified in subparagraphs 1, 2, 3 and 4 of paragraph 12 hereof.

Therefore, it is clear from Article 3(12)(4) that acquisitions of more than 25 per cent of assets or voting rights fall within the definition of control. Even though acquisitions of less than 25 per cent of assets or voting rights do not fall within the definition of control, if the minority shareholder could be shown to exercise decisive influence on the target, then it might also fall within the definition of control.

According to Article 10(1) of the Law on Competition:

> The intended concentration must be notified to the Competition Council and its permission shall be required where combined aggregate income of the undertakings concerned is more than LTL 30 million for the financial year preceding concentration and the aggregate income of each of at least two undertakings concerned is more than LTL 5 million for the financial year preceding concentration.

v. *Other Member States*

(a) Italy

In Italy the relevant merger control legislation is Law No 287 of the Italian Competition Act (ICA), which came into force in 1990. In particular, sections 5–7 and 16–19 set forth the rules for merger control. Section 1(4) ICA requires that the national competition rules and merger control must be interpreted in accordance with the principles of EU competition law. In practice, the Commission's Consolidated Jurisdictional Notice is generally applied by the ICA when assessing national merger cases.

The definition of concentration is given in section 5(1) ICA. A concentration occurs when:

(a) two or more undertakings merge (two or more undertakings amalgamate into a new undertaking (merger in the strict sense), or one or more undertakings are absorbed by another (merger through incorporation));
(b) undertaking or a physical person already controlling an undertaking acquire direct or indirect control of the whole or parts of one or more undertakings; or
(c) two or more undertakings create a joint venture through the establishment of a new company, provided that the joint venture is not of co-operative nature.

The notions of 'undertaking' and 'control' under the ICA are substantially construed in accordance with the EU Merger Regulation. In particular, the definition of control includes any legal or factual situation whereby one undertaking can exercise (including jointly with another party) a *decisive influence* on the strategic commercial behaviour of another undertaking. Therefore, the acquisition of a minority shareholding does not amount to a consolidation according to the ICA. The latter applies to the acquisition of minority shareholdings only when they confer de jure or de facto control over another undertaking.

A minority shareholding may confer joint control over an undertaking by virtue of the provisions which have been laid down in the shareholding agreement or in other contractual arrangements. It may confer sole control over an undertaking if, for example, the remaining shares of the undertaking are widely dispersed or the minority shareholder could exercise a decisive influence over the strategic behaviour of the victim.

Section 5(2) ICA states that the acquisition of a purely financial interest does not constitute a concentration. A purely financial interest is defined as an acquisition involving a financial institution acquiring shares in an undertaking with the intention of reselling those shares on the market. The same holds in France, where

> a purely temporary acquisition of securities by financial institutions with a view of reselling them to a third party within a maximum of one year after their acquisition does not constitute a concentration.[50]

The jurisdictional thresholds for the application of merger control in Italy are (a) the turnover of all the companies' Italian operations exceeds €482 million and (b) the turnover of the target companies in Italy exceeds €48 million (section 16 ICA).

As already noted, Italy has recently adopted Law Decree 6/2011, ratified by amendments by Law 214/2011, which came into force on 28 December 2011, in order to deal with interlocking directorships in the financial sector. In particular, section 36 of the Law prohibits interlocking directorships on the boards of credit, insurance and financial companies in order to improve competitiveness in the financial sector. Section 31(1) of the Law declares that:

> 1. No member of management boards, supervisory boards and statutory board of auditors, as well no executive officer, of companies or corporate groups which are active on the markets for banking, insurances and finance shall, at the same time, serve in 'corresponding' positions in competing companies or corporate groups.
> 2. For the purpose of Paragraph 1, 'competing companies or corporate groups' shall mean companies or corporate groups which are not in any relationship of control within the meaning of Section 7 of the Italian Antitrust Law and which are active on the same product and geographic markets.
>
> 2 bis. Where paragraph 1 is applicable, the person concerned shall have an option to choose [one of the offices] within 90 days from the appointment;[51] where the option is not exercised, the person concerned shall be dismissed from any of such offices; the termination shall be declared by the competent corporate bodies within 30 days from the expiration of the above time-limit or from the date the infringement was acknowledged. In case of failure to act by the competent corporate body, the termination shall be declared by the Surveillance Authority of the market concerned.
>
> 2 ter. For the first application of the Decree, the 90 days time-limit is extended to 120 days as from the entry into force of the ratifying Law.[52]

The introduction of this law has raised some concerns and critical questions regarding the exact definition of the competing companies or the relevant market under scrutiny.

[50] See C Lemaire and S Naudin, *France—Merger Control 2014* (London, ICLG, 2014).

[51] Though for the first application of the Decree this time-limit is extended to 120 days as from the entry into force of the ratifying law.

[52] See also A Baccini and L Marrni, 'In the Shadow of the Interlocking Directorates Regulation. A Comparative Case Study' (2013) 683 *Quaderni del Dipartimento di Economia Politica E Statistica, Universita di Siena* 1, 4.

However, this topic is beyond the scope of this book and we will not analyse it further here. Reader who are interested in this topic may consult the working paper by Baccini and Marrni[53] and the footnotes therein.

Articles 5–7 and 16–19 of Law No 287 of 10 October 1990 contain the merger control regime in Italy. Article 7 provides a definition of control which refers to the notion of controlled companies in the Italian civil code. According to Article 7, the term 'controlled companies' refers, inter alia, to 'companies in which another company has, directly or indirectly, including through fiduciary companies, sufficient voting rights to exercise a dominant influence in its shareholders' meetings; and companies that are under dominant influence of another company by virtue of contractual links'.

Recently Italy has adopted Law Decree 6/2011, ratified by amendments by Law 214/2011 which came into force on 28 December 2011, in order to deal with interlocking directorships in the financial sector. Even though in Italy it is acknowledged that competitive effects may arise from the presence of pre-existing minority shareholdings, the merger guidelines do not take these into account.

(b) Poland

In Poland minority interests, both minority shareholdings and interlocking directorships, constituted legal concentrations for the period from 2000 to 2007. In particular, the Act of 2000 stated that a concentration is defined, inter alia, if:

(a) taking over or acquisition of stocks or shares of another undertaking resulting in achieving at least 25 percent of votes at a general assembly or assembly of partners;
(b) assuming by the same person the function of a member of the managing or controlling body of the competing undertakings.

During the period 2000–07 only 10 per cent of all merger cases fell into the category of passive minority interests.[54] However, the introduction of the new Antimonopoly Act in 2007 (AA)[55] removed both minority shareholdings and interlocking directorships from the notification obligation.

(c) Ireland

In Ireland the relevant merger control legislation is the Competition Act 2002 (CA). Section 16(1) CA provides that a consolidation occurs if:

two or more undertakings, previously independent of one another, merge;

one or more individuals or other undertakings who or which control one or more undertakings acquire direct or indirect control of the whole or part of one or more other undertakings; or

the result of an acquisition by one undertaking (the first undertaking) of the assets, including goodwill, (or a substantial part of the assets) of another undertaking (the second undertaking) is to place the first undertaking in a position to replace (or to substantially replace) the second

[53] Ibid.
[54] See OECD, *Definition of Transaction for the Purpose of Merger Control Review* (2013), DAF/COMP(2013)25, 1, 142.
[55] See Arts 4(4) and 13(2) of the Act on Competition and Consumer Protection 2007 (Journal of Laws of 2007, no 50, item 331).

> undertaking in the business or, as appropriate, the part concerned of the business in which that undertaking was engaged immediately before the acquisition.[56]

The definition of merger control in the AC follows the EU Merger Regulation and EU practice in interpreting the meaning of merger control. Therefore, merger control will arise where *decisive influence* can be exercised in relation to the activities of the undertaking acquired.

Mergers and acquisitions are subject to mandatory notification to the Competition Authority (The Competition Authority and the National Consumer Agency merged in October 2014 to form the Competition and Consumer Protection Commission). The jurisdictional thresholds for such a notification are the following (section 18(1)(a) CA, as substituted by section 55(a) of the Competition and Consumer Protection Act 2014):

> (a) the aggregate turnover in the State of the undertakings involved is not less than €50,000,000, and,
> (b) the turnover in the State of each of two or more of the undertakings involved is not less than €3,000,000.[57]

As already noted, the CA acknowledges the competitive effects that may arise from the presence of pre-existing minority shareholdings. In particular, section 1.11 of the merger guidelines states that:

> The Authority's analysis of a notified merger will also consider competitive effects that may arise where any one or more of the merging parties have non-controlling minority shareholdings in third parties prior to the merger.

(d) France and Belgium

In all the other competent authorities across the EU an acquisition of a minority shareholding is treated as a consolidation only if it leads to a change of the control over the target. For example, merger control in France follows the basic pillars of the EU Merger Regulation. Control is defined as the possibility of exercising a decisive influence over the conduct of an undertaking and an acquisition of a minority shareholding amounts to a consolidation if it results in a change of control. The same holds in Belgium. An acquisition of a minority shareholding is caught by the Code of Economic Law (CEL), which defines the Belgian merger control regime, if it gives rise to a change of control, ie if the acquisition confers veto rights over strategic company decisions such as the business plan and the budget.[58]

(e) Greece

Greek merger control follows the legislation and practice of the EU Merger Regulation. Law 3959/11 (on the protection of free competition)[59] is the new competition law in Greece,

[56] See also T Burke, N Collins and J Kettle, 'Ireland' in *Getting the Deal Through—Merger Control* (London, Law Business Research, 2013).

[57] See Irish govt website (www.tca.ie/EN/Mergers--Acquisitions/When-to-Notify.aspx).

[58] See also the definition of control in s 12(a) of the Danish Competition Act.

[59] See P Fotis, 'Merger Enforcement: Law and Statistical Evidence Worldwide' (2013) 5 *International Journal of Economics and Business Research* 272, 273.

replacing law 703/1977.[60] The merger control applicable in the media sector (television, radio, newspapers and magazines) is law 3592/2007, which sets out specific provisions applicable in relation to transactions in this sector, the calculation of turnover and market share.

Merger control under Law 3959/11 is dealt with in Articles 5–10.[61] According to Article 5(2) a concentration arises where (a) there exists a merger between two or more previously independent undertakings (or parts of such undertakings); and (b) one or more persons already controlling at least one undertaking, or one or more undertakings, acquire, directly or indirectly, control over the whole or parts of one or more other undertakings. In addition, under Law 3959/11, the acquisition of control over a 'full-function' joint venture constitutes a concentration which must be notified to the competition authority where the relevant jurisdictional thresholds are met.

Article 5(3) of Law 3959/11 defines that control is derived from rights, contracts or other means which, either separately or in combination, and having regard to the considerations of fact or law involved, confer the possibility of exercising decisive influence on the activities of an undertaking.

A minority shareholder may be deemed to have sole control on a de facto basis (a) when a minority shareholder is given specific rights or (b) when a minority shareholder is highly likely to achieve a majority at the shareholders' meeting (eg where the balance of shares is widely spread).

An acquisition of a minority shareholding gives rise to a concentration if it confers de facto sole control or confers sole or joint control, since a minority shareholder has the power to block actions which determine the strategic behaviour of the target.

A concentration is applicable to merger control in Greece if certain jurisdictional thresholds are satisfied. In particular, Article 6(1) of the merger control system states that a transaction must be notified to the Hellenic Competition Commission (HHC) if:

(a) the combined aggregate worldwide turnover of the participating undertakings amounts to at least 150 million euro; and
(b) each of at least two of the participating undertakings has an aggregate turnover of at least 15 million euro in Greece.

Regarding transactions in the media sector, Law 3592/2007 states that the turnover thresholds in (a) and (b) above are €50 million and €5 million, respectively.

(f) The Remaining Member States

The same notions of concentration, control and minority interests as in France, Belgium and Greece are found under the Competition Act (Law 19 2012) in Portugal; under the Law on Protection of Competition in Bulgaria; under the Control of Concentrations between Undertakings Law 22(I) of 1999 in Cyprus (107(I) 1999, 154(I) 2000); under the merger control regime set out in Act No 143/2001 (on the Protection of Competition) in the Czech Republic; under the Merger Regulation in the Competition Act (Consolidation Act No 700 of 18 June 2013, as amended by Acts No 620 of 12 June 2013 and No 639 of 12 June 2013) in

[60] Law 3959/11 was amended by law 4072/2012; however, the amendments concerning merger control only relate to certain sanctions for failure to cooperate with the Hellenic Competition Commission's inquiries.

[61] Ibid, paras 273–75.

Denmark; under the amended Competition Act in June 2013 in Finland; under the merger control system in the Competition Act (Act LVII of 1996 on the Prohibition of Unfair and Restrictive Market Practices) in Hungary; under the Republic of Latvia Competition Law; under the merger legislation laid down in the Competition Act in the Netherlands; under the Competition Act of 2013 in Croatia; under the merger control legislation in Romania;[62] under the merger control legislation set out in the Act on the Protection of Competition (Act No 136/2001), as amended, in Slovakia; under the merger control legislation contained in the Prevention of the Restriction of Competition Act of 2008 in Slovenia; under the merger control legislation contained in the Competition Act on Defence of Competition (Law 15/2007 of 3 July) in Spain; under the merger legislation in the Competition Act (Konkurrenslag (2008:579)) in Sweden; under the Competition and Consumer Affairs Authority Act (Chapter 510 of the Laws of Malta) in Malta; and under the Competition Act (Konkurentsiseadus) which came into force in October 2001, and was amended in July 2013, in Estonia.

The merger control legislation in Luxemburg is contained in the Law on Competition (Mémorial A 2011, no 218 p 3755), which came into force in February 2012. The Law of Competition of 2011 has replaced the corresponding Law of 2004. The 2011 Law contains no specific provisions regarding concentrations or minority interests. Concentrations that lead to an abuse of a dominant position and joint ventures that lead to an agreement prohibited by Articles 3 and 5 of the 2011 Law are examined under it. Additionally, in the 2011 Law there are no provisions regarding the notion of control or specific jurisdictional thresholds. Sanctions may be imposed if a concentration violates the 2011 Law.

In conclusion, passive minority interests are subject to merger control in only four Member States: Germany, the UK, Austria and Lithuania. Table 1 summarizes the merger control regimes with respect to minority interests in these four Member States.

C. The Treatment of Minority Shareholdings Around the World

The enforcement practice of minority shareholdings varies around the world. Some national authorities impose notification thresholds and other agencies may intervene on a case-by-case analysis even though they 'do not confer control and are not in and of themselves notifiable'.[63]

Some national authorities require a filing of an acquisition of any level of minority interest and others require a filing of an acquisition of a minority interest if certain thresholds or other criteria are met. We begin by looking at merger control systems involving the first type of filing, and then present the second type of filing of an acquisition of a minority interest.

[62] Such as law no 21/1996 on competition, as amended, Regulation on concentrations ('Merger Regulation') approved by the Romanian Competition Commission (RCC) order no 385/2010, as amended, and various guidelines approved by the RCC (nos 386/2010, 387/2010, 400/2010, as amended, nos. 419/2010, 420/2010, 688/2010, 421/2011, as amended), and Regulations approved by the RCC (no 426/2011, as amended, and no 668/2011).

[63] See P Lugard, 'Minority Shareholdings under Antitrust Law: A Regulatory Gap?' (2012) 1 *CPI Antitrust Chronicle* 1, 8.

Table 1: Passive minority interests under merger control regimes in Germany, the UK, Austria and Lithuania

Member States	Concentration—Control	Jurisdictional thresholds
Germany	1. 25% (section 37(1) no 3(b) ARC)—*legal concentration* 2. <25% (section 37(1) no 4 ARC)	1. €500 million (worldwide consolidated turnover of all participating undertakings); and 2. €25 million (domestic turnover of at least one undertaking); and 3. €5 million (domestic turnover of at least one other participating undertaking)
UK	1. Material influence control (section 26(4) EA)	1. £70 million (the turnover test—target's turnover in the UK); and 2. 25% share of supply of goods or services (the share of supply test—ie the share of supply created due to a merger in the UK)
Austria	1. 25% (section 7 CA)—*legal concentration* 2. The establishment of interlocking directorships whereby at least half of the management or members of the supervisory boards of two or more undertakings are identical 3. Any other concentration by which a controlling influence over another undertaking may be exercised	1. €300 million (worldwide consolidated turnover of all participating undertakings); and 2. €30 million (consolidated turnover of all participating undertakings in the Austrian market); and 3. €5 million each of at least two participating undertakings (worldwide consolidated turnover)
Lithuania	1. 25% (Article 3(12) LC)—*legal concentration* 2. <25% (decisive influence)	1. more than LTL (litras) 50 million (combined aggregate income of the undertakings concerned); 2. more than LTL (litras) 5 million (aggregate income of each of at least two undertakings concerned)

Notes: ARC, Act against Restraints of Competition; EA, Enterprise Act; CA, Cartel Act; LC, Law on Competition.

i. Ecuador

In Ecuador merger control legislation is contained in section 4 (Articles 14–24) of the Organic Law for Regulation and Control of Market Power (OLRCMP). The notion of concentration includes (a) mergers; (b) assignment of all 'effects of a trader'; (c) direct or indirect acquisition of the ownership of or any right in shares, equity shares or debt securities that give any rights of being converted into shares or equity shares or have any influence on the decisions of the person who issued when such acquisition gives the acquirer the control of or substantial influence over that person; (d) an interlocking joint administration; and (e) any other agreement or deed that may transfer factually or legally to a person or 'economic group' assets of an economic operator or gives it 'control' or influence over the adoption of ordinary or special management decisions of an economic operator.

The jurisdictional thresholds provided by the OLRCMP are classified into two categories: in the case where the companies are horizontal competitors a concentration must be notified if after its clearance the merged entity holds 30 per cent or more of the relevant product or service market in the country, or in a defined geographic market within the country. In addition, a concentration must also be notified if the combined turnover of the concerned companies in the concentration in Ecuador exceeds, in the accounting year previous to the transaction, the level of basic unified salaries (*salarios básicos unificados*) established by the Regulation Board. 'Unified basic remunerations are a measure of value linked to the regime of salaries in Ecuador and are expressed in US dollars—the legal tender in Ecuador.'[64]

ii. El Salvador

In El Salvador merger control is contained in the country's Competition Law (CL), which came into force in 2007. Chapter 4 of the CL states in Article 31 that:

> [M]erger and acquisitions are considered to exist when:
>
> (a) Economic agents that have been independent from each other enter into: acts, contracts or agreements, with the purpose of totally of *partially*[65] merging, acquiring, consolidating, integrating, or combining their businesses; and,
>
> (b) when one or more economic agents who control at least one other economic agent acquire through any means whatsoever, the direct or indirect, total or partial control of more economic agents.

The definition of control is given in Article 32 CL. In particular,

> For the legal effects, control shall be understood as the capability of an economic agent to exert influence over another by exercising property rights, or the right of use, of all or part of the economic agent's assets or by means of agreements that grant a substantial influence in the composition, voting or decision making of the Boards and management bodies or the legal representatives of the economic agent.

Both notions of a merger and control indicate that any part of the assets of the victim must be notified to the Superintendence, the competition authority in El Salvador.

The jurisdictional thresholds for a pre-merger notification, which is mandatory in El Salvador, are given in Article 33 CL. In particular,

> Mergers or acquisitions whose combined total assets exceed fifty thousand minimum urban annual wages in the industrial sector or whose total income exceeds sixty thousand minimum

[64] See D Pérez-Ordóñez and J Urízar in IK Gotts (ed), *Merger Control Review*, 4th edn (London, Law Business Research, 2013) 113.

[65] Emphasis added.

urban annual wages in the industrial sector shall request the Superintendence their prior authorization.[66]

iii. Egypt

In Egypt,

> Article 19-2 of the Competition Law introduced as an amendment to the original text of Law 3/2005 by virtue of Law 190/2008, each party having an annual turnover of more than E£100 million that acquires assets [approx USD 18,7000,000], proprietary rights, usufruct, shares or sets up a union, a merger, an amalgamation or a joint management transaction must notify the ECA [Egyptian Competition Authority] of the transaction within 30 days from its completion. Failure to notify the ECA will expose the acquiring party or the surviving entity of the merger in question to a fine that ranges between E£10,000 and E£100,000.[67]

iv. Brazil

Let us now present the type of filing of an acquisition of a minority interest when certain thresholds or other criteria are met. Especially, in Brazil Law No 8884/94 has been replaced by a Brazilian antitrust law (BAL, Law No 12.529/2011), which came into force on May 2012 and applies to all sectors of the economy. Merger control is contained in the BAL and in Resolution 1/2012 by the Administrative Council for Economic Defence (CADE).

According to Article 90 BAL, a concentration occurs if:

> (i) two or more companies or further independents merge; (ii) one or more companies acquire the control of a company or parts of a company, directly or indirectly, by purchasing or exchanging shares or assets; (iii) one or more companies incorporate other company or companies; and (iv) two or more companies enter into a contract of association or joint venture.
>
> According to article 9 of the mentioned Resolution, the acquisition of a shareholding shall be submitted to CADE for review in the following situations: (i) when the transaction results in control acquisition; (ii) when the transaction does not result in control acquisition, but the 'de minimis' rule established in article 10 is met; and (iii) when the acquisition is made by the controlling party.
>
> Regarding the mentioned 'de minimis' rule, article 10 of the mentioned Resolution defines that if the target company is not a competitor of the buyer and does not have activities in the upstream or downstream market, only acquisitions of 20 per cent or more shall be submitted for merger control review. The same article states that if the target company is a competitor of the buyer or has activities in the upstream or downstream market, only acquisitions of 5 per cent or more shall be submitted for merger control review.[68]

[66] Assets or revenue must be domestic. If the acquiring company is a foreign entity, but the victim company is domestic, the acquirer must get the Superintendency's authorisation. Notification is not needed if the companies have no domestic sales.

[67] See FE Samad in IK Gotts (ed), *Merger Control Review*, 3rd edn (London, Law Business Research, 2012) 158.

[68] See NO Felix and OF Advogados, *Brazil—Merger Control 2014* (London, ICLG 2014), available at http://www.iclg.co.uk/practice-areas/merger-control/merger-control-2014/brazil. See also OECD, *Definition of Transaction for the Purpose of Merger Control Review* (2013), DAF/COMP(2013)25, 1, 21. See also 'Merger Control: The International Regulation of Mergers and Joint Ventures in 77 Jurisdictions Worldwide' [2015] *Global Competition Review*, 1, 74.

> According to article 88 of Law n. 12.529/2011, Concentration Acts shall be submitted to CADE for review whenever the following objective criteria is present: (i) at least one of the groups involved in the transaction has had gross annual revenues or volume of business, in Brazil, larger than $750,000,000.00 reals in the preceding fiscal year; and (ii) at least one other group involved in the transaction has had gross annual revenues or volume of business, in Brazil, larger than $75,000,000.00 reals in the preceding fiscal year.[69]

It should be mentioned that CADE proposed in 2014 certain amendments in public consultation regarding its resolutions. Public Inquiry No 1 of 2014 proposed changes to CADE Resolution No 2 of 2012 and concerns, inter alia, notification of acquisitions of convertible bonds.

In particular, Public Inquiry No 1 of 2014 proposed the inclusion of a new Article 11 in CADE Resolution No 2 of 2012 concerning the notification of corporate bonds/debentures:

> [The] proposed new resolution establishes that such type of transaction must be notified to CADE if, upon conversion of the debentures, the transaction will meet the criteria applicable for notification of acquisition of shares, as currently set forth in CADE's resolution No 2/2012. In addition to the acquisition of convertible debentures, the proposed new resolution also provides CADE with the possibility to require, at its own discretion, the notification of the conversion of the debentures as well.[70]

The new Article 11 states that:

> The acquisition of bonds convertible into shares must be mandatorily notified at all times the future conversion into shares fits any of the events in items I or II of Article 10.
>
> 1. In the event of initial public offering of convertible bonds into shares, the bonds' acquisition is not conditional on receiving CADE's previous approval to close the deal, but the exercise of any political rights in connection with the acquired bonds is prohibited until the approval of the transaction by CADE.
> 2. Upon analyzing the transactions of bonds acquisition addressed by this Article, CADE may, by considering its convenience and opportunity, also establish the mandatory previous notification of the transaction of bonds' conversion.[71]

v. *India*

In India merger legislation is contained in the Competition Act of 2002 as amended in 2011. In addition, regulations concerning the concerned companies and general regulations of the Competition Committee in India, as amended in 2013 and 2011 respectively, accompany the merger legislation.

According to the Competition Act, section 5(a)(i) and (ii), the definition of control indirectly states that, except for a merger or amalgamation between companies, a transaction

[69] See especially 'Merger Control', ibid.

[70] See http://www.mayerbrown.com/publications/detailprint.aspx?publication=10075.

[71] Submission Regarding the Public Inquires No 1, 2 and 3/2014 International Bar Association Antitrust Committee (2014), available at http://www.ibanet.org/Document/Default.aspx?DocumentUid=339EB802-2A1B-4160-9A2C-CBEF08DA4AC9.

must be notified to the Competition Committee if control, shares, voting rights or assets of a company are being acquired by another company. This broad definition of concentration suggests that any acquisition of minority interest is subject to merger control. However, the Competition Commission of India (Procedure in Regard to the Transaction of Business Relating to Combinations) Regulations 2011, as amended up to 4 April, 2013, Schedule I, states that 'share acquisitions of up to 25 per cent are exempted if they are solely for investment purposes and do confer on the purchaser control over the target'.[72] Also,

> share acquisitions of up to 5 per cent in the target, where the purchaser already holds a 25 per cent or greater interest in the target, but only up to a 50 per cent interest and only if the incremental share acquisitions do not confer on the purchaser control over the target.[73]

However, 'an acquisition of an insignificant shareholding in a target could be notifiable if competing activities are carried out within the buyer's group'.[74]

The jurisdictional thresholds for a mandatory pre-notification system in India are as follows:[75]

(a) India Asset[76] Test: Whether the assets of (Acquirer + Target)/(Merging or Amalgamating parties) is greater than or equal to INR 1500 crore[77] (approximately USD 249.75 million or Euro 182.46.48 million) in India; or
(b) India Turnover Test: Whether the turnover of (Acquirer + Target)/(Merging or Amalgamating parties) is greater than or equal to INR 4500 crore (approximately USD 749.25 million or Euro 547.38 million) in India; or
(c) India Group[78] Asset Test: Whether the asset of [(Acquirer Group)/(Group to which merged/amalgamated parties will belong), including direct/indirect subsidiaries + Target company] is greater than or equal to INR 6,000 crore (approximately USD 999.01 million or Euro 729.84 million) in India; or
(d) India Group Turnover Test: Whether the turnover of [(Acquirer Group)/(Group to which merged/amalgamated parties will belong), including direct/indirect subsidiaries + Target company] is greater than or equal to INR 18,000 crore (approximately USD 29,970.014 million or Euro 21,895.14 million) in India; or
(e) Worldwide including India Asset Test: Whether the assets of (Acquirer + Target)/(Merging or Amalgamating parties) is greater than or equal to USD 750 million (worldwide) including at least INR 750 crore (approximately USD 124.88 million or Euro 91.23 million) in India; or

[72] OECD, *Definition of Transaction for the Purpose of Merger Control Review* (2013), DAF/COMP(2013)25, 25.

[73] Ibid, fn 59.

[74] See T Reeves and D Harrison, 'India's New Merger Control Regime: When Do You Need to File?' (2011) 26(1) *Antitrust* 94, 97.

[75] See A Kumar and F Sorabjee, *India—Merger Control 2015* (London, ICLG, 2014), available at http://www.iclg.co.uk/practice-areas/merger-control/merger-control-2015/india.

[76] The book value of the assets as of the financial year prior the notification of the transaction, as reduced by any depreciation.

[77] India's national currency, the rupee, is often given as crores, tens of millions (written 1,00,00,000) and lakhs, hundreds of thousands (written 10,00,000).

[78] A Group contains two or more companies which, directly or indirectly, are in a position to exercise 50 per cent or more of the voting rights in the other enterprise; or appoint more than 50 per cent of the members of the board of directors in the other enterprise; or control the management or affairs of the other enterprise. See s 5 of the Competition Act.

(f) Worldwide including India Turnover Test: Whether the turnover of (Acquirer + Target)/(Merging or Amalgamating parties) is greater than or equal to USD 2250 million (worldwide) including at least INR 2,250 crore (approximately USD 374.62 million or Euro 273.67 million) in India; or

(g) Worldwide including India Group Asset Test: Whether the asset of [(Acquirer Group)/(Group to which merged/amalgamated parties will belong) including direct/indirect subsidiaries + Target company] is greater than or equal to USD 3 billion (worldwide) including at least INR 750 crore (approximately USD 124.88 million or Euro 91.23 million) in India; or

(h) Worldwide including India Group Turnover Test: Whether the turnover of [(Acquirer Group)/(Group to which merged/amalgamated parties will belong) including direct/indirect subsidiaries + Target company] is greater than or equal to USD 9 billion (worldwide) including at least INR 2,250 crore (approximately USD 374.62 million or Euro 273.67 million) in India.[79]

However, there exists a target exemption from the provisions of section 5 of the Competition Act of 2002 for small targets if their assets are less than INR 250 crore (approximately US$43.75 million or €33.41 million) or their turnover is less than INR 750 crore (approximately US$131.23 million or €100.24 million) in India.[80]

vi. Japan

In Japan merger review is under the charge of the Merger and Acquisition Division, which is part of the Economic Affairs Bureau of the General Secretariat of the Fair Trade Commission of Japan (JFTC). Merger legislation is governed by the Antimonopoly Law (AL). More specifically, Article 9 AL prohibits a merger or an acquisition which may cause excessive concentration of economic power, while Article 11 AL prohibits a financial company (bank or insurance company) from acquiring more than 5 or 10 per cent, respectively, of the voting rights in a Japanese company, unless otherwise provided in the law (the notion of 'general concentration of economic power').

As well as the general concentration of economic power, there is also the notion of 'specific concentration' under the Antimonopoly Law, which is prohibited by this law since a specific concentration may substantially restrain competition in a particular field of trade (Article 10 AL).[81] A specific concentration may be divided into the following categories:

1. acquisition of stock (ie voting rights);
2. interlocking directorates;
3. merger (amalgamation);
4. acquisition of the entire or an important part of business/assets for business, etc;
5. company split involving a business combination;
6. joint stock transfer involving a business combination.

[79] Above n 72, 105.

[80] For more exemptions from the provision of s 5 of the Competition Act 2002, see ibid, 108–09.

[81] http://www.jftc.go.jp/en/legislation_gls/amended_ama09/amended_ama09_04.html.

A minority shareholding is deemed to be in a legal merger under the Antimonopoly Law in Japan if the following prerequisites are met:[82]

1. when the voting right ratio[83] held by the acquiring company in the acquired company exceeds 50 per cent;
2. when the voting right ratio held by the acquiring company in the acquired company exceeds 25 per cent, and the acquiring company stands alone as the leading holder of voting rights; or
3. when the voting right ratio held by the acquiring company, in the acquired company, exceeds 10 per cent, the acquiring company is ranked among the top three voting right holders, and a combination between the party companies is formed, maintained or strengthened through the given acquisition, which is determined by taking into consideration, among other things: (i) the extent of the ratio of voting rights to be held by the acquiring company; (ii) the rank as a voting right holder, differences in and distribution of the voting right ratios held among the holders; (iii) interlocking directorate; and (iv) transactions between such party companies.

For the filing requirements, 20 per cent is a minimum threshold for the voting right ratio … under the Antimonopoly Law. Therefore, minority shareholders may not be exempt from the filing requirements solely because they are a minority voting right holder.

Article 13 AL (interlocking directorates) states that:

1. Neither an officer[84] nor an employee (meaning in this article a person other than officers engaged in the business of a company on a regular basis) of a company shall hold at the same time a position as an officer of another company where the effect of such an interlocking directorate may be substantially to restrain competition in any particular field of trade.
2. No company shall coerce another company in competition with it in Japan through unfair trade practices, admit its officers concurrently to the position of officer or employee of the latter company, or admit its employees concurrently to the position of officer of the latter company.

In addition, Article 16 AL (mergers) states that:

1. No company shall perform an act falling under any of the following acts, where the effect of such an act may be substantially to restrain competition in any particular field of trade, or through unfair trade practices:
   (i) Accepting assignment of the whole or a substantial part of the business of another company
   (ii) Accepting assignment of the whole or a substantial part of the fixed assets used for the business of another company
   (iii) Taking on a lease[85] of the whole or a substantial part of the business of another company

[82] See E Watanabe, N Ohno and Tsunematsu, *Japan—Merger Control 2014* (London, ICLG, 2014), available at http://www.iclg.co.uk/practice-areas/merger-control/merger-control-2014/japan.

[83] The ratio of voting rights held by an acquiring company to the overall shareholder's voting rights of a target's issued capital.

[84] According to Art 2(3) AL an officer is 'a trustee, director, executive, partner with unlimited liabilities and executive power, an auditor or any person with a similar position, a manager or other employee in charge of the business of the main or branch office'.

[85] The concept of a lease is analysed in ch 2.

(iv) Undertaking the management of the whole or a substantial part of the business of another company
(v) Entering into a contract which provides for a joint profit and loss account for business with another company.

The filing requirements regarding the acquisition of voting rights are the following:

(i) the amount of the domestic turnover of the acquiring company's corporate group exceeds 20 billion yen;
(ii) the amount of the domestic turnover of the target company and its subsidiaries exceeds 5 billion yen; and
(iii) the ratio of voting rights of the acquiring company's corporate group in the target company exceeds 20 per cent or 50 per cent, respectively, through the contemplated stock acquisition.[86]

In the event that the thresholds are met, notification in Japan is mandatory. The filing must be made 30 days prior to the closing of the transaction. After the filing, the JFTC issues an acceptance notice to confirm the filing date, and the parties then have to wait for 30 days (Phase I). Nevertheless, once this waiting period has expired, the parties can legally close the transaction; the right of the parties to close the transaction exists, even if the JFTC has not completed its substantive review. In the event that the JFTC requires one or more parties to the transaction to submit additional material or information before the expiry of the waiting period, a second phase (Phase II) may be opened. The JFTC provides written confirmation of the clearance after both phases have been completed.

vii. Korea

In Korea the merger legislation is contained in Articles 7 and 12 of the Monopoly Regulation and Fair Trade Act (MRFTA). Merger filing requirements are subject to two jurisdictional tests: the size-of-transaction test and the size-of-party test.[87] The types of 'combinations of enterprises'[88] that are notifiable under the MRFTA are given in Articles 7(1) and 12(1) of this Act, as follows:[89]

1. 'Acquisition or ownership of 20 per cent or more of the shares of another company (or 15 per cent for companies listed on the Korea Exchange).'[90]
2. 'Acquisitions of additional shares in a company where the acquiring party already holds 20 per cent or more of the shares in the company (15 per cent for companies listed on

[86] See above n 82.
[87] See SR Yun, SJ Lee, CS Chung and KY Kim, 'Korea' in IK Gotts (ed), *Merger Control Review*, 3rd edn (London, Law Business Research, 2012).
[88] That is, 'the combination of capital, human resources and enterprise organizations, which leads to integration of decision making on business activities while eliminating the independence of the relevant individual enterprises'. See the KFTC website: http://eng.ftc.go.kr/policyarea/competitionpolicy_review.jsp?pageId=0201.
[89] See MRFTA, ch 3: 'Restriction on the Combination of Enterprises and Suppression of Economic Power Concentration'.
[90] 'Where not less than 20/100 (in the case of any listed corporation, 15/100) of the total number of stocks issued (excluding stocks without voting rights provided by Article 370 of the Commercial Act; hereinafter the same shall apply) by other company is held.'

the Korea Exchange) and the acquisition results in the acquiring party becoming the largest shareholder.'[91]

3. 'Interlocking directorate (where an officer or employee holds an officer's position in another company).'[92]
4. 'Merger with other companies.'
5. 'Acquisition by transfer of business (or sometimes substantial assets).'
6. 'Participation in the establishment of a new company or a joint venture'.[93]

However, according to Article 7(2):

> The provisions of Paragraph (1) shall not apply if the Fair Trade Commission deems that a combination of enterprises meets any of the requirements described below. In this case, the parties concerned must prove that they meet such requirements.
>
> 1. The promotion of efficiency attainable through the combination of enterprises is greater than the negative effect produced by the restricted competition.
> 2. A combination is with a nonviable company meeting the requirements prescribed by the Presidential Decree, for instance, a company whose total capital in its balance sheet is less than its paid-in capital for a reasonable period of time.[94]

The MRFTA classifies the above-mentioned transactions into five categories (Table 2).

Table 2: Categories of M&A under the MRFTA

Category	Description
Acquisition or ownership of stocks	Where a company acquires or owns stocks of another company
Concurrent holding of an executive position	Where an executive or employee of a large company concurrently holds an executive position in another company
Merger	Where a company merges with another company
Acquisition of business	Where a company acquires the business of another company
Participation in the establishment of a new company	Where a company participates in the establishment of a new company

Source: KFTC website (see also Table 5 in ch 4).

[91] 'Where anyone who holds stocks issued by other company not less than the ratio falls under subparagraph 1 becomes the largest equity investor by additionally acquiring stocks of the relevant company after making a report on the corporate combination.'

[92] The practice of a company's officers or employees (referring to those other than the officers and who have continued to work in the company; the same shall apply hereinafter) serving on the boards of multiple corporations.

[93] See also Art 12(2) MRFTA (Special Cases concerning Reporting Combination of Enterprises).

[94] According to Art 12(3) MRFTA, 'In case of financial institutions specialized in venture or property investment through share acquisition such as Small and Medium-sized Enterprise Start-up Investment Companies, New Technology-based Investment companies and Real Estate Investment Trusts, the KFTC regards such share acquisitions as solely for investments and exempts them from merger notification.' See OECD, *Antitrust Issues Involving Minority Shareholdings and Interlocking Directorates* (2008), DAF/COMP(2008)30, 1, 139.

The guidelines for the combination of enterprises provide criteria for determining whether a controlling relationship exists.[95] According to these guidelines:

> [I]n case of acquisition of stock, interlocking directorate, or establishment of a new company, a controlling relationship shall be established when the Acquiring Party, etc, meet the conditions set forth under subparagraphs 1–3 in relation to the Acquired Party.
>
> A) In case the shareholding ratio of the Acquiring Party, etc, is 50 per cent or more, a controlling relationship is formed. Even if the shareholding ratio of the Acquiring Party, etc, is less than 50 per cent, a controlling relationship is formed if the Acquiring Party can influence the Acquired Party considering the following in general:
> (1) Shareholding ratio of each stockholder, distribution of shares, mutual relationship among stockholders
> (2) Whether the Acquired Party gets its main raw materials from the Acquiring Party
> (3) Interlocking directorate between the Acquiring Party and the Acquired Party
> (4) The existence of transaction relation, money relation, or affiliation relation between the Acquiring Party and Acquired Party
>
> B) A dominating position shall be recognized to be established if an acquiring company, etc, though they could not form a dominating position for itself, could influence its acquired company's practical administrative issues in association with other parties (existing shareholders or persons who try to own the acquired company's stocks jointly).
> (1) ratio of holding stocks or voting right
> (2) possession of the right to designate an officer
> (3) possession of the right to veto budget plans, business or investment plans and other major decisions
> (4) existence of an agreement on joint voting-right exercise
> (5) possession of an administrative right to pursue business operation.

If interlocking directorships among firms exist the following criteria are used to determine whether a controlling relationship exists:

> A) If the Acquiring Party exercises substantial influence on the overall management of the Acquired Party considering the following, a controlling relationship shall be deemed to have been formed:
> (1) The number of directors at the Acquiring Party, etc, with interlocking directorate with the Acquired Party (hereinafter referred to as 'Interlocking Director') exceeds one third of all directors at the Acquired Party.
> (2) The interlocking director concurrently holds such position as the chairman of the board of directors at the Acquired Party, which grants the power to exercise substantial influence on the overall management of the company.
>
> B) This also applies if the criteria for determining whether a controlling relationship exists can be applied.

Regarding the participation in the incorporation of a new company the guidelines for the combination of enterprises provide that:

> A) In the case of participation in new company establishment, two or more participating companies shall engage in a dominating relationship with the newly founded company.

[95] The guidelines are available at http://eng.ftc.go.kr.

B) The standard for dominating position related to stockholding shall be complied with in determining if there exists any dominating relationship between merging parties and a newly established company.

Article 13 MRFTA also states that:

> (1) Companies belonging to an enterprise group subject to the limitations on mutual investment or on debt guarantees shall submit to the Fair Trade Commission a report on the status of ownership of their stockholders, financial standing, and status of their ownership of other domestic companies' stocks under conditions prescribed by Presidential Decree.
>
> In case of the establishment of a new joint venture company, the size-of-transaction test is satisfied if the acquirer acquires 20 per cent or more of the total issued and outstanding voting shares of the joint venture company. A business transfer involving the transfer of only a portion, not all, of the business at issue is also subject to the size-of-transaction test, which is satisfied if the value of the business transfer is (1) KRW5 billion or more, or (2) 10 per cent or more of the total assets of the transferor according to its financial statements at the end of the most recent fiscal year.[96]

A merger filing is required by the Korean Fair Trade Commission (KFTC) if the size-of-party test applies. Even though there are specific notification thresholds concerning foreign companies,[97] the general thresholds for the application of this test are the following:

1. One of the companies involved in the transaction has worldwide assets or turnover (annual) of at least KRW200 billion.
2. The other company in the transaction has total assets or turnover (annual) of at least KRW20 billion.[98]

A transaction that satisfies the jurisdictional tests and the specific notifications threshold concerning foreign companies may not need to be notified to the KFTC if the following exemptions apply:

1. An interlocking directorate exists between the concerned companies.
2. The share acquisition is among companies that are 'related', ie affiliates, to each other.
3. The acquirer or the target are investment companies or funds.

However, if a transaction satisfies the jurisdictional tests and the specific notifications threshold concerning foreign companies and at the same time does not qualify for an exemption, then a pre- or post-merger notification system applies. A pre-merger notification system applies if 'either the acquirer or the target has consolidated worldwide assets or sales of at least 2 trillion won'. For all other transactions a post-merger notification system applies.

In March 2009 the KFTC abandoned the shareholding cap, a policy in the Large Business Group Schemes in operation since 1986. The Large Business Group Schemes were introduced in order to prevent economic power concentration and the shareholding cap was employed so as to curb attempts by large business groups to concentrate economic power by buying each other's stocks.

[96] Above n 89.

[97] When a foreign company acquires another foreign company or a Korean company acquires a foreign company, then these transactions must be notified to the KFTC if the companies involved have sales revenues of at least KRW20 billion in the Korean market.

[98] These two thresholds have been established by the Enforcement Decree of the MRFTA.

According to the 2012 KFTC annual report:

> Under the scheme, companies (with asset amount of KRW 2 trillion or over) belonging to a business group with a combined asset amount of KRW 10 trillion or over, are not allowed to invest more than 40 per cent of their net asset value to other firms. In 1999, the scheme was re-employed after being suspended in 1998 and much relieved in 2007.

The KFTC's abandonment of the shareholding cap in March 2009 was in line with the trend that as the domestic market opened to growing global competition, Korean firms were increasingly turning their focus on profitability rather than upsizing based on financial leverage. This shift led Korea to see the importance of monitoring the market itself, which effectively undermined the raison d'être of the shareholding cap and ultimately put an end to it.

viii. Taiwan

In Taiwan merger control legislation is governed by the Taiwan Fair Trade Act (TFTA) as amended on 23 November 2011. The Taiwan Fair Trade Commission (TFTC) is the relevant enforcement authority in Taiwan.

According to the TFTA (Article 6), a concentration is broadly defined as (a) a merger; (b) an acquisition of one-third or more of the voting shares of or interest in another company; (c) a transfer or lease of the whole or a substantial part of a company's business or assets, a contractual arrangement with another company for the creation of a joint venture on a regular and ongoing basis, or the management of another company's business under a contract of entrustment, and direct or indirect control over the business operation or personnel management of another company.

The establishment of a joint venture, whether it is a newly incorporated enterprise or an existing enterprise, will be subject to merger control review if it constitutes a concentration under Article 6 TFTA.

A transaction may follow a pre-merger notification system (a notification must be filed with the TFTC prior to the closing of the proposed transaction) if, excluding certain exemptions and simplified procedure,[99] any one of the following thresholds are met (Article 11 TFTA): (a) as a result of the concentration, the merged entity will have a market share of at least one-third; and (b) if one of the companies participating in the concentration holds a market share of at least one-quarter or the preceding fiscal year's turnover of a company participating in the combination exceeds the following amounts:

1. For a concentration between non-financial enterprises, one of the companies generated an annual turnover of at least NT$10 billion, while the other company generated an annual turnover of at least NT$1 billion.
2. For a concentration between financial enterprises, one of the companies generated an annual turnover of at least NT$20 billion, while the other company generated an annual turnover of at least NT$1 billion.[100]

[99] Arts 7 and 8 TFTA provide special thresholds and exceptions relating to simplified filings.

[100] See also 'Merger Control: The International Regulation of Mergers and Joint Ventures in 77 Jurisdictions Worldwide' [2015] *Global Competition Review* 1, 401.

ix. Israel

In Israel mergers and acquisitions are regulated by the Restrictive Trade Practices Law (RTPL), which came into force in 1988. Concentrations are defined as either (a) the acquisition by one entity of most of the assets of another entity, or (b) the acquisition by one entity of shares in another entity, which gives the acquiring entity

1. more than 25 per cent of the nominal value of the target's issued capital or the voting power;
2. the right to appoint more than 25 per cent of the target's directors; or
3. the right to participate in more than 25 per cent of the target's profits.[101]

A merger requires the prior approval of the Director General of the Israeli Antitrust Authority (IAA) and must be notified to the IAA if one or more of the following criteria are met:

1. As a result of the merger, the share of the merged entity in the total production, sale, marketing or purchase of a particular asset or service and a similar asset or service, would be regarded as a monopoly (in Israel a market share that exceeds 50 per cent is regarded as a monopoly).
2. In the fiscal year preceding the merger, both the:
   a) concerned companies' aggregate sales turnover in Israel exceeded 150 million shekels; and
   b) sales turnover in Israel of at least two of the concerned companies exceeded 10 million shekels each.
3. One of the merging entities or a subsidiary, a controlling company, or a subsidiary of the controlling entity has a monopoly in any relevant (product and geographic) market.

A merger between non-Israeli entities falls within the scope of the RTPL if these entities conduct business in Israel and meet the necessary thresholds (in relation to their activities in Israel only).

x. South Africa

In South Africa mergers are regulated in terms of sections 11–18 of the Competition Act, No 89 of 1998 (CA), as amended.

In South Africa, even though there is no legal definition of a concentration regarding minority interests, section 12(2)g of the Competition Act, No 89 of 1998 (CA) stipulated that 'it is possible for a firm which does not have de jure control for example as a result of its majority shareholding in a firm to have the ability to control the firm as if it were a de jure controller'.[102]

[101] As above 224. This constitutes a passive right which 'generally refer[s] to the right to receive dividend payments and financial profit'. See OECD, *Antitrust Issues Involving Minority Shareholdings and Interlocking Directorates* (2008), DAF/COMP(2008)30, 1, 204, fn 4.

[102] Ibid, 162.

A transaction constitutes a merger when 'one or more firms directly or indirectly acquire or establish direct or indirect control over the whole or part of the business of another firm'. Such a concentration may be achieved in any manner, including through the

1. purchase or lease of shares;
2. an interest or assets of the other concerned company or amalgamation or other transaction with the other company in question.[103]

Section 12(2) CA states that the notion of control is defined, inter alia, if a person or a company:

1. beneficially owns more than one-half of the issued share capital of the victim;
2. is entitled to vote a majority of the votes that may be cast at a general meeting of the victim or has the ability to control the voting of a majority of those votes, either directly or through a controlled entity of the victim;
3. is able to appoint or to veto the appointment of a majority of the directors of the victim;
4. is a holding company, and the firm is a subsidiary of that company; or
5. has the ability to influence materially the policy of the victim.[104]

Therefore, the acquisition of a minority shareholding, coupled with veto rights in respect of important decisions such as the approval of budgets and business plans, and the appointment of executive and senior management, is generally considered an acquisition of control and a concentration.

There are two types of concentrations that require notification in South Africa: intermediate and large mergers. Regarding an intermediate merger, the combined assets or turnover of the acquiring firm and the target firm assets or turnover (whichever combination is the higher) must be at least ZAR 560 million[105] and the target firm must have assets or turnover (whichever is the higher) of at least ZAR 80 million.[106] Regarding a large merger, the acquiring firm and the victim firm must have combined assets or turnover (whichever combination is the higher) of at least ZAR 6.6 billion[107] and the victim firm must have assets or turnover (whichever is the higher) of at least ZAR 190 million.[108]

Concentrations that do not meet these thresholds constitute small concentrations,[109] which are not required to be notified.

xi. Indonesia

In Indonesia the agency supervising mergers is Commission for the Supervision of Business Competition (KPPU). Articles 28 and 29 of Antimonopoly Law No 5 of 1999

[103] See also http://uk.practicallaw.com/2-504-5969#.
[104] Ibid.
[105] Approximately US$54,309 or €42,301.
[106] Approximately US$7,759 or €6,043.
[107] Approximately US$640,074 or €498,553.
[108] Approximately US$18,426 or €14,352.
[109] The combined annual turnover/asset value (whichever is the greater) of the acquirer and the target is less than ZAR560 million; and the target's annual turnover/asset value (whichever is the greater) is less than ZAR80 million. Above n 103.

(AL) as well as Government Regulation No 57 of 2010[110] constitute the merger legislation in Indonesia.

Mergers and acquisitions between formerly independent companies and acquisitions of shares are transactions that are subject to merger legislation. However, acquisition of assets and joint ventures are not currently subject to merger legislation.

Minority interests are subject to merger control only if they change the nature of control in the acquired company. For instance, if the acquiring company has a relatively small number of shares, eg ownership of 50 per cent or less of shares of voting rights of a particular company, but has the ability to determine the management policy of the acquired company,[111] then the acquiring company has to notify the acquisition to the KPPU if certain thresholds are met (see below). Interlocking directorships do not constitute legal concentration, but constitute part of unfair business under the AL. Regarding merger control, interlocking directorships are analysed when the potential unfair business level of competition in the market under scrutiny is assessed.

However, it should be noted that:

> [P]rohibition on interlocking directorate is written in the Article 26 of the [AL], which says: anyone who is Directors or Commissioners of a Company, at the same time is prohibited to be directors or commissioners in another company, if the companies:
>
> — are in the same market; or
> — have a close relation in the same business scope and or business type
> — with together might dominate a particular goods and or service market.[112]

Such interlocking directorships 'may cause monopolistic practices and or unfair business competition'.[113]

This is based on the argument that the management of limited liability companies in Indonesia (*perseroan*) is performed by the board of directors/commissioners, which is generally lead by the president director—thus, Directors have interlocking tasks and authorities, namely to manage and represent the *perseroan*. The authorities of the directors cover every legal action related to the objective of *perseroan*, as written in its articles of association. The authority to represent the company is not limited to lead and implement daily activities, but also to take any initiatives and make future plans for the Company. The authority of the directors is not limited to the legal actions written in the articles of associations but includes any secondary actions that regularly, properly and generally comply with the objective of the company. Thus, the board of directors is an independent legal subject.

However, it is also important to understand that Indonesian competition law does not give any clear definition of what constitutes the board of directors/commissioners, and accordingly, this issue has to be referred to another related law. In other words, the positions

[110] The regulation sets out specific details of both the mandatory post-merger notification and the voluntary pre-merger consultation procedure.

[111] The criteria to determine the situation where a company influences the management policy of another company are not clearly defined in the AL. Therefore, the situation is determined on a case-by-case analysis by the KPPU. See also the analysis of the case *Asuransi Dharma Bangsa/AXA SA* (ch 5).

[112] Above n 101, 1, 213.

[113] Ibid.

of directors and commissioners are closely related to share ownership in two or more companies. Therefore, indirectly, an interlocking position will closely relate to the conditions on share ownership and on the merger and acquisition of companies.[114]

A concentration has to be notified to the KPPU if certain thresholds are met. If (a) total assets resulting from the merger exceed 2.5 trillion rupiah (approximately US$280 million) or (b) the total turnover of the merging entity exceeds 5 trillion rupiah (approximately US$560 million), then the transaction must be notified to the KPPU. For bank mergers the threshold of total assets is increased to 20 trillion rupiah.

xii. Norway

In Norway the merger control regime is contained in chapter 4 of the Norwegian Competition Act (CA) of 2004. Even though the CA applies the same definition of concentration as the EU Merger Regulation, section 16(1) CA states that the Norwegian Competition Authority may intervene against acquisitions of minority shareholdings by holdings in a firm even if this minority does not confer control over it. In particular, section 16(1) states: 'The Competition Authority shall intervene against a concentration[115] if the Competition Authority finds that it will create or strengthen a significant restriction of competition, contrary to the purpose of the act.' The purpose of the Act is defined in section 1: 'The purpose of the Act is to further competition and thereby contribute to the efficient utilization of society's resources. When applying this Act, special consideration shall be given to the interests of consumers.'[116]

Furthermore, section 16(2) states that

> The Competition Authority shall, on the same conditions as set forth in the first paragraph, intervene against an acquisition of holdings in an undertaking even if the acquisition will not lead to control of that undertaking. If an acquisition has been made through successive purchases, the Competition Authority may intervene against the transactions that have taken place within two years from the date of the most recent acquisition.[117]

xiii. Russian Federation

In the Russian Federation merger legislation is contained within chapter 7 of the Law of 26.07.2006 No 135-FZ on Protection of Competition (PC). According to Article 28 PC, a transaction should be notified if it involves:

1. acquisition by a person (a group of persons) of more than 25, 50, 75 per cent of voting shares of a Russian joint-stock company;
2. acquisition by a person (a group of persons) of more than 1/3, 50 per cent, 2/3 shares of a Russian limited liability company;

114 Ibid. Interlocking directorships are also prohibited in law no 19/2003 (state-owned enterprises), Art 22 of Central Bank Regulation No 2.7.2000 and Regulation of Capital Market Supervisory Agency No V.A.1 regarding License of Securities Company, Attachment of Regulation of Bapepam No Kep-24/PM/1996 dated 17 January 1996, as amended by the Regulation No Kep-45/PM/1997 dated 26 December 1997.

115 If such a concentration exists, a submission by the firms involved must notified within three months from the completion of the final agreement. See especially 'Merger Control: The International Regulation of Mergers and Joint Ventures in 77 Jurisdictions Worldwide' [2015] *Global Competition Review* 1, 311.

116 Ibid.

117 Ibid.

3. acquisition of more than 20 per cent of the fixed production assets and intangible assets of a management company;
4. acquisition of other rights of control in relation to the Russian economic entity (for example, establishment of indirect control, receiving functions of the management company);
5. acquisition of more than 50 per cent of stocks (shares) of a foreign legal entity that carries out deliveries of goods to the Russian market.

The jurisdictional thresholds in order for the above-mentioned transactions to be notified are as follows:

1. the total sum of assets of the group of the purchaser and the group of the acquired entity exceeds 7 billion roubles (US$233.3 million);
2. the total proceeds of the specified persons from realization of goods exceed 10 billion roubles (US$333.3 million);
3. one of the persons stated above is included in the register of the economic entities having a share in the market of certain goods in a size of more than 35 per cent.

An acquisition of a minority shareholding constitutes a legal concentration according to the PC. In particular:

> Acquisition by a[n] [entity] (a group of [entities]) of more than 25, 50, 75 per cent of voting shares of a Russian joint stock company (more than 1/3, 50 per cent, 2/3 shares respectively—for a limited liability company) is performed both upon a pre-merger notification or a post-merger notification (in the presence of terms established).[118]

In addition, an acquisition of the rights of ownership, use or possession of more than 20 per cent of fixed production assets or intangible assets of another economic company or an acquisition of fixed production assets and exclusive rights to the results of intellectual property, provided the volume of transferred property is over 20 per cent of the balance value of fixed production assets and non-material assets of a transferring person, are subject to merger control.[119]

xiv. Chinese Taipei

In Chinese Taipei minority interests in victims are consider as legal concentrations. In particular, merger legislation is contained in the Fair Trade Act (FTA), in which, inter alia, a merger is defined as when (a) an enterprise holds or acquires the shares or capital contributions of another enterprise to an extent of more than one-third of the total voting shares or total capital of such other enterprise; (b) an enterprise is assigned by or leases from another enterprise the whole or the major part of the business or properties of such other enterprise; or (c) an enterprise directly or indirectly controls the business operation or the appointment or discharge of personnel of another enterprise.

The notion of control is defined as where:

> 1) a company holds more than 50 per cent of the total outstanding voting shares or total capital contributions of another company; 2) a company directly or indirectly controls the personnel, financial or business management of another company; 3) more than half of the executive

[118] See OECD, *Definition of Transaction for the Purpose of Merger Control Review* (2013), DAF/COMP(2013)25, 1, 154.

[119] Ibid, 155.

> shareholders, or members of the board of directors are the same between companies; 4) more than 50 per cent of the total outstanding voting shares or capital contributions of the acquiring company and another company are held by the same shareholders or investors; 5) a company that controls another company in accordance with subparagraph 3 and 4 of Paragraph 1, Article 6 of the FTA.[120]

Therefore, the above-mentioned provisions of the FTA reveal that the control of management, interlocking directorships as well as a minority shareholding of more than one-third of the total voting shares or total capital constitute a legal concentration. In order for all these types of concentrations to be notified to the Fair Trade Commission (FTC), certain jurisdictional thresholds must be met. In particular, according to Article 11(1) FTA a transaction must be notified to the Commission if:

> 1) as a result of the merger the enterprise(s) will have one third of the market share; 2) one of the enterprises in the merger has one fourth of the market share; or 3) sales for the preceding fiscal year of the enterprises in the merger exceeds the threshold [of TWD 10 billion in sales volume for an acquiring enterprise—raised to TWD 20 billion for financial institutions—and, as a cumulative condition, TWD 1 billion for the acquisition target].[121]

xv. Ukraine

In Ukraine Article 22 of the Law of Ukraine on Protection of Economic Competition (PEC) is responsible for merger review. In particular, pursuant to Article 22 PEC a concentration is defined as:

> a) direct or indirect (through third persons) acquisition of control by one or several undertakings over one or several undertakings or parts of undertakings, b) establishing by two or more economic entities of an economic entity [(a merger entity or the establishment of a new business entity)][122] which will for a long period of time independently perform economic activities, but at the same time such creation does not lead to coordination of the competitive behaviour between the economic entities that have created this economic entity, or between them and the newly created economic entity, c) direct or indirect (through other entity) acquisition, or other form of acquiring into ownership of or obtaining for management shares (stocks) that allow to achieve or exceed 25 or 50 per cent of votes in the supreme management body of the economic entity.

According to Article 24 PEC, the Antimonopoly Committee of Ukraine must be notified if: the worldwide aggregate value of assets or sales over the last financial year, by the concerned parties in the merger, taking into account their control companies, exceeds an amount equivalent to €12 million and (a) the worldwide aggregate value of assets or sales, by at least two parties involved in the merger, taking into account their control companies, exceeds an amount equivalent to €1 million and (b) the aggregate value of assets or sales, in Ukraine by at least one company involved in the merger, taking into account its control companies, exceeds an amount equivalent to €1 million.

In addition, a notification is required if either a company involved in the merger has a market share over 35 per cent, or when the combined market share of the parties in the merger exceeds 35 per cent and the merger takes place in the same market or in adjacent markets.

[120] See Art 6(2) FTA.
[121] See OECD, *Investigations of Consummated and Non-notifiable Mergers Chinese-Taipei* (2014), DAF/COMP/WP3/WD(2014)3, 1, 2.
[122] See above n 100, 418.

xvi. Canada

The ninth part of the Competition Act (CA), a federal statute that applies across Canada, describes the type of transactions and the jurisdictional thresholds for merger control. A merger is defined in the Canadian CA as the acquisition of a significant interest in the whole or a part of a company. In particular, according to CA paragraph 91, a merger is:

> [T]the acquisition or establishment, direct or indirect, by one or more persons, whether by purchase or lease of shares …, of control over or significant interest in the whole or a part of a business of a competitor, supplier, customer or other person.

Therefore, the crucial point to be clarified is the type of 'significant interest' that may trigger merger review under the CA. Following paragraph 1.5 of the Merger Enforcement Guidelines (MEG) of the Canadian Competition Bureau,[123] a significant interest is established when the acquiring company or person has the ability, through its interest, to influence materially[124] 'the economic behaviour of the target business, including but not limited to decisions relating to pricing, purchasing, distribution, marketing, investment, financing and the licensing of intellectual property rights'.[125]

For the purposes of Canadian merger control and regarding the acquisition of voting and non-voting shares, the factors that determine if a minority interest confers material influence on the strategic/economic behaviour of the victim are the following:

1. voting rights attached to the acquirer's shareholdings or interest in a combination;
2. the status of the acquirer of partnership interests (eg, general or limited partner) and the nature of the rights and powers attached to the partnership interest;
3. the holders and distribution of the remaining shares or interests (whether the target business is widely or closely held, and whether the acquirer will be the largest shareholder);
4. board composition and board meeting quorum, attendance and historical voting patterns (whether the acquirer will be able to carry or block votes in a typical meeting);
5. the existence of any special voting or veto rights attached to the acquirer's shares or interests (eg, the extent of shareholder approval rights for non-ordinary-course transactions);
6. the terms of any shareholder or voting agreements;
7. the dividend or profit share of the minority interest as compared to the acquirer's equity ownership share;
8. the extent, if any, of the acquirer's influence over the selection of management or of members of key board committees;
9. the status and expertise of the acquirer relative to that of other shareholders;
10. the services (management, advisory or other) the acquirer is providing to the business, if any;
11. the put, call or other liquidity rights, if any, that the acquirer has and may use to influence other shareholders or management;
12. the access the acquirer has, if any, to confidential information about the business; and
13. the practical extent to which the acquirer can otherwise impose pressure on the business's decision-making processes.[126]

[123] As of October 2011, available at http://www.competitionbureau.gc.ca/eic/site/cb-bc.nsf/eng/03420.html.

[124] The concept of material influence is comprehensively analysed under UK merger control in section I.B of this chapter.

[125] Above n 118, 206 and the footnotes therein.

[126] See Merger Enforcement Guidelines 2011 Bureau de la concurrence, Canada, 2–3, 'It is generally the combination of factors—not the presence or absence of a single factor—that is determinative in the Bureau's assessment of material influence.' (http://www.competitionbureau.gc.ca/eic/site/cb-bc.nsf/vwapj/cb-meg-2011-e.pdf/$FILE/cb-meg-2011-e.pdf)

However, following paragraph 1.10 of the MEG,

> [i]n the absence of other relationships, direct or indirect ownership of less than 10 per cent of the voting interests in a business does not generally constitute ownership of a significant interest. While inferences about situations that result in a direct or indirect holding of between 10 per cent and 50 per cent of voting interests are more difficult to draw, a larger[[127]] voting interest is ordinarily required to materially influence a private company than a widely held public company.

In particular:

> The Bureau typically requires disclosure of all holdings that account for 10 per cent or more of the voting interests in a business, and may seek information respecting other minority holdings in the course of a merger review.[128]

These provisions of merger control in Canada reveal that a minority shareholding constitutes a legal concentration subject to the CA if the direct or indirect minority shareholding is more than 10 per cent and confers material influence in the strategic/economic behaviour of the victim.

Regarding convertible securities or options, paragraph 1.12 of the MEG states that:

> [A] significant interest may be acquired or established when these securities are first purchased or created, or at the time they are converted or exercised.[[129]] To determine whether a purchase constitutes a significant interest, the Bureau examines the nature of and circumstances in which the rights (or potential rights) attached to these securities may be exercised, and the influence that the acquirer may possess through their exercise, or threat of exercise, with reference to the factors outlined in paragraph 1.6 and any other relevant factors.'

In terms of asset transactions, the Canadian Competition Bureau treats these 'as the acquisition or establishment of a significant interest in that business'.[130]

As regards interlocking directorships the CA does not explicitly define them as legal concentrations.[131] However, '[a]n interlocking directorate is generally of interest under section 92 of the Act only when the interlocked firms are competitors, are vertically related, or produce complementary or related products'.[132]

A transaction follows a pre-merger notification system if (a) the parties to the transaction satisfy the 'size of parties' threshold; (b) the proposed transaction fits into one of five specific categories and exceeds the 'size of transaction' threshold; and (c) the proposed transaction is not otherwise exempt from the pre-merger notification system.

The 'size of parties' threshold is set at C$400 million. That is, there is a requirement to provide a pre-merger notification to the concerned companies to the transaction, including

[127] The acquisition of more than 20 per cent of a public company and of more than 35 per cent of a private company suffices to trigger a notification obligation. See 'Merger Control: The International Regulation of Mergers and Joint Ventures in 77 Jurisdictions Worldwide' [2015] *Global Competition Review* 1, 84.

[128] Above n 126, 4.

[129] 'A convertible security is a bond, debenture, preferred share or other security that may be exchanged by the owner, usually for common shares of the same company, in accordance with specified conversion terms. An option is a right to buy or sell specific securities or properties at a specified price within a specified time.'

[130] Above n 128, 5.

[131] See National Competition Law Section, Canadian Bar Association (2010) 7–8, available at http://www.competitionbureau.gc.ca/eic/site/cb-bc.nsf/vwapj/Comments-TheCanadianBarAssociation-MEGs-Dec-2010.pdf/$FILE/Comments-TheCanadianBarAssociation-MEGs-Dec-2010.pdf.

[132] Above n 130, 5.

their affiliates, if they have assets in Canada that exceed C$400 million in aggregate book value or have annual gross revenues from sales in, from or into Canada that exceed C$400 million in aggregate value in the most recently completed fiscal year.

The 'size of transaction' threshold 'includes a requirement that assets in Canada or annual gross revenues from sales in or from Canada exceed C$80 million, the 2013 threshold'.[133] The threshold varies according to the type of transaction (ie asset acquisition, acquisition of voting shares, amalgamation, merger, etc).

xvii. Republic of Armenia

In the Republic of Armenia the merger control regime is contained in section 4 of the Law of Protection of Economic Competition (POC), which came into force in 2009. The POC covers all acquisitions of 20 per cent of assets or shares if

> the total gross income of the parties to the concentration has made more than USD 4 million's equivalent in AMD in the year preceding the creation of the concentration or if at least one of the parties to the concentration is entered on the register of economic entities with dominant position on the given commodity market.[134]

xviii. Hong Kong

In Hong Kong only the telecommunications and broadcasting sectors are subject to competition regulations. The applicable merger control rules are contained in section 7P of the Telecommunications Ordinance (TO).[135]

Under the TO a merger must be notified to the Communication Authority (CA), an independent statutory body which replaced the dissolved broadcasting and telecommunication authorities and conducts investigations under the TO if there has been a change in the carrier licensee. Such a change takes place if a person or persons acquires or acquire 15, 30 or 50 per cent of the voting shares in the carrier license, or the said person, through the acquisition, confers the power to influence the affairs of the carrier license.

More specifically, under the TO, a merger takes place if:

1. Previously independent undertakings cease to be independent of each other (and one of them holds a carrier licence or controls an undertaking holding a carrier licence).
2. Any person/undertaking acquires direct or indirect control (as defined in the Ordinance) of the whole or part of one or more other undertakings (and the person/undertaking acquiring control or the undertaking of which control is acquired holds a carrier licence or controls an undertaking that holds a carrier licence), and this includes the creation of a joint venture to perform, on a lasting basis, all the functions of an autonomous economic entity.
3. An asset (including goodwill) is acquired leading to the acquiring undertaking replacing or substantially replacing the target in the business in which the target was engaged immediately before the acquisition (and the acquiring undertaking or the acquired undertaking holds a

[133] AF Baldanza, HA Do and L Milton, 'Canada: Merger Control' [2013] *Asia-Pacific Antitrust Review* 1, 42.

[134] See the 2000 law, ch 4 (Art 9(1)).

[135] Chapter 106 of the Laws of Hong Kong. '*The Guidelines on Merger and Acquisitions in Hong Kong Telecommunications Markets published by the Office of the Telecommunications Authority (OFTA) in May 2004 are also relevant*.' See http://uk.practicallaw.com/3-526-0086?qp=&qo=&qe=.

carrier licence or controls an undertaking that holds a carrier license, and the relevant business conducted by the acquired undertaking immediately before the acquisition was conducted under a carrier licence).[136]

The Competition Ordinance (CO),[137] the first competition law that applies to the entire economy of Hong Kong, was enacted in June 2012 and will be phased in fully throughout 2015.[138] Once in force, the Ordinance will repeal the competition-related provisions in the TO, including section 7P. Schedule 9 of the Ordinance provides for transitional arrangements.[139]

Once in full force the CO, inter alia, will prohibit direct and indirect mergers involving telecommunications carrier licensees. Although the Merger Rule only applies to mergers in the telecommunications sector, the Commerce and Economic Development Bureau 'has previously stated its intention that the scope of the Merger Rule's application should be reviewed, following the initial period of enforcement of the Ordinance'.[140] The CO will be enforced by the Competition Commission and Competition Tribunal.

xix. Australia

In Australia the main merger provision is section 50 of the Competition and Consumer Act (CCA), which came into force in 2010. It is enforced by the Australian Competition and Consumer Commission (ACCC). Even though there is no definition of control in the CCA it is assumed that any acquisition of shares of assets which lead to a substantial lessening of competition is applicable under section 50 CCA.

An acquisition below the level of delivering control of the acquired firm, ie the acquisition of a minority shareholding, may be considered by the ACCC in order to determine whether this acquisition is sufficient to deliver control over the acquired firm or raises competition issues. Concerning the latter, the ACCC examines if there exists a lessening of the degree of competition among the firms with minority shareholdings or an enhanced likelihood for coordinated conduct among them.[141]

xx. Argentina

In Argentina mergers fall under the Competition Act 25,156 (CA), as amended by decrees 89 and 396 of 2001. It is currently enforced by the National Commission for the Defence of Competition (NCDC) and the Internal Trade Secretariat (ITS). Both of these will be replaced by the National Tribunal for the Defence of Competition (NTDC).

Section 6 CA provides the definitions of control. Even though there is no definition or provision in the law regarding minority interests, the NCDC has set forth a principle that an acquisition of a minority interest will account for an acquisition of control if it is accompanied by specific veto rights for the purchaser in relation to the competitive strategy of

136 Ibid.
137 Chapter 619 of the Laws of Hong Kong.
138 At the date of writing not all phases of the CO have yet been implemented.
139 Above n 135.
140 See www.freshfields.com/en/knowledge/An_overview_of_the_Hong_Kong_Competition_Ordinance/.
141 See ACCC, Merger Guidelines [2008], 59–62.

the acquired firm.[142] However, if the purpose of the acquisition of a minority interest is to protect the investment[143] of the purchaser, then veto rights will not be subject under section 6 CA.

xxi. Namibia, Nigeria, Swaziland, Zambia and New Zealand

In Namibia, Nigeria, Swaziland and Zambia the law defines, inter alia, control as the power to veto the appointment of the majority of the directors of the acquired firm.[144] In New Zealand the Commerce Commission's working approach regarding minority interests is the following:

- a minority interest of less than 15 per cent of the issued capital of the acquired firm does not confer the ability to control it;
- a minority interest of between 20 and 30 per cent of the issued capital of the acquired firm is likely to give the purchaser the ability to control the acquisition if there exist factors that enable the purchaser to influence the firm's strategic policy;
- a minority interest of between 30 and 50 per cent of the issued capital of the acquired firm is likely to give the purchaser the ability to control the firm, ie to influence substantially its strategic policy.[145]

xxii. Chile

In Chile the Competition Act (CA) no 211 of 17 December 1973, as last amended in 2009,[146] does not explicitly provide the means to deal with minority interests. In fact, merger control in Chile is not established by law, but is based on the provisions of the CA and especially Articles 1, 3, 18(2) and 26.[147]

However, the Merger Guidelines of the National Economic Prosecutor's Office (NEPO)[148] define a horizontal concentration as

> 'the acquisition of stock, the acquisition of assets, associations and, in general, any arrangements or transactions that have as their object or effect for two or more independent economic entities to become a single entity, to make decisions in a coordinated manner, or to integrate the same corporate group.' According to the [NEPO], 'this definition is grounded on economic concepts' and directed towards 'the *change in incentives*[149] that occurs when, eg, two independent economic entities, through some contractual or factual arrangement, align their incentives in order

[142] See, for instance, the cases examined in ch 5 for a detailed analysis of specific veto rights which may influence the competitive strategy of the acquired firm.

[143] For instance, a veto right which requires the approval of the purchaser for capital increases of the acquired firm or distribution of dividends, etc.

[144] As above n 101, 228, 307, 388, 448, 498.

[145] Ibid, 198. See also Commerce Commission New Zealand, Mergers and Acquisitions Guidelines (2013), attachment C.

[146] See law no 20.361 of 13 July 2009.

[147] See also OECD, *Assessment of Merger Control in Chile Report by the OECD Secretariat* (2014), 1, 14–15, available at http://www.oecd.org/daf/competition/chile-merger-control-2014-en.pdf.

[148] Fiscalva Nacional Economica.

[149] Emphasis added.

to maximise their joint profits, diminish their level of autonomy, or alter the way in which they take competitive decisions'.[150] This broad definition of horizontal concentrations allows NEPO to review any form of horizontal transaction such as 'joint participation in a business (eg joint ventures), the direct and indirect acquisition of a minority interest, overlaps in the management of a competing company, etc.[151]

In conclusion, passive minority interests are subject to merger control in Ecuador, Brazil, Japan, Korea, Taiwan, Israel, South Africa, Indonesia, the Russian Federation, Chinese Taipei, Ukraine, Canada, Republic of Armenia, Hong Kong, Namibia, Nigeria, Swaziland and Zambia. Table 3 summarizes merger control regimes regarding passive minority interests in these countries.

Table 3: Passive minority interests under merger control regimes across the globe

Countries	Interlocking directorship	Minority shareholding
Ecuador	Interlocking joint administration (section 4 OLRCMP)	
Brazil		20% for conglomerate minority shareholdings, 5% for horizontal and vertical minority shareholdings (Article 10 Resolution 1/2012)
Japan	Interlocking directorship (article 13 AL)	Acquisition of stock (20% is the minimum threshold of the voting right ratio) (Article 10 of AL)
Korea	Interlocking directorship (Article 7(1) MRFTA and the Guidelines for the combination of enterprises)	15% for companies listed on the Korean Stock Exchange; 20% for all other companies (Article 7(1) MRFTA and the Guidelines for the combination of enterprises)
Taiwan		Acquisition of one-third or more of the voting shares of or interest in another company (Article 6 TFTA)
Israel	The right to appoint >25% of the target's directors (RTPL)	25% of the nominal value of the target's issued capital or the voting power; the right to participate in more than 25% of the target's profits (RTPL)

(continued)

[150] See also OECD, *Assessment of Merger Control in Chile: Report by the OECD Secretariat* (2014), 1, 19.
[151] Ibid.

Table 3: ***(Continued)***

Countries	Interlocking directorship	Minority shareholding
South Africa	Veto the appointment of a majority of the directors of the victim (section 12(2) CA)	
Indonesia	Prohibition of interlocking position merely to the board of directors and or board of commissioners (Article 26 Antimonopoly Law)	
Russian Federation		25% of the voting rights—1/3 of the shares—25% of the production assets and intangible assets (Article 28 PC)
Chinese Taipei	More than half of the executive shareholders, or members of the board of directors (FTA)	More than 1/3 of the total voting shares or total capital (FTA)
Ukraine	>25% or >50% of votes in the supreme management body of the economic entity (Article 22 PEC)	
Canada	Material influence control (paragraph 1.5 MEG)	
		Material influence control: >10–20% of the voting interests
Republic of Armenia		20% of assets or shares (section 4 POC)
Hong Kong		Acquisition of 15%, 30% or 50% of the voting shares in the carrier license (TO)
Namibia	Veto the appointment of a majority of the directors of the victim	
Nigeria	Veto the appointment of a majority of the directors of the victim	
Swaziland	Veto the appointment of a majority of the directors of the victim	
Zambia	Veto the appointment of a majority of the directors of the victim	

Notes: OLRCMP, Organic Law for Regulation and Control of Market Power; AL, Antimonopoly Law; MRFT, Monopoly Regulation and Fair Trade Act; TFTA, Taiwan Fair Trade Act; RTPL, Restrictive Trade Practices Law; CA, Competition Act, No 89; PC, Protection of Competition; FTA, Fair Trade Act; PEC, Protection of Economic Competition; MEG, Merger Enforcement Guidelines; POC, Protection of Economic Competition; TO, Telecommunication Ordinance.

D. The Treatment of Minority Shareholdings in the US

The treatment of minority interests under US law involves both minority shareholdings and interlocking directorships. In terms of the former the law (section 7 of the Clayton Act, 15 USC § 18) applies to any part of the equity of a victim firm.[152] Regarding the latter, section 8 of the Clayton Act prohibits a member of a firm from serving as a member of a competitor's board of directors.[153] 'Section 8 has been interpreted as establishing a per se prohibition, so that no anticompetitive effect need be shown to establish a violation.'[154] The per se approach dates back to the first judicial development in the case of *United States v Sears, Roebuck & Co.*[155] The court (US District Court for the Southern District of New York) in this case stated that the liability occurred whether or not the interlocked firms were or had been competitors and for any of the provisions and for any of the antitrust laws.

Following the introductory guide II of the Hart–Scott–Rodino Act (HSRA) premerger notification programme,[156]

> For the Act to apply to a particular transaction, it must satisfy three tests: the commerce test of Section 7A(a)(1) as well as the size of transaction test and the size of person test of Section 7A(a)(2). An acquisition will satisfy the commerce test if either of the parties to a transaction is engaged in commerce or in any activity affecting commerce. The size of transaction test[[157]] is met if, as a result of the transaction, the acquiring person will hold an aggregate amount of voting securities, non-corporate interests ('NCI') and assets of the acquired person valued at more than $50 million (as adjusted). … The size of person test[[158]] is met if one of the parties has sales or assets of at least $100 million (as adjusted) and the other party has sales or assets of at least $10 million (as adjusted). …[159] The size of person test is not applicable if, as a result of the transaction, the acquiring person will hold an aggregate amount of voting securities, NCI and/or assets of the acquired person valued in excess of $200 million.[160]

HSRA provides an exemption for 10 per cent or less of an issuer's voting securities made only for investment purposes.[161] However, the strength of this exemption is limited in the case where the firms involved in the transaction are direct competitors. Also, if the victim

[152] However, a court has held an acquisition of at least 15 per cent of a minority interest to be in violation of section 7. See, inter alia, SR Miller, ME Raven and D Went, 'Antitrust Concerns From Partial Ownership Interest Acquisitions: New Developments in the European Union and United States' (2012) 1 *CPI Antitrust Chronicle* 1, 5.

[153] See also 15 USC §18a(a)(2).

[154] ME Jacobs, 'Combating Anticompetitive Interlocks: Section 8 of the Clayton Act as a template for Small and Emerging Economies' (2014) 30 *Fordham International Law Journal* 643, 646. However, the per se approach in the US contradicts that adopted regarding interlocking directorships in Japan, Korea and Indonesia.

[155] *United States v Sears, Roebuck & Co*, 111 F (1953).

[156] Available at http://www.ftc.gov/sites/default/files/attachments/premerger-introductory-guides/guide2.pdf.

[157] 'The size of transaction test, as its name suggests, is concerned with the value of what is being acquired. … [T]he Rules generally require that assets, voting securities or NCI of the acquired person that have already been acquired must be aggregated with those that will be acquired in the proposed transaction. When what has previously been purchased plus what will be bought in the present acquisition meets the size of transaction criteria, the transaction becomes reportable unless an exemption applies.' Ibid, n 113, 4.

[158] The size of person test 'determine(s) the size of the persons you have defined as the ultimate parent entities of the parties. The basic size of person test [is] established by Section 7A(a)(2) of the Act.' Ibid, 12.

[159] Ibid, 2.

[160] Ibid, 2, fn 4. See also § 7A (a)(2) of the Act.

[161] See also 15 USC § 18(a)(c)(9); 16 CFR § 802.9 and 16 CFR §801.1(i)(1).

firm or person is an institutional investor, then a minority interest cannot be more than 15 per cent.[162]

In addition to acquisitions of securities, the HSRA covers acquisitions of assets. The acquired assets may include a firm, tangible assets that do not comprise a firm and/or intangible assets such as patents or licenses.[163] All in all, during the competitive economic analysis in US merger and minority interest cases any minority shareholding is subjected to the same test as US full mergers, namely whether the complete or partial share acquisition leads to substantially less competition.

On 21 January 2015, as applicable after 4 February 2015, the Federal Trade Commission (FTC) announced revised jurisdictional and filing fee thresholds under the Hart–Scott–Rodino (HSR) Antitrust Improvements Act of 1976 (Revised Jurisdictional Thresholds for Section 7A of the Clayton Act). Table 4[164] presents the thresholds for 2015 regarding the size of transaction and person tests.[165]

If the acquired person or firm acquires additional voting securities from the same victim, then notification will be required if the value of the acquisition exceeds the following thresholds: $76.3 million; $152.5 million; $762.7 million; 25 per cent of the voting securities if their value exceeds $1,525.3 million; 50 per cent of the voting securities if their value exceeds $76.3 million.[166]

Section 8 of the Clayton Act states that

> No person[167] shall, at the same time, serve as a director or officer in any two corporations (other than banks, banking associations, and trust companies) that are … by virtue of their business and location of operation, *competitors*,[168] so that the elimination of competition by agreement between them would constitute a violation of any of the antitrust laws … if each of the corporations has capital, surplus, and undivided profits aggregating more than $10,000,000 as adjusted pursuant to paragraph (5) of this subsection.[169]

[162] See also 16 CFR § 802.64.

> Neither this exemption nor the one provided by § 802.9 applies to acquisitions of what are classified for HSR Act purposes as 'non-corporate interests' (eg, partnership interests or limited liability company membership interests). On the other hand, an acquisition of non-corporate interests is not reportable under the HSR Act unless it confers 'control' of the target, 16 CFR § 801.13(c)(2) which, in the case of an unincorporated entity, is defined as 'having the right to 50 percent or more of the profits of the entity, or having the right in the event of dissolution to 50 percent or more of the assets of the entity,' 16 CFR, 801.1(b)(1)(ii).

[163] See also OECD, *Definition of Transaction for the Purpose of Merger Control Review* (2013), DAF/COMP(2013)25, 1, 198.

[164] http://www.antitrustunpacked.com/siteFiles/BlogPosts/014_hsr_thresholds_for2015.pdf. See also Federal Register, vol 80, no 13, Wednesday, 21 January 2015, Notices, available at https://www.ftc.gov/system/files/documents/federal_register_notices/2015/01/150121hsrthreshol-ds7a.pdf and https://www.ftc.gov/news-events/press-releases/2015/01/ftc-announces-new-thresholds-clayton-act-antitrust-reviews-2015.

[165] These revised jurisdictional thresholds will remain in effect until the next adjustment issued by the FTC, which is expected in the first quarter of 2016. The FTC is required to revise the filing thresholds annually, based on the change in the gross national product.

[166] See above n 164, 2.

[167] Or corporation. See especially 15 USC § 12(a) (2012).

[168] Emphasis added. For instance, for the delineation of competitors under s 8 of the Clayton Act, case *TRW, Inc v Federal Trade Commission*, 647 F.2d 942 (1981).

[169] § 19(a).

Table 4: HSR filing thresholds for 2015

Size of transaction test*		Reportability
Up to and including $76.3 million		Not reportable
Above $76.3 million up to and including $305.1 million		Reportable if: (1) satisfies the *size of person test*, and (2) no exemption applies
Size of person test		
Acquiring or acquired person		Other person
$152.5 million (in total assets or annual net sales)	*and*	$15.3 million (in total assets or annual net sales of a person engaged in manufacturing)
	or	
$151.7 million (in total assets or annual net sales)	*and*	$15.3 million (in total assets of a person not engaged in manufacturing)
	or	
$15.2 million (in total assets or annual net sales)	*and*	$152.5 million (in total assets or annual net sales)
In excess of $305.1 million		Reportable absent an exemption

* Based on the value of voting securities and assets the acquiring person will hold as a result of the acquisition, including the value of any previously acquired voting securities.

Source: Antitrust Unpacked blog, Antitrust Law Block, Sherman & Sterling LLP (http://shearmanantitrust.com/)

The word 'competitors' means that section 8 applies only to horizontal interlocking directorships. It does not apply to other types of business entities,[170] such as partnerships between bank and non-bank corporations,[171] and between parent corporations and their wholly owned subsidiaries.[172]

In terms of procedural law, since the proposed transaction has been notified, it cannot be executed before the completion of the filing and the expiration of the 30-day waiting period (or 15 days in the case of a cash tender offer or a transfer in bankruptcy). In US law, there is no provision for voluntary filings as such, but parties to non-reportable transactions have the possibility, if they so wish, to bring their transaction to the attention of the agencies. In addition, if there is no action by the agencies after the notification of the transaction, it may be completed when the waiting period has expired. 'In any case, the agencies do not issue a formal decision clearing a transaction.'[173]

[170] For instance, s 8 of the Clayton Act does not apply in sports league (see *North Am Soccer League v NFL*, 670 F2d 1249, 1262 (2d Cir 1982)). Also, the statue applies only to officers and directors and not to employees or agents.

[171] See *Bankamerica Corp v United States*, 462 US 122, 128 (1983).

[172] ME Jacobs, 'Combating Anticompetitive Interlocks: Section 8 of the Clayton Act as a Template for Small and Emerging Economies' (2014) 30 *Fordham International Law* Journal 643, 663. See *Burnup & Sims, Inc v Posner*, 688 F Supp 1532, 1534 (SD Fla 1988) and *Copperweld Corp v Independence Tube Corp*, 467 US 752, 771–74 (1984).

[173] See para 78 in the Annex to the Commission Staff Working Document, 'Towards More Effective EU Merger Control'.

In *United States v Sears, Roebuck & Co* the court rejected the defendant's argument, according to which

> section 8 required a showing that a hypothetical merger between the two firms would violate section 7 of the Clayton Act, which prohibits mergers between firms only when 'the effect of such acquisition may be substantially to lessen competition, or to tend to create a monopoly'.[174]

The court stated that

> This conclusion is compelled because of the futility of trying to decide whether a given hypothetical merger would violate the pertinent sections of the antitrust laws. Such a decision would involve a consideration of many factors ... [which] can be applied only in an actual case and not in a hypothetical situation. ... This difficulty suggests that the merger test would result in complete nullification of the law prohibiting interlocking directorates in all but the rawest situation. This conclusion is compelled because of the futility of trying to decide whether a given hypothetical merger would violate the pertinent sections of the antitrust laws. Such a decision would involve a consideration of many factors ... [which] can be applied only in an actual case and not in a hypothetical situation. ... This difficulty suggests that the merger test would result in complete nullification of the law prohibiting interlocking directorates in all but the rawest situation.[175]

Furthermore, in *Protectoseal Co v Barancik* the court considered that 'it did not believe Congress intended the legality of an interlock to depend on the kind of complex evidence that may be required in a protracted case arising under § 7'.[176]

In *Reading International v Oaktree Capital Management LLC* an equity firm president's served on the board of a theatre chain, while an equity's principal served on the board of another competitor theatre chain. The court specifically stated that:

> To hold otherwise would be to allow corporations (and individuals) to evade antitrust liability simply by designating agents to serve their bidding on the boards of competing businesses. The purposes of the statute, "to avoid the opportunity for the coordination of commercially sensitive information by competitors," would be ill-served by such a cramped reading.[177]

On 21 January 2015, as applicable after 4 February 2015, the FTC announced the revised thresholds for interlocking directorates required by the 1990 amendment of section 8 of the Clayton Act. In particular,[178]

> Section 8 prohibits, with certain exceptions, one person from serving as a director or officer of two competing corporations if two thresholds are met. Competitor corporations are covered by Section 8 if each one has capital, surplus, and undivided profits aggregating more than $10,000,000, with the exception that no corporation is covered if the competitive sales of either corporation are less than $1,000,000. Section 8(a)(5) requires the Federal Trade Commission to revise those thresholds annually, based on the change in gross national product. The new thresholds, which take effect immediately, are $31,084,000 for Section 8(a)(1),[179] and $3,108,400 for Section 8(a)(2)(A).[180]

[174] Above n 172, 665.

[175] Ibid, 666.

[176] Ibid.

[177] Ibid, 671–72 and *Oaktree Capital*, 317 F Supp 2d, 331.

[178] See also https://www.ftc.gov/system/files/documents/federal_register_notices/2015/01/150121-hsrthresholds8.pdf.

[179] That is, it prohibits a person from serving on the board of directors of competing companies valued at about $31 million.

[180] That is, section 8 does not apply if the two companies have annual sales in competition with each other of less than about $3.1 million.

Also, section 8 of the Clayton Act does not apply if the competitive sales of either firm involved in the transaction amount to less than 2 per cent of that firm's total sales; or the competitive sales of each firm involved in the transaction amount to less than 4 per cent of each firm's total sales. Competitive sales means the gross revenues for all products and services sold by one firm in competition with the other, determined on the basis of annual gross revenues for such products and services in that firm's last completed fiscal year. Total sales mean the gross revenues for all products and services sold by one firm over that firm's last completed fiscal year.

II. Minority Shareholdings in the Context of Articles 101 and 102 TFEU

In the previous section we focused on the treatment of minority shareholdings under various merger laws around the world (inside and outside the EU). We were mainly interested in (a) searching whether national laws regarding mergers and acquisitions have incorporated the notion of minority interests and (b) identifying the qualitative and quantitative criteria under which minority interests must be notified for further investigation by the competition authority.

In this section our primary concern is to connect the notion of minority interests with Articles 101 and 102 TFEU. In section II.A we will present the links between an acquisition of minority shareholding and Articles 101 and 102 TFEU, while in section II.B we will try to show whether interlocking directorships can or cannot facilitate implicit collusion. In section II.C we will try to illustrate the differences between an ex ante and an ex post analysis and the possible gap between the two of these analyses in the context of minority shareholdings. First, however, we briefly present Articles 101 and 102 TFEU and Council Regulation 1/2003 of 16 December 2002 on the implementation of the rules on competition laid down in Articles 81 and 82 of the Treaty.[181]

In particular, the consolidated version of Article 101 TFEU (ex Article 81 TEC) states that[182]

1. The following shall be prohibited as incompatible with the internal market: all agreements between undertakings, decisions by associations of undertakings and concerted practices which may affect trade between Member States and which have as their object or effect the prevention, restriction or distortion of competition within the internal market, and in particular those which:
   a) directly or indirectly fix purchase or selling prices or any other trading conditions;
   b) limit or control production, markets, technical development, or investment;
   c) share markets or sources of supply;
   d) apply dissimilar conditions to equivalent transactions with other trading parties, thereby placing them at a competitive disadvantage;

[181] [2003] OJ L1/1.

[182] [2012] OJ C326/47, Title VII 'Common Rules on Competition, Taxation and Approximation of Laws', ch 1, s 1, 88–89.

e) make the conclusion of contracts subject to acceptance by the other parties of supplementary obligations which, by their nature or according to commercial usage, have no connection with the subject of such contracts.

2. Any agreements or decisions prohibited pursuant to this Article shall be automatically void.
3. The provisions of paragraph 1 may, however, be declared inapplicable in the case of:
— any agreement or category of agreements between undertakings,
— any decision or category of decisions by associations of undertakings,
— any concerted practice or category of concerted practices, which contributes to improving the production or distribution of goods or to promoting technical or economic progress, while allowing consumers a fair share of the resulting benefit, and which does not:
    a) impose on the undertakings concerned restrictions which are not indispensable to the attainment of these objectives;
    b) afford such undertakings the possibility of eliminating competition in respect of a substantial part of the products in question.

Article 102 TFEU (ex Article 82 TEC) states that:[183]

> Any abuse by one or more undertakings of a dominant position within the internal market or in a substantial part of it shall be prohibited as incompatible with the internal market in so far as it may affect trade between Member States.
>
> Such abuse may, in particular, consist in:
>
> (a) directly or indirectly imposing unfair purchase or selling prices or other unfair trading conditions;
> (b) limiting production, markets or technical development to the prejudice of consumers;
> (c) applying dissimilar conditions to equivalent transactions with other trading parties, thereby placing them at a competitive disadvantage;
> (d) making the conclusion of contracts subject to acceptance by the other parties of supplementary obligations which, by their nature or according to commercial usage, have no connection with the subject of such contracts.[184]

Articles 101 and/or 102 TFEU may apply to passive minority shareholdings in situations where there is evidence of an anticompetitive agreement or concerted practice among the investigated firms or the firms that are engaged in the acquisition of non-controlling stakes and/or one or more firms have a dominant position.

There are voices which believe that Articles 101 and 102 TFEU may address the competitive concerns raised by the acquisitions of minority shareholdings. For instance, during the public consultation of the DG Competition in 2013 some stakeholders argued in favour

[183] Ibid, 89.

[184] Art 106 TFEU (ex Art 86 TEC) states that:

> 1. In the case of public undertakings and undertakings to which Member States grant special or exclusive rights, Member States shall neither enact nor maintain in force any measure contrary to the rules contained in the Treaties, in particular to those rules provided for in Article 18 and Articles 101 to 109.
> 2. Undertakings entrusted with the operation of services of general economic interest or having the character of a revenue-producing monopoly shall be subject to the rules contained in the Treaties, in particular to the rules on competition, in so far as the application of such rules does not obstruct the performance, in law or in fact, of the particular tasks assigned to them. The development of trade must not be affected to such an extent as would be contrary to the interests of the Union.
> 3. The Commission shall ensure the application of the provisions of this Article and shall, where necessary, address appropriate directives or decisions to Member States.

of this. They particularly stated that antitrust rules constitute appropriate tools in order to assess the anticompetitive harm potentially arising from such acquisitions.[185] However, others believed that antitrust rules may not cover all cases involving minority shareholdings and therefore the current Merger Regulation system must be updated in order to make the competitive assessment by Commission more effective.[186]

In its White Paper and the accompanying Commission Staff Working Paper of July 2014 the Commission states that an acquisition of a minority shareholding may not constitute an agreement which by object or effect restricts competition. As a consequence, it may not be possible to intervene in cases that involve potentially anticompetitive minority shareholdings. Regarding Article 102 TFEU, the Commission states the same argument unless the acquirer or the victim or both of them have a dominant position in the markets under scrutiny.[187]

Article 9 of Regulation 1/2003 states that

1. Where the Commission intends to adopt a decision requiring that an infringement be brought to an end and the undertakings concerned offer commitments to meet the concerns expressed to them by the Commission in its preliminary assessment, the Commission may by decision make those commitments binding on the undertakings. Such a decision may be adopted for a specified period and shall conclude that there are no longer grounds for action by the Commission.
2. The Commission may, upon request or on its own initiative, reopen the proceedings: (a) where there has been a material change in any of the facts on which the decision was based; (b) where the undertakings concerned act contrary to their commitments; or (c) where the decision was based on incomplete, incorrect or misleading information provided by the parties.

The Commission recently stated that:

> Regulation 1/2003 equipped the Commission with an enhanced set of enforcement tools, notably, the ability to take decisions making commitments offered by parties binding and enforceable under Article 9. This power has since been rolled out for virtually all NCAs, meaning that prohibition and commitment decisions are the principal tools used in the ECN.
>
> The primary purpose of commitment decisions is to preserve effective competition by addressing the potentially anti-competitive practices and to ensure a quick outcome on the market. Commitment decisions allow for the quicker resolution of competition concerns on a more cooperative basis. Such decisions have often been adopted in fast-moving markets and/or in markets that are in the process of liberalisation. Whether an authority follows a particular enforcement route is based on a number of factors. A prohibition decision may be adopted if the case calls for the imposition of fines to sanction past behaviour, if the only remedy available is the cessation of the anti-competitive behaviour or if there is a need for a clear legal precedent. Equally, the use of commitment decisions depends on whether the parties offer effective, clear and precise commitments.[188]

[185] See, for instance, the opinion by MEDEF available at http://ec.europa.eu/competition/consultations/2013_merger_control/medef_en.pdf.

[186] See, for instance, the opinion by ABI available at http://ec.europa.eu/competition/consultations/2013_merger_control/abi_en.pdf.

[187] See para 40 of the White Paper ('Towards More Effective EU Merger Control' COMP(2014) 449 final). See also p 6 of the Annex II of the Commission Staff Working Document ('Towards More Effective EU Merger Control' SWD(2013) 239 final) and para 62 of the Commission Staff Working Document ('Towards More Effective EU Merger Control' SWD(2014) 221 final).

[188] EC Communication from the Commission to the European Parliament and the Council, 'Ten Years of Antitrust Enforcement under Regulation 1/2003: Achievements and Future Perspectives', COM(2014) 453, paras 20–21.

In the light of its enforcement power that stems from Article 9 of Council Regulation 1/2003 the Commission has intervened in particular sectors to assess profit-sharing joint ventures that may restrict competition.[189] In particular,

> In the transport sector the Commission has been particularly vigilant regarding revenue sharing joint ventures that may restrict competition to the detriment of a large number of consumers. In both the British Airways/American Airlines/Iberia case and the Star Alliance case, the Commission intervened and accepted entry facilitating commitments by a number of international air carriers that had formed joint ventures for their transatlantic flights.[190] Those joint ventures affect a large number of European consumers and businesses for whom the Commission's intervention brings about direct benefits in ensuring competition on economically important travel routes.[191]

But how are minority interests as well as interlocking directorships connected with anti-trust rules? This issue will be addressed in the next section.

A. Are Articles 101 and 102 TFEU Suitable for Dealing Effectively with Anticompetitive Minority Shareholdings? General Remarks

Meadowcroft and Thompson found that 15 per cent of cases in their research were *proxy agreements*, ie acquisitions of minority shareholdings as a substitute for agreements infringing competition law.[192] Precisely, proxy agreements are 'holdings which support, or substitute for contractual agreements in continuing trading relationships'.[193] They may either improve the efficiency of trading relationships or they may restrict competition, depending on the circumstances.[194]

During the Commission's 2013 public consultation a number of stakeholders, such as law firms and business associations, had the opportunity to answer the question whether the limited number of problematic transactions would justify broadly extending the Merger Regulation's scope. Some stakeholders had the opinion that the rules on restrictive agreements and abuse of dominance, set out in Articles 101 and 102 TFEU, respectively, constituted adequate substitutes, since they could capture many of the problematic transactions.

Nevertheless, 'the Commission's ability to use Article 101 and Article 102 TFEU to intervene against anti-competitive minority shareholdings may be limited'.[195] More specifically,

[189] Profit-sharing joint revenues can be seen as arrangements that link the fortunes of actual or potential competitors, producing a positive correlation among their profits. See the paper by RJ Reynolds and BR Snapp, 'The Competitive Effects of Partial Equity Interests and Joint Ventures' (1986) 4 *International Journal of Industrial Organization* 141, which is analysed in ch 4, section I.A below and BA Hawk and HL Huser, '"Controlling" the Shifting Sands: Minority Shareholdings under EEC Competition Law' (1994) 17 *Fordham International Law Journal* 294, 295.

[190] For example, COMP/39.595 *Continental/United/Lufthansa/Air Canada*, decision of 23 May 2013 and COMP/39.596 *BA/AA/IB*, decision of 14 July 2010. Both cases are analysed in ch 5, section II.B below.

[191] See p 11, para 30 of the Commission Staff Working Document, 'Ten Years of Antitrust Enforcement under Regulation 1/2003', accompanying the document Communication from the Commission to the European Parliament and the Council, 'Ten Years of Antitrust Enforcement under Regulation 1/2003: Achievements and Future Perspectives' SWD(2013) 230/2.

[192] S Meadowcroft and D Thompson, *Minority Share Acquisition: The Impact upon Competition* (Luxembourg, Office for Official Publications of the European Communities, 1986) 1.

[193] Ibid, 8.

[194] Ibid, 10.

[195] See para 62 of the Commission Staff Working Document accompanying the White Paper, 'Towards More Effective EU Merger Control' SWD (2014) 221 final.

as far as it concerns Article 101 TFEU, 'it is not clear whether acquiring a minority shareholding would constitute an "agreement" having the object or effect of restricting competition within the meaning of Article 101 TFEU in all cases'.[196]

More specifically, it has been observed that regarding acquisitions of a series of shares via the stock exchange, the application of Article 101 TFEU might present a number of conceptual difficulties such as whether or not an agreement exists. In the event that there is an agreement, the Commission would still have to define whether such an agreement would have the object or effect of deterring competition and, in the case of a positive answer, which purchase agreement specifically does impede competition. The same questions probably concern the application of the articles of association of a firm, the purpose of which is generally to define and make clear 'the corporate governance of the company and the relationship between it and its shareholders'.[197]

As far as the application of Article 102 TFEU is concerned, 'its provision requires that the firm acquiring a minority shareholding already hold a dominant position and that the acquisition would constitute an abuse of that dominant position'.[198] Consequently, the necessary circumstances under which the Commission has the authorization to 'intervene against competitive harm arising from acquisitions of minority shareholdings are therefore quite narrow'.[199] The *Aer Lingus* case constitutes an indicative relevant example.

These specific theories relevant for a competition assessment of minority shareholdings are similar to those arising from acquisitions of control (ie horizontal, non-coordinated and vertical effects), since they focus on structural changes in the market. For these reasons, the SIEC test applied in the Merger Regulation seems to be much more appropriate than the tests applied in Articles 101 and/or 102 TFEU.

In addition, a confirmed contradiction ought to be underlined: while some respondents to the public consultation claim that Articles 101 and 102 TFEU should be applied, the same respondents also emphasise the significance of legal certainty for firms making investments. The procedures laid down in Council Regulation (EC) No 1/2003[200] for the appropriate enforcement of Articles 101 and 102 TFEU essentially require undertakings to self-assess whether they comply with the competition rules and offer the Commission and NCAs the legal power to intervene a posteriori against any anticompetitive conduct without any time restriction. This self-assessment-based procedure appears to provide less legal certainty for enterprises and, therefore, in comparison with the procedural framework of the Merger Regulation, it is less appropriate for examining the effect of lasting acquisitions of minority shareholdings. Under this approach, the Commission should make a decision within a short, legally binding deadline.

To sum up, the Commission seems to support the need to extend Regulation 139/2004 to the acquisition of non-controlling minority shareholdings and that 'it is appropriate to apply the substantive test of the Merger Regulation. While it is expected that only a limited

[196] Ibid.

[197] Ibid.

[198] Ibid.

[199] See Case T-411/07 *Aer Lingus v Commission* [2010] ECR II-3691, in particular para 104, and Case 6/72 *Europemballage and Continental Can v Commission* [1973] ECR 215, [1973] 8171 CMLR 199.

[200] Council Regulation (EC) No 1/2003 of 16 December 2002 on the implementation of the rules on competition laid down in Articles 81 and 82 of the treaty [2003] OJ L1/1, as already amended.

number of cases would be examined, past cases have shown that this initiative would demand a relevant enforcement activity.'[201]

In the subsequent sub-sections we will extensively analyse the potential links under which minority shareholdings may be investigated through the antitrust rules. In particular, in sub-section II.B we try to present the links, if any, between minority shareholdings and Articles 101 and 102 TFEU, giving precise examples from existing economic theory. In sub-section II.C we analyse the potential links between interlocking directorships and explicit or tacit/implicit collusion. Last but not least, in sub-section II.D we present the differences between ex ante and ex post analyses in the context of minority shareholdings.

B. The Link Between Minority Interests and Antitrust Rules

There are three possible ways by which antitrust rules may be used for the assessment of anticompetitive minority interests:

i. There Exists an Agreement which by Object or Effect Restricts the Effective Competition and Violates Article 101 TFEU

The difficulty with this approach is that in some cases such an agreement does not exist. For instance, acquisitions of minority interests via a stock exchange may not contain an agreement among the firms of the sellers and the buyers. In this case a memorandum among shareholders and/or particular firms' articles covering their relationship may be viewed as an agreement under Article 101 TFEU. Therefore, a firm's 'constitution takes effect as an agreement among shareholders and between shareholders and the company[202]'.[203] However,

> This is far-fetched, as their [ie articles of association] purpose is to organise the corporate governance of a legal person. Also, it would affect parties to the agreement who have not pursued any anti-competitive objectives, such as the seller of a shareholding or the other shareholders of the target company.[204]

Generally speaking, stock market acquisitions of minority shareholdings involve an agreement between the firm, who acts as a purchaser, and the shareholder(s) of a firm, who act as the seller(s) in the transaction. In this transaction the difficulty which arises for assessing the potential anticompetitive effects of such an acquisition is that the firm is not a participant in the transaction. Therefore, an agreement between the two firms does not exist.[205]

[201] Above n 191, para 65.

[202] 'For example, Section 25 of the Irish Companies Act 1963 and Section 33(1) of the UK Companies Act 2006'.

[203] A Burnside, 'Minority Shareholdings: An Overview of EU and National Case Law' [2013] *e-Competitions* 56676, 1, 3.

[204] *EC Minority Power—EU Merger Control and the Acquisition of Minority Shareholdings* (2014), Competition Policy Brief 15, 1, 2–3.

[205] On the other hand, an agreement between the two firms does exist if the corporate bodies of the two firms are involved directly in the transaction. See F Caronna, 'Article 81 as a Tool for Controlling Minority Cross-Shareholdings between Competitors' (2004) 29 *European Law Review* 485.

Gilo, Moshe and Spiegel have shown

> that a controlling shareholder (whether a person or a parent corporation) can facilitate tacit collusion further by making a direct passive investment in rival firms. Such investment particularly facilitates collusion if the controller has a relatively small stake in his own firm.[206]

ii. The Establishment of Coordinated Effects which Enhance the Coordinated Behaviour of the Competitors and Violate Article 101 TFEU

The establishment of coordinated effects as a consequence of an acquisition of minority interests implies that the firms engaged in the transaction coordinate their strategic behaviour, ie they raise prices and harm effective competition. Coordination may occur by firms that prior to the acquisition did or did not coordinate their behaviour. In the former case a minority shareholding may make coordination more effective and easier.

An acquisition of a minority shareholding may serve as an instrument for influencing the commercial or strategic policy of a direct competitor (especially in the case where reciprocal minority shareholdings exist)[207,208] or it may enable the acquiring firm to acquire control over the acquired firm at a later stage. In that case, even though the acquisition of minority shareholding does not lead by itself to a restriction of competition for the purposes of Article 101 TFEU, ie it has neither the object, nor the effect of distorting competition by creating the premises for cooperation and/or exchange of commercially sensitive information among the engaged firms,[209] its potential impact on competition in the long run can be seen as an agreement which violates Article 101.[210] As a consequence such structural links may eliminate the incentives of the competitors to compete with each other in the market(s) in which they carry out business.[211]

As well as potential commercial cooperation among firms engaged in a minority shareholding transaction, there are other factors that may serve in this direction. For instance, providing that the market under scrutiny is an oligopolistic market, such factors are barriers to entry[212] and the ability of the acquiring firm to achieve effective control (legal or de facto) over the commercial and strategic policy of the acquired firm.

[206] D Gilo, Y Moshe and Y Spiegel, 'Partial Cross Ownership and Tacit Collusion' (2006) 37(1) *Rand Journal of Economics* 81, 82.

[207] See also OECD, *Antitrust Issues Involving Minority Shareholdings and Interlocking Directorates* (2008), DAF/COMP(2008)30, 1, 20. For the definition of reciprocal minority interests, see ch 2, section II.B above.

[208] The Commission has clearly differentiated the rights to determine the commercial or strategic behaviour of a competitor from the rights that enable the minority shareholder to protect the value of its investment. See, for instance, *PepsiCo/General Mills*, cited in [1992] OJ C228/6; Case IV/M.232 (Eur Comm, 5 August 1992) 7; *Eridania/ISI*, cited in [1991] OJ C204/12; Case IV/M.062 (Eur Comm, 20 July 1991) 3–5.

[209] See, for instance, Case IV/34.857 *BT/MCI* in ch 5, section II.A below. In this case the Commission admitted that Art 101 TFEU does not apply to agreements for the sale and the purchase of shares.

[210] See, for instance, the judgment of the European Court of Justice in the *Philip Morris* case in ch 5. See also Cases 142/85 and 156/84 *British American Tobacco Company Limited and RJ Reynolds Industries Inc v Commission* [1987] ECR 4487 (*'Philip Morris'*) 37–38.

[211] See also N Levy, 'Expanding EU Merger Control to Non-Controlling Minority Shareholdings: A Sledgehammer to Crack a Nut?' [2014] December (1) *CPI Antitrust Chronicle* 1, 3 and M Friend, 'Regulating Minority Shareholding and Unintended Consequences' (2012) 33(6) *European Competition Law Review* 303, 303.

[212] Above n 207, 20.

In particular, the level of concentration in the market under scrutiny plays a critical role in the existence or not of coordinated behavior. The higher the level of concentration, the lower the number of the effective firms in the market and the higher the likelihood of cooperation among them. This depends crucially on the magnitude of the influence of the strategic behavior of the acquired firm, since the more the acquiring firm knows about the target firm, the easier it is to coordinate with it in order to enhance the profits of both firms.

A concentrated market enhances coordination among its players without the need for an agreement that may violate Article 101 TFEU. However, two factors that independently contribute to such an enhancement must be considered: firstly, the existence of reciprocal and indirect minority shareholdings among the firms in the market; and secondly, the existence or not of a maverick firm.[213]

The existence of reciprocal and indirect minority shareholdings among the firms in the market enhances the ability of the acquiring firm to monitor the strategic behaviour of the target firm and at the same time the strategic behaviour of all the other firms that are connected with it via the existence of minority shareholdings.[214] Let us consider the simple case shown in Figure 4 in chapter 2. In this market with three competing firms the cooperation among all the firms in it is easier due to the existence of the indirect minority shareholding of firm A in firm C (a passive minority shareholding of firm B in firm C).

The picture is more complex in Figure 3 in chapter 2. Suppose reciprocal minority shareholdings between upstream firms A and B. The existence of all the direct, indirect and reciprocal minority shareholdings in the upstream and downstream markets enables its players to coordinate their behaviour better and more easily given the fact that the 10 per cent equity shareholding provides them with enough knowledge for such a conduct.[215]

The economic literature has shown mixed results regarding the link between passive minority interests and tacit collusion. Flath states that for more than two firms in the market as firms expand its passive minority interests in the rivals' issued capital the perfect cartel scenario is not attained.[216] The author also states that independent authorities must pay more attention to direct than to indirect minority shareholdings. In addition, Flath has indicated that the cartel outcome can be reached only when the passive minority interests are small.[217]

[213] Maverick firms are defined as 'firms that have a greater economic incentive to deviate from the terms of coordination than do most of their rivals'. See D Gilo, Y Moshe and Y Spiegel, 'Partial Cross Ownership and Tacit Collusion' (2006) 37(1) *Rand Journal of Economics* 81, 82 (fn 4). See also J Baker, 'Mavericks, Mergers, and Exclusion: Proving Coordinated Competitive Effects Under the Antitrust Laws' (2002) 77 *New York University Law Review* 135.

[214] Tables 15–20 in ch 7 below present different types of minority shareholdings for various markets across the world.

[215] See also RA Struijlaart, Minority Share Acquisitions below the Control Threshold of the EC Merger Control Regulation: An Economic and Legal Analysis' (2002) 25(2) *World Competition* 173, 178, who states that: 'The effects of the Reynolds–Snapp theorem will be modest where a few firms are linked by relatively small holdings. When more firms become linked by larger shareholdings, the effects on competition may however be significant.' The paper by Reynolds and Snapp is presented in ch 5 below.

[216] See the analysis presented in ch 4, section II.C below. See also D Flath, 'Horizontal Shareholding Interlocks' (1992) 13 *Managerial and Decision Economics* 75.

[217] Ibid. See also D Flath, 'When Is it Rational for Firms to Acquire Silent Interests in Rivals?' (1991) 9, *International Journal of Industrial Organization* 573.

Malueg has shown that repeated interaction among firms may reduce the likelihood of collusion. The author, however, indicates that increasing the value of minority shareholdings among rivals leads to a decreased net gain from cheating as the collusive outcome decreases, and results in a lower punishment level for collusive members. Therefore, the net effect of minority shareholdings on tacit collusion is unambiguous.[218] Kühn and Rimler, on the other hand, have shown that minority shareholdings positively affect the collusive outcome which dominates the deviated profits in markets with intense price competition.[219]

> When several competitors have structural links in a third firm, this may facilitate collusion even in case the third firm is active in another market. In the case a minority shareholder deviates from the collusive behaviour, firms may revert to less collaborative behaviour in the jointly owned firm. The deviating minority shareholders are therefore punished by participating in the losses of the jointly owned firm.
>
> In order for the passive investment to serve as an effective commitment not to deviate, it is necessary that other colluding parties believe that the transaction is effective. For example, this may be the case if the transaction can be publicly observed.[220]

Gilo, Moshe and Spiegel in 'the context of an infinitely repeated Bertrand homogeneous product symmetric n-firm oligopoly model in which both firms and shareholders may hold a complex, not necessarily identical, partial financial interests in rivals' show that 'that partial financial interests can facilitate collusion by reducing the incentive of target firms to deviate from the coordinated arrangement because the increased deviation profit is shared with the acquiring firm(s)'.[221]

The existence of a maverick firm in a market prevents effective coordination among the remaining firms in this market. Ignjatovic and Ridyard have stated that:

> [U]nless structural links are widespread throughout the industry to aid coordination with any firms other than the parties to the transaction, or the target is a 'maverick' firm that has prevented effective coordination among the remaining competitors, enhancing the ability to reach a coordinated agreement between only two firms in the market is rarely likely to lead to effective coordination across the market as a whole.[222]

Gilo, Moshe and Spiegel[223] note that when firms in a market exhibit symmetric marginal costs of production, then an increase in the partial financial interest between two firms, *r*, the acquiring firm, and *s*, the acquired firm, facilitate coordination if and only if

— each firm in the industry holds a stake in at least one rival;
— the maverick firm in the industry has a direct or an indirect stake in firm *r*;
— firm *s* is not the industry maverick.

[218] Ibid. See also DA Malueg, 'Collusive Behavior and Partial Ownership of Rivals' (1992) 10 *International Journal of Industrial Organization* 27.

[219] K Kühn and M Rimler, 'The Comparative Statics of Collusion Models' (2006) CEPR Discussion Paper No 5742.

[220] See p 13, paras 57–58 of the Annex of the Commission Staff Working Document, 'Towards More Effective EU Merger Control' SWD(2013) 239 final.

[221] See the analysis presented in ch 4, section II.C below. See also D Gilo, Y Moshe and Y Spiegel, 'Partial Cross Ownership and Tacit Collusion' 37(1) (2006) *Rand Journal of Economics* 81.

[222] B Ignjatovic and D Ridyard, 'Minority Shareholdings, Material Effects?' (2012) 1 *CPI Antitrust Chronicle* 1, 6–7.

[223] Above n 221.

Gilo, Spiegel and Temurshoev show that when firms in a market exhibit different marginal costs of production, an increase in the passive minority interest of a firm in a rival facilitates collusion if and only if:

— the maverick firm in the industry has a direct or an indirect stake in the acquiring firm,
— the target firm is not the industry maverick.[224]

The role of the maverick firm in sustaining effective coordination among firms in a market has also been indicated in the context of mergers by the European Commission. In particular, the Commission states that:

> [A] merger may also increase the likelihood or significance of coordinated effects in other ways. For instance, a merger may involve a 'maverick' firm that has a history of preventing or disrupting coordination, for example by failing to follow price increases by its competitors, or has characteristics that gives it an incentive to favour different strategic choices than its coordinating competitors would prefer. If the merged firm were to adopt strategies similar to those of other competitors, the remaining firms would find it easier to coordinate, and the merger would increase the likelihood, stability or effectiveness of coordination.[225]

Gilo, Moshe and Spiegel, by considering the target firm not to be the maverick firm in a market, imply that in the case of passive minority interests a maverick firm may not have the incentive to prevent effective coordination among firms in a market if the latter hold a passive minority interest in the maverick firm.

Ferreria and Waddle[226] have also shown that for Bertrand competition with goods with low heterogeneity some degree of tacit collusion is possible. Ferreria and Waddle also examined firms that compete like Bertrand competitors with homogeneous products and indicate that any price between cost and the monopolistic price can be the collusive price and therefore tacit collusion between the two firms can be achieved.[227]

iii. *The Abuse of a Pre-existing Dominant Position either by the Acquiring or the Target Firm which Violates Article 102 TFEU*

Article 102 TFEU applies only in the case where the engaged firms in the transaction under scrutiny hold a dominant position, either independently or collectively, in the concerned relevant market(s). Therefore, an acquisition of minority shareholding requires the existence of a dominant position between the parties that engaged in it. However, as we have already stated above, an abuse of a dominant position requires that an acquisition of a minority shareholding may serve as an instrument for influencing the commercial or strategic policy of a competitor, especially in the case where there exist reciprocal minority shareholdings in the relevant market under scrutiny.

[224] See also the analysis presented in ch 4, section II.C below and D Gilo, Y Spiegel and U Temurshoev, 'Partial Cross Ownership and Tacit Collusion under Cost Asymmetries', mimeo (2009).

[225] Guidelines on the assessment of horizontal mergers under the Council Regulation on the control of concentrations between undertakings [2004] OJ C31/5, para 42.

[226] See also the analysis presented in ch 4, section II.C and JL Ferreria and R Waddle, 'Strategic Profit Sharing Leads to Collusion in Bertrand Oligopolies' (2010) 6(4) *International Journal of Economic Theory* 341.

[227] Ibid.

As a matter of fact this was the judgment of the Court of Justice in the *Phillip Morris* case. Furthermore, in the *Gillette* case the firm abused its dominant position in the relevant market of disposable razors by acquiring a minority shareholding over its direct competitor, Wilkinson Sword. Gillette had become the main shareholder and creditor of Eemland (the owner of Wilkinson Sword) and could have used its rights to prevent future concentration plans that Eemland would have had, and Gillette would not have approved of. Therefore, in the *Gillette* case the European Commission established an infringement of Article 102 TFEU since the transaction had altered the structure of the market under investigation.

The question that arises is why a dominant firm acquires a passive minority interest in a competitor where from the outset it is questionable whether this investment will lead to increased profits. It is generally the final outcome in cases of full merger acquisitions, but in cases of passive minority shareholdings dominant firms are less likely to follow such a strategic policy. In addition, dominant firms, which already charge the monopoly price or almost the monopoly price, have an interest in eliminating their exposure to antitrust review and prefer to limit their partial acquisitions in smaller firms in the market.

However, the acquisition of a minority shareholding in a fringe firm by a dominant firm is more likely to happen in reality but such a transaction cannot be assessed under Article 102 TFEU.

C. Interlocking Directorships as Facilitator of Tacit or Explicit Collusion

In the previous section we focused on the possible ways in which antitrust rules may be used to assess anticompetitive minority interests. One way is the information exchange between firms engaged in the transaction and its subsequent effect on the degree of transparency between the firms in the market.[228]

We have already mentioned in chapter 2 that interlocking directorships refer to situations where competitors either in horizontal or vertical markets share one or more directors. These groupings can be classified as active or passive, horizontal or vertical, direct or indirect, and one-way or reciprocal. In addition, shareholdings with access to crucial information refer to the situation where the owner of the passive minority shareholding has the right to put a member of its firm, eg a director, an executive or non-executive member of the board of directors or a manager, onto the board of directors of its competitor with the right to have access to commercial or confidential information. This right emerges from the shareholder agreement regarding the acquisition of the passive minority shareholding. This is a mixed form of minority interest, but is very important in terms of competition concerns since its owner not only holds a financial interest, but also enjoys the right to draw upon crucial information about its competitors.[229]

Giving the owner of the minority shareholding the opportunity to know the commercial activities of the acquired firm enhances the degree of transparency in the market. The enhancement depends crucially on the type of minority shareholding: if they are reciprocal

[228] See also OECD, *Antitrust Issues Involving Minority Shareholdings and Interlocking Directorates* (2008), DAF/COMP(2008)30, 1, 30.

[229] See also ch 2, section II.C.ii above.

and exist between all the players of the market under scrutiny, then the acquiring firm or the owner of the minority shareholding not only has the opportunity to monitor the behaviour of the target firm but also to stipulate coordinated behavior among all the firms involved.

In the case of minority shareholdings and directorships the degree of transparency is higher than in any other case of minority interests. The owners of such interests are granted sufficient rights to enable them to coordinate their behaviour. The presence of interlocking directorships reduces the degree of competition in the market. Even though in the case of financial interests a certain amount of information exchange between the acquiring and the 'victim' firm should exist as the owner of the interest may have access to information regarding the plans of strategic expansion of the latter which otherwise would not have the ability to obtain them.

The degree of independence of competing firms with respect to their boards affects in one way or another way the corresponding quality of their business decisions. Effective competition implies the existence of independent decisions among firms in a market. The presence of interlocking directorships reduces the incentive of firms to compete independently, either horizontally or vertically. In the former case firms are engaged in horizontal cooperation and in the latter case firms act in favour of some suppliers or customers in both markets.

D. The Differences Between Ex Ante and Ex Post Analyses in the Context of Minority Shareholdings

In the previous two sub-sections we focused on the potential link between antitrust rules and minority shareholdings. We showed that Articles 101 and 102 TFEU as well as Regulation 1/2003 may be used to assess the anticompetitive effects of minority interests. The established antitrust law offers the ability to competition authorities to deal with a large number of, though not all, passive minority acquisitions.

The difference between an acquisition of a minority shareholding and a case concerning antitrust law is that the former is an acquisition and the latter is not. This implies that the method of assessment is completely different for these two situations. In particular, assessment of an acquisition (or a merger) follows an ex ante investigation of the potential unilateral and coordinated effects that might occur in the relevant market under scrutiny. Even though the long-run (coordinated) effects can be assessed by antitrust law, we cannot say the same for the short-run (unilateral) effects.

With an ex ante investigation the priority is to find the anticompetitive mechanisms that the firms engaged in the transaction will use in their own favour and against consumers. As soon as these mechanisms have been revealed, it is then possible to prevent their establishment in markets where the firms are active. Therefore, the main scope of the ex ante analysis is to prevent a hypothetical scenario by which the acquisition restricts effective competition and makes consumers worse off.

This ex ante investigation can be useful within the so-called 'structure–conduct–performance paradigm'. According to this, the interaction of firms is affected/caused by the structure of the market in which these firms are active. Therefore, the potential structure of a market, which is measured by firms' market shares in it, can be used as a proxy in order to predict the effect of an enhanced concentration level[230] on the market.[231]

However, an ex post investigation assesses an already established situation in which the firms engaged in the transaction may or may not have infringed antitrust law. Therefore, the main focus is not to prevent the emergence of the above-mentioned mechanisms, but to stop them should they exist and to enhance the level of competition in the investigated market.

From the analysis so far it seems that an ex ante analysis may postpone or cancel an ex post analysis. That is, an effective ex ante analysis may prevent the emergence of market characteristics or conduct by firms that enable the restriction of effective competition.

Another crucial issue with ex ante analysis is the assessment of the short-run effects of an acquisition on competition. These obviously cannot be assessed from their outset by an ex post analysis since this kind of analysis is beyond the spirit and letter of antitrust law. From established case law and economic theory it is well known that the unilateral effects of an acquisition can dampen consumer surplus by increasing the price of the product and decreasing the quantity produced in the market. This scenario can obviously be prevented by an ex ante analysis, but can only be terminated under an ex post analysis. This means that until their termination, unilateral effects, if any, may harm consumers and establish market conditions in such a way that it may be difficult for a competition authority to assess these effects in a later stage.

All in all, the two methods of analysis have differences regarding their assessment of minority shareholdings. Both approaches are effective from the competition policy perspective, but ex ante analysis is more effective since it precedes ex post analysis.

[230] Which is measured by the Herfindahl–Hirschman Index (*HHI*), the sum of the squares of the market shares of all firms present on a particular market. It ranges from zero (perfect competition) to 10,000 (monopoly). For more details see the analysis presented in ch 4 below.

[231] See also DW Carlton and JM Perloff, *Modern Industrial Organization* (New York, Harper Collins, 1994).

4

The Economics of Minority Interests

I. Theoretical Literature Review of Minority Shareholdings

The economic literature has shown that passive minority shareholdings can harm competition either unilaterally or via coordinated effects. The magnitude of the damage depends crucially on the share of the target's profits that the acquiring firm is actually entitled to as a result of the acquired minority shareholding, and the ability of the acquirer to influence materially the target's strategic behavior. The first of these two criteria implies that the higher the financial interest, the higher the harmful effects of minority shareholdings on competition; while the second one examines the role of corporate rights on the ability of the acquiring firm to influence significantly the competitive policy of the target firm. If both criteria exist, ie financial interests are accompanied by corporate rights,[1] then such structural links may alter the competitive behaviour of both acquiring and target firm.

A. Horizontal Unilateral Effects

The anticompetitive effects of structural links are higher at the horizontal level than at the vertical level. When firms engaged in such links are direct competitors, their silent interests in each other alter their strategic choice in favour of coordination among them. For instance, the acquiring firm may have the incentive to compete less aggressively with its competitor by raising its product price or restricting its output (*horizontal unilateral effects*). The acquiring firm captures part of the diverted sales of its competitor through its minority shareholding. In this scenario the important issues are the degree of competition between the two firms and the level of sales diverted to the competitors. The greater the competition between firms, ie the more the products are close substitutes, the greater the level of lost or diverted sales of the acquiring firm that are captured by the target firm after an increase in the acquiring firm's product. This is called the 'diversion ratio'. The latter in absolute terms is the ratio of the cross-elasticity of demand for firm j's product when firm i raises the price divided by the own-elasticity of demand for firm i's product multiplied by the ratio of unit sales by firm j divided by the unit sales by firm i.[2] In the absence of such

[1] See, for instance, the notion of minority shareholdings with crucial information discussed in ch 2 above.

[2] See, inter alia, C Shapiro, 'Mergers with Differentiated Products' [Spring 1996] *Antitrust* 23 and J Hausman, S Moresi and M Rainey, 'Unilateral Effects of Mergers with General Linear Demand' [2011] *Economics Letters* 119, 119. For the mathematical formula of diversion ratio see equation (20) below.

a minority shareholding the diverted sales of the acquiring firm after an increase of its product price may hinder it from proceeding with such an increase. As a result, the acquiring firm earns profit, the magnitude of which depends on the percentage of its minority shareholding in the issued capital of the target firm.

Let us present a simple example of the effect of a passive minority shareholding on both profits and diversion ratio. Suppose that in the case of a hypothetical merger between firms 1 and 2 the diversion ratio has been estimated to be 20 per cent, ie 20 per cent of the sales of the acquiring firm (1) will be captured by the target firm (2) after an increase in the acquiring firm's price. Suppose now that firm 1 acquires a 25 per cent minority shareholding in the issued capital of firm 2. After the acquisition of the financial interest the former will benefit from only one-quarter of the profits of the target firm attributed to the diverted sales from firm 1 and the diversion ratio between the two firms will equal 5 per cent, ie one-quarter of the estimated diversion ratio in the case of a hypothetical merger between the two firms. Therefore, both horizontal unilateral effects and profits depend on the amount of the minority shareholding. Moreover, it is evident from the above simple blackboard example that the unilateral effects are less pronounced when purchasing a minority shareholding than in a full merger.

B. Coordinated Effects

In most cases structural links enable the firms involved to coordinate their conduct (*coordinated effects*). Coordination between firms stems from the fact that the acquiring firm internalizes part of the target's profit. Moreover, the level of transparency is enhanced in the presence of corporate rights. In particular, when a one-way direct type of passive interest is under scrutiny the one-way exchange of information (from the target to the acquiring firm) enables the latter to monitor the commercial policy of the former. However, when a reciprocal minority shareholding is under scrutiny,[3] then the exchange of information is reciprocal between the firms involved and therefore the level of transparency is enhanced.

The level of transparency in a market is enhanced further in the case where indirect minority shareholdings with their associated corporate rights are under examination.[4] Indirect passive interests are of great importance to antitrust authorities since they strengthen information exchange and increase the ability of firms to coordinate their actions. These two critical characteristics enlarge the scope of coordination and enable the coordinated players to detect possible deviations from the common aim of maximizing the monopoly profits.[5]

[3] See Figure 2 in ch 2 above.
[4] See Figures 3–6 in ch 2 above.
[5] This is the case where all the firms of the market are engaged in the coordinated group of firms. If, however, a competitive fringe of firms maximizes their profits independently from the coordinated group of firms, then the common target of the coordinated firms is the maximization of the collusive profits.

C. Non-Horizontal Unilateral Effects

The anticompetitive effects of non-horizontal minority shareholdings are also a prominent feature of the economic literature (*non-horizontal unilateral effects*). Even though these can be categorized into vertical and conglomerate minority shareholdings, the former may lead more to enhanced competition concerns such as input or customer foreclosure than the latter. Conglomerate minority shareholdings raise anticompetitive issues only in cases where the acquiring firm acquires a minority stake in the target firm which is active in a market related to that of the acquiring firm. In such a case a conglomerate minority shareholding may facilitate firms to make sales of one product contingent on the sales of others via bundling,[6] tying[7] or similar practices such as exclusive dealing[8] or full-line forcing.[9]

Vertical minority shareholdings, ie acquisitions of passive minority interests between firms that are active at another level of the supply chain, can harm competition by imposing input[10] or customer[11] foreclosure.[12] The minority shareholding gives the incentive to the acquiring firm to foreclose competitors from markets where the target firm is active and, if it is accompanied by corporate rights, then the acquiring firm may gain the ability to foreclose the target's competitors from its input and customer base.

[6] Bundling and tying refer to commercial strategies. However, in terms of competition law, bundling usually refers to the way products are offered and priced by the dominant undertaking. The same holds for tying (see below). In the case of pure bundling the products are only sold jointly in fixed proportions. In the case of mixed bundling, often referred to as a multiproduct rebate, the products are also made available separately, but the sum of the prices when sold separately is higher than the bundled price. See [2009] OJ C45/7, para 48.

[7] 'Tying' usually refers to situations where customers that purchase one product (the tying product) are required also to purchase another product from the dominant undertaking (the tied product). Tying can take place on a technical or contractual basis. [2009] OJ C45/7, para 48 (fn 2) states that: 'Technical tying occurs when the tying product is designed in such a way that it only works properly with the tied product (and not with the alternatives offered by competitors). Contractual tying occurs when the customer who purchases the tying product undertakes also to purchase the tied product (and not the alternatives offered by competitors).'

[8] Ibid, para 32: 'A dominant undertaking may try to foreclose its competitors by hindering them from selling to customers through use of exclusive purchasing obligations or rebates, together referred to as exclusive dealing.' [2009] OJ C45/7, para 32 (fn 4) states that: 'The notion of exclusive dealing also includes exclusive supply obligations or incentives with the same effect, whereby the dominant undertaking tries to foreclose its competitors by hindering them from purchasing from suppliers. The Commission considers that such input foreclosure is in principle liable to result in anti-competitive foreclosure if the exclusive supply obligation or incentive ties most of the efficient input suppliers and customers competing with the dominant undertaking are unable to find alternative efficient sources of input supply.'

[9] When firms use bundling as a vertical restraint, then this is known as full-line forcing. Generally speaking, in a full-line forcing arrangement, distributors are contractually obligated to sell a supplier's product line in its entirety. See also K Ho, J Ho and JH Mortimer, 'The Use of Full-Line Forcing Contracts in the Video Rental Industry' (2012) 102(2) *American Economic Review* 686 (formerly published as NBER Working Paper No 16318).

[10] In the case of a merger input foreclosure is 'where the merger is likely to raise the costs of downstream rivals by restricting their access to an important input'. See [2008] OJ C265/10, para 30.

[11] In the case of a merger, costumer foreclosure is 'where the merger is likely to foreclose upstream rivals by restricting their access to a sufficient customer base' (ibid).

[12] In the case of a merger foreclosure is used 'to describe any instance where actual or potential rivals' access to supplies or markets is hampered or eliminated as a result of the merger, thereby reducing these companies' ability and/or incentive to compete. As a result of such foreclosure, the merging companies—and, possibly, some of its competitors as well—may be able to profitably increase the price … charged to consumers. These instances give rise to a significant impediment to effective competition and are therefore referred to hereafter as "anticompetitive foreclosure"' (ibid, para 18).

The acquiring firm's incentives to foreclosure are higher with corporate rights than with sole financial interests. When the acquiring firm has access to commercial data of the target firm, then the gains from foreclosure are higher than in the case of a vertical merger. This happens due to the fact that this approach internalizes the whole stream of profits that are coming from the other levels of supply chain and at the same time incurs only a small portion of the costs caused by the anticompetitive strategy. However, when the minority shareholding includes only a financial interest, then the acquiring firm has no access to appropriate data in order to proceed to a successful foreclosure.[13]

D. Entry Effects

Passive minority interests may sometimes deter entry either for potential entrants which are not active or for active firms which are interested in expanding their product range. In addition, the acquiring firm may hinder another firm from getting access in the capital stock of the target firm.

As we have already mentioned above, the acquiring firm partially internalizes the costs that the target firm incurs. The losses of the acquiring firm from entry are limited to the amount of its minority shareholding. It therefore has an increased incentive to deter entry by credibly committing it to the potential entrant.[14] If the financial interest is accompanied by corporate rights that influence the competitive behaviour of the target firm, then this issue prevents a potential entrant from entering.

E. Arguments in Favour of Minority Interests

It has been argued that passive minority interests may also result in efficiencies. The fact that the acquiring firm incurs only the part of the cost amounting to its minority shareholding is an argument in support of this approach. The acquiring firm may potentially influence the competitive policy of the target firm by incurring only a minimum cost from its daily activity. Ono et al have argued that passive minority interests facilitate the transfer of technology and managerial skills and the creation of cost-synergies which positively influence firms' profits.[15]

[13] 'In Germany, typical examples concern the energy sector where the Bundeskartellamt assessed the foreclosure effects of energy companies acquiring minority stakes in downstream utilities. An example at the EU level concerns the *IPIC/MAN Ferrostaal* case where MAN Ferrostaal held a minority stake in Eurotecnica, a provider of technology and engineering services. The Commission was concerned that MAN Ferrostaal would determine the technology licenses distribution by Eurotecnica and thus exclude competitors. The remedy included the divestiture of the minority share held by MAN Ferrostaal in Eurotecnica.' See JP Schmidt, 'Germany: Merger Control Analysis of Minority Shareholdings–A Model for the EU?' (2013) 2 *Concurrences* 207, 209–10. Regarding *IPIC/MAN Ferrostaal*. See also ch 5, section B(ii).

[14] For economic models of entry deterrence, see especially A Dixit, 'A Model of Duopoly Suggesting a Theory of Entry Barriers' (1979) 10(1) *Bell Journal of Economics* 20 and AM Spence, 'Entry, Capacity, Investment, and Oligopolistic Pricing' (1977) 8 *Bell Journal of Economics* 534.

[15] See H Ono, T Nakazato, C Davis and W Alley, 'Partial Ownership Arrangements in the Japanese Automobile Industry; 1990–2000' (2004) 7(2) *Journal of Applied Economics* 355, 356.

Amundsen and Bergman have noted that expected synergies, such as cost reduction through sales cooperation and learning, ie acquiring information about the production process, are inter alia motives that enable a firm to acquire minority shareholdings in their rivals.[16]

In vertical minority shareholdings the acquiring firm may avoid problems which arise from issues such as double marginalization and incomplete information.[17] However, the economic literature in section II.B of this chapter shows that the double marginalization problem is eliminated only in the case of controlling vertical integration and not in the case of passive minority interests.[18]

Lastly, arguments in favour of minority shareholdings among non-rival firms have also been raised in the literature. Ouimet states, inter alia, that minority acquisitions are more common when the target firm owns a large number of patents, while full acquisition ameliorates the incentives of a firm to invest in assets 'whose value depends on trades with its partner firm'.[19] Obviously this is a cost of full acquisition and a type of synergy of minority shareholdings among non-rival firms.[20]

This chapter is organized as following: in section II.A we present the unilateral effects, while in section II.B we analyse the coordinated effects of minority shareholdings. In both of these sub-sections we will focus our analysis on transactions that take place among direct and indirect competitors. In section II.C we examine the entry effects of minority shareholdings.

II. Unilateral Effects of Minority Shareholdings

A. Horizontal Unilateral Effects

Reynolds and Snapp[21] in their study of a Cournot market with homogeneous products[22] evaluated the competitive effects of reciprocal partial equity interests, ie 'the ownership of any security, ['such as bonds, some kinds of leases, and other financial instruments as well

[16] ES Amundsen and L Bergman, 'Will Cross-Ownership Re-estabish Market Power in the Nordic Power Market?' (2002) 23(2) *Energy Journal* 73, 77.

[17] Commission Staff Working Document, 'Towards More Effective EU Merger Control', annex I, 1, 6, 19.

[18] We are aware about the potential effects of minority shareholdings on corporate governance. However, this analysis is beyond the scope of this book. See, inter alia, E Berglof and E Perotti, 'The Governance Structure of the Japanese Financial Keiretsu' (1994) 36 *Journal of Financial Economics* 259.

[19] See PP Ouimet, 'What Motivates Minority Acquisitions? The Trade-offs between a Partial Equity Stake and Complete Integration' (2012) 26(4) *Review of Financial Studies* 1021, 1023.

[20] See also S Grossman and O Hart, 'The Costs and Benefits of Ownership: A Theory of Lateral and Vertical Integration' (1986) 94 *Journal of Political Economy* 691.

[21] See also RJ Reynolds and BR Snapp, 'The Economic Effects of Partial Equity Interests and Joint Ventures' (1982), US Department of Justice, Antitrust Division, Economic Policy Office Discussion Paper.

[22] See A Cournot, *Recherches sur les principes mathématiques de la théorie des richesses* (Paris, 1838).

as common and preferred stocks'],[23] asset or claim for which the return is positively related to the issuing firm's profitability'.[24]

Reynolds and Snapp assumed a market with high concentration level but not too high to enable its participants to engage in tacitly collusive behaviour.[25] Generally speaking, according to Reynolds and Snapp:

> [I]n markets where entry is difficult, partial ownership arrangements could result in less output and higher prices than otherwise. These effects arise solely because these arrangements link the fortunes of actual or potential competitors, producing a positive correlation among their profits. In this sense, the effects are purely structural: they arise not because of increased opportunities for collusion or changes in the concentration of control, but because the linking of profits gives each firm an incentive to compete less vigorously and adopt behavior more conducive to joint profit maximization than otherwise would be the case.[26]

Their main finding is that without entry, ie entry is blocked efficiently, if Cournot competitors increase the level of partial equity interests in their competitors, then the level of equilibrium market output will decline. The output decrease will be higher for big rather than for small firms, but smaller for high-cost rather than for low-cost firms.

In particular, let us assume that the i th firm in the market controls quantity q_i from plant i[27] (the case of joint ventures).[28] Firm i maximizes its profits according to the following equation:[29]

$$\pi_i = \left(1-\sum_{j}^{j\neq i} mi_{j,i}\right)(p-c)q_i + \sum_{j}^{j\neq i} mi_{i,j}(p-c)q_j \quad (1)$$

where π_i are the profits of the ith firm in the market, $(p-c)q_i$ are the profits of firm i from plant i, $\left[\sum_j^{j\neq i} mi_{j,i}(p-c)q_i\right]$ are the profits which are going to the jth firm in the market due to its partial equity interest ($mi_{j,i}$) in firm i and $\sum_j^{\neq i} mi_{i,j}(p-c)q_j$ are the profits which are going to firm i due to its partial equity interest ($mi_{i,j}$) in firm j.

[23] See RJ Reynolds and BR Snapp, 'The Competitive Effects of Partial Equity Interests and Joint Ventures' (1986) 4 *International Journal of Industrial Organization* 141, fn 1.

[24] Ibid.

[25] However, the authors also state at the end that minority shareholdings may enhance collusive conduct among firms since cheating on a cartel is less desirable for its members due to profit losses they incur upon their competitors.

[26] Above n 23, 142.

[27] A plant is assumed to be a producer of output to be sold in the market price, while a firm is assumed to be decision making unit.

[28] The Commission has experience of profit-sharing joint ventures. See Cases COMP/39.595 *Continental/United/Lufthansa/Air Canada*, decision of 23 May 2013 and COMP/39.596 *BA/AA/IB*, decision of 14 July 2010 presented in ch 5, section II.B below.

[29] See also U Merlone, 'Shareholding Interlocks: Profit Formulations and Cartelizing Effects' (2007) 10(1) *Journal of Interdisciplinary Mathematics* 99, 102 and A Matsutomo, U Merlone and F Szidarovszky, 'Dynamic Oligopoly with Partial Cooperation and Antitrust Threshold' (2009) 73(2) *Journal of Economic Behavior and Organization* 299, 302, 305. In the case of passive minority interests the joint venture formulation is $\pi_i = \left(1-\sum_j^{j\neq i} mi_{j,i}\right)(p-c)q_i + \sum_j^{j\neq i} mi_{i,j}\left[(p-c)q_i + mi_{i,j}(p-c)q_j\right]$, where $[mi_{i,j}(p-c)q_i]$ are the profits which are going to firm i due to its partial equity interest ($mi_{i,j}$) in firm j. See also the analysis of the article by Flath (1991) later in this section.

Equation (1) simply states that firm *i* maximizes its own profits net of those going to firm *j* as well as the profits from the partial equity interests. If one or more of the Cournot competitors increases its amount of partial equity interest in the rival, then the equilibrium market output which is linked with the increased partial equity interest is higher than otherwise.

The plants' output decisions, even where these are joint ventures, are always set by one firm/controller, and the profits are subsequently divided between each equity holder in proportion to the size of the holding. However, the presence of one controller precludes the existence of joint control over the joint ventures.[30] Given this modelling setting the profits generated from partial equity interests will be positive if entry is blocked or at least if it constitutes a process which discourages potential entrants from entering the market. However, if entry is easy, then profits will be eliminated since higher profits will attract new players in the market.

Table 5 shows the levels of reduction of the output market with respect to the number of the firms in the market with partial equity interests in their rivals and the level of passive interest (small or big).

Table 5: The effect of partial equity interests on market output: Cournot competition with homogeneous products

Number of firms in the market	**% reduction of the market output**		
	$ms = \mathbf{0.05}$	$ms = \mathbf{0.10}$	$ms = \mathbf{0.20}$
10 (1→1)	–	0.1	–
5 (1→1)	–	0.2	–
10 (1↔1)	–	0.2	–
5 (1↔1)	–	0.4	–
2 (2↔2)	1.7	3.6	7.7
5 (5↔5)	4	10	40
10 (10↔10)	6.9	45	–

Notes: The percentage reduction of the market output is given by the expression:

$$\left[\left(\frac{Q_{COURNOT(ms=0)} - Q_{QURNOT(ms\neq0)}}{Q_{COURNOT(ms=0)}}\right) * 100\right]$$

(1→1): direct passive interest if one of five or ten equally sized and previously unlinked firms acquired a 10 per cent interest in one competitor.
(1↔1): direct passive interest between two of five or ten equally sized and previously unlinked firms if each acquires a 10 per cent interest in the others.
(2↔2) (5↔5) (10↔10): all the firms in the market have reciprocal passive interests in each other.
ms, passive equity interest.

Source: RJ Reynolds and BR Snapp, 'The Competitive Effects of Partial Equity Interests and Joint Ventures' (1986) 4 *International Journal of Industrial Organization* 141.

30 See also RA Struijlaart, 'Minority Share Acquisitions Below the Control Threshold of the EC Merger Control Regulation: An Economic and Legal Analysis' (2002), 25(2) *World Competition* 173, 177.

In the case where the firms acquire the maximum level of partial equity interest, ie $ms = \frac{1}{n}$, where n is the number of the firms in the market, regardless of the number of firms in it the market equilibrium output is the monopoly output, $Q_{COURNOT(ms \neq 0)} = \left(\frac{1}{2}\right) * \left(\frac{a-c}{b}\right)$.[31]

In Cournot competition with homogeneous products and equally sized firms the relationship between the Lerner index (L), the own price elasticity of demand (η) and the Herfindahl–Hirschman index (HHI) is given by the following equation:

$$L = \frac{1}{\eta} * HHI \tag{2}$$

where $L = \frac{P(Q) - MC(Q)}{P(Q)}$ is the market monopoly power index, $HHI = \sum_{i=1}^{n} s_i^2$ where s is the market share, and $\eta = \left(\frac{\Delta q}{\Delta p}\right) * \left(\frac{p}{q}\right)$ is the own price elasticity of demand in absolute terms.

It should be noted here that the HHI is defined as the sum of the squares of the market shares over all the firms within the market. When the market shares are expressed as fractions, the HHI ranges from 0 to 1.0, moving from a huge number of very small firms (0) to a single monopolistic producer (1.0). Increases in the index indicate a decrease in competition and an increase of market power, whereas decreases indicate the opposite. If whole percentages are used, the index ranges from 0 to 10,000. For instance, an index of .25 when the market shares are expressed as fractions is the same as 2,500 if whole percentages are used.

However, Reynolds and Snapp[32] showed that in the presence of partial equity interests among firms in the market the relationship shown in equation (2) is given by:

$$L = \frac{1}{\eta} * \left(HHI * \frac{\left(1 - \sum_{j}^{j \neq i} mi_{j,i} + \sum_{j}^{j \neq i} mi_{i,j}\right)}{1 - \sum_{j}^{j \neq i} mi_{j,i}} \right) \tag{3}$$

where $\sum_{j}^{j \neq i} mi_{j,i}$ and $\sum_{j}^{j \neq i} mi_{i,j}$ are given by equation (1). Therefore, the adjusted HHI ($AHHI$) is:

$$AHHI = HHI * \frac{\left(1 - \sum_{j}^{j \neq i} mi_{j,i} + \sum_{j}^{j \neq i} mi_{i,j}\right)}{1 - \sum_{j}^{j \neq i} mi_{j,i}} \tag{4}$$

In the presence of partial equity interests, $AHHI > HHI$.

Bresnahan and Salop extended Reynold and Snapp's work by developing the modified HHI ($MHHI$) in order to examine the effects of financial interests on competition by

[31] Suppose that the market demand is $P = a - bQ$, where P the price of the homogeneous product, Q is the market output and a, b are parameters of the demand function (the constant and the slope coefficient, respectively). Note that c is the constant marginal cost of production.

[32] Above n 23.

analysing a horizontal joint venture among competitors in a Cournot market with homogeneous products.[33] The profits of a joint venture are shared among parent firms and so the private incentive of each parent firm to expand its output and reduce the price of the product is limited.

Let us examine first a joint venture with *n* production units the profits of which are shared between two firms, 1 and 2. Neither firm 1 nor firm 2 own any form of control over the joint venture. The *MHHI* is given by the following equation:

$$MHHI = HHI + ms_1 s_1 s_n + ms_2 s_2 s_n \tag{5}$$

where s_1 is the market share of firm 1, s_2 is the market share of firm 2 and S_n is the market share of the joint venture in the market.

If firm 1 has control over the joint venture given its financial interest, then the *MHHI* is given by:

$$MHHI = HHI + \left(\frac{1}{ms_1} + ms_1\right) s_1 s_n + ms_2 s_2 s_n \tag{6}$$

If firm 1 has full control (100 per cent) of the joint venture, ie $ms_1 = 1$ and $ms_2 = 0$, then *MHHI* becomes:

$$MHHI = HHI + 2 s_1 s_n \tag{7}$$

Equation (7) is simply the post-merger formula for the *HHI*.[34] In the case where parent firms 1 and 2 have joint control over the joint venture, then the *MHHI* is given by:

$$MHHI = HHI + (1 + ms_1) s_1 s_n + (1 + ms_2) s_2 s_n \tag{8}$$

When firms 1 and 2 jointly maximize their profits, then the *MHHI* is given by:[35]

$$MHHI = HHI + 2*(s_1 s_2 + s_1 s_n + s_2 s_n) \tag{9}$$

Farrell and Shapiro[36] used the 'structure–conduct–performance' paradigm[37] to examine the effects of asset ownership on prices, output and market concentration. They analysed passive interests in a Cournot market with *n* firms, homogeneous products and efficient barriers to entry. Under constant returns to scale[38] the authors examined capital stocks

[33] TF Bresnahan and SC Salop, 'Quantifying the Competitive Effects of Production Joint Ventures' (1986) 4 *International Journal of Industrial Organization* 155, 155.

[34] See also M Whinston, 'Antitrust Policy toward Horizontal Mergers' in M Armstrong and R Porter (eds), *Handbook of Industrial Organization*, vol 3 (Amsterdam, North-Holland, 2007), ch 36, 2370, for the post-merger formula of *HHI* in a duopoly.

[35] See TF Bresnahan and SC Salop (n 33), 161–67 for the formula of MHHI in the cases of 'competitor-based output formula', 'transfer-price formula with control by distributing parent' and 'transfer-price formula with limited joint control'.

[36] See J Farrell and C Shapiro, 'Asset Ownership and Market Structure in Oligopoly' (1990) 21 *Rand Journal of Economics* 275.

[37] JA Fairburn and P Geroski, 'The Empirical Analysis of Market Structure and Performance' in JA Fairburn and JA Kay (eds), *Merger and Merger Policy* (New York, Oxford University Press, 1989) 175.

[38] If output increases by the same proportional change as all inputs change, then production exhibits constant returns to scale.

among firms in a market and stated that, in general, if all firms in the market have access to the same technology, then the sale of a capital stock from a smaller to a larger firm increases market concentration ratio.[39]

In particular, based on certain assumptions about the cost and demand functions Farrell and Shapiro stated that divestures of small capital stocks from smaller to larger firms decrease output and increase product price. The gain for firms that engage in the divesture is related to their combined size in the market: the higher their size, the higher the anticompetitive effect (increased price) of the divesture. Moreover, if other firms' size in the market is higher than the size of the engaged firms in the divesture,[40] then they also gain from it since they expand their output and markups. Hence, anticompetitive acquisitions of small capital stocks may be welfare enhancing for all the firms in the market.

The last conclusion depends on two critical issues: the first is the total capital stock in the market and the second is the level of the *HHI*. The higher both are, the greater the welfare increase. The intuition behind the second argument is as follows: in a concentrated market the welfare benefits of output expansion by the large firms that do not participate in the divesture are greater than otherwise.[41]

In terms of acquisitions of share in rivals issued capital (ie financial interests), Farrell and Shapiro state that if a firm with a direct minority shareholding slightly increases it, then total output will decrease even though the other firms in the market which do not hold a passive minority shareholding increase their output.

In addition, the profits of the firm that acquires the minority shareholding fall, while the profits of all the other firms in the market, including the target firm, increase after its acquisition. The acquiring firm will find it profitable to buy a share of the capital stock of the target firm if it is a small firm in the market.

The effect of a minority shareholding on total welfare depends on the size of the firm and the amount of the shareholding. If a small firm acquires a minority shareholding in a firm in which it previously had no interest at all, then welfare may increase. Lastly, if a small firm increases its output while the remaining firms in the market do not alter their, then total welfare increases and the *HHI* decreases.

Flath developed a model in which firms purchase equity shares through an efficient stock market before the strategic decision regarding production takes place.[42] An efficient stock market 'is one in which stock prices fully reflect available information'.[43] It is assumed to be (a) weakly efficient if it full incorporates the information in past stock prices,[44]

[39] At the beginning of the article the authors are interested in capital stock acquisitions that alter the production possibilities among firms in the market.

[40] The same argument holds for mergers. See J Farrell and C Shapiro, 'Horizontal Mergers: An Equilibrium Analysis' (1990) 80(1) *American Economic Review* 109.

[41] See J Farrell and C Shapiro, 'Asset Ownership and Market Structure in Oligopoly' (1990) 21 *Rand Journal of Economics* 275, 290.

[42] See D Flath, 'When Is it Rational for Firms to Acquire Silent Interests in Rivals?' (1991) 9 *International Journal of Industrial Organization* 573, 573.

[43] See SA Ross, RW Westerfield and J Jaffe, *Corporate Finance*, 5th edn (New York, McGraw-Hill, 1999) 1, 319.

[44] If the stock prices follow the equation $p_t = p_{t-1} + Expected\ Return + Error$, then they are said to follow a random walk. The latter is assumed to be synonymous with weak form efficiency, even though it is a more restrictive hypothesis since it requires that stock returns are identically distributed through time.

(b) semi-strongly efficient if stock prices incorporate all available public information and (c) strongly efficient if stock prices incorporate all available, public or private, information.

The model comprises two stages: in the first stage firms decide whether or not to acquire a share in their rivals, while in the second stage firms decide the level of production given the passive minority shareholding in the first stage. Let us assume a duopoly game. The profit function of firm i in the market is $\pi_i = (p - c)q_i + mi_{i,j}(p - c)q_j$, where $[mi_{i,j}(p - c)q_i]$ are the profits which are going to firm i due to its partial equity interest $(mi_{i,j})$ in firm j and $(p - c)q_i$ are the profits of firm i due to its operation. In the first stage the profits of firm i are equal to $\pi_i = (p - c)q_i$.[45]

Firms do not acquire a passive financial interest in their rival unless it causes an increase in their operating income. If in the second stage firms are engaged in a Cournot competition with homogeneous products, then it is not strategically efficient for each firm to acquire a passive minority interest in its rival. Even though each firm's production is contracted by the acquisition, the reaction curve of its rival is not affected by it. On the contrary, rivals are induced to choose a larger level of production as a result of the acquisition.[46] Therefore, it is not profitable for each firm to proceed with such an acquisition.[47]

However, the industry profits of the duopoly are enhanced after the acquisition of the passive minority interest. The market monopoly power index is given as follows:[48]

$$L = \frac{P(Q) - MC(Q)}{P(Q)} = \frac{\left(1 - mi_{i,j} + mi_{j,i}\right)}{\bar{\eta}\left(2 - mi_{i,j} - mi_{j,i}\right)} \qquad (10)$$

where $\bar{\eta}$ is the constant elasticity of demand, which is equal to or greater than one $(\bar{\eta} \geq 1)$.

Following Flath, '[t]he unique subgame perfect outcome of share trading is that neither firm acquires shares in the other, even though cross-shareholding by either would be in the combined interest of both'.[49]

If in the second stage firms are engaged in a Bertrand competition with homogeneous products, ie firms choose their prices to maximize their profits (prices are the strategic variables), then due to the fact that prices are perfect substitutes, both firms set their prices equal to their marginal costs regardless the level of the acquired passive minority interest.[50]

[45] In this stage the profits of firm i equal the profits in the first stage minus the net depletions from the acquisition of the minority shareholding through the stock exchange. Given the fact that an efficient stock market implies that the net depletions equal the minority shareholding of firm i times the profits of firm j, ie $mi_{i,j}(p - c)q_j$, it is straightforward to calculate that $\pi_i = (p - c)q_i$.

[46] Firm i's market share is $s_i = \frac{\left(1 - mi_{i,j}\right)}{\left(2 - mi_{i,j} - mi_{j,i}\right)}$. The higher the passive minority interest in firm's j issued capital, the lower its market share. In mathematical terms this implies $\frac{\partial s_i}{\partial ms_{i,j}} < 0$.

[47] See also D Reitman, 'Partial Ownership Arrangements and the Potential for Collusion' (1994) XLII(3) *International Journal of Industrial Organization* 313 and WA Alley, 'Partial Ownership arrangements and Collusion in the Automobile Industry' (1997) XLV(2) *Journal of Industrial Economics* 191.

[48] For the market monopoly power index for the triopoly case (three firms in the market), see especially D Flath, 'Horizontal Shareholding Interlocks' (1992) 13 *Managerial and Decision Economics* 75, 76.

[49] Above n 42, 579.

[50] In the economic literature this is called the 'Bertrand paradox'. See especially J Bertrand, 'Théorie mathématique de la richesse sociale' [1883] *Journal des Savants* 499.

However, if in the second stage firms are engaged in a Bertrand competition with differentiated products, then due to the fact that prices are strategic complements,[51] both firms set higher prices after the acquisition of the passive minority interest. Firms will continue to increase the level of the financial interest in the rival's issued capital until they achieve a cartel in the market.[52]

Flath also examined the cartelized effects of indirect passive minority interests[53] in a market where n firms are engaged in a Cournot competition with homogeneous products. If all firms face constant returns to scale and $mi_{i,j} = m$ if $i \neq j$ and $mi_{i,j} = 0$ if $i = j$,[54] ie the case of symmetric passive minority interests, apart from the cartelized effects which will be discussed in later sections of this chapter, the market monopoly power index is given by the following equation:[55]

$$L = \frac{(1+mi)}{\bar{\eta}n\left(1-mi(n-2)\right)^2} \tag{11}$$

However, if firms ignore indirect passive minority shareholdings, then the market monopoly power index is given by:

$$L = \frac{1+(n-1)mi}{\bar{\eta}n} \tag{12}$$

From equations (11) and (12) it can be calculated that:

$$\frac{1+(n-1)mi}{\bar{\eta}n} < \frac{(1+mi)}{\bar{\eta}n\left(1-mi(n-2)\right)^2} \tag{13}$$

Therefore, 'the price–cost margin is greater when firms do consider the indirect shareholding links than when they ignore them'.[56]

Reitman[57] considered a symmetric Cournot competition in which firms can acquire partial ownership arrangements by purchasing claims to competitor's profits in order to engage in less aggressive competition. When the market consists of more than two firms engaging in quantity competition, passive minority interests are never individually rational for all participants. Moreover, when the nature of competition in the market becomes more rivalrous than Cournot competition, then there exist individually rational partial ownership arrangements in which any number of firms can participate.

[51] See especially J Bulow, J Geanakoplos and P Klemperer, 'Multimarket Oligopoly: Strategic Substitutes and Complements' (1985) 93 *Journal of Political Economy* 488.

[52] The authors reach this conclusion by employing a Hotelling-type competition in the second stage of the game. See especially H Hotelling, 'Stability in Competition' (1929) 39 *Economic Journal* 41.

[53] See also D Flath, 'Indirect Shareholding within Japan's Business Groups' (1992) 38 *Economics Letters* 223.

[54] Passive minority shareholding is $0 \leq mi < \frac{1}{(n-1)}$.

[55] See also E Dietzenbacher, B Smid and B Volkerink, 'Horizontal Integration in the Dutch Financial Sector' (2000) 18 *International Journal of Industrial Organization* 1223, 1229.

[56] D Flath, 'Horizontal Shareholding Interlocks' (1992) 13 *Managerial and Decision Economics* 75, 77.

[57] D Reitman, 'Partial Ownership Arrangements and the Potential for Collusion' (1994) 42 *Journal of Industrial Economics* 313.

The rationale behind Reitman's conclusion is that partial ownership arrangements benefit firms that do not engage in such arrangements more than they benefit the investing firms. That is, there exists a free-rider problem which makes firms not acquire passive minority interests. However, this problem seems to disappear as soon as the symmetric firms in the market compete more aggressively with each other.

Dietzenbacher, Smid and Volkerink[58] state that either in Cournot or in Bertrand markets passive minority interests are anticompetitive. In particular, they show that when shareholdings are absent among firms which engage in Bertrand competition with differentiated products, then the price–cost margin equals the monopolist's margin. In the case of shareholdings among the same firms the monopolist's margin is the lower bound for the market monopoly power index in absolute terms. That is $L \geq \frac{1}{\eta}$.[59]

If the firms compete à la Cournot with homogeneous products, then the market monopoly power index ranges from $\frac{1}{n\eta}$, if the shareholdings are absent, to $\frac{1}{\eta}$ which is the monopolist's margin when the firms hold minority shareholdings in each other.[60] The latter also holds for the case of n identical firms in the market which hold a minority shareholding of $\frac{1}{(n-1)}$ in each other.[61] Dietzenbacher et al also stated that under Cournot competition, when firms increase the level of minority shareholdings in each other, their price–cost margins also increase.

Malueg examined a special case of the Cournot competition described by Reynolds and Snapp where the market demand is given by the following equation:[62]

$$p(Q) = (1 - Q)^a \tag{14}$$

where $Q = q_1 + q_2$ and $a > 0$ is a parameter of demand function. If $0 \leq mi < \frac{1}{2}$, then the symmetric quantity of production of the two firms is:

$$Q_{COURNOT} = \frac{(1-mi)}{(2[(1-mi)+a])} \tag{15}$$

and the symmetric profits are:

$$\pi_{COURNOT} = Q_{COURNOT}*(1 - 2Q_{COURNOT})^{\alpha} \tag{16}$$

O'Brien and Salop examined the competitive effects of passive financial interests (a) by extending 'the *MHHI* to a broader range of corporate control scenarios'[63] in Cournot markets with homogeneous markets and (b) by extending Shapiro's 'diversion ratio' to develop the percentage price increase (PPI) in Bertrand markets with differentiated products.

58 Above n 55.

59 It is assumed here that the own-price elasticity is greater or equal to 1 and the market demand exhibits constant elasticity.

60 It is assumed that the own-price elasticity of demand is equal for all the n firms in the market.

61 See also above n 32.

62 DA Malueg, 'Collusive Behavior and Partial Ownership of Rivals' (1992) 10 *International Journal of Industrial Organization* 27, 29.

63 DP O'Brien and S Salop, 'Competitive Effects of Partial Ownership: Financial Interest and Corporate Control' (2000) 67 *Antitrust Law Journal* 559, 594.

O'Brien and Salop developed revised *MHHI* formulas in a duopoly Cournot market where firm 1 acquires a 20 per cent financial interest in firm 2. Prior to the partial acquisition, firm 1 holds a 20 per cent (s_a) and firm 2 a 10 per cent (s_b) market share. Table 6 exhibits different changes (deltas) of *MHHI* which correspond to different scenarios of control and silent financial interest.

Table 6: Different formulas for *MHHI* deltas for different types of control and silent financial interest

Types of 'control'	*MHHI* deltas	Results
Full merger	$\Delta = 2s_a s_b$[1]	400
Silent financial interest	$\Delta = mi * s_a * s_b$	40
Total control	$\Delta = \left(\frac{mi+1}{mi}\right) * s_a * s_b$	1040
One-way control	$\Delta = (1 + mi) * s_a * s_b$	240
Coasian joint control	$\Delta = 2s_a s_b$	400
Proportional control	$\Delta = \left(\frac{mi+mi}{\left((1-mi)^2+mi^2\right)}\right) * s_a * s_b$	99

[1] See also the second term on the right-hand side of equation (7).

Notes:

Silent financial interest: 'a silent financial interest is one in which the acquiring firm is entitled to a share of the acquired firm's profits but has no power to control or even influence the decisions of the acquired firm'.

Total control: 'a governance structure that leads to the acquiring firm having total control over the significant competitive decision making of the acquired firm'.

One-way control: 'refers to a scenario in which the acquiring firm has enough power over the acquired firm to force the acquired firm to maximize joint profits and not secretly cheat. However, this joint profit maximization only applies to the acquired firm. The acquiring firm continues to act in its own self interest;'

Coasian joint control: 'the managers of the acquiring firm try to maximize the joint profits of both the acquired firm and the acquiring firm. The managers of the acquired firm act similarly.' (See also ch 2, section I.A.)

Proportional control: 'refers to a slightly different scenario in which the Board and managers of the acquiring firm take into account their shareholders' interests in other firms. However, rather than trying to maximize joint profits, they take the shareholders' interests into account in proportion to their financial interests in the acquired firm.'

Source: DP O' Brien and S Salop, 'Competitive Effects of Partial Ownership: Financial Interest and Corporate Control' (2000) 67 *Antitrust Law Journal* 559.

It is evident from Table 6 that the highest *MHHI* delta is for the case of 'total control' since the acquiring firm, without having to pay for the full cost of merging, is able to exert total control over significant competitive decisions of the acquired firm. Conversely, the lowest *MHHI* delta is for the case of 'silent financial interests', indicating that this interest does not influence the incentives of the target firm. When $mi = 1$ all the scenarios, except from the 'silent financial interest' scenario, converge to the 'full merger' scenario.

O'Brien and Salop also derived a general formula for the *MHHI* by modelling firms with multiple owners. In particular, they state that the manager of a firm maximizes the profits of the owners of the firm who may have different objectives for it. For instance, a competitor with a financial interest in a firm has different objectives to the other owners of the firm. Therefore, the objective function of the manager is determined by

> each shareholder's influence over decision-making within the firm. A parsimonious way to model shareholder influence is to assume that the manager of the firm maximizes a weighted sum of the shareholder's returns. … Under this formulation, a higher weight on the profit of a particular owner is associated with a greater degree of influence by that owner over the manager.[64]

Thus, the general formula for the *MHHI* is given by the following equation:

$$MHHI = HHI + \sum_{j}\sum_{j \neq k}\left(\frac{\sum_{i} c_{i,j} mi_{i,k}}{\sum_{i} c_{i,j} mi_{i,j}}\right) \tag{17}$$

In equation (17) $c_{i,j}mi_{i,k}$ is the degree of control of owner i in firm j and $mi_{i,k}$ is the ownership share of firm k owned by owner i. Correspondingly, $c_{i,j}mi_{i,j}$ is the degree of control of owner i in firm j and $mi_{i,j}$ is the ownership share of firm j owned by owner i.

> [T]he MHHI is equal to the HHI plus a set of terms reflecting the competitive effects of cross-ownership within the industry. Starting from a position of zero partial ownership interests, the MHHI delta for a particular new ownership structure can be measured by the summation term in [equation 17].[65]

Let us now consider the duopoly game described by Flath, and in particular the second stage of the game. The profit function of firm i which holds a passive minority interest in firm j is $\pi_i = (p - c)q_i + mi(p - c)q_j$.[66] The corresponding profit function without the passive interest is $\pi_i = (p - c)q_i$.

According to O'Brien and Salop, the equilibrium prices of firm i with or without the acquisition of passive minority interest are given by equations (18) and (19), respectively:

$$p_i = \left(\frac{\eta_i}{\eta_i - 1}\right) * c_i \tag{18}$$

$$p_i = \left[\left(\frac{\eta_i}{\eta_i - 1}\right) * c_i\right] + \left[\left(\frac{\eta_i}{\eta_i - 1}\right) * mi * \left(p_j - c_j\right) * DR_{i,j}\right] \tag{19}$$

where η_i is the own price elasticity of demand of firm i, c_i is the marginal cost of production of firm i, $p_j - c_j$ is the margin earned by firm j for each unit sold and $D_{i,j}$ is the diversion ratio:[67]

$$D_{i,j} \equiv \frac{\eta_{j,i}}{\eta_{i,i}} \frac{q_j}{q_i} \tag{20}$$

64 Ibid, 609–10.

65 Ibid, 611.

66 In the profit function we use mi rather than $mi_{i,j}$ since in our analysis we will focus on symmetric minority interests among firms.

67 See also Hausman et al (n 2) fn 3.

Given equations (18) and (19), and assuming that all the firms in the market, except firm *i*, do not alter their pricing policy after the acquisition of the passive minority interest, the percentage increase in firm *i's* product price is called the *PPI* delta and is given by the following equation:

$$\Delta PPI_i = mi * D_{i,j} * \frac{(p_j - c_j)}{c_i} \quad (21)$$

If the acquisition of the minority interest leads to cost reductions (Δc_i), then equation (21) becomes:

$$\Delta PPI_i = \Delta c_i + mi * D_{i,j} * \frac{(p_j - c_j)}{c_i} \quad (22)$$

The corresponding ΔPPI for firm *j* is calculated in a similar way:

$$\Delta PPI_j = mi * D_{j,i} * \frac{(p_i - c_i)}{c_j} \quad (23)$$

In the case where firm *i* does not exercise control over firm *j*, then ΔPPI_j=0 (see Table 7 for the case of silent financial interest). However, if firm *i* has total control[68] over firm *j*, then ΔPPI is given by the following equation:

$$\Delta PPI_j = \frac{1}{mi} * D_{j,i} * \frac{(p_i - c_i)}{c_j} \quad (24)$$

Table 7 shows the modified ΔPPIs for different control scenarios.

Table 7: Different formulas for *PPI* deltas for different types of control and silent financial interest

Types of 'control'	*PPI* deltas for firm *i*	*PPI's* deltas for firm *j*
Full merger	$\Delta = D_{i,j} * \frac{(p_j - c_j)}{c_i}$	$\Delta = D_{j,i} * \frac{(p_i - c_i)}{c_j}$
Silent financial interest*	$\Delta = mi * D_{i,j} * \frac{(p_j - c_j)}{c_i}$	0
Total control*	$\Delta = mi * D_{i,j} * \frac{(p_j - c_j)}{c_i}$	$\Delta = \frac{1}{mi} * D_{j,i} * \frac{(p_i - c_i)}{c_j}$

(continued)

68 See Table 6.

Table 7: *(Continued)*

Types of 'control'	***PPI* deltas for firm *i***	***PPI's* deltas for firm *j***
One-way control*	$\Delta = mi * D_{i,j} * \frac{(p_j - c_j)}{c_i}$	$\Delta = mi * D_{j,i} * \frac{(p_i - c_i)}{c_j}$
Coasian joint control*	$\Delta = D_{i,j} * \frac{(p_j - c_j)}{c_i}$	$\Delta = D_{j,i} * \frac{(p_i - c_i)}{c_j}$
Proportional control*	$\Delta = mi * D_{i,j} * \frac{(p_j - c_j)}{c_i}$	$\Delta = \left(\frac{mi}{\left((1-mi)^2 + mi^2\right)} \right) * D_{j,i} * \frac{(p_i - c_i)}{c_j}$

Notes: See Table 6.

Source: DP O' Brien and S Salop, 'Competitive Effects of Partial Ownership: Financial Interest and Corporate Control' (2000) 67 *Antitrust Law Journal* 559, Table 6.

Choi, Ahn and Park examined whether cross-ownership (equal or unequal shares of each firm's equity) of wireline and wireless communications carriers is socially beneficial or harmful.[69] In their model, firms produce different but closely related services. They concluded that if the wireline and wireless industries are monopolistic, then the allowance of cross-ownerships among firms produces social gains if the services are complementary and social losses if the services are substitutes. However, if one of the two industries is competitive, then allowing cross-ownerships produces little or no social losses irrespective of whether the services are complements or substitutes.

Ono et al developed a *n*-firm industry in which firms participate in a two-stage game of Cournot competition.[70] In the first stage of the game the firms choose the optimal, in terms of profits, minority shareholdings and in the second stage of the game they maximize their profits by choosing the profit-maximizing quantities.

In the first stage of the game the optimum minority shareholding is chosen by the firms. They maximize their profits in the form of equation (1) by Reynolds and Snapp given the constraint that the total funds available to firms in order to acquire minority shareholdings in competitors minus the total amount of funds which are actually used for the acquisition of minority shareholdings are higher or equal to zero. Given this constraint. the equilibrium minority shareholding is equal to the ratio of the net profits that firms derive from the acquisition of the minority shareholdings over the effect of technology transfers on firms' own profits as a result of ownership in other firms.[71]

[69] See B-S Choi, B-H Ahn and Y-S Park, 'Cross Ownership of Wireline and Wireless Communications Carriers: Synergy or Collusion?' (2003) 15 *Information Economics and Policy* 485.

[70] See H Ono, T Nakazato, C Davis and W Alley, 'Partial Ownership Arrangements in the Japanese Automobile Industry; 1990–2000' (2004) 7 *Journal of Applied Economics* 355, 356.

[71] In equation (11) in ch 7 below we define equilibrium minority shareholding as the ratio of the influence of a firm that acquires minority shareholdings on the profits of other firms through technology transfers over the effect of technology transfers on a firm's own profits as a result of ownership in other firms.

Clayton and Jorgensen[72] built on Flath's work and analysed reciprocal minority shareholdings in a duopoly Cournot market. First, they analysed a model with two stages: in the first stage firms choose the level of minority shareholding by maximizing their operational profits;[73] and in the second stage they choose their product values in order to maximize their total profits (operational and minority shareholdings' profits), ie $\pi_i = (p - c)q_i + mi_{i,j}(p - c)q_j$.[74] Secondly, they examined a model with three stages in order to analyse the effect of passive minority interests on entry.

Suppose that a positive(negative) externality is generated among firms i and j if $\frac{\partial \pi_j}{\partial q_i} > 0 \left(\frac{\partial \pi_j}{\partial q_i} < 0 \right)$, ie as firm i increases its production, the operating profits of firm j increase in case of positive externality, and decrease in case of negative externality. Given this, Clayton and Jorgensen considered that:

> [L]ong (short) positions induce value-maximizing firms to increase (decrease) the operational decision causing the positive externality. With a short position, the firm can make additional profits by decreasing the value of the corresponding firm. This occurs if the firm decreases its operational decision that has a positive externality. In the case of negative externalities, the opposite results obtain. The optimal cross holding depends on the effect of the externality on the marginal profitability of each firm. Assuming that a positive externality increases the marginal profitability associated with operational decisions, we find that firms which trigger positive externalities optimally hold long positions. Thus, cross holding among firms internalizes the externality and allows firms to increase their profits. When operational decisions trigger negative externalities that also decrease marginal profitability, a Prisoner's Dilemma type problem arises: firms choose short positions to commit to a more aggressive operational decision, which in turn decreases profits relative to the absence of cross holdings.'[75]

Moreover:

> When products are substitutes ..., an increase in the equity position of firm i induces firm i to decrease quantity, which has a positive effect on the profits of firm [j] .... Likewise, when products are complements ..., an increase in the equity position of firm i induces firm i to increase quantity, which also has a positive effect on the profits of firm [j] .... In both cases, added profitability induces firm [j] to increase its quantity.[76]

In addition, if the products are complements (substitutes) the equilibrium level of reciprocal minority shareholdings consists of a long (short) equity position. In any case the quantity increases and the price and profits decrease as long as the level of substitution in the market increases.

[72] See MJ Clayton and BN Jorgensen, 'Optimal Cross Holding with Externalities and strategic Interactions' (2005) 78(4) *Journal of Business* 1505. For a blackboard example which built on the paper by Clayton and Jorgensen see OFT, 'Minority Interests in Competitors: A Research Report prepared by DotEcon Ltd' (2010) OFT1218.

[73] As in Flath (n 42) the stock market is characterized as an efficient stock market (no uncertainty, no discounting and the investors have rational expectations). See also SJ Grossman and OD Hart, 'Takeover Bids, the Free-Rider Problem, and the Theory of the Corporation' (1980) 11(1) *Bell Journal of Economics* 42.

[74] In fact, the firms' managers maximize the equity value of their firms. Equity value and shareholder value do not coincide all the time. See especially RG Hansen and JR Lott, 'Externalities and Corporate Objectives in a World with Diversified Shareholder/Consumers' (1996) 31 *Journal of Financial and Quantitative Analysis* 43.

[75] Above n 72, 1506.

[76] Ibid, 1513.

Regarding the welfare implications of minority shareholdings, Clayton and Jorgensen note that firms' profits decrease with substitute products. Consumer surplus and economic welfare increase when minority shareholdings are allowed rather than when they are prohibited. Therefore regulation against passive minority interests decreases consumer surplus.

Karle, Klein and Konrad examined a differentiated Bertrand market 'in which an investor initially owns a controlling stake in one of two competing firms and may acquire a non-controlling or a controlling stake in a competitor, either directly using her own assets, or indirectly via the controlled firm'.[77] In particular, in a symmetric duopoly one of the two firms is controlled by a block-holder who may acquire a portion of the competitor's issued capital either by acquiring a minority shareholding (in the authors' jargon via 'cash flow rights') or by acquiring the right to control the competitor's strategies ('control rights').

Karle et al employed a two-stage game in which in the first stage of the game the block-holder's investment decisions are determined; and in the second stage of the game the equilibrium prices and the reduced form profits are characterized. In the first stage of the game Karle et al 'distinguish between two polar cases, namely that the shares in the target firm and/or the remaining shares in the firm already controlled are held by either one block holder, or by very small dispersed shareholders'.[78] The block-holder may directly, via the controlled firm or via a combination of both of them, acquire shares in the competitor. The competitor and the acquiring firm are assumed to be financially unconstrained.

In the second stage of the game the process of maximizing the firms' profits is determined according to the type of owners of the shares in the two competitors. If the firms are owned by dispersed shareholders their profits are maximized by the management of both firms without taking into account the choice of the block-holders. However,

> if controlling shares of that firm are owned by a block holder, that block holder, after deciding about the direct or indirect acquisition of stakes in both firms, uses the price(s) of the firm(s) controlled by her to maximize the sum of profits in both firms weighed by her cash flow interests in these firms.[79]

The results show that even though the optimum strategy for the block-holder is to get full control of the competitor via its acquisition by the firm it controls, ie not by its own funds, eventually the monopoly outcome is not the one chosen by the block investor. In generally, there are situations where the block-holder does not even acquire full control in both firms and prefers to acquire a non-controlling stake in the competitor.

Willig calculated the upward pricing pressure (*UPP*) and the gross upward pricing pressure index (*GUPPI*) in the case where a firm acquires a partial equity stake in a competitor.[80] *UPP* measures the net effect of a merger, ie the upward pricing pressure from the elimination of competition among the firms that engage in it and the downward pricing pressure from the efficiencies generated by it. Mathematically, if the diversion ratio of product 1 with respect to product 2 multiplied by the price–cost margin of product 2 is higher than the

[77] See H Karle, TJ Klein and SO Konrad, 'Ownership and Control in a Competitive Industry', Center for European Economic Research (2011) ZEW, Discussion Paper No 11-071.

[78] Ibid, 3.

[79] Ibid, 7–8.

[80] See R Willig, 'Unilateral Competitive Effects of Mergers: Upward Pricing Pressure, Product Quality, and Other Extensions' (2011) 39 *Review of Industrial Organization* 19. The *UPP* and *GUPPI* methodologies are based on Bertrand competition with differentiated products.

efficiencies associated with product 1 (eg reduction of the variable cost of product 1 as a result of the merger), then it is assumed that the merger creates an incentive for the merging firm to increase the price of product 1.[81]

The *GUPPI* is an index which measures the upward pricing pressure without taking into account other sources that might affect this pressure. Following Moresi, the *GUPPI* is the diversion ratio of product 1 with respect to product 2 multiplied by the variable profit margin of product 2 as a fraction of revenue and the relative price of product 2 to product 1.[82]

Recently, Brito et al[83] have calculated general version of *HHI* and *GUPPI* which can deal with many forms of acquisitions such as direct or indirect, which may or may not correspond to control, and others. Fotis, Polemis and Eleftheriou[84] have derived a formula for the *GUPPI* used on duopoly markets with differentiated products, under unilateral equity stakes (expressed as a function of the victim's market share) to be endogenously determined. The authors conclude that:

> [W]hen … m[i][85] continues to be exogenous then Willig's *GUPPI* exhibits a downward biasness. The level of this biasness is measured by the elasticity of m[i] with the respect to target firm's pre-acquisition market share. More specifically, the higher the elasticity, the higher the downward biasness of Willig's *GUPPI*.[86]

So far we have tacitly assumed that equity and shareholder value coincide. However, this coincidence holds only in the case where the shareholders do not hold minority shareholdings in the issued capital of the rivals and are not consumers of firms' products. Moreover, if the shareholders are diversified, ie they hold direct minority shareholdings in firms, then they may not behave as Bertrand oligopolists but rather as cooperative 'competitors' that aim to maximize their joint profits.[87]

Assume two firms the shareholders of which control direct minority shareholdings in both firms. Under full diversification among shareholders they prefer to maximize joint profits and passive minority interests do not enhance further their level of profitability. If diversification does not exist, ie shareholders of each firm hold shares in either firm but not both, or at least they hold small shares of the issued capital in rival firms, then equity and shareholder values coincide. However, when a large portion of shares constitute minority shareholdings in the rival firm,then the incentives of the shareholders of both firms do not coincide and voting rights in them play a crucial role in determining their strategic interaction.

Brito, Cabral and Vasconcelos[88] have argued that consumer surplus is enhanced by turning voting shares (shares with control rights) into non-voting shares (shares with no control

[81] Ibid, 23. See also P Fotis, 'Economic Tools for Merger Appraisal: A Theoretical and Empirical Standpoint' (2014) 3 *Journal of Reviews on Global Economics* 24.

[82] See S Moresi, 'The Use of Upward Price Pressure Indices in Merger Analysis' (2010) 1 *Antitrust Source* 6. Also see Fotis (n 81).

[83] See D Brito, A Osório, R Ribeiro and H Vasconcelos, 'Unilateral Effects Screens for Partial Horizontal Acquisitions: The Generalized HHI and GUPPI' (2015), available at http://ssrn.com/abstract=2627103.

[84] P Fotis, M Polemis and K Eleftheriou, 'Upward Pricing Pressure Formulations with Logit Demand and Endogenous Partial Acquisitions' (2015), MPRA Paper No 66049 (http://mpra.ub.uni-muenchen.de/66049/).

[85] That is, minority interest.

[86] Above n 84, 4.

[87] Above n 76, 1516.

[88] DL Brito, L Cabral and H Vasconcelos, 'Divesting Ownership in a Rival' (2014) 34 *International Journal of Industrial Organization* 9.

rights). Moreover, the sale of voting shares to a new large shareholder is better than their sale to a series of small shareholders. Under certain conditions, the sale of voting shares is worse than turning those shares into non-voting shares and even worse than not doing anything. That is, complete divestiture of voting stock leads to greater consumer surplus if it takes place by sale than if it takes place by a switch to preferred stock.[89]

In particular, Brito et al considered an industry with two firms and *n* shareholders. Each firm's objective function is a weighted sum of voting shareholders' payoffs, where the weights are given by those shareholders' voting shares.[90] One preliminary result is the following: financial interest affects the incentives of both acquiring and acquired firms, while a passive minority interest which confers control over the acquired firm affects its incentives. Therefore, the authors agree with the main results of O' Brien and Salop, but also consider that a financial interest affects not only the incentives of the acquiring firm, but also the incentives of the acquired firm.[91]

Foros, Kind and Shaffer (2011) have compared

> the profitability of a merger between two firms in which one firm fully acquires another and the profitability of a partial ownership arrangement in which the acquiring firm, although owning less than 100 percent of the acquired firm, is nevertheless able to obtain corporate control over all pricing decisions.[92]

They mainly found 'that joint profit can be higher in the latter case because it may result in a greater dampening of competition with respect to an outside competitor when the partial ownership arrangement is publicly observable'.[93]

In particular, Foros et al examined a three-firm Bertrand model with differentiated products, which are imperfect substitutes for each other. In their setting partial ownership is viewed as a commitment device which can affect a rival's pricing behavior. Assuming that firm 1 acquires a controlling stake in firm's 2 issued capital, then if firm 3's price is a decreasing function of the acquired minority shareholding, the joint profits of firms 1 and 2 are higher than in the case where firms 1 and 2 merge.

After the acquisition of the controlling stake in firm's 2 issued capital by firm 1 the former has an incentive to raise the prices of both products produced by the two firms. However, firm 1 has an incentive to set the price of firm 2's product higher than what it would set it in the case of a merger between the two firms. This result is due to the fact that with a partial arrangement firm 1 does not fully internalize the costs of diverted sales of firm 2's product after the increase of its price. If the rival in the market anticipates this, then it may find it profitable to keep the price of its product at a high level as well.

Foros et al considered that:

> If firm 1 owns a sufficiently small share of firm 2, it will therefore find it optimal to maximize the profitability of good 1 by not selling good 2. … [However,] the higher is firm 1's share of ownership in firm 2, the more firm 1 will internalize the negative effects on firm 2's profit of setting an

[89] See also proposition 3. Ibid, 18–19.

[90] Ibid, 10.

[91] The authors apply the theoretical results on the divesture of Portugal Telecom's 58 per cent ownership in PT multimedia to PT's shareholders in 2007. See especially ibid, 17–19.

[92] See Ø Foros, HJ Kind and G Shaffer, 'Mergers and Partial Ownership' (2011) 55(7) *European Economic Review* 916.

[93] Ibid.

> artificially high [price of firm 2's product]. ... all other things being equal, firm 1 will charge a higher price on good 1 the more it owns of firm 2.[94]

Regarding the issue of profitability between a partial arrangement versus a merger, Foros et al considered that for some levels of minority shareholdings, including the 100 per cent acquisition of a rival's share, a partial arrangement is more profitable than a merger since as the level of a minority shareholding increases the product price of the rival decreases.

Shelegia and Spiegel have shown that under cost asymmetries (different levels of constant marginal costs) among firms with passive ownership stakes in each other the equilibrium price may be as high as the monopoly price of the most efficient firm in the market.[95]

In particular, in a $n \geq 2$ Bertrand model with homogeneous product, Shelegia and Spiegel demonstrated that:

> [W]henever the second most efficient firm (firm 2)[96] has a direct or indirect stake in the most efficient firm (firm 1), the model admits multiple Nash equilibria. In all equilibria, firm 1 serves the entire market, but the upper bound on its equilibrium price increases with firm 2's stake and can be as high as the monopoly price of firm 1.[97]

Jain and Pal (2012) examined the effects of minority shareholdings on privatization in mixed duopoly, and showed that:

> [C]ross-ownership is profitable to the private firm only if the level of privatization of the public firm is sufficiently high. In equilibrium, cross-ownership does not take place even if there is partial privatization. However, the possibility of cross-ownership significantly limits the socially optimal level of privatization in most of the situations.[98]

Jain and Pal argue that 'the possibility of cross-ownership in post-privatization regime limits the prospect of privatization in most of the situations'.[99] They examined a Cournot duopoly with either homogeneous or differentiated products. Firm 1 is a public firm owned by the state and firm 2 is a private firm. Firm 1 is assumed to be less efficient than firm 2. The game setting involves three stages: in the first stage the government chooses the level of privatization, in the second stage firm 2 chooses the level of minority shareholding in firm 1 and in the third stage both firms maximize their profits by choosing their outputs.

The main results reported by Jain and Pal in their article are the following:

— Privatization of the public firm does not necessarily lead to an increase in private firm's output ...
— In case of homogeneous products mixed duopoly with identical DRS[100] technologies, partial privatization of the public firm is socially optimal ...
— In case of homogeneous products private duopoly with identical DRS technologies, full cross-ownership emerges in the equilibrium.

94 Ibid, 924.

95 See S Shelegia and Y Spiegel, 'Bertrand Competition when Firms Hold Passive Ownership Stakes in One Another' (2012) 114 *Economics Letters* 136.

96 The most efficient firm in the market exhibits the lowest marginal cost of production compared to all the other players in it. Therefore, efficiency is ranked according to firms' marginal costs.

97 Above n 95, 136.

98 See R Jain and R Pal, 'Mixed Duopoly, Cross-Ownership and Partial Privatization' (2012) 107 *Journal of Economics* 45.

99 Ibid, 47.

100 That is, decreasing returns to scale.

- — In case of homogeneous products mixed duopoly with DRS technologies, cross-ownership is not always profitable to the private firm unlike as in case of private duopoly. …
- — In case of homogeneous products mixed duopoly with identical DRS production technologies, (i) full nationalization is socially optimal unless firms' marginal cost of production increases at a low rate with the increase in production, and (ii) partial privatization is socially optimal only if the rate of increase in marginal cost due to increase in production is low. …
- — When the public firm is relatively less efficient than the private firm, it is optimal for the private firm to fully own the privatized portion of the public firm, if the level of privatization is sufficiently large. …
- — If the public firm is relatively inefficient than the private firm, cross ownership does not emerge in equilibrium and partial privatization of the public firm is socially optimal. …
- — In case of differentiated products mixed duopoly, it is not always optimal for the private firm to have as large stake as possible in its rival partially privatized firm. …
- — Partial privatization of the public firm is socially optimal. (b) Cross ownership does not occur in equilibrium…[101]

Bitro, Ribeiro and Vasconcelos[102] provided a structural approach to horizontal partial acquisitions (either financial interests or corporate control—direct or indirect). In particular, they present an empirical methodology for stimulating the unilateral effects of partial acquisitions and especially the effects of the latter on prices, market shares, firm profits and consumer welfare. The empirical methodology consists of four steps: in the first step the degree of substitutability between the competing products is examined by estimating the consumer demand. In the second step supply-side competition with both direct and indirect partial acquisitions is modelled following the approach of Salop and O' Brien. In the third step marginal costs are recovered through demand estimates and Bertrand equilibrium, and in the fourth step the unilateral effects of partial acquisitions are evaluated.[103]

In the second step[104] '[e]ach firm's aggregate profit is distributed among shareholders proportionally to the total stock owned, regardless of whether it be voting stock or preferred stock … [while] [t]he manager of the firm maximizes a weighted sum of the shareholders' returns.[105]

In the third step each firm maximizes its profits in Bertrand–Nash markets. The existence of reciprocal minority shareholdings, either financial interests or corporate control, eliminates any degree of competition in the product market. Given the first-order conditions of the equilibrium and the cross- and own-price elasticity estimates from the pre-partial acquisitions demand system, the marginal costs are recovered.

In the fourth step the price of the product after the partial acquisition is calculated and is used in order 'to examine the (unilateral) impact of partial acquisitions on market shares,

[101] Above n 98, 50–63.

[102] Above n 88.

[103] See also A Nevo, 'Mergers with Differentiated Products: The Case of the Ready-to-Eat Cereal Industry' (2000) 31(3) *RAND Journal of Economics* 395.

[104] The analysis of the first step of the methodology is given in pp 29–30 of the article by Bitro et al (n 102).

[105] Ibid, 24–25.

firm profits and consumer welfare'.[106] The methodology implies that the marginal costs and the market conduct among firms in the market remain constant before and after the partial acquisition. However, as Bitro et al state, the setting of the model can be easily extended so as to capture possible efficiencies and coordinated effects.[107]

B. Vertical Unilateral Effects

The effect of minority interests on input or customer foreclosure, ie upward and downstream foreclosure respectively, depends crucially on the level of concentration of the vertical markets under scrutiny. The more concentrated the markets, the greater the concern that either of these types of foreclosure will occur. The economic literature on the vertical unilateral effects of minority interests is based on examining whether partial vertical integration raises fewer anticompetitive concerns about each type of foreclosure than full vertical integration.

In the case of full vertical integration these two types of foreclosure may be or may be not prove to be successful strategies for a vertical firm. Salinger[108] considered a market of homogeneous products and concluded that a vertical merger eliminated the number of upstream firms from which independent downstream firms can buy, and limited the double marginalization[109] within the integrated firm which expands its output to final consumers. The former effect causes an increase in the final price of the product, while the latter possibly causes a decrease. Therefore, the second effect benefits consumers, while the first effect does not a priori worsen the consumer welfare since the other independent upstream firms contract their output as a response to the expansion of output of the vertically integrated firm.

Suppose now that two independent upstream firms sell a homogeneous input to two independent downstream firms and a vertical merger between an upstream and downstream firm occurs. Following the vertical merger the merged entity has an incentive to foreclose the other downstream firm since the latter raises the price of the final product and therefore gains ultimately gains a strategic advantage over it.[110] However, Hart and Tirole have argued that the merged entity's commitment not to deliver to the independent downstream firm is not available in the market and is unlikely be credible.[111] Moreover, Reiffen has argued that the foreclosure strategy proposed by Ordover, Salop and Saloner is not

[106] Ibid, 26.

[107] The authors empirically examine the partial acquisition of 22.9 per cent of the non-voting shares of Wilkinson Sword by Gillette Company in 1989 in the United States as well as the full acquisition of Wilkinson Sword by Warner-Lambert Company from Eemland in 1993. See also the analysis of the case in ch 5 below.

[108] M Salinger, 'Vertical Mergers and Market Foreclosure' (1988) 103(2) *Quarterly Journal of Economics* 345.

[109] 'The double marginalization problem, first formulated by Spengler (1950), arises when both a supplier and a distributor earn positive profits margins on their respective sales. The resulting retail price then is higher than it would be under full vertical merger and retail price in the final market is above the monopoly level.' See especially D Gilo and Y Spiegel, 'Partial Vertical Integration in Telecommunication and Media Markets in Israel' (2011) 9(1) *Israel Economic Review* 29, 48 and J Spengler, 'Vertical Integration and Antitrust Policy' (1950) 58 *Journal of Political Economy* 347.

[110] J Ordover, S Salop and G Saloner, 'Equilibrium Vertical Foreclosure' (1990) 80 *American Economic Review* 127.

[111] O Hart and J Tirole, 'Vertical Integration and Market Foreclosure', Brookings Papers on Economic Activity: Microeconomics (1990) 205.

credible for the merged entity since if the other upstream firm raises its offered input price to the independent downstream firm, the merged entity has an incentive to offer the input to it at a slightly lower price and make profits. The independent downstream firm accepts the offer from the merged entity since its cost is negligible relative to the cost that will be incurred if it accepts the offer of the independent upstream firm.[112]

Ordover et al in their reply to Reiffen point out that:

> The notion that vertically integrated firms behave differently from nonintegrated ones in supplying inputs to downstream rivals would strike a business person, if not an economist, as common sense.[113]

Suppose now that in the upstream market there is one firm and in the downstream market there are two independent firms.[114] Both downstream firms invest an equal amount in order to increase their profits from the selling of the final product and hence the probability of buying the input is equally shared between them. Finally, the downstream firm with the higher profits gets input from the monopolist in the upstream market since it has the ability to pay more for the input than the other downstream firm.

If a vertical integration takes place, the vertically merged entity enhances the level of its investment, while the independent downstream firm lowers it (the investments are assumed to be strategic substitutes). Therefore, the probability of buying the input now is not equally shared between them; in fact, it is less than 50 per cent for the independent downstream firm. The foreclosure strategy in the models proposed by Bolton and by Riordan stems from the effect of a vertical merger on the incentives of the two downstream firms to invest. The independent downstream firm is foreclosed if there is an output contraction and the willingness to pay for the input is higher for the merged entity than for the independent.

Stefanadis has stated that if a firm in the upstream market is characterized by dynamic economies of scale in the form of competition in Research & Development (R&D), then may be preferable for it to have a captive downstream firm in order to force its rivals to use low-scale production technology and to discourage them from innovating. Under such circumstances a downstream firm may be persuaded to sign an exclusive contract since it is offered favourable terms from the innovative upstream firm in relation to its rivals and hence a downstream input foreclosure takes place which harms consumers.[115]

Chen has stated that if the merged entity produces the input more efficiently than the other independent upstream firms, then the downstream firms may choose to buy the input from it even though they have to pay a higher price than the input price that is charged by the other independent upstream firms. Therefore, a foreclosure strategy takes place because of the preferences of downstream firms to choose the merged entity as their input supplier. Vertical integration softens the competition in the downstream market, but also eliminates the double marginalization problem.[116]

[112] D Reiffen, 'Equilibrium Vertical Foreclosure: Comment' (1992) 82 *American Economic Review* 694.

[113] J Ordover, S Salop and G Saloner, 'Equilibrium Vertical Foreclosure: Reply' (1992) 82 *American Economic Review* 698.

[114] See especially P Bolton and M Whinston, 'The Foreclosure Effects of Vertical Mergers' (1991) 147 *Journal of Institutional and Theoretical Economics* 207, and P Bolton and M Whinston, 'Incomplete Contracts, Vertical Integration and Supply Assurance' (1993) 60(1) *Review of Economic Studies* 121.

[115] C Stefanadis, 'Downstream Vertical Foreclosure and Upstream Innovation' (1997) 45(4) *Journal of Industrial Economics* 445.

[116] Y Chen, 'On Vertical Mergers and their Competitive Effects' (2001) 32(4) *RAND Journal of Economics* 667.

Allain, Chambolle and Rey have examined 'the impact of vertical integration on competition and performance in markets where firms need to exchange sensitive information in order to interact efficiently with their suppliers or customers'.[117] They considered 'a bilateral duopoly framework in which, to develop an innovation, firms must share with their suppliers some information, which cannot be protected by traditional intellectual property rights',[118] and showed that vertical integration leads to foreclosure which discourages the rival's innovation efforts and increases the vertically integrated firms' profit at the expense of independent rivals. Foreclosure harms consumers and reduces the overall benefit.

Nocke and Rey considered a model of interlocking bilateral relationships between upstream firms of differentiated products and downstream firms that compete imperfectly for consumers.[119] According to Nocke and Rey, both exclusive dealing and vertical integration between an upstream and a downstream firm lead to vertical foreclosure, to the detriment of consumers and society. Moreover, they show that firms have incentives to sign such contracts or to integrate vertically.[120]

i. Controlling Partially Vertical Minority Interests

In the case of partial vertical integration there are two main categories. In the first category the partial acquisition gives the acquirer a non-controlling stake in the target's capital, ie a passive minority interest. In the second category the partial acquisition gives the acquiring firm a controlling stake in its target, ie an active minority interest. Regarding the second category, Gilo and Spiegel have stated that:

> [D]ownstream foreclosure which diverts profits from the input market to the final market is more likely to be profitable if the distributor controls the supplier with a partial ownership stake, and is less likely to be profitable if the supplier controls the distributor with a partial ownership stake. Likewise, upstream foreclosure that diverts profits from the final market to the input market is more likely to be profitable if the supplier controls the distributor with a partial ownership stake, but is less likely to be profitable if the distributor controls the supplier with a partial ownership stake.
>
> Apart from the size of the partial controlling stake, the incentive to engage in vertical foreclosure also depends on the market shares of the merging firms. There are two reasons for this. First, the larger the market share of the firm that benefits from the foreclosure, the greater is the incentive to foreclose competing firms, both because the benefit of foreclosure is larger and because the cost of foreclosure is smaller (competing firms have smaller market shares so the lost profit from not selling to them is limited). Second, the larger the market share of the foreclosing firm, the more severe is the resulting anticompetitive effect.[121]

[117] M-L Allain C Chambolle and P Rey, 'Vertical Integration, Information and Foreclosure', Toulouse School of Economics, Working Paper 11-237.

[118] Ibid, 3.

[119] V Nocke and P Rey, 'Exclusive Dealing and Vertical Integration in Interlocking Relationships' (2014), CEPR Discussion Paper No DP10176.

[120] The economic literature on the effects of fully partial integration on foreclosure is vast. A review of it is provided by P Rey and J Tirole, 'A Primer on Foreclosure' in M Armstrong and R Porter (eds), *Handbook of Industrial Organization*, vol 3 (Amsterdam, Elsevier, 2007) ch 33, 2145; M Riordan, 'Competitive Effects of Vertical Integration' in P Buccirossi (ed), Handbook of Antitrust Economics (Cambridge, MA, MIT Press, 2008) 145, and D Gilo and Y Spiegel, 'Partial Vertical Integration in Telecommunication and Media Markets in Israel' (2011) 9(1) *Israel Economic Review* 29. See also the literature review in Allain, Chambolle and Rey (n 115).

[121] See Gilo and Spiegel (n 109) 33–34. See also W Baumol and J Ordover, 'On the Perils of Vertical Control by a Partial Owner of a Downstream Enterprise' (1994) 69(3) *Revue d'Économie Industrielle* 7 and S Dasgupta and Z Tao, 'Bargaining, Bonding, and Partial Ownership' (2000) 41(3) International Economic Review 609.

There are two main types of partial vertical integration: partial forward integration, which means a partial acquisition of the issued capital of a downstream firm by an upstream firm; and partial backward integration, which constitutes a partial acquisition of the issued capital of an upstream firm by a downstream firm.

Regarding partial forward integration, the larger the market shares of both upstream and downstream firms, the easier and lower cost the foreclosure and limitation of consumer surplus, respectively. Moreover, partial forward integration does not solve the problem of double marginalization, which full vertical integration removes. The same arguments hold for partial backward integration. However, in contrast with partial forward integration, partial backward integration does solve the problem of double marginalization.

Table 8 summarizes the effects of forward and backward vertical integration in relation to full vertical integration on foreclosure.

Table 8: The effects of forward and backward partial vertical integration in relation to full vertical integration on foreclosure

	Partial forward integration	Partial backward integration
Downstream/costumer foreclosure	–	+
Upstream/input foreclosure	+	–

Notes: +, the incentive to foreclosure is stronger under partial than full vertical integration; –, the incentive to foreclosure is weaker under partial than full vertical integration.

Source: D Gilo and Y Spiegel, 'Partial Vertical Integration in Telecommunication and Media Markets in Israel' (2011) 9(1) *Israel Economic Review* 29, 36.

Table 8 shows that when an upstream firm has vertical corporate control over a downstream firm, the upstream firm has a stronger incentive to foreclose its upstream rivals than its competing downstream firms relative to full vertical integration. However, when a downstream firm has vertical corporate control over an upstream firm, the downstream firm has a stronger incentive to foreclose its downstream rivals than its competing upstream firms (after the acquisition of the partial interest) relative to full vertical integration. Therefore, it is evident that in either type of partial vertical integration the firm that holds the minority interest has a stronger incentive to foreclose its 'original' competitors, ie firms that were horizontal competitors prior to the acquisition of the corporate control, than to foreclose potential' competitors, ie firms that become horizontal competitors after the acquisition of corporate control.[122]

Gilo, Levy and Spiegel[123] have examined the incentive of firms to acquire partial, controlling, interests in vertically related firms and then foreclose downstream rivals. They note that:

> [P]artial acquisition of an upstream supplier (partial backward integration) is more likely to occur and lead to foreclosure than full vertical merger, especially when initially, the upstream supplier is

[122] See also R Fiocco, 'The Strategic Value of Partial Vertical Integration' (2014), GESY Discussion Papers No 455.

[123] D Gilo, N Levy and Y Spiegel, 'Partial Vertical Integration, Ownership Structure and Foreclosure', mimeo (2014), available at http://www.fas.nus.edu.sg/ecs/events/seminar/seminar-papers/24Mar14.pdf.

> held by dispersed shareholders. By contrast, partial acquisition of a downstream customer (partial forward integration) is less profitable than full vertical merger, especially when initially, the downstream customer has a controlling shareholder whose controlling stake is small, and is never profitable when the downstream customer is initially held by dispersed shareholders.

The authors also considered that:

> [P]artial backward integration, followed by foreclosure of a downstream rival is less likely when the downstream customer holds a toehold in the upstream supplier, more likely when the acquisition is made by the controlling shareholder of the downstream customer rather than the firm itself, and is as likely when two downstream customers compete for the acquisition of control in the upstream supplier.

Spiegel examined a four-stage game as described by Bolton and Whinston, and considered that:

> [P]artial vertical integration affects both vertical externalities that arise because downstream investments boost the willingness of downstream firms to pay for the input, as well as horizontal externalities that downstream firms impose on each other. Partial vertical integration allows firms to (partially) internalize these externalities and this in turn affects the incentive of the downstream firms to invest. Moreover, when the partial backward integration gives the integrated downstream firm control over the upstream supplier, the price at which the input is sold to the non-integrated downstream firm increases.[124]

Spiegel also noted that:

> From an antitrust perspective, the analysis shows that partial backward integration leads to more foreclosure of non-integrated rivals than full vertical integration, while partial forward integration leads to less foreclosure. Moreover, passive vertical integration … always leads to less foreclosure than controlling vertical integration, though it is not necessarily better for consumers than controlling vertica[l] integration.[125]

ii. Non-Controlling Partially Vertical Minority Interests

Regarding the economic literature on the effects of passive minority interests on competition, Flath has noted that if Cournot competitors hold symmetric passive minority interests in each other, then vertically related Cournot oligopolies produce more output in the case of partial forward integration, particularly when the equity shares are exclusive in the sense that no two upstream firms own shares in the same downstream firm. The case of partial backward integration has either the opposite effect on output or no effect. The author state that the reason for the asymmetry is that upstream firms are first movers and downstream firms are second movers. Moreover, according to Flath, minority interests may enhance the mark-up of firms and could then be detrimental to competition, contrary to the result of controlling vertical integration which, as we have shown earlier, eliminates the double marginalization problem.

[124] Y Spiegel, 'Backward Integration, Forward Integration, and Vertical Foreclosure' (2013), CEPR Discussion Paper No DP9617.

[125] Ibid.

Greenlee and Raskovitch, extending inter alia, the work of Flath and Salinger, have examined partial backward integration with passive minority interests.[126] In particular, they explored a two-stage game in which, given the passive minority interest in the upstream firm (monopolist) by downstream firms, in the first stage of the game the upstream firm maximizes its profits by choosing a uniform essential input price,[127] and in the second stage downstream firms maximize their profits by choosing final product prices or quantities.

In the second stage each downstream firm maximizes its profits given by the following equation:

$$\pi_i(\theta, m, mi) \equiv p_i(\theta)q_i(\theta) + mi_i\Pi(\theta, m, mi) - mx_i(q_i(\theta), m, mi) - y_i(q_i(\theta), m, mi) \qquad (25)$$

where i represents values for downstream firm i, $\pi_i(\theta, m, mi)$ are the profits of downstream firm i, θ is the strategic variable which maximizes the profits of downstream firm i (price, quantity, advertisement, etc), m is the input price of the upstream firm which maximizes its profits, mi is the passive minority interest in the issued capital of upstream firm by downstream firm i, $p_i(\theta)q_i(\theta) + mi_i\ \Pi(\theta, m, mi)$ are the total profits of downstream firm i including the profits from the partial acquisition, $(mi_i\Pi(\theta, m, mi))$, $\Pi(\theta, m, mi)$ are the profits of the upstream firm, $mx_i(q_i(\theta), m, mi)$ is the cost of buying x units of input from the upstream firm by downstream firm i, $y_i(q_i(\theta), m, mi)$ is the cost of buying y units of input from the upstream firm by downstream firm i,[128] and $x_i(q_i(\theta), m, mi)$ $y_i(q_i(\theta), m, mi)$ are i's demand functions for inputs x and y, respectively.

In the second stage the upstream firm maximizes its profits according to the following equation:

$$\Pi(\theta, m, mi) = (m - c)\sum x_i\left(q_i(\theta), m, mi\right) \qquad (26)$$

where c is the marginal cost of production of input x.

Generally speaking, under a homogeneous Cournot setting as well as under a symmetric and differentiated Bertrand setting, in the downstream market, Greenlee and Raskovitch find that partial backward integration does not affect the price or quantity choices of downstream firms, and thus does not affect social welfare.

In particular, the main results of Greenlee and Raskovitch may be summarized into two contradicting effects: on the one hand if downstream firm i increases its passive minority interest in the upstream firm, this will reduce the input price and hence will force the downstream firm to expand its output. However, since outputs are strategic variables the other downstream firms except i will reduce their output by less than i's output expansion and therefore the total output in the downstream market will increase. Given this increase, the upstream firm faces a greater demand for its input and therefore increases its price. On the other hand, the upstream firm's input price increase will lower the downstream firms' demand for its input, which in turn reduces their output. Therefore, Greenlee and Raskovitch conclude that the two effects cancel out and the price of the final product remains unchanged. This conclusion is not detrimental for competition since consumer welfare is not affected by the partial backward integration.

[126] P Greenlee and A Raskovich, 'Partial Vertical Ownership' (2006) 50 *European Economic Review* 1017.

[127] That is, no price discrimination occurs among downstream firms.

[128] Input y is the input of all the other upstream firms except from the upstream firm under scrutiny. Since the authors focus on one upstream firm, y's price is normalized to 1 without loss of generality.

Gonçalves considered some slightly different assumptions about the upstream market in order to allow for the possibility of price discrimination by the upstream monopolist. Gonçalves considered that 'it is profit-maximizing for the upstream firm to discriminate against its retail shareholder. Compared to a vertical separation scenario, this partial vertical integration induces input foreclosure, higher retail prices and lower social welfare.'[129]

Hunold, Röller and Stahl[130] examined a three-stage game in which there are two Bertrand competitors in the downstream market that produce differentiated products. In the upstream market there are two upstream firms that produce a homogeneous input used for the downstream production. The one supplier is more efficient than the other supplier in terms of marginal cost of production and can price discriminate between the two downstream firms. Hunold et al examined partial backward integration with perfect information among the firms.

In the first stage of the game the downstream firms simultaneously acquire passive minority interests in the two upstream firms. Both downstream firms want to hold a passive stake in the more efficient upstream firm. Let us assume that at the beginning only one downstream tries to acquire a passive stake in the more efficient upstream firm. Gains from trading stakes will arise if the joint profits of the two firms after the partial acquisition are higher than without it. Moreover, an increase of the passive stake by the downstream firm will cause an overall increase of their joint profits as well as an increase in the market profits if upstream competition is sufficiently intense or effective (the *competition softening effect*). The same argument holds if both downstream firms hold a passive stake in the more efficient upstream firm.[131]

In the second stage determination of the input prices under partial backward integration takes place. The most efficient upstream firm supplies both downstream firms for any given level of ownership, since it can offer an input price as high as its marginal cost, while the less efficient upstream firm cannot profitably sell at a price below its marginal cost. If the upstream competition is intense or effective, then the input price is equal to:

$$\omega_i^* = \frac{c}{\left(1 - mi_i\right)} \tag{27}$$

where i denotes the two downstream firms.

According to Hunold et al:

> (i) both equilibrium downstream prices … increase … for any non-controlling ownership structure (ii) the increase is stronger when the downstream products are closer substitutes.
>
> Any increase in passive ownership in [the most efficient firm] by one or both downstream firms is strictly anti-competitive.[132]

In stage three, downstream firms buy their inputs from the upstream supplier who offers the lowest effective input price. 'If both [upstream firms] charge the same effective input

[129] R Gonçalves, 'Backward Partial Vertical Integration with Discriminatory Pricing' (2013), mimeo, available at http://www3.eeg.uminho.pt/economia/nipe/PEJ2014/Ricardopercent20GonpercentC3percentA7alves.pdf.

[130] M Hunold, L-H Röller and K Stahl, 'Backwards Integration and Strategic Delegation' (2012), CEPR Discussion Papers 8910.

[131] This means that the marginal cost of production is sufficiently small between the two upstream firms and hence the efficient upstream firm is constrained by the less efficient upstream firm. Ibid, 11.

[132] Ibid, 7.

price, we assume that downstream firms buy all inputs from the efficient upstream firm as that supplier could slightly undercut to make its offer strictly preferable.'[133]

Suppose now that one of the downstream firms merges with the efficient upstream firm. Then, due to the fact that the double marginalization problem is eliminated within the vertically integrated firm, the merger decreases both downstream prices as compared to without the merger. Hence, a vertical merger is procompetitive, while a partial backward integration via a passive minority interest in the efficient upstream firm is anticompetitive since it increases all the downstream prices.

In terms of profitability and assuming that the competition is intense or effective, the downstream firms acquire maximal backwards passive interests in the efficient upstream firm since the profits are higher than full vertical integration.[134]

C. Coordinated Effects of Minority Shareholdings

Flath[135] has shown that in the cartel case the passive minority shareholding is given by the following equation:

$$mi = \frac{1}{(n-1)} \tag{28}$$

where n is the number of firms in the market. As mi approaches $\frac{1}{(n-1)}$,[136] then

$$L = \frac{1}{\bar{\eta}} \tag{29}$$

Recall that equation (28) exhibits the monopoly power index in the case of a monopolist.

Moreover, from equation (12) Flath states that when there are more than two firms in the market, as firms expand their passive minority interests in the rivals' issued capital the perfect cartel scenario is not attained. That is, equation (29) becomes:

$$L = \frac{1}{n\bar{\eta}} \tag{30}$$

Flath concludes that:

> The cartelizing effects of horizontal shareholding interlocks are compounded if firms are mindful not only of direct shareholding but also of indirect shareholding. In considering the antitrust implications of shareholding links, attention to indirect shareholding is certainly warranted on theoretical grounds. However, the effects of indirect shareholding are likely to be an order of magnitude smaller than those of whatever direct shareholding links are present.[137]

[133] Ibid, 6.

[134] The authors also offer some extensions of the basic model regarding key issues of it such as the presence of (a) ineffective competition, (b) non-discriminatory upstream prices, (c) simultaneous price setting in both upstream and downstream markets and (d) two-part tariffs. See particularly ibid, 11–15.

[135] Above n 56.

[136] $\bar{\eta}$ is the constant elasticity of demand which is equal to or greater than one ($\bar{\eta} \geq 1$).

[137] Above n 135, 77.

We have stated in section II.A of this chapter that firms engaged in a Bertrand competition with differentiated products will continue to increase the level of the financial interest in the rival's issued capital until they attain the cartel outcome in the market. The cartel outcome can be achieved only when the passive minority interests are small and the 'difference between cartel prices and those that would prevail in the absence of cross-shareholding must also be small'.

Malueg[138] noted that repeated interaction among firms may reduce the likelihood of collusion, and showed that for a particular set of demand functions a high level of cross-ownership may entail a lower likelihood of collusion compared to the absence of cross-ownership. In particular, by examining a symmetric Cournot oligopoly model, Malueg demonstrated that

> for some demand conditions, increasing the degree of cross ownership in the market may decrease the case or likelihood of collusion. … [I]ncreasing cross ownership among rivals has two effects: first, it reduces the gain from cheating on a collusive agreement; second, it softens the punishment that would follow cheating. The first effect makes collusion more likely; the second effect makes collusion less likely. The net result of these two forces is ambiguous.[139]

The repeated model is based on the static model of Reynolds and Snapp. In order to examine whether collusion can be sustained as an equilibrium solution of the repeated model Malueg examined if the monopoly outcome can be supported in each period by the firms in the market, given the threat that 'if this "cooperation" ever breaks down, both firms will forever after set their outputs equal to the static Cournot equilibrium outputs'.[140]

If the market demand is given by equation (14) and both firms choose the monopoly output level in each period of the model, then the present discounted value of each firm's profit equals:

$$\Pi^M \equiv \frac{\pi^M}{(1-\delta)} \tag{31}$$

where δ is the (intertemporal) discount factor. However, if the firms follow the trigger strategy, then the discounted payoff resulting from this optimal deviation is:

$$\Pi^D \equiv \pi^D + \frac{\delta\pi_{COURNOT}}{(1-\delta)} \tag{32}$$

where π^D is the one-period profit generated for the trigger strategy, $\frac{\delta\pi_{COURNOT}}{(1-\delta)}$ is the profit generated after the cheating, ie the one-period profit and $\pi_{COURNOT}$ is the Cournot profit from equation (16).

In the absence of passive minority interests the fully collusive outcome, ie where each firm chooses the monopoly price and the monopoly profits are equally shared among the

138 Above n 62.

139 Ibid, 28.

140 Ibid, 31. In game theory this is called the 'trigger strategy'. See, inter alia, R Porter, 'Optimal Cartel Trigger-Price Strategies' (1983) 29(2) *Journal of Economic Theory* 313.

collusive members, is sustained if the intertemporal discount factor is as large as given by the following equation:[141]

$$\bar{\delta} = 1 - \frac{1}{n} \tag{33}$$

Malueg showed that when passive minority interests are present, the collusion is sustained as an equilibrium outcome of the model if $\Pi^M \geq \Pi^D$. The latter holds if the discount factor is as large as:

$$\delta^C = \frac{\left(\pi^D - \pi^M\right)}{\left(\pi^D - \pi_{COURNOT}\right)} \tag{34}$$

where *C* stands for cooperation.[142]

Gilo, Moshe and Spiegel[143] extended the infinitely repeated Cournot homogeneous-product symmetric duopoly model of Malueg in which each firm's single shareholder holds an identical partial minority interest in the rival

> to the context of an infinitely repeated Bertrand homogeneous product symmetric[144] n-firm oligopoly model in which both firms and shareholders may hold a complex, not necessarily identical, partial financial interests in rivals, and follow grim-trigger strategies that, should any single firm in any past period deviate from the coordinated arrangement, reverts permanently to the static Bertrand–Nash equilibrium. In this framework, the static Nash equilibrium is not impacted by partial acquisitions, which allows the authors to focus the impact analysis on the first (positive) effect identified in Malueg (1992): that partial financial interests can facilitate collusion by reducing the incentive of target firms to deviate from the coordinated arrangement because the increased deviation profit is shared with the acquiring firm(s). They show that partial financial interests do facilitate coordination if and only if a set of conditions is satisfied cumulatively.[145]

In particular, the fully collusive outcome can be sustained in the equilibrium if the generated profits from the collusive outcome discounted by the discount factor δ are higher than or equal to the profits generated from the trigger strategy. This holds if:

$$\delta \geq \overline{\delta(A)} \tag{35}$$

Given the fact that $\overline{\delta_i(A)} = 1 - \frac{\pi_i^M(A)}{\pi_i^D(A)}$, where $\pi_i^M(A)$ are the profits generated from the collusive outcome and $\pi_i^D(A)$ are the profits generated from the trigger strategy for firm *i*, then it follows that:

$$\overline{\delta_i(A)} \leq \bar{\delta} = 1 - \frac{1}{n} \tag{36}$$

[141] J Tirole, *The Theory of Industrial Organization* (Cambridge, MA, MIT Press, 1988) ch 6.

[142] Above n 140, 32. Equation (34) displays the discount factor for collusion when the demand function is convex ($a = 2$).

[143] See especially D Gilo, Y Moshe and Y Spiegel, 'Partial Cross Ownership and Tacit Collusion' (2006) 37(1) *RAND Journal of Economics* 81.

[144] Each firm has the same marginal cost.

[145] D Brito, R Ribeiro and H Vasconcelos, 'Quantifying the Coordinated Effects of Partial Horizontal Acquisitions' (2013), CERP Discussion Paper No 9536, 3.

$\bar{\delta}$ is given by equation (33). From equation (35) it also follows that in the presence of passive minority interests firm i has the same or even stronger incentives to collude with the other firms in the market than they have in the absence of these passive minority interests. Moreover, if firm i does not invest in any rival in the market, then it is the industry maverick[146] and $\overline{\delta_i(A)} = \bar{\delta} = 1 - \frac{1}{n}$.

Suppose that firm r holds a passive minority interest in a rival firm s. The partial financial interests do facilitate coordination according to the following statement:

> [A]n increase in the partial financial interest of firm r in a rival s do facilitate coordination 'if and only if (i) each firm in the industry holds a stake in at least one rival, (ii) the maverick firm in the industry (the firm with the strongest incentive to deviate from a collusive agreement)[147] has a direct or an indirect stake in firm r, and (iii) firm s is not the industry maverick'.[148]

If firms in the market hold identical passive minority interests $\overline{mi} < \frac{1}{(n-1)}$, then the fully collusive outcome is not sustained in the equilibrium if the number of firms in the market increases and the aggregate passive minority stake in rivals is small, ie

$$\overline{MI} < \frac{1}{2} \tag{37}$$

where $\overline{MI}$ is the aggregate passive minority stake in rivals which is equal to $(n-1)\overline{mi}$. However, if

$$\overline{MI} > \frac{1}{2} \tag{38}$$

then the fully collusive outcome is facilitated.[149]

> Kühn and Rimler (2006)[150] show that structural links may be particularly conducive to collusion when firms can credibly recur (or have recurred in the past) to aggressive deterrent strategies in case of deviations from a collusive scheme. Without structural links, the means of punishing deviators are limited because firms can effectively avoid heavy losses by maintaining prices close to marginal costs (and thus reducing their output if market prices fall below their costs). The absence of a severe punishment therefore restricts firms' possibilities to collude. If instead colluding firms have minority shareholdings in their competitors, then they indirectly suffer also from losses incurred by their competitors. Hence, more aggressive punishment strategies can be implemented and thus collusive schemes may be more easily sustained. This concern is most relevant in industries where there have been past episodes of intense price wars (as a result of which market participants incurred losses),

146 A firm with a minimal ratio $\frac{\pi_i^M(A)}{\pi_i^D(A)}$ is called an industry maverick. There may be several maverick firms in the industry.

147 See The Horizontal Merger Guidelines of the US Department of Justice and Federal Trade Commission.

148 Above n 145, 4.

149 In the rest of the article the authors examine the effect of passive minority interests of controllers of firms in rivals. See especially 90–93.

150 K Kühn M Rimler, 'The Comparative Statics of Collusion Models' (2006), CEPR Discussion Paper No 5742.

> or where aggressive punishment are likely to be implemented in the future (if coordination breaks down). Note that largely passive minority shareholdings and thus the absence of significant control is actually a contributing factor for sustaining collusion in this way.[151]

Gilo, Spiegel and Temurshoev[152] extended the article by Gilo and Spiegel by introducing cost asymmetries among firms in the market. They showed that when firms in the market exhibit different marginal costs of production an increase in the passive minority interest of a firm in a rival facilitates collusion if and only if (a) the maverick firm in the industry has a direct or an indirect stake in the acquiring firm, and (b) the target firm is not the industry maverick.

Matsumoto, Merlone and Szidarovszky (2008) assumed 'that the [competition] authorities use the Herfindahl–Hirschman Index in order to detect the anticompetitive behavior of the coalition, and that the firms in the coalition cooperate unless their behavior is likely to attract the antitrust authorities' attention'.[153] They examined an n-firm Cournot model where some of the firms in the markets partially cooperate by each other. The profit function of the ith firm in the market is the same as noted by Flath. The partially cooperating firms have identical output in equilibrium, which is different from the identical non-cooperating output. If we suppose that all the firms in the market are N and a subset of them, m, partially cooperate with each other, then the *HHI*[154] is given by the following equation:

$$HHI^C = \frac{(N-m)\left[(a-c_q)\left(1+(m-1)mi-(c_q-c_q^C)m\right)\right]^2+m\left[(a-c_q^C)+(c_q-c_q^C)(N-m)\right]^2}{\left[(a-c_q)(N-m)\left(1+(m-1)mi\right)+(a-c_q^C)m\right]^2} \tag{39}$$

where c_q is the marginal cost of production of the non-cooperating firms and c_q^C is the marginal cost of production of the cooperating firms. However, if all of the firms in the market maximize the monopoly profits, ie all the firms join the cooperative coalition, then regardless of the value of the passive minority interest the *HHI* is given by:

$$HHI^C = \frac{1}{n} \tag{40}$$

Since the value of HHI^C in equation (40) is the minimum value of the index for an N-firm non-cooperative symmetric industry, then it is quite difficult for a competition authority to reveal 100 per cent cooperation in the market. According to Matsumoto et al, this constitutes a limitation of the measure given by equation (39).[155]

151 See especially p 13, para 56 of the annex of the Commission Staff Working Document, 'Towards More Effective EU Merger Control' SWD(2013) 239 final.

152 D Gilo, Y Spiegel, and U Temurshoev, 'Partial Cross Ownership and Tacit Collusion under Cost Asymmetries', mimeo (2009).

153 A Matsutomo, U Merlone and F Szidarovszky, 'Cartelizing Groups in Dynamic Linear Oligopoly with Antitrust Threshold' (2008) 10(4) *International Game Theory Review* 399, 418. For an extension of this model, see A Matsutomo, U Merlone and F Szidarovszky, 'Cartelizing Groups in Dynamic Hyperbolic Oligopoly with Antitrust Threshold' [2010] *Australian Economic Papers* 289.

154 See also equation (2) of this chapter.

155 Above n 153, 404.

Given an exogenously determined *HHI* by the competition authorities the cooperative firms stop cooperating if:

$$\overline{HHI} < \frac{(N-m)q^2 + mq_C^2}{\left((N-m)q + mq_C\right)^2} \tag{41}$$

where q is the quantity of the non-cooperating firms and q_c is the quantity of the cooperating firms. The cooperating firms restart cooperation otherwise. In addition, the *HHI* in the case of non-cooperation is given by the following equation:

$$HHI^{NC} = \frac{(N-m)\left[\left(a-c_q\right)-\left(c_q-c_q^C\right)m\right]^2 + m\left[\left(a-c_q^C\right)+\left(c_q-c_q^C\right)(N-m)\right]^2}{\left[\left(a-c_q\right)(N-m)+\left(a-c_q^C\right)m\right]^2} \tag{42}$$

From equations (40) and (42) we see that $HHI^{NC} < HHI^C$ for $mi > 0$. If the competition authorities select a $\overline{HHI}$ lower than HHI^{NC}, then they cannot detect if a subset of firms in the market are violating the antitrust law, ie 'the detection method is incorrect and it will always show violation even if the firms are non-cooperative'.[156] Therefore, it always holds that $\overline{HHI} = HHI^{NC}$. Other cases to be scrutinized are $HHI^C < \overline{HHI}$ and $HHI^{NC} < \overline{HHI} < HHI^C$.

When $\overline{HHI} = HHI^{NC}$ cooperation does not take place among firms in the market. In the case where $HHI^{NC} < \overline{HHI} < HHI^C$ whether or not cooperation occurs depends on the value of the $\overline{HHI}$ chosen by the competition authorities, 'possibly sanctioning the anticompetitive behavior of the cooperative firms'.[157]

Ferreria and Waddle[158] extended the work of Reitman[159] and examined two symmetric firms which during the first stage of the game give away part of their profits, ie they endogenize the degree of passive interest in their operational profits (the stage of profit sharing) and at the second stage of the game compete like Cournot or Bertrand competitors with heterogeneous products. The results show that this approach

> is more likely to allow for tacit collusion when choice variables are strategic complements and when monopolistic profits are big compared to the non-cooperative equilibrium in the oligopoly. In fact, they find that for Bertrand competition with goods with low heterogeneity some degree of tacit collusion is possible. However, their methodology relies on the differentiability of the profits functions, and cannot be applied to Bertrand competition with homogenous goods.[160]

[156] Ibid, 412.

[157] Ibid, 416. See also A Matsutomo, U Merlone and F Szidarovszky, 'Dynamic Oligopoly with Partial Cooperation and Antitrust Threshold' (2009) 73(2) *Journal of Economic Behavior and Organization* 299.

[158] JL Ferreria and R Waddle, 'Strategic Profit Sharing Leads to Collusion in Bertrand Oligopolies' (2010) 6(4) *International Journal of Economic Theory* 341.

[159] The basic contribution of the article in relation to the article by Reitman (1994) is that 'the choice of how much of the profits to share does not need to be part of an agreement between two firms, as we only need that the level of profit sharing be decided by the giving firm'. See especially JL Ferreria and R Waddle, 'Strategic Profit Sharing Leads to Collusion in Bertrand Oligopolies', mimeo, 2–3, available at http://e-archivo.uc3m.es/bitstream/10016/9795/1/we1036.pdf.

[160] Ibid, 1.

Ferreria and Waddle[161] examined the same strategy in the first stage of the game as above, but at the second stage of the game the firms compete like Bertrand competitors with homogeneous product. Their main finding was that any price between cost and the monopolistic price can be sustained in the equilibrium and therefore tacit collusion between the two firms can be achieved.

Brito, Riberiero and Vasconcelos quantified the coordinated effects of horizontally passive or active, direct or indirect minority interests in differentiated product industries.[162] In particular, they presented an empirical methodology for stimulating the coordinated effects of partial acquisitions and especially the effects of the latter on prices, market shares, firm profits and consumer welfare.

> The proposed methodology relates to two strands of the literature. The first strand of literature examines the theoretical impact of partial competitor ownership on the likelihood of a tacit coordinated agreement. ... The second strand of literature relates to the quantitative evaluation of the impact of mergers on coordinated effects. ... We use a procedure similar to Davis (2006)[163] and Davis and Huse (2010)[164] to simulate firms' counterfactual static profits under the different elements of the coordination model (agreement, defection and punishment), which are then incorporated in the repeated game [where oligopolistic firms interact repeatedly, by playing an infinite sequence of ordinary static games over time and across markets][165] to identify the minimal threshold for the discount factor that sustains coordination.[166] The procedure can be used to examine the impact of partial acquisitions involving only financial interests, corporate control or both.[167]

The empirical methodology consists of six steps similar to those Davis and Davis and Huse: in the first step the degree of substitutability between the competing products is examined by estimating the consumer demand. In the second step differentiated product industries and competition between asymmetric multiproduct firms with both direct and indirect partial acquisitions is modelled, while in the third step marginal costs are recovered through demand estimates. In the fourth stage of the game firms play a repeated game in which they interact repeatedly, by playing an infinite sequence of ordinary static games over time and across markets. In steps five and six the likelihood of coordinated conduct among firms before the acquisition of the minority interest is addressed, while in the seventh stage of the game this likelihood is addressed after the acquisition of the minority interest.

In particular, in the fifth stage the recovered marginal costs along with the demand estimates are used in order to simulate the static profits of the firms prior the partial acquisition. In the sixth step the static profits are used so as to calculate the minimum threshold

[161] Ibid.

[162] D Brito, R Riberiero and H Vasconcelos, 'Quantifying the Coordinated Effects of partial Horizontal Acquisitions' (2013), CERP Discussion Paper No 9536.

[163] P Davis, 'Coordinated Effects Merger Simulation with Linear Demands' (2006) Competition Commission, available at http://www.biicl.org/files/2757_peter_davis_-_coordinated_effects_merger_simulation_with_linear_demands.pdf.

[164] P Davis and C Huse, 'Estimating the Coordinated Effects of Mergers' Competition Commission' (2010), available at http://catalogue.polytechnique.fr/site.php?id=298&fileid=1759.

[165] BD Bernheim and MD Whinston, 'Multimarket Contact and Collusive Behavior' (1990) 21 *RAND Journal of Economics* 1.

[166] For a critical review on the economics of tacit collusion in a dynamic environment, see M Ivaldi, B Jullien, P Rey, P Seabright and J Tirole, 'The Economics of Tacit Collusion', Final Report for DG Competition, Commission (IDEI, Toulouse, 2003).

[167] Above n 162, 2–3, 5, 6.

of discount factor that sustains collusion among firms. Lastly, in the seventh step the procedure in steps five and six are repeated for different ownership structures in the market, either for other actual or hypothetical partial acquisitions.

In the second stage of the game '[e]ach firm's aggregate profit is distributed among shareholders proportionally to the total stock owned, regardless of whether it be voting stock or preferred stock'.[168] Moreover, '[t]he manager of the firm maximizes a weighted sum of the shareholder's returns'. In stage three firms compete in prices and the Bertrand–Nash equilibrium is calculated. By assuming constant marginal costs the marginal costs are recovered from the first-order conditions and the demand estimates in the first stage. In stage four a setting similar to that proposed by Friedman is adopted in order to introduce dynamic conduct among firms in the market. Firms adopt the following trigger strategy:

> [E]ach firm chooses to set coordinated prices in period 1 and trust each other to continue to do so indefinitely. In face of this coordinated conduct, individual firms may be tempted to increase static profit for a period or so by deviating from the arrangement. However, should any single firm in any past period choose something different …, trust vanishes and each firm reverts permanently to a position in which no firm has any short-term temptation to deviate: the Bertrand–Nash equilibrium in prices.[169]

In fifth stage Brito et al empirically computed the aggregate profits of the firms under three different scenarios: (a) coordinated arrangement, (b) deviation from the coordinated arrangement and (c) punishment of deviation which would forever after trigger a Nash reversion punishment by rivals. The benchmark case for the two first scenarios is full (all the firms in the market) tacit collusion. Given the latter it is assumed that '[t]he managers of tacitly coordinating firms maximize the joint weighted sum of the shareholder's returns'.[170]

In the sixth stage the coordinated conduct is supported in the equilibrium if firms are sufficiently patient in the sense that they give more weight to future profits rather than profits that generated in the short term. For this the discount factor, the rate of time preference, must be high and exceeds a critical value given by the following equation:

$$\delta^{TH-PRE} = \frac{\Pi^{D}_{pre} - \Pi^{C}_{pre}}{\Pi^{D}_{pre} - \Pi^{BNE}_{pre}} \tag{43}$$

where Π^{D}_{pre} are the one-shot aggregate profits of a firm if it decides to deviate from the coordinated arrangement, Π^{C}_{pre} are the infinitely repeated aggregate profits of a firm if it decides to follow the coordinated arrangement and Π^{BNE}_{pre} are the aggregate profits of a firm from the Bertrand–Nash equilibrium. Therefore, coordination is sustained in the equilibrium if:

$$\delta^{C} > \delta^{TH} \tag{44}$$

In the seventh stage of the game the post partial acquisition values are computed and equations (40) and (41) are evaluated once again in order to consider whether the partial

168 Ibid, 10, 12. Above n 63, 609.
169 Ibid, 17.
170 Ibid, 19.

acquisition has altered the coordinated conduct of the firms. Equations (43) and (44) become equations (45) and (46), respectively:

$$\delta^{TH-POST} = \frac{\Pi^{D}_{post} - \Pi^{C}_{post}}{\Pi^{D}_{post} - \Pi^{BNE}_{post}} \tag{45}$$

$$\delta^{C} > \delta^{TH-POST} \tag{46}$$

D. Entry Effects of Minority Shareholdings

Clayton and Jorgensen[171] considered a game with three stages where in the first stage firm *j* examines whether or not to enter and the other two stages remain the same as in the case where entry is not allowed. In particular, given entry, the presence of minority shareholdings will enhance firms' profits if the products are complementary. Therefore, entry is more likely to occur when minority shareholdings are permitted rather than when they are prohibited.

If reciprocal minority shareholdings are prohibited, then entry will be deterred (promoted) if products are complements (substitutes). With complementary products, consumer surplus and firms' profits are enhanced more when minority shareholdings are allowed rather than when they are prohibited. With substitute products, firms' profits are enhanced when minority shareholdings are prohibited rather than when they are allowed, whereas consumer surplus is enhanced when minority shareholdings are allowed.

Therefore, with substitute products the overall effect of permitted reciprocal minority shareholdings on consumer surplus depends on entry costs. For instance, with small entry costs entry occurs regardless the existence of minority shareholdings and consumer surplus is enhanced. With intermediate entry costs and higher minority shareholdings, entry does not occur and consumer surplus decreases.

> Hansen and Lott (1995) demonstrate that cross holding can affect the entry decision. They analyze equity positions taken prior to entry and demonstrate that a firm considering entry can profit from trading in an incumbent firm's stock because the prospective entrant has private information about its own entry decision. They assume that, if the entrant does enter the product market, the stock price of the incumbent falls and otherwise it rises. The potential entrant earns profits by taking a short position in the stock prior to entering the product market and otherwise taking a long position. Thus, their rationale for trading in equity is to profit from private information about the incumbent's future stock price.[172]

In particular, if the market constitutes a passive incumbent[173] and

> [i]f short and long positions offer equal profits to the entrant (for the same change in incumbent value), the possibility of cross-trading has a smoothing effect on the probability of entry. If the

[171] Above n 72.

[172] Ibid, 1507–08.

[173] That is, the authors 'assume that there is one incumbent firm already established to serve a one-period market and that there is one potential entrant that would incur a fixed, non-recoverable entry cost of FC if it entered the market'. See RG Hansen and JR Lott, 'Profiting from Induced Changes in Competitors' Market Values: The Case of Entry and Entry Deterrence' (1995) 18 *Journal of Industrial Economics* 261, 264.

> perceived probability of entry is less than $\frac{1}{2}$ without cross-trading, then it will be higher with cross-trading, and vice versa.[174]

If the market constitutes an entry-deterring incumbent and

> suppose that without cross-trading the optimum probability of entry chosen by the incumbent is less than or equal to $\frac{1}{2}$ [, then with] cross-trading, the marginal benefit of increasing the entry-deterring bond must fall. Thus, the incumbent will be motivated to lower the bond and therefore the probability of entry will increase. If, in the absence of cross-trading, the optimum probability of entry is greater than $\frac{1}{2}$, then cross-trading might increase or decrease the marginal benefit of increasing the bond and therefore increase or decrease the optimum probability of entry.[175]

> Hansen and Lott (1996) investigate the proper objective of a firm when operational decisions generate externalities and demonstrate that maximizing firm value need not to be in the best interest of shareholders. Instead, fully diversified shareholders prefer joint value maximization. However, if some shareholders are not diversified, this leads to a conflict among the shareholders as to the preferred operating activities. Nonetheless, if managers are compensated with stock or stock options, their incentives lead them to maximize equity value over shareholder wealth. We show that cross holding leads the firm to internalize these externalities and can allow value maximization to become more aligned with the intent of diversified shareholders.[176]

[174] Ibid, 267.
[175] Ibid, 271–72.
[176] See above n 172.

5

Case Law Regarding Minority Interests

In section I we provide selected cases regarding minority interests under merger law. For this reason in section I.A we will present case law regarding selected active minority shareholdings, pre-existing merger cases and cases involving veto rights under the Merger Regulation. In section I.B we will present case law regarding minority shareholdings across Member States and in section I.C we present selected cases of minority interests across the globe. In section I.D we present selected cases of minority interests in the US.

In section II we provide selected cases concerning minority interests under Articles 101 and 102 TFEU and show how the Commission applies Council Regulation 1/2003 on profit-sharing joint ventures in the air transport sector. The Commission has been particularly vigilant regarding revenue-sharing joint ventures in the air transport sector since these may restrict competition to the detriment of a large number of consumers.

In particular, in section II.A.i we present the treatment of minority interests under Article 101 TFEU by providing a thorough analysis of critical cases. In section II.B.ii we present the treatment of minority interests under Article 102 TFEU by providing a critical analysis of selected cases. Finally, in section II.B we provide an application of Council Regulation 1/2003 regarding profit-sharing joint ventures in the air transport sector.

I. Merger Case Law Regarding Minority Shareholdings

A. Active and Pre-Existing Minority Shareholdings Under the Scope of the EC Merger Regulation

Under Council Regulation (EEC) 4064/89 the notion of 'decisive influence' constitutes transactions which enable the acquiring firm to control (solely or jointly) the acquired firm. Such transactions include full mergers, 100 per cent acquisitions and acquisitions of the majority of interests of the acquired firm. The *Philip Morris* case enhances the notion of decisive influence by including a broad array of acquisitions of minority shareholdings which violate Article 85 TFEU (see section II.A below).

In particular, *Philip Morris* involved a number of minority interests in the 25 and 40 per cent range. Therefore, the lower boundary of the influence standard was a 25 per cent interest; acquisitions of minority interests above this standard fell within it, given that particular agreements allocated sufficient control rights to the acquiring firm, while acquisitions of minority interests below it appeared to fall within the 'no influence' standard.

In the post-*Philip Morris* era the *Gillette* case seemed to expanded the lower boundary below 25 per cent by utilizing the notion of 'some influence' (see also section II.A below). In this sub-section we will thoroughly analyse how the Commission used its experience from the *Philip Morris* and *Gillette* cases in order to deal with certain types of minority interests (active, pre-existing and veto rights) from the outset of the implementation of the Merger Regulation 4064/89 until the application of Regulation 139/2004.

i. Active Minority Shareholdings

(a) IV/M.025 *Arjomari-Prioux-SA/Wiggins Teape Appleton plc* and IV/M.072 *Sanofi/Sterling Druf*

Case IV/M.025 *Arjomari-Prioux-SA/Wiggins Teape Appleton plc* was an early transaction/decision by the Commission under Council Regulation (EEC) 4064/89.[1] It was notified on 8 November 1990 and concerned the combination of business between Arjomari-Prioux-SA and Wiggins Teape Appleton plc. In particular, Arjomari-Prioux-SA transferred to Arjomari Europe, its wholly owned subsidiary, most of its assets, liabilities and undertakings. Subsequently, Arjomari-Prioux-SA transferred to Wiggins Teape Appleton plc almost its entire shareholding (99 per cent) in Arjomari Europe in exchange for 39 per cent of Wiggins Teape Appleton's ordinary shares.

The Commission stated that the acquisition of 39 per cent of Wiggins Teape Appleton's issued share capital by Arjomari-Prioux-SA constituted a concentration within the meaning of Article 3 of Regulation 4064/89[2] since:

> Arjomari will be able to exercise decisive influence on WTA because the remainder of [Wiggins Teape Appleton]'s shares are held by about 107.000 other shareholders none of whom own more than 4 percent, with only three shareholders having over 3 percent of the issued share capital.[3]

The Commission followed its Notice on the Notion of Concentration[4] which stated that sole control existed, inter alia, where the minority shareholder has the ability to achieve a majority in a shareholders' meeting, given that the remaining shares are widely dispersed among a number of shareholders (the case of a qualified minority shareholding).

However, the Commission concluded that the concentration did not have a Community dimension. Therefore, it 'decided that the concentration did not fall within the scope of Council Regulation No 4064/89 and adopted a decision under Article 6, 1(a) of the Regulation'.[5]

In case IV/M.072 *Sanofi/Sterling Druf* the Commission argued that the minority shareholder of 30 per cent of the share capital of a joint venture shared joint control with the largest shareholder, even though the decisions were taken by simple majority votes and the majority of the joint venture board's directors (five out of eight) were named by the largest shareholder.

[1] See also BA Hawk and HL Huser, '"Controlling" the Shifting Sands: Minority Shareholdings under EEC Competition Law' (1994) 17 *Fordham International Law Journal* 294, 306.

[2] See http://eur-lex.europa.eu/LexUriServ/LexUriServ.do?uri=CELEX:31989R4064:EN:HTML.

[3] See para 4 of Commission decision of 10 December 1990 declaring a concentration to be compatible with the common market (Case IV/M.0025 *Arjomari-Prioux SA/Wiggins Teape Appleton*) according to Council Regulation ([1990] OJ C321).

[4] See [1994] OJ C385, 5, para 14.

[5] See above n 2.

(b) COMP/JV.55 *Hutchison/RCPM/ECT*

On 3 November 1999 Hutchison Atlantic Ltd, Rotterdam Container Participatie Maatschappij BV and ABN AMRO Effecten Compagnie BV notified an agreement falling within the scope of Regulation (EC) 1216/1995 (Case COMP/37.688/D2 *RCPM + Hutchison + ABN AMRO*). On 24 October 2000 the Commission found that:

> Hutchison Altantic Ltd (through its subsidiary Hutchison Ports Netherlands BV (Hutchison)) and RMPM (through its subsidiary [Rotterdam Container Participatie Maatschappij BV]) had acquired de facto joint control of [Europe Combined Terminals BV] and that the notified transaction therefore constituted a concentration within the meaning of Article 3(1)(b) of the Merger Regulation. … The Commission took the view that Hutchison Altantic Ltd and RMPM had acquired joint control of [Europe Combined Terminals BV] on the basis of a number of elements, which, taken collectively, indicated that the two parties would act together when exercising their voting rights in [Europe Combined Terminals BV].'[6]

On the Commission's view the concentration constituted a joint venture (joint control of Europe Combined Terminals BV by the two notifying parties, Hutchison Atlantic Ltd and Rotterdam Container Participatie Maatschappij BV), ie the creation of

> a new holding company, [Europe Combined Terminals BV] Beheer BV ([Europe Combined Terminals BV] Beheer) which holds 100 percent of the share capital of [Europe Combined Terminals BV]. [Hutchison Atlantic Ltd] and RMPM/[Rotterdam Container Participatie Maatschappij BV]… each have 35 percent of the shares in [Europe Combined Terminals BV] Beheer, with ABN holding 28 percent and an employees' trust (Star) holding the remaining 2 percent.[7]

The Commission based its decision mainly on several factors indicating a common strategic behaviour between the two entities. In particular, the Commission stated that the two shareholders of the joint venture had strong common interests and hence when voting would not act against each other. Paragraph 15(b) of the Commission's decision stated that:

> [T]he structure of the shareholdings and voting rules, which seem to have been tailored in such a way as to allow the two parties to exercise joint control over [Europe Combined Terminals BV]. [Hutchison Atlantic Ltd] and RMPM [Rotterdam Container Participatie Maatschappij BV] together have 70 percent of the shares and voting rights, with a 60 percent majority being required for most decisions; … they also have four out of five seats on the Board of Supervisory Directors. … Although ABN would theoretically be able to form a voting majority with either of the strategic investors, the evidence shows that this was not the intention when the voting rights and rules were decided.

Also, paragraph 15(c) of the Commission's decision stated:

> [A] high degree of mutual dependency as between the two strategic investors regarding the success of their respective investments in [Europe Combined Terminals BV]. [Hutchison Atlantic Ltd] thus counts on RMPM [Rotterdam Container Participatie Maatschappij BV] to ensure the approval of future [Europe Combined Terminals BV] development plans, RMPM [Rotterdam Container Participatie Maatschappij BV] in turn expects [Hutchison Atlantic Ltd] to provide expertise and capital. In the former respect, RMPM [Rotterdam Container Participatie Maatschappij BV] has stated that it has chosen [Europe Combined Terminals BV] to be the one and only stevedore in the

[6] See paras 7 and 8 of the Commission's decision.

[7] Ibid, 13.

> western part of the port of Rotterdam (Maasvlakte) to receive and handle large vessels. [Hutchison Atlantic Ltd]'s expectation that RMPM [Rotterdam Container Participatie Maatschappij BV] will give preference to [Europe Combined Terminals BV] when considering applications for further expansion in Rotterdam must accordingly be regarded as well founded. Expansion is vital if [Europe Combined Terminals BV] is to maintain its position as the leading container terminal operator in Northern Europe. … Equally essential is access to expertise and capital. [Hutchison Atlantic Ltd], as the world's leading container terminal operator and financially well endowed, is indisputably well placed to assist.

Lastly, paragraph 15(d) stated that:

> [A] common guarantee provided by the strategic investors for the benefit of the financial investor. The common guarantee takes the form of a clause (Clause 11(5)) in the shareholders' agreement by which the two strategic investors undertake to maintain a minimum shareholding of at least 24 percent each in ECT for a period of five years following Closing. The evidence shows that this clause serves a dual purpose: on the one hand it provides each strategic investor with reassurance as to the seriousness of the other's commitment to [Europe Combined Terminals BV], on the other hand it provides an assurance to the financier, ABN, that its exposure on loans to [Europe Combined Terminals BV] Beheer is limited by the backing of the Hutchison Whampoa Group and the Port of Rotterdam. Clause 11(5) must be read in conjunction with provisions in the credit agreement (the Term Loan Agreement.) that give ABN the right to call in the loans granted to [Europe Combined Terminals BV] Beheer should the strategic investors. shareholding fall below the agreed minimum level.[8]

(c) IV/M.159 *Mediobanca/Generali*, IV/M.229 *Thomas Cook/LTV/West LB* and IV/M.239 *Avesta/British Steel/NCC/AGA/Axel Johnson*

On 27 November 1991 Mediobanca-Banca di Credito Finanziario Spa notified to the Commission the acquisition of 6.86 per cent of the issued share capital of Assicurazioni Generali SpA. Prior to the notified transaction Mediobanca-Banca di Credito Finanziario Spa owned 5.98 per cent of the issued share capital of Assicurazioni Generali SpA. Therefore, the total participation of Mediobanca-Banca di Credito Finanziario Spa in the share capital of Assicurazioni Generali SpA increased to 12.84 per cent.

The Commission considered whether this increase constituted an acquisition of sole control within the meaning of Council Regulation (EEC) 4064/89. Given the fact that the minority shareholding was the largest minority interest in the share capital of Assicurazioni Generali SpA the Commission compared the size of this interest to the normal overall shareholder participation in shareholder meetings. The Commission found that in the previous five years, between 32 and 42 per cent of total shareholder interests had voted at ordinary shareholder meetings, a percentage range that did not enable Mediobanca-Banca di Credito Finanziario Spa to exercise sole control over Assicurazioni Generali SpA. The firms involved in the transaction claimed that the acquired firm did not enjoy any special rights over the target firm, while the Commission found that there was no separate agreement among them for block voting or evidence of joint control of the target firm by its shareholders.[9]

[8] See also Case IV/M.042 *Alcatel/Telettra* [1991] OJ L122/48.

[9] See also Hawk and Huser (n 1).

However, the Commission considered that the notified transaction did not fall within the meaning of Merger Regulation and as consequence did not constitute concentration. The Commission's consideration was based on the fact that Mediobanca-Banca di Credito Finanziario Spa could not exercise sole or joint control over Assicurazioni Generali SpA.

In case IV/M.229 *Thomas Cook/LTV/West LB*[10] a travel agency acquired 90 per cent of the share capital of another travel agency and the remaining shares were acquired by a bank. The Commission deemed that the two shareholders exercised joint control over the travel agency given the fact that the shareholders' agreement gave to the bank control rights over it. In particular, the shareholders's agreement stated that

> The bank had (i) the right to name five of the entity's ten directors, the 90 percent shareholder had the right to name only two directors and the remaining three directors were to be jointly named; and (ii) a further right to name the chairman of the board, who would have a casting vote. The consent of both shareholders was required for strategic, commercial, and competitive decisions, such as approval of the acquired entity's annual and five-year business plans, material changes in the entity's business, major financial and acquisition/divestiture proposals and hiring/firing of senior employees. The bank also loaned most of the funds to allow the other parent to acquire its 90 percent interest.[11]

In Case IV/M.239 *Avesta/British Steel/NCC/AGA/Axel Johnson* a joint venture was formed in which the larger shareholder owned 40 per cent of its share capital. Even though the shareholders' agreement provided that approval was required of each of the two major and only one of the minor shareholders (7–8 per cent) for strategic decisions by the joint venture, the Commission found that the four largest and the two minor shareholders could be able to exercise joint control over it.[12]

(d) IV/M.258 *CCIE/GTE*, IV/M.292 *Ericsson/Hewlett-Packard*, IV/M.331 *Fletcher Challenge/Methanex* and IV/M.343 *Société Générale de Belgique/Générale de Banque*

In case IV/M.258 Citicorp Capital Investors Europe Limited bought shares in International Lighting Division's subsidiaries from GTE Corporation through its subsidiary EDIL International Lighting BV. After the clearance of the proposed concentration Citicorp Capital Investors Europe Limited owned 19 per cent of the voting rights of EDIL International Lighting BV. The other shareholder of EDIL International Lighting BV. was at the time of notification an independent investment banking company.

The Commission considered that after the completion of the concentration Citicorp Capital Investors Europe Limited exercised control over EDIL International Lighting BV based on the following criteria:

— The firm had a permanent seat on EDIL International Lighting BV's board and will appoint the Chairman and CEO.
— The Citicorp Capital Investors Europe Limited 'director's prior written approval will be required for all significant decisions (such as appointments and removal of board

[10] Case IV/M.229 *Thomas Cook/LTU/West LB* [1992] OJ C199/12.

[11] See especially Hawk and Huser (n 1) 309. See also Case IV/M.249 *Northern Telecom/Matra Telecommunication* [1992] OJ C240/15.

[12] See also Case JV/M.293 *Philips/Thomson/SAGEM* [1993] OJ C 22/2.

members, engagement and dismissal of senior employees, material capital expenditure, disposal of significant assets and approval of the annual budget)'.[13]
— The same veto right as above held for the shareholders' meeting.

In case IV/M.292 *Ericsson/Hewlett-Packard*[14] the majority shareholder had the right to name four of the acquired firm's seven board members. Even though the majority of board and shareholder's votes were by simple majority, the Commission stated that the majority and minority shareholders were able to confer joint control over the acquired firm since certain issues (approval of business plans and budget decisions) required unanimity.

In addition, in case IV/M.331 *Fletcher Challenge/Methanex*[15] Metallgesellschaft AG ('MG') owned 32 per cent of the share capital of Methanex, with the remaining shares widely dispersed among the public.

> Fletcher Challenge ('Fletcher') and Methanex agreed that Fletcher would contribute its worldwide methanol business to Methanex in exchange for a stock issue that would give Fletcher a 44 per cent interest in Methanex and dilute MG's interest to 10 per cent.[16]

Even though Fletcher nominated five Methanex's directors and MG only three, the remaining (three) directors would be jointly nominated by the two firms and the fact that board's decisions were subject to simple majority vote meant that

> the shareholders agreement also provided that (i) Fletcher and MG would jointly name the Chairman and Deputy Chairman of the board; ... (ii) Fletcher and MG would vote together at shareholders meetings in favour of all simple, non-extraordinary proposals made by the board that were subject to shareholder approval; and (iii) Fletcher and MG had mutual rights of first offer and refusal, as well as take along rights, regarding transfers of the other's interest. ... These minimal control rights were deemed sufficient to enable MG, with its mere 10 percent interest, to exercise joint control over Methanex.[17]

In the light of these provisions the Commission found that the shareholders conferred joint control over the acquired firm.

The Commission also investigated the minority shareholding of Société Générale de Belgique (SGB) in the share capital of Générale de Banque (GDB).[18] In particular, the former increased its minority shareholding in the share capital of the latter from 20.94 to 25.96 per cent by acquiring voting stock from GDB's larger shareholder whose minority shareholding declined from 14.69 per cent to below 5 per cent. The Commission argued that before the increment of SGB's shareholding in SDB's share capital no entity exercised control over GDB since at the last three shareholders' meetings of the firm the 20.94 per cent minority shareholding represented less than 50 per cent of the total shares voted at these meetings.

After the completion of the transaction SGB argued that the 25.96 per cent minority shareholding would represent the 56.62 per cent of the total shares voted at the meetings, if all its shareholders vote at the meetings and all other shareholders would vote the same percentage of their interests as at previous shareholder meetings. The Commission, even though it did not accept or reject SGB's assumptions, agreed that SGB would be likely to

13 See para 8 of the Commission's decision.
14 Case IV/M.292 *Ericsson/Hewlett-Packard* [1993] OJ C83/5.
15 Case IV/M.331 *Fletcher Challenge/Methanex* [1993] OJ C98/12.
16 See especially Hawk and Huser (n 1) 313.
17 Ibid.
18 See also Case IV/M.343 *Société Générale de Belgique/Générale de Banque*.

be able to exercise more than 50 per cent of the voting rights at the meetings and therefore would be able to confer control over GDB. The Commission's view was reinforced by the fact that the majority vote by the shareholders was determined the composition of the GDB's board of directors and as a consequence its decisions concerning business plans and budget.[19]

(e) IV/M.754 *Anglo American Corporation/Lonrho*

The proposed concentration concerned the acquisition by Anglo American Corporation of South Africa Limited ('Anglo American') of a 24.98 per cent shareholding in Lonrho plc. Through the concentration Anglo American acquired sole control of Lonrho plc within the meaning of Merger Regulation No 4064/89. After the Commission's investigation of the proposed concentration it was concluded that Anglo American, in conjunction with De Beers Consolidated Mines Limited and Central Holdings International Limited, was in a position to control a 27.47 per cent minority shareholding in Lonrho plc's issued share capital.

The Commission had to decide whether this minority shareholding conceded sole or joint control over Lonrho plc. Given the Commission's Notice on the Notion of Concentration[20] it investigated Lonrho shareholders' meetings during the period 1993–96 and concluded that:

> [T]he 27,47 percent shareholding would have amounted to a majority of the votes cast at all these meetings with the exception of the 1995 AGM. ... [I]n the past three years, the number of shares voted at the general meetings of shareholders has represented less than 55 percent of the share capital.[21]

On the contrary, Anglo American had 'argued that the only reliable method to test the influence of a shareholder is by reference to resolutions on contentious matters'.[22] According to the firm's point of view such an influence did not exist and therefore did not control, within the meaning of Merger Regulation, the acquired firm. However, the Commission had argued that exceptional resolutions on contentious matters are not relevant for the assessment of the case under scrutiny.[23]

Anglo American also argued that in the future the proportion of institutional shareholders will be increased in Lonrho plc's issued share capital with a consequence that its shareholding 'would not be expected to represent more than 50 percent of the votes cast'.[24] The Commission could not verify this tendency from the facts of the scrutinized case.

Furthermore, Anglo American argued

> that convertible bonds due in 2004 and 2006 and potentially representing 57 590 096 shares (7.4 percent of the current share capital) have been issued. These bonds have the potential to further dilute [it]'s shareholding, since [it] does not hold any of these bonds.[25]

[19] See also Case IV/M.613 *Jefferson Smurfit group plc/Munksjo AB*; Case IV/M.731 *Kvaerner/Trafalgar*; Hawk and Huser (n 1) 307–08 and the Greek coastal navigation case discussed in ch 6 below.

[20] Para 14 of the Commission's notice on the concept of a concentration under Council Regulation (EEC) No 4064/89 on the control of concentrations between undertakings ([1998] OJ C66, 5). See also Case IV/M.0025 *Arjomari Prioux SA/Wiggins Teape Appleton plc.*

[21] See para 32 of the Commission's decision. See also the analysis in Case COMP/M.3330 *RTL/M6*.

[22] Ibid, 33.

[23] Ibid, 34.

[24] Ibid, 35.

[25] Ibid, 36.

The Commission responded that the convertible price was far higher than the actual price of the bonds and that Anglo American 'would be able to adjust its own shareholding correspondingly by purchasing shares in the market'.[26]

Lastly but not least, Lonrho plc argued that its board 'could resist any attempt by [Anglo American] to nominate a majority of the board by rallying the support of institutional investors, other shareholders and the financial press'. The Commission's investigation regarding the role of institutional investors in Lonrho plc indicated that the volatility of their composition might negatively affected the above-mentioned support. The Commission stated in paragraph 37 of its decision that: 'This cannot be taken for granted, since even the body of institutional shareholders can change quite dramatically within a short period of time.'

Other factors that played a crucial role concerning the nature of control over Lonrho plc are the following:[27]

— the position of other large shareholders in Lonrho plc (the next largest shareholder in Lonrho plc was SA Mutual with a 3 per cent share of its issued capital).[28]
— The fact that Anglo American was the only industrial mining shareholder with a significant share in Lonrho plc.
— The fact that Lonrho plc's directors would not vote against Anglo American.[29]

(f) COMP/M.2283 *Schneider Electric/Legrand*

According to the Commission's press release:

> Schneider's proposed takeover of Legrand was notified to the Commission on 16 February 2001, and a second-stage detailed investigation was initiated on 30 March 2001. The public offer of exchange of shares announced by Schneider on 15 January 2001 was closed on 25 July 2001, and Schneider holds some 98 percent of Legrand's shares.[30]

The Commission prohibited the above-mentioned concentration since it would have considerably weakened the operation of the market[31] in a number of countries, notably France. In particular, the Commission declared that the concentration was incompatible with the common market since it raised competition concerns:

(i) in the market for electrical switchboards, where the merged parties would have had a combined market share of between 40 and 70 per cent in several countries;
(ii) in the market for wiring accessories, in which the combined market share would increase to 90 per cent in a number of countries.

[26] Ibid.
[27] Ibid, 38.
[28] Also, there existed cross-minority shareholdings among the concerned parties in the concentration and SA Mutual.
[29] The Commission reached the same conclusion concerning the effect of the proposed concentration in the London context and especially Anglo American Corporation of South Africa Limited's influence in Lonrho Platinum Division. See especially paras 40–43 of the Commission's decision.
[30] The press release is available at http://europa.eu/rapid/press-release_IP-01-1393_en.htm. This case was one of the arguments of Aer Lingus in *Ryanair/Aer Lingus*. Aer Lingus argued that the Commission's decision was not in line with its decision in the *Schneider/Legrand* case and this created a gap in European merger enforcement.
[31] The market for low-voltage electrical equipment.

The parties proposed commitments on 24 September 2001 in order to remove any concerns of the Commission primarily in the market of low-voltage electrical equipment. However, the Commission stated that 'Schneider's proposals did not provide any effective solution as regards a number of geographic markets and/or product markets on which competition problems had been identified'.[32]

On 15 January 2002 the Commission informed the parties of the broad lines of the draft of its decision on 30 January 2002 as submitted to the Advisory Committee on Concentrations. This decision set out the demerger arrangements to be made within a certain period of time.[33]

In particular, the Commission ordered Schneider to divest all its shareholdings in Legrand above 5 per cent in order to restore the conditions of effective competition. It considered that by keeping a significant minority shareholding in Legrand, Schneider would control it. Moreover, the Commission indicated that if Schneider were to be allowed to keep a significant minority shareholding, the number of investors interested in taking over Legrand would decrease significantly.

(g) COMP/M.2416 *Tetra Laval/Sidel*

> On 18 May 2001, the Commission received a notification ... pursuant to Article 4 of Council Regulation (EEC) No 4064/89 ... of a proposed concentration by which Tetra Laval SA, France, belonging to the group Tetra Laval BV ..., The Netherlands, acquired within the meaning of Article 3(1)(b) of the Merger Regulation control of the French company Sidel SA ('Sidel') by way of a public bid announced on 27 March 2001. After examination of the Original Notification, the Commission concluded that the notified operation fell within the scope of the Merger Regulation and that it raised serious doubts as to its compatibility with the common market and the EEA Agreement. On 5 July 2001, the Commission decided in accordance with Article 6(1)(c) of the Merger Regulation to initiate proceedings in this case. On 30 October 2001, the Commission declared the operation incompatible with the common market, following an in-depth investigation (the 'Decision'). By judgement ... delivered on 25 October 2002, the Court of First Instance of the European Communities[34] ... annulled the Commission's Decision in its entirety.[35]

However, in 2005, the European Court of Justice upheld the Commission's judgment against Tetra Laval.[36]

In particular, Tetra Laval was a major player in the aseptic carton packaging equipment and consumables market while Sidel was a major producer of polyethylene terephthalate (PET) packing equipment.[37] The Commission prohibited the proposed concentration on the grounds that Tetra Laval's minority shareholding would allow it to dominate the PET market since post-merger there would be a reduction in competition in the supply of stretch blow moulding machines.

[32] The Commission's analysis of the proposed commitments by the parties is presented in paras 788–850 of its decision.

[33] The Commission's decision on 30 January 2002 is available at http://ec.europa.eu/competition/mergers/cases/decisions/m2283_20020130_1240_en.pdf.

[34] See Case T-5/02 *Tetra Laval v Commission* ('*Tetra Laval I*') [2002] ECR II-438.

[35] See paras 1–3 of the Commission's decision on 13 January 2003 available at http://ec.europa.eu/competition/mergers/cases/decisions/m2416_62_en.pdf.

[36] See Case C-12/03 P *Commission v Tetra Laval* ('*Tetra Laval II*') [2005] ECR I-00987.

[37] In particular, a producer of stretch blow moulding machines which make the PET bottles used to package water and carbonated soft drinks.

In contrast to case COMP/M.2283 *Schneider Electric/Legrand* the Commisssion ordered Tetra Laval to divest all its minority shareholdings in Sidel. The Commission's argument was based on the fact that by retaining a minority shareholding in Sidel, Tetra Laval would be likely to take into account its expected revenue stream generated by its financial interests in Sidel and would therefore be likely to consider how its actions would affect Sidel's profit stream.[38] As a consequence of this the incentives of Tetra Laval to compete would therefore be eliminated as a result of the minority shareholding.

(h) COMP/M.3330 *RTL/M6*

On 2 and 3 February of 2004 Suez Lyonnaise des Eaux divested its minority shareholding (29.2 per cent) in the share capital of Métropole Télévision SA. Prior to this divestment the two major shareholders of Métropole Télévision SA were RTL Group SA, which owned 48.4 per cent of the equity capital and 34 per cent of the voting rights of Métropole Télévision SA, and Suez Lyonnaise des Eaux, which owned 37.6 per cent of the equity capital of Métropole Télévision SA.

After the completion of the transaction RTL Group SA continued to own the minority shareholding and voting rights of Métropole Télévision SA, but Suez Lyonnaise des Eaux owned only less than 5 per cent of Métropole Télévision SA's share capital. Its remaining participation was sold to a large number of investors through public placement.

The Commission concluded that the divestment of Suez Lyonnaise des Eaux constituted a passive acquisition of sole control of Métropole Télévision SA by RTL Group SA. That is, the Commission stated that RTL Group SA, as a minority shareholder in Métropole Télévision SA, had sole control over it on a de facto basis.[39]

Commission's conclusion was based on the fact that the remaining shares in Métropole Télévision SA were widely dispersed, given the facts that emerged from the investigation of previous shareholders' meetings.[40] According to paragraph 9 of the Commission's decision

> In the present case, the CSA[41] has limited [RTL Group SA]'s voting rights to 34 percent, even though RTL owns 48.39 percent of [Métropole Télévision SA's] shares. M6 itself holds 0.91 percent of its shares without any voting rights. The remaining 50.7 percent of shares and votes are widely dispersed among a large number of small shareholders.

ii. Cases Involving Veto Rights

(a) IV/M.017 *Aérospatiale/MBB*

On 24 January 1991 the French state-owned company Aérospatiale and the German Messerschmitt-Bölkow-Blohm GmbH merged their helicopter activities by transforming their divisions into legally independent companies owned by Eurocopter SA. Even though Aérospatiale owned a 60 per cent and Messerschmitt-Bölkow-Blohm GmbH a 40 per cent

[38] See also D Brito, R Ribeiro and H Vasconcelos, 'Measuring Unilateral Effects in Partial Horizontal Acquisitions' (2014) 33 *International Journal of Industrial Organization* 22, 22 where '[f]inancial interest refers to the right of the (partial) owner to receive the stream of profits generated by the operations and investments of the target firm'.

[39] See the analysis in Case IV/M.754 *Anglo American Corporation/Lonrho* and the footnotes therein.

[40] See also Case IV/M.343 *Société Générale de Belgique/Générale de Banque*, Case IV/M.754 *Anglo American Corporation/Lonrho*, Case IV/M.1157 *Skanska/Scancam* and the Greek coastal navigation case discussed in ch 6 below.

[41] That is, Conseil Supérieur de l.Audiovisuel.

of the share capital of Eurocopter SA, 'strategic decisions will require the unanimity of both partners in the supervisory board and the executive functions will be exercised by two managing directors (one from AS and one from MBB) who will act on a consensus basis'.[42]

Therefore, the proposed concentration constituted a joint control over Eurocopter SA by its two shareholders.

(b) IV/M.093 *Apollinaris/Schweppes*

On 20 May 1991 Brau und Brunnen AG and Cadbury Schweppes plc notified their agreement to establish a joint venture. The primary business plan of the joint venture was to manufacture, prepare, bottle, distribute and sell mineral waters and soft drinks in several European countries.

According to the agreement, Brau und Brunnen AG owned 72 per cent and Cadbury Schweppes plc owned 28 per cent of the share capital of the joint venture.[43] However,

> [T]he managing directors of the JV shall be elected by unanimous vote of both parties, and its supervisory board shall be composed of six members, two nominated by B&B and two by CS, the remaining two being representatives of the employees. It is also agreed that certain actions and decisions of the JV shall require the prior consent of the shareholders, including the approval of long range business, loans and annual budgets. It can therefore be concluded that the JV will be jointly controlled by the parents.[44]

(c) IV/M.397 *Ford/Hertz*

According to paragraph 1 of the Commission's decision, the Ford Motor Company offered 'to purchase from Commerzbank 5 percent of the share capital of The Hertz Corporation'. Following the transaction, the Ford Motor Company would own the 54 per cent of the shares of Hertz Corporation.

The notified transaction, even though it gave the Ford Motor Company de jure control of Hertz Corporation by obtaining the majority of its voting rights as well as board representation, did not imply a modification in the quality of Ford's decisive influence on the conduct of the business of Hertz Corporation.

Prior to the notification of the transaction, the Ford Motor Company owned 54 per cent of the shares of Hertz Corporation and possessed de facto sole control of it. Even though the Ford Motor Company did not have the majority of votes on the board and its veto rights 'did not include essential matters related to the conduct of Hertz's businesses such as the establishment of the business plan and the budget and decisions regarding major capital expenditure',[45] it was granted by an agreement with all the other shareholders in Hertz Corporation the power 'to increase its representation on Hertz's Board to an absolute majority with the addition of two other directors'.[46]

[42] See para 1 of the Commission's decision.

[43] Cadbury Schweppes plc's intention was to increase its shareholding up to 50 per cent of the share capital of the joint venture within the first five years of its operation. See para 6 of the Commission's decision.

[44] Ibid.

[45] See para 6 of the Commission's decision. Ford Motor Company's veto rights 'should be viewed as primarily aimed to protect Ford's financial investment in Hertz. These matters included inter-alia the issuance of shares, changes to the company statutes, acquisitions or divestitures and vehicle supply agreements.' See para 5 of the Commission's decision.

[46] See para 7 of the Commission's decision.

In fact, the above-mentioned agreement gave the right to the Ford Motor Company 'to convert, at its sole discretion and at any time, part of its Class C shares into Class B shares, … Ford's conversion rights could be exercised in a matter of hours and did not require any further cash disbursement'.[47]

(d) IV/M.970 *TKS/ITW Signode/Titan*

The notified concentration on 20 November 1997 constituted the acquisition of the joint control of the German company Titan Umreifungstechnik GmbH by the German companies Thyssen Krupp Stahl GmbH and ITW Signode Holding GmbH.[48]

ITW Signode Holding GmbH and Thyssen Krupp Stahl GmbH intended to acquire all of the shares of Titan Umreifungstechnik GmbH and so to form a joint venture. The former owned 65 per cent of the share capital of Titan Umreifungstechnik GmbH, while Thyssen Krupp Stahl GmbH owned the remaining share capital of the joint venture.

ITW Signode Holding GmbH appointed the managing directors of the joint venture, given the unanimous consent of its shareholders' assembly. In addition, ITW Signode Holding GmbH appointed two of the three members of the board of administrators, the role of which was to 'to supervise the Board of Directors and to determine the business policy of the joint venture'.[49]

However, the following veto rights required the unanimous consent of the joint venture's shareholders' assembly:

- the approval of the annual financial and business plans including investments and their modification;
- the approval of the extension of the powers of the board of directors;
- the appointment of the managing directors.

According to the Commission's decision,[50] these veto rights[51] were 'related to strategic commercial and financial decisions on the future joint venture's business policy and surpass the usual rights protecting the financial rights of minority shareholders'.

The Commission concluded that Thyssen Krupp Stahl GmbH 'ha[d] rights within the meaning of Article 3(3) of the Merger Regulation which confer[red] the possibility of exercising decisive influence on the strategic behaviour of the joint venture'.

(e) IV/M.2763 *Toray/Murata/Teijin*

With the proposed concentration on 22 January 2002 Toray Engineering Co Ltd, Murata Machinery Ltd and Teijin Seiki Co Ltd acquired joint control of the newly created joint venture TMT Machinery Inc (all Japanese firms) by way of a share purchase. Toray and Teijin each owned 33 per cent and Murata 34 per cent of the share capital of TMT Machinery Inc.

The notifying firms argued that the parent firms of the joint venture would not be able to exercise joint control of the joint venture since none of them had a veto power at the board

[47] Ibid.
[48] See also Case IV/M.925 *Krupp-Hoesch/Thyssen* and Case IV/ECSC1243.
[49] See para 8 of the Commission's decision.
[50] Ibid, para 9.
[51] See especially Case IV/M.897 *Stinnes/Haniel Reederei.*

of directors 'where decisions regarding the annual business plan and budget and important investment are to be taken'.[52]

However, the Commission noted that at the level of the shareholders' meeting unanimity was required for the adoption of decisions regarding the strategic policy of the joint venture, and therefore the scope and practice of the board of directors were reduced. The Commission argued that in the case of a joint venture with limited parents, where none of the three firms own a majority share, 'there's a strong likelihood that the JV will be operated with the parent's agreement on the most important strategic decisions, even if there is no express provision for any veto rights'.[53]

(f) IV/M.3101 *Accor/Hilton/Six Continents*

On 27 September 2002 Accor.Com SA, Ladbroke Group International Limited (controlled by Hilton), InterContinental Hotels Limited (controlled by Six Continents plc) and Worldres.Com Inc notified their acquisition of joint control of newly established joint venture WorldRes Europe Limited.

The Commission, after examination of the proposed concentration, concluded that given the participation of each parent firm in the share capital of the joint venture (each owned 31.25 per cent of it and Hilton initially held 6.25 per cent of joint venture's issued share capital, but also owned an option to increase its participation up to 31.25 per cent) and their veto rights, all parent firms, included Hilton, exercised joint control over the joint venture.

iii. Pre-Existing Minority Shareholdings

The Commission is limited to reviewing pre-existing structural links of the parties to a notifiable transaction. This is the reason why the Commission's scrutiny is limited, since many transactions do not fall within the scope of the Merger Regulation. This happens because the creation of a structural link by itself without including a change of control does not constitute a notifiable transaction under the Merger Regulation. The cases that will be presented below constitute examples where a party to a transaction has pre-existing structural links to competitors or other firms and where the parties quite often offered to divest these minority shareholdings with the intention of remedying the competition concerns raised by the transactions.

Furthermore, according to the point of view expressed in paragraph 8 of Annex II of the Commission Staff Working Document (Towards More Effective EU Merger Control, SWD(2013) 239 final), as was also demonstrated by the *Ryanair/Aer Lingus* case, the Commission's power to order the unwinding of a concentration declared incompatible with the internal market is limited, since the Commission has no legal means to request the undertakings to divest fully or partially a minority shareholding. The reason is that since the change of control[54] in the case examined has been avoided due to the Commission's decision, the role of the Commission has been accomplished.

[52] See para 12 of the Commission's decision.

[53] Ibid, para 13. See also [1998] OJ C66, point 34.

[54] At this point it should be repeated that sole control exists in cases where only one shareholder is able to veto strategic decisions of a company, although he is not the only one with power to impose such decisions (negative sole control).

(a) COMP/M.4439 *Ryanair/Aer Lingus*

On the end of October 2006, the proposed concentration by which Ryanair[55] was to acquire, for the purposes of paragraph (1)(b) of Article 3 of the Merger Regulation 139/2004,[56] control of Aer Lingus by public bid was notified to the Commission in accordance with Article 4 of the above-mentioned merger regulation. Almost two months later, by e-mail of 19 December 2006, Ryanair informed the Commission that its share acquisitions constituted part of its plans to gain control of Aer Lingus.

In its decision of 20 December 2006, ie the day after receiving the above-mentioned e-mail, the Commission found that the notified concentration raised serious doubts regarding its compatibility with the common (already unified) market and therefore decided to initiate a detailed examination procedure, in accordance with paragraph (1)(c) of Article 6 of the Merger Regulation.[57,58]

On 3 April 2007 a Statement of Objections was sent by the Commission to Ryanair in accordance with Article 18 of the Merger Regulation.[59] In its reply[60] to the Statement of Objections, Ryanair informed the Commission of its commitment to 'refrain from exercising the voting rights attached to its Aer Lingus shares until the conclusion of the detailed examination procedure', while noting that those shares 'did not enable it to exercise control over Aer Lingus in any event'.

[55] See case COMP/M.4439.

[56] [2004] OJ L24/1: '1. A concentration shall be deemed to arise where a change of control on a lasting basis results from: ... (b) the acquisition, by one or more persons already controlling at least one undertaking, or by one or more undertakings, whether by purchase of securities or assets, by contract or by any other means, of direct or indirect control of the whole or parts of one or more other undertakings.'

[57] '1. The Commission shall examine the notification as soon as it is received. ... (c) Without prejudice to paragraph 2, where the Commission finds that the concentration notified falls within the scope of this Regulation and raises serious doubts as to its compatibility with the common market, it shall decide to initiate proceedings. Without prejudice to Article 9, such proceedings shall be closed by means of a decision as provided for in Article 8(1) to (4), unless the undertakings concerned have demonstrated to the satisfaction of the Commission that they have abandoned the concentration.'

[58] See recital no 7 in the preamble of this decision, where it was mentioned that: 'As Ryanair acquired the first 19 [per cent] of the share capital of Aer Lingus within a period of less than 10 days before launching the public bid, and the further 6 [per cent] shortly thereafter, the entire operation comprising the acquisition of shares before and during the public period as well as the announcement of the public bid itself is considered to constitute a single concentration within the meaning of Article 3 of the merger regulation.'

[59] '1. Before taking any decision provided for in Article 6(3), Article 7(3), Article 8(2) to (6), and Articles 14 and 15, the Commission shall give the persons, undertakings and associations of undertakings concerned the opportunity, at every stage of the procedure up to the consultation of the Advisory Committee, of making known their views on the objections against them.

2. By way of derogation from paragraph 1, a decision pursuant to Articles 7(3) and 8(5) may be taken provisionally, without the persons, undertakings or associations of undertakings concerned being given the opportunity to make known their views beforehand, provided that the Commission gives them that opportunity as soon as possible after having taken its decision.
3. The Commission shall base its decision only on objections on which the parties have been able to submit their observations. The rights of the defence shall be fully respected in the proceedings. Access to the file shall be open at least to the parties directly involved, subject to the legitimate interest of undertakings in the protection of their business secrets.
4. In so far as the Commission or the competent authorities of the Member States deem it necessary, they may also hear other natural or legal persons. Natural or legal persons showing a sufficient interest and especially members of the administrative or management bodies of the undertakings concerned or the recognised representatives of their employees shall be entitled, upon application, to be heard.'

[60] Of 17 April 2007.

Pursuant to paragraph 3 of Article 8 of the Merger Regulation,[61] the Commission stated[62] that 'the notified concentration was incompatible with the common market (already internal market)'.[63]

Aer Lingus Group plc, ie the applicant, raised two pleas in law in support of its action. The first plea alleged an infringement of paragraphs 4[64] and 5[65] of Article 8 of the Merger Regulation and the second was based on an infringement of Article 21 paragraph 3[66] of the same Regulation. Given that the applicant presented the second plea in a way that was closely related or combined to the first, a fact that was confirmed at the hearing at which the applicant stated that the second plea could be regarded as part of the first, the General Court decided to examine the two pleas together.

Regarding the first plea, alleging an infringement of paragraphs 4 and 5 of Article 8 of the Merger Regulation, the applicant submitted that, in the contested decision, the Commission infringed those provisions by finding, following the Ryanair decision prohibiting implementation of the proposed concentration, that firstly it did not have the power to require Ryanair to divest its minority shareholding in Aer Lingus, and secondly it did not take appropriate measures to restore the situation prevailing before the merger or did not take any interim measures.

According to the Commission's point of view,[67] '[i]n the present case, [the] negative effects [on competition] cannot occur, since Ryanair has not acquired, and may not acquire,

[61] 'Where the Commission finds that a concentration fulfils the criterion defined in Article 2(3) or, in the cases referred to in Article 2(4), does not fulfil the criteria laid down in Article 81(3) of the Treaty, it shall issue a decision declaring that the concentration is incompatible with the common market.'

[62] On 27 June 2007.

[63] Decision C(2007) 3104, Case COMP/M.4439 *Ryanair/Aer Lingus* ('the Ryanair decision'). This specific decision was the subject of Case T-342/07 *Ryanair v Commission*, in which Aer Lingus intervened in support of the Commission. The main issues examined by the Court of First Instance (now the General Court) in this case were the following: (a) decision declaring a concentration to be incompatible with the common market, (b) assessment of the effects of the concentration on competition, (c) barriers to entry, (d) efficiency gains, (e) commitments.

[64] '4. Where the Commission finds that a concentration: (a) has already been implemented and that concentration has been declared incompatible with the common market, or (b) has been implemented in contravention of a condition attached to a decision taken under paragraph 2, which has found that, in the absence of the condition, the concentration would fulfil the criterion laid down in Article 2(3) or, in the cases referred to in Article 2(4), would not fulfil the criteria laid down in Article 81(3) of the Treaty, the Commission may:

— require the undertakings concerned to dissolve the concentration, in particular through the dissolution of the merger or the disposal of all the shares or assets acquired, so as to restore the situation prevailing prior to the implementation of the concentration; in circumstances where restoration of the situation prevailing before the implementation of the concentration is not possible through dissolution of the concentration, the Commission may take any other measure appropriate to achieve such restoration as far as possible,
— order any other appropriate measure to ensure that the undertakings concerned dissolve the concentration or take other restorative measures as required in its decision.

In cases falling within point (a) of the first subparagraph, the measures referred to in that subparagraph may be imposed either in a decision pursuant to paragraph 3 or by separate decision.'

[65] '5. The Commission may take interim measures appropriate to restore or maintain conditions of effective competition where a concentration: (a) has been implemented in contravention of Article 7, and a decision as to the compatibility of the concentration with the common market has not yet been taken; (b) has been implemented in contravention of a condition attached to a decision under Article 6(1)(b) or paragraph 2 of this Article; (c) has already been implemented and is declared incompatible with the common market.'

[66] 'No Member State shall apply its national legislation on competition to any concentration that has a Community dimension.'

[67] Para 12, last phrase.

control of Aer Lingus by way of the proposed concentration'. The applicant challenged this statement: according to its point of view,[68] Ryanair's shareholding had significant negative effects on competition

> and if, in such circumstances, the Commission did not have power under Article 8(4) and (5) of the merger regulation to eliminate those effects, there would be a serious lacuna in the merger regulation and in the Community's competence to secure 'undistorted competition'.[69]

More specifically, according to the applicant's claims, the significant negative effects on competition resulting from Ryanair's shareholding in Aer Lingus included the following: it would be possible for Ryanair, using its shareholding, to have access to Aer Lingus's confidential strategic plans and business secrets; in addition, according to the applicant, Ryanair blocked a special resolution relating to an increase in Aer Lingus's capital and imposed two extraordinary general meetings in order to change strategic decisions adopted by Aer Lingus. Furthermore, Ryanair had used its position as a shareholder to mount a campaign against Aer Lingus's management and to threaten its directors with litigation for breach of their statutory duties. The applicant considered that 'those facts weaken Aer Lingus as an effective competitor of Ryanair'.[70]

One of the most interesting arguments of the applicant was the following:[71] from an economic point of view, the specific type of minority shareholding between (actual and not just potential) competitors 'in a duopoly inherently distorts competition'.[72] More specifically, Ryanair had less incentive to compete with Aer Lingus since, as a shareholder, it preferred to maintain the value of its shareholding and ensure that Aer Lingus would be profitable. Such a type of shareholding changed the interests of the parties involved by encouraging price increases and tacit collusion, which distorts competition. Consequently, the market and financial attractiveness of Aer Lingus was also reduced as a result of Ryanair's shareholding.

According to the applicant's claims regarding the arguments about the *Tetra Laval/Sidel*[73] and *Schneider/Legrand*[74] cases, the statement challenged by Aer Lingus was also contrary to the Commission's previous practice. The first case, COMP/M.2416 *Tetra Laval/Sidel*,[75] ie Decision 2004/103/EC,[76] set out measures to restore conditions of effective competition pursuant to paragraph 4 of Article 8 of Council Regulation 4064/89 on the control of concentrations between undertakings; according to the Commission's point of view, Tetra Laval should not be allowed to retain a shareholding in Sidel. The second case, COMP/M.2283 *Schneider/Legrand*,[77] ie Decision 2004/276/EC,[78] required undertakings to be separated pursuant to paragraph 4 of Article 8 of Council Regulation 4064/89.

[68] See para 45 of the General Court's decision no T-411/07.
[69] Ibid.
[70] Ibid, para 46.
[71] Ibid, para 47.
[72] Ibid, para 47.
[73] See also section A(g) below.
[74] See also section A(f) below.
[75] [2004] OJ L38/1.
[76] Of 30 January 2002.
[77] [2004] OJ L101/134.
[78] Of 30 January 2002.

In this second case,[79] according to the Commission's point of view, Schneider's shareholding of less than 5 per cent of Legrand's capital would not lead to negative effects on competition. In that regard, the applicant challenged the Commission's opinion,[80] according to which the situation in the Ryanair case was different from those in *Tetra Laval* and *Schneider*, since in those two cases 'the public bid had already been fully implemented and the purchaser had acquired control of the target'.[81] The applicant stated that this specific distinction was not relevant and demanded a different interpretation;[82] according to this interpretation, in *Tetra Laval* and *Schneider* the Commission took precisely the opposite view, 'namely that even if the relevant shareholdings were reduced to a level which did not allow the exercise of "control", a minority shareholding would still result in an unacceptable distortion of competition'.[83] Furthermore, the concentration at issue still constitutes a *prospective concentration*. The point is that whether or not the public bid lapsed was immaterial since Ryanair continued to maintain its intention of acquiring Aer Lingus. Different national rules applicable to public bids should not be used as an excuse in order to justify those cases where one acquirer is able to maintain a minority shareholding while another is required to dispose of it. In both cases the effect on competition was the same.[84]

It is remarkable that a kind of rule of reason approach was attempted by the applicant; the applicant claimed that paragraph 4 of Article 8 of Merger Regulation 139/2004 ought to be interpreted as applying in this case to Ryanair's shareholding acquired as part of the prohibited concentration. Under this angle, the application of the same reasoning is profitable, mutatis mutandis, regarding the Commission's competence to adopt interim measures under paragraph 5(c) of Article 8 of the same regulation. More specifically, interpretation of the Merger Regulation must follow a teleological approach. In the applicant's point of view, the settled case law had 'indicated that the narrower interpretation would deprive the merger regulation of its effectiveness, whereas the broader interpretation was consistent with the text of the merger regulation, even if that was not explicitly stated'.[85] Therefore, the Commission's narrow interpretation of paragraphs 4 and 5 of Article 8 of Merger Regulation 139/2004 was contrary to the Regulation's purpose, which was (and continues to be) to ensure a system of undistorted competition in accordance with Article 3(g) of the EC Treaty. The applicant argued that Ryanair's minority shareholding created a distortion of competition and that the Commission's approach left the EU helpless in the face of that distortion, 'even though that shareholding was acquired as part of a prohibited concentration'.[86]

Furthermore, the applicant argued that preconditions for the application of paragraph 4 of Article 8 of the Merger Regulation, were (a) that a concentration 'has already been implemented' and (b) that it 'has been declared incompatible with the common market'.

[79] Published the same day as the *Tetra Laval/Sidel* decision.
[80] As was expressed in point 13 of the contested decision.
[81] See para 48 of the General Court's decision no T-411/07.
[82] As regards assessing the Commission's statement made in point 12 of its decision that there are no negative effects on competition 'in the absence of control'.
[83] Above n 72, para 48.
[84] The applicant also relied on the example of the United Kingdom Competition Commission: the Authority in October 2007 provisionally found that on the one hand the acquisition by BSkyB of 17.9 per cent of ITV's shares was likely to lessen competition substantially owing to the loss of rivalry between those two competitors and on the other hand to BSkyB's ability to have a material influence on ITV's management.
[85] Above n 83, para 51.
[86] Ibid.

Nevertheless, in the applicant's view, the Commission gave a purely literal interpretation[87] of that provision by stating that 'the concentration assessed in the present case has not been implemented' and that '[t]he transactions that have been carried out during the Commission's proceedings can therefore not be considered as part of an implemented concentration'. That strictly literal interpretation was erroneous, since the Commission adopted the opinion that the 'transactions' under assessment in the contested decision could be examined separately from the concentration examined.

In addition, that interpretation was also erroneous because the Commission equated the term 'implemented' used in paragraph 4(a) of Article 8 of the Merger Regulation with 'acquire control' in the sense of paragraph 2 of Article 3 of the same Regulation. The applicant considered that the concentration was implemented in the *Ryanair* case by means of transactions which formed part of the prohibited concentration and which finally allowed Ryanair to acquire (and to continue to hold) more than 25 per cent of Aer Lingus. The fact that the concentration was never fully completed, because the Commission prevented it, did not mean that the concentration was not implemented, at least partially, through the transactions referred to. In that regard, the Commission's claim that the concept of a concentration being 'partially implemented' did not find support in the wording of paragraph 4 of Article 8 was correct 'but of little assistance, since neither is it possible on the basis of the wording of that provision to require full implementation in the sense of acquiring control'.[88] From the applicant's point of view, the basic principle of paragraph 4 of Article 8 of the Merger Regulation was not the acquisition of control, 'but the need to restore the status quo ante, by reversing transactions forming part of the prohibited concentration'.[89]

In the applicant's view, the term 'implementation' ought to be examined in the light of paragraph 1 of Article 7 of the Merger Regulation:[90] in this paragraph it is provided that a concentration with a Community (now European Union) dimension could not be 'implemented' either before it had been notified or before it had been declared compatible with the common market (now internal market).[91] According to the applicant, the potential conclusion of an assessment of the Commission's practice could be that, according to the specific provision, it was possible to prevent partial implementations, 'including transactions falling short of a transfer of control'.[92]

In the case examined, the Commission obtained an undertaking from Ryanair to postpone the exercise of the voting rights attached to its shareholding in Aer Lingus, despite the fact the exercise of these voting rights was not equivalent to the exercise of control. Thus, it could be concluded that the intention was indeed the prevention of possible negative effects on competition.

[87] It is about an interpretation based on the exact wording.

[88] Above n 86, para 51.

[89] Ibid, para 52.

[90] 'A concentration with a Community dimension as defined in Article 1, or which is to be examined by the Commission pursuant to Article 4(5), shall not be implemented either before its notification or until it has been declared compatible with the common market pursuant to a decision under Articles 6(1)(b), 8(1) or 8(2), or on the basis of a presumption according to Article 10(6).'

[91] Above n 89, para 53, quoting 'A coherent approach to the concept of "implementation" should also examine the meaning of that term.' In the authors' view, regarding the meaning of the term 'implementation', in this specific paragraph there is an attempt at a kind of a rule-of-reason approach.

[92] Ibid.

Furthermore, in the applicant's view, the concept of 'implementation of a concentration' used in paragraphs 4 and 5 of Article 8 and in Article 7 could have three meanings/interpretations: (i) the full implementation of the concentration, or (ii) the partial implementation of the entire concentration or (iii) the full implementation of part of the concentration. This triple meaning was exposed in the case examined, in which the Commission prohibited a concentration which consisted of two parts (on the one hand an acquisition of shares in the market and on the other hand a public bid) 'of which only the former had been implemented'.[93]

Furthermore, the applicant claimed that the Commission's erroneous conclusions concerning the application of paragraphs 4[94] and 5[95] of Article 8 of the Merger Regulation had led it into error regarding the interpretation of paragraph 3 of Article 21[96] of the same Regulation. More specifically, since the Commission had indeed the power to adopt divestment measures in connection with Ryanair's shareholding, the national competition authorities therefore had no such power under paragraph 3 of Article 21. According to the applicant, the 'one-stop shop' principle is supported by that approach. If this approach is considered correct, the Commission, in the contested decision, infringed paragraph 3 of Article 21 of the Merger Regulation, since it failed to state, unequivocally, that the specific provision precluded the intervention of national competition authorities and thereby left open the possibility of such intervention. In the applicant's view, that infringement was more than serious, since the relevant national authorities had already issued conflicting opinions. The applicant believed that the Commission's approach offered Ryanair's shareholding legal immunity from both EU and national law. Nevertheless, a coherent interpretation of paragraphs 4 and 5 of Article 8 of the Merger Regulation would exclude any interpretation of paragraph 3 of Article 21 which would prevent the Member States from applying their national laws to Ryanair's shareholding once the shareholding was examined in isolation from the public bid and which simultaneously would also leave the Commission without power to examine that shareholding under paragraph 4 of Article 8 of the Merger Regulation.

[93] Ibid, para 54.

[94] 'Where the Commission finds that a concentration: (a) has already been implemented and that concentration has been declared incompatible with the common market, or (b) has been implemented in contravention of a condition attached to a decision taken under paragraph 2, which has found that, in the absence of the condition, the concentration would fulfil the criterion laid down in Article 2(3) or, in the cases referred to in Article 2(4), would not fulfil the criteria laid down in Article 81(3) of the Treaty, the Commission may:

— require the undertakings concerned to dissolve the concentration, in particular through the dissolution of the merger or the disposal of all the shares or assets acquired, so as to restore the situation prevailing prior to the implementation of the concentration; in circumstances where restoration of the situation prevailing before the implementation of the concentration is not possible through dissolution of the concentration, the Commission may take any other measure appropriate to achieve such restoration as far as possible,
— order any other appropriate measure to ensure that the undertakings concerned dissolve the concentration or take other restorative measures as required in its decision.

In cases falling within point (a) of the first subparagraph, the measures referred to in that subparagraph may be imposed either in a decision pursuant to paragraph 3 or by separate decision.'

[95] 'The Commission may take interim measures appropriate to restore or maintain conditions of effective competition where a concentration: (a) has been implemented in contravention of Article 7, and a decision as to the compatibility of the concentration with the common market has not yet been taken; (b) has been implemented in contravention of a condition attached to a decision under Article 6(1)(b) or paragraph 2 of this Article; (c) has already been implemented and is declared incompatible with the common market.'

[96] 'No Member State shall apply its national legislation on competition to any concentration that has a Community dimension.'

The Commission challenged the applicant's argument. More specifically, it noted that the Merger Regulation applies only to 'concentrations' which satisfy the definition set out in Article 3 of the Merger Regulation. In that context, according to the Commission's point of view, the acquisition of a minority shareholding, which did not confer 'control' as such, did not constitute a 'concentration' under the Merger Regulation. Furthermore, the Commission submitted that paragraph 3 of Article 21 of the Regulation did not confer any specific duties or powers on it and that it thus did not have the power to offer an interpretation of that provision when called upon to act under Article 265 TFEU (ex Article 232 EC).[97]

Aer Lingus focused on the argument about a partial implementation of the concentration. More specifically, it submitted in essence that the shareholding in Aer Lingus acquired by Ryanair before or during the public bid represented a partial implementation of the concentration declared incompatible by the Commission. Therefore, in order for the conditions for effective competition to be restored, Aer Lingus claimed that the Commission ought to require, pursuant to paragraph 4 of Article 8 of the Merger Regulation, 'the disposal of all the shares acquired by Ryanair'.[98]

In the contested decision,[99] the Commission denied to initiate proceedings against Ryanair under paragraph 4 of Article 8 of the Merger Regulation, since it considered that the concentration notified by that undertaking had not been implemented and that the disputed shareholding did not grant Ryanair control of Aer Lingus. Furthermore, the Commission considered that, in the absence of a concentration which has been implemented as defined by Regulation 139/2004, the perhaps teleological interpretation suggested by the applicant, ie Aer Lingus, went beyond the limits of its powers.

In order to assess the legality of the contested decision in the light of the Commission's power to require an undertaking to dissolve a concentration, in particular through the disposal of all the shares acquired in another undertaking, the benchmark should be the relevant moment established by paragraph 4 of Article 8 of the Merger Regulation, which foresaw 'concentration' which 'had already been implemented' and which 'had been declared incompatible with the common market'.

The time of declaration by the Commission that the concentration notified by Ryanair was incompatible with the common market should be underlined. At the same time the Commission did not address the issue of Ryanair's minority shareholding in Aer Lingus in the Ryanair decision; the Commission still had the option to do so in a separate

[97] Above n 93, para 56. Art 265 TFEU provides that:

> Should the European Parliament, the European Council, the Council, the Commission or the European Central Bank, in infringement of the Treaties, fail to act, the Member States and the other institutions of the Union may bring an action before the Court of Justice of the European Union to have the infringement established. This Article shall apply, under the same conditions, to bodies, offices and agencies of the Union which fail to act.
>
> The action shall be admissible only if the institution, body, office or agency concerned has first been called upon to act. If, within two months of being so called upon, the institution, body, office or agency concerned has not defined its position, the action may be brought within a further period of two months.
>
> Any natural or legal person may, under the conditions laid down in the preceding paragraphs, complain to the Court that an institution, body, office or agency of the Union has failed to address to that person any act other than a recommendation or an opinion.

[98] Ibid, para 57.

[99] Ibid, para 58.

decision adopted on the basis of the final sentence of paragraph 4 of Article 8 of Regulation 139/2004. Nevertheless, as was correctly stated in the contested decision, the other condition laid down in paragraph 4 of Article 8 of the Merger Regulation was not satisfied, since the notified concentration had not been implemented. In the case examined, from the moment when the decision finding incompatibility with the common market (internal market) was adopted, 'it was no longer possible for Ryanair, de jure or de facto, to exercise control over Aer Lingus or to exercise decisive influence on that undertaking'.[100]

From a legal point of view, the basis for the Commission's powers is provided by the concept of concentration used in the Merger Regulation. More specifically, according to paragraph 1 of Article 1, the Merger Regulation applies to all concentrations with a European (Community) dimension. A definition of the concept of concentration exists in Article 3 of the Merger Regulation. Under paragraph 1 of Article 3, a concentration is created *where there is a change of control on a lasting basis* which results, for instance, from the merger of two enterprises or the acquisition by an enterprise of the control of another enterprise. According to paragraph 2 of Article 3, rights, contracts or any other means which confer the possibility of exercising decisive influence on the undertaking concerned constitute the above-mentioned control.[101]

Thus, for the purposes of the Regulation 139/2004, concentration constitutes any transaction or group of transactions which brings about 'a change of control on a lasting basis' by conferring 'the possibility of exercising decisive influence on the undertaking concerned'. Two main characteristics are common in such types of concentrations: (i) before the merger there are two distinct undertakings (for a given economic activity) and (ii) after the concentration there will only be one. Unlike in the case of a merger in which one of the two undertakings concerned ceases to exist, the Commission thus has to determine whether the result of the implementation of the concentration is to confer on one of the undertakings the power to control the other, that is to say a power which it did not previously hold. That power to control is the possibility of exercising decisive influence on an undertaking, in particular where the undertaking with that power is able to impose choices on the other in relation to its strategic decisions.

It is apparent from the above analysis that the acquisition of a shareholding which does not, as such, confer control in the terms of Article 3 of the Merger Regulation does not constitute a concentration which is deemed to have arisen for the purposes of that Regulation. On that point, European law differs from national law at least in comparison with some of the Member States: more specifically, in some Member States the national authorities are authorized under provisions of national law on the control of concentrations to take action in connection with minority shareholdings in the broader sense.[102]

Contrary to the applicant's claims, in terms of European law the concept of concentration cannot be extended to cases in which control has not been obtained and the shareholding at issue does not, as such, confer the power of exercising decisive influence on the other undertaking.[103]

[100] Ibid, para 61.
[101] Ibid, para 62.
[102] Ibid, paras 21, 49 and 64.
[103] Nevertheless, it could be considered that it forms part, in a broader sense, of a notified concentration examined by the Commission and declared incompatible with the common market following that examination, without having been any change of control within the above meaning.

It is obvious that under the Merger Regulation 139/2004, the Commission has not been granted such a power. More specifically, according to the actual terms used in paragraph 4 of Article 8 of the Merger Regulation, the power to require the disposal of all the shares acquired by an undertaking in another undertaking exists only 'to restore the situation prevailing prior to the implementation of the concentration'. The crucial point is that, in the case that control has not been acquired, the Commission does not have the power to dissolve the concentration. According to the correct teleological approach, *if the legislature had wished to grant the Commission broader powers than those laid down in the Merger Regulation, it would have explicitly enacted a provision to that effect.*

In the case examined, from a factual point of view, it is not disputed that Ryanair's shareholding in Aer Lingus does not give to Ryanair the necessary power to 'control' Aer Lingus.[104] Equally, Aer Lingus does not claim that Ryanair's shareholding of 29.3 per cent in it from August 2007 confers control of the company on it, but merely states that this shareholding gives it 'substantial opportunities to seek to interfere with the management and commercial strategy of Aer Lingus'. Nevertheless, even in such a case, the crucial question still remains: is it enough in order to conclude that Ryanair controls Aer Lingus or even there is a joint control from both companies? In the Commission's view, definitely no.

In addition, in response to the applicant's arguments in relation to the alleged negative effects on competition, the Commission was correct in the contested decision to reject the claim that those effects could actually be assimilated to a form of control in the case examined.[105] In this regard, one made point by the General Court should be underlined: '[T]he merger regulation does not seek to protect companies from commercial disputes between them and their shareholders or to remove all uncertainty in relation to the approval of important decisions by those shareholders'.[106] In addition, the General Court estimated that in case that the management of Aer Lingus considered that Ryanair's conduct as a shareholder was abusive or unlawful, it could bring the matter before the competent national courts or authorities.[107]

In any event, the fact that the data put forward by the applicant suggest that the relations between its management and Ryanair are tense, and that they have opposing views on a number of points, is not enough in itself to prove that it is possible for Ryanair to exercise decisive influence on that undertaking.[108] On the contrary, it could safely be said that the data show that the supposed influence (if is it accepted that there is such) of Ryanair is definitely not decisive.

There was also a claim that Ryanair used its shareholding to seek access to Aer Lingus's business secrets and confidential strategic plans. Nevertheless, the only evidence provided in support of that claim was a letter in which Ryanair requested, in general terms, a meeting to be held with the management of Aer Lingus. However, there was no evidence at all that confidential information was actually exchanged during such a meeting. Furthermore,

[104] Above n 102, para 67. In addition to the information given in points 10 and 11 of the contested decision, Aer Lingus states that '[it] accept[s] the assumption, made in paragraph 11 of the [c]ontested [d]ecision, that Ryanair did not, as at 27 June 2007, have "control" within the meaning of Article 3(2) [of the merger regulation]'.

[105] See point 11 of the contested decision.

[106] Above n 104, para 68.

[107] Ibid.

[108] Ibid, para 69. This is required for the Commission to be able to have recourse to Art 8(4) of the Merger Regulation. See relevant thoughts on the Sea Star case discussed in ch 6 below.

the General Court clearly stated that 'in any event, such an exchange of information would not be a direct consequence of the minority shareholding, but would constitute subsequent conduct on the part of the two companies which could potentially be examined under Article 81 EC [now Article 101 TFEU]'.[109]

Concerning whether or not Ryanair was in a position to impose its will, the fact is that there was a claim that Ryanair voted against a special resolution that, if passed, would have allowed the board of directors to issue shares without having first to offer them to existing shareholders. Nevertheless, the first offer to existing shareholders is a usual term which generally required under national company law. Besides, it is apparent from the comments of Aer Lingus's CEO that the failure of the above-mentioned resolution did not have a significant impact on the company.[110]

Furthermore, there was a claim that Ryanair demanded two extraordinary general meetings having the intention of the reversing strategic decisions adopted by Aer Lingus. However, the Commission stated on the one hand that the board of directors of Aer Lingus rejected these two requests, and on the other hand that the planned decisions were implemented despite Ryanair's opposition. Furthermore, these two facts were not contradicted by the applicant. These factual examples illustrate 'the fact that, contrary to the applicant's claims, Ryanair is not in a position to be able to impose its will'.[111]

As regards the campaign mounted by Ryanair against Aer Lingus's management, the relevant claim should be understood as connected to the two extraordinary general meetings demanded by Ryanair.[112] In addition, the Commission clearly established in its pleadings that Aer Lingus rejected those two requests and implemented its decision as planned. Hence, even if it was accepted that Ryanair had disrupted the management of Aer Lingus for several weeks, this fact by itself would still not prove that Ryanair was able to exercise decisive influence on Aer Lingus within the meaning of the Merger Regulation.[113] Moreover Ryanair did not exercise a kind of negative veto, since the delay in making managerial decisions was only temporary.

One of the main arguments made by Aer Lingus was that in a duopoly market there is an inherent connection of a minority shareholding with a distortion of competition: Aer Lingus's point was that the undertaking with a minority shareholding has less incentive to compete with an undertaking in whose profitability it is interested. In response to this argument, it must be observed that this claim was not confirmed by the facts. More specifically, after the acquisition of its shareholding in Aer Lingus, Ryanair's competitive policy became more 'aggressive', since it entered four routes previously served only by Aer Lingus and, in addition, increased its frequencies on six other routes where it competed with Aer Lingus.[114] Consequently, the theoretical argument that in a duopoly market there is an inherent connection of a minority shareholding with a distortion of competition is not

[109] Ibid, para 70.

[110] See 'Ryanair Blocks Aer Lingus Bid to Reduce Holding', *Irish Times* 7 July 2007. This is also cited by the Commission without being disputed by the applicant.

[111] Above n 109, paras 71 and 72.

[112] About the correspondence and the related public statements, above n 109, paras 71 and 72.

[113] Above n 111, para 73.

[114] This argument was stated by the Commission, without being contradicted by Aer Lingus (the applicant). See also Ryanair's two press releases 'Ryanair Announces 6 New Routes from Dublin' (15 August 2007) and '31st New Route from Shannon Base and 3 New Routes from Dublin' (25 October 2007).

confirmed and therefore, it is not adequate, 'in any event, to show, as such, a form of control by Ryanair of Aer Lingus able to justify the divestment of the minority shareholding at issue in the present case'.

Another argument made by Aer Lingus was that Ryanair's shareholding had a material impact on Aer Lingus's shares, in a way that it made them less attractive to potential buyers.[115] Nevertheless, in principle, it should not be ignored or underestimated that the attractiveness of Aer Lingus both financially and on the stock market is not based solely on Ryanair's minority shareholding; on the contrary, it ought to take into account the entire capital of this enterprise, in which it is quite possible that other significant shareholders have a stake. In addition, even supposing that Ryanair's shareholding may affect Aer Lingus's attractiveness, this hypothetical case would not by itself be sufficient to show that there is control within the meaning of the Merger Regulation. Therefore,control and influence on attractiveness are absolutely different things. The limit of power that the Commission has for the purposes of merger control would be exceeded in the case that it was accepted that the Commission has the authorization to decide the dividing of a minority shareholding on the sole base either of the theoretical existence of an economic risk when there is a duopoly, or of a disadvantage for the attractiveness of the shares of one of the undertakings creating the abovementioned duopoly.[116]

Furthermore, the Commission's previous practice in relation to the treatment of minority shareholdings under paragraph 4 of Article 8 of the Merger Regulation cannot usefully be cited to question the criteria laid down in the provision of this article. More specifically, an examination of the Commission's previous practice shows quite clearly that all the decisions adopted to date by the Commission under paragraph 4 Article 8 of the merger regulation concern concentrations which have already been implemented, in which the target company—after the merger—had ceased to be an independent competitor of the purchasing company (in the case of a horizontal merger) or generally an independent undertaking in comparison with the purchasing company (in the case of a vertical or a conglomerate merger). In contradiction with the case examined, the above-mentioned decisions did not concern the applicability of paragraph 4 of Article 8 to the concentration at issue; they concerned merely the measures appropriate to restore the competition which had been eliminated by the implementation of the concentration.[117] Since those measures are not the same but, on the contrary, may vary from one case to the next depending on the circumstances of the specific case, a case-by-case analysis is demanded. Consequently, as regards the case examined, the Commission cannot be accused of infringing paragraph 4 of Article 8 of the Merger Regulation because on the one hand no concentration had been implemented and, on the other hand, it did not have the power to require Ryanair to dispose of its shareholding in Aer Lingus. Only if such a shareholding was in a position to enable Ryanair to control Aer Lingus by exercising de jure or de facto decisive influence on it, would the Commission have had such a power under the Merger Regulation; but, this is not the case here.[118]

Also, concerning the timing of the examination procedure, it does not matter that the Commission considered, during the examination procedure, that the shareholding acquired by Ryanair on the market just before and during the public bid—which, in its

[115] Above n 113, para 75.
[116] Ibid, para 76.
[117] Ibid, para 77.
[118] Ibid.

words, constituted a 'single concentration'—should be regarded as falling within the scope of that bid. This means that the Commission is not concerned during the examination procedure with the issue of 'restoring the situation prevailing prior to the implementation of the concentration'. Those concerns arise under the previous precondition that a final decision, ie a decision after the examination procedure,[119] has been adopted 'and when it is necessary to draw consequences from that decision after it becomes apparent that the situation at hand is not in accordance with it'.[120]

Furthermore, during the examination procedure, the Commission seeks rather to prevent the implementation of a concentration which might still be declared incompatible with the common market (already single market). That is the main purpose of Article 7 of Regulation 139/2004, which seeks to ensure that one of the founding principles of the Regulation is respected, namely that concentrations with a single market dimension cannot be implemented without first being notified to, and finally declared compatible with the single market, by the Commission.[121]

More specifically, according to paragraph 1 of Article 4 of the Merger Regulation,[122] concentrations defined in the Regulation 139/2004 are to be notified to the Commission prior to their implementation and following the conclusion of the agreement, the announcement of the public bid, or the acquisition of a controlling interest. The same principle is also set out in Article 7 of the Merger Regulation.[123] As already mentioned in the previous paragraph, under paragraph 1 of Article 7 of the Merger Regulation, a concentration with a single market dimension is not to be implemented either before its notification or until it has been declared compatible with the common market (already single market). In addition, in paragraph 2 of Article 7 it is stated that the purpose of paragraph 1 is not to prevent the implementation of a public bid or of a series of transactions in securities, by which control within the meaning of Article 3 is acquired from various sellers, under the prior precondition that the concentration under assessment is notified to the Commission pursuant to Article 4 without delay and that the buyer does not exercise the voting rights attached to the securities in question or does so only to maintain the full value of its investments based on a derogation[124] that the Commission has granted.[125]

It should be observed that the obligation to postpone the implementation of the concentration until it has been declared compatible by the Commission is subject to an automatic derogation in the case of public bids or acquisition of control by means of a series of

[119] Only a decision after the examination procedure could be considered as a final decision.

[120] Above n 118, para 79.

[121] Ibid, para 80. See mainly para 1 of Art 7 of the Merger Regulation: 'A concentration with a Community dimension as defined in Article 1, or which is to be examined by the Commission pursuant to Article 4(5), shall not be implemented either before its notification or until it has been declared compatible with the common market pursuant to a decision under Articles 6(1)(b), 8(1) or 8(2), or on the basis of a presumption according to Article 10(6).'

[122] Which is entitled 'Prior notification …'.

[123] Which is entitled 'Suspension of concentrations'.

[124] See P Fotis, M Polemis and N Zevgolis, 'Stock Price Performance as an Argument for Derogation from Suspension of Concentrations: Reality or Myth?' (2009) 30 *European Competition Law Review* 216. For the Greek market, see also P Fotis, M Polemis and N Zevgolis, 'Robust Event Studies for Derogation from Suspension of Concentrations in Greece during the Period 1995–2008' (2011) 11 *Journal of Industry, Competition and Trade* 67–89.

[125] Above n 121, para 81.

transactions in securities involving various sellers.[126] To be able to benefit from that derogation, the interested parties ought to notify the Commission of the concentration without delay and, cumulatively, not exercise the voting rights attached to those securities.[127] As the Commission mention in its pleadings, that derogation effectively transfers the risk of having the operation prohibited to the acquirer.[128] In the case that, after the examination procedure, the Commission considers that the notified merger operation must be prohibited, the securities acquired to implement this concentration have to be disposed of, as is illustrated in *Tetra Laval*[129] and *Schneider.*[130]

In that regard, the acquisition of a shareholding, even if it does not, as such, confer control for the purposes of Article 3 of Regulation 139/2004, may nevertheless fall within the scope of Article 7, ie suspension of concentrations. The Commission's approach can logically be explained as using the concept of 'single concentration' forward looking

> to limit the risk of finding itself in a situation in which a decision finding incompatibility would need to be supplemented by a decision to dissolve in order to put an end to control acquired even before the Commission has taken a decision on its effects on competition.[131]

The only reason for the Commission requesting Ryanair not to exercise its voting rights,[132] was that otherwise Ryanair would be exposed in such circumstances that it would be implementing a merger liable to give rise to a measure adopted on the basis of paragraphs 4 and 5 of Article 8, if found to be incompatible with the single market.

For the above-mentioned reasons, the Commission was correct to consider[133] that Ryanair's minority shareholding in Aer Lingus could not be considered, in the case examined, as the 'partial implementation' of a merger liable to give rise to a measure adopted on the basis of paragraphs 4 and 5 of Article 8,[134] if found to be incompatible with the single market.

[126] It should be noted that in cases where a derogation has been requested, the Commission—in order to decide whether or not the realization of the concentration should be permissible—is obliged to balance not only the interest of the merging parties and that of interested third parties, but also the possible harm to competition as a consequence of the immediate completion of the merger. This is the reason why 'such a derogation may be made subject to conditions and obligations in order to ensure conditions of effective competition'. See G Karydis, 'Le contrôle des concentrations entre entreprises en vertu du règlement 4064-89 et la protection des intérêts légitimes des tiers' [1997] No 1(2) *Cahiers de droit Européen* 81, 92, point 24.

[127] Above n 125, para 82.

[128] Ibid.

[129] Case COMP/M.2416 *Tetra Laval/Sidel* [2004] OJ L38, 1 ('the *Tetra Laval* decision').

[130] Case COMP/M.2283 *Schneider/Legrand* [2004] OJ L101, 134 ('the *Schneider* decision').

[131] Above n 128, para 83.

[132] Besides, in any case, the Commission also pointed out that those voting rights did not grant Ryanair control of Aer Lingus.

[133] See mainly paras 12 and 13 of the contested decision.

[134] '4. Where the Commission finds that a concentration: (a) has already been implemented and that concentration has been declared incompatible with the common market, or (b) has been implemented in contravention of a condition attached to a decision taken under paragraph 2, which has found that, in the absence of the condition, the concentration would fulfil the criterion laid down in Article 2(3) or, in the cases referred to in Article 2(4), would not fulfil the criteria laid down in Article 81(3) of the Treaty, the Commission may:

— require the undertakings concerned to dissolve the concentration, in particular through the dissolution of the merger or the disposal of all the shares or assets acquired, so as to restore the situation prevailing prior to the implementation of the concentration; in circumstances where restoration of the situation prevailing before the implementation of the concentration is not possible through dissolution of the concentration, the Commission may take any other measure appropriate to achieve such restoration as far as possible,

Since Ryanair did not actually take control of Aer Lingus, the disputed shareholding cannot be assimilated to a 'concentration' which 'has already been implemented', even in the case that the operation by which that shareholding was acquired has been declared incompatible with the single market.[135]

According to the General Court, none of the arguments raised by the applicant in its pleadings or at the hearing[136] was capable of calling the Commission's assessment into question.[137] Furthermore, the General Court considered that 'the Commission justified to the required legal and factual standard, in the contested decision, its decision not to adopt a measure pursuant to Article 8(4) of the merger regulation'.[138] In addition, the same reasoning is valid for paragraph 5 of Article 8[139] of Regulation 139/2004.[140]

Furthermore, the General Court (ex Court of First Instance) clarified[141] that paragraph 3 of Article 21 of the Merger Regulation merely imposing an obligation on the Member States, it did not confer any specific duties or powers on the Commission.[142] Therefore, the Commission correctly considered that it did not have the legal power to give a binding interpretation of that provision and that it was not in a position to act in response to Aer Lingus's request for an interpretation.[143]

However, the General Court clarified that paragraph 3 of Article 21 of the Merger Regulation states that '[n]o Member State shall apply its national legislation on competition to any concentration that has a Community dimension' and this is the reason why the Commission does not have the power to adopt a measure producing binding legal effects of such a kind as to affect Aer Lingus's interests. So, the Commission should not be criticised

— order any other appropriate measure to ensure that the undertakings concerned dissolve the concentration or take other restorative measures as required in its decision.

In cases falling within point (a) of the first subparagraph, the measures referred to in that subparagraph may be imposed either in a decision pursuant to paragraph 3 or by separate decision.

5. The Commission may take interim measures appropriate to restore or maintain conditions of effective competition where a concentration: (a) has been implemented in contravention of Article 7, and a decision as to the compatibility of the concentration with the common market has not yet been taken; (b) has been implemented in contravention of a condition attached to a decision under Article 6(1)(b) or paragraph 2 of this Article; (c) has already been implemented and is declared incompatible with the common market.'

135 Above n 131, para 85.

136 Arguments essentially reproducing the theory which the contested decision had already addressed.

137 Above n 135, para 86.

138 Ibid, para 87. Despite the fact that Commission found in its Ryanair decision that 'there was a single concentration and the finding that the concentration was incompatible with the internal market'.

139 'The Commission may take interim measures appropriate to restore or maintain conditions of effective competition where a concentration: (a) has been implemented in contravention of Article 7, and a decision as to the compatibility of the concentration with the common market has not yet been taken; (b) has been implemented in contravention of a condition attached to a decision under Article 6(1)(b) or paragraph 2 of this Article; (c) has already been implemented and is declared incompatible with the common market.'

140 The applicant raised the same challenges to the Commission's analysis on this point in the contested decision, which reproduced, mutatis mutandis, the analysis made in relation to para 4 of Art 8 ECMR. Above n 138, para 88.

141 As the Commission stated.

142 'No Member State shall apply its national legislation on competition to any concentration that has a Community dimension.

The first subparagraph shall be without prejudice to any Member State's power to carry out any enquiries necessary for the application of Articles 4(4), 9(2) or after referral, pursuant to Article 9(3), first subparagraph, indent (b), or Article 9(5), to take the measures strictly necessary for the application of Article 9(8).'

143 Above n 140, para 89.

for doing something self-evident, ie having reiterated, in its response, the legal framework applicable to the case examined and the consequences to be drawn from it, in particular regarding the actions provided for in Article 258 TFEU[144] (ex Article 226 EC) and Article 267 TFEU[145] (ex Article 234 EC).[146]

Since the conclusions of the Commission as far as the application of paragraphs 4 and 5 of Article 8 of the Merger Regulation in the case examined are not erroneous, as was claimed by the applicant, and, furthermore, there is no concentration with a European dimension, 'the Member States remain free to apply their national competition law to Ryanair's shareholding in Aer Lingus in accordance with the rules in place to that effect'.[147]

For all the above mentioned reasons, the General Court decided that the action must be dismissed in its entirety.[148]

Last but not least, the Commission states in paragraph 3 of the Annex II of the Commission Staff Working Document (Towards More Effective EU Merger control, SWD(2013) 239 final) that:

> This section also pays attention to certain situations in which the acquisition of a minority stake succeeds the acquisition of control and therefore the Commission has no competence under the Merger Regulation to deal with any competition concern that these structural links might lead to. These limitations under the current EU merger control regime became particularly apparent in the Ryanair/Aer Lingus case, where the Commission could not act against Ryanair's structural link in Aer Lingus in view of the limitations of the Merger Regulation—a reasoning which was subsequently confirmed by the General Court in 2010.

However, in our view and following the above-mentioned analysis, in the *Ryanair/Aer Lingus* case the specific acquisition of a minority stake did not result in the acquisition of control. On the contrary, the reason why in this case the Commission decided—and the Court confirmed—that it had no competence under the Merger Regulation to deal with any competition concern was that the acquisition of control by Ryanair had not been successful.

[144] 'If the Commission considers that a Member State has failed to fulfill an obligation under the Treaties, it shall deliver a reasoned opinion on the matter after giving the State concerned the opportunity to submit its observations.

If the State concerned does not comply with the opinion within the period laid down by the Commission, the latter may bring the matter before the Court of Justice of the European Union.'

[145] 'The Court of Justice of the European Union shall have jurisdiction to give preliminary rulings concerning:

(a) the interpretation of the Treaties;

(b) the validity and interpretation of acts of the institutions, bodies, offices or agencies of the Union;

Where such a question is raised before any court or tribunal of a Member State, that court or tribunal may, if it considers that a decision on the question is necessary to enable it to give judgment, request the Court to give a ruling thereon.

Where any such question is raised in a case pending before a court or tribunal of a Member State against whose decisions there is no judicial remedy under national law, that court or tribunal shall bring the matter before the Court.

If such a question is raised in a case pending before a court or tribunal of a Member State with regard to a person in custody, the Court of Justice of the European Union shall act with the minimum of delay.'

[146] Above n 143, para 90.

[147] Ibid, para 91.

[148] Ibid, para 92.

iv. Other Pre-Existing Minority Shareholdings Except for the Ryanair/Aer Lingus *Case*

There are many other cases apart from *Ryanair/Aer Lingus* in which the Commission has dealt with pre-existing minority shareholdings. In paragraph 12 of the Annex II of the Commission Staff Working Document (Towards More Effective EU Merger Control, SWD(2013) 239 final) it is mentioned that 'Since then [1991], in at least 53 merger cases scrutinised by the Commission, structural links[149] were relevant for the assessment of the competitive effects of the transaction.'

The major anticompetitive scenarios that have been raised from the investigation of the scrutinized cases are the following:

1. enhanced degree of concentration by either merging parties;
2. unilateral effects;
3. coordinated effects;
4. foreclosure effects;
5. entry effects.

(a) IV/M.042 *Alcatel/Telettra*

The notified concentration concerned 'the acquisition by Alcatel NV from Fiat Spa of a controlling interest of 69.2 percent of the shares of Telettra Spa'.[150] The major anticompetitive concern raised by this concentration was its impact 'on the markets for line transmission equipment and microwave equipment (the transmission markets) in Spain'.[151] Figure 11 presents the position of the merging parties in the transmission markets before and after the clearance of the acquisition.

Regarding the presence of minority shareholdings between the merging parties and Telefonica de España, the owner of the acquired firm, the decision stated that:

> [T]here are vertical links between Telefonica and its major equipment suppliers and in particular Alcatel and Telettra, by means of minority shareholdings. Vertical links between telecommunications operators and their suppliers can distort normal conditions of competition by giving those suppliers a privileged position on the market. This can be the case even where telecommunications operators only have minority shareholdings, since such links would normally put other suppliers without such links at a disadvantage.[152]

In order to remove any vertical minority shareholding between the merging parties and Telefonica de España,

> Alcatel ... entered into a commitment vis-à-vis the Commission whereby Alcatel will acquire from Telefonica the minority shareholdings in Telettra and Telettra España SA and will enter into negotiations to acquire from Telefonica the minority shareholding in Alcatel Standard Electrica SA.[153]

[149] That is, minority shareholdings.

[150] According to the decision (see para 1 in http://ec.europa.eu/competition/mergers/cases/decisions/m42_en.pdf): 'Telettra will in turn acquire 100 percent of Alcatel Face Spa, which is a subsidiary of Alcatel. Fiat will still own 25.4 percent of Telettra. The balance of the shares in Telettra are currently owned by the Spanish telecommunications operator, Telefonica de España (Telefonica).'

[151] See para 36 of annex II of the Commission Staff Working Document, 'Towards More Effective EU Merger Control' SWD(2013) 239 final.

[152] Ibid, para 34.

[153] Ibid, para 45.

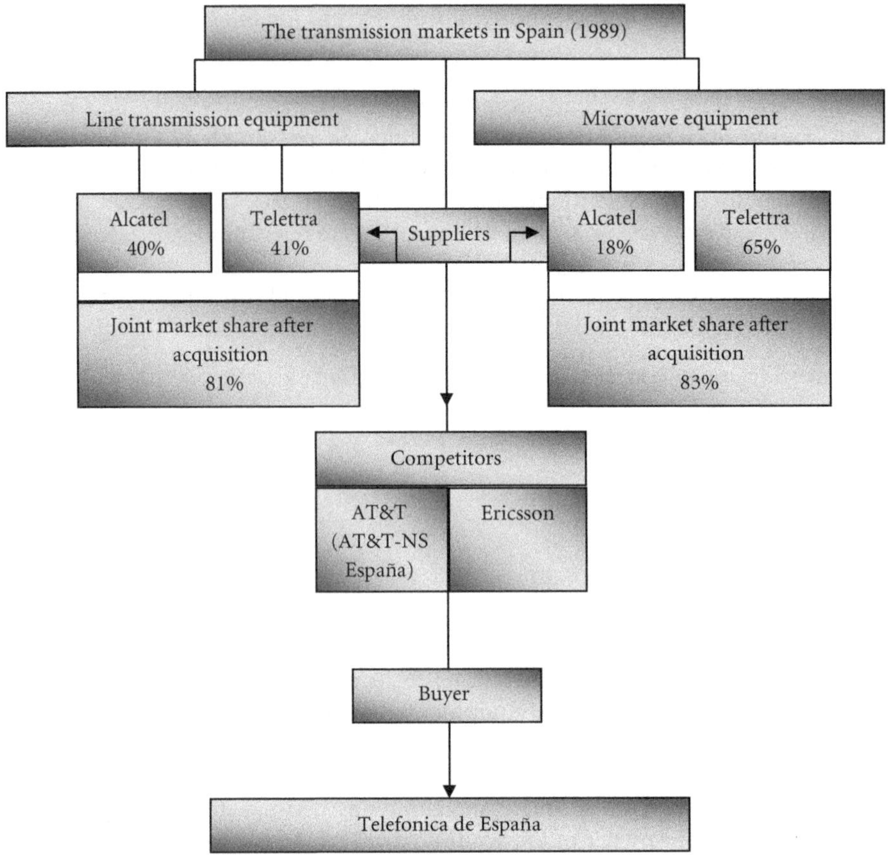

Figure 11: Market shares of Alcatel NV and Telettra Spa in the transmission markets in Spain (1989)

(b) IV/M.113 *Courtaulds/SNIA*

The proposed concentration constituted the creation of a joint venture (Novaceta Limited) in the acetate filament yarn sector by Courtaulds plc and SNIA Fibre SpA. At the time of notification (19 November 1991) Courtaulds plc was a publicly quoted company.

According to paragraph 6 of the Commisson's decision Courtaulds plc held 'a minority interest (12 percent of the shares and the appointment of one director) in INACSA SA, a Spanish manufacturer of acetate yarn which has 9 percent of the Western European market'. However, Courtaulds plc was 'in the process of terminating … this interest in INACSA'.

Given the above-mentioned divesture the Commission concluded, inter alia, that the new joint venture would face strong competition, either from actual or future players of the market of acetate filament yarn and therefore declared the proposed notification compatible with the common market.

(c) IV/M.833 *The Coca-Cola Company/Carlsberg A/S*

On 25 March 1997, the Commission received a notification of a proposed concentration pursuant to Article 4 of Council Regulation (EEC) No 4064/89 by which the Coca-Cola Company and Carlsberg A/S[154] intended to set up a jointly owned company named Coca-Cola Nordic Beverages (to be owned 51 per cent by Carlsberg A/S and 49 per cent by the Coca-Cola Company).

The Commission found that the concentration would have lead 'to the elimination of both actual and potential competition from Carlsberg in both Denmark and Sweden'.[155] The Commission's position was based on, inter alia, the minority shareholdings (active or passive) that Carlsberg A/S held in many competitors as well as interests in other companies in both Denmark and Sweden. In particular, it had sole control over Dansk Coladrik, which owned and bottled Jolly Cola, the third largest cola brand in Denmark. It also held 37 per cent of the shares and 48 per cent of the votes in Jyske Bryg,[156] which in turn held, direct and indirectly, 62 per cent of the shares and 49 per cent of the votes of Bryggerigruppen, the second largest brewer and bottler of soft drinks in Denmark and a direct competitor to the Coca-Cola Company since it was the brand owner of Faxe Kondi, a carbonated lemon-lime drink that competed directly with the Coca-Cola Company's Sprite brand.

The Commission stated that 'Carlsberg ha[d] substantial influence over Bryggerigruppen and therefore that Bryggerigruppen offers reduced competition to Carlsberg'[157] since

> [i]f a disagreement were to arise between Jyske Bryg and Faxe Bryg, the leading position of Carlsberg in the beer and [carbonated soft drinks] markets would play an important role in any negotiations to resolve the differences. It would be in the economic interests of Bryggerigruppen, and its shareholders, to find an accommodation with Carlsberg to avoid retaliation in the markets where Bryggerigruppen operates and Carlsberg has market leadership.[158]

In the light of the above evidence regarding the minority interests of Carlsberg in other companies, the latter had committed to the Commission to divest its shareholdings in Jyske Bryg and Dansk Coladrik 'to one or more viable industrial undertakings unconnected to Carlsberg A/S or The Coca-Cola Company'.[159] The Commission 'consider[ed] that the proposed undertakings [were] adequate to prevent the strengthening of a dominant position as a result of which effective competition would be significantly impeded'.[160]

[154] At the time of the Commission's decision Carlsberg was the Danish-registered parent of a group of companies that were active primarily in the production and wholesale distribution of beer, but also in other drinks-related operations, including non-alcoholic beverages. One of Carlsberg's subsidiaries, Dadeko A/S, was the largest bottling company of carbonated soft drinks in Denmark. In addition Carlsberg had interests in other soft-drink and brewing companies in both Denmark and Sweden.

[155] See para 51 of Case IV/M.833 *The Coca-Cola Company/Carlsberg A/S*.

[156] The Commission, after examination of the last three annual general meetings of the Jyske Bryg's shareholders, concluded that 'Carlsberg has cast more than 50 percent of the votes present at the meetings' and therefore it has 'the possibility of exercising decisive influence and consequently control over Jyske Bryg'. Ibid, para 60.

[157] Ibid, para 62.

[158] Ibid.

[159] Ibid, para 109.

[160] Ibid, para 112. In Case IV/M.1080 *Thyssen/Krupp* the merger between Thyssen and Krupp created the likelihood of links being established between Thyssen and Kone, since Krupp held a 10 per cent minority shareholding in Kone, with the right of appointing one member of the board of directors. The Commission cleared the merger under the condition that Krupp's minority shareholding in Kone would be disconnected of the right to appoint the member of the board of directors.

(d) IV/M.890 *Blokker/Toys 'R' Us (II)*

On 23 January 1997 the Dutch government pursuant to Article 22 of Council Regulation (EEC) No 4064/89 requested the Commission to examine the acquisition of the Dutch operations of Toys 'R' Us by Blokker.

> On 21 February 1997 the Commission adopted a decision under Article 6(1)c in conjunction with Article 22 of the Merger Regulation finding that the request was admissible in accordance with Article 22, that the request had been made within the one-month period provided for in Article 22(4) and that the concentration raised serious doubts as to its compatibility with the common market.[161]

The relevant product market of the proposed concentration was the retail of toys through specialized toy retail outlets.

The Commission, after examination of the effects of the proposed concentration on the above-mentioned relevant product market, stated that prior to the concentration Blokker hald a dominant position in this market and as a consequence the clearance of the acquisition would enhanced Blokker's ability to exercise its market power irrespective of its competitors' reaction, ie it would further strengthen its dominant position.

In the light of the Commission's statement the concerned parties in the concentration offered the following undertakings in order to ameliorate the possible anticompetitive doubts raised by the Commission:

> Blokker undertakes to transfer to its wholly owned subsidiary Speelhoorn BV (Speelhoorn): (i) all of Blokker's rights and obligations pursuant to the Franchise agreement, (ii) all of Blokker.s rights and obligations pursuant to the Marketing subsidy agreement, and (iii) all the assets acquired by Blokker pursuant to the Asset purchase agreement.
>
> Blokker undertakes as soon as practical after the notification of this decision, to begin negotiations with interested third parties with a view to transferring at least 60 percent of the share capital of Speelhoorn to a viable and independent undertaking not connected to either Blokker or Toys 'R' Us, which is capable of maintaining the Dutch Toys 'R' Us on the market and fulfilling the social commitment made by Blokker. The choice of such an independent third party will be subject to the Commission's reasonable approval.
>
> Blokker undertakes not to retain a minority shareholding in Speelhoorn that exceeds 20 percent. Blokker undertakes to transfer to Toys 'R' Us a minority shareholding corresponding to its own shareholding. Blokker and Toys 'R' Us will both be entitled to a maximum of one seat on the board of Speelhoorn which will comprise five members. Furthermore, Blokker and Toys 'R' Us will not be granted any special rights beyond those typically provided to minority shareholders. Blokker undertakes that it will not interfere with Speelhoorn.s freedom to determine independently its commercial policy.
>
> Prior to the completion of the transfer of a majority shareholding in Speelhoorn to a third party, Blokker will ensure that Speelhoorn and the Dutch Toys 'R' Us stores are managed as distinct and saleable undertakings with their own management accounts. During this period, Blokker will ensure the continued viability and market value of those stores and will provide sufficient financial resources to this end in the ordinary course of business.[162]

[161] See para 2 of the Commission's decision.

[162] Ibid, paras 121–24.

The Commission decided that '[t]he concentration by which Blokker Holding BV acquires the Dutch operations of Toys 'R' Us Inc is declared incompatible with the common market and with the functioning of the EEA Agreement' and ordered, inter alia, Blokker to undertake the following steps:

(a) to transfer the following assets, rights and obligations to its wholly owned subsidiary Speelhoorn BV: (i) all of Blokker's rights and obligations pursuant to the Franchise Agreement dated 3 February 1997, between Blokker and Toys 'R' Us, (ii) all of Blokker's rights and obligations pursuant to the Marketing subsidy agreement of 3 February 1997 between Blokker and Toys 'R' Us, and (iii) all the assets acquired by Blokker pursuant to the Asset purchase agreement of 3 February 1997 between Blokker and Toys 'R' Us. This transfer must be implemented as soon as practical after the notification to Blokker of this Decision and in any event no later than the date on which Blokker enters into a binding letter of intent with a third party on the sale of a majority shareholding in Speelhoorn BV;

(b) to divest itself of at least 80 percent of the total share capital of Speelhoorn BV in the following way. Up to 20 percent of the total share capital of Speelhoorn BV shall be transferred to Toys 'R' Us. At least 60 percent of the total share capital of Speelhoorn BV shall be transferred to a third party. The third party shall be given the possibility to purchase the total share capital of Speelhoorn BV or at least the 80 percent held by Blokker. The third party must be an independent undertaking unconnected to the Blokker group and must be able to maintain and develop Speelhoorn BV as a viable and active competitive force in the market for specialized toy retailing. Blokker may hold one seat on the management board of Speelhoorn BV on condition that the third party has at least three seats and Toys 'R' Us has one seat. Blokker may hold the seat no longer than for a period of ... years, following the transfer of a majority shareholding to a third party.[163]

The Commission argued

> that in the circumstances of the case that the continued presence of Blokker in the form of a 20 percent minority shareholding in combination with the active presence of Blokker on the management board of Speelhoorn can, at least for a certain period of time, serve both to demonstrate the confidence of Blokker in the future viability of the company and to guarantee the development of the company into a viable business within this period. (paragraph 132)

However, the Commission decided to limited the interlocking directorate to a specific time period and explained that

> [a]lthough Blokker undertakes not to interfere with Speelhoorn's freedom to determine independently its commercial policy, the presence of Blokker on the board will still give it access to information on the commercial decisions which it could use for its own competitive strategy and also in relation to the competitive strategy of the Toys 'R' Us business operated by Speelhoorn. This possibility is to be evaluated especially in the light of the fact that, for a certain period of time, Blokker will have been operating the Toys 'R' Us business on its own and that, even after the implementation of the divestiture as set out in the proposals, Blokker has a dominant position on the market. Therefore the Commission considers it necessary in order to ensure that effective competition is restored on the market, that Blokker's active presence on the management board should be eliminated once the viability of the company is established. (paragraph 133)[164]

[163] Ibid, pp 24–25 of the Commission's decision.

[164] See OECD, *Antitrust Issues Involving Minority Shareholdings and Interlocking Directorates* (2008), DAF/COMP(2008)30, 1, 50 (fn 112).

(e) IV/M.1082 *Allianz/AGF*

On 19 March 1998 the Commission received notification of a proposed concentration by which Allianz AG[165] acquired sole control over AGF, a firm active in the credit insurance market (Figure 12).[166]

The major concern of the Commission regarding the possible anticompetitive effects of the proposed concentration focused on so-called 'del credere' credit insurance which comprises domestic credit insurance, export credit insurance and capital goods insurance.[167] In particular, on a European level and prior to the clearance of the proposed concentration Allianz AG and AGF possessed an approximately 39–46 per cent market share of the market, while Coface, the second player of the market possessed a 16 per cent market share.

Coface, prior to the proposed concentration, was a subsidiary of AGF since the latter possessed a 58.06 per cent stake. AGF, via contractual arrangements with the other shareholders of Coface, was supposed to reduce its participation in Coface to 24.9 per cent and at the same time to relinquish its sole control over it.

However, the Commission was interested in the relationship between AGF, Coface and SCOR, a major reinsurer of AGF and the biggest reinsurer of Coface. Figure 12 depicts the relationship between the three firms.

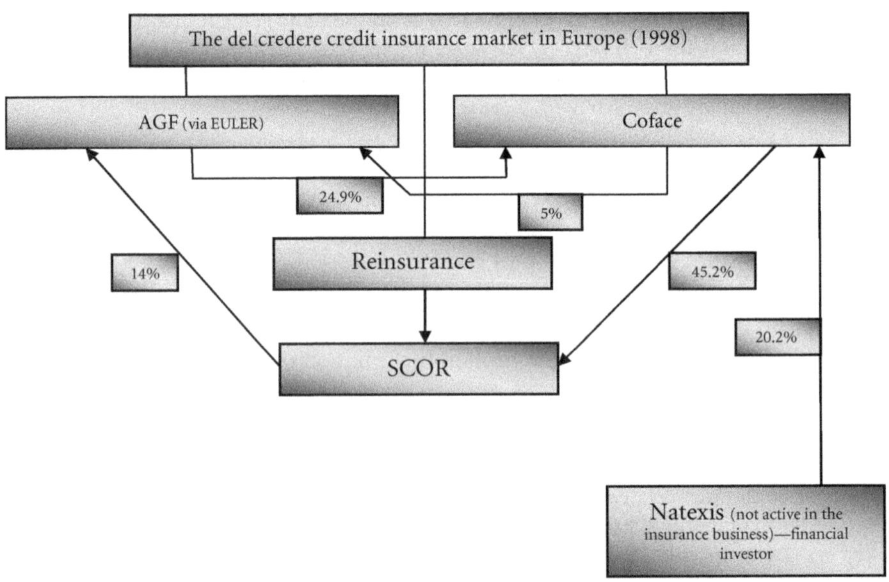

Figure 12: Minority shareholdings in the del credere credit insurance market in Europe (1998)

165 At the time of the Commission's decision Allianz AG was the 'leader of a group of insurance companies active in all sectors of private insurance business and is one of the largest industrial insurers in the EEA and third countries'. See para 2 of the Commission's decision.

166 According to para 16 of the Commission's decision 'the [proposed concentration] in the life and non-life insurance market—except credit insurance—does not create or strengthen a dominant position as a result of which effective competition would be significantly impeded in the EEA or any substantial part of that area'.

167 See Cases IV/M. 812-*Allianz/Vereinte* and IV/M. 813-*Allianz/Hermès*.

The Commission stated that:

> Although there is no shareholder agreement between SCOR and AGF, there is the risk that AGF and SCOR could exercise a decisive influence on the company by pooling their voting rights. The special situation of business interests between the re-insurer and its clients is appropriate to discourage competition between AGF/Euler and Coface. Those aspects are strong indications for a likely de facto joint control of AGF and SCOR over Coface.
>
> The fact that SCOR and AGF are the only shareholders in Coface disposing of a sufficient experience in del credere business provides a further incentive for SCOR and AGF to act in agreement as regards strategic decision marking process in Coface.[168]

The Commission's view regarding the nature of control of Coface was enhanced by the existence of strong interlocking directorships between AGF and Coface. As paragraph 51 of the Commission's decision stated: 'Several members of the management board of AGF are members of the management or supervisory board of Coface, while members of Coface are also represented in the management board of AGF/Euler.'

Given the above-mentioned issues as well as the minority shareholdings at a national level (France and Italy)[169] and the fact that there were several cooperating links between the two firms,[170] the parties, according to Article 6(2) of the Merger Regulation, offered commitments to the Commission. According to them

> AGF after clearance of the present concentration will sell ... shares in Coface to buyers not belonging to the AGF/Allianz group. Furthermore, ... the members of the managing board of AGF will leave the management board of Coface. Any other personal links existing between companies owned/controlled by one of the parties and companies belonging to Coface will be removed.[171]

The Commission, in the light of these commitments, decided not to oppose the notified concentration and declared it compatible with the common market.

(f) IV/M.1378 *Hoechst/Rhône-Poulenc*

Paragraphs 1–3 of the Commission's decision explained in detail the concerns of the Commission regarding the proposed concentration and the commitments that the parties to it undertook in order to alleviate these concerns:

> On 24.06.1999 Hoechst and Rhône-Poulenc notified their concentration (which led to the creation of Aventis) to the Commission. The Commission cleared the transaction on 09.08.1999 subject to commitments. In one of the commitments, Rhône-Poulenc committed to divest its chemical activities by selling its 67.3 percent stake in Rhodia and to keep the management of Rhodia separate from Wacker-Chemie until the date of the Rhodia divestiture (the Rhodia Commitments.).
>
> The merged entity retained the chemical activities of Hoechst in Wacker-Chemie, a 50/50 joint venture with the Wacker family. The Rhodia Commitments were intended to remove competition concerns over the overlap markets for silicone sealant, silicone elastomer, and polymer powder, made up of the chemical activities of Rhodia controlled by Rhône-Poulenc and those of Hoechst in Wacker-Chemie.

168 See paras 49–50 of the Commission's decision.

169 Ibid, paras 56–58.

170 Ibid, paras 52–55.

171 Ibid, para 66.

> The Rhodia Commitments were designed to address the competition concerns over the overlap markets by means of a structural remedy requiring the exit of Rhône-Poulenc from Rhodia and the maintenance of the independence of Rhodia from Wacker-Chemie in the meantime. The purpose of the latter limb of the Rhodia Commitments was to ensure that there will be no risk of co-ordination of the competitive behaviour of these entities whilst awaiting the severance of the structural link created between previously entirely independent undertakings by the merger of Hoechst and Rhône-Poulenc.[172]

(g) M.1383 *Exxon/Mobil*

On 3 May 1999 the Commission received notification of a proposed merger between the US undertakings Exxon Corporation and Mobil Corporation. On 9 June 1999 the Commission initiated proceedings in this case pursuant to Article 6(1)(c) of the Merger Regulation.[173]

Both merging parties were active in the exploration, development and production of crude oil and natural gas and even though at the outset the Commission had expressed serious doubts on these markets, it concluded that 'the concentration will not lead to the creation or strengthening of a dominant position on the markets for the exploration, development, production and sale of crude oil and natural gas'.[174]

Regarding the competitive impact of the concentration on motor fuel retailing the Commission considered the participation of Mobil in Aral (28 per cent) along with the participation of the other two major players of the market, ie Veba (56 per cent) and Wintershall (15 per cent), and found that 'Mobil, together with Veba and Wintershall have de facto joint control over Aral'.[175]

Due to this merger, the parties' activities in the German gas market were combined; however, the German gas market was already susceptible 'to coordination through a complex network of controlling or non controlling stakes among the major wholesale suppliers of gas in Germany, similar to the German electricity market in the VEBA/VIAG case'.[176] The merger, if approved as such, would definitely have further reduced the already existing weak competition between Ruhrgas, BEB, EGM and Thyssengas and others, since it would bring together Exxon's and Mobil's respective pre-existing (controlling and non-controlling) links in some of these competing gas suppliers. Hence, inevitably the merger between the parties, if approved as such, it would have led to the strengthening of individual dominant positions in some regional markets and coordinated effects in others, unavoidably further reducing the already weak competition.

In particular, the Commission concluded that:

> [T]hrough this stake, Mobil can exercise a relevant influence over Aral commercial policy. It has the same voting rights as the other main shareholders, and it appoints the same number of members of

[172] See also OECD (n 164).

[173] Art 6(1)(c) of the Merger Regulation states that: 'The Commission shall examine the notification as soon as it is received. ...Without prejudice to paragraph 2, where the Commission finds that the concentration notified falls within the scope of this Regulation and raises serious doubts as to its compatibility with the common market, it shall decide to initiate proceedings. Without prejudice to Article 9, such proceedings shall be closed by means of a decision as provided for in Article 8(1) to (4), unless the undertakings concerned have demonstrated to the satisfaction of the Commission that they have abandoned the concentration.'

[174] See para 39 of the Commission's decision.

[175] Ibid, paras 459–60.

[176] Above n 151, para 37.

> the supervisory committee, which in turn elects the management board. Finally, Mobil has access to a large amount of strategic information which is exchanged within Aral's decision making bodies. It is thus clear that the existence of this link is likely to reduce Mobil's incentives to compete against Aral and vice versa. With such an important interest of the former in the capital of the latter, competition between the two operators seems to be seriously weakened.[177]
>
> In response to the Commission's conclusion that the concentration will create or strengthen oligopolistic dominance over Austria, French toll motorways, Germany, Luxembourg, the Netherlands and the UK, the parties have undertaken to dispose of Mobil's share in Aral and to terminate Mobil's participation in the fuels part of the BP/Mobil Joint Venture.[178]

According to the Commission's decision, this commitment by the merging parties 'removes the incentives for Exxon or BP/Mobil and Aral to co-ordinate their competitive behaviour and therefore eliminate[s] the objections raised by the Commission'.[179]

Furthermore, in the Dutch wholesale transmission market the parties agreed on the sale of Mobil Europe Gas Inc to an independent purchaser. In particular, '[Mobil Europe Gas Inc] is the Mobil entity that sells natural gas in competition with Gasunie on the Dutch market. This company shall be sold with its contracted supply portfolio.'[180] Given the specific conditions of the sale of Mobil Europe Gas Inc, which are reported in paragraph 829 of the Commission's decision, the latter concluded that: '[T]he status quo ante to the transaction will be re-established so that the transaction will, subject to fulfilment of the commitment, not lead to the strengthening of Gasunie's dominant position in the Dutch wholesale transmission market.'[181]

In the German long-distance wholesale transmission market(s) the merging parties agreed to reach an agreement 'on the sale of Exxon's 25 percent equity interest in Thyssengas GmbH to a third party approved by the Commission'.[182] In particular, '[t]he Commission considers that, overall, the divestiture of Exxon's equity interest in Thyssengas compensates for the strengthening of the dominant positions that would otherwise have occurred as a consequence of the merger'.[183]

In addition, the merging parties

> shall use their reasonable best efforts to obtain the agreement of the other shareholders in [Erdgas Münster] to reallocating a certain percentage of the voting rights currently held by Mobil to such shareholders (pro rata to their current voting rights) so that BEB and Mobil (or Exxon Mobil) combined will hold less than 50 percent of the voting rights in [Erdgas Münster]. The commitment contains a re-allocation for both legal entities within [Erdgas Münster].[184]

With this commitment the Commission considered that '[Erdgas Münster] maintains the possibility to develop into a potential competitor on the long-distance wholesale transmission market in a future liberalised environment'.[185]

[177] Above n 175, para 461.
[178] Ibid, para 848.
[179] Ibid, para 852.
[180] Ibid, para 829
[181] Ibid.
[182] Ibid, para 830.
[183] Ibid, para 831.
[184] Ibid, para 835.
[185] Ibid, para 837.

(h) M.1453 *AXA/GRE*

On 18 February 1999 the Commission received notification of an operation by which AXA took over the Guardian Royal Exchange via a public tender offer for the ordinary shares in the latter.

The concentration considered many relevant product markets, among them the market for life and non-life insurance. In Luxemburg AXA was active at the time of notification while Guardian Royal Exchange was holding 'a 34.8 percent interest in the leading insurer Le Foyer Finance Compagnie Luxembourgeoise SA[186]'.[187]

The merging parties argued that the participation of Guardian Royal Exchange in Le Foyer Finance Compagnie Luxembourgeoise SA was not strategic but constituted a purely financial minority interest. Furthermore, they stated that:

> [Guardian Royal Exchange] has only 4 representatives in the managing board whereas Groupe L[188] has 7 members. They further say that the shareholder representing Le Foyer's 33 percent stake in Luxempart[189] is a member of Groupe L. The parties thus conclude that GRE and Groupe L do not exercise joint control over Le Foyer but that the company is solely controlled by Groupe L.

It is interesting to depict the complex system of minority shareholdings among competitors in the market for life and non-life insurance in Luxemburg at the time of notification (Figure 13).

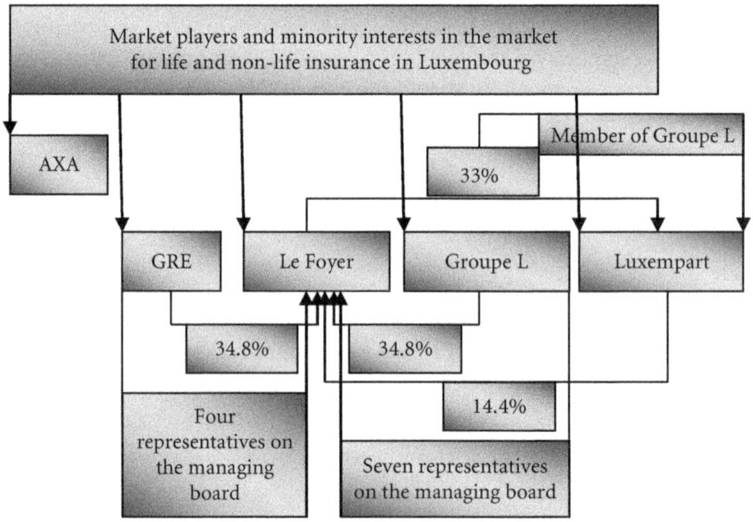

Figure 13: Minority interests in the relevant product market for life and non-life insurance in Luxembourg (1999)

186 It was the leading insurer in Luxembourg.

187 See para 20 of the Commission's decision.

188 Groupe L held a 34.8 per cent in Le Foyer which consisted of a block of several individuals.

189 Luxempart was at the time of notification a Luxembourg company which held a 14.4 per cent interest in Le Foyer Finance Compagnie Luxembourgeoise SA. At the same time the latter held a 33 per cent interest in the former and its shareholder who represented its interest in Luxempart was a member of Le Foyer.

The Commission decided to leave open the question of control for reasons that are quite evident: the takeover of GRE's shares and voting rights in Le Foyer by AXA would produce important structural links between undertakings which were competitors. Consequently, AXA would have had an important financial interest in Le Foyer. Furthermore, and simultaneously, AXA would have been represented in the management bodies of its competitor, and thus unavoidably it would be involved in the strategic business decisions of its rival.

It should be underlined that the relevant market was highly concentrated (ie there were only a few active undertakings, all large in size). Hence, the Commission found that the examined link between GRE and Le Foyer would result in possible anticompetitive effects in wider non-life insurance market in Luxembourg and any relevant sub-segments. In reality, the transaction examined would result in a situation where in a highly concentrated market,[190] two of the three largest rivals, ie AXA and Le Foyer, would have been closely linked.

Given the above-mentioned facts and the examination of the market shares in the relevant product market for life and non-life insurance the Commission concluded that 'the [transaction], in its notified form, would raise serious doubts as to the creation or strengthening of a single or joint dominant position between the market leaders in several non-life insurance markets'.

Given this statement, the merging parties proposed two alternative commitments: the first consisted in the sale of Guardian Royal Exchange's participation in Le Foyer to buyers independent of AXA, and the second consisted in the divestiture of certain of AXA's insurance portfolios. The Commission believed that such commitments represented

> a sufficient remedy to eliminate any concern as regards the effect of the remaining structural link between AXA and Le Foyer. The proposed commitments will either eliminate this link and thus any risk that AXA could exercise decisive influence over Le Foyer as a result of the concentration, or ensure in any event the maintenance of a strong independent competitor to the market leaders.[191]

(i) IV/M.1673 *VEBA/VIAG*

It has been proved that horizontal minority shareholdings may lead to *coordinated anti-competitive effects* by increasing the ability and incentive of market participants to create a tacit or explicit collusion with the intention of achieving *supracompetitive profits*. It has been observed that the acquisition of a minority shareholding in a competitor can facilitate such effects by offering the acquiring company a privileged insight into the competitor's commercial activities. Furthermore, it may make the threat of future retaliation[192] more believable and serious, since the acquiring company is in a position to use its rights in an obstructive or hostile way in order to limit the competitive strategies of the 'target' firm. Both effects will influence the ability and incentive of market participants to coordinate. Regarding potential coordinated effects, concerns were raised at the core of VEBA/VIAG case.

[190] Three competitive companies, AXA, Le Foyer and La Luxembourgeoise, held on average 70–80 per cent of the total non-life insurance market.

[191] See para 38 of the Commission's decision.

[192] About retaliation see, for example, I Lianos and D Geradin, *Handbook on European Competition Law: Substantive Aspects* (Cheltenham, Edward Elgar Publishing, 2013) 336–37.

On 14 December 1999 the Commission received notification of a proposed merger in the legal sense (de jure) between VEBA Aktiengesellschaft and VIAG Aktiengesellschaft. On 4 February 2000 the Commission initiated proceedings in this case pursuant to Article 6(1)(c) of the Merger Regulation. The proposed merger concerned mainly the German electricity and chemical sectors.

The German market for electricity supply at the interconnected level (Figure 14)[193] was characterized as a highly concentrated sector. The clearance of the merger created a strong dominant duopoly between the merging parties (VEBA/VIAG) and RWE + VEW.[194] The latter was the leading interconnected firm prior to the completion of merger with a 38.54 per cent (33.1 per cent + 5.44 per cent) share of the electricity supply from the grid. VEBA and VIAG possessed, respectively, 21.2 per cent and 12.1 per cent shares in the same market prior to the completion of the merger. Therefore, after the clearance of the merger both entities (ie the merged entity and RWE + VEW) would possess a 71.84 per cent share of the electricity supply.

The competitors in the market were VEBA, VIAG, RWE, VEW, BEWAG, VEAG, enBW and HBW. However, BEWAG was controlled jointly by Southern Company and VIAG[195] and VEAG was controlled jointly by VEBA (26.5 per cent), VIAG (22.5 per cent) and RWE (26.5 per cent). 'The remaining shares [were] held by the other interconnected power companies VEW, EnBW, BEWAG and HEW.'[196] Moreover, VIAG controlled a minority shareholding in VEW, so after the declaration of the merger between VEW and RWE it controlled a minority shareholding in the merged entity.

> VEAG cannot be regarded as a competitor of the duopoly.[197] The company is owned 26.25 percent by RWE Energie AG, 26.25 percent by VEBA and 22.5 percent by Bayernwerk. The remaining shares are held by the other interconnected power companies VEW, EnBW, BEWAG and HEW. … VEAG is controlled jointly by RWE, VEBA and VIAG. … VEAG generates electricity using almost exclusively east German lignite and is dependent for its supplies on LAUBAG [see below], which in turn is dependent on the duopoly.[198]

Furthermore, the merging parties possessed a 45 per cent share in LAUBAG AG, the largest lignite producer in eastern Germany. The remaining capital share of LAUBAG AG was possessed by BBS-Braunkohle-Beteiligungsgesellschaft mbH. BBS was owned 18.2 per cent by a group of companies consisting of BEWAG, HEW, VEW and a subsidiary of EnBW and by RWE (through direct and indirect participation in its capital share). The Commission considered that since LAUBAG AG is the supplier of VEAG, both of them formed an economic unit for the purposes of the notified concentration.

[193] 'It comprise[d] (in Germany) the generation of power at interconnected level and electricity imports, which are delivered over extra high voltage and high voltage lines to different customer groups, such as regional distributors, the larger municipal electricity undertakings, electricity traders and large industrial special customers'. See para 19 of the Commission's decision.

[194] At the same period with the merger under scrutiny RWE and VEW notified their intention to merge. Therefore, the Commission treated the two entities as one entity.

[195] According to para 92 of Commission's decision '[t]he company is owned approximately 26 percent by Southern Company, approximately 26 percent by VIAG and 23 percent by VEBA, which has 20 percent of the voting rights'.

[196] See para 79 of the Commission's decision.

[197] That is, the merging parties (VEBA/VIAG) and RWE + VEW.

[198] Ibid.

Of great importance was the Commission's consideration regarding the direct and indirect minority interests of VEBA group in Rhenag Rheinische Energie AG, a supplier of gas and a regional supplier of electricity. As the Commission stated in paragraph 79 of its decision:

> Rhenag is 54.1 percent owned by RWE Energie AG and 41.3 percent by Thüga AG, in which the VEBA group has a shareholding of 56.29 percent. … The VEBA group has a substantial interest in the success of this RWE subsidiary to the extent of its abovementioned shareholding. It is represented on Rhenag's supervisory board and therefore has inside knowledge of its corporate strategy.

STEAG AG, a producer of electricity by lignite and the main electricity supplier of RWE and VEW, is '26 percent owned by Gesellschaft für Energiebeteiligung mbH, which in turn is owned 49.7 percent by RWE Energie AG and 50.3 percent directly and indirectly by VEBA'.[199] Also, 'Envia, a RWE group member company, has several minority holdings in municipal electricity undertakings in Saxony in which the VEBA group member company Thüga also has a minority holding'.[200]

Another striking feature that emerged from the established interrelationships among the competitors in the German market for electricity supply at the interconnected level was the existence of minority shareholdings and directorships of VEBA in HEW. Following chapter 2, section II.E, the term minority shareholdings and directorships refers to the situation where the owner of a passive minority shareholding has the right to put a member of its firm, such as a director, an executive or non-executive member of the board of directors, or a manager, on to the board of directors of a competitor with the right to have access to this competitor's commercial or confidential information. The right turns out from the shareholder agreement regarding the acquisition of the passive minority shareholding. This is a mixed form of minority interest, but very important in terms of competition concerns since its owner does not only hold a financial interest, but also enjoys the right to draw upon crucial information about its competitors.

The Commission in paragraph 92 of its decision stated that:

> VEBA holds a 15.4 percent share in HEW directly and another 15.4 percent share indirectly through Sydkraft, in which it has a 17.6 percent interest. HEW is a small interconnected power company with limited production capacities and only a small transmission grid. … Although HEW will be jointly controlled by Vattenfall and the municipality of Hamburg, as a minority shareholder with a seat on the supervisory board VEBA is privy to HEW's main decisions and strategies. Its shareholding enables it to obtain information on HEW's price strategy and on any quantities purchased, together with the prices, through, for example, VEBA's interconnector with Denmark.

Regarding the minority shareholding and directorship of VIAG in VEW, the Commission states in the same paragraph that 'VIAG has by reason of this shareholding a seat on VEW's supervisory board and hence is privy to its corporate strategy'.

Figure 14 presents the complex system of active and passive minority shareholdings among competitors in the German market for electricity supply at the interconnected level.

[199] See para 79 of Commission's decision.
[200] Ibid.

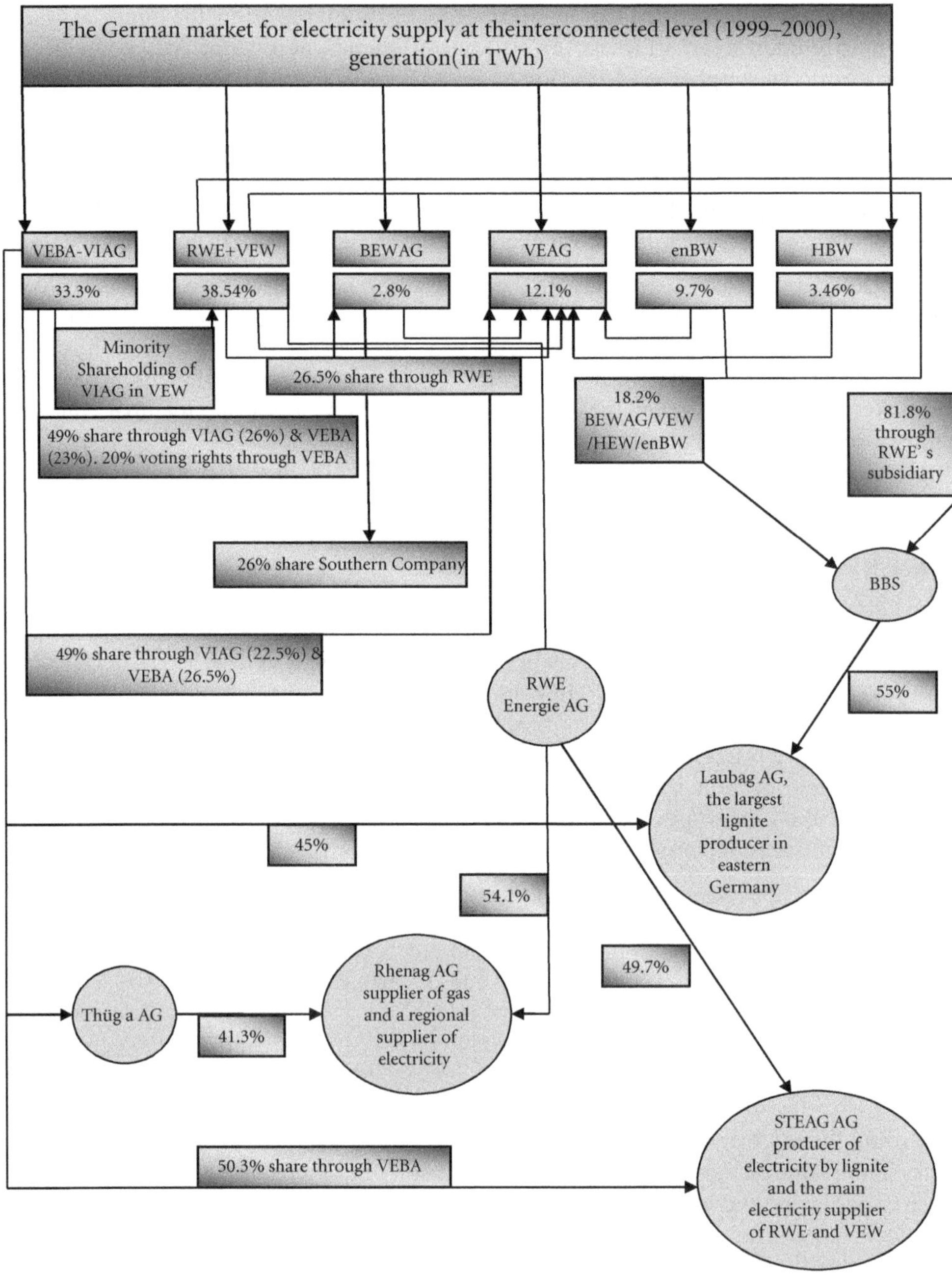

Figure 14: Minority interests in the German market for electricity supply at the interconnected level (1999–2000)

Given the above-mentioned interrelationships, the Commission considered that:

> After the merger, VEBA/VIAG and RWE would therefore have a long lead over their nearest competitors. The position of these interconnected power companies is even weaker than is apparent from their market shares as VEBA/VIAG and RWE hold substantial interests in most of their competitors. Meaningful competition is not therefore to be expected from these interconnected power companies.[201]

The merging parties, in order to ameliorate the concerns of the Commission regarding the existence of minority shareholdings, proposed to divest their shareholdings in VEAG and LAUBAG and 'to transfer the rights which the latter owns in the mining of east German lignite to the acquirer of the shareholdings in VEAG'.[202] In addition, they proposed to divest their shareholdings in BEWAG.[203] Moreover,

> VIAG undertakes to divest the shares it holds directly and indirectly in VEW and RWE should the merger between RWE and VEW be completed before the divestment of its shareholding in VEW. … VEBA undertakes to divest its direct shareholding in HEW … to terminate its existing alliance with RWE within Rheinische Energie AG (Rhenag).[204]

The Commission approved the proposed commitments from the merging parties, stating that '[t]he commitments thus improve conditions on the market for the supply of electricity at the interconnected level in such a way that all market operators are placed on a comparable footing'.[205]

(j) IV/M.1940 *Siemens/Framatome/Cogéma*

On 10 July 2000 the Commission received notification of a proposed full-function joint venture[206] between Framatome SA, Siemens AG and Cogéma SA. On 11 August 2000 the Commission initiated proceedings in this case pursuant to Article 6(1)(c) of the Merger Regulation. According to the Commission's decision,

> Framatome and Siemens will contribute most of their nuclear activities to NewJV [ie the new joint venture]. The business activities of Cogema will not be contributed to NewJV. However, Cogıma will have influence in NewJV as far as MOX fuel business and technology aspects are concerned through arrangements in the shareholders agreement. Framatome will hold 66 percent and Siemens 34 percent of the shares in NewJV. Cogema will have one special share with particular rights attached. … NewJV will be jointly controlled by the three parent companies, according to

201 Ibid, para 96.
202 Ibid, para 215.
203 Ibid, para 217.
204 Ibid, paras 218–20.
205 Ibid, para 248.
206 A full-function joint venture can 'perform, on a lasting basis, all the functions of an autonomous economic entity. Joint ventures which satisfy this requirement bring about a lasting change in the structure of the undertakings concerned. … They are referred to in this Notice as "full-function" joint ventures.' See especially Commission Notice on the concept of full-function joint ventures under Council Regulation (EEC) No 4064/89 on the control of concentrations between undertakings [1998] OJ C66, para 11 and N Levy, *European Merger Control Law: A Guide to the Merger Regulation*, 9th edn (Newark, NJ, LexisNexis, 2012) vol I. See also Cases IV/M.527 *Thomson CSF/Deutsche Aerospace*, COMP/M.2903 *DaimlerChrysler/Deutsche Telekom*, COMP/M.3003 *Energia Italia/Interpower*, IV/JV.15 *BT/AT&T* and COMP/M.6905/Neos/Solvay.

the initial notification, as strategic business decisions require the unanimous approval of all board members.[207]

The concentration mainly concerned fuel assembly, instrumentation and control, and handling spent fuel rods in the nuclear sector. Concerning the supply of PWR fuel assemblies in France, Edf, a competitor of Framatome SA in this market, agreed to give up its minority shareholding in the latter in order to implement its new strategic policy independently from Framatome's strategic decisions. This commitment, among others, seemed to be crucial for the Commission to state: 'It may therefore be concluded that the modified operation would not lead to the creation or strengthening of a dominant position.'[208]

(k) COMP/M.1980 *Volvo/Renault*

On 24 July 2000 the Commission received notification of a proposed acquisition of sole control of Renault Vehicule Industriels by AB Volvo. 'After examination of the notification, the Commission has concluded that the notified operation falls within the scope of the Merger Regulation and does not raise serious doubts as to its compatibility with the common market and with the EEA Agreement.'[209]

The proposed notification concerned the relevant markets of

— heavy trucks and medium trucks;
— city buses, intercity buses and touring coaches.

In order for the Commission to reach the above-mentioned conclusion 'Volvo ... committed vis-à-vis the Commission to divest its shareholding [45 per cent of the capital and just over 30 per cent of the votes] in Scania'[210] and 'Renault ... committed vis-à-vis the Commission firstly to rescind the Irisbus joint venture, and, secondly, to sell an ongoing bus business equalling Volvo's French bus activities'.[211] Also, '[t]he parties commit to sell [Renault Vehicule Industriels]'s share in Hansa. Following the implementation of this commitment, Volvo will therefore not have the decisive influence on the sales and marketing of Sisu trucks that RVI has had so far'.[212]

(l) COMP/M.2050 *Vivendi/ Seagram*

The proposed notified concentration concerned the acquisition of Seagram by Vivendi. Seagram is a Canadian based company, and in 1998, acquired Universal and Polygram (IV/M.1219 *Seagram/Polygram*). According to paragraph 5 of the Commission's decision 'Vivendi [was, inter alia] active in cinema and television through its 49% equity interest in Canal+,[213] its 25% equity interest in BSkyB (a British pay-TV operator), and its 100% of Havas Images'.

207 However, in the end Cogema SA gave up its shareholding participation in the joint venture along with 'rights that confer influence on the decisions of [n]ew [joint venture] or otherwise confer joint control of [n]ew [joint venture] within the meaning of the Merger Regulation' in order to remove the impact of its vertical relationships in it. See especially para 98 of the Commission's decision.

208 See para 100 of the Commission's decision.

209 See para 2 of the Commission's decision.

210 Ibid, para 4.

211 Ibid, para 6.

212 Ibid, para 53.

213 Vivendi had sole control of Canal+.

After examination of the proposal, the Commission initiated proceedings in this case pursuant to Article 6(1)(c) of the Merger Regulation. Serious doubts regarding the anti-competitive effects of the concentration were raised in many relevant product markets. In one of them, in the pay-TV market,[214] Canal+ was dominant in France, Spain, Italy, Belgium and The Netherlands, and also had a strong position in the Nordic countries. Universal was not present in retail pay-TV in any other Member State. According to paragraph 42 of the Commission's decision:

> Given its current dominant position in a number of Member States, in particular in terms of customer base, given its links through its share holding interest in BSkyB with the pay-TV operators in Europe, given its ability to leverage its combined European leading position in the negotiation of output deals with the US majors, Canal+ was, already before the proposed merger, ideally placed to renew its existing contracts with the majors. In this context it must be stressed that the price of pay-TV rights is usually determined by reference to the total numbers of subscribers, subject to a stated minimum. Consequently, Canal+'s competitors face additional disadvantages because of their relatively limited customer base compared to that of Canal+.

Post merger the Commission investigated that Canal+ would be

> in a even better position than pre-merger both to renew its existing contracts with the majors and to enter into new output deals with the other US studios. This will result from the different structural links and arrangements such as film co-financing that the other major US studios have with Universal.[215]

The notifying party (Vivendi) undertook to implement a structural remedy. In particular divesting its minority shareholding in BSkyB. As the Commission stated in its decision:

> The severing of this link with both Fox, as a film supplier, and BSkyB as a potential competitor will significantly reduce the impact of the acquisition of Universal as a partner to UIP[216] and to existing and future co-financing deals. ... The set of proposals reduces considerably Canal+ access to Universal's films and neutralises the negative competitive effects of the operation.[217]

(m) COMP/M.2567 *Nordbanken/Postgirot*

The proposed concentration concerned the acquisition of control of the whole of the Swedish undertaking Postgirot Bank AB by the Swedish undertaking Nordbanken AB by way of a purchase of shares.

In the relevant market of services provided by payment systems there were two payment systems that could provide giro payment systems in Sweden at the time of the notified concentration: the acquired firm and Bankgirot, which was, in terms of total annual transaction value 40–50 per cent larger than Postgirot Bank AB based on outgoing payments and approximately 30–40 per cent based on incoming payments.

---

[214] Regarding pay-TV market see Commission's decisions IV/M.410 *Kirch/Richmond/Telepiù*, IV/M.469 *MSG Media Service*, COMP/M.1574 *Kirch/Mediaset* and COMP/JV.37 *B SKY B/Kirch Pay-TV*.

[215] See para 44 of the Commission's decision.

[216] A joint venture between Universal, MGM, and Paramount Universal, which conducted theatrical distribution around the world including Europe.

[217] See para 75 of the Commission's decision.

The acquired firm Nordbanken AB held a 27 per cent minority shareholding in Bankgirot and had the ability to be represented on Bankgirot's board of directors. According to the Commission's decision:

> The shareholding in Bankgirot enables Nordbanken, inter alia, … to veto the issuance of new shares or securities, the reduction of share capital, amendment of the articles of association as well as any merger plans. Through its Board representation and participation in committee meetings, Nordbanken would, in addition, have access to confidential business information of its competitor. It would thus exert significant influence on strategic decisions by both competing giro systems.[218]

The Commission also stated that:

> The 27 percent shareholding also gives Nordbanken a joint-majority of capital together with either SEB or Handelsbanken.[219] Third parties noted that there is significant commonality of interest between the four large banks[220] vis a vis smaller competitors, which would increase Nordbanken's chances of mustering support from either SEB or Handelsbanken for strategic decisions in its competitor Bankgirot.

Therefore, the Commission concluded that:

> [T]here is a serious risk that the structural link between Postgirot and Bankgirot resulting from the operation would enable the two payment systems to coordinate their pricing structure and conditions. The operation, hence, creates serious doubts with regards to the creation of a jointly-dominant position by Postgirot and Bankgirot on the market for payment systems services in Sweden.[221]

In the relevant market of technical services, 'Nordbanken having a strong influence on the main competitor to Postgirot through its shareholding and representation on the Board and other governing bodies of Privatgirot, creating a serious risk that a jointly-dominant position is created'.[222]

In order to remove the competition concerns raised by the concentration in relation to the market for payment systems services and related technical services the acquiring firm undertook to reduce its influence in Bankgirot to 'no more than 10 percent and refrain from any shareholder rights going beyond minority protection rights safeguarding the financial value of its stake'.[223] In addition, it undertook 'to cease to exercise any rights it derives from its participation to the Bankgirot Shareholders' agreement and from its shareholding in Bankgirot'.[224] 'Regarding Privatgirot, Nordbanken undertakes to cease to exercise its voting rights attached to its shareholding, to cease to be represented on the Board of Directors and to withdraw from any working groups and other for a within Privatgirot.'[225]

Given the above-mentioned commitments the Commission concluded that, 'the undertakings submitted by Nordbanken are sufficient to remove the serious doubts raised by this concentration as far as the markets for payment systems services and technical services are concerned'.[226]

[218] See para 53 of the Commission's decision.
[219] The other shareholders of Bankgirot.
[220] That is, SEB, Handelsbanken, Nordbanken and Postgirot.
[221] See para 55 of the Commission's decision.
[222] Ibid, para 57.
[223] Ibid, para 59.
[224] Ibid, para 60.
[225] Ibid, para 61.
[226] Ibid, para 63.

(n) COMP/M.3547 *Banco Santander/Abbey National Transactions*

On 13 August 2004 the Commission received notification of a proposed acquisition by which Banco Santander Central Hispano SA acquired within the meaning of Merger Regulation 139/2004 control of the whole of Abbey National plc by way of purchase of shares.

Before the proposed notification Banco Santander Central Hispano SA and UK-based Royal Bank of Scotland (a direct competitor of Abbey National plc in the UK) decided to modify their strategic cooperation arrangement. According to paragraph 11 of the Commission's decision:

> In particular, [Royal Bank of Scotland] and Banco Santander agreed to terminate the representation on each others' Board of Directors, the commercial cooperation, as well as any cooperation in joint venture operations in Europe as set out in the Agreement. The termination of cooperation in these areas is conditional only upon the implementation of the notified operation. Pending the implementation of the notified operation Banco Santander and [Royal Bank of Scotland] have each procured that their respective representatives on the Boards of Directors of the other bank do not attend any board meetings.

At the same time Banco Santander Central Hispano SA reduced its minority shareholding in Royal Bank of Scotland from 5.06 to 2.54 per cent, while the latter continued to hold a minority shareholding of 2.83 per cent of Banco Santander's share capital.

Given the above modifications of the strategic cooperation arrangement between Banco Santander Central Hispano SA and Royal Bank of Scotland and in the light of the reciprocal minority shareholding between the two companies the Commission indicated that the banking activities of Banco Santander Central Hispano SA in the UK were limited and therefore adopted a phase I decision, ie the proposed concentration did not raise serious doubts as to its compatibility with the common market.

(o) COMP/M.3653 *Siemens/VA Tech*

On 10 January 2005 the Commission received notification of a proposed acquisition of control by a public takeover bid of the company VA Tech AG by Siemens Österreich AG (Austria), which was controlled by Siemens AG. On 14 February 2005 the Commission adopted a decision pursuant to Article 6(1)(c) of the Merger Regulation. On 22 April 2005 the Commission sent a statement of objections to the notifying parties, while on 25 May 2005 Siemens Österreich AG offered commitments designed to remove any existing competition concerns.

This case concerned the acquisition of the Austrian engineering group VA Tech by Siemens. It was about a horizontal overlap between SMS Demag, a company in which Siemens held a 28 per cent (non-controlling) minority shareholding, and one of VA Tech's subsidiaries. Due to SMS Demag's shareholder agreement, Siemens had the opportunity to obtain certain information, consultation and voting rights. Siemens had at the time of the Commission decision already exercised a put option to sell its stake in SMS Demag to the latter's main shareholder. Nevertheless, the sale had not yet been put into effect due to ongoing litigation about the appropriate purchase price. As a result, the Commission found that, given Siemens's 28 per cent share in SMS Demag, competition would be reduced in the metal plant-building market by the proposed merger.

In order to resolve these concerns identified by the Commission, Siemens proposed commitments. In particular, on 25 May and 13 June 2005 the notifying party submitted commitments under Article 8(2) of the Merger Regulation regarding its minority shareholdings in the markets for equipment for hydroelectric power stations and in the markets for metal plant building. According to the commitments in the markets for equipment for hydroelectric power stations, the notifying party undertook 'to sell VA Tech Hydro GmbH & Co ("VA Tech Hydro"), a power-generation company forming part of VA Tech, to a suitable buyer that is independent of the parties and subject to the Commission's approval'.[227] The Commission considered that: 'The sale of VA Tech Hydro removes entirely the overlap for competition purposes between Siemens and VA Tech in the market for equipment for hydroelectric power stations.'[228] In addition, customers and competitors of VA Tech AG and Siemens Österreich AG 'considered that Siemens' divestment of VA Tech Hydro was an entirely effective measure to remove the competition concerns raised by the proposed merger as originally notified'.[229]

According to the commitments in the markets for metal plant building, the notifying party, Siemens, undertook the following commitments:

> (1) Siemens will exercise its right to be represented on the shareholders' committee of SMS, as enshrined in the SMS shareholders' agreement, by appointing as its representative an independent trustee, with the Commission's approval; in the period up to the appointment of the trustee, Siemens will not take part in meetings of the shareholders' committee.
>
> (2) Siemens will do its utmost to ensure that the seats it holds on SMS' supervisory board pursuant to the shareholders' agreement and the concomitant legal status are assumed by two independent trustees appointed by Siemens, with the Commission's approval. The trustees will also exert all other information rights, consultation rights and administrative rights, including voting rights, instead of Siemens. …
>
> (3) Siemens will ensure that only the aforementioned trustees and not Siemens will receive information from SMS that is not publicly available. The only exceptions to this obligation are as follows:
> — information required by Siemens to meet its legal obligations regarding financial reporting and drawing up the group's financial statement …;
> — information on the valuation of Siemens' holding in SMS at 31 December 2004 and relating solely to the period up to that date ….
>
> (4) Siemens will not contest, cancel or revoke the exercise of the put-option at 31 December 2004; 262 for a specified period it will not acquire any shares in SMS, unless the Commission has found that the market structure has changed in such a way that this undertaking is no longer necessary.[230]

The Commission considered that:

> The commitments ensure that Siemens cannot use its position as minority shareholder … to obtain any strategic knowledge about SMS' business policy. In addition, Siemens' voting rights will be transferred to the trustee or trustees to be appointed. Furthermore, the commitments ensure that Siemens will permanently and irrevocably sell its holding in SMS by exercising the put-option or by other means. There is therefore no reason for any weakening of competition between Siemens/VAI and SMS in the markets affected, something which would be expected in the absence of such commitments.[231]

[227] See para 490 of the Commission's decision.
[228] Ibid, para 492.
[229] Ibid.
[230] Ibid, para 491.
[231] Ibid, para 493.

(p) COMP/M.3696 *E.ON/MOL*

On 2 June 2005 the Commission received notification of a proposed acquisition of control by way of purchase of shares of the companies (a) MOL Földgázellátó Rt (Hungary), (b) MOL Földgáztároló Rt (Hungary), currently solely controlled by MOL Hungarian Oil and Gas Rt (Hungary) and (c) MOL's shareholdings in Panrusgáz Magyar-Orosz Gázipari Rt (Hungary), a joint-venture company between OAO Gazprom (Russia) and MOL by E.ON Ruhrgas International AG, a solely controlled subsidiary of E.ON Ruhrgas AG.[232]

Moreover, 'MOL is … granted a put option under which MOL can require [E.ON Ruhrgas International AG] to purchase a 25 percent plus 1 share or a 75 percent minus 1 share interest in [MOL Földgázszállító Rt]'.[233] MOL Földgázszállító Rt is a solely controlled subsidiary of MOL and the Commission stated that:

> [T]he put option foreseen by the agreements will be considered in the competitive assessment of the transaction in view of the crucial importance of access to the gas transmission network. … the Commission notes that the change in control that may result from the exercise of the put option would at any rate constitute a concentration for merger control purposes and would thus be closely scrutinised by the competent competition authorities (either the Commission or national competition authorities).[234]

After an in-depth inquiry, the Commission found that the proposed deal, if permitted as planned, would have given rise to vertical foreclosure effects in the gas and electricity wholesale and retail markets in Hungary. More specifically, the minority stakes which MOL would have retained in MOL WMT and MOL Storage simultaneously with the existence of MOL's put option to sell the shareholding of MOL Transmission to E.ON would unavoidably lead to the creation of structural links between E.ON and MOL, since in reality the ability and the incentive for MOL to discriminate against the parties' competitors for access to domestic gas, gas transmission services and new gas storage facilities was provided in the notified deal. In addition, because of MOL's remaining shareholding in MOL WMT, another consequence would be that the transaction would also maintain structural links between MOL's domestic gas production and MOL WMT, giving MOL an incentive to discriminate against MOL WMT's downstream competitors when granting access to the transmission network.

In order to remove the competition concerns described above on the gas and electricity markets, on 20 October 2005 E.ON submitted a package of commitments. On 15 November 2005 E.ON submitted revised commitments. E.ON submitted final commitments on 8 December 2005.[235]

As an appropriate measure to avoiding this undesirable situation, MOL agreed to divest its remaining shareholdings in MOL Storage and MOL WMT. Furthermore, MOL made a commitment not to acquire direct or indirect minority stakes in MOL WMT and MOL Storage for a period of 10 years as long as E.ON was a majority shareholder of those companies. MOL also committed not to exercise the put option to require E.ON to buy a minority

[232] The concentration affected the gas and electricity sectors.

[233] See para 8 of the Commission's decision. An option may be either call option or put option (see ch 2, section I above). The owner of a call option has the right to buy stocks or bonds in the future at a predetermined value and the owner of a put option has the right to sell stocks or bonds in the future at a predetermined value.

[234] See paras 13 and 14 of the Commission's decision.

[235] Ibid, para 734.

stake in MOL Transmission in order to relieve the concerns that could stem from E.ON's opportunity for further integration in the gas transmission market. However, in the authors' view, especially regarding this last commitment, E.ON should also have been obliged not to integrate further in the gas transmission market for several years.

In particular, paragraphs 735–40 of the Commission's findings summarize the main features of the commitments which were submitted by the parties involved in the concentration:

(i) Ownership unbundling

> (735) Under the agreements concluded between MOL and E.ON, MOL would remain a minority shareholder in MOL WMT and MOL Storage (25 [per cent] + 1 share in each) and enjoy a 5-year put option under which it can require E.ON to purchase these minority interests.
>
> (736) Pursuant to the undertakings, MOL will divest its remaining shareholdings of 25 [per cent] + 1 share in MOL Storage and MOL WMT within six months following the transaction. The buyer of the shares will be subject to the Commission's approval. In addition, MOL will not acquire direct or indirect minority stakes in MOL WMT and MOL Storage for a period of 10 years as long as E.ON is a majority shareholder of those companies.
>
> (737) The objective of the ownership unbundling remedy is to alleviate the competition concerns raised by the Commission as regards MOL's incentives (in particular through its subsidiary MOL Transmission and its branch MOL E&P) to favour MOL WMT (for access to the transmission network) and MOL Storage (for access to future storage sites).

(ii) Put option related to MOL Transmission

> (738) Under the agreements concluded between MOL and E.ON, MOL would be granted a 2-year put option under which it can require E.ON to purchase a 25 per cent + 1 share or a 75 [per cent]—1 share interest in MOL Transmission.
>
> (739) Pursuant to the undertakings, MOL will not exercise the put option for the 25 [per cent] + 1 share interest in MOL Transmission. In addition, MOL will not sell to E.ON or any of its affiliates, for a period of 10 years as long as E.ON is a majority shareholder of MOL WMT and MOL Storage, a share interest in MOL Transmission that would not result in the acquisition of sole control over MOL Transmission by E.ON or of joint control over MOL Transmission by E.ON and MOL.
>
> (740) The objective of the undertaking related to the put option for MOL Transmission is to ensure that any acquisition of a share interest in MOL Transmission by E.ON will be subject to merger control review by the relevant competition authority.

(q) COMP/M.4150 *Abbott/Guidant*

On 23 February 2006 the Commission received notification of a proposed concentration by which Abbott acquired control of Guidant's interventional cardiology and endovascular device businesses.[236] Abbott, at the time of notification, developed, manufactured and sold interventional cardiology and endovascular devices, and Guidant at this time was active in the design and development of cardiovascular medical products.

[236] That is, it acquired all assets, rights and stock related to Guidant's vascular intervention and endovascular businesses.

According to paragraph 98 of the Commission's decision:

> In order to remove the serious doubts resulting from the proposed transaction in the interventional cardiology and endovascular businesses, and in particular in the DES markets, Boston Scientific and Abbott have proposed the following modifications of the Transaction Agreement:
>
> ...
>
> — Regarding the minority stake[237] of Abbott in Boston Scientific[238], Abbott commits (i) to exercise its voting rights proportionately with the votes cast by all other Boston Scientific stockholders, (ii) not to have any representation on the Board of Directors, and (iii) to dispose of the minority stake within 30 months of the date of closing of the transaction.

In particular, paragraph 7 of the annexed commitments stated that:

> (a) As of Closing and for as long as Abbott or any of its affiliates shall own such shares, with respect to any matter to be voted on by stockholders of BSC, such shares shall be voted proportionately with the votes cast by all other Boston Scientific stockholders entitled to vote and voting on such matter.
> (b) Abbott shall not have any representation on BSC's Board of Directors as part of the Abbott Minority Stake.
> (c) Abbott will sell, transfer or otherwise dispose of the Abbott Minority Stake no later than 30 months following Closing.

(r) COMP/M.4153 *Toshiba/Westinghouse*

On 31 July 2006, the Commission received notification of a proposed concentration by which Toshiba Corporation (Japan) acquired by way of purchase of shares control of Westinghouse Electric UK Limited and BNFL USA Group Inc, both forming the Westinghouse group. Business related to nuclear power plants was the focus of the proposed concentration.

Westinghouse was active in the nuclear sector. Simultaneously, Toshiba held already a pre-existing minority shareholding in Global Nuclear Fuels (GNF); GNF was a joint venture active in the markets for pressurized water reactor (PWR) and boiling water reactor fuel assemblies, constituting one of the two most important competitors to Westinghouse (alongside French company Areva) in both the European Economic Area (EAA) and worldwide markets for the design and manufacture of nuclear fuel assemblies. As a consequence, the notified transaction would have led to an overlap between Westinghouse's activities and Toshiba's non-controlling shareholding in the joint venture.

Toshiba held 24.5 per cent of the voting rights in GNF. Furthermore, Toshiba could exercise a number of veto rights that it could use to prevent GNF from expansions into fields in which it would compete with Toshiba/Westinghouse, as well as certain information rights and representation on various boards of GNF and its subsidiaries.[239]

The Commission noted that in this case 'competition concerns arising from a minority shareholding might be relieved not only by a full divestiture, but also by non-structural remedies regarding voting rights and access to information'.

[237] Shares of common stock.
[238] That is, the seller of Guidant.
[239] Above n 176, para 24.

The Commission decided that Toshiba 'd[id] not have control pursuant to Article 3(2) of the Merger Regulation over GNF or GENUSA'.[240] That is, 'Toshiba [wa]s not able to exercise decisive influence on the composition, voting or decisions of the organs of any of these companies.'[241]

The Commission found that the transaction examined could lead to a possible elimination of competition. More specifically, the Commission found that Toshiba was in a position to use its veto rights in GNF and its subsidiaries to prevent GNF from expansion into fields in which they would compete with Toshiba/Westinghouse. In addition, Toshiba was in a position easily to obtain sensitive confidential information which would help it to make GE's expansion more difficult through its information rights and its representation on various boards of GNF and its subsidiaries.

In particular, the Commission stated that:

> The remaining veto rights Toshiba holds pursuant to section [...] of the GNF Formation Agreement [...] might allow Toshiba to block some specific decisions (such as the expansion into new business areas). However, these rights cannot be regarded as conferring control to Toshiba, since they correspond to veto rights normally accorded to minority shareholders in order to protect their financial interests as investors in the joint venture.[242]

On 14 September 2006 the notifying party offered commitments to the Commission in order to remove the latter's serious doubts in the field of PWR fuel assembly markets. The commitments concerned (a) Toshiba's board representation in GNF, (b) Toshiba's veto rights in GNF under the GNF Formation Agreement and (c) Toshiba's access to non-public GNF information. The Commission decided that: 'Altogether, the remedies provide an effective and sufficiently clear-cut solution to remove all identified competition problems on all potentially affected markets.'[243] Nevertheless, it is quite impressive that 'Toshiba was not prevented from receiving strictly limited information'.

(s) COMP/M.5096 *RCA/MAV Cargo*

On 25 August 2008 the Commission received notification of a proposed concentration by which Rail Cargo Austria acquired by way of purchase of shares sole control of the whole of MÁV Cargo Árufuvarozási Zártkörűen Működő Részvénytársaság.[244] Following paragraph 1 of the Commission's decision, Rail Cargo Austria AG 'concludes the acquisition within a consortium together with Raab-Ödenburg-Ebenfurter Eisenbahn Aktiengesellschaft (GySEV). ... GySEV will acquire a non-controlling minority stake of MÁV Cargo at the closing of the transaction.'[245] According to paragraph 4 of the same decision, 'GySEV is

[240] See para 76 of the Commission's decision.

[241] Ibid.

[242] Ibid, para 79.

[243] Ibid, para 118.

[244] 'The notified transaction concerns the acquisition of MÁV Cargo by RCA through (or by) a consortium with GySEV and will be effected by a share purchase agreement for at least [90–100 per cent] plus one share. RCA will acquire [80–90 per cent] plus one share and GySEV [5–10 percent] of MÁV Cargo.' See para 5 of the Commission's decision.

[245] 'In the consortium contract between RCA and GySEV from October 2007, GySEV has the unilateral, non-transferrable and irrevocable right to acquire up to [20–30 per cent] plus 1 share of MÁV Cargo from RCA after the closing of the transaction. Due to MÁV Cargo's corporate agreements, exerting this option will give GySEV certain veto rights in MÁV Cargo (eg business plan) which may be considered as giving it joint control over MÁV Cargo.' Ibid, para 6.

jointly controlled by the Republic of Hungary (61 percent of the shares) and the Republic of Austria (33.3 percent of the shares). RCA holds through a subsidiary a 5.7 percent non-controlling share of GySEV.'

The proposed concentration concerned rail freight services (freight transport) in Austria, Hungary and other Member States. In particular, in the market for cross-border rail freight transport

> The following structural and contractual links have been identified between RCA/MÁV Cargo and GySEV:
>
> (i) Participation of GySEV in the acquisition of MÁV Cargo by RCA (including the acquisition of [5–10] [percent] of MÁV Cargo at the closing of the transaction, and a call option for up to [20–30] [percent] plus one share post closing of the transaction).
> (ii) RCA holds via its 100 percent subsidiary Speditions Holding GmbH a non-controlling minority shareholding of 5.7 [percent] in GySEV.
> (iii) …
> (iv) GySEV and RCA are shareholders of Raabersped Speditionsgesellschaft mbH, and GySEV, RCA and MÁV Cargo hold shareholdings in the following same freight forwarding companies Intercontainer Austria GmbH, Hungarokombi Kft, and Hungaria Intermodal Kft.
> (v) GySEV is jointly controlled by the Republic of Austria (33.3 [percent] of the shares) and the Republic of Hungary (61 [percent] of the shares), the ultimate parents of RCA and MÁV Cargo respectively. Post-transaction, a strong structural link would remain between the new entity and GySEV via the Republic of Austria as ultimate shareholder in both companies. Moreover, following a capital increase due to infrastructure investments, the shareholding of the Republic of Austria might increase to approximately [30–40] [percent].[246]

'On 4 November 2008 Declarations of the Austrian Minister of Transport on behalf of the Republic of Austria and of the Hungarian Minister of Transport on behalf of the Republic of Hungary, respectively, were communicated to the Commission.'[247] The declarations considered:

(i) Changing the ownership structure in the merged entity in such a way that GySEV will no longer acquire any shares in MÁV Cargo;
(ii) Procuring a review and, if necessary, modification of the co-operation agreements between RCA/MÁV Cargo and GySEV;
(iii) Procuring the acquisition by RCA of GySEV's shareholdings in 6 freight forwarding and rail terminal companies with common shareholdings of RCA and/or MÁV Cargo and GySEV;
(iv) Diminishing the influence of the Republic of Austria over GySEV's cargo business via (a) amendment of the Articles of Association and the current Syndicate Agreement in such a way that the voting rights of the Republic of Austria with respect to GySEV's cargo operations would not go beyond the statutory minority rights of a minority shareholder in GySEV under Hungarian law; and (b) the re-organisation of GySEV's cargo business as a separate legal entity, in which the Republic of Austria is not represented by board members.[248]

[246] Ibid, para 94.
[247] Ibid, para 101.
[248] Ibid, para 102.

In addition, RCA submitted on 22 September 2008 commitments in order to remove potential competition concerns arising from the proposed concentration. According to these,

> RCA committed touse its best endeavours to procure that GySEV agrees to
>
> (i) sell its [5–10] [percent] shareholding in MÁV Cargo at the completion of the transaction;
> (ii) to sell all shares transferred as a result of employee share offering; and
> (iii) not to acquire any further shares in MÁV Cargo for a period of [...] years following the decision.[249]

On 4 November 2008 RCA proposed further commitments in order to 'strengthen GySEV as a potential competitive constraint on the merged entity by removing structural and contractual links between GySEV and the merged entity'.[250] RCA proposed the following commitments:

> (i) Divest its 5.7 [percent] minority shareholding held by its subsidiary Speditions Holding in GySEV;
> (ii) Procure that GySEV exits from the acquisition transaction of MÁV Cargo (This includes (a) selling to RCA the [5–10] [percent] interest GySEV would acquire in MÁV Cargo at closing of the transaction; (b) selling any shares in MÁV Cargo transferred to GySEV as a result of the employee share offering; and (c) not acquiring any further shares in MÁV Cargo.);
> (iii) Review and, if necessary, modify co-operation agreements between RCA/MÁV Cargo and GySEV; and
> (iv) Acquire GySEVs shareholdings in the 6 freight forwarding and terminal companies with common shareholdings of RCA and/or MÁV Cargo and GySEV.[251]

The Commission considered that the commitments are suitable to remove all competition concerns identified from the notified transaction.

(t) COMP/M.5406 *IPIC/MAN Ferrostaal*

Apart from horizontal transactions which may raise competition concerns, non-horizontal may also may raise similar concerns. More specifically, non-horizontal transactions may raise competition concerns which are related to input foreclosure. Minority shareholdings may make input foreclosure possible, since the acquiring firm only incorporates a part, rather than all, of the target company's profits. It ought to be underlined that at least in some cases, the risk of foreclosure created by a minority shareholding is actually higher in comparison with the risk from a fully integrated firm.

On 23 January 2009 the Commission received notification of a proposed concentration by which International Petroleum Investment Company acquired sole control of the whole of the undertaking MAN Ferrostaal AG. At the moment of notification International Petroleum Investment Company's, 'principle activity [wa]s to invest on a long-term basis in energy and energy-related companies outside of the United Arab Emirates concentrating on petroleum refining and related upstream and downstream distribution and service network'[252] and 'MAN Ferrostaal's business [were] divided into two divisions, namely the Projects Division and the Services Division'.[253]

[249] Ibid, para 107.
[250] Ibid, para 110.
[251] Ibid, para 111.
[252] See para 2 of the Commission's decision.
[253] Ibid, para 3.

The main anticompetitive concern of the notified transaction was a 'vertical link concerning the market for the production of melamine and the melamine production technology market because of a minority shareholding of MAN Ferrostaal'.[254] The latter held 30 and 19.5 per cent minority shareholdings in Eurotecnica and Methanol Holding Trinidad Limited, respectively.

According to the Commission's decision, the 30 per cent MAN Ferrostaal minority shareholding in Eurotecnica in the market of melamine production technology enabled it to exclude inputs, ie to exclude other competitors in the market from technology for the production of melamine.

In addition, in reality it was considered by the Commission that there was a potential problem regarding the contestability of the relevant market, since a foreclosure strategy towards DSM or potential new entrants/competitors for the production of melamine[255] could be expected. Furthermore, the Commission also found that due to the high concentration[256] of the melamine market (because of the existence of two main producers with similar market shares, namely AMI, a subsidiary of International Petroleum Investment Company, and DSM) and its transparent nature (which consisted mainly in published contract prices and well-known costs), there was an increased risk of coordination between the two market leaders, ie AMI and DSM. Furthermore, it should not be forgotten or underestimated that the production of melamine constitutes a billion euro European market. Hence, a foreclosure strategy towards DSM or potential new entrants in the same product and geographical market could be expected.

Although it was about a minority stake, this participation of 30 per cent gave MAN Ferrostaal significant influence on the decision making concerning Eurotecnica's melamine licensing and engineering business: according to the shareholders' agreement, certain decisions ought to be taken by super-majority. In addition, the shareholders' agreement provided that all shareholders should have broad information rights. The Commission found that this was likely to have a substantial deterrent effect on the licensing practice for current and future customers of Eurotecnica, since a significant amount of information was exchanged between a prospective client and Eurotecnica; it was about crucial information which finally might end up in the hands of a competitor of these clients, namely AMI.[257]

In particular, the Commission was very concerned about the information rights that emerged from the shareholders' agreement. Indeed, the Commission stated that such information rights were

> likely to have a substantial deterrent effect on the licensing practice for current and future customers if it is known that the voluminous information which needs to be exchanged between a prospective client and Eurotecnica might end up in the hands of a competitor of these clients.[258]

On 20 February 2009 the notifying party offered commitments in order to remove the Commission's doubts regarding the possible anticompetitive effects of the notified acquisition. These commitments provided the full divestment of MAN Ferrostaal's minority

[254] Ibid, para 6.
[255] It is emphasized that this concerns a billion euro European market.
[256] High concentration means existence of very few firms with big size.
[257] Above n 239, para 20
[258] Ibid, para 39.

shareholding in Eurotecnica from Eurotecnica. The Commission considered them suitable for remedying its serious doubts as to the compatibility of the concentration with the common market.

(u) COMP/M.6541 *Glencore/Xstrata*

On 2 October 2012 Glencore International plc, the world's leading metals and thermal coal trader and the largest supplier of zinc metal in the EEA through a 7.79 per cent minority shareholding (vertical relationship) in Nyrstar, the world's largest zinc metal producer, acquired by way of purchase of shares Xstrata, the world's fifth largest metals and mining group. The notified concentration, inter alia, enhanced the ability and incentive of the merged entity to control zinc metal supplies in the EEA via its minority shareholding in Nyrstar.

According to the Commission's investigation, the merger examined, as initially notified, gave rise to competition concerns through unilateral effects, increasing the merged entity's capacity, and at the same time giving this entity the possibility to control the level of zinc metal supplies in the EEA.[259]

Glencore sought to remove these concerns; therefore it committed inter alia to terminate its exclusive (long-term) contractual agreement with Nyrstar, to the extent that this agreement was related to commodity zinc products produced by Nyrstar in the EEA. Furthermore, 'On 30 October, 13 November and 19 November 2012, the parties proposed remedies in order to address the competition concerns raised with respect to the EEA zinc metal market.'[260] According to the first remedy the parties committed, inter alia, to divest Glencore's 7.79 per cent minority stake in Nyrstar.[261] The remedy proposals of 13 and 19 November 2012 concerned various agreements between Glencore and Nyrstar. The Commission finally considered the commitments suitable for remedying the serious doubts as to the compatibility of the concentration with the common market and decided not to oppose the proposed concentration.

(v) COMP/M.6662 *Andritz/Schuler*

This case concerns the acquisition of the German press manufacturer Schuler by the Austrian plants and equipment manufacturer Andritz. It should be mentioned that, prior to the notification examined, Andritz already held a 24.99 per cent shareholding in Schuler. The Commission carried out a thorough investigation into the effects of the merger on the market for mechanical single presses (tools for forming metal parts from sheet metal) for sheet metal forming, where both companies were active before concluding that there were no relevant competition concerns. Nevertheless, it ultimately cleared the merger in phase I based on the result that the market structure would not be significantly changed.

However, it is observed that such competition scrutiny by the Commission was possible only under the precondition of the previous notification by Andritz which notified the acquisition of control and not at the time when the initial structural link of 24.99 per cent was created; nevertheless, this quite high percentage could have raised very similar competition concerns at the time it was created.

259 Above n 257, paras 15 and 16.
260 See para 482 of the Commission's decision.
261 Ibid, para 484.

B. Treatment of Minority Shareholdings Across Member States

In the following sub-sections we present selected cases involving minority shareholdings in the EU Member States UK, Germany, Austria, Lithuania as well as various nations around the world. We also present a study by DG Competition which used the Zephyr Database in order 'to make a rough but conservative approximation of the number of cases of structural links that are above the turnover thresholds of the Merger Regulation and might potentially merit competition scrutiny'.[262]

i. UK

The Office of Fair Trading (OFT) considers as a general policy that a minority shareholding of more than 25 per cent of the issued share capital of the acquired firm which enables the acquirer to block special resolutions is likely to confer sufficient power to influence the commercial policy of the acquired firm. This policy has been applied in cases where the remaining shares of the acquired firm are held by one or more than one shareholder(s).

Therefore, the critical issue under examination in the case where the minority shareholding is above 25 per cent is the ability of the acquirer to influence materially the management of the acquired business. That is, the question that has to be answered is whether the acquirer has the ability to influence materially the competitive conduct of the acquired firm and therefore its strategic interaction in the market and its ability to achieve its commercial goals.[263]

However, when the minority shareholding is below 25 per cent of the issued share capital of the acquired firm, then the phase I authority considers other factors in order to determine if control, ie material influence, exists. Such factors are (a) distribution of shareholdings, (b) voting power, (c) representation on the board of directors and (d) various commercial arrangements.[264]

Cases involving minority shareholdings in the UK represent approximately 5 per cent of all notified mergers.[265] Meadowcroft and Thompson analysed the characteristics of minority shareholdings in the UK for the years 1980 and 1984. Their research reveals that 459 minority shareholdings existed among 367 firms in 1984. The sectors with the highest activity volume were mechanical engineering, textiles, leisure and overseas traders. In 1980 the corresponding sectors were brewing and chemicals. Regarding the size of shareholdings, a 155 of them were between 5 and 10 per cent, 87 were between 10 and 15 per cent, 61 were between 25 and 30 per cent, and 54 were between 15 and 20 per cent. The average holding was 17.7 per cent. Concerning the type of minority shareholding, '[a]bout a half of holdings are horizontal, broadly a third are conglomerate, and only a small number are vertical'.[266]

[262] See also Commission Staff Working Document, 'Towards More Effective EU Merger Control', annex 2, 1, 18.
[263] See Cases ME/4694/10, ME/1633/04 and ME/3128/07.
[264] See Case ME/2811/06.
[265] Above n 262, 15.
[266] S Meadowcroft and D Thompson, *Minority Share Acquisition: The Impact upon Competition* (Luxembourg, Office for Official Publications of the European Communities, 1986) 1, 21.

(a) ME/1633/04 *Emap/Scottish Radio*

On 13 May 2004 the OFT[267] decided to clear, ie not to refer to the Competition Commission (CC), the completed acquisition by Emap plc of a 27.8 per cent share in Scottish Radio Holdings plc. Even though both firms in the transaction stated that the minority shareholding would not conferred to them any rights or any representation on the Scottish Radio Holdings board, the authority decided to consider the transaction as a concentration under section 26(1)[268] and (4)[269] of the Enterprise Act (EA) since it met the supply test in section 23(4) EA.[270]

The OFT decided that the concentration under scrutiny may not be expected to result in a substantial lessening of competition within the markets under consideration in UK and therefore did not refer it to the CC under section 22(1) EA.[271]

(b) ME/1962/05 *Creative/BBC*

As in case ME/1633/04 *Emap/Scottish Radio* the OFT decided not to refer to the CC the completed acquisition by Creative Broadcast Services Limited of BBC Broadcast Limited. Even though the OFT considered that in the light of the notified transaction Creative Broadcast Services Limited had conferred sole control over BBC Broadcast Limited and the turnover test had been met since the UK turnover of BBC Broadcast Limited exceeded £70 million, the authority believed that the concentration under scrutiny may not be expected to result in a substantial lessening of competition within the markets under consideration in the UK.

(c) ME/2811/06 *BSkyB/ITV*

On 27 April 2007 the OFT reported and advised the Secretary of State for Business, Enterprise and Regulatory Reform[272] that the completed acquisition by British Sky Broadcasting

[267] As we have already mentioned in ch 3, section I.B.ii the OFT and CC were responsible for protecting consumer interests throughout the UK until the end of March 2014. Both of them closed on 1 April 2014 with their responsibilities passing to the Competition and Market Authority (CMA). Throughout this book and for reasons of convenience we will use the terms OFT, CC and CMA interchangeably.

[268] Under s 23(1) EA enterprises cease to be distinct enterprises if they are brought under common ownership or control.

[269] Under s 23(1) EA 'a person or group of persons may be treated as bringing an enterprise under his or their control if (a) being already able to control or materially to influence the policy of the person carrying on the enterprise, that person or group of persons acquires a controlling interest in the enterprise or, in the case of an enterprise carried on by a body corporate, acquires a controlling interest in that body corporate; or (b) being already able materially to influence the policy of the person carrying on the enterprise, that person or group of persons becomes able to control that policy.'

[270] Section 23(4) EA states that 'the supply of services of that description in the United Kingdom, or in a substantial part of the United Kingdom, is to the extent of at least one-quarter (a) supply by one and the same person, or supply for one and the same person; or (b) supply by the persons by whom the enterprises concerned are carried on, or supply for those persons.'

[271] Section 22(1) EA states that 'The OFT shall, subject to subsections (2) and (3), make a reference to the Commission if the OFT believes that it is or may be the case that— (a) a relevant merger situation has been created; and (b) the creation of that situation has resulted, or may be expected to result, in a substantial lessening of competition within any market or markets in the United Kingdom for goods or services'.

[272] Secretary of State for Trade and Industry. Prior to this (26 February 2007), 'the Secretary of State issued a notice ("the intervention notice") to the Office of Fair Trading ("OFT"), pursuant to section 42 of the Enterprise Act 2002 ("the Act"), stating that he believed it was or may have been the case that the public interest consideration contained in section 58(2C)(a) of the Act was relevant to a consideration of the merger situation'. See para 7 of the Final Decisions by the Secretary of State for Business, Enterprise & Regulatory Reform on British Sky Broadcasting Group's acquisition of a 17.9 per cent shareholding in ITV plc, 29 January 2008.

Group plc (BSkyB), the leading pay-TV provider in the UK, of a 17.9 per cent minority shareholding in ITV plc, a leading commercial free-to-air broadcaster, on 17 November 2006 had met the reference criteria to the CC, according to sections 44(3),(4) and 22 EA.[273]

The OFT considered that a merger situation had been created since BSkyB had acquired material influence over ITV. That is, the minority shareholding would substantially lessen competition in an all-TV market through BSkyB's ability to influence the strategic decision making of ITV. OFT's consideration was based, inter alia, on the following facts:

- The attendance of BSkyB at ITV shareholder meetings. OFT considered that this was evidence that the former represented more than 25 per cent of the votes and therefore could have the ability to block special resolutions at these meetings.
- The ability of the acquirer to obtain representation in ITV.

More specifically, it was considered that, although BSkyB would be unlikely to be able to get board representation, it would through veto rights[274] be able to limit the strategic options of ITV. This was the reason why the UK authorities found it likely that the acquisition would result in a substantial lessening of competition and therefore identified the following possible effects: reduction in the quality on offer, and a lessening in innovation combined possibly with an increase in the price of audiovisual services in the all-TV market. The case was cleared under the precondition of diminishing the crucial shareholding down to 7.5 per cent; this percentage was considered adequate to eliminate the key veto rights of BSkyB.

Regarding the substantive competitive assessment of the proposed concentration, some third parties considered that the completion of the acquisition would create an incentive to foreclose the acquirer's competitors from access to the Digital Terrestrial Television (DTT) multiplexes and to ITV's content. Even though BSkyB and ITV offered commitments in order to alleviate the OFT's competitive concerns, the latter considered them as insufficient to enhance the competitive level in the relevant market under consideration.

On 24 May 2007 the Secretary of State for Business, Enterprise and Regulatory Reform announced his decision to refer the proposed concentration to the CC under section 45(2) EA.[275] According to paragraph 9 of the summary of CC's decision, the authority

> formed the view that BSkyB, through its acquisition of a stake in ITV, was looking to preserve its options as regards the future of ITV. We thought it unlikely that BSkyB would have chosen to invest in ITV purely as an investment vehicle.

Following paragraph 11 of the summary of the CC's decision, the authority

> found that the size of BSkyB's holding both in absolute and relative terms was such that on the basis of past voting patterns it would be able to block special resolutions proposed by ITV's management. BSkyB's ability to block a special resolution would limit ITV's strategic options, for example its ability to raise funds. BSkyB's importance and stature as an industry player, together with its position as the largest shareholder, would give additional weight to its views, increasing its ability to influence other ITV shareholders.

[273] Above n 265.

[274] It is acceptable that sole control exists in cases where only one shareholder is able to veto strategic decisions of a company, although he is not the only one with power to impose such decisions (negative sole control). In this case, a single shareholder possesses the same degree of influence usually possessed by one shareholder, who jointly controls a company, including the power to block strategic decisions.

[275] According to the summary of the CC's decision this was the first reference under chapter 2 of part 3 of the Enterprise Act regarding public interest cases. See para 1 of the summary of the CC's decision.

Therefore, the CC concluded that:

> BSkyB had acquired the ability materially to influence the policy of ITV which gives rise to common control for the purposes of section 26 of the Act. The turnover test under section 23(1) of the Act was satisfied. We concluded that a relevant merger situation had been created.[276]

In the light of the above-mentioned conclusion the CC proposed two remedies in order to address the lessening of competition in the relevant markets under scrutiny:

> (i) full divestment of the whole of BSkyB's shareholding in ITV and (ii) partial divestment with BSkyB being required to divest its shares down to a level below 7.5 [per cent] combined with undertakings not to seek or accept representation on ITV's Board and not to re-acquire shares in ITV.[277] The Competition Commission ha[d] recommended the second of these on the grounds that partial divestment [was] less intrusive than full divestment and [was], therefore, a more proportionate remedy.[278]

BSkyB and ITV proposed some alternative remedies, among them the placement of all BSkyB's shares in ITV

> in an independent voting trust which would [have] complete freedom over decisions on how to vote the shares, and/or undertaking not to vote their shareholding. BSkyB suggest[ed] that this would be equally effective in remedying any substantial lessening of competition that may be deemed to arise since it would [have] remove[d] the scope for them to block special resolutions of shareholders. They argue[d] that this type of remedy should be adopted on the grounds that it represent[ed] the least intrusive measure that provides an effective remedy.[279]

On 14 December 2007 the CC referred its final report to the Secretary of State for Business, Enterprise and Regulatory Reform in accordance with the section 50 EA. On 29 January 2008 the Secretary of State took his final decisions in accordance with sections 54 and 55 EA. Accordingly, the Secretary of State accepted the decisions of the CC that a concentration had been created. Regarding the remedies proposed by the CC with its final report, the Secretary of State saw 'no reason to depart from the Competition Commission's recommendations which [we]re based on an analysis of the level at which, on cautious assumptions, BSkyB would not be able to block a special resolution presented to ITV shareholders'.[280]

According to the judgment of the Tribunal on 29 September 2008[281] on the application of BSkyB for a review under section 120 EA of the decision of the CC and the Secretary of State, BSkyB's arguments were rejected regarding the CC's findings of the existence of concentration and its anticompetitive effects in the relevant markets. In addition, the judgment of the Tribunal rejected BSkyB's arguments concerning the CC's remedy of partial

[276] See para 12 of the summary of CC's decision.

[277] There were arguments against this proposed remedy by the CC on the grounds that BSkyB was a major player in the market and at the same time could not be the major shareholder of ITV with a minority shareholding of less than 7.50 per cent.

[278] Therefore, the CC concluded that partial divestiture could be as effective as full divestiture in addressing the lessening of competition from the concentration. See paras 21 and 22 of the final decisions by the Secretary of State for Business, Enterprise & Regulatory Reform on British Sky Broadcasting Group's acquisition of a 17.9 per cent shareholding in ITV plc (29 January 2008).

[279] Ibid.

[280] Ibid.

[281] See Case *1095/4/8/08 British Sky Broadcasting Group plc v (1) Competition Commission (2) The Secretary of State* [2008] CAT 25. In this case the CC had been supported by Virgin Media Inc.

divestment of BSkyB's minority shareholding in ITV. In particular, BSkyB argued that the CC had acted irrationally by selecting a level of 7.50 per cent.

Furthermore, on the same day as the above-mentioned judgment of the Tribunal, the latter declared a decision regarding the application of Virgin Media Inc applied against the CC and the Secretary of State, supported by BSkyB, relating to the public interest provisions of sections 58 and 58A EA and the remedial proposition of the CC.

Concerning the latter the Tribunal rejected Virgin's arguments that the CC should have required complete divestiture of BSkyB's minority shareholding in ITV. Concerning the former the Tribunal invited the parties involved in the concentration to submit further facts in order to address the lessening of competition in the relevant markets of the concentration.

On 21 January 2010 the Court of Appeal[282] 'allow[ed] its [BskyB] appeal on the media plurality issue and also the Respondent's Notices of the Commission and the Secretary of State'.[283]

(d) ME/3128/07 *Caisse du dépôt/Interconnector*

On 22 June 2007 Caisse du dépôt acquired from British Gas plc a 25 per cent minority shareholding in Interconnector. On 31 July 2007 the OFT decided not to refer the notified concentration to the CC.

The OFT believed that even though a concentration had been created since Caisse du dépôt and Interconnector came under common control for the purpose of section 26 EA as a result of the former acquiring the ability materially to influence the policy of the latter and the turnover test had met, it was not expected to result in a substantial lessening of competition within the markets under consideration in UK. Therefore, the authority did not refer the concentration to the CC under section 22(1) EA.

(e) ME/4519/10 *RREEF/Kelda*

On 21 June 2010 the OFT decided that the transaction notified on 28 April 2010 regarding the acquisition of a minority shareholding of Saxon from Kelda did not constitute a concentration within the meaning of the Enterprise Act.

In particular, on 23 March 2010 Saxon, a wholly owned subsidiary of RREEF, acquired a minority shareholding of around 21 per cent of the issued share capital in Kelda, the ultimate parent company of the water company Yorkshire Water Services Limited. Given the fact that the ultimate parent of RREEF was Deutsche Bank AG, which owned 'interests in a number of companies that ultimately own shares in Sutton and East Surrey Water Company',[284] the OFT initiated an investigation in order to clarify whether Deutsche Bank AG would be the ultimate parent of the two water firms.

According to the OFT's decision, Saxon had the right to appoint 'two of the 12 directors on the board of Kelda in line with its equity stake in Kelda'.[285] However, it would not have the ability to out-vote matters before the board of directors since board decisions were taken by simple majority. In addition, Saxon would not have the ability to block strategic commercial decisions (ie, acquisitions and disposals, financing structures, appointing and

[282] See also *In the Court of appeal (Civil Division) on Appeal from the Competition Appeal Tribunal (Mr Justice Barling, Prof Peter Grinyer and Mr Peter Clayton)* [2008] CAT 25, [2010] EWCA Civ 2.

[283] Ibid, para 124.

[284] See para 5 of the OFT's decision of 21 June 2010.

[285] Ibid, para 10.

dismissing directors and approval or adoption of the Business Plan) since decisions for these matters required approval of at least 60.6 per cent of the votes. Regarding minority shareholder protection matters (ie, insolvency proceedings, fundamental changes to the company's existing lines of business and changes to the dividend policy), these required at least 90.1 per cent of the votes.[286]

Given also the fact that no director of the firms concerned in the transaction was member of the board of East Surrey Water Company and also the fact that Saxon's directors in Kelda would not have any particular influence in its day-to-day management, the OFT declared that Saxon did not control Kelda.[287]

(f) ME/4694/10 *Rynair/Aer Lingus*

The *Ryanair/Aer Lingus* case is characterized as 'one of the most prominent and long-running European cases on minority shareholdings'.[288] Between 2006 and 2008, Ryanair gradually increased its share in Aer Lingus to a current level of 29.82 per cent (Table 9). The acquisition of this percentage constituted part of Ryanair's attempt eventually to take over Aer Lingus entirely. In October 2010, the Commission ruled that the minority shareholding did not constitute a concentration under Merger Regulation 139/2004, and that for this reason it did not have jurisdiction to examine the issue.

Table 9 presents the evolution of Ryanair's minority shareholdings in Aer Lingus's total issued share capital from 2006 until the publication of the OFT's decision.[289]

Table 9: Evolution of Ryanair's minority shareholding in Aer Lingus, 2006–12

Date	Minority shareholding (%)
5 October 2006	19.2
28 November 2006	25.2
20 August 2007	29.4
2 July 2008–15 July 2010	29.8

Source: Table 1, OFT statement on its investigation of Ryanair's minority shareholding in Aer Lingus, 2 (https://assets.digital.cabinet-office.gov.uk/media/532acf5140f0b60a76000374/Ryanair.pdf).

Ryanair became the largest shareholder of Aer Lingus, followed by the Irish government with a minority shareholding of around 25 per cent.

The OFT subsequently took the decision to initiate its own investigation into the minority shareholding of Ryanair in Aer Lingus.[290] In particular, the OFT had to consider two main issues regarding:

(i) whether the OFT has jurisdiction under the Enterprise Act 2002 to review the acquisition as a relevant merger situation. This will include considering whether Ryanair has

[286] Ibid, para 12.

[287] See also the Case ME/4540/10 *Sports Direct/Blacks*.

[288] See 'Who Calls the Shots? Minority Shareholdings in Merger Control' [2014] *Oxera, Agenda* March.

[289] That is, 5 July 2012.

[290] See especially press release 112/10, 29 October 2010, OFT statement on its investigation of Ryanair's minority shareholding in Aer Lingus, available at http://webarchive.nationalarchives.gov.uk/20140402142426/http://www.oft.gov.uk/news-and-updates/press/2010/112-10.

the ability to exercise material influence over the commercial policy of Aer Lingus (see Note 4) as well as whether the OFT is within the statutory time period available to it to investigate the acquisition and, if need be, refer it to the Competition Commission (see Note 5) and

(ii) if so, whether the acquisition raises competition issues that give rise to a duty to refer the acquisition to the Competition Commission under the 'substantial lessening of competition' test set out in the Enterprise Act 2002.[291]

On 15 June 2012 the OFT took a decision to refer the case under section 32 EA. Its main concern was that the minority shareholding would enable Ryanair to weaken Aer Lingus as a competitor.

On 13 August 2013[292] the CC largely confirmed the OFT's position:[293] CC took the severe measure of requiring Ryanair not only to reduce its shareholding in Aer Lingus to 5 per cent but also not to accept or seek any board representation in Aer Lingus or even acquire further shares.

Let us here examine the CC's methodology in the *Ryanair/Aer Lingus* case.

It is remarkable that the CC had no serious concerns about 'traditional' unilateral effects relating to potential price increases. Furthermore, there was no evidence that Ryanair's pricing had been affected by the shareholding; on the contrary, the CC accepted evidence that strong competition remained between the two airlines during the period of Ryanair's shareholding.[294] In addition, due to the absence of board representation from Ryanair, the CC did not expect that the shareholding would affect Aer Lingus's incentives to take into account Ryanair's interests. The result was that classical concerns about unilateral effects were excluded.

Instead, the CC, like the OFT, chose to focus mainly on potential ways in which Ryanair's minority shareholding could (theoretically) affect Aer Lingus's commercial policy and strategy, and thereby weaken Aer Lingus as a competitor. More specifically, the CC's main concern was that the shareholding would enable Ryanair to prevent Aer Lingus from combining with another airline (either through a merger/acquisition or through a joint venture)[295] and its concerns were reinforced by the recent trend towards oligopoly in the airline industry. The CC identified a number of mechanisms through which Ryanair could theoretically weaken Aer Lingus as a competitor. At this point it should be mentioned that sole control exists in cases where only one shareholder is able to veto strategic decisions of a company, although he is not the only one with the power to impose such decisions (negative sole control).

Thus, in the case examined, the CC found that Ryanair's minority shareholding would provide it with sufficient votes to block special resolutions/decisions which (because of

[291] Ibid.

[292] On 18 June 2012 the CC announced its investigation of the completed acquisition by Ryanair Holdings plc of a minority stake in Aer Lingus Group plc. See also http://webarchive.nationalarchives.gov.uk/20140402141250/http://www.competition-commission.org.uk/media-centre/latest-news/2012/Jun/cc-to-investigate-ryanair-stake.

[293] See the final report in Competition Commission, 'Ryanair Holdings plc and Aer Lingus Group plc. A Report on the Completed Acquisition by Ryanair Holdings plc of a Minority Shareholding in Aer Lingus Group plc', 28 August 2013, available at http://webarchive.nationalarchives.gov.uk/20140402141250/http://www.competition-commission.org.uk/media-centre/latest-news/2013/Aug/cc-requires-ryanair-to-sell-shareholding.

[294] In fact, according to the evidence suggested, competition had intensified!

[295] The CC was of the view that a combination could enable Aer Lingus to reduce its unit costs through economies of scale.

their significance) require approval by at least 75 per cent of shareholders at a general meeting and constitute a necessary precondition for certain types of transactions. Furthermore, the CC was concerned that having a competitor of Ryanair's size and reputation as a shareholder would make Aer Lingus less attractive to potential buyers. Simultaneously, the CC expressed several other (secondary) concerns. For instance, it considered that the minority shareholding (by itself) would provide Ryanair with sufficient control to restrict Aer Lingus's ability to manage effectively its portfolio of Heathrow slots.

Because of the above-mentioned reasons, the CC decided that only through a (partial) divestment of Ryanair's shares could its concerns be diminished. According to the CC' s point of view, in order to specify the size of the required divestment, an assessment of Ryanair's *effective voting power*[296] was considered necessary. In this framework, the CC defined a range of potential outcomes that could increase Ryanair's effective voting power. These outcomes were the following:

— The Irish government, the other major shareholder in Aer Lingus, with a stake of 25.1 per cent, refrains from attending a shareholders' meeting.
— Limited attendance by other shareholders.[297]
— What is going to be the result, if on the one hand the Irish government sells its stake sometime in the (unknown) future, and on the other hand its shares are dispersed to the general public (thereby potentially reducing the gathering of people or legal persons for those shares). However, the reply to this hypothetical question is that even if in the unknown future the Irish government decides to sell its stake, it does not necessarily mean that its shares will be dispersed to the general public. On the contrary, it is quite possible that a new investor-enterprise will decide to buy this stake. Hence, in our view, this hypothesis of the CC is absolutely theoretical and therefore constitutes in reality an impossible scenario.
— Some shareholders (characterized as 'allies' by the CC) vote in line with Ryanair on a particular issue. Nevertheless, in our view, the crucial question is what the result of such voting is.

The CC's analysis is based on scenarios obtained by combining the above-mentioned outcomes in several ways. The CC also took into account estimates of historical voter attendance being based in Aer Lingus's shareholders' meetings. While the analysis relies primarily on the average historical turnout estimate of 37.2 per cent, other scenarios were also considered:[298] more specifically, the historical minimum attendance (23.4 per cent) and the maximum attendance (41.4 per cent) were considered by the CC. Furthermore, a 'full participation' scenario, ie with 100 per cent attendance, was considered as well.

For each of the scenarios considered in the CC's analysis, the minimum level of shareholding that theoretically would allow Ryanair to block special resolutions/decisions was calculated. According to the CC's theoretical analysis, special resolutions could be blocked by a shareholder or group of shareholders holding 25 per cent of the votes actually cast. If, for instance, half the shareholders do not actually vote, a 12.5 per cent stake would equate

[296] It is about the number of votes available to Ryanair relative to the total number of votes actually submitted at a given shareholders' meeting.

[297] That is, other than Ryanair and the Irish government.

[298] Above n 288.

to 25 per cent of the votes actually cast; consequently, it is about a percentage which would be enough to block a special resolution/decision.[299]

Based on the above analysis, the CC concluded that, in order to ensure that Ryanair would not be able to prevent Aer Lingus from participating in a combination with another airline (either through a merger/acquisition or through a joint venture) in most of the scenarios examined, Ryanair's shareholding ought to be reduced to 5 per cent. Furthermore, according to the CC's view, a reduction to 5 per cent would offer an adequate solution for most of its other concerns (eg the disincentive created for potential Aer Lingus 'allies').

It should be emphasized that the CC's economic analysis/approach to the nature of Ryanair's influence on Aer Lingus provides a conceptual underpinning not only for its assessment of the minority shareholding in this specific case, but also in general. Nevertheless one of the main questions is whether or not the principle of proportionality was applied by the CC; more specifically, it is not at all clear whether the magnitude of the divestment remedy that the CC derives from its economic analysis is proportionate given the behavioural remedies that Ryanair offered, including a commitment not to block special resolutions.[300]

In addition, the CC's assessment that merger efficiencies between Aer Lingus and Ryanair[301] would not be probable was so vague that it could not be excluded that similar findings could apply to a potential merger between Aer Lingus and another airline. Moreover, the truth is that there were only a few realistic takeover candidates, all of which had stated that they were not interested in combining with Aer Lingus at that time, but without simultaneously declaring the existence of Ryanair's shareholding as a reason for this decision.

Thus, the result is that the CC's concerns in the *Ryanair/Aer Lingus* case were not based directly on 'typical' economic theories of harm in relation to minority shareholdings. On the contrary, the CC put forward a more novel theory of harm: the main problem is that, if this theory applied consistently, it will create, in the authors' view, novel and perhaps unresolved problems, since in reality it would create a per se rule, by preventing most minority shareholdings above 5–10 per cent between competitors. Thus, in such a case, the 'map' for mergers is not changed de jure but de facto, since the CC's approach may therefore send a crystal-clear negative message to undertakings interested in engaging in partial acquisitions more generally. Consequently, in the authors' view, the CC's recent decision in the *Ryanair/Aer Lingus* case does not constitute an example to follow. On the contrary, it is an inappropriate example, which, if adopted, would create novel and perhaps resolved problems in merger issues.

On 23 September 2013 Ryanair filed an application with the Competition Appeal Tribunal (CAT) challenging the findings of the CC's Report of 28 August 2013. In particular, Ryanair challenged the lawfulness of this report on six grounds. Firstly, Ryanair stated that the CC's decision to require divesture of its minority interest in Aer Lingus would undermine any future cooperation between the two undertakings and especially Ryanair's intention to acquire the entire capital stock of its competitor.

299 Ibid.

300 Ibid. As is quoted in *Oxera, Agenda*: 'In other words, the CC drew the remedies line close to the final rows in the table, whereas there were also arguments to draw it further to the top'.

301 It should be mentioned that Aer Lingus and Ryanair were considered to be each other's closest competitors.

Secondly, Ryanair believed that it was unfair to keep secret facts (material and evidence) which the CC had relied upon in reaching its decision and in particular evidence concerning the assessment of the passive partial acquisition at the horizontal level. Thirdly, it argued that the CC had followed a wrong approach by comparing the acquisition of the minority stake with a situation where such an acquisition does not exist. Fourthly, it argued that the CC's conclusions were irrational since the CC had relied upon sophisticated theories of harm without any support from the evidence. Fifthly, it submitted that the report inappropriately imposed the divesture. Sixthly, it argued that the CC did not have the 'jurisdiction to impose requirements on Ryanair, an Irish company which does not carry on business in the UK'.[302]

Three of these arguments were relevant to Ryanair's appeal in the CAT. Briefly, these three grounds are the following:

(1) it was procedurally unfair for the CC to have refused to disclose to Ryanair (or its external lawyers) the material allegations and evidence relied upon by the CC in reaching the conclusion that Ryanair might affect Aer Lingus's ability to participate in a combination with another airline. Particular weight was attached to the evidence of other airlines but their identities and the underlying evidence were withheld from Ryanair despite its requests for their disclosure. It was therefore denied a fair opportunity to respond;
(2) the decision to require divestiture of all but 5 [per cent] of the minority stake involved a breach of the duty of sincere co-operation under Article 4(3) of the Treaty on European Union ('TEU') because of a material risk of conflict between the order and a future decision of the [Commission] (following the appeal to the General Court) that Ryanair should be permitted to bid for 100 [per cent] of Aer Lingus; and
(3) the divestiture remedy was disproportionate and was imposed by the CC on the basis of a misdirection as to the degree of risk of an SLC[303] occurring that has to be found before a remedy can be imposed and which dictates the type of remedy required.[304]

The CAT by its decision on 7 March 2014 dismissed Ryanair's application.

On 12 February 2015 Ryanair filed an application with the Competition and Markets Authority (CMA) requesting that it consider whether there has been a material change of circumstances since the CC report of 28 August 2013. It should be noted that until the day of Ryanair's application both the CAT and the Court of Appeal's judgments had upheld the findings in the CC report.

In particular, Ryanair in its application stated that:

> The findings in the Final Report have now been contradicted and disproven by events, which demonstrate conclusively that Ryanair's shareholding in Aer Lingus does not prevent Aer Lingus from merging with, being acquired by, or otherwise entering into combinations with other airlines, and which fatally undermine the lawfulness of the proposed divestment remedy.[305]

Ryanair argued that the Irish government represented the only obstacle to Aer Lingus's combination with another firm and an example of this was its reaction to a recent attempt by International Consolidated Airlines Group SA (IAG) to acquire it. It should be mentioned here that IAG had stated in the past that its purpose was not to acquire Aer Lingus with a

[302] Case 1219/4/8/13 *Ryanair Holdings plc v Competition and Markets Authority* [2014] CAT 3, 7 Mar 2014.
[303] Substantial lessening of competition.
[304] England and Wales Court of Appeal (Civil Division) Decisions, *Ryanair Holdings plc v The Competition and Markets Authority & Anor* [2015] EWCA Civ 83.
[305] *Ryanair/Aer Lingus Merger Inquiry Application to the Competition and Markets Authority* (2015), para 5.

significant ongoing minority shareholder. Also, one of the major arguments of the CC for ordering the divestment of Ryanair's minority shareholding was that its presence 'prevented Aer Lingus from merging with, being acquired by, or otherwise entering into combinations with other airlines'.[306] The significance of this argument was also recognized later by the CAT.[307]

In the light of the above evidence Ryanair made the following recommendations to the CMA:

— The CMA is obliged to investigate these developments, which have materially changed the environment assessed by the Competition Commission in ways that contradict its conclusions, and to reach a reasoned decision on their implications before imposing remedies on Ryanair—particularly where the remedy in question would be irreversible.
— Circumstances have changed materially since the Competition Commission published the Final Report in August 2013, meaning that the CMA no longer has the power to impose a divestment remedy.
— Whatever the CMA's conclusion on whether a divestment remains appropriate, a Final Order in the form currently envisaged (requiring a Trustee to sell Ryanair's shares in a pre-determined manner) would be unworkable. It is highly doubtful whether any Trustee would be prepared to accept the CMA's mandate at this time and, even if it did, it is inconceivable that the mandate could be fulfilled.[308]

On 3 March 2015 Aer Lingus responded to Ryanair's application stating that 'In Aer Lingus' respectful view, the application by Ryanair is transparently little more than a device to achieve further delay.'[309] It also argued that Ryanair's application

> is based on a deliberate mischaracterisation of the facts, and does not begin to provide a plausible basis for re-examining the Report of the Competition Commission. Rather, it is clearly Ryanair's intent to manufacture the basis for yet another—fourth!—challenge in the CAT[310]

and urged the CMA to reach a final decision regarding Ryanair's new application.

On 11 March 2015 IAG responded to the CMA regarding Ryanair's application and announced its intention to take control of Aer Lingus. IAG stated that its proposal to acquire one of its major competitors was subject to the acceptance of the CC's demand that Ryanair divest its Aer Lingus shares and the acceptance of the proposal by the Minister of Finance of Ireland—Ryanair and the Irish government constituted the two major shareholders of Aer Lingus, together holding 54.98 per cent of Aer Lingus's share capital. Concluding, IAG stated to the CMA that since Ryanair had not divested its minority shareholding in Aer Lingus at the time of the consultation there had been no material change since the time of preparation of the CC's final report. Therefore, IAG proposed to the CMA to dismiss Ryanair's application against its final report of 28 August 2013.[311]

[306] Ibid, para 1.

[307] See especially Case 1219/4/8/13 *Ryanair Holdings plc v Competition and Markets Authority* [2014] CAT 3, 7 Mar 2014, para 159.

[308] Above n 299, para 6.

[309] See especially Completed Acquisition by Ryanair Holdings plc of a Minority Interest in Aer Lingus plc, Competition and Markets Authority, Consultation Response Submission by Aer Lingus, 2.

[310] Ibid.

[311] See also Ryanair Holdings plc/Aer Lingus Group plc (minority shareholding): invitation to comment (2015), IAG, available at https://assets.digital.cabinet-office.gov.uk/media/5508105c40f0b613e9000009/IAG_response_to_consultation.pdf.

On 17 March 2015 Ryanair sent its responses to the consultation by the CMA indicating that 'Ryanair's shareholding does not deter other airlines from combining with Aer Lingus. Rather, it is the Irish Government that has placed obstacles in the way of the proposed takeover and which deters potential merger partners.'[312] Ryanair's response was based on the facts that (a) IAG remained committed to making a public bid for Aer Lingus as soon as the Irish government was prepared to accept it on reasonably commercial terms, (b) Aer Lingus's board was ready to accept the public bid by IAG, (c) the Irish government was the institutional body which was obstructing Aer Lingus's amalgamation with any other airline and (d) Ryanair continued to state that 'will consider any offer for its shareholding in Aer Lingus if the price offered is attractive'.[313]

Ryanair also stated that the facts from the final report of the CC onwards also reveal that Aer Lingus and IAG remain in favour of their merger and that Ryanair's minority shareholding was not deterring any competitor from acquiring Aer Lingus share capital with a view of eventually controlling the company.

In a later document Ryanair stated that both airlines (Ryanair and Aer Lingus) continued to compete intensely after the CC's final report as they had done for the seven years prior to that. In particularly, Ryanair stated that:

— Aer Lingus has entered two new routes in competition to Ryanair, namely Dublin to Leeds–Bradford and Dublin to Newcastle.
— Over the same period, the combined traffic on Ryanair and Aer Lingus routes between Dublin and Great Britain increased by over 24 [per cent], while the airlines combined capacity between Dublin and Continental Europe has increased by 36 [per cent].
— There has been a significant shift in market shares held by each of the two airlines. Ryanair's share has increased on most of the routes on which the two airlines operate, but where Aer Lingus has entered new routes, it has successfully won market share from Ryanair.
— Looking beyond Great Britain, Ryanair and Aer Lingus are competing intensely on a large number of routes between Dublin and other European cities.
— There are examples of Ryanair entering new European routes in direct competition to Aer Lingus and successfully winning market share, ie, Dublin–Alicante, Dublin–Lisbon, Dublin–Prague, and Dublin–Nice.
— Ryanair also entered the Dublin–Bucharest route, previously operated by Aer Lingus'.[314]

The intense competition between the two airlines was also further evidence for Ryanair that the circumstances had changed materially since the CC's final report.

On 17 April 2015 the CMA provisionally decided that there had been no material change in circumstances or special reason for it not to implement the remedies in the Ryanair/Aer Lingus inquiry. In particular, the CMA, after considering the views of the participants in its consultation concerning Ryanair's application on 12 February 2015, upheld its view in

[312] Ryanair/Aer Lingus Merger Inquiry, Response to Consultation by the Competition and Markets Authority (2015) para 5.

[313] Ibid, para 4.

[314] Ryanair/Aer Lingus Merger Inquiry, Ryanair's Observations on Responses to the CMA's Consultation on a Material Change of Circumstances (2015) para 32.

the CC's final report. Its provisional decision was based on the assessment of two critical propositions which were advanced in Ryanair's application, namely:

(a) the fact that IAG is willing to make a bid for the entirety of Aer Lingus (and the fact that the Irish Government has so far declined to give IAG an irrevocable commitment in respect of its 25.11 [per cent] shareholding) 'fatally undermines' the CC's argument that Ryanair's minority shareholding deters other airlines from combining with Aer Lingus; and
(b) the passing of time since publication of the Report, and the fact that Aer Lingus has been able to continue to compete with Ryanair during that period despite Ryanair's continued presence as a minority shareholder, in and of itself constitutes a MCC.[315]

Regarding the first proposition, the CMA stated that Ryanair would have an incentive not to sell its minority shareholding since a potential merger between Aer Lingus and IAG would strengthen the level of competition in the market. After the merger Aer Lingus would be a potentially stronger competitor for Ryanair and this is an issue that the CMA had already considered. Additionally, the CMA indicated that in its final report the CC had stated that Ryanair's incentives as competitor would generally outweigh its incentives as a shareholder of Aer Lingus due to profit flows from the latter to the former and the fact that Ryanair would have to bear only a share of Aer Lingus's cost in proportion to the value of its minority shareholding. According to the CMA this incentive had not changed in the previous two years and especially after the final report of the CC.

At the same time IAG's intention was and continues to be the acquisition of 100 per cent, or at least above 90 per cent, of Aer Lingus's share capital.[316] This means that the transaction will not be contemplated as soon as Ryanair continues to be a major shareholder in Aer Lingus with enhanced abilities to block certain decisions.

The CMA also stated in paragraph 52 of its provisional decision regarding Ryanair's application on 12 February 2015 that:

> [I]n addition to the finding that Ryanair's shareholding would affect Aer Lingus's ability to combine with another airline by requiring Ryanair's approval for certain types of transactions, the CC found that Ryanair's influence over Aer Lingus, combined with its incentives as a competitor, would create significant execution risk for airlines considering Aer Lingus as a potential partner, and would therefore be likely to deter some airlines from entering into, pursuing, or concluding discussions with Aer Lingus. … This remains true.

Regarding the second proposition under scrutiny CMA stated that:

> [W]e have provisionally concluded that to the extent that there has been a continuation of that competition (or even an intensification as noted by Ryanair) between the airlines since the publication of Report this does not materially affect the findings in the Report. Consequently, we provisionally decided that there was no reason why the passage of a further 17 months, in addition to the preceding period over which Ryanair has held its minority shareholding in Aer Lingus, provided any evidence of an MCC such that the CMA should consider departing from the findings in the Report.[317]

[315] Ryanair/Aer Lingus Merger Inquiry, Provisional Decision of Possible Material Changes of Circumstances (2015) para 45.

[316] The acquisition will not be terminated since it will not be possible for IAG to initiate squeeze-out procedures if its capital participation in Aer Lingus is less than 90 per cent.

[317] Ryanair/Aer Lingus Merger Inquiry, Provisional Decision of Possible Material Changes of Circumstances (2015) para 57.

The CMA's provisional decision on 17 April 2015 was confirmed by its decision on 11 June 2015. In its decision the CMA stated that there had been no material change and therefore Ryanair must sell its shares in Aer Lingus down to 5 per cent. In particular, in its report in the same day[318] the CMA gave effect to the remedies identified by the decision of the CC.

On 15 July 2015 the CAT dismissed Ryanair's latest appeal regarding its shareholding in Aer Lingus. One day earlier the Commission had decided to approve IAG's bid for Aer Lingus subject to conditions, while the CMA has also moved to grant Ryanair the necessary approvals to sell its 29.8 per cent stake to IAG. The chairman of the Ryanair/Aer Lingus inquiry group stated, inter alia, that by

> [d]ivesting its shareholding removes that concern and we note that the [Commission] has accepted commitments from IAG to address its potential concerns over the deal. We have therefore agreed to give the necessary permissions to allow Ryanair to sell its shareholding by accepting the IAG offer.[319]

ii. Germany

Section 37(1) of German Competition Act (CA) is explained in detail in chapter 3, section I.B. In general, a concentration arises when the acquirer acquires 25 per cent of the capital or the voting rights of the victim firm, or by a notified transaction the acquirer directly or indirectly exercises a competitively significant influence (*wettbewerblich erheblicher Einfluss*)[320] on the victim firm. The first criterion is independent of the second qualified criterion and vice versa.

It is assumed that a minority shareholder with 25 per cent of the issued capital of a firm may block certain corporate decisions such as the amendment of the statutes of the corporation, capital increases, and mergers and liquidation. The second criterion came into force in 1990 since many minority shareholding cases below 25 per cent escaped the German CA. Prior to this amendment, and after the introduction of German merger control, the legislature added a provision by which minority shareholding transactions of less than 25 per cent of the capital or the voting rights of the victim may also subject to merger control. According to this provision, a concentration is established if an 'acquirer attained, through contract, statutes, articles of association or resolution, the legal position of a shareholder in a stock corporation holding more than 25 [percent] of the voting rights'.[321]

The notion of competitively significant influence is demonstrated under the following prerequisites:[322]

— The existence of an acquisition of a shareholding.
— Other factors that in cooperation with the minority shareholding enable the acquirer to influence the target firm.

[318] The title of the order is 'The Ryanair Holdings plc and Aer Lingus Group plc Inquiry Order 2015'.

[319] See also https://www.gov.uk/government/news/cma-welcomes-cat-judgment-on-ryanair-and-moves-to-approve-shareholding-sale.

[320] See Bundesgerichtshof, KVR 26/03, WuW/E DE-R 1419, *Deutsche Post/trans-o-flex*, 21 December 2004 and OLG Düsseldorf, VI-2 Kart 10/04 (V), WuW/E DE-R 1390, KG Wochenkurier, 24 November 2004.

[321] See also S Barthelmess, 'Minority Shareholdings in Competing Companies—Lessons from Germany?', 18th St Gallen International Competition Law Forum (2011) 1, 11, available at http://ssrn.com/abstract=2416217.

[322] Also called 'plus factors'. Ibid, 12.

- Veto rights[323]
  - de facto blocking minority of more than 25 per cent of the issued capital of the target firm concerning key corporate decisions of the target firm (in conjunction with the level of dispersion of the remaining shares of the target firm);
  - shares with special rights;
  - contractual veto rights;
  - rights to appoint supervisory board members.
- Board representation
  - management board of the competitors;
  - supervisory board of the competitor.
- Access to sensitive information.
- Composition of remaining shares of the target firm.
- Option or pre-emptive rights.[324]
- Financial instruments such as loans that are linked with the minority shareholding
- The competitive relationship between the minority shareholder and the target firm
  - the minority shareholder is actual competitor of the target firm;
  - either the minority shareholder is an upstream supplier or a downstream customer of the target firm (vertical relationship).[325]
- The minority shareholder acts in concert with the target firm regarding a project that influences the commercial activities of both of firms.[326]

The size of the minority shareholding that gives control to the acquiring firm requires a case-specific analysis. The Bundeskartellamt (the German Federal Cartel Office) has considered minority shareholdings below 10 per cent (1 and 9 per cent) as sufficient to give control to the acquiring firm.[327]

Notified transactions regarding minority shareholdings represented 10 per cent of all notified transactions from 1990 to 2010. Furthermore, the Bundeskartellamt prohibited four minority shareholding cases from 2005 to 2012, representing 12.5 per cent of all prohibitions in that period (4 out of 32), while the corresponding proportion from 1990 to 2009 was 11 per cent.[328]

> However, while for transactions involving the acquisition of a 25 [per cent] participation … account for about 10 [per cent] of both notifications and prohibition, transactions notified under

[323] See also OLG Düsseldorf, Kart 5/08 (V), WuW/E DE-R 2462, *A-TEC Industries/Norddeutsche Affinerie*, 12 November 2008.

[324] As it concerns pre-emptive rights see, inter alia, B6-106/04 *Volksfreund-Druckerei/TW Wochenspiegel*, WuW/E DE-V 1072; *Mainova/Aschaffenburger Versorgungs GmbH*, WuW/E DE-V 983; B6-27/04, DMS/BZ, WuW/E DE-V 968; B8-27/04; B8-107/02 *Stadtwerke Eberswalde*, WuW/E DE-V 707; B5-42/90, *Gillette/Wilkinson* (1992) AG 363.

[325] See Federal Court (BGH), Decision of November 21, 2000, KVR 16/99 *ASV/Stilke*, WuW/E DE-R 608.

[326] See B8-27/04 *Mainova/Aschaffenburger Versorgungs GmbH*, WuW/E DE-V 983.

[327] See Activity Report 2001/2002 of the Bundeskartellamt and Barthelmess (n 321) 12.

[328] See JP Schmidt, 'Germany: Merger Control Analysis of Minority Shareholdings—A Model for the EU?' (2013) 2 *Concurrences* 207, 208–09 and footnotes therein.

> the 'competitively significant influence' criterion ... account for only ca 0.6 [per cent] of all notified cases but of about 11 [per cent] of all mergers prohibited.[329]

In the *Xella Baustoffe* case the Bundeskartellamt considered that a 50 per cent call option on the shares of the target firm in relation to the fact that the acquirer had the right to appoint a member in the management of the acquired firm sufficed to create significant influence over it.[330]

The energy and media sectors in Germany are characterized by a high degree of active and passive minority shareholdings: 34 per cent of cases notified because of competitively significant influence concerned the energy sector and 19 per cent the media sector.[331]

In July 2001 E.ON AG—the largest electricity company in Germany—proposed to acquire an active minority shareholding in Gelsenberg AG[332] and later on in the same year it notified to the Bundeskartellamt its intention to acquire Bergemann GmbH.[333] E.ON's ultimate aim was to control Ruhrgas—the largest German gas supplier with a dominant market share of about 60 per cent (of supply) in the German gas market—since Gelsenberg AG and Bergemann GmbH held, respectively, 25 and 34.8 per cent minority shareholdings in Ruhrgas.[334]

In January 2002 the Bundeskartellamt, aiming to prevent E.ON's acquisition of the 25 per cent stake in Ruhrgas, prohibited E.ON's purchase of a controlling interest in Gelsenberg; the Bundeskartellamt considered that it would have strengthened E.ON's dominant positions in both the gas and electricity sales markets. For similar reasons, one month later,[335] the Bundeskartellamt also prohibited E.ON's acquisition of Bergemann.[336]

Following the Bundeskartellamt's prohibition, E.ON and Ruhrgas applied to the Federal Ministry for Economic Affairs and Technology for a ministerial authorization under paragraph 42 Gesetz gegen Wettbewerbsbeschränkungen in der Fassung der Bekanntmachung (GWB):[337] the expected authorization was granted on 5 July 2002, but the Ministry's decision placed a series of obligations on E.ON/Ruhrgas, specifically, a number of sales of shareholdings, including minority shareholdings, in vertically related undertakings, such as the divestiture of E.ON's 27.4 per cent stake in EWE AG, E.ON's 80.5 per cent stake in Gelsenwasser AG, E.ON's 22 per cent capital interest/24.1 per cent voting rights in swb AG, and E.ON's 22 per cent stake in Bayerngas GmbH. In addition, 'E.ON was obliged to ensure that Ruhrgas would effectuate legal unbundling of its gas transmission network by 1 January 2004 and put in place a gas release program of a volume of 75 billion kWh.'[338]

The Bundeskartellamt in 2002 cleared with remedies the creation of the joint venture Stadtwerke Eberswalde GmbH.[339] In particular, EWE AG and E.DIS AG (a subsidiary of E.ON), which each held 22.5 per cent of the issued capital of Stadtwerke Eberswalde

[329] Above n 151, para 46.
[330] See Activity Report 2007/2008 of the Bundeskartellamt.
[331] Above n 329, para 47.
[332] B8-109/01 *E.ON/Gelsenberg*.
[333] B8-149/01 *E.ON/Bergemann*.
[334] Above n 331, para 62.
[335] In February 2002.
[336] Above n 334, para 63.
[337] The German Competition Act.
[338] Above n 336, para 64.
[339] Above n 337, paras 58–61.

GmbH, increased their participation to 37.5 per cent each and therefore together held 75 per cent of the firm along with the ability jointly to control it. Both firms had the majority of the votes in the board of the directors and as a consequence joint approval of the supply contracts of the joint venture.

The gas supplier EWE AG, the electricity supplier E.DIS AG (a subsidiary of E.ON), the City of Eberswalde and Stadtwerke Remscheid GmbH constituted the four significant shareholders of Stadtwerke Eberswalde GmbH. EWE AG was Stadtwerke Eberswalde GmbH's gas supplier, holding 22.5 per cent, E.DIS AG was Stadtwerke Eberswalde GmbH's electricity supplier with the same shareholding, the City of Eberswalde held 51 per cent and Stadtwerke Remscheid GmbH 4 per cent. According to the new scheme proposed, EWE and E.DIS would increase their shareholding to 37 per cent each, Stadtwerke Remscheid GmbH would exit the scheme as shareholder, and the City of Eberswalde would retain a reduced stake of 26 per cent. Furthermore, as a result of the new shareholder structure EWE and E.DIS would have also had six out eight representatives on the board. The Bundeskartellamt had to decide on the above-mentioned proposed shareholding structure.

Under the new system, EWE and E.DIS would have been in a position jointly to approve the supply contracts, since they would have jointly had the majority on the board. In addition, since the conclusion of supply contracts would have been subject to the approval by the board on the basis of a simple majority vote, the two main shareholders, ie EWE and E.DIS, would have been in a position jointly to approve these contracts. The same result also concerned a number of other decisions. Hence, the acquisition of a further 14.5 per cent stake each would have increased EWE's and E.DIS's de jure and de facto influence on Stadtwerke Eberswalde, notably with regard to its commercial decisions, mainly concerning purchasing.

As far as it concerned the wholesale market for electricity, it was accepted that the transaction would probably have little reinforcing effect on the collective dominance by E.ON (which controlled E.DIS) and RWE. Nevertheless, the Bundeskartellamt stated that in cases where a high level of concentration already exists, competition needs to be protected against further restrictions, even by way of small reinforcing effects, which simply means that in these cases even small reinforcing effects could be extremely harmful.

The Bundeskartellamt considered that a high degree of concentration already existed in the electricity market and competition had to be protected from further transactions that might restrict it. EWE and E.DIS offered remedies limiting their respective influence on the appointment of Stadtwerke Eberswalde's management as well as the conclusion of energy supply contracts. These remedies were considered sufficient to prevent a reinforcement of the existing collective dominant position and the Bundeskartellamt cleared the transaction.

In the *Springer/Stilke* case in 2000[340] Axel Springer Verlag (ASV) had the intention of acquiring a 24 per cent participation combined with extensive information rights in the Hamburg newsagent Stilke; Stilke was the owner of numerous bookshops located in train stations. Valora, an undertaking active in the Swiss kiosk business, intended to acquire the remaining 76 per cent of Stilke. The Bundeskartellamt found that the transaction, if permitted, would result in a competitively significant influence by ASV over Stilke and therefore prohibited the acquisition of the 24 per cent stake by ASV in Stilke.

[340] See BGH, judgment of 21 November 2000, KVR 16/99.

The Bundeskartellamt's finding was confirmed by the Bundesgerichtshof (Federal Court of Justice): the transaction, if permitted, would have reinforced the already existing dominant position of ASV in the Hamburg newspaper and newspaper advertisements markets. It should be underlined that, according to the Bundesgerichtshof, newspaper publishers were currently not involved in the press retail business, guaranteeing a certain neutrality of the retail side towards publishers. The existence of this characteristic of the specific market ought to be continued. Hence, in light of this, the Court emphasized that the entry of ASV into the press retail level, if it took place, it would have changed competitive conditions to the disadvantage of ASV's competitors.

In the *A-Tec Industries/Norddeutsche Affinlerie* case[341] A-Tec acquired a 13.75 per cent minority shareholding of the issued capital of Norddeutsche Affinerie. Norddeutsche Affinerie was a copper producer, and this share purchase granted A-Tec a competitively significant influence over Norddeutsche Affinierie; the Bundeskartellamt ordered the dissolution of the merger. The relevant analysis of the Bundeskartellamt is extremely interesting: taking into account the generally low presence at Norddeutsche Affinierie's shareholders meetings, A-Tec's 13.75 per cent share, if permitted, would have granted it a de facto blocking minority under corporate law 'comparable with the legal position granted by an acquisition of a 25 percent stake'.[342] Furthermore, no other shareholder had any strategic long-term objectives directed at the competitive behaviour of Norddeutsche Affinierie. On the contrary, A-Tec was active by itself in all of Norddeutsche Affinierie's essential business sections, and it was the only other participant there.

In particular, the Bundeskartellamt concluded that this share acquisition would give the acquirer the ability to exert a competitively significant influence over the target firm. The decision was based on the following facts:

- A-Tec's minority shareholding was de facto able to block major decisions of Norddeutsche's shareholder meetings.
- A-Tec had an interest of the competitive behaviour of Norddeutsche.

Since A-Tec and Norddeutsche Affinierie were the largest competitors in the manufacture and distribution of oxygen-free copper billets in the EEA with a combined market share of well over 85 per cent, the Bundeskartellamt prohibited the concentration on the grounds that it would have led to the creation of a dominant position in the market for oxygen-free copper billets.[343] As a consequence the two firms involved in the concentration would have the ability to coordinate their behaviour. Before the merger, buyers of oxygen-free copper billets were able to choose between two equal suppliers, active competitors, independent of one another. Should the merger proceed, the Bundeskartellamt expected the two parties to coordinate their behaviour in the marketplace, with the most probable result being that customers would have no real alternative suppliers.

341 B5-198/07 *A-Tec Industries AG/Norddeutsche Affinerie AG.*

342 Above n 339, para 49.

343 At the time of the decision the Bundeskartellamt followed the dominance test (DT) as the substantive test and not the SIEC test for the appraisal of concentrations. Dominance was viewed as a necessary but not sufficient condition. For more details of both tests, see also P Fotis, 'Merger Enforcement: Law and Statistical Evidence Worldwide' (2013) 5(3) *International Journal of Economics and Business Research* 272, 275–76 and L-H Roller and M De la Mano, 'The Impact of the New Substantive Test in European Merger Control' (2006) 2(1) *European Competition Journal* 9, 12.

In addition, A-Tec was a minority shareholder with knowledge of Norddeutsche's business and markets and given the fact that the interests of the other shareholders of Norddeutsche were not directly affected A-Tec and Norddeutsche's interests, this reinforced A-Tec's incentive to influence further the decision process of its competitor.[344]

In case B6-27/04 Bonner Zeitungsdruckerei/DuMont Schauberg the Bundeskartellamt prohibited the acquisition of 18.03 per cent of the shares in Bonner Zeitungsdruckerei by DuMont Schauberg on the grounds that this minority shareholding would reinforce the dominant position of Bonner Zeitungsdruckerei in the regional reader (market of daily newspaper in neighbouring Bonn) and advertising markets.[345]

The decision of the Bundeskartellamt was not altered even when the concerned parties reduced the minority shareholding from 18.03 to 9.015 per cent. However, the Court of Appeal annulled the authority's prohibition decision since it considered that a competitively significant influence did not result from a 9.015 per cent minority shareholding.

The Bundeskartellamt also prohibited the acquisition of a 17.5 per cent minority shareholding of the issued capital of Aschaffenburger by Mainova.[346] Both firms were active in the gas sector. Mainova was a supplier and Aschaffenburger (previously wholly municipally owned) was a retailer of gas. Therefore, the acquirer was active in the upstream market and the acquired firm was active in the downstream market of gas in Germany.

The Bundeskartellamt found that this planned acquisition, if allowed, would have led on the one hand to vertical foreclosure of upstream suppliers (as it concerned customer foreclosure), and on the other hand to restriction of potential competition in the regional and local gas supply markets. Simultaneously, E.ON, a wholesale supplier of a much larger scale than the parties, already indirectly held a 24.4 per cent stake in Mainova. Because of this significant stake held by E.ON in Mainova, the vertical foreclosure effects would be further reinforced through the risk of favouring supply through the E.ON group, causing harm to other suppliers.

The minority participation, if permitted, would have given de facto influence, reinforcing Mainova's existing supplier position towards AVG and increasing its chances of agreeing the signing of new supply contracts with AVG. Potential upstream competitors of Mainova would have been discouraged by AVG's incentives to give Mainova a privileged supplier position; more specifically, Mainova would have an information advantage and a possibility to compensate losses (by charging lower prices to AVG) through participation in AVG's profits. The moderate level of the shareholding at 17.5 per cent was not sufficient to alter this finding, since Mainova had a superior knowledge of the energy sector, taking into account that AVG's majority shareholder, the City of Aschaffenburg, lacked any sector-specific know-how. AVG had already a dominant position in the local retail gas market which would be further reinforced due to the link with Mainova, because of which Mainova's incentive to enter downstream would be reduced. Hence, in the absence of appropriate remedies, the notified transaction was finally prohibited.

The Bundeskartellamt prohibited the concentration on the grounds that, were it to be cleared, it would have led to foreclosure issues. In particular, the competition authority

[344] See OLG Düsseldorf, Decision of November 12, 2008, VI-Kart 5/08 (V), *A-TEC/Norddeutsche Affinerie*. See also Federal Court (BGH), Decision of December 21, 2004, KVR 26/03, *Deutsche Post/trans-o-flex*, WuW/E DE-R 1419.

[345] Above n 342, para 54.

[346] B8-27/04 *Mainova AG/Aschaffenburger Versorgungs AG.*

considered that the minority shareholding could have resulted in the vertical foreclosure of other gas suppliers from the upstream market.

In the *Avacon/Energiewerke Isernhagen* case the Bundeskartellamt allowed the acquisition of a minority shareholding by an E.ON[347] subsidiary in Energiewerke Isernhagen.[348] The competition authority approved the concentration on the grounds that the acquisition of a minority shareholding in downstream municipal providers was a practice employed by several energy providers in the past.[349]

However, a few months earlier the Bundeskartellamt had prohibited the acquisition of a 33 per cent minority shareholding by E.ON in another downstream municipal utility, Stadtwerke Eschwege. 'On November 11, 2008, the German Supreme Court confirmed [the] decision adopted by the German competition authority.'[350]

The German Supreme Court investigated the possible collective dominance of the two leading players in the German energy market, ie E.ON and RWE, and considered that 'the other two German providers, Vattenfall and EnBW,[351] do not effectively constrain E.ON and RWE'. The Court further considered, inter alia, the level of transparency in the market and whether there existed a mechanism of deterrence/retaliation. Other criteria also considered by the Court were the following:

- symmetry of the parties with regard to their respective product portfolios, employed technologies and cost structures;
- potential entry barriers;
- buyer power of customers;
- demand side price elasticity;
- constraints on product and quality competition due to product homogeneity;
- existing links between oligopoly members; and
- the rate of customers switching between oligopoly members.[352]

Given the investigation of the above-mentioned factors the German Supreme Court considered that:

> [I]f E.ON were to acquire the minority interest in one of its customers, the Stadtwerke Eschwege, E.ON's and RWE's joint dominant position would be strengthened. In this context, the Court also found that both market leaders had pursued a strategy of acquiring minority interests in municipal utilities and other energy providers to secure their customer bases; E.ON and RWE hold shareholdings in excess of 10 per cent in 204 out of 900 German utility providers (E.ON: 134, RWE: 70).[353]

As mentioned earlier, the representation of a minority shareholder in the management and supervisory bodies of the 'victim' firm may be considered as a right that enables this shareholder to influence competitively in a significant manner the decision process of the target firm. On the one hand, the Bundeskartellamt decided that when a minority shareholder has the right to be represented on the management board of the competitor, then this, almost

[347] E.ON was the largest energy provider in Germany at the time of the decision.

[348] B8-46/09 *E.ON Avacon/Energiewerke Isernhagen*.

[349] See also T Gaspary, 'German Supreme Court Confirms Prohibition of Minority Investment (E.ON/Stadtwerke Eschwege)' (2009) 6 *European Competition Law Review* 307, 308.

[350] Ibid, 307.

[351] Energie Baden Württemberg AG.

[352] Above n 350.

[353] Ibid.

per se, enables it to exert significant competitive influence on the target firm.[354] On the other hand, the competition authority also considered that when a minority shareholder has the right to be represented on the supervisory board of the competitor, then this may not per se enable it to exert significant competitive influence on the target firm.[355] In the latter case the examination of other factors such as 'the actual specific powers of the supervisory board (notably the board's approval rights with respect to decisions impacting the competitive behavior of the company), and the composition of the remaining members'[356] play a crucial role in determining what influence the minority shareholder may exert on the target firm.

On 6 July 2009 the Bundeskartellamt cleared, subject to conditions, the plans by Energie Baden Württemberg AG to acquire a 26 per cent minority shareholding in EWE Aktiengesellschaft.[357] The competition authority considered that in the electricity sector '[Energie Baden Württemberg AG did] not satisfy the necessary criteria recently confirmed by the Federal Court of Justice in its decision on the municipal utility "Stadtwerke Eschwege" (B8-21/03)'. That is,

> [T]he Bundeskartellamt's investigations did not produce any evidence which would indicate that EnBW, together with E.ON and RWE, is a member of a dominant oligopoly in the domestic markets for the first-time sale of electricity and its supply to industrial customers.[358]

On the contrary, in the gas sector

> the concentration would have led to a strengthening of dominant positions held by associated companies of [Energie Baden Württemberg AG] and [EWE Aktiengesellschaft] in eastern Germany. ... The merger was also expected to strengthen the dominant positions of [ENSO Energie Sachsen Ost AG] and [DREWAG Stadtwerke Dresden GmbH] in the supply of distributors and end consumers in their regional and local gas markets, as any potential competition provided by [Verbundnetz Gas AG] in these markets would have been weakened.[359]

The Bundeskartellamt considered that:

> In order to prevent a prohibition of the concentration, [EWE Aktiengesellschaft] and [Energie Baden Württemberg AG] have agreed to either divest [EWE Aktiengesellschaft]'s participation in [Verbundnetz Gas AG] or sell [Energie Baden Württemberg AG]'s associated company GESO within a certain period of time.[360] Both divestitures are of equal competitive value because they both prevent a strengthening of the dominant positions of [Verbundnetz Gas AG], [ENSO Energie Sachsen Ost AG] and [DREWAG Stadtwerke Dresden GmbH] in the relevant gas markets as a consequence of the planned merger.[361]

On 19 May 2009 the Bundeskartellamt announced its decision that:

> RheinEnergie AG ... [has] abandoned its plans to acquire a 41.53 percent stake in the utility Stadtwerke Bonn Beteiligungs-GmbH from BRS Beteiligungsgesellschaft Bonn/Rhein-Sieg

354 See, inter alia, B8-263/00 *Fair Energie*, WuW/E DE-V 460; B8-279/00 *Easyplus*, WuW/E DE-V 467.

355 See, inter alia, B6-159/01 *Radio L12*, WuW/E DE-V 599; Federal Court (BGH), Decision of December 21, 2004; KVR 26/03 *Deutsche Post/trans-o-flex*, WuW/E DE-R 1419; OLG Düsseldorf, Decision of November 12, 2008, VI-Kart 5/08 (V) *A-TEC/Norddeutsche Affinerie.*

356 See also Barthelmess (n 321) 13.

357 B8-96/08 *EnBW/EWE.*

358 Ibid, 1.

359 Ibid, 2.

360 See Bundeskartellamt's decision on 26 February 2010 [B8—23/10 EnBW/CESO].

361 Ibid.

> mbH. … Based on the results of its investigations, the Bundeskartellamt concluded that the concentration project would have created a dominant position on the local public passenger services market.[362]

On 31 January 2012 the Bundeskartellamt cleared the acquisition of a minority shareholding in VNG Verbundnetz Gas AG by Gazprom Germania GmbH.[363] In particular, the acquirer increased its minority shareholding in the target firm from 8.64 to 10.52 per cent and at the same time obtained the right to have one seat on the supervisory board of it. After the clearance of the concentration Gazprom Germania GmbH and Wintershall (a member of BASF SE) jointly exercised competitively significant influence over VNG Verbundnetz Gas.

The competition authority considered that the concentration would not strengthen or create a single and joint dominant position of Gazprom Germania GmbH in the market for the development, production and sale of mineral gas and the markets for 'the supply of regional distributors by long-distance wholesale transmission companies, the supply of load profile end consumers by long-distance wholesale transmission companies and … also underground gas storage facilities'.[364]

On 3 April 2013 the Bundeskartellamt announced its intention to terminate divesture proceedings for the non-notified mergers between Barmherzige Brüder Trier eV, Waldbreitbacher Franziskanerinnen and Marienhaus.

Notably, '[t]he divestiture proceedings focused in particular on the markets for in-patient hospital treatment in the Trier region and in northern Saarland'. In July 2003 Waldbreitbacher Franziskanerinnen acquired 38 per cent of the voting rights, ie 5 out of 13 votes in the general assembly of cari-tas trägergesellschaft eV. In July 2006 the same firm gained sole control over the same target firm, while in 2008 Marienhaus and Barmherzige Brüder Trier eV jointly established the Hildegard Foundation, and the latter indirectly exercised competitively significant influence over cari-tas trägergesellschaft eV.

After the initiation of divesture proceedings by the Bundeskartellamt the concerned firms in the non-notified concentrations began to divest certain minority shareholdings and interlocking directorships in order to remove the competitive concerns raised by the competition authority.[365]

iii. Austria

Between 1 July 2000 and 30 June 2001 11.46 per cent of all concentrations notified to the Bundeswettbewerbsbehörde (the Austrian competition authority) concerned acquisitions of minority shareholdings (29 out of 253 cases).[366] Furthermore, in 2011 15.04 per cent of all concentrations (226 cases) notified to the Austrian competition authority concerned acquisitions of minority shareholdings (34 cases below 50 per cent of the issued capital of the acquired firm).[367]

[362] B9-202/08 *RheinEnergie/Stadtwerke*.

[363] B8-116/11 *Gazprom/VNG*.

[364] Ibid, 2. In July 2012 the Düsseldorf Higher Regional Court validated the Bundeskartellamt's decision since it withdrew the appeals against the decision by two third parties.

[365] See also the case *Springer/Stilke* (2000) and the BGH judgment of 21 November 2000, KVR 16/99.

[366] See OECD Annual Report on Competition Policy Austria (2000–01) 1, 6 (http://www.oecd.org/austria/39553596.pdf).

[367] Above n 338, para 68.

In 1998 the joint committee on cartel matters investigated the acquisition of a 26 per cent minority shareholding in Michelfeit Einrichtungshaus AG by Kika-Leiner after an application for review by the Federal Chamber of Labour.[368] After a thorough examination of the acquisition the joint committee decided to clear the acquisition subject to commitments, and finally, the cartel court decided not to prohibit it.

In August 2004 the cartel court cleared the creation of a joint venture, Morawa Grosso, between Morawa Pressevertrieb GmbH and Mediaprint Zeitungs- und Zeitschriftenverlag GmbH & Co KG.[369] Morawa Pressevertrieb GmbH held 75.1 per cent and Mediaprint Zeitungs- und Zeitschriftenverlag GmbH & Co KG held 24.9 per cent of the issued capital of the joint venture. The clearance was subject to certain 'Chinese walls':[370] Mediaprint reduced its influence on the joint venture by not participating in the operation of it and by not obtaining access to critical data and information offered by the joint venture to its customers and to competitors of Mediaprint.

In February 2011 Mediaprint notified a 30 per cent acquisition of the issued capital of Niederösterreichische Gratismedien, 'a company publishing a free newspaper in the region of Lower Austria'.[371] By this notification Niederösterreichische Gratismedien would have been jointly controlled by Mediaprint and Niederösterreichisches Pressehaus. However, a shareholder of Mediaprint already owned 20 per cent of the joint venture.

The main concern with this vertical concentration was, inter alia, reduced pluralism in the media sector. That is, Mediaprint, by acquiring a minority shareholding in the joint venture, would be able to influence further the joint venture's commercial policy and to restrict its independence in the media sector. In the light of an in-depth examination of the notified concentration (phase II examination of the concentration) by the cartel court, it was withdrawn by the firms involved.

In 2011 a proposed acquisition of a 25 per cent minority shareholding in Vossloh AG, a rail vehicle manufacturer, by Mr Heinz Hermann Thiele (conglomerate merger) took place.[372] The Austrian competition authority cleared the concentration without referring it to the Commission.[373]

[368] See OECD Annual Report on Competition Policy Austria (1998–99) 1, 6 (http://www.oecd.org/austria/2408907.pdf).

[369] See OECD Annual Report on Competition Policy Developments in Austria (2003–04) 1, 14 (http://www.oecd.org/austria/34720199.pdf).

[370] Chinese walls may have eliminated concerns regarding an exchange of information among competitors. See especially I Lianos and D Geradin, 'Handbook of European Competition Law' (2013) 1, 162 and footnotes therein.

[371] See OECD Annual Report on Competition Policy Developments in Austria (2010) 1, 14 (http://www.oecd.org/officialdocuments/publicdisplaydocumentpdf/?cote=DAF/COMP/AR(2011)23&docLanguage=En).

[372] Above n 367, para 68.

[373] In August 2012 the acquisition of a 24.9 per cent minority shareholding by Gewista in Ankünder (advertising sector) was considered to be part of the notified concentration among Ankünder GmbH and three subsidiaries of Gewista-Werbegesellschaft mbH, even though as a standalone transaction would have not fulfilled the turnover thresholds. See also OECD Annual Report on Competition Policy Developments in Austria (2010) 1, 13–14 (http://www.oecd.org/officialdocuments/publicdisplaydocumentpdf/?cote=DAF/COMP/AR(2013)26&docLanguage=En). Concerning the turnover thresholds in Austria, see ch 3, section I.B.iii above.

iv. Lithuania

In 2003 Rokiškio sūris acquired a 35.3 per cent minority shareholding in Panevėžio pienas. A major shareholder of the target firm was Pieno žvaigždės, which owned 50.2 per cent of its shares and votes. At the time of notification both firms were active in the dairy sector.[374]

The competition authority considered that the acquisition of the minority shareholding would enable the acquiring firm to control the general meeting of shareholders of the target firm by exercising its veto rights. Given the control of the general meeting of shareholders of the target firm and other issues that emerged from the analysis of the proposed transaction, the competition authority concluded that Panevėžio pienas was jointly controlled by its major shareholders. The authority decided to allow the concentration subject to certain commitments.[375]

In 2012 two notified transactions were withdrawn after a preliminary investigation by the competition authority. The notified minority shareholdings were 45 and 49 per cent of the issued capital of the target firms.[376] The competition authority in Lithuania considered that the degree of competition in the markets concerned would have been reduced if the mergers were implemented.

In 2013 the Competition Council terminated a non-notified merger in the banking sector.[377] The Council concluded that the implementation of a credit agreement between Swedbank, AB Alita and the Company Group Alita AB enabled Swedbank to control the risk of the target firms, but not to gain control of them.

v. Further Evidence

The Netherlands Competition Authority (NMa) investigated in 2004 the existence of direct interlocking directorships in several major sectors of the Dutch economy, such as the financial sector, the construction sector and the energy sector, and direct interlocking directorships between firms listed on the Amsterdam stock exchange (AEX).[378] The results from the NMa's investigation are the following:

(a) A direct interlocking directorship, ie when two firms share the same director, is relatively uncommon.
(b) The construction sector had been heavily fined by the NMa 'without the need to go explicitly into the subject of interlocking directorates'.[379]
(c) 'The relatively high number of interlocks at the level of AEX firms is in itself neither surprising nor alarming, since most of the firms are not competing in the same relevant market'.[380]

[374] See OECD, *Antitrust Issues Involving Minority Shareholdings and Interlocking Directorates* (2008), DAF/COMP(2008)30, 1, 211.

[375] Ibid, 213.

[376] See OECD Annual Report on Competition Policy Developments in Lithuania (2012) 1, 11 (http://www.oecd.org/officialdocuments/publicdisplaydocumentpdf/?cote=DAF/COMP/AR(2013)12&docLanguage=En) and Competition Council of the Republic of Ireland Annual Report (2012) 1, 13 (http://kt.gov.lt/en/index.php?show=annual.

[377] See Competition Council of the Republic of Lithuania Annual Report (2013) 7 (http://kt.gov.lt/en/annual/2013_eng.pdf).

[378] Above n 374, 143.

[379] Ibid, 144.

[380] Ibid.

Given the above-mentioned facts the NMa considered that it 'did not find reason to act only on the basis of the above figures[381]'.[382]

A study in 2006 in Norway[383] by the Institute for Research in Economics and Business Administration (SNF)[384] indicated, based on standard concentration indices, that the Norwegian electricity market was concentrated. The study, inter alia, analysed the effects of passive minority shareholdings among electricity producers on the level of concentration in the electricity market in Norway. The existence of passive minority shareholdings in the Norwegian electricity market was complex and constituted direct, indirect and cross minority shareholdings.[385]

In particular, the study examined the market shares of electricity producers and how their capacity was affected by passive minority shareholdings. The results showed that both the market shares of the firms and the Herfindahl–Hirschman index (*HHI*)[386] of the electricity market was almost doubled by the inclusion of passive minority shareholdings in the analysis.[387]

Furthermore, the study also examined the hypothesis that the level of capacity controlled by a producer is in proportion to its voting power with other companies/producers. The results indicated that the *HHI* increased with respect to its corresponding level when only corrected for passive minority shareholdings.[388]

The Norwegian Competition Authority, following section 16(2) of the Competition Act in Norway, has intervened in the electricity market in order to examine the ownership structure among electricity producers. In 2002 the authority prohibited the acquisition of approximately 46 per cent of the shares of Agder Energi by Statkraft, the major Norwegian electricity producer, which had direct or indirect minority shareholdings in a great number of other electricity producers. The authority considered that the partial acquisition under scrutiny, along with various agreements between the firms concerned, would enable Statkraft to gain significant influence and to coordinate its actions with these of Agder Energi.[389]

In 2003 the Norwegian Competition Authority ordered the Statkraft group of companies, Agder Energi, Skagerak Energi and BKK, to notify all acquisitions of power plants and minority shareholdings of at least 20 per cent in southern, mid and northern Norway. The order of the Norwegian Competition Authority expired in 2007. Given the nature of the notifications it received, the authority considered that the electricity market was

381 That is, the figures as above in Table 1 regarding interlocking directorships.

382 Above n 380.

383 The study was commissioned by the Norwegian Competition Authority.

384 B Singh and F Skjeret, 'Ownership Relations and Cooperation in the Norwegian Power Market' (2006) SNF Report No 35/06, Institute for Research in Economics and Business Administration, available at http://www.konkurransetilsynet.no/iKnowBase/Content/427168/SNF-06-35_KRYSSEIE_KRAFT.PDF.

385 Ibid, 6 (figure 2). See the passive minority shareholdings of one of the major electricity producers Statkraft.

386 See section II.A in ch 4 above.

387 The same result holds with the price–cost margin of the firms engaged in acquisitions of minority shareholdings. See the article by D Flath, 'Indirect Shareholding within Japan's Business Groups' (1992) 38 *Economics Letters* (section II.A in ch 4 above).

388 The study also examined cooperative issues among the electricity producers. Above n 385, 31–40.

389 The decision was appealed by the concerned firms and the Ministry of Labour and Government Administration in October 2002 cleared the partial acquisition subject to commitments. Based on the latter, Statkraft was required to sell its 20 per cent minority shareholding and had to resign from the board of directors in E-CO Vannkraft AS.

characterised by high ownership concentration. Therefore, it decided in 2008 to order Statkraft, Agder Energi, Skagerak Energi and BKK to notify all their concentrations as well as minority shareholdings below 20 per cent of the issued capital of the acquired firm. Also, in 2003 the Ministry of Labour and Government Administration upheld the authority's intervention concerning the prohibition of the 100 per cent acquisition of the shares in Trondheim Energiverk by Statkraft.

In chapter 3, section I.B.v(a) we note that the merger control regime in Italy does not take into account minority interests. 'Therefore in merger cases the problem of minority shareholding and interlocking directorates can only be addressed in the context of remedies, so as to impede a dominant position to be created or strengthened.'[390]

However, Law Decree 6/2011 deals with interlocking directorships in the financial sector. The reason for this is the existence of a great number of passive minority interests, both minority shareholdings and interlocking directorships, especially in the banking sector. The Italian Competition Authority has addressed antitrust issues regarding minority shareholdings through its investigation of a great number of concentrations in the banking sector.[391]

Furthermore, the ownership and control of Italian listed companies has changed during the period 1990–2005.[392] In particular, the largest shareholder among all listed companies has decreased on average from 55 per cent in 1990 to 45 per cent in 2005, while the largest shareholder in relation to the size of the company has also decreased from 48 per cent in 1990 to 29 per cent in 2005.[393] At the same time the percentage of minor shareholders (less than 2 per cent of equity) increased from 28 to 38 per cent.

The largest shareholder among private non-financial listed companies has decreased on average from 52 per cent in 1990 to 46 per cent in 2005. At the same time the percentage of minor shareholders increased from 29.4 to 35.6 per cent. Lastly, the largest shareholder among listed companies in the banking sector has decreased on average from 64.7 per cent in 1990 to 31.9 per cent in 2005, while the percentage of minor shareholders increased from 23.9 to 49.6 per cent. It is notable that during the same period companies were generally controlled by coalitions, either through agreements or formal coalitions. Informal coalitions, ie coalitions in which 'the three largest shareholders together owned more than 20 per cent of equity,[394] have also played a significant role in the evolution of the ownership structure.

It is also quite interesting to note the number of directors who sit on one or more boards. Statistics show that in 2006 there were 327 such directors, 'though not all of them can be considered as interlocking directorates because these firms do not operate in the same markets and thus they cannot be considered as truly competitors'.[395]

Recently the ownership structure of Telecom Italia has become of great importance.[396] In September 2013 the Spanish telecoms company Telefonica increased its share in the Italian

[390] Above n 374, 125.

[391] Ibid. For instance see the concentrations of Banca Intesa and Sanpaolo IMI, BPU and Banca Lombarda and Piemontese (UBI), Unicredit and Capitalia.

[392] See OECD, *Related Party Transactions and Minority Shareholder Rights* (2012) 1, 108.

[393] That is, the larger the company the lower the percentage.

[394] See also M Bianchi and M Bianco, 'Italian Corporate Governance in the Last 15 Years: From Pyramids to Coalitions?' (2006) ECGI Finance Working Paper No 144/2006.

[395] Above n 390, 126.

[396] See M Scott, 'Battle for Control of Telecom Italia Heats Up', *New York Times*, 19 December 2013, available at http://www.nytimes.com/2013/12/20/business/international/battle-for-control-of-telecom-italia-heats-up.html?_r=0.

telecommunications company Telco (to 46 per cent) and owned an option to acquire a controlling share of the issued capital of the holding company. The latter owned a 22.4 per cent minority shareholding in Telecom Italia, while the second largest shareholder was BlackRock, which owned a 10 per cent minority shareholding but only a 5.9 per cent voting share. The minority shareholders of Telecom Italia, such as Findim, considered that the scope of Telco and eventually Telefonica's strategic movement was to sell Telecom Italia's operations in Brazil (TIM Participações), a direct competitor to Telefonica, in order to reduce its debt and increase its credit rating.

Furthermore, the antitrust authorities in Brazil considered that Telefonica should reduce its market share in the Brazilian cellphone market. Telefonica, as well as its minority shareholding in TIM Participações, also controlled the Brazilian direct competitor Vivo.

Until 2008 the Czech Competition Authority 'ha[d] not dealt with any case in which acquisition of minority share[holding]s was being investigated as a prohibited agreement or as abuse of dominant position'.[397] Even though Czech Competition Law[398] did not contain any provisions regarding interlocking directorships, the Competition Authority had dealt with these in several merger cases.

In particular, in 2002 under a privatisation scheme, ČEZ company, a dominant producer of electrical energy, acquired five companies (STE, VČE, SČE, ZČE and SME) and at the same time it was to acquire a minority shareholding of 35 per cent in other three companies (JME, JČE and PZE). The consolidation was approved with certain commitments given the fact that it could distort the markets of power production and distribution in Czech Republic. The commitments were the following:

- The first condition was the sale of 34 percent minority share owned by the ČEZ company in the ČEPS company (monopoly operator of the distribution network) prior to the realization of this transaction, for the purpose of a complete separation of the power distribution network and the dominant producer of electricity.
- The second condition was the sale of the minority share owned by the ČEZ company in the three distribution companies (JME, JČE and PZE), for the purpose of assurance of full independence of other market players—who are ČEZ's competitors.
- The last condition was the sale of one of the five distribution companies to a third legal entity, this was to serve as a minimal structural measure that would prevent the creation of a strong and dominant merged undertaking and that was to provide the strengthening of competitive environment and to increase the possibilities of market success to independent producers and providers of electrical energy.[399]

In 2002 the Competition Authority also approved with conditions 'the merger of RWE GAS AG (RWE) with the Transgas company and with eight gas distribution companies'.[400] The commitments were focused on two main issues: firstly, the Commission was aware of the risk that RWE GAS AG (RWE) would take control over over the two main distribution companies for gas, heat and electric energy, while it was also aware about potentially coordinated effects among firms taking part in the merger.

[397] Above n 392, 106.
[398] Act on the Protection of Competition.
[399] Above n 395, 107–08. During the privatization of Izmir port in western Turkey the competition authority examined the minority shareholdings possessed by the acquiring firm and eventually decided to block it. Above n 388, 160.
[400] Ibid, 108.

In November 2007 the competition authority approved subject to commitments the merger between Telefonica and Deltax Systems:

> Th[e] commitment was related to the assurance of the withdrawal of the DELTAX company from the participation on the realization of public contract—the Information system for the administration of interactive forms (IS ASDM) for the Czech Telecommunication Office (ČTÚ).[401]

In Sweden competition law makes no reference to passive minority interests. However, in the past decade the Swedish competition authority intervened in the nuclear power industry (electricity market) in order to investigate alleged infringements of the Competition Act (CA).

In particular, in 2007 the competition authority considered taking action against anticompetitive cooperation among the major energy firms over their joint management of Swedish nuclear power firms. In addition, the competition authority was sceptical about the importance of minority shareholdings among the energy companies. Even though the authority did not take a decision against the energy firms, it informed the minister responsible for the energy sector in Sweden.

Concerning interlocking directorships, in 2000 the competition authority surveyed nine sectors of the Swedish economy and concluded that such directorships occurred in five of these nine sectors and only 16 per cent of them were related to control.

In addition, the authority examined minority shareholdings under section 5 CA, which prohibits the abuse of a dominant position. However, for share acquisitions performed in the open market, it would be difficult to apply section 5 CA.[402]

Until 2002 the competition authority in Ireland had dealt with a great number of minority shareholdings among non-competitors.[403] In 1994 it investigated an acquisition of a minority shareholding between two major firms in the press industry under section 5 of the Competition Act. It was considered by the authority that the minority shareholding was of sufficient size to enable the acquiring firm to influence the commercial behaviour of the acquired firm.[404]

In Turkey minority shareholdings have been mainly examined under Articles 4 and 5 of the Competition Act (CA).[405] They have also been examined under the merger control regime (Act No 4054 on the Protection of Competition & Communiqué No 1997/1). During the privatization of Izmir port in western Turkey the competition authority examined the minority shareholdings possessed by the acquiring firm and eventually decided to block the transaction.[406]

The Romanian Competition Council (RCC) has dealt with pre-existing minority shareholdings in several cases. For instance, during the examination of a case in the oil market the RCC considered the effects of a minority shareholding of the acquiring firm in a third independent firm in two affected markets. In order to obtain a clearance for the notified

[401] Ibid, 109.

[402] Ibid, 155–57.

[403] Up until this date minority shareholdings were possibly viewed as practices which violated section 4 (concerning anticompetitive agreements) and section 5 (concerning anticompetitive abuse of dominant position) of the Competition Act in Ireland. Given the fact that up until 2002 a notification system for agreements existed in Ireland, the Irish Competition Authority made a large number of decisions on share purchases. Ibid, 119.

[404] Ibid.

[405] See, for instance, the cases *Nevşehirliler Turizm* (28.9.2006; 06-67/909-263), *Aerated Cartel* (30.5.2006; 06-37/477-129), *Ulusoy and UN Ro-Ro* (13.7.2005 05-46/668-170). Ibid, 162.

[406] See the case *Privatization of İzmir Port* (20.6.2007; 07-53/615-204).

transaction the acquiring firm undertook to divest its minority shareholding, which was considered by the RCC to be an adequate commitment.[407]

vi. The Zephyr Database

DG Competition carried out an analysis of certain information contained in the Zephyr Database,[408] including information on transactions resulting in changes of ownership in listed undertakings ('ownership transactions') within the EU for the period between 2005 and 2011. The purpose of this analysis was to have at least a first understanding about the frequency of the creation and changes of structural links in the internal market. In addition, it could offer answers about the question whether certain transactions that are currently not subject to merger control would on a preliminary basis have been deemed worthy of competition scrutiny.[409]

The Zephyr database contains information on the total number, the value and the corresponding participation percentages of ownership transactions in listed companies registered in all 27 (now 28) EU Member States. Furthermore, information is contained on buyer and target companies,[410] resulting to the identification of intra-sector and inter-sector transactions. In this way, the Zephyr database can yield a coarse but conservative approximation of the number of cases of 'structural links that on the one hand are above the turnover thresholds of the Merger Regulation and on the other hand might potentially merit competition scrutiny'.[411]

Only a sub-sample of the EU economy and the relevant structural links are covered by the Zephyr database. The database for the most part covers only listed companies, though transactions between listed and private companies are included. However, transactions between two private companies are not included. Furthermore, the Zephyr database covers only transactions involving both a buyer and target registered in the EU. Consequently, transactions involving, for example, a non-European buyer and a European target are not included in this database. Nevertheless, in the case that a non-EU buyer purchases the stake through its EU-based subsidiary, this transaction is included. In addition, DG Competition analysed only those transactions taking place between 2005 and 2011. For the above-mentioned reasons, the actual number of transactions is certainly underestimated by the dataset and the methodology used. Despite this inadequacy, the analysis applied nevertheless offers a useful initial indication regarding the importance (and the size) of relevant structural links, 'in particular by indicating a *confirmed minimum number of structural links between competitors*'.[412]

— The DG Competition investigated whether an enforcement gap regarding minority shareholdings existed under the current Merger Regulation 139/2004. It used the following criteria in order to identify transactions among the 27 EU countries which

[407] For a case involving coordinated effects, see above n 404, 220–21.

[408] The Zephyr database constitutes an international dataset containing information on data on listed companies' ownership change transactions within the EU.

[409] See para 91 in the annex to the Commission Staff Working Document, 'Towards More Effective EU Merger Control'.

[410] For instance, name, code, nationality, country code, legal status, turnover, sectorial activity are usually included.

[411] Above n 409, para 92.

[412] Ibid, para 93 (emphasis added).

were capable during the years 2005–2011 of being scrutinized under the Merger Regulation.: Annual turnover of the target is at least €10 million.

— Buyer acquires up to 49 per cent of the target.
— Only horizontal transactions (as expressed by the firms' NACE code) which were able to fulfil the turnover thresholds of the Merger Regulation[413] were included in the analysis.
— Purely financial investments (venture capitalists or investment funds), purely risk diversification investments and intra-group transactions were excluded from the analysis.[414]

In particular, due to the information contained in the Zephyr database, DG Competition managed to identify *transactions involving structural links potentially meriting competition scrutiny* based on the following methodology:

— Annual turnover of the target was at least €10 million and the buyer acquired up to 49 per cent of target. Nevertheless, it should be mentioned that this criterion did not determine whether a participation of 49 per cent or less would lead to control within the meaning of the Merger Regulation (eg either in the form of joint control or de facto sole control).
— However, the sample covered only non-reviewed transactions. This means that already reviewed transactions either by DG Competition or by EU national competition authorities were excluded from the sample.
— The buyer and target are active in the same economic sector,[415] ie constituted active or potential competitors. Consequently, non-horizontal transactions, ie vertical or conglomerate transactions, are for the most part excluded from the analysis.
— Venture capitalists or investment funds were also excluded from the sample. Hence, if the buyer and target were not financial investors, *acquisitions of shareholdings considered to be purely risk diversification investments were excluded as well.*
— Since the purpose was to exclude intra-group transactions, only those companies involved in an acquisition which are independent in the sense of the Zephyr database were retained. By this concept were included those companies with known recorded shareholders, in which none of the shareholders had more than a maximum of 25 per cent of direct or total ownership.

Nevertheless, a certain number of proxies had been taken into account, in order to avoid scenarios of de facto control as much as possible. Information accumulated from the database and from companies' annual reports was used in order to establish on a preliminary basis whether the shareholdings examined lead to situations of de facto control.

Lastly, by the addition of another criterion, the sample was reduced to cases that would potentially have an EU dimension under the precondition that structural links were covered by the Merger Regulation:

— The turnover thresholds of the Merger Regulation are possibly fulfilled by the transaction (ie a combined global turnover of at least €2.5 billion and an individual turnover of at least €100 million).

413 A combined global turnover of at least €2.5 billion and an individual turnover of at least €100 million.

414 Also, transactions already reviewed by DG Competition or by EU national competition authorities were excluded from the sample.

415 As expressed by their respective NACE code.

By applying the above-mentioned methodology, DG Competition has tried to identify those transactions that might justify competition scrutiny and simultaneously would meet the turnover thresholds of the Merger Regulation. In particular, this potentially interesting sub-sample constitutes in reality a sub-set of the representative structural links meeting the jurisdictional filters only.

According to the above-mentioned methodology,[416] 91 transactions of varying size and value potentially meriting competition scrutiny were identified by DG Competition. The average value of the transactions was €139 million. Furthermore, the average turnover of the buyer was €7.2 billion and of the target €3.2 billion. The average level of the initial shareholding was 6.9 per cent. However, the average shareholding post-transaction was 14.3 per cent. Generally, final shareholdings vary from 1 to 44.7 per cent. Furthermore, for some industry sectors, 'minority shareholding transactions appear to take place more often than in others'.[417]

It is underlined that 43 of these 91 transactions fulfilled the additional criterion, according to which they were likely to have an EU dimension and fall under the Merger Regulation, under the precondition that this Regulation covers structural links.[418]

These transactions constitute about 5 per cent of all cases decided by the Commission during the same period 2005–2011 under the Merger Regulation following the normal procedure (Table 10).[419] The largest number of transactions concerns primarily the banking sector (ie 14 transactions) and then the gas, water and electricity sectors (7 transactions). Furthermore, taking into account that the dataset and methodology used were designed to underestimate rather than overestimate the real importance of transactions involving structural links, this finding according to DG Competition suggests that 'there is a significant scope of cases with a potential EU dimension that would warrant competition scrutiny but currently fall outside the scope of the Merger Regulation because they do not involve a change of control'.[420]

Table 10: Non-justification of enforcement gap concerning passive minority interests

	27 EU Member States	UK	Germany	Austria
2005–2011	5%			
		5%*		
1990–2010			10%** 0.6%***	
2000–2001				11.46%
2011				15.04%

* Commission Staff Working Document, 'Towards More Effective EU Merger Control', Annex 2, paras 92–105.
** Section 37 (1) No 3(b) ARC.
*** Section 37 (1) No 4 ARC.

[416] Above n 412, para 94.
[417] Ibid, para 97. For instance, the maritime transports services in Greece constitute a sector where minority shareholding transactions appear quite often.
[418] Ibid, para 95.
[419] That is, excluding cases dealt with under the simplified procedure.
[420] Above n 418, para 99.

Among the transactions identified, two indicative examples are further explained below in order to underline the kind of potential competition issues raised by these cases.

(a) *LVMH/Hermès* Case (2010/2011)

Through a series of transactions that took place between 2010 and 2011, LVMH managed to increase its shareholding in Hermès from 14.2 to 22.28 per cent (representing 16 per cent of voting rights); these transactions had a total value €1.6 billion.[421] As a direct consequence of these transactions, a majority holding was created by the Hermès family, controlling 50.2 per cent of the company's shares.

LVMH constituted the world's biggest luxury group with an annual turnover of €20.3 billion in 2010 and net profit of €3.3 billion. Hermès constituted a smaller luxury player with a turnover of €2.4 billion in 2010 and net profit of €421.3 million. LVMH and Hermès were close/active competitors in luxury markets and, given the level of LVMH's shareholding (combined with the small size of Hermès, compared with LVMH), it could not a priori be excluded that the minority shareholding enabled LVMH to influence decisions of Hermès in relation to key competitive parameters or obtain sensitive commercial information.

(b) *Salini Construttori SpA/Impregilo SpA* Case (2011/2012)

Salini Construttori constituted an unlisted Italian construction group that bought through a series of transactions a minority stake in Impregilo. Impregilo constituted Italy's leading engineering and general contracting company in civil construction and was active internationally.[422] In January 2013 Salini's stake amounted to 29.83 per cent of Impregilo's share capital. Impregilo, as Italy's leading constructor, had an annual turnover of €1.1 billion. Simultaneously, Salini Construttori's turnover amounted to €457.5 million.

The rest of Impregilo's shareholding was widely dispersed between a large number of companies, most of which were investment funds and banks. The largest of Impregilo's shareholdings included IGLI SpA[423] (29.96 per cent), Amber Capital LP[424] (7.26 per cent) and UBS AG (2.5 per cent).

Since both Salini and Impregilo operated in the Italian construction sector, they could be actual or potential competitors in the sector of construction tenders and thus a weakening of competition in the specific tenders cannot be a priori excluded, in particular through access to information on the other tenderer's bid.[425] In addition, this potential effect could even be reinforced by the presence (through IGLI) of other competitors in the construction sector acquiring Impregilo share capital. The specific case examined could also constitute a useful case study indicative of a situation where a smaller competitor's stake in a much larger player is able ultimately to change the former's competitive behaviour in such a (cooperative) way, so as to 'ultimately benefit from the larger operator's profits'.[426]

[421] Ibid, para 101.

[422] Ibid, paras 102–05.

[423] IGLI was a holding company owned by the multinational steel, engineering and construction group, Technit. Ibid, para 103.

[424] Amber Capital was an engineering and construction company, part of the Technit Group.

[425] Above n 423, para 104.

[426] Ibid.

Whilst it cannot be stated without specific proof that the above examples would necessarily lead to competition concerns, it is generally accepted that they provide good real-world examples of cases where it would seem justified to scrutinize the impact of the minority shareholding on competition. Even though the number of scrutinized cases involving passive minority interests is not large enough over the period under consideration (Table 10), it should be emphasized here once again that the Zephyr database provides a conservative approximation regarding the number of cases of structural links that are above the turnover thresholds of the Merger Regulation and might potentially merit competition scrutiny.

C. Cases Regarding Minority Shareholdings Around the World

i. Japan

In Japan the acquisitions of shares according to Article 10 of the Antimonopoly Act constitute the majority of cases of notified business combinations. For instance, the years 2010, 2011 and 2012 constituted approximately 70, 81.5 and 81.7 per cent of all notified cases, respectively.[427] However, cases involved minority shareholdings are rare.[428]

In 2000 NTT Communications Corp, a dominant company dealing in private line services using ground networks, proposed an acquisition of shares (18.6 per cent) in JSAT Corp, a satellite communications provider. The Japanese Fair Trade Commission considered that the minority shareholding would enhance JSAT's power in private line services using satellites; the firms concerned in the notified transaction responded that:

- NTT Communications and JSAT would trade with each other under the same fair and appropriate conditions as those with other satellite communications providers;
- They would not jointly conduct material procurement, so that JSAT could not use NTT Communications' buying power;
- NTT Communications would not support JSAT through its unfair use of NTT Communications' selling power; and
- They would not tie up their advertisements. In addition, when JSAT made advertisements, NTT Communications would not support JSAT by using NTT Communications' advertising power, for example with NTT Communications' logo.[429]

In the light of the above commitments the Japanese Fair Trade Commission considered that this acquisition would not restrain competition in the product/service market under scrutiny.

In 1997 a firm intended to restrict and stabilize the financial condition of a competitor which at the time of notification had a minority shareholding of 30 per cent of its issued capital. In return it obtained the right to put two members on to the board of the competitor. The Japanese Fair Trade Commission considered that the two firms had engaged in a joint relationship which would have reduced the level of completion in the product/service markets concerned. In the light of this evidence the firm agreed not to exercise its right

[427] See Japan Fair Trade Commission, 'Major Business Combination Cases in Fiscal Year 2012', http://www.jftc.go.jp/en/policy_enforcement/mergers/index.files/MajorBusinessCombinationCasesFY2012.pdf.

[428] Above n 404, 137.

[429] Ibid, 138.

regarding the interlocking directorships, while the competitor agreed to reduce its minority shareholding in the firm to less than 25 per cent of its issued capital.[430]

ii. Korea

In Table 2 of chapter 3 we showed different categories of mergers & acquisitions (M&A) under the Monopoly Regulation and Fair Trade Act (MRFTA) in Korea. During the period from 1991 to 2013 the Korean Fair Trade Commission (KFTC) examined 11,587 M&A cases in Korea, of which 1,761 cases constituted cases involving interlocking directorships issues and 4,329 cases constituted stock acquisitions (Table 11).

Table 11: M&A enforcement in Korea, 1991–2013

Period	M&A (total)	Interlocking directorships	Stock acquisitions
1991	154	5 (3.2%)	37
1992	149	2 (1.3%)	34
1993	123	2 (1.6%)	29
1994	195	2 (1.0%)	77
1995	325	4 (1.2%)	142
1996	393	16 (4.1%)	159
1997	418	27 (6.5%)	130
1998	486	32 (6.6%)	192
1999	557	42 (7.5%)	146
2000	703	104 (14.8%)	268
2001	644	177 (27.5%)	234
2002	602	143 (23.8%)	215
2003	589	167 (28.4%)	215
2004	749	236 (31.5%)	263
2005	658	138 (21%)	295
2006	744	141 (19%)	355
2007	857	144 (16.8%)	402
2008	550	80 (14.5%)	216
2009	413	46 (11.1%)	119
2010	499	62 (12.4%)	186
2011	543	68 (12.5%)	208
2012	651	62 (9.5%)	189
2013	585	41 (10.4%)	218
Total	11.587	1.761	4.229

Source: Fair Trade Commission Republic of Korea, Annual Reports, 2009, 2013 (http://eng.ftc.go.kr/bbs.do?command=getList&type_cd=53&pageId=0301).

[430] Ibid.

It is evident from Table 11 that in 2004 cases involving interlocking directorships issues reached a peak (236) which constituted the 31.5 per cent of all examined M&A cases in this year (749). Figure 15 presents the evolution of examined cases involving interlocking directorships issues from 1991 to 2013.

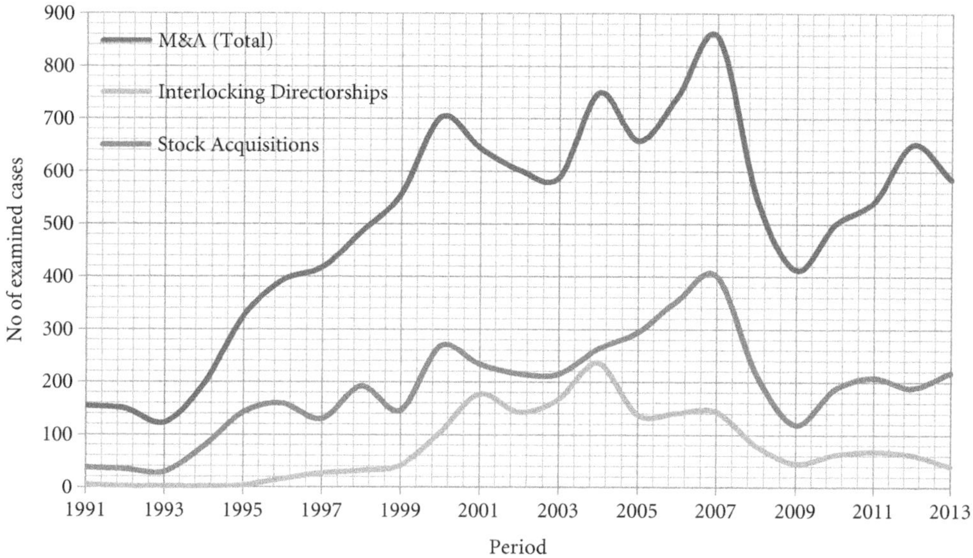

Figure 15: Evolution of M&A enforcement in Korea, 1991 to 2013
Source: Table 11 in this volume

Stock acquisitions constituted approximately 37 per cent of total cases during the whole period. They reached a peak (402) in 2007 which approximately constituted 47 per cent of all examined M&A cases in that year (857).

There were on average approximately 157 cases involving interlocking directorships each year during the period from 2000 to 2007. In all the other years in the period under scrutiny there were fewer than 100 such cases, with the lowest levels being found in the period from 1991 to 1995.

In 2004 the KFTC prohibited the merger between Samick Musical Instrument Co, Ltd. and Young Chang Co, Ltd. On 12 March 2004 the former acquired 48.13 per cent minority shareholding and gained a controlling interest in the latter as well as taking control over Young Chang's management by appointing Young Chang directors and executives.[431]

The KFTC decided not to allow the merger between the two firms after its post-acquisition investigation. The competition authority considered that after the merger both firms had jointly raised prices as a consequence of the interlocking directorate between the two of them.

[431] See Decision No 2004-271 of the KFTC.

iii. Indonesia

In November 2011 AXA SA notified to the KPPU (Indonesia's Commission for the Supervision of Business Competition) the acquisition of a 40 per cent share of the issued capital of Asuransi Dharma Bangsa.[432] The KPPU considered that this minority shareholding conferred control over Asuransi Dharma Bangsa since it gave AXA SA the power to nominate two of the three directors of Asuransi. Furthermore, the KPPU, in its assessment regarding the issue of control over Asuransi Dharma Bangsa, took into account the fact that AXA SA was active in the same market as Asuransi Dharma Bangsa, ie the insurance market, while the majority shareholder was active in the banking industry.[433]

In case no 5/KPPU-L/2002 the KPPU investigated the existence of interlocking directorships among the firms CIF, SPE and NSR. The competition authority decided that these firms had not violated Article 26 of the Antimonopoly Law (AL)[434] since it concluded at the end of its investigation that it did not have enough evidence that the interlocking directorships had caused anticompetitive practices. In fact, the firms involved in the investigation reduced their interlocking positions between each other before the KPPU has published its conclusions.[435]

In case no 4/KPPU-2/2003 the KPPU assessed a situation where a horizontal competitor of two firms with dominant influence in the market which there were active (port service market) had the power to appoint their president directors. Since the firms concerned were active in the same markets, the KPPU assessed whether there existed a violation of Article 26 AL. The KPPU considered that such a violation existed since their existence 'appeared to create unfair business competition'.[436]

iv. Brazil

Under law no 8884/94 the Brazilian competition authority has examined minority shareholdings in several cases. In case no 08012.010293/2004-48[437] Ideiasnet SA was incorporated through stock acquisitions into several firms, all of them controlled by the Pactual Internet Stock Investment Fund, and the latter acquired a 36.12 per cent minority shareholding in the capital stock of Ideiasnet SA. Given the fact that none of the shareholders of Ideiasnet SA held individual or shared control of Ideiasnet SA nor was there a stockholder agreement defining a specific bloc of controlling stockholders, the Administrative Council for Economic Defence (CADE)[438] examined the capital structure before and after the transaction in order to consider whether a concentration had taken place.

The examination showed that the majority of Ideiasnet's shares after the transaction was concentrated in the hands of its four largest shareholders, while before its implementation this majority was concentrated in the hands of the five largest shareholders. In addition, CADE considered that the remaining shares were dispersed among various shareholders

[432] The remaining 60 per cent was owned by an Indonesian state-owned bank.

[433] See also J Davies (ed), *Merger Control: The International Regulation of Mergers and Joint Ventures in 77 Jurisdictions Worldwide* (Global Competition Review, Law Business Research, London, 2015) 1, 213.

[434] See section C(ix) in I in ch 3 above.

[435] Above n 430, 199–200.

[436] Ibid, 200–01.

[437] Ibid, 192.

[438] See section I.C in ch 3 above.

without the existence of a shareholder agreement which enabled them to infer influence or block the decisions of the majority.

Furthermore, the CADE also examined past shareholder's meetings and concluded that no single shareholder could exercise control. The decisions were taken with significant participation and unanimous vote by the shareholders. Given, inter alia, these facts the Brazilian competition authority considered that the transaction did not fall under the provisions set out in Article 54(3) of law no 8884/94.

In case no 08012.010786/2004-88[439] Holcim acquired several concrete production units from Geral de Concreto. The acquiring firm had also minority shareholdings in two firms (15 and 22 per cent) that were active in the market for the production and supply of concrete. The main question that had to be answered in this transaction was if it was a horizontal or a conglomerate merger. In the first case the two firms in which Holcim held minority shareholdings were supposed to be members of Holcim's group of companies and in the second case the two firms were not supposed to be members of Holcim's group of companies.

After an examination to see whether Holcim exerted a relevant influence on the two firms, ie whether it influenced the commercial policies of Topmix and Brasmix, the CADE, following the approach of the Secretariat for Economic Monitoring (SEAE), considered that both companies were considered as belonging to the Holcim group and decided to calculate their shares of the market for the production and supply of concrete for the purposes of the concentration under scrutiny.

In 2010 the CADE did not allow a 'transaction in the industry of concrete services based on a conservative presumption of economic group by summing minority equity interest in companies with small cross-sharing'.[440] Moreover, in 2012 the CADE did not clear a concentration in the construction sector between Votorantim and Cimpor.[441]

v. Israel

The acquisition of 30 per cent of the right to profits and about 12 per cent of the voting rights in Yedioth Ahronot by the Baron-Fishman Group was initially blocked by the Israeli Antitrust Authority (IAA).[442] From an economic point of view the IAA considered that:

> [T]he fact that one competitor had the right to receive over a third of its competitor's profits, creates a very significant financial interest for the acquiring firm in its acquired competitor. The IAA also took into account, in that particular case, the fact that Yedioth (whose shares were acquired) was also a declared monopoly in the Hebrew daily newspapers market. It was explained, as mentioned earlier, that the acquiring firm would take into account the combined profits of both firms, rather than focus on maximizing its own profits. In addition, the decision mentioned that acquisition of right to profits in a competitor could function as a way of signalling. The signal allows the latter to take into account the fact that the acquiring firm takes both firms' profits into account when conducting its business. This signal, the IAA stated, has special importance in an oligopoly

[439] Above n 437, 194.

[440] See also http://www.concurrences.com/Bulletin/News-Issues/October-2010/The-Brazilian-CADE-vetoes?lang=fr.

[441] See also http://www.concurrences.com/Bulletin/News-Issues/July-2012/The-Brazilian-Administrative?lang=fr.

[442] See section I.C.vii in ch 3 above.

> market where competitors are few, and a supra-competitive equilibrium might be established or maintained.[443]

Finally, the competition authority and the firms concerned in the concentration agreed the acquiring firm should divest any share entitling over 25 per cent of the acquired firm's profits and in the meantime to eliminate its influence on Yedioth through the exercise of interlocking directorships.

The Antitrust Tribunal on 13 January 2004 upheld the IAA's decision on the grounds that the acquisition was notified due to the acquisition of passive rights and not due to acquisition of any active rights such as the existence of interlocking directorships in the acquired firm. In particular, '[t]he Antitrust Tribunal … explained that a solely passive financial investment, with no management rights whatsoever was indeed different from acquiring passive rights by a party who has active management rights'.[444] Finally,

> [T]he Antitrust Tribunal emphasized the significant effect that interlocking directorates inflict on the competitive outcome of the merger. A director in a competitor's board, the Tribunal stated, may have access to sensitive corporate information in terms of competition, and may also encourage collusion between the competing firms.[445]

vi. South Africa

In South Africa passive minority interests have been scrutinized under both antitrust and merger regulation. In the case *Pro Sano v Community Hospital Group and Netcare Hospital Group* (Case No 2005Jun1659) the Commission considered that Netcare and Community Hospital Group did not constitute a single economic unit even though the former held a 43.7 per cent of minority shareholding in the latter.

In particular, Pro Sano complained that this minority shareholding violated section 4(5)(b) of the Competition Act (CA).[446] However, the Commission concluded that there was no relationship between the two firms. Also, the Commission stated that the Community Hospital Group did not constitute a joint venture between Netcare and Community Healthcare Holding Limited which also held 43.75 per cent of its issued capital.

Regarding merger legislation, in the merger between Primedia and Capricorn (the acquiring firm) and Nail (the acquired firm), the target firm held a minority shareholding of 24.9 per cent in Kaya FM (an radio station active in the regional market of Gauteng) and the acquiring firm Primedia also held significant radio minority interests in the same regional market. Following its investigation, the South African Competition Commission considered that the merger would create coordinated effects among direct competitors and therefore it decided to approve it subject to certain conditions, including prohibiting Primedia from appointing a representative on Kaya's board of directors.

The merging firms challenged the Commission's decision at the Competition Tribunal[447] which decided in favour of them since it considered that the acquiring firm could not

[443] Above n 439, 206.
[444] Ibid, 205.
[445] Ibid, 207.
[446] See section I.C.viii in ch 3 above.
[447] See case no 39/AM/MAY06, 12 February 2007.

exercise control over Kaya FM. The Commission intervened against the Competition Tribunal's decision.[448]

In the *Two Rivers Platinum Ltd* case, a joint venture between Impala and Avmin, and Assmang (Case No 54/LM/SEP01, 15 November 2001), the Competition Tribunal considered that the minority shareholdings 'would unquestionably facilitate intelligent forecasting of one's competitors supply responses'.[449] The Commission has also considered interlocking directorships in several cases.[450]

vii. Chile

In 1996 Arauco (Celulosa Arauco y Constitucin SA), a major firm in the forestry products industry, complained that its main competitor, Carter Holt Harvey, had sought to appoint a representative to Arauco's board so as to gain access to confidential information, inter alia, the strategic plans of the firm.[451] After investigation of the complaint by the Competition Tribunal in Chile the latter dismissed it on the grounds that Arauco was actually a subsidiary of Carter Holt Harvey since the acquisition of 50 per cent of its issued capital by Carter Holt Harvey. Therefore, as a parent company of Arauco, Carter Holt Harvey had the right to appoint a representative to the former's board.

In the *Fusion entre VTR y Metropolis Intercom* case[452] the Competition Tribunal,[453] during its review of the merger between VTR, a firm active in Chile's cable television industry, and its main competitor, Metropolis Intercom, prohibited the merged entity from '"engag[ing] directly or indirectly, or through related persons … in the ownership of companies operators via satellite or microwave in Chile … participat[ing], directly or indirectly" in certain dominant companies in the fixed telephony market'.[454] Specifically, the parent company of VTR Liberty was obliged to divest its 10 per cent minority shareholding in Sky Multi-Country Partners, the parent company of satellite television provider Sky Chile.

In 2011 the National Economic Prosecutor's Office (NEPO) confronted interlocking directorships among department store chains while reviewing the acquisition of one of these chains by one of the largest Chilean's retail conglomerates. In particular, during the review of the merger between Cencosud SA, the owner of one of Chile's largest department store chains, and Johnson's, a competing department store, the NEPO raised concerns about the potential coordinated conduct between Cencosud SA and Ripley Corp SA, which owned the remaining issued capital (14 per cent) of Johnson's.

> In order to address the FNE's concerns and to decrease the chances of coordinated action between Ripley and Cencosud, the two companies established a series of measures, which included a commitment by the minority shareholders in Johnson's not to participate in the management and

[448] Competition Appeal Court decision in *African Media Entertainment Limited and David Lewis NO and others*, CAC case no 68/CAC/MAR/07/Tribunal case no 39/AM/MAY06, 19 November 2007.

[449] Above n 445, 226 and Competition Tribunal case number 54/LM/SEP01, 15 November 2001, 10.

[450] See, inter alia, Competition Tribunal case no 54/LM/SEP01, 15 November 2001 and Competition Tribunal case no 14/LM/feb06, 14 September 2006.

[451] See also Comision Resolutiva [Antitrust Commission], Resolucion 458.

[452] Tribunal de Defensa de la Libre Competencia (TDLC) 25 octubre 2004, *Liberty Comunicaciones de Chile Uno Ltda y Cristalchile Comunicaciones SA*, Resolucion 1/2004. See also ME Jacobs, 'Combating Anticompetitive Interlocks: Section 8 of the Clayton Act as a Template for Small and Emerging Economies' (2014) 30 *Fordham International Law Journal* 643, 660.

[453] That is, the Tribunal de Defensa de la Libre Competencia (TDLC).

[454] Resolucion 1/2004 (n 452), 50.

administration of Johnson's or any other company in the Cencosud group, as long as they maintained their holdings in Ripley.[455]

In addition, the target firm agreed to eliminate the existence of common directors with a direct competitor.[456]

During 'an investigation of an alleged market allocation agreement between competitors in [the wood pulp market]'[457] the NEPO examined a minority shareholding of 11.03 per cent and the holding of a directorship in Copec SA by the Matte Group. During the investigation the NEPO discovered an interlocking directorship between the Matte Group and CMPC Celulose and the fact that Copec SA was the parent company of Arauco, a main competitor of CMPC Celulose in the wood pulp market. However, the NEPO did not further examine the various structural links between the firms since it considered that they were insufficient to establish an agreement between the main competitors in the relevant market.

In the *SMU SA y Supermercados del Sur SA* case[458] the Competition Tribunal ordered the supermarket chain SMU to divest its 40 per cent minority shareholding in Supermarket Montserrat, a supermarket chain store that did not participate in the merger, since it considered that anticompetitive concerns emerged from the passive minority interest.[459]

Recently, the NEPO undertook a study in order to examine how anticompetitive interlocking directorships might be incorporated into the CA.[460] The study was undertaken due to the fact that certain passive minority interests were and continue to be a common feature in major sectors of Chilean economy.[461]

viii. Canada

In Canada the Federal Competition Act constitutes the relevant statute for the control of mergers. According to the substantive provisions of this law, structural links might be caught because a merger is defined there to include any transaction by which a party acquires a 'significant interest' in the business of another person. In this regard, according to the Merger Enforcement Guidelines, the acquisition of a 'significant interest' could exist either as a 10 per cent ownership interest or without an equity interest under the precondition that 'contractual or other circumstances allow material influence to be exercised over the business of another person'.[462]

[455] Above n 452, 661.

[456] For the opinion of NEPO, see Operacion de Concentracion Cencosud-Johnson's, Fiscalia Nacional Economica (FNE, National Economic Prosecutor's Office) (22 December 2011), available at http://www.fne.gob.cl/2011/12/22/operacion-de-concentracion-cencosud-johnson's.

[457] Above n 455, 661 and Informe de Archivo de la Investigacion, 27 noviembre 2012, Rol-1533-09.

[458] TDLC, 12 diciembre 2012, Consulta de SMU sobre los efectos en la libre competencia de la fusion de las sociedades SMU SA y Supermercados del Sur SA, Resolucion 43/2012.

[459] Ibid.

[460] See Fiscalva Nacional Economica, Division de Fusiones y Estudios, Participaciones Minoritarias y Directores Comunes entre Empresas Competidoras (2013), available at http://www.fne.gob.cl/wp-content/uploads/2013/11/Participaciones-minoritarias.pdf.

[461] See, for instance, Pontificia Universidad Catolica de Valparaíso, Mercado de la Salud Privada en Chile 46–48 (2012), available at http://www.fne.gob.cl/wpcontent/uploads/2012/11/INFORME-PUCV-MERCADO-SALUD.pdf.

[462] See also ch 3, section I.D above.

The acquisition of Fairmont Hotels by Kingdom Hotels International and Colony Capital, and Torstar Corporation's acquisition of a partial interest of 20 per cent in Bell Globemedia constituted cases where interlocking directorships and minority interests were examined and assessed in detail by the Competition Bureau. Both cases were examined in 2006. During its investigation, the Competition Bureau initially estimated each transaction as a full merger, but it also took into account the nature of the interlocking directorships and minority interests in order to assess whether the transactions under assessment were likely to result in unilateral and/or coordinated effects. For both cases, the Bureau concluded the same result: the transaction was not likely to result in a substantial lessening of competition.

D. Cases Regarding Minority Shareholdings in the US

In the US any acquisition of minority shareholding is subject to the jurisdiction of the antitrust agencies.[463] Acquisition of assets or shares where the effect of such acquisition may be substantially to lessen competition or to tend to create a monopoly is prohibited by section 7 of the Clayton Act. The main consequence of this specific provision is that such a general prohibition may apply to structural links as well as to full mergers, even in cases where the acquisition is not sufficient to acquire control and irrespective of whether or not the examined structural links appear to be a step towards control. Hence, this is (inevitably) a great opportunity for US judges.

The legal and teleological scope of section 7 has been clarified by the US courts in a number of cases. However, some legal certainty issues exist, since no settled case law exists; the US courts have not set a standard in case law for how large a percentage of share capital must be acquired in order to raise competition concerns about the impact of the acquisition on competition: in reality, there have been cases where structural links have been held to violate section 7 and the acquisitions of shareholdings were at least 15 per cent. Nevertheless, there were also cases where remedies have been ordered even for minority acquisitions smaller than 15 per cent.[464]

According to US law, a notification requirement is triggered by any acquisition of voting securities or assets that meets the transaction-size threshold (and the person-size threshold, if applicable),[465] provided that no exemption set forth in the Hart–Scott–Rodino (HSR) Act is met. Nevertheless, the HSR Act constitutes a safe harbour for acquisitions of 10 per cent or less of a company's share capital solely for the purpose of investment: these specific cases are exempted from such pre-merger notification obligation.[466]

As far as it concerns the competitive assessment of structural links, the same level of scrutiny in the case of structural links as in full mergers is applied by the US agencies. Therefore, *the main criterion is whether there is or not a reasonable probability of a substantial lessening of competition*. The truth is that the competitive concerns arising from structural links are in

[463] See, for instance, cases *Denver & Rio Grande W RR Co v US*, 387 US 485, 501 (1967) ('A company need not acquire control of another company in order to violate [§7]'), *US v EI du Pont de Nemours & Co*, 353 US 586, 592 (1957) ('Any acquisition of all or any part of the stock of another corporation, competitor or not, is within the reach of [§7]').

[464] See, for instance, *Time Warner Inc*, 61 Fed Reg 5, 0301 (25 September 1996).

[465] See especially ch 3, section I.D above.

[466] Ibid.

terms of quality the same as in a full merger, ie by offering the acquirer the potential opportunity to influence the target firm's competitive policy, either by competing less aggressively or by coordinating its conduct with that of the acquiring firm; by diminishing the incentive for the acquiring firm to compete, by giving rise to unilateral competitive effects (although the effect is likely lessened since the ownership is partial); and by offering to the acquiring firm access to sensitive information in the target, which, even in the absence of any ability to influence the conduct of the target, could however jeopardize competition conditions, since it is able to lead to adverse unilateral or coordinated effects.

Between 1996 and June 2011, for instance, 18 cases involving minority acquisitions were detected, in which the Department of Justice (DoJ) raised concerns. In some of these cases the minority acquisition was considered as having the effect of 'transforming' a strong competitor into an investor, and consequently eliminating either potential or actual competitors, to the detriment of competition. In cases that were found to violate section 7 of the Clayton Act the minority shareholdings were at least 15 per cent.[467] Among these, the *Primestar* and *Dairy Farmers* cases constitute good examples of this effect.

O'Brien and Salop presented several cases with minority shareholdings of less than 30 per cent of a firm's issued capital prior to 2000.[468] The experience so far has shown that there are three categories of examined cases regarding minority shareholdings:[469]

> Transactions in which the acquiring firm is a direct competitor of the target itself or of the target firm's partial ownership interest.[[470]]

[467] See also Commission Staff Working Document, 'Towards More Effective EU Merger Control', annex 2, 1, 17.

[468] See DP O'Brien and SC Salop, 'Competitive Effects of Partial Ownership: Financial Interest and Corporate Control' (2000) 67 *Antitrust Law Journal* 559, 565–66, fn 21–22: '*United States v. E.1. du Pont de Nemours & Co.*, 353 U.S. 586, 602–07 (1961) (23 percent stock acquisition violates § 7); *Denver & Rio Grande*, 387 U.S., at 501–04 (20 percent stock acquisition warrants ICC assessment of anticompetitive effects under § 7); *American Crystal Sugar Co. v. Cuban-American Sugar Co.*, 259 F.2d 524, 526, 53] (2d Cir. 1958) (23 percent stock acquisition violates § 7); *Crane Co. v. Harsco Corp.*, 509 F. Supp. 115, 123–25 (D. Del. 1981) (20 percent stock acquisition analyzed under § 7 for horizontal and vertical effects); *United Nuclear Corp. v. Combustion Eng'g, Inc.*, 302 F. Supp. 539, 540, 552–55 (E.D. Pa. 1969) (21 percent stock acquisition violates § 7); *Hamilton Watch Co. v. Benrus Watch Co.*, 114 F. Supp. 307, 313, 317 (D. Conn.) (24 percent stock acquisition violates § 7), aJfd, 206 F.2d 738 (2d Cir. 1953); *United States v. Gillette Co.*, Proposed Final Judgment, Stipulation, and Competitive Impact Statement, 55 Fed. Reg. 12,567, 12,569 (1990) (imposing restrictions to sterilize acquisition of 23 percent non-voting shares); *Medtronic, Inc., Analysis to Aid Public Comment*, 63 Fed. Reg. 53,919, 53,920 (1998) (restrictions imposed to make passive 10 percent holding of voting stock); *United States v. Rockwell Int'l Corp.*, Proposed Final Judgment, Stipulation, and Competitive Impact Statement, 45 Fed. Reg. 69,314 (1980) (full divestiture of 29 percent stock holding); *United States v. AT&T Corp.*, Proposed Final Judgment, Stipulation, and Competitive Impact Statement, 64 Fed. Reg. 2506 (1999) (full divestiture of 23.5 percent stock holding); *United States v. MCI Communications. Corp.*, Proposed Final Judgment, Stipulation, and Competitive Impact Statement, 59 Fed. Reg. 33,009 (1994) (restrictions imposed on 20 per cent stock holding); *Time Warner, Inc., Proposed Consent Agreement with Analysis to Aid Public Comment*, 61 Fed. Reg. 50,301, 50,308 (1996) (requiring divestiture of 7.5 percent equity position or acceptance of capped non-voting shares); *Shell Oil Co., Analysis to Aid Public Comment*, 62 Fed. Reg. 67,868, 67,871 (1997) (full divestiture of either a 14 percent interest or a separate 24 percent stock interest); U.S. Dep't of Justice Press Release, "American Airlines Cleared to Acquire Stock in Argentine Airline" (8 July 8, 1998) (restructuring to create an 8.5 percent passive investor)'.

[469] See especially ME Jacobs, 'US Antitrust Enforcement Involving Minority Shareholding' (2013), available at http://www.fne.gob.cl/wp-content/uploads/2013/11/Minority-Shareholding-in-the-US.pdf.

[470] '(1) Clear Channel Communications Inc's purchase of AMFM, Inc which controlled a 28.6 percent interest in a direct competitor of Clear Channel; (2) AT&T's purchase of TCI, which held a 23.5 percent interest in a direct competitor of AT&T in wireless phone service; (3) US West's purchase of Continental Cablevision, which held a 20 percent interest in a direct competitor of US West; (4) American Airlines' purchase of 8.5 percent of its direct competitor, Aerolineas Argentinas; (5) TCI's purchase of 7.5 percent of its direct competitor, Time Warner's equity,

Transactions in which the acquiring firm has a controlling interest in a direct competitor of the target firm itself or of an investment of the target firm ....[471]

Transactions in which the acquiring firm has a non controlling interest in a direct competitor of the target firm.

In particular:

On December 20, 1989, the Gillette Company, contracted to acquire the wet shaving businesses of Wilkinson Sword trademark outside of the 12-nation European Community (which included the United States operations) from Eemland Management Services BV (Wilkinson Sword's parent company) for $72 million. It also acquired a 22.9 percent of the nonvoting equity shares of Eemland for about $14 million.

On January 10, 1990, the DoJ instituted a civil proceeding against Gillette. The complaint alleged that the effect of the acquisition by Gillette may have been substantially to lessen competition in the sale of wet shaving razor blades in the United States. Shortly after the case was filed, Gillette voluntarily rescinded the acquisition of Eemland's wet shaving razor blade business in the United States. Gillette said it decided to settle the case to avoid the time and expense of a lengthy trial. However, Gillette still went through with the acquisition of 22.9 percent nonvoting equity interest in Eemland and of all worldwide assets and businesses of Wilkinson Sword trademark from Eemland, apart from the United States and the European Community.

The DoJ (1990) allowed the acquisition provided that:

> Gillette and Eemland shall not agree or communicate an effort to persuade the other to agree, directly or indirectly, regarding present or future prices or other terms or conditions of sale, volume of shipments, future production schedules, marketing plans, sales forecasts, or sales or proposed sales to specific customers ... (page 7)
>
> In other words, the DoJ approved Gillette's 22.9 percent stake in Wilkinson Sword after being assured that this stake would be passive. Indeed, Gillette claimed it was merely making an investment.[472]

In the *Time Warner/Turner* case[473] TCI, a shareholder of Turner, acquired a 9 per cent minority shareholder in Time Warner. The Federal Trade Commission (FTC) cleared the concentration on the condition that TCI not reveal sensitive information from Time Warner's day-to-day management and reduce TCI's ability to influence Time Warner's strategic behaviour.[474]

with an option to purchase another 7.5 percent; and (6) Lockheed Martin's purchase of Loral Corp's defense-related business, which included a 20 percent interest in Loral Space & Communications, which in turn owned a 33 percent interest in Space Systems/Loral, a direct competitor of Lockheed.' See also the cases *United States v Dairy Farmers of America* (2006) and *Kinder Morgan, Inc/Carlyle Group/Riverstone Holdings LLC* (2007) which are discussed below.

471 'AT&T's proposed acquisition of MediaOne, in which both companies maintained partial ownership interests in competitors in the residential broadband market (AT&T with 26 percent of Excite@HomeCorp, and MediaOne with a 34 percent interest in the company that operated RoadRunner).'

472 D Brito, R Ribeiro and H Vasconcelos, 'Measuring Unilateral Effects in Partial Horizontal Acquisitions' (2014) 33 *International Journal of Industrial Organization* 22, 26–27.

473 See also *Time Warner Inc*, 61 Fed Reg 5, 0301 (25 September 1996).

474 Above n 468, 560. For more details, see also SM Besen, EJ Murdoch, DP O'Brien, SC Salop and J Woodbury, 'Vertical and Horizontal Ownership in Cable TV: Time Warner-Turner (1996)' in JE Kwoka Jr and LJ White (eds), *The Antitrust Revolution: Economics, Competition, and Policy*, 3rd edn (New York, Oxford University Press, 1999) 452–75, available at http://global.oup.com/us/companion.websites/fdscontent/uscompanion/us/pdf/kwoka/0195120159_19.pdf.

Furthermore, in the *Primestar/ASkyB* satellite services case[475] in 1998 Primestar (a satellite television service) proposed to acquire a 'Direct Broadcast Satellite slot owned by News Corporation and MCI'.[476] ASkyB constituted a joint venture owned by News Corp and MCI. In exchange a 20 per cent non-voting equity share inPrimestar would be received by News Corp/MCI.

According to the DoJ's decision, this project, if permitted, it would transform ASkyB from a possible entrant into the relevant market into an investor to the detriment of competition. That is, the DoJ was mainly concerned by the elimination of potential or actual competition in the market of satellite services since Primestar and the new satellite service offered from the slot would be competitors.

In some cases the final decisions by the agencies responsible for competition in the US have limited the level of minority shareholding below 30 per cent of the issued capital of the target firm.[477] Moreover, in other cases the agencies have considered that the acquisition of a minority shareholding does not influence the target's commercial strategy. For instance, in the *United States v Tracinda Inv Corp* case,[478] even though the acquirer stated the acquisition was solely for investment purposes, the court considered that '[t]he ultimate definitive factor the courts have looked to … is whether the stock was purchased for the purpose of king over the active management and control of the acquired company'.

In *Anaconda Co v Crane Co*[479] the court considered if there were subsequent agreements between the firms involved which limited the use of the acquired stocks in the target firm, while in *Hamilton Watch Co v Benrus Watch Co*[480] the court has examined other factors such as the level of the portfolio's diversification of the acquirer and the price paid for the minority shareholding in relation to its market value. 'From 1914 to 1965 the DOJ had filed only ten cases alleging violations of section 8, while the FTC filed thirteen lawsuits in that time, with all but one resulting in dismissal upon voluntary dissolution of the interlock.'

Following enforcement of section 8 of the Clayton Act, experience so far has shown that the types of commitments that have been enforced in cases that violated it are:

— the resignation of the director[481] in one of the two or more firms involved;
— the divesture of the part of the firm so the firms concerned are no longer competitors.

The investigation by the FTC regarding the interlocking directorship of Google and Apple led to the resignation of the common directors in both firms in 2009.[482] In particular, the

[475] Complaint, *United States v Primestar, Inc*, No 1:98CV01193 (JLG) (DDC, 12 May 1998).

[476] Above n 474, 560–61.

[477] See, for instance, *US v Gillette Co, Proposed Final Judgment, Stipulation and Competitive Impact Statement*, 55 Fed Reg 12,567, 12,569 (1991); *US v MCI Comm Corp, Proposed Final Judgment, Stipulation and Competitive Impact Statement*, 59 Fed Reg 33,009 (1994); *Time Warner Inc, Proposed Consent Agreement with Analysis to Aid Public Comment*, 62 Fed Reg 67,868, 67,871 (1996); *US v AT&T Corp*, Proposed Final Judgment, Stipulation and Competitive Impact Statement, 64 Fed Reg 2506 (1999).

[478] *United States v Tracinda Inv Corp*, 477 F Supp 1093, 1098 (CD Cal 1979).

[479] *Anaconda Co v Crane Co*, 411 F Supp 1210, 1219 (SDNY 1975).

[480] *Hamilton Watch Co v Benrus Watch Co*, 114 F Supp 307, 316 (D Conn 1953).

[481] The time period until the resignation of the director is one year. See 15 USC § 19(b).

[482] FTC, 'Statement of Bureau of Competition Director Richard Feinstein Regarding the Announcement that Google CEO Eric Schmidt Has Resigned from Apple's Board' (3 August 2009), available at http://www.ftc.gov/opa/2009/08/googlestmt.shtm, and FTC, 'Statement of Chairman Jon Leibowitz Regarding the Announcement that Arthur D Levinson Has Resigned from Google's Board' (12 October 2009), available at http://www.ftc.gov/opa/2009/10/google.shtml.

FTC considered that both firms were active competitors in the market for mobile devices, after the introduction of the iPhone and Android mobile device platforms in 2007.

In the *United States v CommScope* case in December 2007[483] the DoJ raised concerns regarding the minority shareholding of 30 per cent in the issued capital of Andes by Andrews and its accompanying rights such as the right to appoint several members of Andes's doard of directors. Given the fact that CommScope had acquired Andrews and Andes was a direct competitor, the DOJ considered that 'both the incentive and the ability to coordinate its activities with those of Andes, and/or to undermine Andes' ability to compete on price and innovation'.[484] Therefore, the DoJ required the concerned firms to abandon the specific rights.

Below we present some selected cases of minority shareholdings in the United States.

i. Univision Communications Inc/Hispanic Broadcasting Corp *(2003)*

The acquisition of Hispanic Broadcasting Corp by Univision Communications belongs to the third category of transactions regarding minority shareholding by which the acquiring firm has a non-controlling interest in a direct competitor of the target firm. Univision Communications held a minority shareholding of 30 per cent in Entravision, a direct and principal competitor of Hispanic Broadcasting Corp and the rights to appoint two members to its board of directors and to veto certain of Entravision's business decisions (the issuance of equity or debt, or acquisitions over $25 million).

The main concern of the DoJ was the elimination of the degree of competition in the market of Spanish-language radio advertising time. In the light of the DoJ's concerns the acquiring firm agreed (a) to limit its minority shareholding in Entravision to no more than 15 per cent for six years after the transaction was cleared, and (b) to abandon its interlocking directorship on Entravision's board of directors.

ii. United States v Dairy Farmers of America *(2006)*

On 24 April 2003

> '[t]he United States and the Commonwealth of Kentucky filed a civil antitrust Complaint under Section 15 of the Clayton Act, 15 USC 25, alleging that the acquisition by Dairy Farmers of America, Inc. ('DFA') of its interest [50 percent] in Southern Belle Dairy Co, LLC ('Southern Belle') violated Section 7 of the Clayton Act ('Section 7'), 15 USC 18. … An Amended Complaint[485] was filed on May 6, 2004.[486]
>
> The Amended Complaint alleged that DFA's acquisition of its interest in Southern Belle would lessen competition substantially in the sale of school milk in each of the school districts identified in the Amended Complaint. These districts receive school milk bids from Southern Belle and dairies operated by National Dairy Holdings, LP ('NDH'), a dairy holding company also 50 percent-owned by DFA. Some affected districts and groups of districts also receive bids from a third supplier. One of the NDH-operated dairies that serves the affected school districts is the Flav-O-Rich dairy,

[483] See Competitive Impact Statement at *United States v CommScope, Inc*, 2008 WL 3978124 (No 07-2200) (DDC 2008) 7.

[484] Ibid, 8.

[485] It alleged that the acquisition may substantially lessen competition for the sale of milk sold to schools in 100 school districts in eastern Kentucky and Tennessee.

[486] See also United States District Court, Eastern District of Kentucky, London Division, Civil Action No 6:03-206-KSF.

> located in London, Kentucky, only 30 miles from the Southern Belle plant in Somerset, Kentucky. The transaction lessened competition for school districts receiving milk contract bids from both Southern Belle and NDH because, as a result of the transaction, both Southern Belle and NDH were 50 percent-owned by DFA. Since any contracts won by Southern Belle from NDH, or vice versa, through aggressive bidding would likely reduce DFA's profits, reduced competition between Southern Belle and NDH is in DFA's interest.
>
> In 45 of the school districts listed in the Amended Complaint, the effect of the acquisition has been to establish a monopoly, with only Southern Belle and Flav-O-Rich (or another NDH dairy) as possible milk suppliers. In these districts, the acquisition would give DFA the incentive and ability to encourage, facilitate, or enforce cooperation between Southern Belle and NDH to raise prices or decrease the level or quality of service provided to these school districts. In 55 school districts listed in the Amended Complaint, the acquisition has reduced the number of independent competitors from three to two, making it likely that the remaining bidders will bid less aggressively against each other.
>
> The Amended Complaint also alleged that entry into the affected markets by other dairies or distributors would not be timely, likely, or sufficient to deter the anticompetitive effects caused by the acquisition. Dairies or distributors not currently competing in the affected markets would be unlikely to start bidding as a result of a small but significant increase in school milk prices.[487]

Given these critical reasons the US government found that the proposed acquisition would violate section 7 of the Clayton Act. The government's judgment was reinforced by the fact that 'after the transaction, bids to districts where Southern Belle and Flav-O-Rich were the only bidders who were higher than bids received by other districts with only two bidders, though this was not true before the transaction'.[488] That is, the acquisition, if permitted, would have the effect of eliminating the already small competitive pressure on the specific oligopolistic dairy market.

The amended complaint of 6 May 2004 required DFA (a) to divest its interest in Southern Belle and (b) to use commercial efforts to cause AFLP to divest its interest in Southern Belle. After the divestures Southern Belle must be a viable, independent and ongoing business in the relevant product market (sale of school and fluid milk in Kentucky and Tennessee). The proposed divestures would, inter alia, 'eliminate the possibility of anticompetitive effects as a result of DFA's ability to influence AFLP, its long-time business partner'.[489]

All in all, '[t]he divestitures required by the proposed Final Judgment eliminate the harm to competition identified in the Amended Complaint by making Southern Belle completely independent from DFA and NDH, including the Flav-O-Rich dairy'.[490]

iii. Kinder Morgan, Inc/Carlyle Group/Riverstone Holdings LLC *(2007)*

On 28 August 2006 Kinder Morgan, Inc (KMI)[491] announced a merger agreement under which a group of investors, including the Carlyle Group and Riverstone Holdings LLC,[492]

[487] Ibid.
[488] Ibid.
[489] Ibid.
[490] Ibid.
[491] KMI is a midstream energy firm whose business includes, directly or through affiliates, the terminalling of gasoline and other light petroleum products.
[492] Private equity funds managed by the Carlyle Group and Riverstone Holdings LLC (a) members of KMI management, including Chairman and Chief Executive Officer Richard Kinder, (b) Goldman Sachs Capital Partners and affiliates, (c) American International Group and affiliates, (d) Carlyle Partners IV, LP, a private equity fund managed and controlled by respondent Carlyle; and (e) respondent CR-III, a private equity fund jointly managed and controlled by respondents Carlyle and Riverstone.

would acquire all outstanding shares of KMI for approximately $14.4 billion plus the assumption of more than $7 billion in debt (22.6 per cent).[493] As a result of the acquisition, Carlyle and Riverstone, would jointly hold approximately a total equity interest of 22.6 per cent of KMI.

Additionally, as a result of their interest in KMI held through CR-III and Carlyle Partners IV, LP, Carlyle and Riverstone may appoint representatives to the board of directors of KMI and receive non-public competitively sensitive information from and about KMI.

The relevant product market of the proposed minority interest is the provision of terminals of gasoline and other light petroleum products.

> Terminals are specialized facilities with large storage tanks used for the receipt and local distribution of large quantities of gasoline and other light petroleum products. Terminals receive deliveries of gasoline and other light petroleum products from pipelines or marine vessels, store the products in large tanks, and redeliver them into tank trucks for ultimate delivery to retail gasoline stations or other buyers. There are no substitutes for terminals for the storage and local distribution of gasoline and other light petroleum products.[494,495]

The major anticompetitive effects of the proposed acquisition of the minority interest were the following:[496]

(a) elimination of competition 'between KMI and Magellan in the terminaling of gasoline and other light petroleum products in the relevant sections of the country',
(b) enhanced likelihood of 'collusion or coordinated interaction between KMI and Magellan, or between KMI, Magellan and other providers of terminaling services, in the relevant sections of the country',
(c) enhanced likelihood of exercising market power KMI and Magellan in the relevant sections of the country.

Given the above-mentioned jurisdictional findings and issues the FTC in 2007 ordered the firms involved in the acquisition to terminate their interlocking directorships.[497] In particular, the Commission's decision, inter alia, ordered the acquirers to undertake the following steps so as to ensure that firms involved in the acquisition operate independently of, and in competition with, each other, and to remedy the lessening of competition:

— to remove all the directors from the 'victim' firm';
— not to have the ability to elect or appoint a director to the victim's board of directors;
— not to have officer, partner, employee, agent or representative on any victims' board;
— not to attempt to influence, directly or indirectly, by voting or otherwise, the victim's operating entities, or the management or operation of the victim's operating entities;
— not to attempt to influence, directly or indirectly, the victim's investment entities, or the management or operation of the victim's investment entities;

493 See also United States of America before Federal Trade Commission, Docket No C-4183.
494 Ibid.
495 'Magellan and KMI both own competing terminals in each of the following metropolitan areas in the southeastern United States: (a) Birmingham, Alabama; (b) Albany, Georgia; (c) Atlanta (Doraville), Georgia; (d) Charlotte, North Carolina; (e) Greensboro, North Carolina; (f) Selma, North Carolina; (g) North Augusta, South Carolina; (h) Spartanburg, South Carolina; (i) Knoxville, Tennessee; (j) Richmond, Virginia; and (k) Roanoke, Virginia.' Each one of these metropolitan areas constitutes distinct relevant product markets for the purpose of the proposed acquisition. Ibid, paras 28 and 30.
496 Ibid, para 35.
497 See also United States of America before Federal Trade Commission, Public Record Version, 0610197.

- not to receive or attempt to receive, directly or indirectly, any non-public information of, from or relating to the victim's operating entities;
- not to discuss with, or provide, disclose or otherwise make available to any of their directors, directly or indirectly, any non-public information of, from or relating to the victim;
- to prohibit any director in acquired firms from discussing with, or providing, disclosing or otherwise making available to, their directors, directly or indirectly, any non-public information of, from or relating to victim;
- to institute procedures and requirements throughout their various entities to ensure that non-public information is protected,

In addition, the acquired firms shall not attempt, directly or indirectly, acquire any stock, share capital, equity or other interest in victim other than the minority interest acquired through the proposed acquisition.

II. Antitrust and Abuse of Dominant Position Case Law Regarding Minority Shareholdings

In this section we provide selected cases regarding minority interests under antitrust and abuse of dominant position law. Particularly, in section II.A we provide selected cases of minority shareholdings under Articles 101 and 102 TFEU. In section II.B we demonstrate how the Commission applied Council Regulation 1/2003 to assess two cases regarding profit-sharing joint ventures in the air transport sector.

A. Selected Cases of Minority Shareholdings Under the Scope of Antitrust and Abuse of Dominant Position Law in the EU

In this sub-section we describe cases in which the Commission has challenged minority shareholdings under Articles 101 and 102 TFEU. In section A.i we present cases under Article 101 TFEU and in section A.ii we present cases under Article 102 TFEU. From the cases provided it is evident that in recent years the Commission has not sought to apply these two TFEU articles to challenge passive minority shareholdings.

i. The Treatment of Minority Shareholdings Under Article 101 TFEU

(a) The *Philip Morris* Case

Before we proceed with the presentation and analysis of the agreements let us first introduce the parties involved. Rembrandt Group Limited ('Rembrandt') was at the time a South African investment company with no presence in the EU. It owned all the issued capital of Rothmans Tobacco Holdings Ltd ('Rothmans Holdings'), an investment company with its seat in the United Kingdom. Rothmans Holdings owned in turn the 43.8 per cent of the shares and 58.3 per cent of the voting rights of the Rothmans International plc ('Rothmans

International'),[498] a public limited company with its seat in the United Kingdom. Its main activity was the manufacture and sale of cigarettes and other tobacco products with market shares of 12–15 per cent in the EU and 50 per cent in the Benelux countries. Philip Morris Incorporated ('Philip Morris') was a US company which was active in the sales of cigarettes, beer and other soft drinks. Its market share in the EU was 11–14 per cent though slightly lower in the Benelux countries.[499]

In April and May 1981 Rembrandt concluded specific agreements whereby Philip Morris acquired half of the shares and half of the convertible Rothmans International's bonds held by Rembrandt. Philip Morris also agreed to buy certain Rothmans International trade mark rights in the Americas and South Africa and the parties additionally agreed each to appoint half of the members to the board of directors of Rothmans Holdings.[500] Philip Morris paid US$350 million for this agreement.

This agreement between Rembrandt and Philip Morris gave Rembrandt the ability to retain the control of Rothmans International's commercial activities. However, a specific clause in the agreement revealed the intention of the parties to cooperate in their activities:

> The parties will endeavor to exploit the potential benefits which would be derived from cooperation in areas such as joint distribution, joint manufacture, technical know-how and research, etc. The seller will cause Rothmans International to join such efforts of cooperation.[501]

As a consequence of the agreement in 1981 Philip Morris acquired a share of 29.81 per cent of the profits of its competitor Rothmans International. Figure 16 illustrates the capital stock and the shareholders of Rothmans International after the agreement in 1981.

On May 1981 RJ Reynolds Industries Inc ('RJR'), a US manufacturer of cigarettes and other products with a market share of 3–4 per cent in the EU, and 10 per cent in the Netherlands and Germany, filed a complaint against the 1981 agreements considering that they were in breach of both Articles 85 and 86 EEC. The same complaint was raised almost a year later by British American Tobacco Company Ltd ('BAT'), the biggest US tobacco manufacturer in the Western world with a market share of about 10 per cent in the EU and 25 per cent in the Netherlands and Germany.

Given the complaints of the two competitors and 22 days after the complaint from RJR the parties to the agreements modified them in order to obtain a negative clearance or an exemption. On May 1982 the Commission found that these agreements infringed both

[498] Rothmans's Holdings' voting rights were limited to half less one given some articles of association of Rothmans International. However, the wide dispersion of the remaining voting rights among the public gave Rothmans Holdings the ability to exercise effective control over substantial issues regarding Rothmans International.

[499] In the *Philip Morris* case the Court of Justice held 'that the creation of structural links could constitute an abuse of a dominant position provided "the shareholding in question results in effective control of the other company or at least in some influence on its commercial policy"'. See N Levy, 'Expanding EU Merger Control to Non-Controlling Minority Shareholdings: A Sledgehammer to Crack a Nut?' (2014) 1 *CPI Antitrust Chronicle* 1, 3 and Cases 142/85 and 156/84 *British American Tobacco Company Limited and RJ Reynolds Industries Inc v Commission* [1987] ECR 4487 ('Philip Morris') 65.

[500] The agreements, however, provided that since both firms were active in the same markets, the flow of information from each direction would not include sensitive data regarding the competitive nature of them.

[501] See especially Report for the Hearing, delivered in Joined Cases 142 and 156/84, 4493. The same clause was part of an independent agreement between the two parties which was in force from September 1981 to April 1983.

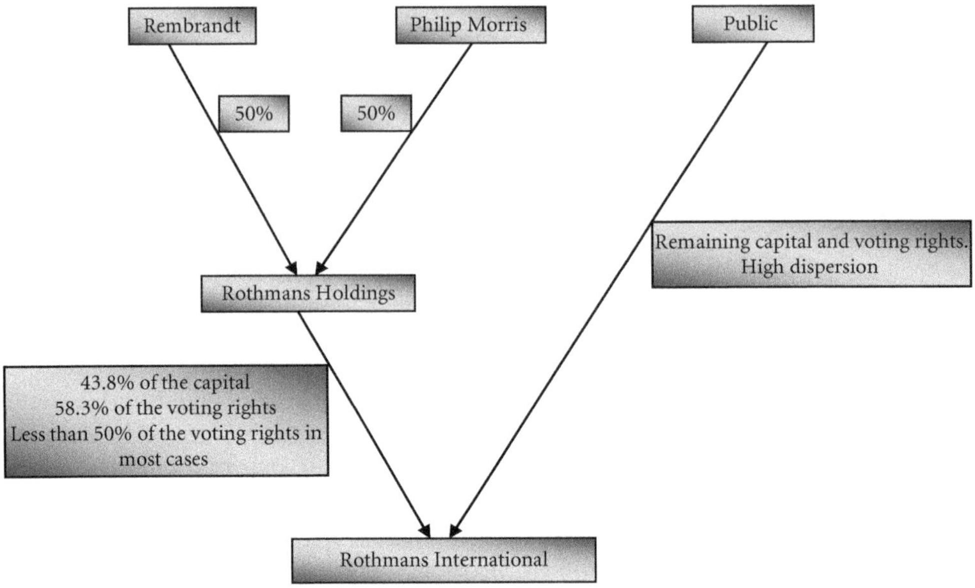

Figure 16: The 1981 agreement between Rembrandt and Philip Morris

Articles 85 and 86 EEC. In particular, the main conclusion of the Commission's statement was as follows:

> The Commission made the preliminary observation that the acquisition by Philip Morris of shares and bonds in Rothmans International placed Philip Morris in a position of absolute parity with Rembrandt. ...... [F]rom 1976 to 1980 the Community cigarette market was stagnant in volume terms and oligopolistic, and in the absence of significant price competition or research breakthroughs, advertising and corporate acquisition came to be seen as the principal means of increasing market share. Several studies carried out in recent years showed that advertising, rather than increasing overall cigarette sales and consumption, served to maintain or increase market share. Furthermore, since the market was dominated by large undertakings with considerable resources and expertise, and advertising was of paramount importance, barriers to entry were very high.
>
> As regards the acquisition of shares in Rothmans Holdings by Philip Morris, ... [t]he Philip Morris and Rothmans International groups of companies were normal competitors in the Community cigarette market prior to the events giving rise to the proceedings. When, as a result of an agreement, two actual or potential competitors together owned a subsidiary which sold its products on the same market, the fact that it was contrary to the economic interests of each of the parent companies to compete with their subsidiary (and therefore pro tanto with each other) was an effect of the agreement on competition within the meaning of Article 85 (1).
>
> ... Thus, an undertaking which had made a major direct or indirect investment in another undertaking would be certain to refrain from any action which might harm it, lest the value of the investment should be endangered. Moreover, the undertaking making the investment would acquire an influence in the management and conduct of the undertaking in which it had invested, enabling it to ensure that its own business interests were not injured by the activities of the latter undertaking. Similarly, an undertaking in which such an investment had been made could not but adapt its conduct and plans to take account of the interests of the investor and the former controlling

> shareholder in that undertaking could not exercise its remaining rights and powers without regard to the interests and policies of the acquirer.
>
> … Philip Morris's and Rembrandt's joint control of Rothmans Holdings was reinforced by the agreement concerning the appointment of the members of the board of directors and that the lack of a chairman's casting vote ensured that no board decision might be taken without the consent of both of them. In the light of Rothmans Holdings's control of Rothmans International, the power to appoint directors served to strengthen the anti-competitive effect of the share acquisition. The provisions granting rights of first refusal or designed to maintain the parity of interest on the part of Philip Morris and Rembrandt in Rothmans Holdings ensured that no major uncoordinated manoeuvres were possible.
>
> As regards Article 86, … Rothmans International, whose 1980 market share was 47.8 percent in Belgium and Luxembourg and 49 percent in the Netherlands, had a dominant position in two substantial parts of the common market.
>
> The joint force of those two undertakings [Rothmans International and Philip Morris] committed to anti-competitive coordination enabled them to act with an appreciable degree of independence of competitors and customers. Philip Morris and Rembrandt were therefore jointly dominant in two substantial parts of the common market. Philip Morris abused its dominant position by buying Rothmans International shares, thereby triggering the cooperation agreement and intensifying its policy of coordination with Rothmans International in the relevant markets. The strengthening of joint dominance thus brought about substantially fettered competition.[502]

After the Commission had issued its Statement of Objection to the involved parties, the latter agreed to modify drastically the agreement which was finally concluded in 1984. According to the new agreement, Philip Morris did not acquire 50 per cent of the issued capital of Rothmans Holdings in exchange for an acquisition of 30.8 per cent of the issued capital or 24.9 per cent of the votes of Rothmans International. In addition, Philip Morris agreed not to increase its voting power above 25 per cent in Rothmans International by exercising its power to convert the firm's convertible bonds. At the same time Rembrandt's minority shareholding in Rothmans International dropped to 30.8 per cent of its issued capital which represented 43.6 per cent of its votes (Figure 17).

Furthermore,

> Philip Morris undertakes not to have any representative on the board or any management body of Rothmans International or any member of the Rothmans International group having an interest in tobacco operations in the European Communities. Philip Morris also undertakes neither to seek nor accept from Rothmans International or Rembrandt any information regarding the Rothmans International group that might influence the competitive behaviour of any Philip Morris group company within the European Community or which might otherwise affect the Philip Morris group's competitive activities towards the Rothmans International group or the competitive relationship between the Philip Morris and Rothmans International groups within the European Community.[503]
>
> After explaining the content of the new agreements, the Commission stated that Philip Morris and Rembrandt no longer had machinery to coordinate their activities in respect of the Rothmans International group and that Philip Morris's position as a minority shareholder in Rothmans International, unaffiliated with any other shareholder, did not seem to give rise to apprehension of any

[502] Ibid, 4497–500.
[503] Ibid, 4496.

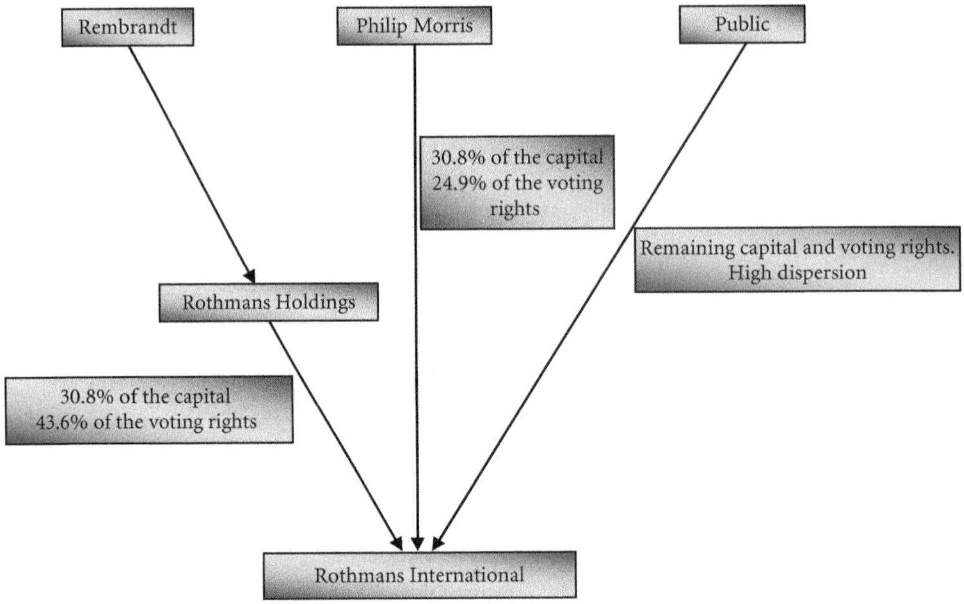

Figure 17: The 1984 agreement between Rembrandt and Philip Morris

appreciable anticompetitive impact on its or Rothmans International's behaviour in the Community cigarette market. In particular, Philip Morris and Rembrandt had abandoned their partnership agreement and the instrument of corporate control which gave Philip Morris influence in Rothmans International. There was therefore no longer any restriction of competition within the meaning of Article 85 of the Treaty or any abuse of dominant positions within the meaning of Article 86.

The Commission also stated that the agreements to be concluded contained provisions relating to disposal and acquisition of Rothmans International shares, but that it had informed Philip Morris that implementation of those clauses was, under the then foreseeable circumstances, incompatible with the competition rules. It stated that the parties had given undertakings enabling the Commission to take appropriate measures urgently, if the need arose, in the event of any future change in the structure of ownership of Rothmans International.[504]

On 4 and 20 June 1984 BAT and RJR sought annulment of the Commission's decision regarding the agreement between Rembrandt and Philip Morris of 22 March 1984.[505] The two parties involved in the agreement intervened in favour of the Commission's decision. 'The submissions of the applicants concern the administrative procedure, the Commission's assessment of the agreements and the statement of the reasons for its decisions.'[506]

In particular, concerning the Commission's assessment of the agreements,

'[t]he applicants argue[d] that in the decisions at issue the Commission applied Articles 85 and 86 of the Treaty incorrectly and was guilty of manifest error inasmuch as it considered that the

[504] Ibid, 4502. See also Cases IV/30.342 and IV/30.926.

[505] See Judgment of the Court (Sixth Chamber) of 17 November 1987, Joined cases 142 and 156/84.

[506] Above n 504, 4571.

undertakings entered into by Philip Morris and Rembrandt were sufficient in order to avoid an infringement of those articles.[507]

The Court preliminarily stated that:

> It must be pointed out first of all that the decisions at issue concern only the 1984 agreements and not the 1981 agreements, which are relevant only in so far as they reveal the original intentions of the parties. *The main issue in these cases is whether and in what circumstances the acquisition of a minority shareholding in a competing company may constitute an infringement of Articles 85 and 86 of the Treaty*[508].[509]

Regarding the violation of Article 85 of the Treaty (now 101 TFEU), BAT and RJR argued that:

> [I]n substance that where a company acquires a substantial shareholding, albeit a minority one, in a competing company it must be presumed that there will be a restrictive effect on competition. The acquisition of such a shareholding inevitably has an influence on the commercial behaviour of the companies concerned, particularly in a stagnant and highly oligopolistic market such as that for cigarettes, where any attempt to increase the market share of one company will be at the expense of its competitors. The establishment of links between two of the largest firms on the market for cigarettes will destroy the competitive balance.
>
> According to the applicants, the transaction in question not only has the effect of restricting competition but was intended to do so. That is clear from the relationship between the agreements in issue and the original 1981 agreements which provided for commercial cooperation between the parties. It was by means of the rights which it obtained under the original agreements that Philip Morris was able to acquire a direct shareholding in Rothmans International, and there is no indication that the idea of commercial cooperation was abandoned, especially since the price paid by Philip Morris remained the same. The intention of Philip Morris and Rothmans International to cooperate on the Community market is confirmed, moreover, by the fact that they have agreements to cooperate in Indonesia, Malaysia and the Philippines.
>
> The applicants also submit that the anti-competitive effect and intention of the agreements at issue are reinforced by the clauses providing for a right of first refusal in the event that one of the parties should wish to dispose of its shareholding in Rothmans International. Those clauses are intended to preserve for Philip Morris the possibility of acquiring control of Rothmans International, and show that its acquisition of an equity interest is not a simple passive investment. The fact that the exercise of the rights granted by those clauses would be contrary to Article 85 is sufficient in itself to justify a finding that the object of the agreements is to restrict competition.
>
> Finally, the undertakings required by the Commission are, according to the applicants, in no way sufficient to rid the agreements of their anti-competitive nature. First of all, the undertakings regarding the existing management of Rothmans International do not prevent Philip Morris from exerting informal influence in its capacity as a substantial shareholder in Rothmans International. Furthermore, the undertakings regarding the separation of the interests of Philip Morris and Rothmans International should Philip Morris exercise its right of first refusal concern the period following an infringement of Article 85 and would not even apply if Philip Morris gained effective control of Rothmans International on the sale of Rembrandt's shareholding to at least 10 purchasers independent of each other and of Philip Morris.[510]

[507] Ibid, 4575.
[508] Emphasis added.
[509] Above n 507, 4575.
[510] Ibid, 4575–76.

The Court argued that:

> Although the acquisition by one company of an equity interest in a competitor does not in itself constitute conduct restricting competition, such an acquisition may nevertheless serve as an instrument for influencing the commercial conduct of the companies in question so as to restrict or distort competition on the market on which they carry on business.[511]

The Court identified several ways for the last mentioned to be true, such as (a) the acquiring company obtains legal or de facto control over the target firm, (b) the agreement provides or creates for commercial cooperation among the firms involved in it, (c) the agreement enables the acquiring firm in the near future to strengthen its position and to take effective control of the target firm, (d) the elimination of the competitive structure of the relevant markets, (e) the multinational dimension of the parties involved in the agreement which cannot be ignored.

The Court, inter alia, considered 'whether, in the circumstances of this case, Philip Morris's shareholding in Rothmans International requires the companies involved to take into consideration the other party's interest when determining their commercial policy, as the applicants argue'.[512] It stated that:

> The Commission submits that Rembrandt retains its interest in deriving the greatest possible profit from its investment in Rothmans International and that through its voting rights and its traditional management links with Rothmans International it is in practice able to control Rothmans International's commercial policy without taking into account Philip Morris's interests. Although Philip Morris has sufficient votes to block certain special resolutions, that possibility is too hypothetical to amount to a real threat which might have an influence on Rembrandt in the management of Rothmans International. There is no reason to suppose that the management and employees of Rothmans International do not have an interest in making that company as profitable as possible.
>
> Although Philip Morris, because of its share in the profits of Rothmans International, has an interest in the success of that company, its first preoccupation must, according to the Commission, remain that of increasing the market share and turnover of its own companies. Philip Morris thus retains a considerable interest in limiting any increase in Rothmans International's market share by its own industrial and commercial efforts. The Commission therefore considers that the acquisition by Philip Morris of a minority shareholding in Rothmans International does not in itself result in any change in the competitive position on the Community cigarette market.[513]

The Court concluded that:

> There is nothing in the evidence before the Court to invalidate that assessment by the Commission. In particular, there is no ground for the conclusion that the acquisition of a shareholding might result in a sharing of the market on the basis that Philip Morris, without itself losing market share, could concentrate on one specific sector of the market, thus allowing Rothmans International to increase its activities in another sector of the market.[514]

It is worth mentioned here that Philip Morris did not hold a dominant position in the market of manufacture and sale of cigarettes and other tobacco products. In the case *Warner-Lambert/BIC SA v Gillette and others*, presented in sub-section A.ii below, Gillette held a

511 Ibid.
512 Ibid, 4579.
513 Ibid, 4579–80.
514 Ibid, 4580.

dominant position in the market for wet shaving products, both in the Union as a whole and in each Member State, and this constituted the determinant difference for the Commission's decision as regards its assessment of Article 86 of the Treaty (now 102 TFEU).

In the post-*Philip Morris* era the Commission challenged a number of cases regarding acquisitions of minority shareholdings. The *Philip Morris* case had enlarged the standard definition of influence in such acquisitions and the willingness of the Commission to challenge them. In particular, in the *Mitchell, Cotts/Sofiltra* case[515] Sofiltra intended to acquire a 25 per cent minority shareholding in a competitor and the right to name two of the competitor's five board members as well as the right to name half of the members of the competitor's shareholder committee.[516] The Commission, after investigation of these arrangements, concluded that the acquisition fell within Article 85 of the Treaty (now 101 TFEU).

The proposed acquisition of a 66 per cent minority shareholding in Sofreb by Carnaud SA, two French competitors in the can industry, was not eventually fulfilled since the Commission raised serious doubts concerning the risk of cooperation between the competitors. In the light of the Commission's objections Carnaud SA agreed to buy the remaining shares in Sofreb and eventually acquire sole control of it.[517] In another case, the Commission opposed the proposed acquisition of a 40 per cent minority shareholding in a Dutch operator by KLM as well as KLM's right to appoint two of the competitor's five board members.[518]

In *Mecaniver/PPG*, [1985] OJ L35/54 the Commission granted a negative clearance regarding the sale by Mecaniver of 81 per cent of share capital of its subsidiary Boussois to PPG, a major worldwide producer of flat glass, while at the same time retaining a 20 per cent minority shareholding in a Spanish competitor. The Commission stated that the proposed transaction did not fall under Article 85(1) of the Treaty (now 101(1) TFEU) since:

> (i) Mecaniver could not influence the competitive behavior of either Boussois or the Spanish entity given that full and effective (ie sole) control was vested in the majority shareholder of each entity; (ii) the majority shareholder in each entity had an option to acquire Mecaniver's minority interests; and (iii) the Commission perceived Mecaniver's minority interests as temporary because Mecaniver had announced its intent to withdraw from the flat glass industry.[519]

(b) Case IV/31.846 *Enichem/ICI*

The Commission decision of 22 December 1987 relating to a proceeding under Article 85 TFEU concerned agreements between Enichem and ICI under which the firms on 12 February 1986 set up European Vinyls Corporation ('EVC'), a jointly operated firm (50/50) active in the vinyl chloride monomer (VCM) and polyvinylchloride (PVC) product markets. The decision also concerned agreements between the two firms to restructure production in certain plants and facilities.

[515] See also *Mitchell Cotts/Sofiltra* [1987] OJ L41/31, [1988] 4 CMLR 111.

[516] In addition, there was a separate agreement between the competitor and Sofiltra by which the former would manufacture via technology licensed by Sofiltra.

[517] See also Commission, Nineteenth Report on Competition Policy (1990) 69.

[518] See also Commission, Twenty-First Report on Competition Policy (1992) 90.

[519] BA Hawk and HL Huser, '"Controlling" the Shifting Sands: Minority Shareholdings under EEC Competition Law' (1994) 17 *Fordham International Law Journal* 294, 302.

Enichem, a subsidiary of the Italian company ENI, was active in the energy sector (petrochemichals). At the time of the decision Enichem was one of the largest global petrochemical firms. ICI was a British firm and its main business was chemicals, especially petrochemicals and thermoplastics. The products under scrutiny were the derivatives of ethylene and either chlorine or hydrogen chloride.

The agreements covered these firms' activities in the VCM and PVC product markets. In particular, they concerned the distribution of primary and secondary plasticizers, both of which are used in the PVC processing industry.[520] In 1986 Enichem and ICI held a 15 per cent market share in the manufacture of PVC. Enichem did not hold any interests in the share capital of other firms in the same market (as well as the market for manufacturing VCM). However, ICI held minority interests in three other firms outside Western Europe which were capable of supplying the European market, and a minority shareholding (25.45 per cent) in a Spanish producer and distributor of VCM/PVC, a subsidiary of Solvay, a major competitor of Enichem and ICI. In addition, ICI, but not Enichem, held some interests in downstream PVC processing firms.

According to the Commission's decision the agreements required the engaged firms: (a) to rationalize their respective VCM/PVC businesses;[521] (b) to close down substantial VCM/PVC production capacity over the years 1986–1988 (requiring a global restructuring of their production plans;[522] and (c) to reduce the combined production capacity (estimated at about 22–23 per cent for PVC and 15 per cent for plasticizers). It should be mentioned here that in 1985 and for the first nine months of 1986 the PVC competitors of the firms involved in the agreement supplied 78 per cent of the EU market, 50 per cent of the Italian market, 57 per cent of the UK market and 88 per cent of the German market.

In the light of the above facts the Commission adopted a decision regarding Article 85(3) of the Treaty (now 101(3) TFEU). According to this:

> [T]he provisions of Article 85 (1) of the EEC Treaty are hereby declared inapplicable, for the period 26 March 1986 to 25 March 1991, to the agreements between Enichem SpA (Enichem) and Imperial Chemical Industries pic (ICI), dealing with the setting up of a jointly-owned company, European Vinyls Corporation (EVC), to operate their VCM and PVC sectors, and the agreement concerning the distribution of PVC primary and secondary plasticizers.[523]

The Commission also stated that:

> The declaration of exemption contained in Article 1 shall be subject to the condition that, in respect of the products covered by the agreements, Enichem, ICI and EVC shall not maintain either directly or indirectly any interests in competing producer or distributor undertakings within the common market of a kind likely to serve as an instrument for influencing the commercial conduct of such undertakings.[524]

Article 2 of the Commission's decision clearly shows that the Commission was worried about any possible link between the engaged firms and other horizontal competitors or downstream distributors in the markets concerned by the agreements. At the time of its

[520] See also Commission Decision of 22 December 1987 relating to a proceeding pursuant to Art 85 of the EC Treaty (IV/31.846 *Enichem/ICI*), [1988] OJ L50/18, para 6.
[521] Ibid, para 18.
[522] Ibid, para 19.
[523] Ibid, Art 1 of the Decision.
[524] Ibid, Art 2 of the Decision.

decision Enichem, ICI and EVC had become one of the largest, if not the largest, manufacturer in the PVC market and the Commission was interested in keeping a record of its future strategic decisions. As a consequence, its decision (under Article 3) required the firms involved in the agreements to

> each individually, inform the Commission in advance of any initiative planned by them or their subsidiaries or associated companies with reference to the products under consideration in this Decision or to other products of the upstream, and/or downstream markets.

(c) Cases IV/M.353 and IV/34.857 *BT/MCI*

Case IV/M.353 concerned agreements under which British Telecommunications (BT) intended, inter alia, to acquire 20 per cent of the outstanding shares of common stock in MCI Communications Corporation (NCI) and to create a joint venture entitled Newco in which BT would hold 75.1 per cent of the capital and MCI the remaining shares. By the acquisition of the minority shareholding BT would have been the largest shareholder in MCI with board representation.[525]

The Commission in its decision on 13 September 1993 stated that the creation of the joint venture would be cooperative rather than concentrative in nature and therefore did not constitute a concentration within the meaning of the Council Regulation (EEC) 4064/89.

Regarding the acquisition of the minority shareholding the Commission stated that BT would hold 'normal minority shareholder protection rights [which] do not constitute a power of veto over competitive behaviour and commercial strategy'.[526] In addition, the Commission concluded that this acquisition would not give BT positive control over MCI and as a consequence it did not constitute a concentration within the meaning of Merger Regulation 4064/89.

Subsequently, the parties involved in the agreements converted the notification under Article 3 of the Merger Regulation into a notification for negative clearance and/or exemption pursuant to Regulation 17.[527,528] The parties stated that:

> [T]he creation of Newco and the investment of BT in MCI are steps taken by the two parent companies to pre-position themselves for when full liberalization is in place, steps that are being followed by many TOs who are creating sets of products comparable to those of Newco.[529]

Regarding the minority shareholding in MCI by BT, the Commission stated that under Article 7(1) of the investment agreement between the two parties, BT cannot exceed 20 per cent until the 10th anniversary of the closing date and furthermore could not seek to control or influence MCI (Article 7(3) of the agreement). After the 10-year period and pursuant to Article 7(4) of the investment agreement BT could only exceed 35 per cent of the

[525] Following para 15 of Commission's Decision, 'It will be entitled to three out of fifteen seats on MCI's board and will hold a veto over certain decisions such as the issuance of fresh equity, substantial acquisitions or disposals and borrowings taking the company over a certain gearing threshold.'

[526] Ibid. As a result BT would not be able to exercise negative control over MCI.

[527] Council Regulation No 17 (EEC), First Regulation implementing Arts 85 and 86 of the Treaty [1962] OJ N L013.

[528] See Commission Decision of 27 July 1994 relating to a proceeding pursuant to Art 85 of the EC Treaty and Art 53 of the EEA Agreement (Case IV/34.857 *BT-MCI*) [1994] OJ N L223/86, para 1.

[529] Ibid, para 14.

equity capital of MCI 'by a tender offer or business combination that has been approved by a majority of the independent directors and by a majority of the shareholders'.[530]

The Commission also noetd that pursuant to Article 9(12) of the investment agreement if either of the parties engaged in the core business of the other, then the engaging party would lose specific rights such as the conversion of BT's shares into common stock and the subsequent loss of its rights. This provision was limited by a number of exceptions in Article 12(b) and (d).

The legal assessment of the Commission concerning the minority shareholding of BT in MCI concluded that 'the investment by BT in MCI does not fall within the scope of Article 85(1) of the EC Treaty or Article 53(1) of the EEA Agreement' since 'the [investment agreement] has been drafted in such a way that BT does not have the possibility to seek to control or influence the [MCI]'.[531]

(d) Case IV/34.410 *Olivetti/Digital*

On 30 July 1992 Digital Equipment Corporation (Digital) and Ing C Olivetti & C SpA (Olivetti) notified to the Commission a technological agreement in the field of computer systems, for the purpose of obtaining negative clearance or/and exemption pursuant to Article 85(3) of the Treaty.[532] This agreement was accompanied by 'the acquisition by Digital of approximately 8 percent of Olivetti's share capital … and by the proportional representation of Digital on Olivetti's board of directors'.[533] However, on 24 August 1994 Olivetti sold all its shares to Digital and as a consequence the Commission's assessment regarding the presence of minority shareholding and directorship was only for the period for which these agreements were in force.

Following the share purchase agreement and the shareholders' agreement Digital was able to have one representative on Olivetti's board of directors 'for so long as Digital owned at least 25 million shares of Olivetti's common stock'.[534] Also,

> Digital was free to exercise the voting rights pertaining to its Olivetti shares. It could not, however, purchase any interest in Olivetti which would have resulted in a holding of more than 10 percent. Digital could not deposit its shares in any voting trust or enter into any other arrangements with third parties with respect to the holding of its Olivetti shares or the exercise of its voting rights.[535]

Given the above and the fact that Digital did not hold any voting rights for controlling Olivetti, which remained under the control of CIR, an Italian holding company and Olivetti's parent company, the Commission concluded that 'Digital's minority share acquisition of Olivetti would not have led to a change in the control of Olivetti'.[536] Furthermore, the parties involved in the agreement claimed that

> the board of directors of Olivetti has delegated all of its operative functions to Olivetti's Chairman and General Manager. … With the exception of the Chairman, the Vice-Chairman and

[530] Ibid, para 30.
[531] Ibid, para 44.
[532] See also Commission Decision of 11 November 1994 relating to a proceeding pursuant to Art 85 of the EC Treaty (IV/34.410 *Olivetti-Digital*) [1994] OJ N L 309/24, para 1.
[533] Ibid, para 2.
[534] Ibid, para 15.
[535] Ibid, para 16.
[536] Ibid, para 26(a).

the Managing Director of Olivetti, none of the board members has an operational function at Olivetti. … Olivetti's board is not involved in decisions on the development of new products or their pricing.[537]

As a consequence, the Commission is of the opinion that, in so far as the functions of Olivetti's board of directors were confined to those described above, it is unlikely that Digital's representation on Olivetti's board of directors would have led to a coordination of competitive behaviour or to an exchange of competitive information.[538]

(e) Case IV/35.617 *Phoenix/GlobalOne*

The Commission issued a decision on 22 December 1996 relating to a proceeding under Article 85 of the Treaty (now 101 TFEU) concerning agreements made by Phoenix on 5 March 1996. In particular, these agreements

consist of two main transactions involving two Community telecommunications organizations (TOs) and one United States telecommunications operator:

(i) [France Telecom] (FT) and [Deutsche Telekom] (DT) each acquired an equity stake [common stock][[539]] of approximately 10 [percent] in Sprint, worth United States $3.7 billion. Both FT and DT obtained proportionate board representation and investor protection as minority shareholders in Sprint; … provisions have been included in the investment agreement to prevent DT and/or FT, either separately or jointly, from controlling or influencing Sprint; and

(ii) Atlas and Sprint created a joint venture, Phoenix, for the provision of non-reserved global telecommunications services and other telecommunications services to corporate users, carriers and consumers. The Phoenix joint venture is structured into groups of operational entities under the strategic supervision of a Global Venture Board (collectively referred to as the 'Phoenix entities'). … The Global Venture Board shall take decisions on matters of policy only and not engage in the management of individual operational entities created pursuant to the Phoenix agreements.[540]

According to the decision (paragraph 17), the acquisition of the minority shareholding in Sprint by DT and FT (amounting to 20 per cent) was a strategic decision by the state-owned companies to consolidate a new strategic alliance in the global telecommunications market and especially to extend their services into new market segments. Also, as is stated in paragraph 18 of the Commission's decision, 'Phoenix in 1993 [held] a … market share of 12.2 percent in the global market for customized packages of corporate telecommunications services'. Concerning the market for travelling services, Phoenix was

the largest calling card services provider in the Community (23 percent market share) in terms of subscriber numbers, ahead of AT&T and BT with a 21 percent and 17.8 percent market share respectively. In terms of calling card traffic within the Community, the aggregate market shares of FT (21 percent) and DT (3 percent) are equal to BT's market share of 24 percent.[541]

[537] Ibid, para 26(b).

[538] Ibid.

[539] See also Commission Decision of 17 July 1996 relating to a proceeding pursuant to Art 85 and Art 53 of the EEC Agreement (IV/35.617 *Phoenix/GlobalOne*) [1996] OJ N L239/57, para 26(2).

[540] Ibid, para 2.

[541] Ibid, para 22.

In the market for carrier services Phoenix was the third largest global switched transit provider behind AT&T and BT.[542]

Regarding the minority shareholding in Sprint, the agreements between FT and DT further stated that:

> (b) The standstill agreement binds FT and DT for a period of 15 years not to acquire additional shares in Sprint which would increase their combined aggregate voting rights to more than 20 [percent].
> (c) The registration rights agreement is required in order for each party to consummate the transactions contemplated by the investment agreement.
> (d) The investor confidentiality agreements between Sprint and DT, and Sprint and FT, respectively, provide for the maintenance of the confidentiality of all Sprint proprietary information received by DT and FT as a result of the investment agreement and in particular by the DT and FT representatives on the Sprint board of directors, which may be used by DT and FT only for the purposes of exercising their rights under such agreement.[543]

Concerning the rights and board representation of FT and DT with respect to Sprint, article 27(2) of the Commission's decision states that:

> FT and DT have the right to elect directors to the Sprint board in proportion to their shareholding, provided that each has the right to elect at least one director. Neither FT nor DT have access to confidential, competitive information on Sprint's activities in the EEA through their representation on Sprint's board. Nor may these representatives provide Sprint with confidential information that FT or DT may have obtained from United States competitors through correspondent relationships.
>
> As the sole holders of Sprint's class A common stock, FT and DT have been granted substantial consensual rights with respect to certain corporate actions of Sprint, which nevertheless fall considerably short of control. These actions include major equity issuances, disapproval of investments in Sprint by major competitors, participation rights in transactions involving change of control, and other bilateral corporate transactions. FT and DT have a right of first offer with respect to long-distance assets of Sprint for a fixed period of time.

The Commission considered that the Phoenix agreements eliminated competition in the relevant product markets and restricted trade among Member States. Regarding the applicability of Article 85(1) EEC and Article 53(1) of the EEA Agreement to DT and FT's investment in Sprint, the Commission decided that 'DT and FT's investment in Sprint falls outside the scope of Articles 85 (1) of the EC Treaty and 53 (1) of the EEA Agreement'.[544] In particular:

> The Commission and the Court of Justice do not consider Article 85 (1) of the EC Treaty applicable to agreements for the sale or purchase of shares unless these agreements affect the competitive behaviour of the parties to the transaction. The Commission analysed whether the appointment of DT and FT representatives to Sprint's board and subsequent access to confidential business data could give rise to coordination of the competitive behaviour of all three undertakings. The Commission found that (i) the investment agreement signed on 31 July 1995 does not afford DT and FT the possibility of exercising a controlling influence over Sprint and (ii) United States corporate and antitrust laws are designed to prevent access to and misuse of Sprint's confidential information

[542] Ibid, para 23.
[543] Ibid, para 27(1).
[544] Ibid, para 51.

by DT and FT. Sprint and DT, and Sprint and FT, respectively, set out an additional prohibition to misuse such information in two investor confidentiality agreements signed on 31 January 1996.[545]

ii. The Treatment of Minority Shareholdings Under Article 102 TFEU

(a) *Warner-Lambert/BIC SA v Gillette and others*

In section I.D above we discussed the way in which the DoJ dealt with the acquisition of Eemland's wet shaving businesses bearing the Wilkinson Sword trade mark outside of the 12-nation European Community (which included operations within the US) and the acquisition of 22.9 per cent of its non-voting equity shares by the Gillette Company. The DoJ after its civil proceedings against Gillette on 10 January 1990 and the abandonment of the acquisition of Eemland's wet shaving businesses by Gillette, approved Gillette's 22.9 per cent stake in Wilkinson Sword after being assured that this acquisition would be passive.

Shortly after the DoJ initiated its civil proceedings against Gillette (on 12 February 1990) the European Commission received a

> complaint from Warner-Lambert Company concerning the sale of the Wilkinson Sword wet-shaving business. Warner-Lambert allege[d] that the transaction and related agreements involving Gillette constitute an infringement of Article 85 (1) of the EEC Treaty on the part of Gillette and Eemland and an infringement of Article 86 on the part of Gillette. A second complaint relating to the same matter was filed on behalf of [La Société Bic SA (BIC SA)] on 14 March 1990.[546]

Warner-Lambert was at the time of the decision a US company and it was 'active on the wet-shave market through its Schick brand of razors and blades'.[547] BIC SA was at that time a French company and it was 'active on the wet-shave market through its own brand of razors and blades'.[548] It is worth mentioning here that the Commission's decision came after the DoJ's decision. Therefore, at the time of the European decision Eemland had 'retained [its] wet-shaving products business, principally under the Wilkinson Sword brand name, in the Community and the United States of America'.[549]

Gillette had played a crucial role during the sale of Stora Kopparbergs Bergslags AB's consumer product division to Eemland in 1989. According to the agreements signed at that time, this purchase was achieved by means of a leveraged buy-out, using Eemland as a cell company. Gillette, among other investors, financed this transaction and the company stated that it had acted thus in order to acquire Eemland's wet shaving division outside the EU.

Moreover, at the time of the Commission's decision Gillette owned 22 per cent loan stock of Eemland's issued equity and quasi-equity capital. Gillette's loan stock

> confer[ed] no voting rights, no representation on the Board, no representation at shareholders' meetings and no access to internal information. Gillette [would] never be entitled to nominate any director of the Board of Eemland, and [undertook] that it would not exert or attempt to exert any influence over the Board or any member of the Board. There [were] certain circumstances in which

545 Ibid.

546 See especially Commission Decision of 10 November 1992 relating to a proceeding pursuant to Arts 85 and 86 of the EEC Treaty (Cases IV/33.440 *Warner-Lambert/Gillette and Others* and IV/33.486 *BIC/Gillette and Others*) [1992] OJ N L116/21, para 2.

547 Ibid, para 4(v).

548 Ibid, para 4(vi).

549 Ibid, para 11.

Gillette [might] acquire voting rights in Eemland (on a conversion of its loan stock into ordinary shares) namely on a winding up of Eemland or a listing of the ordinary shares of the company or the sale of the company's equity to a third party.[550]

Gillette also held loans which represented 13.6 per cent of Eemland's total financing.[551]

Regarding Article 86 TEC, the Commission stated that:

The change in the structure of the wet shaving market[552] brought about by Gillette's participation[553] in the overall arrangement [would] have an adverse effect on competition in that market in the Community and therefore Gillette's involvement constitute[d] an abuse of its dominant position.[554]

Gillette ha[d] not only become a major shareholder in Eemland but ha[d] also become its largest creditor and ha[d] acquired important pre-emption and conversion rights and options in Eemland. The position of Gillette [was] a matter which the management of Eemland [would] be obliged to take into account and consequently it [was] a factor which [would] influence the commercial conduct of Eemland. It follows that Gillette [would] have at least some influence on Eemland's commercial policy.[555]

Of great importance was also the fact that Gillette was a major creditor of Eemland and therefore the latter was financially dependent upon Gillette. Also, Gillette had substantial pre-emption rights and convention rights which impeded other competitors in the market to improve their positions through a potential acquisition of Eemland. The Commission viewed these rights 'as a strategy by Gillette to weaken the competitive position of Eemland and correspondingly to strengthen Gillette's own position'.[556]

The Commission also regarding Article 85 EEC considered that:

[T]he non-Community sale and the intellectual property agreements between Gillette and Eemland restrict[ed] competition on the wet-shaving market in the Community in so far as they relate[d] to neighbouring markets in Europe. For the reasons set out in recital 32 above and in view of the marketing policies of large buyers of wet-shaving products who buy on a Europe-wide basis, these agreements [would] affect trade between Member States.[557]

For all the above-mentioned reasons the Commission ordered the parties involved to bring to an end the infringement of Article 86 by disposing of Gillette's minority shareholding and its interest as a creditor in Eemland to an independent third party. In addition, the Commission ordered the parties to bring to an end the infringement of Article 85 'by re-assigning to Eemland the Wilkinson Sword businesses including trade marks in the former German Democratic Republic, Czechoslovakia, Hungary, Poland, Turkey, the former Yugoslavia and the EFTA countries'.[558]

[550] Ibid, para 14.

[551] Ibid, para 15. Given the equity holders' agreement and under certain exceptions no shareholder of Eemland was entitled to dispose its shareholding prior to 1 January 1993. Gillette also held a pre-emption right to acquire the whole or a substantial part of the wet-shaving business from Eemland.

[552] In which Gillette held a dominant position at the time of Commission's decision.

[553] That is, the participation of Gillette in the buy-out of the Wilkinson Sword business.

[554] See especially Commission Decision of 10 November 1992 (n 551) para 23.

[555] Ibid, para 24.

[556] Ibid, para 28.

[557] Ibid, para 39.

[558] Ibid, Art 5 of the Decision.

iii. A Comparison Between the Judgments in Philip Morris *and* Gillette

Without any doubt Gillette carefully structured its buy-out in order to fall below the influence threshold of 25 per cent outlined in the *Philip Morris* case. A careful examination of these two cases shows that Gillette held pre-emptive rights over other shareholder interests, had no board representation in the acquired firm and implemented Chinese walls like Philip Morris. Unlike Philip Morris, Gillette held a 22.9 per cent non-voting equity shareholding while Philip Morris held 24.9 and 30.8 per cent voting and non-voting equity shareholdings, respectively. In addition, Gillette held 13.6 per cent of Eemland's total debt, although Philip Morris held 50 per cent of Rothmans International's outstanding convertible bonds. The main difference between the two cases was Gillette's commercial agreements with Eemland outside the EU which seemed to influence more trade within the Community than in the *Philip Morris* case.

However, the Commission stated that Gillette may be able to exercise 'some influence', rather than 'influence' as in the *Philip Morris* case, over Eemland's commercial activities violating Article 86 TEC. The Commission's decision was based on the Court's *Philip Morris* judgment, in which the Court used this term with respect to Article 86, whereas it used the term 'influence' with respect to Article 85.[559]

Hence, with its decision the Commission seemed to expand the lower boundary of 25 per cent in the *Philip Morris* case (under Article 85 TEC) for application of Article 86 to acquisition of minority shareholdings. At the same time it clearly distinguished acquisitions of minority interests which fell under the two Articles by creating a lower safe harbour for cases under Article 86 TEC.

B. Application of Council Regulation 1/2003 Regarding Profit-Sharing Joint Ventures in the Air Transport Sector

Economic theory has used the case of joint ventures as a good example of a group of firms where each one holds a partial equity interest and maximizes its profits net of those which are going to the competitor due to the existence of the minority interest. Reynolds and Snapp showed that the anticompetitive effects of such arrangements arise mainly because the profits of the members of a joint venture are linked to each other and this makes them compete less vigorously and to adopt behaviour more conducive to joint profit maximization than would otherwise be the case.[560] In addition, the behaviour of these members becomes more conductive the higher the entry barriers in the market. In the case where entry is blocked efficiently, then if competitors increase the level of partial equity interests in their competitors the level of the equilibrium market output will decline. The output decrease will be higher for big rather than for small firms, but smaller for high-cost rather than for low-cost firms.[561]

[559] Ibid, para 24.

[560] See also the analysis of horizontal unilateral effects in ch 4, section II.A above. See the paper by RJ Reynolds and BR Snapp, 'The Competitive Effects of Partial Equity Interests and Joint Ventures' (1986) 4 *International Journal of Industrial Organization* 141.

[561] A Matsutomo, U Merlone and F Szidarovszky, 'Dynamic Oligopoly with Partial Cooperation and Antitrust Threshold' (2009) 73(2) Journal of Economic Behavior and Organization 299, 302.

In this section we present how the European Commission applies Council Regulation 1/2003 in two cases regarding profit-sharing joint ventures in the air transport sector. The first case is COMP/39.595 *Continental/United/Lufthansa/Air Canada* and the agreement between Air Canada, United Airlines, Continental Airlines Inc and Lufthansa in relation to the establishment of a profit-sharing joint venture which covered, inter alia, all passenger air transport services of the parties on routes between Europe and North America. This agreement provided for extensive cooperation between the firms party to it, which included pricing, capacity and scheduling coordination, as well as the sharing of revenues.

The second case is COMP/39.596 *BA/AA/IB* which involved a set of agreements establishing cooperation on all routes served by British Airways, American Airlines and Iberia between Europe and North America. As in the former case, the parties to the agreements agreed to coordinate prices, capacity, schedules, marketing and sales, as well as to share revenues.

i. COMP/39.595 Continental/United/Lufthansa/Air Canada

On 19 June 2008, Air Canada (AC), United Airlines (UA), Continental Airlines (CO) and Lufthansa (LH), announced their intention to form a revenue-sharing joint venture covering all their transatlantic passenger air transport services. Within the joint venture, AC, UA, CO and LH would cooperate on key parameters of competition such as pricing, capacity, schedules and marketing.[562] On 25 July 2008 the Commission opened an ex officio investigation of the cooperation between the firms engaged in the joint venture according to Article 9 of Council Regulation (EC) No 1/2003 of 16 December 2002 on the implementation of the rules on competition laid down in Articles 81 and 82 EC.[563]

On 10 October 2012 the Commission adopted a preliminary assessment within the meaning of Article 9(1) of Regulation (EC) No 1/2003 and 'raised concerns as to its compatibility with Article 101 of the Treaty, and raised preliminary concerns in relation to the Frankfurt–New York route for premium passengers'.[564]

The main features of Commission's preliminary decision may be summarized as follows:

(a) in the absence of the agreement the parties would be competitors on the Frankfurt–New York route;
(b) the joint venture would be likely to restrict competition (by object) on the Frankfurt–New York route (premium passengers)
    1. price inelastic passengers
    2. low buying power
(c) elimination of previously existing competition, especially between LO and CO;
(d) substantial barriers to entry (competition cannot be replaced)
    1. slot constraints at New York and Newark Liberty airports and probably also at Frankfurt airport
    2. hub advantages at Frankfurt, New York and Newark Liberty airports
        (i) economies of scale

[562] As is stated in para 2 of the Commission's Decision of 23 May 2013 (COM(2013) 2836 final), 'Since July 2011, the cooperation in the A++ joint venture extends to the fully-owned Lufthansa subsidiaries Austrian Airlines AG and Swiss International Air Lines Ltd, and since March 2012 to Brussels Airlines SA/NV.'

[563] See also [2012] OJ C396/21, paras 1–2.

[564] See especially Commission's Decision of 23 May 2013 (n 543) para 4.

(ii) brand name recognition
(iii) power of firms' frequent flyer programme
(iv) access to feeder traffic
(v) ability to attract corporate contracts compared to their actual or potential competitors without such a hub advantage
(vi) firms offer higher quality of service than their actual or potential competitors due to frequencies operated on the Frankfurt–New York route
(vii) customers pay higher prices due to the absence of buying power.

On 11 December 2012, in response to the preliminary assessment, the firms engaged in the joint venture offered commitments to the Commission. The initially submitted commitments for the Frankfurt–New York route were as follows:

> (a) [the parties will] make arrival and departure slot pairs available at Frankfurt airport and/or New York JFK/Newark Liberty airports—at the competitor's choice—to allow to operate up to seven additional frequencies weekly (and up to 21 weekly frequencies should existing third party services on the route be withdrawn). The offer is subject to a number of conditions, including that the competitor has exhausted all reasonable efforts to obtain the necessary slots through the general slot allocation process. The parties also do not have to release more than one slot at New York JFK airport;
> (b) [the parties will] enter into fare combinability agreements with competitors for premium passengers. Eligible competitors are all competitors which operate or have started to operate new or increased non-stop services on the Frankfurt–New York route, and do not operate a hub/focus-city airport at both ends of the route;
> (c) [the parties will] enter into special prorate agreements for traffic with a true origin and a true destination in Europe/Israel or North America/the Caribbean/Central America, provided that part of the journey involves the Frankfurt–New York route. Eligible competitors are all competitors which have started to operate new or increased non-stop services on the Frankfurt–New York route, and alone or in combination with their alliance partners do not operate a hub/focus-city airport at both ends of the Frankfurt–New York route;
> (d) [the parties will] open their frequent flyer programmes [FFPs] to a competitor which commences or increases services on the route, if such competitor does not have a comparable programme of its own and does not participate in any of the parties' FFPs.[565]

The duration of the proposed commitments was 10 years with the ability of the Commission to review them five years after the adoption of its final decision (review clause).

On 4 February 2013 the Commission stated regarding the observations made by interested third parties on the initial commitments that:

> [T]hose comments did not identify new competition concerns and contained no points such as to make the Commission reconsider the concerns it expressed in the preliminary assessment. The respondents did not question the general aim of the initial commitments to lower the barriers to entry and expansion on the Frankfurt–New York route for premium passengers by making slots available and providing the possibility to conclude fare combinability, FFP agreements and SPAs with the parties on this route. The respondents, however, made several comments on the exact scope and the way the initial commitments could operate in an efficient manner to achieve the general aim.[566]

[565] Ibid, para 11.
[566] Ibid, para 99.

On 15 May 2013, after the consultation of the Advisory Committee on Restrictive Practices and Dominant Positions on 7 May 2013, the firms submitted updated commitments. Overall, the Commission concluded that:

> The final commitments are sufficient to address the concerns identified by the Commission in its preliminary assessments. The slot commitment offered by the parties remedy the loss of one daily competitive frequency operated by CO precooperation. With the released slots at Frankfurt, and if applicable at New York, new entrants or existing competitors can operate or increase up to one daily new or additional frequencies (seven weekly frequencies) on the Frankfurt–New York route.

The revision also

> ensures the proportionality of the slot commitment but at the same time always enables the parties' competitors to maintain at least three daily competing frequencies—the number of daily frequencies by LH's competitors that were available before the implementation of the [joint venture]. The number of slots to be released by the parties may be increased or decreased according to the number of frequencies operated by the parties' competitors.[567]

Given the fact that the principle of proportionality held for the remaining provisions of the final commitments by the firms involved in the joint venture (fare combinability, FFP agreements and SPA),[568] the Commission considered that there were no longer fears of violation of Article 101 TFEU and the case was brought to an end.[569]

ii. COMP/39.596 BA/AA/IB

On 8 April 2008 Virgin Atlantic Airways (VA) lodged a complaint with the European Commission against an agreement between British Airways plc (BA), American Airlines Inc (AL) and Iberia Líneas Aéreas de España SA (IB) to cooperate for all routes served by them between Europe and North America. In particular, they agreed to coordinate prices, capacity, schedules, marketing, sales and share revenues. On 8 April 2008 the Commission opened proceedings regarding this agreement(s) and on 29 September 2009, through a statement of objections, it expressed its concerns regarding six routes between Europe and North America—namely London–Dallas (premium and non-premium market); London–Boston (premium and non-premium market); London–Miami (premium and non-premium market); London–Chicago (premium market); London–New York (premium market); and Madrid–Miami (premium and non-premium market)—and the compatibility of firms' agreements with Article 101 TFEU and Article 53 of the EEA.

Between December 2009 and January 2010 the firms involved offered commitments in order to address the concerns identified by the Commission. On 26 February 2010 the firms offered revised commitments, which were amended on 12 May and 25 June 2010. In the light of the final commitments by the firms the Commission informed VA that 'there would not be a sufficient degree of European Union interest for conducting a further investigation into the alleged infringement'.[570]

[567] Ibid, paras 142–43.

[568] Ibid, para 140. According to this, the principle of proportionality 'requires that the measures adopted by the Institutions of the European Union must be suitable and not exceed what is appropriate and necessary for attaining the objective pursued'. See also Case T-260/94 *Air Inter v Commission* [1997] ECR II-997, para 144 and Case T-65/98 *Van den Bergh Foods v Commission* [2003] ECR II-4653, para 201.

[569] Ibid, para 149.

[570] See especially Commission's Decision of 14 July 2010 relating to a proceeding under Art 101 of the Treaty on the Functioning of the European Union and Art 53 of the EEA Agreement, Case COMP/39.596 *BA/AA/IB*, para 14.

The main concerns of the Commission expressed in its statement of objections may be summarized as follows:

(a) the agreements appreciably affect trade between Member States;
(b) extensive cooperation in relation to key parameters of airline competition
    1. fares
    2. capacity
    3. schedules
    4. sales (sell each other's products and services without regard to which party is operating the aircraft)
    5. marketing
(c) elimination of competition (by object) between the firms involved with respect to prices, capacity and other key strategic decisions;
(d) strong anticompetitive effects on transatlantic routes in which the firms involved
    1. hold a strong position
    2. there are extensive barriers of trade
    3. face low constraint from actual or potential competition.

The engaged firms in the agreement(s) argued that these will create efficiencies in favour of customers. Particularly, the joint venture will result in lower fares, due to elimination of double marginalization and cost savings as well as it will provide higher quality services 'in terms of scheduling, reciprocity of FFPs, fare combinability, and joint corporate contracts'.[571] However, the Commission stated that 'the parties had not produced sufficient evidence demonstrating that their agreements met all the criteria for application of Article 101(3) of the Treaty'.[572]

On 26 February 2010 the firms offered commitments regarding the six routes under investigation by the Commission.[573] On 25 June 2010 the firms submitted their final commitments, as follows:

(a) to increase the number of slots to be released on the London–New York route to enable 21 (instead of 14) weekly frequencies;
(b) to change the duration of the agreements concluded under the Final Commitments, in particular extending the guaranteed duration to 10 years if a relevant commitment is entered into before IATA winter season 2012/13;
(c) to exclude the slot releases/exchanges with third parties signed before the 12 May 2010 from the clauses intended to prevent abuse;
(d) to grant anonymity to the applicants for slots if the applicant so requests;
(e) to introduce a number of amendments into the fare combinability and SPA commitments; and
(f) to introduce a review clause enabling the Commission to review the Final Commitments after five years of operation.[574]

After assessment of these final commitments by the Commission,[575] the latter concluded that: 'The Final Commitments facilitate entry or expansion on the routes of concern by lowering the barriers to entry or expansion and strengthening the services of existing or new competitors with connecting traffic.'[576]

571 Ibid, para 78.
572 Ibid, para 79.
573 Ibid, paras 81–97 of the Commission's Decision.
574 Ibid, para 149.
575 Ibid, paras 102–52.
576 Ibid, paras 150 and 229.

6

Greek Coastal Navigation Case

In this chapter we analyse in detail the Greek coastal navigation case (Decision No 427/V/2009 of the Hellenic Competition Commission (HCC)), the first critical case regarding the role of minority shareholdings on competition in Greece.

The HCC met in plenary session at its premises[1] on 23 October 2008 in order to decide whether the control of unreported, ie non-notified, acquisitions of minority interests under Articles 4–4f of law 703/77, as applied in relation to coastal shipping, by the firm Sea Star Capital plc (the acquiring firm, hereinafter Sea Star) in the firm Anonymous Shipping Company of Crete (the victim firm, hereinafter ANEK), conferred sole or joint or no control of the acquiring firm over the strategic policy of the acquired firm.

In particular, the aim of this meeting of the HCC was to take decisions concerning an ex officio investigation by the Directorate-General for Competition (DGC) into non-disclosure under Articles 4–4f of law 703/77 (now 3959/11),[2] as applicable, of the above-mentioned acquisitions of minority interests. A Coast Guard commander, who had been appointed by the Minister of Development and Merchant Marine, Aegean and Island Policy, attended the meeting though did not have the right to vote.[3]

In the following sub-sections we present the basic merits of the case which constitutes a clear-cut paradigm for future analysis.

I. Greek Coastal Navigation Sector: The Facts

A. The Basic Merits of the Case

i. Introductory Remarks

Since September 2006 several parliamentary questions had been sent to the DGC raising issues over the situation in the field of short-distance sea shipping that may lead to significant distortions of the competition in this sector. Consequently, the DGC launched in October 2006 an ex officio investigation into businesses engaged in providing ferry services. The aim was to investigate potential breaches of Articles 1 and 2 of law 703/77, as amended, and Articles 81 and 82 TEU (now Articles 101 and 102 TFEU) in relevant markets of the

[1] 1A Kotsika Street, Athens.

[2] In accordance with article 17(5) of law 3260/2004 (Gov't Gazette Issue A151/6.8.2004).

[3] Both authors of this book were involved actively in the specific case not only regarding the investigation of the Directorate-General of Competition but also as rapporteurs. However, all the data given here regarding the Greek coastal navigation sector have already been published on the official website of the HCC (www.epant.gr).

this sector (eg transportation of persons, vehicles with classical/conventional boats or high-speed boats).

To this end, a working group was created at the DGC in accordance with the provisions of Article 12 of Presidential Decree 31/2006[4] to undertake an investigation of possible infringements of law 703/77, as applicable to the field of coastal shipping in Greek territorial waters.

ii. Crucial Announcements by the Firms Involved

On 28 August 2007 ANEK announced on its website that:

> The company ANEK announces based on Law 3556/2007 (Article 3 (xvi), (bb) and 21) in combination with decision 1/434/03.07.2007 HCMC and further relevant information to the company, that the company 'Sea Star Capital Plc' proceeded on 24/08/2007 to purchase 19,967,663 common nominal shares of our company at a price of 2.50 euros per share. After this specific purchase the company 'Sea Star Capital Plc' holds 23,495,163 shares representing 14.93 percent of the share capital of the Company and the respective voting rights.

On 11 December 2007 Sea Star acquired through a stock exchange transaction a total of 18,942,487 common registered voting shares, which represented 26.71 per cent of the share capital of Minoan Lines.[5] On the same date, the acquiring firm obtained 26,935,378 common registered voting shares, which represented 34.70 per cent of the share capital of Hellenic Seaways (collectively referred to hereinafter as HSW).

On 28 January 2008 an ANEK press release stated that:

> The company ANEK announces based on Law 3556/2007 (Article 3 § 1 (F) and 21) in combination with decision 1/434/03.07.2007 HCMC that the Company SAINES HOLDINGS LTD where legally represented by Mr I. J. V. (liable person according to article 13 of Law 3340/2005), proceeded on 24/01/2008 to the sale of 2,575,000 common registered shares, with a total net value of Euro 5,793,750.

On the same date a Minoan Lines press release stated that

> The company Minoan Lines SA announces the following: On January 25, 2008, was communicated to us a letter stating that the company 'Sea Star Capital Plc' sold 18.942.487 common registered shares with voting rights in the company 'ATLANTICA Spa Di NAVIGAZIONE' and its quota in the share capital of our company was changed from 26.7 percent to 0.0 percent. On January 25, 2008, was communicated to us a notification of change in shareholder whereby the company 'ATLANTICA Spa Di NAVIGAZIONE' participates in our share capital with 30.0 percent and holds 21,282,000 ordinary registered shares with voting rights.

On 29 January 2008, ANEK informed its shareholders that

> The company ANEK announces based on Law 3556/2007 (articles 9 and 21) in combination with decision 1/434/03.07.2007 of HCMC and following the relevant information from 29/01/2008 to our company, that the company 'SEA STAR CAPITAL PLC' proceeded on 25/01/2008 to purchase of 26,760,003 common registered shares of our company. After this specific purchase 'SEA STAR CAPITAL PLC' owns 52.422.237 shares representing 32.50 percent of the share capital and corresponding voting rights, instead of the percentage 15.90 percent of the share capital of the company and corresponding voting rights that held before the transaction.

[4] Gov't Gazette Issue A'29/14.2.2006.

[5] A competitor of the acquiring firm.

Remarkably, on the same day (29 January 2008) an ANEK press release stated that:

> The company ANEK announces based on Law 3556/2007 (article 9, par and 21) in combination with decision 1/434/03.07.2007 of HCMC and as from 25/01/08 relevant information to our company, that the company 'ATLANTICA SPA DI NAVIGAZIONE' proceeded on 25/01/2008 to the sale of 27,102,750 common registered shares of our company. After this sale the company 'ATLANTICA SPA DI NAVIGAZIONE' holds shares representing 0 percent of the share capital and corresponding voting rights instead the percentage 16,80 percent of the share capital of the Company and the respective voting rights that held before the transaction.

On 30 January 2008, ANEK informed its shareholders via its website that:

> The company ANEK announces based on Law 3556/2007 (article 9, par.a and 21) in combination with decision 1/434/03.07.2007 HCMC and following from 31/01/08 relevant information to our company, that the company 'INTESA SANPAOLO SPA' proceeded on 25/01/2008 to the sale of 27,134,435 common registered shares of our company, acting as custodian of several shareholders. After this sale, the company 'INTESA SANPAOLO SPA' holds for the account of its customers 346,950 shares representing 0.215 percent of the share capital and corresponding voting rights, instead the percentage 17.03 percent of the share capital of the Company and the respective voting rights that held before the transaction.

On the same day a Minoan Lines press release stated that:

> The company Minoan Lines SA announces the following: On January 29, 2008, was communicated to us a notification of alteration of voting rights pursuant to which the company 'INTESA SANPAOLO Spa' holds a stake of 30.85 percent through the acquisition of 21,882,829 shares with voting rights. The above change was held on January 25, 2008. Finally, it is noted that in the above voting rights is included quota 30.0 percent that is held by the company 'ATLANTICA Spa Di NAVIGAZIONE' through the above mentioned 'INTESA SANPAOLO Spa' as custodian.

Following these announcements, the DGC under the ex officio investigation into the coastal shipping sector for possible breaches of the articles of screening concentrations of law 703/77, as applicable, proceeded to scrutinize these transactions in order to determine whether they fell into the provisions of Articles 4–4f of law 703/77, as applicable.

B. The Companies Involved

i. Sea Star Capital plc

According to decision no 427/V/2009 of the HCC, Sea Star, based in Nicosia, Cyprus, is a public company whose shares are listed on the Cyprus Stock Exchange. It was incorporated in Cyprus on 24 August 1987 under the name Sportsman Betting Co Limited as a private limited liability company. On 1 February 2000 it was renamed as Megabet Public Company Limited (Megabet) and on 22 May 2007 as Sea Star Capital Public Limited Company.

According to its statutory purpose, Sea Star conducts global club bets on the results of football matches (eg acts as a bookmaker for bets on games globally) and participates in the issued capital of other companies. Its main activity is the provision of a full range of services and product bets. The main types of bets offered by Sea Star include bets at predetermined prices (fixed odds) and Asian bets, and the services offered are principally providing results in real time (live scores) to subscribers and live streaming of football matches.

The share capital of the company, as announced at the previous general meeting of shareholders (5 June 2008), was €50 million divided into 1.25 billion common shares.

Sea Star's shareholdings in its various subsidiary and connected companies were at that time as follows:

— ANEK (32.5 per cent)
— Hellenic Seaways (34.7 per cent) (and 1.8 per cent through its subsidiary Magnilon Ltd)
— Magnilon Ltd (100 per cent)
— Sea Star Cargo Limited (100 per cent)

According to Sea Star, the company has not developed any activity in Greece so had no turnover in the national territory. The worldwide turnover of the group, again based on Sea Star's own figures, was €12,738,112 in 2007 and €9,396,865 in 2006.

ii. ANEK

ANEK was founded in Chania in 1967 and in 1999 incorporated Rethimnian Naval Tourist Cretan Ferries LC. Its shares are listed on the Athens Stock Exchange. This diversified company was established under the provisions of law 2190/1920 on public limited companies.

ANEK, during the period under examination, was active on routes to Crete (Heraklion–Piraeus, Piraeus–Rethymno and Piraeus–Chania) and to Italy (Patra–Igoumenitsa–Corfu–Ancona/Venice). According to its own data, the company ranked third among the 20 biggest shipping companies in Greece by total assets published in 2006. ANEK's subsidiaries during this period were Lassithi SA (50.11 per cent), ET.AN.AP SA (50.00 per cent), LEUKA ORI SA (62.00 per cent), ANEK Lines Italia srl (49.00 per cent), Champion Ferries Ltd (70.00 percent), ANEK Holding SA (99.00 per cent), TI.SI.Sailing MC (95.00 per cent) and ANEK Lines Luxembourg (100.00 per cent).

The board of directors of ANEK comprised of 15 members, 11 elected and 4 appointed by the statute of the company. These four were the former metropolitan (ie bishop) of Kissamos and Selinos Irenaeus Galanakis (chairman), the mayor of Chania, the mayor of Rethymno and a member of the Association of Professional Finance Scientists of Chania. Before the completion of the non-notification act (acquisition of minority interests), the shareholder structure of ANEK was as follows: public investment: 63.32 per cent; Sea Star: 15.90 per cent; Intesa San Paolo: 15.11 per cent; and Morgan Stanley: 5.67 per cent.

The share capital of ANEK's parent company amounted to 161,299,191.00 shares, divided into 157,360,940 common and 3,938,251 preferred voting shares. Prior to the acquisition of 32.50 per cent of the share capital of ANEK from Sea Star (on 29 January 2008), the company Intesa Sanpaolo SpA, which was controlled by the Italian Grimaldi Group, participated with a significant amount of 15.115 per cent of the share capital of ANEK. The existence of such a level of participation in combination with the fact that the Sea Star had 15.90 per cent of the share capital of ANEK, tends to indicate that the appellant was unable to have exclusive control over ANEK. After completion of the transaction of 29 January 2008, the shareholders holding more than 5 per cent were:

— Sea Star Capital (32.50 per cent);
— Morgan Stanley & Co International plc (7.45 per cent).

The worldwide turnover of the company on a consolidated basis amounted to €254,332,000.00 in 2007 and to €254,718,000.00 in 2006.

iii. Hellenic Seaways plc

Hellenic Seaways plc (HSW) is based in Piraeus and its purpose, according to its amended statute of 17 May 2008 is purely maritime. In particular, the company's operations include only the purchase, lease, shipbuilding and factoring of its own ships and the operation of ships and boats in general, proprietary or otherwise, of any nationality and flag under charter or otherwise, for the transport of persons and goods by sea vehicles.

On 31 December 2007 HSW's shareholding structure was (a) Sea Star 34.7 per cent, (b) Minoan Lines 33.3 per cent, (c) Interamerican 2.9 per cent, (d) Magnilon Ltd (a Sea Star subsidiary) 1.8 per cent and (d) other 29 per cent. The worldwide turnover of the parent company was €162,174,900.67 in 2007 compared to €144,287,496.01 the previous year. On a consolidated basis, the global company's turnover (both national and worldwide turnover) in 2007 amounted to €182,334,699.12 compared to €165,406,163.58 in 2006.

C. Definition of Relevant Markets (Product and Geographic)

The relevant product market comprises all those products and/or services which are regarded by the consumer as interchangeable with or substitutable for each other, because of their characteristics, prices and the use for which they are intended. The relevant product or service may in some cases be composed of individual products and/or services which present largely identical physical or technical characteristics and are interchangeable.

The relevant geographic market comprises the area in which offer or request goods or provide the relevant services the participating undertakings under conditions of competition that are sufficiently homogeneous and which can be distinguished from neighbouring geographic areas, particularly because of the markedly different conditions of competition prevailing in them.

According to the settled practice of the HCC,[6] the relevant product (service) markets in this case are:

(a) The provision of maritime services for persons using classical/conventional O/C-O/C ships.

(b) The provision of marine transportation for vehicles with classical type/conventional F/C/C ships.

(c) The provision of maritime services for persons using fast boats and in particular:
  (i) high-speed passenger hydrofoils capable of speeds over 35 knots (F/Y/C, Flying or Mega Dolphins);
  (ii) new-technology high-speed passenger catamarans capable of speeds over 35 knots (F/C/C Highspeed).

(d) The provision of maritime transport for vehicles using fast new-technology (F/C/C Highspeed) catamarans.

[6] See mainly HCC cases 210/III/2002 and 247/III/2003.

Voyages on the most crowded routes are usually done with conventional vessels (F/F/B) and speedboats (F/S/W), while the number of new-technology fast catamarans (R/C Flyingcat and F/C/C Highspeed) has significantly increased. The fast ferries can run a route in about half time of conventional vessels, but the ticket costs about twice as much, and the fast ferries are more susceptible to bad weather.

Finally, it is worth noting that the market for transport services by sea, despite the possibility of transfers by air and road, is a distinct market because of:

(a) the difference in price (transportation cost) for each mode, which varies depending on how the total cost of transport is calculated (individual expense, family, group, specific categories, one way or round trip, etc);
(b) the different characteristics of each mode of transport, such as the duration of the trip, the speed relative to the distance, safety, comfort, weight limits, ease of approach to the final destination, vulnerability to weather conditions, etc;
(c) the specific reasons for using each mode of transport (business trips, leisure, need to transport large cargo, need to transport vehicles, etc).

However, substitution between different modes of transportation is frequently not possible for most of the destinations served by vessels, since air transport between mainland ports and the Greek islands or between islands is not always possible, due to the absence of airports on many islands, while road transport is clearly irrelevant. Hence, substitution between different modes of transport in this case is merely incidental and therefore negligible and of minor importance.

Regarding the relevant geographical market of services, each specific line that runs each ship constitutes the relevant geographical market for this case and more generally for maritime transport of passengers and vehicles, since the user of the service selects a specific line according to the place of departure and the destination.[7] Partial substitution could be accepted between neighbouring ports if the client could be served by departures from these ports at the same time, with the same type of vessel and reaching the destination at the specified time—conditions that do not exist in the case examined. The choice of service by the user in determined in principle by the domestic route used to serve his/her needs (touristic, business or other) and then by the vessel on which he/she will embark.

Based on the above analysis, it appears that as a separate relevant geographical market in this case ought to be considered based on routes on which the above-mentioned ferry companies are active, namely the individual maritime lines and in particular (a) the Adriatic routes (Ancona, Venice, Bari), (b) the Crete routes (Piraeus–Hania–Rethymnon–Heraklion Lasithi) and (c) the Crete/Cyclades routes (Tables 12–14).

C. Economic Assessment

i. Market Size

If the various routes are categorized, following the National Statistic Service of Greece, at the time of the HCC decision there were 7 general interior–exterior routes, 15 routes

[7] See HCC decision no 210/III/2002.

Table 12: Shipping lines and routes serving Crete, 2001–08

Company	Piraeus–Heraklio						
	2001	2002	2003	2004	2005	2006	2007–08
Minoan	✓	✓	✓	✓	✓	✓	✓
ANEK	✓	✓	✓	✓	✓	✓	✓
Pasifai SC		✓	✓	✓	✓		
Daidalos SC		✓	✓	✓	✓		✓
Venizelos SC			✓	✓	✓		
	Piraeus–Chania						
ANEK	✓	✓	✓	✓	✓	✓	✓
Blue Star			✓	✓	✓		
HSW	✓	✓	✓	✓	✓	✓	✓
Aigiakestransport sc NE		✓	✓				
Venizelos SC			✓	✓	✓		
Melodia SC				✓	✓		
Archaggelos SC							✓
	Piraeus–Rethymno						
ANEK	✓	✓	✓	✓	✓	✓	✓
NEL				✓	✓		✓
HSW							✓

Table 13: Shipping lines and routes serving the Adriatic and western Greece, 2001–08

Company	Patra-Venice						
	2001	2002	2003	2004	2005	2006	2007–08
Minoan	✓	✓	✓	✓	✓	✓	✓
ANEK							✓
Superfast Ferries	✓	✓	✓				
	Patra-Ancona						
Minoan	✓	✓	✓	✓	✓	✓	✓
ANEK	✓	✓	✓	✓	✓	✓	✓
Superfast Ferries	✓	✓	✓	✓	✓	✓	✓
	Patra-Bari						
Minoan			✓				
Blue Star	✓	✓	✓	✓	✓	✓	✓
Superfast Ferries							✓

(continued)

Table 13: ***(Continued)***

Company	**Patra-Venice**						
	2001	2002	2003	2004	2005	2006	2007–08
Minoan	✓						
Blue Star	✓	✓	✓				
Superfast Ferries							✓
	Patra–Igoumenitsa–Corfu						
Minoan	✓	✓	✓	✓	✓	✓	✓
ANEK	✓	✓	✓	✓	✓	✓	✓
Superfast Ferries	✓	✓	✓	✓	✓	✓	

Source: HCC Decision No 427/V/2009.

Table 14: Shipping lines and routes serving the Cyclades, 2001–08

Company	**Piraeus–Siros–Tinos–Mykonos**						
	2001	2002	2003	2004	2005	2006	2007–08
Blue Star	✓	✓	✓	✓	✓	✓	✓
HSW	✓	✓	✓	✓	✓	✓	✓
NEL	✓	✓	✓	✓		✓	
	Paros–Naxos (Piraeus)						
Blue Star	✓	✓	✓	✓	✓	✓	✓
HSW	✓	✓	✓	✓	✓	✓	✓
NEL	✓	✓	✓	✓		✓	✓
SAOS				✓	✓		
GA Ferries	✓	✓	✓	✓	✓	✓	✓
Piraikes Lines SC			✓	✓			
Aegean Jet 2 SC			✓	✓			
Aegean Glory SC				✓	✓		
Mυκonos SC				✓	✓		
Evoikes G SC				✓	✓		
Filippos VE SC				✓	✓		

Source: HCC Decision No 427/V/2009.

on which R/C-O/C boats operated, and 29 local routes operated by conventional ferries. Furthermore, there were no statutory or otherwise clearly defined routes to include a specific range of ports or points approached by the vessel. The routes where cruise lines operate their ships depend on the ports to which they approach, and fit into broader regions, such as the Saronic, Cyclades, Sporades, etc.

The above-mentioned 15 routes are as follows:

1. Patras–Akarnanias–Ionian islands.
2. Piraeus–Saronic Gulf ports.
3. Piraeus–Crete.
4. Piraeus–Mykonos–Tinos–Samos.
5. Piraeus–Dodecanese.
6. Piraeus–eastern Cyclades.
7. Piraeus–Chios–Mytilene.
8. Line Rafina–Evia–Andros–Tinos.
9. Line Volos–Sporades–Kimi.
10. Piraeus–western Cyclades.
11. Line Lavrio–Kea–Kythnos.
12. Piraeus–Peloponnese.
13. Piraeus–Crete–Dodecanese.
14. Piraeus–Dodecanese–south Aegean–Thessaloniki.
15. Other.

Regarding lines serving the Adriatic, it should be emphasized that these present continuous fluctuations in passenger traffic to total traffic kept constant at over 2.6 million passengers per year. The route with the highest number of passenger movements in this market is that connecting western mainland Greece (Patras) with the port of Ancona (Italy) which was the preferred option for 44.6 per cent of passengers in 2006.A similar picture exists for the movement of vehicles on the Adriatic ferry routes.

However, in particular the overall movement of vehicles for over the four years 2003–06 saw a significant reduction of 9.5 per cent (from 1.2 million vehicles in 2003 to 929,000 in 2006). This decrease can be attributed to the fact that large trucks engaged in international transport, which are an important customer group for these routes, preferred to drive through the Balkan countries for cost reasons.[8]

Finally, it is worth noting that according to data covering the first nine months of 2007, an increase of 25.4 per cent was seen in the number of passengers carried on the Greece–Italy route compared with the same period in 2006 (2007: 2,189,559 passengers; 2006: 1,746,089 passengers), while the number of vehicles handled increased by 9.9 per cent (2007: 783,490 vehicles; 2006: 712,602 vehicles).

ii. Market Shares on Domestic Routes

At the corporate level HSW has a significant market share of domestic passenger traffic, carrying 32 per cent of all passengers carried in 2006, while the other companies/competitors (ie Blue Star Ferries, ANEK, Minoan Lines, NEL and Saos) carried the remaining 68 per cent. Of these latter companies, Blue Star Ferries is the most important, since it holds a market share of almost 16 per cent of total passengers carried in 2006, followed by ANEK with a share of 8 per cent. Lastly, Minoan Lines, NEL and Saos present low shares, which together accounted for 10 per cent of total passenger traffic volume in 2006.

[8] The ICAP Group provides a wide range of services that are grouped into the following four service lines: credit risk services; marketing solutions; management consulting; and people and employment solutions (http://www.icap.gr/).

The classification of the companies in terms of market share of transport of vehicles is broadly similar: HSW holds first place (24 per cent), with Blue Star Ferries having 16 per cent of the total market, followed by ANEK with 12 per cent. Finally, Minoan Lines, NEL and Saos together have 12 per cent of the market, with other companies supplying the remaining 36 per cent of the market.

It should be emphasized that, according to a study by ICAP,[9] the national market share of the ANEK Group based on turnover was 14.2 per cent in 2007. It is worth noting that the corresponding market share of the ANEK Group in the Adriatic market was, during the same year, 24.0 per cent. According to the same study, the national market share of HSW based on turnover was 21.3 per cent in 2007.

iii. Market Shares in Foreign Routes

The Attica Group (through its subsidiary Superfast Ferries), Minoan Lines, ANEK and on a small scale HSW are active on the Adriatic routes. In particular, the Attica Group operates five ships (four by Superfast Ferries and one by Blue Star Ferries) on the Adriatic routes, while Minoan Lines has three ships. Finally, ANEK runs two ships on the Adriatic routes.

Based on the turnover for 2006, the ANEK Group and Minoan Lines share 45.5 per cent of the market, with Minoan Lines in first place by number of passengers carried and vehicles with market shares of 22.1 and 26.4 per cent, respectively. In 2007, the ANEK Group held first place with a 24 per cent share in the overall market.

E. The Effects of the Acquired Minority Shareholdings on the Markets Under Scrutiny

i. Horizontal Effects—Reduction of Existing Competition

The main horizontal effects that emerged from the acquisition of minority interests in the present case are the following:

— A competitor disappeared from the Piraeus–Chania route (on which both ANEK and HSW are active).

— Despite the change in routing of ships by ANEK on the Piraeus–Rethymno and on the Paros–Naxos routes, and the entry of HSW on the Piraeus–Rethymno route early in 2007, the acquisition examined further strengthens the presence of the company that will be created from this on the routes serving Crete.

— The acquisition of minority interests will further strengthen the presence of the company that will be created from this on the Paros–Naxos route.

ii. Conglomerate Effects—Reduction of the Intensity of Potential Competition

The main conglomerate effects that emerged from the acquisition of minority interests are the following:

— HSW entered the Piraeus–Heraklio route (through ANEK).

[9] Ibid.

— HSW entered the Adriatic Sea routes (through ANEK).
— ANEK entered the Piraeus–Syros–Tinos–Mykonos route (through HSW).

II. Research of the Directorate General of Competition

A. Law 703/77

The DGC's research was based on a number of specific provisions of law 703/77 (now 3959/11).

According to Article 4a of law 703/77,[10]

1. The Hellenic Competition Commission must be notified of every concentration of undertakings within a month from their completion when: a) the market share of the products or services that this concentration concerns, as this is laid down in article 4(f), represents in the national market or in a considerable part thereof, in correlation with the products' or services' characteristics, at least ten per cent (10 [percent]) of the total turnover that is carried out with the products or services considered as kindred by consumers because of their qualities, prices and the use for which they are destined, or b) the total turnover of all undertakings participating in the concentration, as laid down in article 4(f), amounts, in the national market, to at least fifteen million (15,000,000) euros.
2. Notification is obligatory:

   for each one of the undertakings participating in the concentration, in case the concentration constitutes the object of an agreement between those undertakings, in all other cases, for the natural persons, undertakings or groups of natural persons or undertakings that take control of the whole or parts of one or more undertakings.

3. The notification's specific content is determined and every other relevant issue is regulated by decision of the Hellenic Competition Commission, taken within thirty (30) days from the coming into force of the present law.
4. In case of guilty breach of the obligation for notification, the Hellenic Competition Commission imposes on each one of the bearers of the relevant obligation a fine of at least three thousand (3,000) euros, a sum which cannot surpass five per cent (5 percent) of the total turnover, as this is laid down in article 4(f).

According to Article 4b of law 703/77,[11]

1. The Hellenic Competition Commission must be notified of every concentration of undertakings within ten (10) working days of the conclusion of the agreement or the publication of the offer or of the exchange, or the acquisition of participation that ensures the control of the undertaking when the total turnover of all undertakings participating in the concentration, pursuant to the provisions laid down in article 4(f), amounts, in the global market, to at

[10] As was modified by Art 3, law 3373/2005. This provision had been inserted in this law by Art 2, law 1934/1991, replaced by Art 2(2), law 2296/1995, which was modified by Art 9(1) and (2), law 2741/1999, and abolished by Art 1(3), law 2837/2000.

[11] Inserted by Art 2, law 1934/1991, which was modified by Art 19, law 2000/1991, and replaced by Art 2(3), law 2296/1995, which in turn was modified by and supplemented with Arts 9(3), (4) and (5), law 2741/1999, 1(4) and (5), law 2837/2000, and 4 and 26 case 1, law 3373/2005.

least one hundred and fifty million (150,000,000) euros and at least two of the participating undertakings accomplish, each one separately, a total turnover of more than fifteen million (15,000,000) euros in the Greek market.

2. The ten-day time-limit starts from the oncoming of the first one of the operations laid down in the previous paragraph.
3. Notification is obligatory:
   a) for each one of the undertakings participating in the concentration, in case the concentration constitutes an object of agreement between these undertakings. It is mentioned by oversight 'of the present law' instead of the correct 'of the law 3373/2005'
   b) in all other cases, the natural persons, the undertakings or groups of natural persons or undertakings that take control of the whole or parts of one or more undertakings.

According to Article 4f of law 703/77,[12]

1. The market share laid down in article 4a(1) ... corresponds to the sum of all market shares held by the participating undertakings in the national market or in the part thereof concerned by the concentration.
2. The total turnover, laid down in articles 4a(1b) and (4), 4b(1) and (4), and 4e(1.3) and (4.2), includes the amounts deriving from the sale of products and from services rendered by the undertakings in question, in the national or global market (as the case may be), during the last fiscal year and corresponding to their usual activities, the discounts on sales deducted together with the value-added tax and other taxes directly connected to the turnover.
   In the total turnover of a participating undertaking are not included the transactions carried out between undertakings mentioned in the following paragraph 5.
3. By derogation of the provisions of the previous paragraph 2, when the concentration is carried out by acquisition of parts of one or more undertakings, regardless if these parts constitute legal entities or not, only the turnover and the market share corresponding to the transferred part are taken into account as far as the transferor is concerned.
   If two or more transactions of those laid down in the previous subparagraph are carried out between the same natural persons or undertakings within a period of two (2) years, they are considered as one concentration that is carried out on the date of the last transaction.
4. Instead of the turnover, the following items are taken into account:
   a) For the credit institutions and the other financial organizations, the total sum of the following categories of revenues, as laid down in the provisions of the presidential decree 367/1994 (Government Gazette Issue 200 A′), after deduction, as the case may be, of the value-added tax and other taxes directly connected to the services rendered and products in question:
      aa) revenues from interests and assimilated revenues,
      bb) revenues from titles:
         — revenues from actions, shares and other titles of floating return,
         — revenues from participations
         — revenues from shares in interconnected undertakings
      cc) commissions
      dd) net revenues from money credit transactions,
      ee) other exploitation revenues.
   b) The turnover of a credit or financial institution in Greece includes the revenue items, as laid down above, that are achieved, as the case may be, by a branch or part of this undertaking, established in Greece.

[12] Art 8, law 3373/2005. This provision had initially been inserted into the law by Art 2, law 1934/1991, as Art 4e. It was subsequently replaced (as the new Art 4f) by Art 2(7), law 2296/1995, and modified by Arts 9(8) and (9), law 2741/1999, and 1(6), law 2837/2000.

c) For the insurance companies, the value of the gross premiums that include all amounts collected or to be collected by virtue of the insurance policies that have been concluded by them or on their behalf, including premiums transferred to the reinsurers, as this value emerges after the deduction of taxes and other levies collected on the basis of the amount of premiums or of the total volume of this amount. As far as the calculation of the turnover within Greece is concerned, pursuant to articles 4a and 4b, the items taken into account are respectively the net premiums paid by the natural persons domiciled or residing in Greece.

4. Without prejudice to the provisions of paragraph 3, the turnover and the market share of a participating undertaking, pursuant to articles 4a(1) and (4), 4b(1) and (4) 4e(1.3) and (4.2), results from the sum of the turnovers and market shares of the following undertakings:
   a) of the participating undertaking,
   b) of the undertakings to which the participating undertakings directly or indirectly possess:
      aa) either more than 50 percent of their capital or assets,
      bb) or the majority of the rights of vote,
      cc) or the power to appoint or fire the majority of the members of these undertaking's administrative bodies.
      dd) or the right to manage these undertakings' affairs,
   c) of the undertakings that possess in a participating undertaking the rights or possibilities of influence mentioned in case b),
   d) of the undertakings in which an undertaking mentioned in case c) possesses the rights of influence mentioned in case b),
   e) of the undertakings in which more than one undertaking among those mentioned in cases a) to d), jointly possess the rights or possibilities of influence mentioned in case b).

6. When the undertakings participating in the concentration jointly possess the rights or possibilities of influence mentioned in paragraph 5, case b, when it comes to the calculation of the turnover of the participating undertakings pursuant to articles 4a(1b) and (4), 4b(1) and (4), and 4e(1.3) and (4.2), one must:
   a) not take into account the turnover resulting from product sales or services rendered between the joint undertaking and each one of the participating undertakings or any other undertaking connected to any one of these, in the sense of paragraph 5, cases b) to e),
   b) take into account the turnover resulting from product sales or services rendered between the joint undertaking and any third undertaking. This turnover is equally assessed among the participating undertakings.

According to Article 25 of law 703/77,[13]

1. When it is necessary for the exercise of the Hellenic Competition Commission's powers laid down in the present law, the Hellenic Competition Commission's Chairman or the (thereby) authorized Director or employee of the Directorate General of Competition, may request, by way of a written document, information from undertakings, associations of undertakings or other natural persons or legal entities, or public or other authorities. This document must refer to the provisions of law constituting the foundation of this request, to the time-limit fixed for providing information, which cannot be shorter than five (5) days for information regarding cases of injunction or decisions based on article 4e(3) of the present law, ten (10) days for information concerning cases of concentrations, and twenty (20) days for the rest of the cases, as well as to the sanctions provided in case of non-compliance with the obligation for providing information.

[13] Art 6(2), law 2296/1995, as modified by Art 9(19), law 2741/1999, and Art 26, law 3373/2005. It replaced Art 25, law 703/1977.

The addressees of this document are obliged to immediately, fully and accurately provide the requested information. When the information is requested from undertakings or associations of undertakings, the responsible persons or the competent employees thereof, pursuant to article 30, are obliged to provide it. Those who cannot be examined during criminal trials, pursuant to article 212 of the Code of Criminal Procedure, are not obliged to provide any information, provided that they observe the obligation laid down in paragraph 3 of the same article. The provisions on bank confidentiality are not prejudiced by the provisions of the present paragraph.

2. In case of refusal of, recalcitrance or delay in the supply of the requested information pursuant to the previous paragraph, or in case of supply of inaccurate or incomplete information, without prejudice to the penal sanctions laid down in article 29 of the present law, the Hellenic Competition Commission:
   a) when it comes to undertakings or associations of undertakings, directors or employees thereof, as well as private individuals or public law corporate bodies, imposes a fine of fifteen thousand (15,000) euros with a maximum limit of 1 percent of the turnover, as this is calculated pursuant to article 4f for each one of the those persons or entities and for each infringement,
   b) when it comes to civil servants or employees of public law corporate bodies, refers to the competent authority for the initiation of the disciplinary prosecution for the aforementioned infringements that constitute a disciplinary fault.

B. Research Evaluation

In order to evaluate whether the non-notified acquisition of minority interests between Sea Star and ANEK is subject to the provisions of Articles 4a and 4b of Law 703/77, as applicable, the DGC within its competence sent questionnaires to the participating companies while evaluating the existing material, which was collected for the purposes of routine inquiry in the field of coastal shipping.

Furthermore, the DGC sent a letter to the owner of Sea Star in accordance with the provisions of Article 25 of law 703/77, as applicable, asking him to provide data on the companies in which he held more than 5 per cent. In his letter of reply the owner of Sea Star stated that 'he did not participate or participate as an individual with more than 5 percent in companies of the industry on your investigation'. Furthermore, during the above communication, DGC wrote another letter asking for full details of all the companies outside the coastal shipping industry in which the owner of Sea Star had an interest amounting to more than 5 per cent for the period January 2007 to the date of dispatch of the letter, and his share in each of them.

i. The Issue of Control in Sea Star

According to the DGC's evaluation, the board of directors of Megabet (the former name of Sea Star Capital) decided at a meeting on 22 April 2007 that it was in the interest of both the company and its shareholders to expand its business into new areas, always within the framework of its business objectives. To this end, the board determined to seek business opportunities to make acquisitions of international companies or stakes in international companies whose business would include shipping and the extraction of mineral wealth. New funds were required to implement this expansion, and therefore the Board decided to issue new share capital totalling €100 million to one or more strategic investors, after noting that these strategic investors must ensure the company was able to make the new investments. That issue and sale of shares had to be completed by 31 December 2007.

Five days later, on 27 April 2007, the board of directors of Megabet decided to propose to the upcoming extraordinary general meeting on 22 May 2007 that the company be renamed Sea Star Capital Public Limited Company. A further meeting of the board of directors took place on 1 June 2007 at which the main topic was: 'Talk of a possible amendment of the Articles of Association of the Company'. Eventually it was decided not to proceed to an extraordinary general meeting to amend any of the founding documents, because at that stage it was not thought to be a matter that needed to be resolved immediately. In the context of the specific decision, and after a series of meetings with potential strategic investors, the board of directors decided on 28 June 2007 to accept the interest of two investors (one of them the future owner of Sea Star). The minutes of that board meeting on the subject of 'approval of strategic investor', ie the future owner of Sea Star, state:

> Following contacts conducted by the Company with a number of strategic investors the Board decided unanimously, in first, to accept the interest of [the first investor] for an investment totaling €61 million and [the second investor] for a total of €14m. Subsequently, the Board authorized the Chairman of the Company, with the assistance of legal advisors, to negotiate with the above investors in order to realize this investment.

On 5 July 2007, the following steps were approved by the board of directors of Sea Star:

(a) participation of the company in the acquisition of a similar company and authorized the president to proceed with the relevant investments without the need to refer the matter to the board; and
(b) reorganization of the company's activities so that the existing activities of the company would be transferred to a subsidiary company named Megabet Ltd.

On 25 July 2007 the board of directors of Sea Star decided to ask the company's stockbrokers to conduct an evaluation and assessment study of the ferry company ANEK (which was listed on the Athens Stock Exchange) with the purpose of strategic investment in it. According to the memorandum that was filed for approval with the Cyprus Stock Exchange, after the implementation and completion of the capital share of the company, Sea Star intended to proceed to enlarge the board such that its composition would reflect the shareholder structure and experience in the shipping industry. More specifically, it declare that: 'Indicatively, the two investors, …, the interest of which for investment totaling 75 million euros has been accepted by the Board of Directors, have proven knowledge and experience in this industry.'

On 3 August 2007 an interim investment agreement was signed between Sea Star and the first investor, in which Sea Star's original intention of acquiring shares in ANEK was revealed. More specifically, preamble A of the agreement provided as follows:

> The Company is a public limited liability company registered in Cyprus and its shares are traded on the Cyprus Stock Exchange with a wide range of activities and tasks and hopes to expand its activities in the field of shipping.

In addition, it was stated in point B of the preamble that 'the company in connection with enlargement of its work is in the process to increase the issued capital by 100,000,000 (one hundred million euros) by issuing shares in various strategic investors'.

Section C of the preamble stated that: 'The Investor [ie the first investor] is a businessman who is active in various fields of business and hopes to acquire shares in the capital of the Company amounting up to 61,000,000 (sixty-one million euros).'

This agreement was implemented on the basis of the following conditions:

> 2.3 The company agrees that the sum of the initial commitment will be used exclusively by this for the following purposes:
>
> A) to acquire shares of ANEK, or and
> B) as part of the collateral for a loan or funding the total amount of which shall not exceed 61,000,000 million euros for the purchase of shares of ANEK.
>
> 2.4 … The Parties agree that the Investor will be able by the exchanging of that check to require and receive shares of the share capital of a total value of 61,000,000 Euros without waiting for the issue and the concession by the Company of the New Shares.
>
> 2.5 The Parties agree that the amount of the initial commitment is not provided by the investor to the company in the form of loans or facilities and will not bear interest against the Company.

On 28 August 2007 the board of Sea Star provided the following information:

> (a) Sea Star has come to an agreement with the first investor for the form of payment of 61 million euros. Until then a sum of 30.593.775 euros had been deposit to the Company and has been reported that is guaranteed by the bank a credit facility totaling 55 million euros with a commitment of the amount of 26.5 million euros (cash of the company) and personal guarantees offered by the first investor and
> (b) The company had acquired the 14.93 percent (= 23,495,163 shares) of the listed in the Athens Stock Exchange company with the name ANEK.

On 26 November 2007 the chairman of the board informed the other members that

> he is informed by PROTON BANK SA (the 'Bank') that Mr […] who is client of the Bank seems willing to sell its shareholdings in the share capital of Minoan Lines and Hellenic Seaways. The Board of Directors decides to inform about this development [the first investor], who after the completion of the issue of share capital which is in progress, will become the largest shareholder of the Company.

On 28 November 2007 the members of the board were informed that the largest shareholder of Sea Star

> has been informed and consents to explore the possibility of investing in companies Minoan Lines and Hellenic Seaways, but recommends that the company should appoint professional advisers to study and advise the company on this issue. The Board agrees with the recommendation of Mr […] and decides to appoint and hereby appoints companies Credit Suisse and Deutche Bank, to the position of consultants of the company for this investment.

On 31 December 2007 the board decided to proceed with the issue and concession of 234,615,385 new shares of the company at a price of €61 million in company Estragon Ltd as designated by Mr […], as the means of his participation.

In conclusion, on the basis of the above analysis, it appears that the largest shareholder of Sea Star, following the implementation of the interim agreement on investment (3 August 2007) and his participation through the company Estragon Ltd in the share capital of Sea Star (39.42 per cent), controlled Sea Star, which allowed him to take crucial strategic decisions affecting the company.

ii. Control System of HSW—The Significance of Documents

On 11 December 2007 the board of directors of Sea Star announced the acquisition of a 26.71 per cent stake in the company Minoan Lines and the acquisition of a 34.70 per cent stake in HSW. On the basis of these developments, Sea Star, which already owned 1.8 per cent of HSW through its subsidiary Magnilon Ltd, then owned a total of 36.5 per cent of the shares of HSW. Taking into account that the only other shareholder in HSW was Minoan Lines with 33.5 per cent, the question raised was whether from 11 November 2007 Sea Star had joint or sole control over the HSW.

Even if the initial evidence suggested joint control, subsequent events reinforced the view that Sea Star in fact exercised exclusive control over HSW. In particular, at the HSW board meeting of 18 December 2007 the second vice-president of the company resigned and in his position was elected an attorney, who appeared to cooperate with Sea Star. At the same meeting the agenda was determined regarding HSW's expansion into maritime cargo (containers) on regular routes within the Mediterranean but was not to be discussed before the information of the new shareholder (Sea Star).

Even more indicative of the new state of affairs that arose due to the (controlling) acquisition of Sea Star's 36.5 per cent stake in HSW is the importance its board placed on a number of significant issues raised by one of its members at a meeting on 3 January 2008: (a) continuing the preparation of the company for listing on the Athens Stock Exchange; (b) engaging in company management through joint committees and finalizing confirmation of the merged entity; and (c) preparation/filing of its 2008 budget, under the precondition that the new shareholder of the company, Sea Star, has previously been informed about and approved of this.

In addition, on 17 January 2008 the replacement of the second vice-president of HSW (see above), who had participated in the Maritime Commission-Technical-Procurement Committee and in the Development and New Investment Committee, by the new board member (attorney) was confirmed. Furthermore, the new board member participated on the Commercial-Economic-Assessment-Remuneration and Audit Committees of the company.

As an extension of the same reasoning but with obvious elements of exclusive rather than joint control is the statement by a representative of Minoan Lines on 6 March 2008, according to which

> expressing the view of shareholders of Minoan Lines company has indicated that they claim to participate in the affairs of the company Hellenic Seaways and in what happens therein with the other large shareholder Sea Star. Expressed also the complaint that decisions were taken for route planning—and were introduced in the Committees—in absentia of Minoan Lines.

In addition, the briefing provided to the board by the managing director on this issue is from this perspective revealing, to the extent that compliance with the request of the shareholders of Minoan Lines concerning participation in the management of HSW seems to depend on its potential acceptance by the representative of Sea Star. Specifically, in the minutes of the board of directors meeting on 6 March 2008 it was stated that:

> The CEO Mr [...] informed the Board that has already informed Mr [...] of Minoan Lines that no decision was taken on the merits, but instead he said at the outset to the representative of Sea Star, I.V., with whom he collaborated on several issues of fleet operators the Hellenic Seaways, that what is discussed between them will be discussed by the committees of the Hellenic Seaways, and

> that Mr I.V. brought no objection to this. Mr [...] submitted a request to participate the Minoan Lines to what preliminary occur, exercising their right to equal approximately stake in the company.

Nevertheless, the real nature and extent of the control of Sea Star over HSW progressively emerged as that of sole control. In particular, on 13 March 2008, the company shareholder Sea Star submitted to the board of HSW a draft of major amendments to the statutory text and requested an extraordinary general meeting be convened to adopt these. The proposed amendments included the following:

— widening of the purpose of the company (Article 4) by adding new business lines;
— capital increase through the issue of redeemable shares and prediction of the relevant procedure;
— prediction of the preponderance of the vote of the chairman of the board in case of an even number of votes; and
— provision for meetings of the board within and outside of Greece (Cyprus).

Eventually the extraordinary general meeting convened and all the above-mentioned amendments were adopted, thus confirming the power of the Cypriot influence on the management of the company.

In addition, on 17 April 2008, the largest shareholder of Sea Star was elected CEO of the board of HSW, replacing Mr [...] who had resigned the previous day, while the position of CEO in the company was upgraded as follows:

> The CEO of the company oversees all company services, shows diligence for the compliance with the statutes and decisions of the Board, plans and coordinates the work of all services and performs the control of these, represents the company outwards binding it only with his signature, where no other joint signature is demanded as follows, prepares and introduces to the Board for discussion the agenda and monitors the implementation of its decisions.

In addition, the result of the election of new board members of the company during the subsequent postponed general meeting of shareholders on 17 May 2008 was very significant: 'Members of the Board for three years in accordance with article 18 paragraph 2 of the Statutes were elected eleven persons in the order of their election and depending on the crosses of preference that each one received.'

At this same general meeting the changes to HSW's statutes proposed by Sea Star on 13 March 2008 (see above) were also adopted. Finally, at a meeting on 21 May 2008 of the members of the HSW board, following the proposal of its CEO, the board was unanimously chosen and established as body. It is worth noting that at the same meeting the largest shareholder of Sea Star and CEO of HSW was designated as president, and the duties of the chairman of the board were redefined and upgraded as follows:

> The CEO of the company supervises all company services, shows diligence for the compliance with the statutes and decisions of the Board, plans and coordinates the work of all services and performs the control of these, represents generally the company, prepares and introduces to the Board for discussion the agenda and monitors the implementation of its decisions.

As a result of the above-mentioned voting, and in conjunction with the existing form of the HSW board, the following issues arose:

(a) Despite the participation of Minoan Lines in the postponed extraordinary general meeting of HSW (17 May 2008) for the election of a new board of directors, which was formed in shares equal to 33.3 per cent of the share capital of HSW, not even one member of the board of HSW came from Minoan Lines, even though the latter constituted the second largest (after Sea Star) shareholder of HSW.

(b) More specifically, the Minoan Lines candidates with the names Vavourakis Michail, Mamalakis Kon/nos, Dris Georgios and Xenikakis Ioannis, failed to get elected, in comparison with the last elected candidate, Mr N Mousas, who was the Sea Star candidate.

(c) The lack of representation of the second major shareholder (ie Minoan Lines) on the board of HSW in conjunction with the fact that at least two board members who held important positions of responsibility in the company (president and vice-president, respectively) were representing Sea Star's interests, demonstrated clearly the decisive influence that Sea Star had in critical decision-making such as the election of board members

(d) The entire board of HSW, as elected at the latest general meeting held on 17 May 2008, came from the major shareholder, Sea Star.

(e) The largest shareholder of Sea Star and CEO of HSW had increased powers in HSW, as chairman of the board and especially after the adjustment/increase of his board powers.

It is worth noting that the absence of control in HSW by the Minoan Lines, was inter alia confirmed by statements made by company representatives. More specifically, a representative of Minoan Lines, in a recent interview, stressed that 'Minoan don't participate in the administration of this company [ie HSW]', adding that 'what would happen with the block of shares holding in it will be decided soon by the company (ie Minoan Lines)'.

In support of these findings, the DCG solicited a testimony in accordance with Article 26 of law 703/77, as amended, from a former board member of HSW. More specifically, in his evidence on 10 July 2008, this individual stated the following:

DGC Question: What happened during the general meeting of 17 May 2008?

Answer: There was elected a new Board, which was the main theme of the extraordinary general meeting, and if I'm not mistaken, were adopted the proposed amendments to the Articles of Association of the company which were all included in the application for concurrency from the share Sea Star. It is worth noting that this shareholder and portion of the agreed with her shareholders were represented by about the 52 percent (if I'm not mistaken) of the paid up share capital.

DGC Question: How many and which members proposed Minoan Lines for the Board of Hellenic Seaways, in the meeting of May 17, 2008?

Answer: With a Board decision of Minoan Lines were proposed … who were then all members of the Board of Minoan Lines, of which none was elected, although all the four were exposed as candidates.

DGC Question: How many and which members proposed Sea Star to the Board of the Hellenic Seaways at the meeting of May 17, 2008?

Answer: I am not able to mention them by name, but elected those that were suggested, that means eleven out of eleven.

DGC question: By what process are proposed the candidates for the Board?

Answer: Theoretically all of them had the desire to do so and of these were elected the ones that proposed the majority holder of Hellenic Seaways shareholder, namely the Sea Star.

DGC Question: As Minoan Lines did you participate in the exercise of administration of Hellenic Seaways; When changed the balance regarding the management of the company?

Answer: Until the extraordinary general meeting of Hellenic Seaways, which as I mentioned was held on 17th May 2008, adjourned, Minoan Lines attended the Board of the company (Hellenic Seaways) with four members of their Board. After the extraordinary general meeting there is no representation of Minoan Lines in the Board of Hellenic Seaways. Since then there is no participation of Minoan Lines in the administration and management of the company Hellenic Seaways.

DGC Question: Do you think that the Sea Star can exercise alone the exclusive control over the company Hellenic Seaways;

Answer: As I mentioned on the proposed eleven, Sea Star elected eleven members of the Board.

iii. Distribution of Votes at General Meetings of HSW

All shareholders attended the general meetings held in the years prior to the ex officio investigation by the HCC, and from examination of these meetings the following conclusions arise:

(a) Significant decisions taken at general meetings, such as the election of board members, the approval of annual financial statements, the amendment of the statutes and the issuing of bond, were taken by a majority of the votes in the years 2004–08, during which the entire share capital remained unchanged at 77,615,000 common shares.
(b) A significant proportion of HSW shareholders attended the general meetings; however, according to the statutes, decisions were taken based on a fifth of shareholders (15,523,000 shares) representing the share capital (Article 14 of the statutes).
(c) By 11 December 2007 the total percentage of Sea Star's holding in HSW, including the percentage held by the Magnilon Ltd, which as mentioned above was a 100 per cent subsidiary of Sea Star, was 34.50 + 1.8 = 36.50 per cent.
(d) Even if it could be assumed that theoretically the available from Sea Star percentage of votes is not always adequate for the adoption of critical decisions without the involvement of additional votes from other shareholders, nevertheless in practice the vote on 17 May 2008 showed that in issues of exceptional importance with long-term effects, eg the amendment of the statutes and the election of board members, Sea Star in reality had the support of a large number of shareholders, which together accounted for about 52 per cent of the share capital. Indicatively, during the last general meeting of the company, the CEO of ANEK who is a major shareholder in Sea Star, represented a significant number of common shares of other shareholders, the voting rights of which were exercised according to his own discretion.

Adding together the Magnilon Ltd and Sea Star shareholdings, it is found that the gathered shares represent 46 per cent of the highest number of votes cast at general meetings of HSW from 2004 to 2008.

It follows that from December 11, 2007, the date marking the last change in the shareholder structure of the company Hellenic Seaways (ie before the decision of the Hellenic Competition Commission), the company Sea Star exercised effective control, which, according to all indications, is sole control or at least joint during the period before the election of new members of the Board.

In conclusion, the view that the Sea Star did not have a turnover in 2007 in the national market in accordance with the provisions of Article 4f of law 703/77, as applicable, is found to be in complete contradiction of the fact that the latter exercised control (solely or at least jointly with Minoan Lines) in HSW. Therefore, a turnover of HSW either by 100 per cent, or by 50 per cent respectively, must be attributed to Sea Star.

iv. Control Regime of ANEK

On 24 August 2007 Sea Star acquired 19,967,663 common shares of ANEK, thereby increasing the number of these shares it held to 23,495,163, representing 15.90 per cent of the share capital of the company and the respective voting rights. On 25 January 2008 Sea Star made a new purchase of 26,760,003 common shares of ANEK, thereby gathering a total of 52,422,237 shares representing 32.50 per cent of the share capital of ANEK and corresponding voting rights. Therefore, Sea Star constituted by far the largest shareholder of ANEK (the second largest shareholder, Morgan Stanley & Co International plc, held no more than 7.45 per cent of ANEK' s share capital).

In light of this and in order to investigate the nature and extent of the control exercised by Sea Star over ANEK, the DGC considered it necessary to examine the participation of Sea Star's shareholders in ANEK's general meetings and the persons who control these meetings. For the year 2008 the overall rate of Sea Star shareholdings in ANEK was 32.50 per cent. Therefore, Sea Star with this percentage was in a position to influence critical decisions (election of board members, financial reporting, etc) taken by ANEK. Furthermore, it was emphasized that 'in the company ANEK Mr [...] h[eld] percentage amounting to 1.5 percent and repeatedly is elected to the Board of Directors of the company as CEO since 2001'.

Apart from the majority voting rights Sea Star held in the share capital of ANEK, the dominant influence that the Sea Star exercised through the presence of the largest shareholder of the company in ANEK is reflected in the minutes of discussion of its general meeting. In particular, during the general meeting of ANEK of 25 March 2005, Mr [...] mentioned: 'I would say that today the main reason of our meeting is to vote whether I and my colleagues will continue administrating with the vision that we have.' After the vote, the largest shareholder of Sea Star decided to remain a member of the board of ANEK.

Also, at the general meeting of ANEK held on 3 February 2008 it was mentioned by one of the participants that: 'Today [...] does not exist, he has been replaced by the company Sea Star represented and manipulated by the interests of the CEO of ANEK [...].'

Based on the above analysis, it was concluded that Sea Star with 32.5 per cent of the share capital of ANEK held the necessary majority in general meetings, which could not be influenced by temporary or permanent precarities caused by possible collaboration by other shareholders. This fact, in conjunction with the fact that since 2001 the largest shareholder of Sea Star was the CEO of ANEK, who through Estragon Ltd held 39.42 per cent of the share capital of Sea Star, was sufficient to lead to the conclusion that Sea Star controlled ANEK and could take critical decisions about its future business planes.

Market conditions may affect negatively competition, both in the short as well as in the longer term. More specifically in the present, on the one hand, in the short term, competition decreased because of the *disappearance* of a competitor from the Piraeus–Chania route and the enhanced company that would emerge from acquisition, especially for the Crete and Paros–Naxos routes. On the other hand, in the long term, the intensity of potential competition would be reduced on the Piraeu–Heraklion, Piraeus–Syros–Tinos–Mykonos and Adriatic routes.

On the basis of the data analysed above, it appeared that the control of ANEK by Sea Star came under the provisions of preventive control of concentrations of law 703/77, as amended, and should therefore be notified to the HCC on the basis of Article 4b of that law.

III. Legal Assessment

A. Control of Sea Star Capital by its Largest Shareholder

i. The Issue of Permanent Change of Control

According to the interim agreement which was signed on 3 August 2007, prior to this date Sea Star had no activity at all in the maritime sector. It is worth noting that according to point A of the preamble of the interim agreement:

> [T]he company [Sea Star] is a public limited liability company registered in Cyprus and its shares are traded on the Cyprus Stock Exchange with a wide range of activities and tasks and hopes to expand its activities in the maritime sector.

In addition, point B of the same preamble mentioned that: '[T]he company [Sea Star] in the context of the enlargement of its work is in the process of increasing the issued capital by 100,000,000 (one hundred million euros) by issuing shares in various strategic investors.'

Furthermore, point C declared that:

> The Investor [the first investor and subsequent the largest shareholder of Sea Star] is a businessman who is active in various fields of business and hopes to acquire shares in the capital of the Company amounting up to 61,000,000 (sixty-one million euros).

In fact it was known that this investor was already active in the shipping industry before this acquisition of shares.

One of Sea Star's documents, issued through the assignee law firm, stated that:

> [T]he Company is diversified and there is no shareholder with voting rights that could be able to exercise control of the Company. In this sense, control is exercised by each time formed majority of shareholders in accordance with the conditions laid down in the statutes.

Did the first investor through the acquisition of shares to the value of €61 million in the capital of Sea Star essentially acquire control of this company? For the correct answer to this crucial question, it is important to emphasize that the conceptual content of concentration provides for change of control on a permanent basis. It is remarkable that paragraph 1(b) of Article 3 of Regulation 139/2004 states:

> A concentration shall be deemed to arise where a change of control on a lasting basis results from … the acquisition, by one or more persons already controlling at least one undertaking, or by one or more undertakings, whether by purchase of securities or assets, by contract or by any other means, of direct or indirect control of the whole or parts of one or more other undertakings.

Furthermore, paragraph 20 (1st sentence) of the recital of Regulation 139/2004 states that:

> It is expedient to define the concept of concentration in such a manner as to cover operations bringing about a lasting change in the control of the undertakings concerned and therefore in the structure of the market. It is therefore appropriate to include, within the scope of this Regulation, all joint ventures performing on a lasting basis all the functions of an autonomous economic entity.

On the basis of the above-mentioned critical remarks, firstly it needs to be emphasized that determining whether control has been obtained constitutes a real issue that should be investigated ad hoc. In this context, it is prudent to consider whether permanent change of control has the meaning of *no restitutio in integrum*. The audit findings may result from a combination of different indications. It is considered that acquisition of sole or joint control, directly or indirectly, exists in the case where the contract being considered provides the possibility of decisive influence of one or more undertakings, based on property rights, exploitation rights, etc, or contractual rights (eg shareholder agreements, long-term contracts of economic dependence) or any other means. It is conceivable that the above-mentioned general definition of control can include additional cases in the concept of concentration and not only those which were indicatively listed in Article 4 paragraph 3 of law 703/77.[14]

ii. Economic Dependence

In particular, as referred to in Article 4, paragraph 3(a) of law 703/77, the acquisition of control may be based, inter alia, on the use of all or part of the assets of the business. Furthermore, control may result from relations of economic dependence: according to the practice of the European Commission, it has been accepted that such relations are, for example, long-term supply agreements or credit provided by suppliers or clients—such agreements may lead to one undertaking exercising *decisive influence* over another.[15]

Regarding especially the issue of providing credit, it is recalled, as mentioned in the above economic analysis, that the interim investment agreement between the Sea Star and its largest shareholder signed on 3 August 2007, apart from hinting that the real intention was the acquisition of ANEK's shares by Sea Star, also stated that:

> '[T]he Parties agree that the Investor will be by the encashment of that check to require and receive shares of the share capital of the Company of total value of 61,000,000 (sixty-one million) euros without waiting for issue and concession by the Company of the New Shares. … The Parties agree

[14] 'For the application of the present law, control derives from rights, contracts or other means, which either individually or jointly with other ones, and taking into consideration the relevant factual and legal conditions, offer the possibility of a decisive influence on the activities of an undertaking, and *particularly* [emphasis added] by means of:

(a) rights of property or usufruct on the whole or part of an undertaking's assets,
(b) rights or contracts offering the possibility of a decisive influence on the composition, meetings and decisions of an undertaking's bodies.

1. Control is taken by the natural person or persons, or undertakings that:
   (a) are subjects of these rights or empowered by those agreements or
   (b) without being holders of these rights or beneficiaries of said contracts, they are entitled to make use of the rights emanating there from.'

[15] Cases IV/M.258 *CC IE/GTE*, 25 September 1992, IV/M.697 *Lockheed Martin Corporation/Loral Corporation*, 27 March 1996 and IV/M.286 *Zurich/MMI*, 2 April 1993 are considered as relevant decisions by the European Commission.

> that the amount of the initial commitment is not provided by the investor to the company in the form of loans or facilities and will not bear interest against the Company.

Once again, it should be underlined that *control may be obtained by any means*. Therefore, *purely economic ties can play a decisive role in the acquisition of control*. Indeed, in exceptional cases it cannot be excluded that a situation of economic dependence could lead to de facto control, provided that, for instance, significant long-term supply agreements or supply of credit to suppliers or customers, combined with structural links, ensure decisive influence. It is estimated that the investment by the largest shareholder (either debt security is considered or not) in Sea Star of €61 million constitutes such a case.[16] Regarding in particular the relationship between this shareholder and Sea Star, it should be noted that the privilege of redemption or conversion of shares may not be sufficient to secure exclusive control, *unless it will be exercised in the near future by legally binding agreements, as happened in the case examined here.*

It is emphasized that, according to the practice of the Commission, despite the fact that the privilege generally does not lead by itself to a concentration, it may however be taken into account for the substantial assessment of a relative concentration. Nevertheless, it is underlined that under preconditions it cannot a priori be excluded that this privilege, in combination with other elements, could lead to the conclusion that there was de facto sole control.[17] In the case examined, it was estimated that the final redemption of shares to the amount of €61 million by a subsidiary of the largest shareholder of Sea Star, combined with the expressed intention to invest in ANEK of which the same shareholder continued to be CEO,[18] also considered in connection with the essential change in the statutory purpose of Sea Star which took place simultaneously with the involvement of its largest shareholder in the share capital, could lead the HCC safely to the conclusion that this specific natural person exercised in any case de facto sole control over the Sea Star.

The following points can also help us to reach this conclusion.

iii. Combined Assessment of Economic Dependence with the Expertise of the Same Natural Person: Exclusive Control

In connection with the above investment it is estimated that the confirmed know-how of the largest shareholder of Sea Star concerning the shipping industry by itself created a relationship of economic dependence between Sea Star and this individual, as prior to his involvement in the share capital and then in the administration of it, Sea Star had no connection whatsoever with the shipping industry.

More specifically, it is characteristic that the letter that Sea Star sent to the DGC, through the assignee law firm, mentioned (inter alia) the following decision of its board of directors dated 28 November 2007:

> Mr […] informed the Board members that (the first investor and subsequent its largest shareholder) is informed and consents to explore the possibility of investing in companies Minoan Lines and Hellenic Seaways, but recommends that the company should appoint professional advisers

[16] See also Cases IV/M.794 *Coca-Cola/Amalgamated Beverages GB*, IV/M.625 *Nordic Capital/Transpool*, and IV/M.697 *Lockheed Martin Corporation/Loral Corporation*.

[17] Relevant is the European Commission's decision in Case IV/M.397 *Ford/Hertz*, 7 March 1994.

[18] At the moment of the HCC's decision.

> to study and advise the company on this issue. The Board agrees with the recommendation of [the first investor] and decides to appoint and hereby appoints the companies Credit Suisse and Deutche Bank, to the position of consultants of the Company for this investment.

As noted in this document, the board of Sea Star made no investments unless it had the consent of the strategic investor, and always chose immediately to satisfy his recommendations. It is estimated that the *Gillette/Wilkinson Sword* (*Stora/Swedish Match/Gillette*) case constitutes a similar case encountered by the competition authority in the UK in 1991.[19] Proportionately, a similar phenomenon is observed regarding the position of the first investor in relation to Sea Star: in this case business activities were undertaken by the board only after the approval of the strategic investor.

According to the above-mentioned elements, it is estimated that if in fact the largest shareholder in Sea Star is not in reality the creator of the company, he nevertheless is the only person who controls it. More specifically, according to the above-mentioned general definition of control, which definition may also result even from relationships of economic dependence, it may safely be considered that the largest shareholder through the acquisition of shares in the capital of Sea Star totalling €61 million essentially took control of the company concerned. As was characteristically noted on 2 March 2008: '[T]he company SEA STAR … is represented and manipulated by the interests … of […].' Once again, it is emphasized that prior to the involvement of Mr […] in its share capital Sea Star had not been active in the shipping industry.

iv. Control of HSW by Sea Star–Concept of Control

Under the provision of Article 4, paragraph 3[20] of law 703/77, which resembles Article 3, paragraph 2 of Regulation 139/2004,[21] 'the conceptual content of control is defined as the possibility of exercising decisive influence on the activity of an undertaking'. Therefore it is not necessary to prove that the decisive influence is exercised effectively or that it will be exercised with certainty in the future.

Nevertheless, as illustrated by the relevant case law, *the ability to influence must be real.* In accordance with the above-mentioned provision of Article 4, paragraph 3 of law 703/77, control, ie the decisive influence on an undertaking, may be exercised through rights, contracts or any other means, either individually or in combination and always by taking into account the factual or legal conditions that characterize the case examined.

Consequently, a concentration can be carried out either on a legal basis (de jure) or in fact (de facto). A concentration may also take the form of sole or joint control and extend to all or parts of one or more businesses. In the case examined it was investigated whether Sea Star acquired joint control (with Minoan lines) or had the exclusive control over HSW.

[19] See especially http://webarchive.nationalarchives.gov.uk/20111202195250/http:/competition-commission.org.uk/rep_pub/reports/1991/301storakopparbergs.htm.

[20] Above n 14.

[21] 'Control shall be constituted by rights, contracts or any other means which, either separately or in combination and having regard to the considerations of fact or law involved, confer the possibility of exercising decisive influence on an undertaking, in particular by: (a) ownership or the right to use all or part of the assets of an undertaking; (b) rights or contracts which confer decisive influence on the composition, voting or decisions of the organs of an undertaking.'

v. Acquisition of Control

The degree to which a (business) action leads to acquisition of control depends on a number of legal and/or factual issues. The most usual means of obtaining control is the acquisition of shares, through acquisition of assets or—in the case of joint control—in combination with the agreement of the shareholders.

Control may be acquired on the basis of a contractual relationship. In order to ascertain that this contractual relationship confers the ability to control, the control of the administration and the resources of the other company, as in the case of acquisition of shares or assets, ought to be investigated. It is noted that, according to Article 4, paragraph 3(a) of law 703/77,[22] the content of which corresponds to Article 3, paragraph 2(a) of Regulation 139/2004, control may consist of rights to use the assets of the business.[23] Such contracts may lead to joint control, where the owner of the assets and the company that controls the administration has veto rights on strategic business decisions.[24]

Finally a change of control may occur as a result of the succession of one shareholder or because of the output of a shareholder or even due to a change from joint to sole control.[25] In the case examined here, the output of a shareholder constitutes the most interesting case, especially as far as it concerns the Grimaldi group.

vi. Negative Sole Control as a Form of Exclusive Control

If one single company is in a position to affect significantly another company, it is considered that the first company has acquired sole control of the second. The undertaking that has exclusively control has the power to determine the strategic commercial decisions of the company controlled. This power is usually ensured—though not exclusively—by the acquisition of the voting rights in another company.

Furthermore, sole control exists in cases where only one shareholder is in a position to veto strategic decisions of a company, although he is not in a position to impose such decisions (negative sole control). In this case, the single shareholder has the same degree of influence usually possessed by a shareholder who *jointly* controls a company, including the power to block strategic decisions.

Nevertheless, unlike the case of a jointly controlled company, another shareholder with the same degree of influence does not exist and the shareholder holding negative sole control[26] is not bound necessarily to cooperate with other specific shareholders in order jointly to define the strategic behaviour of the controlled undertaking.

Therefore, that shareholder has the ability to block actions through the acquisition of decisive influence within the meaning of paragraph 2 of Article 3 of Regulation 139/2004, and therefore control within the meaning of the same Regulation. Indeed, as noted in footnote 60 of the Commission Consolidated Jurisdictional Notice, '[s]ince this shareholder is the only undertaking acquiring a controlling influence, only this shareholder is obliged to

[22] Above n 20.

[23] See especially Cases COMP/M.2060 *Bosch/Rexroth*, COMP/M.3136 *GE/Agfa NDT* and COMP/M.2632 *Deutsche Bahn/ECT International/United Depots/JV*.

[24] See also Commission's decisions presented in ch 5 above.

[25] See especially Cases COMP/M.3330 *RTL/M6* and COMP/M.452 *Avesta (II)*.

[26] The notion of negative control is presented in ch 2, section II.B above.

submit a notification under the Merger Regulation'. The aforementioned are applied mutatis mutandis regarding the case of Sea Star in terms of control of HSW, in which—*apart from the joint control*—the *minimum* that can be attributed is that Sea Star exerts *negative sole control over HSW.*

vii. De Facto or De Jure Sole Control

A key element for the acquisition of de jure sole control, but not the only one, is the acquisition of a majority of voting rights. Even if the majority of shares have been acquired, control is not confirmed without the acquisition of the majority of voting rights.

However, a minority shareholder may be deemed to have de facto sole control, mainly—but not exclusively—in the case that he has many chances to ensure a majority at the shareholders' meeting due to his level of participation and the attendance of shareholders at meetings during the previous years.[27] The special case of a joint venture which held participation in a company through which negative sole control was exerted over this[28] constitutes a pertinent example. In addition, in the Commission Consolidated Jurisdictional Notice paragraph 59 provides that in such cases '[b]ased on the past voting pattern, the Commission will carry out a prospective analysis and take into account foreseeable changes of the shareholders' presence which might arise in future following the operation'; eg the European Commission will apply a kind of a forward-looking and predictive approach. The decision of the European Commission in COMP M.4336 *MAN/Scania*, regarding the question of whether Volkswagen had acquired control over MAN decision, is considered relevant.[29]

In this light, the above-mentioned analysis of the majorities that supported important decisions of the general meetings of HSW in the years 2004–08 when the entire share capital of the company remained unchanged at 77,615,000 common shares is considered extremely important. Even if theoretically (eg without taking into account the line with the Sea Star shareholders) the shares created could not guarantee exclusive control for Sea Star, it could nevertheless provide with certainty, beyond joint control, at least negative control over HSW's decisions.

Furthermore, additional analysis regarding the attitudes and the role of other shareholders emphasizes the degree of practical control exercised by Sea Star over HSW. This analysis is mainly based on criteria that include structural, economic or family ties between other major shareholders and the minority shareholder or the existence of strategic or purely economic interests of the other shareholders in the target company. From this point of view the role of two individuals who served on the board of directors of Sea Star, one of them also the vice-president of HSW, is extremely important as this highlights the structural-economic links that these two individuals contribute to promoting the interests of Sea Star in HSW.

[27] See also the European Commission's decisions in Cases COMP/M.3537 *BBVA/BNL*, 20 August 2004 and M.3768 *BBVA/BNL*, 27 April 2005. Also relevant are Cases M.3198 *VW-Audi/VW-Audi Vertriebszentren*, COMP/M.2777 *Cinven Limited/Angel Street Holdings*, IV/M.258 *CCIE/GTE*.

[28] See especially Case COMP/M.3876 *Diester Industrie/Bunge/JV* (http://ec.europa.eu/competition/mergers/cases/decisions/m3876_20050930_20310_fr.pdf).

[29] See especially http://ec.europa.eu/competition/mergers/cases/decisions/m4336_20061220_20310_en.pdf.

Furthermore, on the basis of the created allocation of votes at shareholder meetings, the leadership role of the largest investor in Sea Star, which as already been mentioned, was apparent at the previous general meeting of the company where he represented not only the major shareholder, Sea Star, but also nominative shares registered with voting rights.

It is, therefore, ascertained that despite the fact that Sea Star seemed to constitute the minority shareholder, it ultimately had a stable majority at these important votings and it was therefore deemed to exercise exclusive control over the HSW. In support of this position, it is characteristic when the DGC questioned a representative of Minoan Lines if he believes that the Sea Star could currently exercise alone exclusive control over HSW, his response was positive and absolute ('As I said on the proposed eleven Sea Star elected eleven members of the Board').[30]

This absolute control of the board that established definitively exclusive control of Sea Star over HSW after 17 May 2008, of course, did not cancel the control already exercised frequently by Sea Star prior to that date, but rather confirms it, since it was the result of the relationship of forces that formed the last change in the shareholding structure of HSW on 11 December 2007.

So, since 17 May 2008 joint control of HSW from Sea Star and the only other major shareholder, Minoan Lines, no longer exists. As was said by the representative of Minoan Lines in his deposition to the DGC, after this extraordinary general meeting of 17 May 2008 'there is no representation of Minoan Lines in the Board of Hellenic Seaways. Since then there is no participation of Minoan Lines in the administration and management of the company Hellenic Seaways'.

viii. Control of ANEK by Sea Star—Apparent Control

Under the provision of Article 4, paragraph 4(a) of law 703/77[31] control may be acquired generally by persons or undertakings which are the holders of rights or beneficiaries under contracts that provide them with control.

However, there are also cases in which the apparent owner of a controlling interest does not coincide with the person or business that has substantial de facto power to exercise the rights arising from such participation. This instance may occur when an undertaking uses another person or company in order to acquire a controlling interest and maintains the power to exercise the rights from which derive this control through the particular person or business—ie that person is only typically subject to the rights; in reality he is essentially used simply as a 'vehicle'.

It is obvious that in this case control is acquired by the company behind the entity which exercises de facto power to control the target company. In the case examined it was estimated that the largest shareholder of Sea Star had obtained control over ANEK through the company Sea Star, which, as demonstrated above, he also controlled.

[30] See HCC Decision No 427/V/2009, 32 (in Greek). See also above the deposition of the former board member of HSW in accordance with Art 26 of law 703/77, as amended.

[31] 'Control is taken by the natural person or persons, or undertakings that: a) are subjects of these rights or empowered by those agreements.'

ix. Indirect De Facto Control

It is characteristic that the Court of First Instance in the *Cementbouw* case,[32] applying Regulation 4064/1989 and based on a base proportionate to the provision of Article 3, paragraph 3(a) of Regulation 139/2004, found that the control acquired by commercial companies may be attributed to their sole shareholders, to the majority shareholders or to those who have joint control over the company, given that they comply in any case with the decisions of those shareholders. Therefore it is about an indirect control for the ascertainment of which factors such as, for example, shares, contractual relationships, sources of financing or family links may be taken into account as evidence on the basis of a case-by-case analysis either alone or in combination. A characteristic related example is case M.754 *Anglo American Corporation/Lonrho* (23 April 1997).[33]

This is exactly what happened in the case under scrutiny, where the largest investor exercised sole control over Sea Star through Estragon Ltd, who also exercised sole control over ANEK, which was in turn controlled by Sea Star.

More specifically the following facts should be noted. For the year 2008 the overall percentage of Sea Star's holding in ANEK amounted to 32.50 per cent. Therefore, Sea Star with this percentage was able to take decisive decisions (election of board members, financial reporting, etc) for ANEK. It should also be emphasized that the largest shareholder of Sea Star held 1.5 per cent of ANEK and he had been repeatedly elected to the board of directors of the company as CEO since 2001. In addition, apart from the majority of voting rights that Sea Star seemed to hold in the share capital of ANEK, the dominant influence that Sea Star had—also through the largest shareholder—on ANEK was reflected in the minutes of the general meeting.

In particular, during the general meeting of ANEK of 25 March 2005, the largest shareholder of Sea Star mentioned: 'I would like to say that today the main reason of our meeting is to vote whether me and my colleagues stay and administrate (the company ANEK) with the vision that we have.'

After this vote, it was decided that he would remain as member of the board and therefore the administration of ANEK by him is inferred. In addition, the position of the Minoan Lines representative supported of this conclusion, since at the 3 February 2008 general meeting of ANEK, he stated that '[t]oday [...] does not exist, he has been substituted by the company Sea Star represented and managed by the interests of the CEO of ANEK', without a contrary view being expressed on this.

Furthermore, it appears that prior to the acquisition of 32.50 per cent of the share capital of ANEK from Sea Star (29 January 2008), the company Intesa San Paolo SpA, which is controlled by the Italian Grimaldi Group, held a significant 15.115 per cent in the share capital of ANEK. The existence of such a percentage in combination with the fact that Sea Star then held 15.90 per cent of ANEK tends to the conclusion that Sea Star was unable to exercise exclusive control over ANEK. This finding is reinforced by the fact that a significant

[32] See especially Case T-282/02 *Cementbouw Haniel & Industries v. Commission* [2006] ECR II-319. The decision was confirmed by the ECJ in its decision, reported as C-202/06 P (http://eur-lex.europa.eu/legal-content/EN/TXT/PDF/?uri=CELEX:62006CJ0202&from=GA).

[33] OJ L 149, 20/05/1998, 21–45. See especially the cases of active minority shareholdings analysed in ch 5, section I.A above.

percentage of the share capital of the company (63.32 per cent) is dispersed over a variety of (free floating) investors in the stock market (holding investments that do not exceed 5 per cent of share capital). But this scheme, as has been shown through the above analysis, has today been fundamentally changed.

The above-mentioned data confirm that, at the present time, Sea Star, which holds 32.5 per cent of the equity capital of ANEK, has the required majority in general meetings, even without being subject to temporary or permanent defaults from potential partnerships among the other shareholders. This fact, in combination with the fact that since 2001 the largest shareholder of Sea Star is the CEO of ANEK, who through Estragon Ltd controls 39.42 per cent of the share capital of Sea Star, leads to the conclusion that Sea Star controls ANEK, and is able to take critical decisions about its future business plans.

It ought to be noted that the acquisition of control constitutes an integral part of the concept of concentration. As has been accepted in theory, the *possibility of decisive influence* on the activity of an enterprise is sufficient.[34] This is the reason why it is not required to prove that the controlling undertaking is actually pursuing this option. The potential of using this option in reality is not of critical importance. Many times, it is not necessary even to make use of it, since the controlled undertaking responds by itself to the suspected desires of the controlling company. In addition, the control can be either direct or indirect.

It is stated that the minority interest (eg less than 50 per cent) in order to establish control must provide the acquirer with the power of decisive influence in the activity of the other company. The minority participation by itself is not adequate to offer the above option to the acquiring undertaking, unless special circumstances exist (eg the remaining shares are spread among the general public and the representation of these shares at general meetings is small, so that the majority of board members and the major decisions on the trade policy of the controlled company are determined by the holder of the minority stake). Under these preconditions, a minority stake below 25 per cent is in a position to exercise control.

Furthermore, it should be mentioned that the European Commission has also accepted that, in such circumstances, minority shareholdings are adequate to companies with share capital for the acquisition of control over another company.[35] Consequently, according to the above-mentioned data, it is clear that despite the fact a change in control of ANEK has been established, the HCC was not informed about this change, since the merger committed was not notified under the provisions of Article 4b[36] of law 703/77.

x. *Concluding Remarks*

According to the above-mentioned analysis, the conclusions of the legal assessment coincide with those of the economic analysis. In particular, it is noted that regarding the acquisition of control of ANEK through Sea Star, there was no notification in accordance with Article 4b of law 703/77.

[34] See, for example, RA Struijlaart, 'Minority Share Acquisitions Below the Control Threshold of the EC Merger Control Regulation: An Economic and Legal Analysis' (2002) 25(2) *World Competition* 173–204, with relevant footnotes.

[35] See, for instance, Case IV/M.343 *Société Générale de Belgique/Générale de Banque*, 20 August 1993, where it was found that it was sufficient for 25.9 per cent of the share capital to exercise control. See also HCC Decision No 360/V/2007.

[36] Above n 11.

More specifically, and bearing in mind the legal issues discussed above, in the light of this analysis, as far as it concerns the existence of the preconditions for preventive control of the merger examined, the following should be noted.

Sea Star had a domestic turnover in 2007, because the turnover of HSW was attributable to Sea Star, either via exclusive control or at least via joint control with Minoan Lines. Furthermore, ANEK had a domestic turnover of €107,855,000.00.[37]

According to paragraph 3 of Article 4b and given the fulfilment of the 'thresholds' provided in the law, as was demonstrated above, the liable (legal) person for the notification in this case (ie acquisition of control of ANEK by Sea Star) is Sea Star.

According to Article 4d, paragraph 1 of law 703/77, 'the Hellenic Competition Commission examines the notified concentration as soon as the relevant notification is submitted'. However, in the present case there was no notification, as required by the law. According to paragraph 3 of the same Article:

> If it is established that the notified concentration, although falling into the scope of application of article 4b(1), does not raise serious doubts about its capacity to significantly restrict competition in the partial markets concerned, the Hellenic Competition Commission, by decision issued within a month from the notification, allows the concentration.

Nevertheless, in the case examined, the failure to notify this de facto merger raised serious doubts about the concentration's compatibility with competition law due to the ability of this merger to restrict competition in the relevant market, as was demonstrated in detail in the above economic analysis.

According to paragraph 4 of Article 4d:

> In case of guilty breach of the obligation for notification, the Hellenic Competition Commission imposes to each one of the bearers of the obligation for notification, as laid down in paragraph 3 of the present article, a fine of at least fifteen thousand (15,000) euros, a sum that does not exceed seven per cent (7 percent) of the total turnover, as this is laid down in article 4(f).

Given the exclusive control of ANEK by Sea Star without prior notification to the HCC, the latter considered it necessary to impose a fine not exceeding 7 per cent of the total turnover of Sea Star as required by law.

Moreover, according to Article 25, paragraph 2 of law 703/77,[38] in the case examined the largest shareholder of Sea Star did not answer the questions raised by the DGC, but gave explanations retrospectively and only on the issues he wanted to address (rather than on the issues for which he was asked by the DGC), and the arguments he invoked to justify his delayed response were judged as unfounded. That said, the HCC imposed on him a fine for refusal to provide the requested information as required by law.

B. Proposal of the Directorate-General for Competition

The DGC produced a brief written proposal in which it announced its intention (a) to impose on Sea Star a fine which shall not exceed 7 per cent of the total turnover, as defined

[37] ANEK's global turnover was considered classified.

[38] Above n 13.

by the law, and (b) to fine the largest shareholder of Sea Star as a specific natural person for his refusal to provide the requested information as required by law.

The attorneys then presented their views, gave explanations and answered questions put to them by the chairman and members of the HCC and requested the rejection of the proposal.[39] After the completion of the hearing and the examination of the witness proposed by Sea Star, the attorneys of the company asked to have until 30 October 2008 to submit supplementary observations; the president of the Commission allowed this request.

The Competition Commission held a conference on 20 November 2008, which was continued and completed during the hearing on 8 January 2009. After taking into account all the documents of the case at issue, the proposal of the DGC, the views expressed orally and in writing by the parties involved at the hearing of the case and the further pleadings made to, as well as what the witness testified at the hearing, the HCC deliberated as follows:

— Imposed on Sea Star a fine of €3,742,945.40, under the provisions of paragraph 4 of Article 4b of law 703/77, as applicable.
— Imposed on Mr [...] a fine of €75,000 for his refusal to provide the information requested under the provisions of paragraph 2 of Article 25 of law 703/77, as applicable.[40]
— Ordered the conduct of an ex officio investigation in the present case under the provisions of Article 4c of law 703/77, as applicable.

The decision was issued on 8 January 2009. The Administrative Appeal Court of Athens rejected the appeal of Sea Star against decision no 427/V/2009 of the HCC with its decision no 1966/2012.

[39] In support of their claims, the attorneys of Sea Star requested the examination of a witness and the HCC, accepting their request, examined the witness under oath.

[40] Regarding this fine, the HCC by decision no 461/V/2009 changed the amount to €15,000 euro instead of €75,000.

7

Empirical Literature Review of Minority Interests

I. Empirical Evidence of Minority Shareholdings

In chapter 4 we provided a review of the theoretical literature on passive minority shareholdings; in this chapter we present an empirical literature review on them. In particular, we present the unilateral and coordinated effects of such shareholdings on competition, analyzing them in different product as well as geographical markets.

We begin with a paper by Flath which examines indirect and direct minority shareholdings in the six horizontal *keiretsu* groups of Japan (Mitsui, Mitsubishi, Sumitomo, Fuyo, Sanwa and Dai-Ichi Kangyo)[1] using 1980 data.[2] In 1980 there were 175 companies compromising about a quarter of all corporate assets in Japan. Examination of the data shows that (a) one quarter of shareholdings were indirect compared to direct; (b) in the groups with the highest direct shareholdings the indirect shareholdings on average were greatest; and (c) the majority of shareholdings, either direct or indirect, were held by financial institutions (bank and insurance companies).

According to Flath, during the 1980s banks and insurance companies in Japan were more inclined to hold direct and indirect minority shareholdings in those clients (firms) that borrowed more from them. The rationale for this strategy was based on the fact that these minority shareholdings were used to resolve agency problems of debt.[3]

Flath provided the following econometric model:

$$mi_{i,j} = \beta_0 + \beta_1 mi_{j,i} + \beta_2 \mathbf{B}_{i,j} + \beta_3 \left(\frac{Debt}{Equity} \right)_j + \beta_4 (same)_{i,j} + \varepsilon_{i,j}, \quad i = 1 \dots n \qquad (1)$$

where $B_{i,j}$ represents the fraction of *j*'s borrowing (both long-term and short-term loans but not discounted notes or other trade credit) that comes from financial institution

[1] Alley has defined *keiretsu* groups as groups of firms that have common financial links to the six groups of firms or other financial institutions which are called financial *keiretsu* (horizontal keiretsu), a group consisting a parent company and its suppliers and its subcontractors which is called a supplier *keiretsu* (vertical *keiretsu*), a group comprising of a parent company and its subsidiaries and affiliated firms (vertical *keiretsu*), and a group comprising of a manufacturer and its affiliated wholesalers and distributors, which is called a distribution *keiretsu* (vertical *keiretsu*). See WA Alley, 'Partial Ownership Arrangements and Collusion in the Automobile Industry' (1997) 45(2) *Journal of Industrial Economics* 191, 191.

[2] D Flath, 'Indirect Shareholding within Japan's Business Groups' (1992) 38 *Economics Letters* 223.

[3] D Flath, 'Shareholding Interlocks in the Keiretsu, Japan's Financial Groups' (1993) 75 *Review of Economics and Statistics* 249.

i, $mi_{i,j}$ and $mi_{j,i}$ are reciprocal minority shareholdings between i and j, $(same)_{i,j}$ is a dummy variable which means that i and j are members in the same *keiretsu* group[4] and $\left(\frac{Debt}{Equity}\right)_j$ is a financial indicator of firm j.

The author examined the following hypotheses:

H1: The greater the fraction of a firm's borrowing that is from a particular financial institution, the greater is the institution's shareholding interest in the firm.

H2: Financial institutions will have stronger equity positions in firms that have greater overall reliance on borrowing.

H3: Financial institutions will have smaller equity positions in firms that hold more of the financial institutions' stock.

Hypothesis 1 (H1) holds if:

$$\frac{\partial mi_{i,j}}{\partial B_{i,j}} > 0 \tag{2}$$

Hypothesis 2 (H2) holds if:

$$\frac{\partial mi_{i,j}}{\partial \left(\frac{Debt}{Equity}\right)_j} > 0 \tag{3}$$

Hypothesis 3 (H3) holds if:

$$\frac{\partial mi_{i,j}}{\partial mi_{j,i}} > 0 \tag{4}$$

The results show that H3 does not hold. There is no clear relation between minority shareholding by firms in financial institutions (banks) and minority shareholding by banks in the firms. Moreover, H1 holds especially for life insurance firms and city banks. H2 is not totally confirmed since it holds for some city banks, but typically overall leverage induces less minority shareholding by trust banks and some life insurance firms.

Flath tried to answer the question why large firms in Japan hold small percentages of stock (5 per cent or less) in their trading partners.[5] He claimed that firms, by holding minority shareholdings in their trading partners, may weaken their bargaining position against them, but for this reason they may penalize them at any time by divesting their partial interest. This particularly deters opportunistic behaviour by the trading partner.[6]

4 Above n 1.

5 D Flath, 'The Keiretsu Puzzle' (1995), Center on Japanese Economy and Business, Columbia University, Working Paper No 93, 1.

6 Opportunism means substituting products of lower quality than claimed or misrepresenting investments that lower the other firm's costs.

In particular, Flath stated that:

> Holding stock in a trading partner slants the bargaining over product market variables in favor of the trading partner. Divesting such a stock interest accomplishes the reverse. The firm that holds shares in a trading partner can credibly threaten to divest should the trading partner behave opportunistically, withdrawing from it the bargaining advantage that the equity position had conferred. In this manner a firm may establish a partial equity position in a trading partner to deter opportunism.[7]

Parker and Röller examined, inter alia,[8] the possibility that minority shareholdings among firms in the telecommunication industry in the US might cause collusive behaviour among them.[9] In particular, they considered the effects of cross-market behaviour on collusion where two wireline operators compete in one market and the same two operators are joint venture partners in a non-operator in another market.

The period they scrutinized was from 1984 to 1988. In the early 1980s the FTC categorized the US into 305 non-overlapping markets in which in each market two firms were awarded licenses in order to provide competing mobile cellular mobile services. During the period from 1983 to 1988 all 305 metropolitan cellular markets had two licensees operating their networks. However, at the beginning of the period some providers enjoyed a monopoly period until the second licensee appeared in the same geographical market.[10]

Parker and Röller estimated via a structural duopoly model at the industry level[11] the degree of collusion for both monopoly and duopolistic periods of time. The degree of collusion or else the conduct parameter was defined as:

$$\theta_{ts} = f(\mu_{ts}) \tag{5}$$

where μ_{ts} are various market characteristics in period t in market s and θ_{ts} is a dummy variable which takes the value 1[12] in the monopoly case or the estimated value in the duopoly case. For instance, if, inter alia, a market characteristic that affects collusion is the presence of minority shareholdings, then equation (5) becomes as follows:

$$\begin{aligned} &\theta_{ts} = \gamma_1 mi_{ts} + \gamma_2 multimarket_{ts} + \gamma_3 lead_{ts} + \gamma_4 age_{ts} + \varepsilon_{ts} \text{ in duopoly case or} \\ &\theta_{ts} = 1 \text{ in monopoly case} \end{aligned} \tag{6}$$

where mi_{ts} is a dummy variable which indicates whether the two providers are joint-venture partners in another market, $multimarket_{ts}$ measures the total number of markets where the two providers compete with each other, $lead_{ts}$ measures the monopoly period (the period until the second provider came into the market) and age_{is} measures the number of months since the introduction of the cellular service into the market.

[7] Above n 5, 3.

[8] For instance, multimarket contact is another source that might enhance collusive behaviour among firms.

[9] PM Parker and L-H Röller, 'Collusive Conduct in Duopolies: Multimarket Conduct and Cross-ownership in the Mobile Telephone Industry' (1997) 28(2) *Rand Journal of Economics* 304.

[10] For instance, the first awarded provider was Ameritech mobile in October 1983 in Chicago. This provider enjoyed a monopoly period of almost 14 months until the second awarded provider, ie Cellular One, entered the market.

[11] See, for instance, TF Bresnahan, 'Empirical Studies in Industries with Market Power' in R Schmalensee and R Willig (eds), *Handbook of Industrial Organization* (Amsterdam, Elsevier, 1989) vol 2, no 2, 1011.

[12] The authors estimated θ_{ts} for the monopoly period 1.079 with a standard error of .17.

The estimation of equation (6) indicates that if the providers jointly operate a license in another market, then this significantly affects the degree of collusion among them, ie they tend to collude more than otherwise. Also, multimarket conduct significantly increases collusion, while the pricing behaviour of the monopolist does not affect prices after the entry of the second provider.

Alley examined econometrically via a conjectural variation model the effects of minority shareholdings in Japanese corporate *keiretsu* on imports, exports, domestic competition and firms' profits.[13] Table 15 presents the passive minority shareholdings that existed among Japanese automobile manufacturers in the years 1979 and 1993.

Alley extended the model of Clarke and Davies[14] in order to incorporate passive minority shareholdings. He also assumed that Japanese automobile manufacturers consider output quantities when maximizing profit and developed a conjectural variation model that allowed for foreign trade. The model was also applied to the US automobile industry. Although collusion was found to occur in the Japanese automobile industry, it was found to be more competitive than the US automobile industry. He also found different effects of imports on firms' price–cost margins.

In particular, Clarke and Davies assumed that in a Cournot competition with a homogeneous product each firm believes that all others firms in the market will react to output changes so as to maintain their market shares. Therefore, the *i*th firm's conjecture with respect to the other firms' output changes is given by the following equation:

$$\lambda_i = \alpha \sum_{j \neq i} \frac{X_j}{X_i} = \alpha \left(\frac{X}{X_i} - 1 \right) \tag{7}$$

where $X = \sum_{i=1}^{N} X_i$ and α is the parameter which represents the degree of collusion in the market. It is assumed that the parameter is the same for all i firms and as α tends to zero we approach the Cournot case while as α tends to 1 we approach the perfect collusion case.

Given the fact that firm i maximizes its profits, ie $\max_{X_i} \pi_i = pX_i - c_i X_i$ where $p = \sum_{i=1}^{N} X_i$ is the price and c_i is the marginal cost of production, firm's i price–cost margin or profitability is given by:

$$L_i = \frac{p - c_i}{p} = \alpha \frac{1}{\eta} + (1 - \alpha) \frac{s_i}{\eta} \tag{8}$$

where η is the own price elasticity of demand.

Equation (8) can be easily estimated using a linear regression of price–cost margin against market shares.[15] Large values of estimated α imply enhanced market power and therefore collusion while low values indicate the opposite.[16]

[13] Alley (n 1) 191.

[14] See R Clarke and SW Davies, 'Market Structure and Price–Cost Margins' (1982) 49(195) *Economics* 277. See also R Clarke, SW Davies and M Waterson, 'The Profitability–Concentration Relation: Market Power or Efficiency?' (1984) 32 *Journal of Industrial Economics* 435.

[15] For an empirical application to the US manufacturing sector, see Clarke et al (n 14) 443–48.

[16] Clarke et al (n 14), 441–42 also derive equations (8) and (9) in the case of product differentiation.

Table 15: Minority shareholdings in the Japanese automobile manufacturing sector in 1979 and 1993 (per cent of total shares of the target/column firm)

Column firm / Row firm	Toyota Motor	Hino Motors	Daihatsu Motor	Isuzu Motors	General Motors	Suzuki Motor	Nissan Motor	Nissan Diesel Motor	Fuji Heavy Industries	Mazda Motor	Mitsubishi Motors	Ford Motor	Chrysler Motors
Toyota Motor	0	7.92–16.05	9.14–11.08										
Hino Motors	0.22–020	0	0.18–0.15										
Daihatsu Motor	0.23–0.21	0.15–0.13	0										
Isuzu Motors				0		0–2.32							
General Motors				34.21–37.05	0	0–3.28							
Suzuki Motor				0–1.07		0							
Nissan Motor							0	46.05–39.82	6.79–4.23				
Fuji Heavy Industries							0.07–0.49		0				
Ford Motor										0–24.54		0	
Chrysler Motors											0–15.0		0

Notes: The table presents minority shareholdings from the row firm to the column firm. The first percentages are the 1979 figures and the second ones are the 1993 figures.

Source: WA Alley, 'Partial Ownership Arrangements and Collusion in the Automobile Industry' (1997) 45(2) *Journal of Industrial Economics* 191, 192, figure 1.

The relationship between industry gross profit–revenue ratio and the *HHI* is given by the following equation:

$$\frac{\Pi}{R} = \alpha\frac{1}{\eta} + (1-a)\frac{HHI}{\eta} \tag{9}$$

where $\frac{\Pi}{R}$ is the gross profit–revenue ratio. If $\alpha = 0$ (the Cournot case), then $\frac{\Pi}{R} = \frac{HHI}{\eta}$, ie the gross profit–revenue ratio is positively related to the *HHI*.

Alley assumed[17] that each of the n firms in the market maximizes the total profit, including a fixed cost F.[18] Given the presence of minority shareholdings, equation (8) becomes as follows:

$$L_i = \frac{p-c_i}{p} = \alpha\frac{1}{\eta} + (1-\alpha)\frac{s_i}{\eta} + \frac{\sum_{j\neq i} mi_{j,i}}{\left[1-\sum_{j\neq i} mi_{i,j}\right]}\frac{s_j}{s_i}\left[\alpha\frac{1}{\eta} + (1-\alpha)\frac{s_i}{\eta} - \alpha\frac{p-c_j}{p}\right] \tag{10}$$

where mi_{ji} is the percentage of firm *j*'s stock owned by firm *i* and where mi_{ij} is the percentage of firm *i*'s stock owned by firm *j*. If $mi_{j,i} = mi_{i,j} = 0$, then we get equation (8) for a closed economy. Also if we assume $\alpha = 0$, then we get the corresponding equation for firm *i* in the Reynolds and Snapp model.[19]

Alley also assumed that passive minority shareholdings create synergies through the transfer of technologies[20] and managerial skills from one firm to another. If these synergies are proportional to the market shares of the firms that are engaged in partial minority acquisitions, then a passive minority interest from firm *i* to firm *j* is given by the following equation:

$$1+\frac{B}{A} = 1+\frac{\sum_{j\neq i} mi_{ji}s_j}{\left(1-\sum_{j\neq i} mi_{ji}\right)s_i} \tag{11}$$

where s_j the market share of firm *j*, s_i the market share of firm *i*, $\frac{B}{A}$ is the ratio of the influence of firm *i* on the profits of other firms through technology transfers over the effect of technology transfers on firm *i*'s own profits as a result of ownership in other firms.

In an open economy with foreign trade in place, equation (10) becomes more complicated since now we have to take into account the price–cost margins of firm *i* in the domestic and foreign markets.[21] The total profits of firm *i* are given by the following equation:

$$\pi_i = L_i p_i q_i = L_i^d p_i^d q_i^d + L_i^f p_i^f q_i^f \tag{12}$$

[17] Above n 13.

[18] That is, the operating earnings of firm *i* become $(p-c-F)q_i$.

[19] See also equation (3) in ch 4.

[20] See especially Alley (n 1) 193.

[21] Ibid, equations (6) and (7).

where d indicates domestic market and f indicates foreign market. Solving for L_i from equation (12), we get:

$$L_i = L_i^d \frac{p_i^d q_i^d}{p_i q_i} + L_i^f \frac{p_i^f q_i^f}{p_i q_i} \tag{13}$$

Therefore, in an open economy the price–cost margin of firm i is the weighted average of its price–cost margin in domestic and foreign markets.

Alley used equation (14) in order to estimate the price–cost margin of firm i in an economy with no imports or exports (ie a closed economy):

$$PCM_i = \alpha_1 \left[1 + \frac{\sum_{j \neq i} mi_{ji} s_j}{\left(1 - \sum_{j \neq i} mi_{ji}\right) s_i} \right] + \alpha_2 s_i \left[1 + \frac{\sum_{j \neq i} mi_{ji} s_j}{\left(1 - \sum_{j \neq i} mi_{ji}\right) s_i} \right] + \varepsilon_i \tag{14}$$

where $\alpha_1 = \frac{\alpha}{\eta}$ and $\alpha_2 = \frac{(1-\alpha)}{\eta}$.

Alley used the following equation to estimate the price–cost margin of firm i in an economy with imports and exports (ie an open economy):

$$\begin{aligned} PCM_i = {} & \alpha_1 \left[1 + \frac{\sum_{j \neq i} mi_{ji} s_j^d}{\left(1 - \sum_{j \neq i} mi_{ji}\right) s_i^d} \right] \frac{p_i^d q_i^d}{p_i q_i} + \alpha_2 s_i^d \left[1 + \frac{\sum_{j \neq i} mi_{ji} s_j^d}{\left(1 - \sum_{j \neq i} mi_{ji}\right) s_i^d} \right] \frac{p_i^d q_i^d}{p_i q_i} + \\ & \alpha_3 s^m \left[1 + \frac{\sum_{j \neq i} mi_{ji} s_j^d}{\left(1 - \sum_{j \neq i} mi_{ji}\right) s_i^d} \right] \frac{p_i^d q_i^d}{p_i q_i} + \alpha_4 \left[1 + \frac{\sum_{j \neq i} mi_{ji} s_j^f}{\left(1 - \sum_{j \neq i} mi_{ji}\right) s_i^f} \right] \frac{p_i^f q_i^f}{p_i q_i} + \\ & \alpha_5 s^f \left[1 + \frac{\sum_{j \neq i} mi_{ji} s_j^f}{\left(1 - \sum_{j \neq i} mi_{ji}\right) s_i^f} \right] \frac{p_i^f q_i^f}{p_i q_i} + \alpha_5 DGR + \alpha_6 EGR + \varepsilon_i \end{aligned} \tag{15}$$

where *DGR* is the domestic growth rate (the rate of economic growth in GDP) and *EGR* is the export growth rate.

Dietzenbacher, Smid and Volkerink[22] examined the effect of horizontal passive minority shareholdings on firms' price–cost margins in the Dutch financial sector in 1997 (Table 16). They stated that if the firms compete in a Cournot fashion the price–cost margins of the firms with minority shareholdings are 13 per cent higher than the corresponding margins of the firms without passive interests. Moreover, if the firms compete in a Bertrand fashion the price–cost margins of the firms with minority shareholdings are 2 per cent higher than the corresponding margins of the firms without passive interests.

[22] See also E Dietzenbacher, B Smid and B Volkerink, 'Horizontal Integration in the Dutch Financial Sector' (2000) 18 *International Journal of Industrial Organization* 1223.

Table 16: Direct minority shareholdings in the Dutch financial sector in 1997 (per cent of total shares of the target firm)

	Aegion	ING	Fortis	ABN AMRO	Rabobank
Aegion	0	6.02	0	9.19	0
ING	5.31	0	8.87	16.57	0
Fortis	0	6.15	0	5.70	0
ABN AMRO	0	0	0	0	0
Rabobank	0	0	5.64	0	0

Source: E Dietzenbacher, B Smid and B Volkerink, 'Horizontal Integration in the Dutch Financial Sector' (2000) 18 *International Journal of Industrial Organization* 1223, 1233, Table 1.

Amundsen and Bergman explored whether the increase of mergers and minority shareholdings between the major power firms in Norway and Sweden positively affects their market power.[23] In 1996 the integration of the two power markets in these two countries had significantly constrained the ability of the power firms to exercise national market power. By assuming Cournot competition, Amundsen and Bergman tried to evaluate if passive minority shareholdings facilitate firms to re-establish the market power that had lost by the integration of the two national markets (Table 17).

Table 17: Passive minority shareholdings in the Nordic power market in 1999 (per cent of total shares of the target/column firm)

Column firm	SydKraft	Birka Energi	Graninge	OSLO Energi	BKK
Row firm					
Sydkraft			20		
Graninge		8			
Statkraft	17			20	26

Notes: The table presents minority shareholdings from the Row Firm to the Column Firm.

Source: ES Amundsen and L Bergman, 'Will Cross-Ownership Re-establish Market Power in the Nordic Power Market?' (2002) 23(2) *Energy Journal* 73, 84, Table 2.

In terms of the impact of minority shareholdings on competition Amundsen and Bergman compared prices and quantities in the Nordic power market with or without the presence of passive minority interests. The results of the calibrated model showed that the presence of passive minority shareholdings decreased the output and increased the prices in Norway, while in Sweden both strategic variables remained unchanged with or without passive interests among the firms.[24]

The effects of passive minority interests on firms' profits were also explored by the model. The results indicated that in Norway, even though the profit of the firm which owns

[23] ES Amundsen and L Bergman, 'Will Cross-Ownership Re-establish Market Power in the Nordic Power Market?' (2002) 23(2) *Energy Journal* 73.

[24] Ibid, 85.

minority interests in other competitors is lower with them than without them, this loss was fully compensated by the share of profit in the target firms.[25] Therefore, the total profit of the acquiring firm was higher with the presence of minority shareholdings than without them.

Ono et al[26] empirically explored the effect of minority shareholdings in the Japanese automobile manufacture sector using data from 11 Japanese automobile manufacturers from 1990 to 2000 (Table 18).

The authors used an approximation of equation (14) and empirically estimated the following equation:

$$PCM_i = \alpha_1 \left[1 + \frac{\sum_{j \neq i} mi_{ji} s_j}{\left(1 - \sum_{j \neq i} mi_{ji}\right) s_i} \right] + \alpha_2 s_i \left[1 + \frac{\sum_{j \neq i} mi_{ji} s_j}{\left(1 - \sum_{j \neq i} mi_{ji}\right) s_i} \right] + \alpha_3 DGR + \varepsilon_i \qquad (16)$$

The results indicated a positive and significant estimation of α_1, a negative and significant estimation of α_2 and a positive but not significant estimation of α_3. Therefore, passive minority shareholdings positively affected the price–cost margin (by almost 2 per cent), but were more advantageous for smaller firms rather than for bigger firms in the market. Also, the rate of economic growth in GDP did not play a crucial role in a firm's decision to acquire a passive minority interest in another firm.

Table 18: Minority shareholdings in the Japanese automobile manufacture sector in 2000 (per cent of total shares of the target/column firm)

Column firm / **Row firm**	**Nissan**	**Mitsubishi**	**Subaru**	**Mazda**	**Suzuki**	**Daihatsu**	**Isuzu**	**Hino**	**Nissan Diesel**
Renault	36.82								
Chrysler		36.01							
GM			24.39		21.00				
Ford				33.39			49.00		
Toyota						52.42		33.80	
Nissan and Renault									45.00

Notes: The table presents minority shareholdings from the Row Firm to the Column Firm.

Source: H Ono, T Nakazato, C Davis and W Alley, 'Partial Ownership Arrangements in the Japanese Automobile Industry; 1990–2000' (2004) 7(2) *Journal of Applied Economics* 355, 366, Table A1.

[25] Ibid, 86.

[26] H Ono, T Nakazato, C Davis and W Alley, 'Partial Ownership Arrangements in the Japanese Automobile Industry; 1990–2000' (2004) 7(2) *Journal of Applied Economics* 355.

Ono et al also explored, via the following equation, the effect of passive minority shareholdings in foreign firms on the price–cost margin of the acquiring firms.

$$PCM_i = \alpha_1 \left[1 + \frac{\sum_{j \neq i} mi_{ji} s_j}{\left(1 - \sum_{j \neq i} mi_{ji}\right) s_i} \right] + \alpha_2 s_i \left[1 + \frac{\sum_{j \neq i} mi_{ji} s_j}{\left(1 - \sum_{j \neq i} mi_{ji}\right) s_i} \right] + \alpha_3 DGR + \alpha_4 dummy_{foreign} + \varepsilon_i \tag{17}$$

The results indicated a positive and significant estimation of α_4. Therefore, an acquisition of a minority shareholding in a foreign firm positively affected the price–cost margin of a Japanese automobile manufacturer.

Lastly, the authors examined the determinants of passive minority shareholdings. They found, inter alia, that (a) foreign firms are interested in short-term profitability but domestic firms are not interested in this; (b) R&D plays a significant (positive) role for domestic but not for foreign firms; (c) a strong brand position negatively affects the acquisition of a passive minority shareholding (Japanese automobile manufacturers seek firms with a weak brand position in order to acquire a silent minority interest); and (d) if a firm acquires more than one-third of the issued capital of another firm, then such a passive minority shareholding positively affects the choice of the firm to be engaged in the partial acquisition.

Trivieri examined the effects of minority shareholdings among Italian banks on competition in the national banking sector.[27] Trivieri applied the methodology of Panzar and Rosse[28] in order to measure the degree of competition in the Italian banking sector. By comparing it among firms with or without minority shareholdings for the period 1996–2000 the author concluded that the credit institutions which engaged in partial acquisitions were less competitive than those not thus engaged. Therefore, minority shareholdings may be seen as anticompetitive strategic decisions. Table 19 presents minority shareholdings (direct and indirect) in the Italian banking sector at the end of the year 2000.

'[T]he statistic of Panzar and Rosse allows us to identify the nature of the market structure in which a firm operates by estimating the sum of the elasticities of the firm's revenues with respect to the firm's input prices.'[29] This statistic is the sum of elasticity of total revenues with respect to input prices:

$$H = \sum_{k=1}^{K} \left(\frac{\partial R_i^*}{\partial \omega_{ki}} \frac{\omega_{ki}}{\partial R_i^*} \right) \tag{18}$$

where ω_{ki} is a vector of k input prices and R_i^* are the equilibrium revenues. The following equation presents the econometric model:

$$\log R_{it} = \sum_{k=1}^{K} \alpha_k \log \omega_{it}^k + \sum_{n=1}^{N} \alpha_n \log X_{it}^n + \sum_{j=1}^{J} \alpha_j \log S_{it}^j + \varepsilon_{it} \tag{19}$$

[27] F Trivieri, 'Does Cross-Ownership Affect Competition? Evidence from the Italian Banking Industry' (2007) 17 *International Financial Markets, Institutions and Money* 79.

[28] JC Panzar and JN Rosse, 'Testing for Monopoly Equilibrium' (1987) 35 *Journal of Industrial Economics* 443.

[29] Above n 27, 84.

Table 19: Minority shareholdings in the Italian banking sector at the end of 2000 (per cent of total shares of the target/column firm)

Column firm / Row firm	Banca Intesa	Unicredit	San Paolo IMI-Banco di Napoli	Banca di Roma-MCC	Banca MPS	Banca Nazionale del Lavoro	Banca Cardine	Bipop-Carire	Banca lombarda EP	CdR Firenze	Carinord	Credem
Fondazione Cariplo	9.917											
Banca Intesa								2.024			31.00*	
Compagnia di San Paolo			16.155*									
San Paolo IMI-BN					2.071	2.032	10.80			19.109		2.057
Fondazione MPS			6.170		66.03*							
Ente CariFirenze			2.592							44.97*		
Mediobanca (via Spafid)		2.471							2.517			
Montedison**				2.109	2.008							
Generali**	6.014					7.620		1.500				
Gruppo Agnelli			4.909	10.05								
Reale Mutua			3.00						6.290			
ABN Amro				10.209								

Notes: The table presents minority shareholdings from the row firm to the column firm and reports the shares held by the major shareholders (>2 per cent).
* *Majority shareholding.*
** *Mediobanca owns the majority of the shares.*

Source: F Trivieri, 'Does Cross-Ownership Affect Competition? Evidence from the Italian Banking Industry' (2007) 17 *International Financial Markets, Institutions and Money* 79, 82, Table 1.

where X_{it}^n are exogenous variables that affect firms' revenues and cost functions, S_{it}^j is a vector of scale variables, i stands for firms and t for the time period.[30] The statistic of Panzar and Rosse is computed from the sum of the estimated coefficients of the variables in the vector $\log\omega_{it}^k$.

According to the value of H the market is characterized as (a) perfectly competitive market if $H = 1$, (b) perfectly collusive oligopoly or monopoly if $H \leq 0$ and (c) monopolistic competition with freedom of entry if $0 \leq H \leq 1$.[31]

> From an econometric point of view, the monopoly model is not consistent with the data when the H < 0 hypothesis is rejected, while the monopolistic competition model is the only one consistent if the hypotheses H < 0 and H = 1 are both rejected. Finally, the rejection of the hypothesis H ≤ 1 rules out all the three models.[32]

For the estimation of the econometric model of equation (18) Trivieri uses data from 503 credit firms for the period 1996–2000. The author concludes the econometric analysis leads to the following two conclusions:

> The first is that, in the 5 year period under consideration, Italian banks taken as a whole operated under conditions of monopolistic competition. …
>
> Secondly, … the Italian banks linked by cross-ownership behaved less competitively than credit firms not involved in the same phenomenon'.[33]

We have already shown in chapter 4 how Foros, Kind and Shaffer[34] examined the main effect of active minority shareholdings on firms' pricing decisions. As an empirical example Foros et al examined the pay-TV market in Norway and Sweden. In both markets the supply and demand conditions are almost the same. There are two pay-TV subscriptions via satellite (Canal Digital and Viasat) and one firm in each country (RTV in Norway and Boxer in Sweden) for the provision of digital terrestrial platforms.

However, the subscription fee for the digital terrestrial platform provider is higher in Norway than in Sweden and the price charged by the two platforms is lower than the price charged by RTV in Norway but is higher than the price charged by Boxer in Sweden. Foros et al considered that the differences in prices in the two markets were based on the different ownership structures in the two countries. The Swedish provider of digital terrestrial platform is independently owned, 'whereas the Norwegian telecommunications incumbent Telenor owns 100 percent of the shares in Canal Digital and 33.3 percent of the shares in RTV'.[35]

[30] The definitions of the variables are presented in Table 2 in Trivieri (n 27).

[31] 'Vesala (1995) proves that the H statistic is an increasing function of the absolute price elasticity of demand, that is an inverse measure of market power exercised on the part of firms. This implies that values of H between 0 and 1 can be interpreted as a continuous measure of level of competition, in the sense that higher values of the statistic indicate stronger competition than lower values (Bikker and Haaf, 2002).' See especially above n 27, 87 and footnotes therein.

[32] Ibid.

[33] Ibid, 98.

[34] Ø Foros, HJ Kind and G Shaffer, 'Mergers and Partial Ownership' (2011) 55(7) *European Economic Review* 916.

[35] Ibid, 917–18.

According to Foros et al:

> [I]f Telenor has corporate control in TV, then Telenor would indeed have an incentive to increase RTV's price—perhaps substantially—in order to reduce the competitive pressure on Canal Digital. If Telenor owned 100 percent of the shares in both companies, Telenor would induce RTV and Canal Digital to set the same (high) prices, other things being equal. However, since Telenor only has 33 percent of the shares in RTV, it will have incentives to set a higher price for the services offered by RTV than for the services offered by Canal Digital in Norway. … This might be true even if consumption of the former has a lower perceived quality.[36]

Nain and Wang examined 579 acquisitions of passive minority shareholdings among rival firms (firms operating in the same four-digit SIC code) across 119 manufacturing industries in the US during the period 1980–2009.[37] The majority of these firms were in chemicals and allied products (218 or 37.68 per cent of the total sample), instruments (85 or 14.68 per cent of the total sample) and electronic and other electrical equipment (73 or 12.61 per cent of the total sample).

Nain and Wang explored if (a) there exists a link between industry concentration[38] and the occurrence of silent partial acquisitions, (b) there exists a link between a decline in the degree of competition and the enhancement of passive minority shareholdings. Concerning the former, they estimated that a 1 per cent decline of the 4-firm concentration ratio (CR-4)[39] enhances the likelihood of silent partial acquisitions by 6.4 per cent. Regarding the latter, Nain and Wang reported that price–cost margins and real producer price indexes are higher in industries after the acquisition of passive minority shareholdings than otherwise. In addition, the enhancement of profitability indicators is observed only in industries with high barriers to entry[40] which supports the view that the increase of prices and profits after the acquisition of silent minority interests is attributable to changes in firms' market power rather than to unobserved exogenous shocks.[41]

Brito, Ribeiro and Vasconcelos[42] provided an empirical application to four (two actual and two hypothetical) silent partial acquisitions in the wet shaving industry. In particular, their primary objective was to quantify the coordinated effects of the following actual (cases a and b) and hypothetical (cases c and d) partial horizontal acquisitions: (a) the acquisition of the 22.9 per cent non-voting equity of Wilkinson Sword by Gillette in 1990 'and of all worldwide assets and businesses of Wilkinson Sword trademark from Eemland, apart

[36] Ibid, 918.

[37] A Nain and Y Wang, 'The Anti-Competitive Effects of Minority Stake Acquisitions' (2012), available at http://www.mcgill.ca/channels/sites/mcgill.ca.channels/files/channels/attach/wang_yan_-_the_anti-competitive_effCommissionts_of_minority_stake_acquisitions.pdf.

[38] The authors use 4-firm and 20-firm concentration ratios and the *HHI* in order to capture industry concentration.

[39] The CR-4 is a concentration index which measures the degree of concentration in the market. It is defined as the sum of the market shares of the four biggest firms in the market (in terms of market shares).

[40] The authors use capital intensity and capital expenditures as proxies for barriers to entry.

[41] Nain and Wang also state that: 'Stock-price reactions of non-participating competitors of the acquirer and target are positive while announcement returns of customer firms are negative. Moreover, announcement returns of competitors are significantly higher and those of customers weakly lower when the acquirer and target are larger firms. These results indicate that equity ownership of rival firms dampens competition in an industry.' A Nain and Y Wang, 'The Product Market Impact of Minority Stake Acquisitions' (2014), available at http://papers.ssrn.com/sol3/papers.cfm?abstract_id=2180996.

[42] D Brito, R Ribeiro and H Vasconcelos, 'Quantifying the Coordinated Effects of Partial Horizontal Acquisitions' (2013), CERP Discussion Paper No 9536, 1.

from the United States and the European Community';[43] (b) the acquisition of 100 per cent voting equity of Wilkinson Sword by Warner-Lambert Company in 1993; (c) the acquisition of 100 per cent voting equity of Wilkinson Sword by Gillette (all worldwide assets and businesses of Wilkinson Sword trademark, apart from the US and the European Union); and (d) the acquisition of the 22.9 per cent voting equity of Wilkinson Sword by Gillette.

A key assumption of their empirical model was that the control that each owner holds over the firm's management equals the percentage of voting shares the owner holds over the issued capital of the target firm. Table 20 presents the shareholding structure of the firms under scrutiny.

'The sample covers 6 brands in 81 stores[44] (across 7 counties in the Chicago metropolitan area) for 104 weeks.'[45] In each store/market Gillette is the dominant brand with an average share of 59.5 per cent, while the second largest brand is a private label with an average share of 20.6 per cent in each store/market. Shick and BIC are in the third and fourth places, respectively, while Wilkinson Sword and ASR Personna have low market shares.

The empirical results regarding the above-mentioned four actual and hypothetical cases were as follows:

— If Gillette acquires 100 per cent voting equity of Wilkinson Sword, then a low price increase occurs (<10 per cent).
— If Gillette acquires 22.9 per cent non-voting equity of Wilkinson Sword, then an extremely low price increase occurs (<0.01 per cent).
— If Gillette acquires 22.9 per cent voting equity of Wilkinson Sword, then a low price increase occurs (<3 per cent).
— If Warner-Lambert Company acquires 100 per cent voting equity of Wilkinson Sword, then a low price increase occurs (<2 per cent).

Concerning the coordinated effects of the partial or full acquisitions, Brito et al stated that 'tacit coordination in the post-(partial or full) acquisition industry is less likely to be sustained'.[46]

Brito et al[47] examined the unilateral effects of the above-mentioned four actual and hypothetical partial acquisitions. For this scope the authors use the same data set and the same two hypothetical partial acquisitions. Table 8 in Brito et al[48] lists changes in consumer welfare, firm aggregate profits and total welfare.[49]

Concerning the impact of partial and full acquisitions on consumer welfare, the empirical results show that if Gillette acquires 100 per cent voting equity of Wilkinson Sword, this the highest negative impact on consumer welfare among all the cases under examination, 'approximately \$20.4 thousand per year'.[50] Moreover, the corresponding numbers regarding the acquisitions of 22.9 per cent non-voting and voting equity of Wilkinson Sword are \$2.1 and \$5.8 thousand per year, respectively. The results concerning firm aggregate profits

[43] Ibid, 23.
[44] Stores play the role of the markets in the empirical model.
[45] Above n 43, 24.
[46] Ibid, 39.
[47] D Brito, R Ribeiro and H Vasconcelos, 'Measuring Unilateral Effects in Partial Horizontal Acquisitions' 33 (2014) *International Journal of Industrial Organization* 22.
[48] Ibid, 35.
[49] The empirical results regarding prices are the same as in Brito, Ribeiro and Vasconcelos (n 42).
[50] Above n 47, 22, 35.

Table 20: Passive minority shareholdings in the wet shaving industry in 1994 (per cent of total stock of the parent firm)

Shareholders / Parent firm	Allsop Venture Partners	Goldman Sachs	Scudder Stevens and Clarck	Equitable*	Grantham Mayo Van Otter	Leucadia Investors	Mezzanine Capital	Bruno Bich	The Capital Group	Wilkinson**	Berkshire Hathaway
American Safety Razor Company	12.40†	7.80†	7.00†	14.40†	5.10†	4.10†	2.00†				
BIC Corporation								77.70†			
Warner-Lambert Company									5.16†	100.00†	
The Gillette Company											10.90‡ (10.70)***

Notes:
† Total stock = voting stock.
‡ Total stock.
* Equitable denotes the cumulative ownership of Equitable Capital Partners LP, Equitable Deal Flow Fund, LP, Equitable Capital Partners (Retirement Fund) LP, and the Equitable Life Assurance Society of the United States.
** Subsidiary.
*** Voting stock.

Source: D Brito, R Ribeiro and H Vasconcelos, 'Quantifying the Coordinated Effects of Partial Horizontal Acquisitions' (2013) CERP Discussion Paper No 9536, 1, 56, Table 4, Appendix B.

mirror those for consumer welfare. Lastly, total welfare decreases more if Gillette acquires 100 per cent voting equity than if it acquires 22.9 per cent non voting equity of Wilkinson Sword. In the former case the negative impact equals $13.3 thousand per year, while in the latter case the corresponding value is $1.6 thousand per year. In the other two cases the negative effect was lower than $3 thousand per year.

So far we have explored the empirical findings of passive and active minority shareholdings among rivals, ie firms that are active in the same market. However, the economic literature has also examined the effects of minority shareholdings among non-rivals. To the best of our knowledge there are three papers in the literature which provide evidence on this issue, namely those by Allen and Phillips,[51] Fee, Hadlock and Thomas[52] and Ouimet.[53]

Allen and Phillips examined long-term block ownership by corporations and performance changes in firms with corporate block owners. They found

> the largest significant increases in targets' stock prices, investment, and operating profitability when ownership is combined with alliances, joint ventures, and other product market relationships between purchasing and target firms, especially in industries with high research and development.[54]

In particular, Allen and Phillips studied 'the changes in investment and operating performance of firms after nonfinancial corporations purchase large equity positions',[55] and also examined 'why corporations might establish these equity positions and propose some alternative explanations'.[56]

The sample studied by Allen and Phillips

> consists of 402 ownership stakes established during the 1980 to 1991 period where corporations hold a minimum of five percent of outstanding shares. Thirty-seven percent, or 150, of the target firms in the sample have explicit business relationships with their corporate blockholders.[57]

The authors

> examine the abnormal stock returns to target firms, purchasing firms, and combined target plus purchaser returns around purchase announcements.[58] [They also] examine changes in investment expenditures and operating performance of target firms following corporate block purchases. [They] examine whether these changes in performance differ for firms based on the existence of product market relationships and whether a firm is likely to be constrained in its ability to finance investments.[59]

[51] WJ Allen and GM Phillips, 'Corporate Equity Ownership, Strategic Alliances, and Product Market Relationships' (2000) 55(6) *Journal of Finance* 2791.

[52] CE Fee, C Hadlock and S Thomas, 'Corporate Equity Ownership and the Governance of Product Market Relationships' (2006) 61(3) *Journal of Finance* 1217.

[53] PP Ouimet, 'What Motivates Minority Acquisitions? The Trade-Offs between a Partial Equity Stake and Complete Integration' (2012) 26(4) *Review of Financial Studies* 1021.

[54] Allen and Phillips (n 51).

[55] Ibid, 2792.

[56] Ibid.

[57] Ibid.

[58] Event studies are quite common in the literature. See especially P Fotis, M Polemis and N Zevgolis, 'Stock Price Performance as an Argument for Derogation from Suspension of Concentrations: Reality or Myth?' (2009) 30(5) *European Competition Law Review* 216; P Fotis and M Polemis, 'The Use of Economic Tools in Merger Assessment' (2011) 7(2) *European Competition Journal* 323; P Fotis, M Polemis and N Zevgolis, 'Robust Event Studies for Derogation from Suspension of Concentrations in Greece during the Period 1995–2008' (2011) 11(1) *Journal of Industry Competition and Trade* 67; P Fotis, 'Competition Policy and Firm's Damages' in J Harrington and Y Katsoulakos (eds), *Recent Advances in the Analysis of Competition Policy and Regulation* (Cheltenham, Edward Elgar, 2012) 116.

[59] Allen and Phillips (n 51) 2793.

The main results reported by Allan and Phillips are the following:

— stock prices of target firms, on average, increase significantly at announcements of corporate block purchases.
— ... block purchases ... accompanied by agreements, alliances, or joint ventures between firms result in significantly larger excess stock returns to target shareholders when compared to block purchases by corporations that are not associated with alliances or joint ventures.
— ... target firms significantly increase investment expenditures and exhibit substantive gains in operating cash flows following block equity purchases by corporations relative to industry peers and the period prior to purchase announcements, especially for target firms that form alliances or joint ventures with corporate blockholders.
— ... target firms operating in industries with high research and development (R&D) and advertising expenses—those most likely to create relationship-specific assets or to be subject to information asymmetries—show significant improvements in industry-adjusted operating cash flows and increases in investment expenditures following corporate equity purchases.
— ... The increase in operating cash flows, however, is concentrated in firms that operate in R&D-intensive industries and most notably in R&D-intensive firms that form alliances or joint ventures with corporate block owners.
— board representation by corporate owners, independent of product market relationships with target firms, has[n't] a positive impact on announcement period stock returns or on subsequent changes in the investment or operating performance of target firms.[60]

Fee, Hadlock and Thomas explored a sample of over 10,000 firms listed on the Center for Research in Security Prices (CRSP) and the Compustat database from 1988 to 2001. They studied whether there exists any efficient argument for the acquisition of minority shareholdings and whether there is a link between it and their size. They also examined whether there is a positive relationship between the partial acquisition and a subsequent trading relationship between the acquiring and the target firm.

The empirical results reveal that minority shareholdings are present in only 3.31 per cent of the whole sample, indicating that it is relatively rare for a customer to acquire a minority shareholding in its supplier. They also suggest that there is a positive link between R&D and acquisition of a minority shareholding as well as supplier's sales to the customer. Also, partial acquisitions are more common in relationships with alliance agreements and in firms with financial (ie cash) constraints than otherwise, but their size is moderate. The last conclusion indicates that suppliers are concerned about customers having too much control over their firms.

Ouimet explored a sample of 1,913 majority and 255 minority acquisitions (less than 50 per cent of the issued capital of the target firm) announced between 1994 and 2006 involving listed US acquirers and targets.[61] He found that 'firms are more likely to engage in minority acquisitions when the loss of a stock price is expected to lead to a greater dilution[62]

[60] Ibid.
[61] Ouimet (n 53) 1029.
[62] As Ouimet mentions, 'the dilution to incentives will be greater, the smaller the relative size of the target' (ibid).

to target managerial equity incentives[63]'.[64] Therefore, 'relatively small public firms are more likely to be targets of minority acquisitions'.[65]

Ouimet also stated that majority acquisitions lower the incentive of the target firms 'to invest in assets whose value depends on trades with its partner firm'.[66] He empirically used the number of patents held by the partner firm as a proxy of a partnership of this type and concluded that 'minority acquisitions are relatively more common when the acquirer has a large number of patents, consistent with the hypothesis'.[67]

Moreover, according to Oiumet,

> A firm operating in a similar marketplace or having strategic relationships with a constrained firm may be better informed about the constrained firm's investment opportunities and thus be able to act as an optimal investor or certify the target in the eyes of other potential investors.[68]

He found empirically that

> financially constrained targets are more likely to be associated with a minority acquisition. Moreover, minority acquisitions are more common when the target firm can benefit most from certification, as proxied by low analyst coverage and the absence of a preexisting blockholder.[69]

Furthermore, the Ouimet proxies the inefficient internal capital markets by using the degree of investment opportunity heterogeneity among firms that are engaged in the acquisition. He empirically estimated that '[m]inority acquisitions are more common when the integration of internal capital markets is expected to be especially costly'.[70] He also suggested that 'as uncertainty regarding the value of the target and related synergies increases, as measured by industry volatility, acquirers exhibit a preference for minority acquisitions, consistent with a real options hypothesis'.[71]

[63] The dilution in target managerial equity incentives is measured by the relative size, which 'is the ratio of the target firm to the size of the combined firms using market capitalizations estimated twenty-eight days before the deal was announced' (ibid, 1031, table 2).

[64] Ibid, 1022.

[65] Ibid.

[66] Ibid, 1023.

[67] Ibid.

[68] Ibid.

[69] Ibid.

[70] Ibid. See also R Rajan, H Servaes and L Zingales, 'The Cost of Diversity: The Diversification Discount and Inefficient Investment' (2000) 55 *Journal of Finance* 35.

[71] Ouimet (n 53) 1023.

8

Commission's White Paper

I. Analysis of the Commission's White Paper

A paper by the European Commission entitled 'Towards More Effective EU Merger Control' (the so-called 'White Paper') was accompanied by a Staff Working Document. Both documents were published on the same date.[1] The Staff Working Document assesses and explains on the one hand the already existing considerations regarding the Commission's analysis of the current functioning of the Merger Regulation,[2] and on the other hand the proposals for possible amendments to the Merger Regulation put forward in the White Paper.

Regarding the reform of the Merger Regulation, the main points had already been discussed in general terms in an earlier Staff Working Document also called 'Towards More Effective EU Merger Control'[3] (the so-called 'Consultation Paper').[4] Interested stakeholders made comments on the Consultation Paper regarding primarily two main issues:

— Certain acquisitions of non-controlling minority shareholdings result in anticompetitive effects. In these cases are merger control rules applicable or not?
— The potential effectiveness of a system according to which merger cases are transferred from Member States to the Commission 'both before and after notification'.[5]

The Commission received approximately 70 replies in response to the Consultation Paper. Furthermore, the DG Competition staff had already engaged in an intensive dialogue not only with Member States—mainly with national competition authorities (NCAs)—but also with private stakeholders as far as it concerns the questions raised in the Consultation Paper. In the Staff Working Document accompanying the White Paper—which will be analysed in this chapter—the Commission took serious account of the extremely useful feedback received during the public consultation in order to develop these areas further.

The first goal of the Staff Working Document is to investigate more broadly the progress of the substantive assessment applied to mergers by the Commission, as well as how to reform the playing field and encourage cooperation and convergence between the

[1] Brussels, 9 July 2014. SWD (2014) 221 final.

[2] Council Regulation (EC) No 139/2004 of 20 January 2004 on the control of concentrations between undertakings [2004] OJ L24/1.

[3] Commission Staff Working Document SWD(2013) 239 final, see http://ec.europa.eu/competition/consultations/2013_merger_control.

[4] The Commission published its Consultation Paper on 25 June 2013.

[5] See para 2 of the Commission Staff Working Document accompanying the White Paper 'Towards More Effective EU Merger control' (n 1).

Commission and NCAs in the field of merger control. The second goal is to explain the way in which it is possible to undertake the main reforms in more detail than the White Paper did. At this point, it should be remembered that the scope chosen for the White Paper did not underestimate additional evaluations of other significant aspects of the EU merger control by the Commission.

A. Non-controlling Minority Shareholdings Under Merger Control Rules: Main Reasons

The application of appropriate and well-designed methods for tackling all sources of harm to competition, and thus to consumers, constitutes probably the main precondition for the achievement of effective and efficient competition policy. Regarding non-controlling minority shareholdings,[6] the following issues are observed.

First of all, it ought to be emphasized that the Merger Regulation only applies to 'concentrations': concentrations are defined as acquisitions of control by one or more person(s) or enterprise(s) over one or more other enterprises or parts of enterprises. For instance, a company acquiring a majority stake in another company qualifies as a concentration. Furthermore, two firms creating a joint venture also qualify as a concentration. If certain threshold requirements are met, such concentrations ought to be notified a priori to the Commission and can only be implemented after the Commission's clearance.

In cases where the acquisition of a minority shareholding does not lead or is not related to acquisition of control, the Commission is not authorized to investigate or intervene against it. In the context of a notified merger concerning a separate acquisition of control, only a concentration party's pre-existing minority shareholding in a competitor or a company which is activated in an upstream or downstream market can be taken into account by the Commission. Nevertheless, in the case that the minority shareholding is acquired after the examination of the acquisition of control by the Commission, there is no competence under the Merger Regulation for the Commission to raise possible competition concerns.

The experience acquired by the Commission, the Member States and third countries has shown that at least in some cases the acquisition of a non-controlling minority shareholding, such as, for example, one firm acquiring a 20 per cent shareholding in a competitor, can harm competition and, consequently, consumers. According to the Commission, this type of minority shareholding can lead to an SIEC which cannot be adequately addressed under the Merger Regulation in its current form.[7]

There are four Member States in the European Union that, according to their national merger control rules, have the competence to review acquisitions of non-controlling minority shareholdings, namely Austria, Germany, the UK and Lithuania. The NCAs in these four Member States have intervened against acquisitions of minority shareholdings that addressed competition concerns. Likewise, structural links under merger control rules are examined by many jurisdictions outside the EU, such as Canada, the US and Japan.[8]

[6] See also BA Hawk and HL Huser, 'Controlling the Shifting Sands: Minority Shareholdings under EEC Competition Law' (1993) 17(2) *Fordham Corporate Law Institute* 294.

[7] Above n 5, para 46.

[8] About Japan, see E Kameoka, Competition Law and Policy in Japan and the EU (Cheltenham, Edward Elgar, 2014) 113–14. See also ch 3, section I.C.vi above.

Furthermore, in both public consultations and recent media reports, recent acquisitions of minority shareholdings have emerged especially in cases where a competitor or a vertically related company acquired the shareholding. The minority stakes acquired by Telefónica in Telecom Italia, by Air France in Alitalia, by Intel in ASML (a manufacturer of lithography systems for the semiconductor industry), by Marine Harvest in Grieg Seafood, or by VW in Suzuki constitute relevant examples. In addition, as far as it concerns minority shareholdings in vertical relationships, relevant examples are the 10 per cent minority shareholding of Nestlé in Givaudan (now sold) or the 15 per cent shareholding of BMW in SGL Carbon (in addition to the 29 per cent shareholding of the Quandt/Klatten family, who control BMW).

B. The Similarity of Theories of Harm Regarding Minority Shareholdings

In the by no means rare case where a minority shareholding is acquired, several types of competition concerns can be raised. The specific competition concerns are mainly based on theories of harm similar to those relevant for acquisitions of control. In addition, in general, they require that the transaction significantly increases market power.

> In both the Horizontal and the Non Horizontal Merger Guidelines[[9]] is relatively observed that effective competition brings benefits to consumers (for instance, low prices, high quality products, a wide selection of goods and services and innovation). Through the mergers control, the [Commission] prevents mergers that would be likely to deprive customers of these benefits by significantly increasing the market power of undertakings. The sense of 'increased market power' means the ability of one or more undertakings to profitably raise prices, reduce output, diminish choice or quality of goods and services, diminish innovation, or otherwise influence parameters of competition. In the same context, the expression 'increased prices' is often used as shorthand for the above mentioned various ways in which a merger may result in competitive harm. With the expression 'increased prices' are also covered situations where, for example, prices are decreased less, or are less likely to decrease, than they otherwise would have without the merger and where prices are increased more, or are more likely to increase, than they otherwise would have without the merger. In general, both suppliers and buyers can have market power. Nevertheless, in the Horizontal Merger Guidelines, for clarity reasons, market power will usually refer to a supplier's market power; in cases where a buyer's market power is the issue, the term 'buyer power' is employed.

The economic effects of minority shareholdings on competition in the market are determined by factors such as the size of the minority shareholding, the resulting financial interests and the corporate rights conferred by them. Financial interests refer to the acquiring firm's right to a share of the target firm's profits; corporate rights refer to the ability to influence the acquired firm's commercial decisions.[10]

The acquisition of a minority shareholding in a competitor firm is able to lead to non-coordinated anticompetitive effects, since, due to such a shareholding, the acquirer's incentive and ability unilaterally to raise prices or restrict output may increase. It has been observed

[9] See the Horizontal and the Non Horizontal Merger Guidelines, paras 8 and 10, respectively.

[10] See also RJ Reynolds and BR Snapp, 'The Competitive Effects of Partial Equity Interests and Joint Ventures' (1986) 4 *International Journal of Industrial Organization* 141.

that, by instinct, where undertakings have financial stakes in their competitors' profits, they will possibly decide to incorporate the positive effects of their own output reductions or price increases on their competitors' profits. This may happen when the minority shareholding is passive, ie its holder is unable to influence the target firm's decisions.[11]

A fortiori, the above-mentioned potential anticompetitive effects may also materialize if a minority shareholding is active, ie its holder may have influence on the target undertaking's decisions.[12] This scenario can become real in the case that the acquirer gains influence over the result of special resolutions at shareholder meetings, which are needed for the approval of certain strategies related to significant investments, eg engaging in mergers and acquisitions, product lines, geographical scope, raising capital and advertising. In this respect, according to economic theory predictions, the acquiring enterprise may be able to influence the target undertaking to increase its prices, since the acquiring firm fully benefits from the positive externalities of the competitor's price increase but receives only part of the costs, *depending on the level of its financial ownership rights*. If the target company is finally forced to stop competing with the acquiring firm, the situation would be similar in reality to a full merger but without any of the cost-saving efficiencies that a merger can create (economies of scale or economies of scope, etc).

According to the Commission and the Member States' findings, competition concerns are more likely to be significant in the case that a minority shareholding grants some degree of influence over the target enterprise's decisions.[13]

C. Proposed Options/Solutions for Controlling the Acquisition of Minority Shareholdings

For the appropriate design of a system for the control of minority shareholdings, it is considered useful to establish the parameters for a system for controlling minority shareholdings at the EU level. The purpose of this system is to answer correctly two fundamental questions: (i) which cases should fall under the Commission's authorization and (ii) which procedure is best suited to meet the Commission's intentions?

A successive system for controlling minority shareholdings at the EU level should strike the right balance between three main principles. First and most importantly, taking into account not only the overall aim of preventing harm to consumers but also the theories of harm analysed above, the system ought to detect and capture the potentially problematic cases.

Secondly, it must avoid unnecessary and disproportionate administrative burdens, not only for undetakings but also for the Commission and NCAs. It should be emphasized that in the public consultation, stakeholders expressed their concerns that the Commission's proposal would constitute a far-reaching system placing a high administrative burden on business, although few transactions would be problematic. Stakeholders often pointed out that most minority shareholdings—eg those acquired only for investment purposes

[11] See also the analysis in ch 2 above.

[12] Ibid.

[13] See, for instance, Cases COMP/M.3653 *Siemens/VA Tech*, *Ryanair/Aer Lingus*, COMP/M.4153 *Toshiba/Westinghouse*, COMP/M.1673 *VEBA/VIAG*, COMP/M.5406 *IPIC/MAN Ferrostaal AG* discussed in ch 5 above.

or during recapitalization or restructuring of problematic undertakings by financial institutions—are perfectly harmless. Subjecting such shareholdings to mandatory review under merger control rules without discrimination might go beyond what is necessary in order effectively to prevent anticompetitive transactions.

While the above-mentioned first two principles are significant for a system of controlling minority shareholdings in any jurisdiction, a third principle is significant for a system for the control of minority shareholdings at the EU level. More specifically, the system ought to fit with the existing merger control systems at both EU and national levels.

The NCAs considered that any system for controlling minority shareholdings at the EU level should be consistent with national systems. The NCAs' point is important given that the Member States that currently control the acquisition of minority shareholdings would lose in such a case the competence to review transactions above the turnover thresholds of the Merger Regulation. More specifically, regarding the outlining of competences between the Member States and the Commission, it would be provided that the turnover thresholds of the Regulation 139/2004 would also apply to the acquisitions of minority shareholdings and that, furthermore, the referral system would apply for minority shareholdings in order to allow for a precise adjustment of case allocation to the 'more appropriate authority' where this is not achieved via the turnover thresholds. Some NCAs also had the opinion that a high level of protection of competition would only be achieved under the precondition that the Commission is at least informed about the fact that a transaction is examined and takes a clear position on whether it will investigate that transaction. In such a case, Member States will be allowed to request a referral in case the Commission was to decide not to investigate a case.[14]

A system for controlling minority shareholdings must also fit without problems into the already existing legal and procedural framework of the Regulation 139/2004 in order to avoid complicating EU merger control in an unnecessary way. This goal can be achieved without necessarily extending the notification system.

D. Potential Alternatives

Regarding the possible design of the procedure, three procedural options for the control of minority shareholdings were put forward in the Consultation Paper: (a) a notification system; (b) a self-assessment system; and (c) a transparency system.[15] The Consultation Paper does not define what constitutes a relevant 'minority shareholding',[16] and it is up to the stakeholders to state which minority shareholdings ought to be controlled. According to many of the replies received, a targeted system which would cover only transactions between competitors or vertically related companies would be preferable. More specifically:

a) Under the notification system proposed, there would be an extension of the current system of ex ante merger control to acquisitions of non-controlling minority shareholdings under certain preconditions. Thus, all acquisitions of shareholdings above a

[14] Above n 7, para 71.

[15] A transparency system actually constitutes a hybrid option.

[16] It should be noted that in the Consultation Paper the term 'structural link' is used.

given 'safe harbour' would have to be notified a priori and could only be implemented after the Commission's clearance decision. Furthermore, the same strict procedural deadlines as for mergers would also apply to minority shareholdings.

b) Under the self-assessment system, the parties involved would not be obliged to notify the acquisition of a minority shareholding a priori and could proceed to the acquisition without prior approval by the Commission. This system, if preferred, would oblige the Commission to rely on its own market intelligence (ex officio process) or complaints for becoming aware of transactions that may raise competition concerns; then the Commission would be free to select the potentially problematic cases (acquisitions below a 'safe harbour' would be excepted) and examine them.

c) Under the (hybrid) transparency system, the parties would be required to submit an *information notice*, with which the Commission would be informed about certain types of transactions. Following the submission of an information notice the Commission would be allowed to decide whether the transaction merited investigation and would allow Member States to assess whether to make a request for a referral.

Those cases that fall within the Commission's authorization remit ought to be closely linked to the theories of harm mentioned above, which means that only transactions between competitors or vertically related firms are potentially anticompetitive. Amongst those, only transactions resulting in some sort of influence over the competitive behaviour of the 'target' undertaking or creating an incentive for the acquiring firm to change its competitive behaviour (eg after taking into account the knowledge gained about the target firm through the minority shareholding) must be captured. Concerning the identification of potentially anticompetitive transactions, further details and criteria will be analysed in the following pages.

There is a direct relation between the scope of the Commission's jurisdiction and the answer to the question as to what procedure is considered to be more appropriate and adequate. For instance, if the Commission's competence covers all acquisitions of minority shareholdings above a certain threshold, ie a 'safe harbour', a pre-merger notification system would create a heavy administrative burden (and cost) on businesses since unproblematic mergers would also be covered. Should the Commission have jurisdiction over all acquisitions of minority shareholdings above a certain threshold, the existence of a self-assessment system might be more appropriate, since, in this case, the Commission would be free to investigate transactions on its own initiative (ex officio investigation). However, the undisputable administrative burden imposed by a notification or transparency system would be much lower in the cases where the Commission's jurisdiction was limited to only potentially problematic transactions. The relationship between the design of the procedural system and the scope of jurisdiction is crystal clear and this is the reason why it was frequently mentioned in responses to the public consultation.

E. The Choice of a Targeted Transparency System

Considering the three principles analysed above and taking into consideration the scope of jurisdiction and the procedure, the Commission proposed focusing the new system on only certain types of minority shareholdings. From the beginning, due to the Commission's authorization under Regulation 139/2004 certain potentially anticompetitive transactions would be limited; this would restrict the number of cases to be assessed under the new system.

Thus, the Commission must define the group of potentially anticompetitive acquisitions of minority shareholdings to be captured. Taking into account the analysis regarding the theories of harm,[17] only transactions between competitors or vertically related firms seem to raise competition issues. In addition, a 'floor', ie a certain minimum level of shareholding and/or certain rights combined with that shareholding, which consequently is in a position to grant the acquirer some influence over the target or access to information, ought to be required.

Furthermore, in view of the theories of harm,[18] according to the Commission's proposal, only transactions meeting the following criteria fall within the Commission's competence and require an information notice. These specific transactions would reasonably create a 'competitively significant link':

- The transaction concerns the acquisition of a minority shareholding in a competitor or vertically related firm (in fact, this is precisely the meaning of a 'competitively significant link').
- Due to the minority shareholding a significant link between the two undertakings is created. Such a link would be assumed if the post-transaction minority shareholding is above a certain threshold (e.g. around 20 per cent): such shareholdings usually are combined with certain corporate rights and change financial incentives. As an alternative, if the minority shareholding is between 5 and 20 per cent, in order for the link to be considered competitively significant, certain rights would need to attach to the shareholding, eg the right to nominate a member of the board might be included. Other relevant indicative examples constitute the exertion of influence, or the obtaining of access to the target's competitively sensitive information.

Transactions involving acquisitions of minority shareholdings below 5 per cent would not be covered by the new competence. However, transactions involving acquisitions of minority shareholdings below 5 per cent might still be captured by the Member States' merger control regimes or, if they constitute part of wider cooperation horizontal or even vertical agreements, by Article 101 TFEU. In the case of pre-existing minority shareholdings which are analysed in the context of a concentration, full divestiture may still be required to ensure a remedy's efficiency or/and effectiveness if, according to the Commission findings, this specific minority shareholding affects the incentives to compete.

Considering the three principles set out above, the targeted transparency system seems to be the most preferable solution/option for the following reasons.

Firstly, with the application of a targeted transparency system, potentially harmful transactions might come to the attention of the Commission and NCAs while innocent transactions, such as those entered into for investment purposes only, might not. Thus, with a targeted transparency system, *cases under investigation are limited to those that are strictly necessary to prevent harm to consumers.*

[17] Above n 14, subchapter 3.1.1.

[18] Ibid.

Secondly, a targeted transparency system limits the administrative burden by eradicating the non-problematic cases and by diminishing the amount of information that under other circumstances would be submitted to the Commission at the first stage. On the contrary, with a targeted notification system, *the parties would have to submit a notification in each and every case.* Nevertheless, with a targeted transparency system, only if the Commission were to decide (either ex officio or after a complaint) to investigate a specific case would the parties involved have to submit full notifications, and in this case only the Commission would have to issue a decision following its investigation. For these reasons, the targeted transparency system is considered administratively lighter for both firms and the Commission.

Last but not least, a targeted transparency system would generally fit with the existing systems for controlling minority shareholdings on a national level. The Member States would be informed of relevant transactions and would be allowed to request a referral. The Commission would take into account the reduced level of information available to Member States when considering whether the criteria for a referral, pursuant to Article 9 of Regulation 139/2004, are met. Under the latter,

1. The Commission may, by means of a decision notified without delay to the undertakings concerned and the competent authorities of the other Member States, refer a notified concentration to the competent authorities of the Member State concerned in the following circumstances.
2. Within 15 working days of the date of receipt of the copy of the notification, a Member State, on its own initiative or upon the invitation of the Commission, may inform the Commission, which shall inform the undertakings concerned, that:
   (a) a concentration threatens to affect significantly competition in a market within that Member State, which presents all the characteristics of a distinct market, or
   (b) a concentration affects competition in a market within that Member State, which presents all the characteristics of a distinct market and which does not constitute a substantial part of the common market.
3. If the Commission considers that, having regard to the market for the products or services in question and the geographical reference market within the meaning of paragraph 7, there is such a distinct market and that such a threat exists, either:
   (a) it shall itself deal with the case in accordance with this Regulation; or
   (b) it shall refer the whole or part of the case to the competent authorities of the Member State concerned with a view to the application of that State's national competition law.

   If, however, the Commission considers that such a distinct market or threat does not exist, it shall adopt a decision to that effect which it shall address to the Member State concerned, and shall itself deal with the case in accordance with this Regulation.

   In cases where a Member State informs the Commission pursuant to paragraph 2(b) that a concentration affects competition in a distinct market within its territory that does not form a substantial part of the common market, the Commission shall refer the whole or part of the case relating to the distinct market concerned, if it considers that such a distinct market is affected.
4. A decision to refer or not to refer pursuant to paragraph 3 shall be taken:
   (a) as a general rule within the period provided for in Article 10(1), second subparagraph, where the Commission, pursuant to Article 6(1)(b), has not initiated proceedings; or
   (b) within 65 working days at most of the notification of the concentration concerned where the Commission has initiated proceedings under Article 6(1)(c), without taking the preparatory steps in order to adopt the necessary measures under Article 8(2), (3) or (4) to maintain or restore effective competition on the market concerned.

5. If within the 65 working days referred to in paragraph 4(b) the Commission, despite a reminder from the Member State concerned, has not taken a decision on referral in accordance with paragraph 3 nor has taken the preparatory steps referred to in paragraph 4(b), it shall be deemed to have taken a decision to refer the case to the Member State concerned in accordance with paragraph 3(b).
6. The competent authority of the Member State concerned shall decide upon the case without undue delay.

   Within 45 working days after the Commission's referral, the competent authority of the Member State concerned shall inform the undertakings concerned of the result of the preliminary competition assessment and what further action, if any, it proposes to take. The Member State concerned may exceptionally suspend this time limit where necessary information has not been provided to it by the undertakings concerned as provided for by its national competition law.

   Where a notification is requested under national law, the period of 45 working days shall begin on the working day following that of the receipt of a complete notification by the competent authority of that Member State.
7. The geographical reference market shall consist of the area in which the undertakings concerned are involved in the supply and demand of products or services, in which the conditions of competition are sufficiently homogeneous and which can be distinguished from neighbouring areas because, in particular, conditions of competition are appreciably different in those areas. This assessment should take account in particular of the nature and characteristics of the products or services concerned, of the existence of entry barriers or of consumer preferences, of appreciable differences of the undertakings' market shares between the area concerned and neighbouring areas or of substantial price differences.
8. In applying the provisions of this Article, the Member State concerned may take only the measures strictly necessary to safeguard or restore effective competition on the market concerned.
9. In accordance with the relevant provisions of the Treaty, any Member State may appeal to the Court of Justice, and in particular request the application of Article 243 of the Treaty, for the purpose of applying its national competition law.

Also, under the transparency system, a 15-working-day waiting period ought also to be considered. Such a waiting period would be compatible with the deadline under Article 9 for a Member State referral request following a full notification. A system like this would ensure that the Member States with notification systems and stand-still obligations do not face transactions a posteriori, ie transactions that have already been implemented before the Member States start their investigations. If a self-assessment system was applied, the Member States would not be in a position to have been informed of transactions and—excluding the case where a transaction were voluntarily notified before implementation—the Member States could not possibly request a referral before the transaction's implementation.

For the above-mentioned reasons, the Commission expressed the opinion that an amendment to the Merger Regulation to cover acquisitions of non-controlling minority shareholdings ought to be based on a 'targeted transparency system', as analysed above. This system should include a provision permitting voluntary notifications—something that many stakeholders seem to have advocated during the public consultation in order to obtain legal certainty. In such cases, the notified case would be investigated by the Commission, which would issue a decision.

According to the Commission's estimations, approximately 20–30 minority shareholding cases per year will meet the above mentioned criteria of the targeted transparency system as well as the turnover thresholds provided in the Merger Regulation.

This number corresponds to approximately 7–10 per cent of the merger cases currently examined by the Commission each year. The specific figures were based on a conclusion coming from the Zephyr database[19] and an assessment based on the annual number of minority shareholding transactions with an EU dimension that were investigated by those Member States that have a system for the control of minority shareholdings. Nevertheless, this assessment assumes in advance that acquisitions of non-controlling minority shareholdings are similarly frequent across different Member States.[20]

F. Analysis of the Criteria for Transactions Creating a 'Competitively Significant Link'

The Commission, basing its analysis on the theories of harm,[21] suggested the following criteria for determining the cases where a transaction creates a 'competitively significant link' and, thus, must fall under its jurisdiction.

Firstly, the minority shareholding ought to be acquired in a competitor firm or in a directly vertically related undertaking. However, for the establishment of the Commission's competence, the concept of 'competitor' would not require a detailed antitrust analysis of the relevant (products/services and geographic) markets. Rather, the concept of 'competitor' would take into account whether the firms are active in the same sector and the same geographic area and, on the basis of a self-assessment analysis of the parties involved, whether the acquirer has a competitive relationship to the target.

The specific approach would also cover an acquisition of a minority shareholding by one firm which itself does not compete with the target, but which already holds a minority stake (or more) in one (or more) other firm(s)/competitor(s) of the same target. The main possible theory of harm applicable in such a case would be one of coordination: for example, the holding firm has a position on the board of several competitors and therefore has access to confidential information which it can share with the other competitors. Although the possibility that such a case would result in raising competition issues may be less in comparison with the case of a direct link between acquirer and target, such transactions would still fall under the Commission's jurisdiction.[22] However, it is remarked that the specific described case could constitute a simple example of a cartel case, in which the Commission would obviously also have competence. In any case, one would further need to assess the turnover calculation and the definition of undertakings concerned for such cases.

Secondly, the link would be considered important in the case that: (i) the acquired minority shareholding is above a 'floor', ie a certain thresholds (eg around 20 per cent of the total share capital); or (ii) the minority shareholding is above 5 per cent, but below the 20 per cent threshold, with the precondition that additional rights are also present.

[19] As has already been mentioned, the Zephyr database is a database containing information on the total number, the value and the corresponding participation percentages of ownership transactions in listed companies registered in 27 EU Member States.

[20] For more detail, see the impact assessment report.

[21] Ibid, and the analysis presented in chs 4 and 7.

[22] Above n 14, para 88.

G. Considerations Applied to the Threshold Levels

Firstly, national corporate law often provides that shareholdings conferring certain levels of voting rights enables these shareholders to block special resolutions. This right offers the shareholder the opportunity to influence the target firm's strategy. The UK and Germany are the two Member States so far that rely on a similar test: in the UK it is called 'material influence', and in Germany 'wettbewerblich erheblicher Einfluss' (ie competitively significant influence). Both Member States take into account whether the shareholding gives rise to equivalent rights to those granted to a minority shareholder of 25 per cent in defining '*significance*', the essence of the shareholding.

The percentage of voting rights that offers the shareholder the ability to block special resolutions is not the same for all Member States and mainly depends on the corporate form; however, it is frequently set at 25 per cent. A shareholding that is around this level may very often have as an (added) result the blocking of other corporate rights. Thus, a 25 per cent shareholding ought to be the higher limit for a threshold. Furthermore, a de facto blocking minority could reach the same threshold due to low attendance rates at the annual shareholder meetings.

Secondly, higher shareholdings more strongly influence or even change financial incentives, so the rights attached to such shareholdings may have less importance during the assessment of whether a minority shareholding is potentially anticompetitive. From the point of view of economic theory, financial incentives that de facto may affect the incentives for companies to compete may be considered important at a threshold significantly lower than 25 per cent.[23] Hence, the Commission must consider approximately *20 per cent as an appropriate starting point for analysing financial incentives.* Alternatively, a 15 per cent threshold could be considered as appropriate. For example, in the UK a threshold of 15 per cent has been set, above which the UK may examine any case.[24] This might also serve as a well-defined, crystal-clear threshold above which a shareholding would be assessed as a 'competitively significant link'.

If the minority shareholding is above 5 per cent but below 20 per cent, additional elements would also have to be demanded in order for a minority shareholding to meet the necessary requirements to be considered a competitively significant link. For instance, a shareholding could qualify if it results in a de facto blocking minority[25] due to the low attendance level at shareholder meetings or because additional rights were granted by the shareholder agreement. A seat on the board (or the agreement or even the likelihood to be elected to the board) and information rights giving access to commercially sensitive information could constitute indicative examples of other elements that would typically be included. For the establishment of the 'additional elements', typically rights stemming from the shareholding itself, corporate law or the shareholder agreement are significant for clarifying whether or not the shareholdings create competitively significant links.

[23] See, for example, the responses to the Consultation Paper received from economic consultancies and academics.

[24] See OFT, *Mergers—Jurisdiction and Procedural Guidance*, para 3.20.

[25] The 2007 UK case of *BSkyB/ITV* constitutes a good example of a de facto blocking minority shareholding as a stake of 17.9 per cent was considered sufficient for a material link on the basis that it allowed BskyB to influence the strategic decision-making of ITV. Therefore, for the clearance of the case, a divestiture of the shareholding down to 7.5 per cent was demanded.

Meanwhile, according to the experience obtained, competitive harm is very rare for shareholdings of 5 per cent or less. However, shareholdings above 5 per cent which are linked with special rights, such as board seats, are in a position to make competitive harm possible, since in these cases the shareholding constitutes something more than mere financial participation for investment purposes. It ought to be noted, for example, that in the US acquisitions of voting securities of 10 per cent or less are exempted from the filing obligation, under the precondition that the acquisition is made 'solely for the purpose of investment'.[26] There is no application of the exemption in the case that the acquirer is a competitor or can nominate a candidate for the board of directors, for instance. Having this in mind, a 'safe harbour' of 5 per cent seems to be appropriate, especially because additional conditions would exist up to the 20 per cent threshold (eg further rights, acquisition of a stake in a competitor or vertically related company).

Other types of agreements, such as horizontal cooperation agreements, joint production agreements, R&D agreements, joint purchasing agreements, off-take agreements and long-term exclusive supply agreements, in some cases coincide with the acquisition of a minority shareholding. If a minority shareholding is *only* acquired for supporting a broader cooperation, the Commission suggests excluding these agreements from the assessment of the question if a transaction creates a competitively significant link and falls within the Commission's jurisdiction. Nevertheless, in line with current practice for mergers, these agreements could be considered in the competitive assessment of the transaction. Realizing the difference between the rights linked to the shareholding itself and commercial agreements ought to increase legal certainty in defining whether or not a minority shareholding results in a competitively significant link.

H. Legislative Application—Proposals for Appropriate Legislative Implementation

The Commission's authorization to cover only acquisitions of minority shareholdings which create a 'competitively significant link' could be defined in the text of the Merger Regulation. The criteria of a 'competitively significant link', for instance that (a) the competence covers only minority shareholdings in competitors and vertically related companies that either (b) the transaction results in a cumulative minority shareholding of around 20 per cent and above, or (c) a minority shareholding between 5 and 20 per cent under the precondition that additional rights are covered would either be added (provided) in the articles of the Merger Regulation, the recitals, and/or a guidelines/notice document.

Another option, perhaps more detailed and technical, would be to implement the Commission's proposals to provide, in the Merger Regulation itself, that the Commission has the competence for acquisitions of minority shareholdings above 5 per cent if added criteria, which ought to be specified by the Commission in an implementing regulation, are

[26] More specifically, see s (c)(9) of the Hart–Scott–Rodino Act (15 USC § 18a). An acquisition is made 'solely for the purpose of investment' if the person holding or acquiring such voting securities has no intention of participating in the formulation, determination, or direction of the basic business decisions of the issuer. See 16 CFR 801.1(i)(1) and 16 CFR 802.9 available at: http://www.ftc.gov/enforcement/premergernotification-program/statute-rules-and-formal-interpretations.

fulfilled. Referring (and analysing) the criteria separately in an implementing regulation would offer the Commission the opportunity to adjust precisely the criteria, in consultation with the Member States, after gaining some experience from the relevant practices applied in the Member States and *without requiring a full amendment of the Merger Regulation.*

I. Amendment of the Banking Clause as a Consequence of Legislative Implementation

The perspective of extending the scope of the Merger Regulation to non-controlling minority shareholdings might also require the modification (or even the repealing) of the so-called 'banking clause', which is provided in Article 3(5)(a)[27] of the Merger Regulation 139/2204: the banking clause currently allows financial institutions to acquire a controlling shareholding in other firms under certain circumstances without being obliged to notify the transaction. In general, a merger is not deemed to arise in the case that the acquiring financial institution does not exercise the voting rights with a view of determining the competitive behaviour of the target firm and in the case also that the securities are disposed of within one year after the acquisition.

In the public consultation, some stakeholders expressed their concerns that the suggested reform should not jeopardize restructuring transactions. For instance, in case of debt-for-equity swaps, business decisions might have to be taken very fast as any waiting period or stand-still obligation would delay and harm such transactions.

The Commission is in a position to avoid this by changing the 'provision in para 5 of Article 3 of the Merger Regulation stating exactly that restructuring transactions, carried out by financial institutions in the normal course of business and for a limited period of time, would not create competitively significant links'.[28]

Hypothetically speaking, the application of such a modified banking clause would likely be restricted, as, according to the targeted approach, only transactions between competitors or vertically related companies in the first place are captured. Nevertheless, the modification would offer reconfirmation to the parties involved.

J. Procedural Issues

The targeted transparency notice could broadly focus on the following:

— According to the above-described criteria, the parties involved self-assess whether, in their opinion, a competitively significant link is created by the transaction.

[27] 'A concentration shall not be deemed to arise where: (a) credit institutions or other financial institutions or insurance companies, the normal activities of which include transactions and dealing in securities for their own account or for the account of others, hold on a temporary basis securities which they have acquired in an undertaking with a view to reselling them, provided that they do not exercise voting rights in respect of those securities with a view to determining the competitive behaviour of that undertaking or provided that they exercise such voting rights only with a view to preparing the disposal of all or part of that undertaking or of its assets or the disposal of those securities and that any such disposal takes place within one year of the date of acquisition; that period may be extended by the Commission on request where such institutions or companies can show that the disposal was not reasonably possible within the period set.'

[28] Above n 14, para 100.

— If such a link is created, the parties submit an information notice to the Commission. As an alternative, in the case that the parties demand legal certainty, they can also voluntarily notify the transaction to the Commission under the normal procedure.
— If the parties submit an information notice, the Commission takes the decision on the basis of the notice if the necessary circumstances are covered so that the case merits a phase I investigation. Under such a scenario, regarding the transaction the Commission would publish a notice allowing, on the one hand, complainants to come forward, and on the other hand, allowing Member States, after having been informed of the notice, to consider a referral request.
— In the case that the Commission considers that the case deserves an investigation, it would request a full notification from the parties involved. In practice this means that there would be an initiation of the phase I procedure as applicable for concentrations. On the contrary, in the case that the Commission does not request a notification, the parties have the possibility to close the transaction either immediately or after a short waiting period and there will be no decision by the Commission on the case.

The information notice should mainly address the following issues: a description of the transaction, information about the parties, the turnover of the undertakings involved, the level of shareholding before and after the transaction, and any rights attached to the minority shareholding if it is below 20 per cent. Furthermore, the notice would have to contain some essential market information about the parties (relevant products and/or services market) and their main competitors (market contestability, barriers to entry, potential competition) or internal documents adequate for an initial competitive assessment.[29] For instance, one possibility would be to require market share information only for the markets where the combined market shares are 20 per cent or above.[30] In addition, another possibility would be to require the submission of internal documents, including any studies, analyses, etc, which were prepared 'for the purpose of evaluating or analysing the acquisition with respect to market shares, competition, competitors, markets, potential for sales growth or expansion into product or geographic markets'.[31]

The Commission is conscious of the difficulty that companies reviewing documents and describing and identifying antitrust markets can face; however, this information might be significant for the Commission's decision of whether or not a transaction warrants investigation. Furthermore, this analysis allows Member States to determine whether to request a referral of the case.

The targeted transparency system must be fully compatible with the Member States' merger control systems. In order to achieve this result, the Commission ought to consider imposing a waiting period, eg 15 working days, once an information notice has been submitted; during this period, the parties would not be able to close the transaction. The referral of a case could be requested by the Member States within this period. Taking into account the current deadlines for Member States to request a referral, the same period,

[29] Another possibility would be to require the submission of internal documents similar to the HSR 4(c) documents in the US, covering any studies, analyses, etc, which were prepared 'for the purpose of evaluating or analysing the acquisition with respect to market shares, competition, competitors, markets, potential for sales growth or expansion into product or geographic markets'.

[30] It is about a precondition similar to what is required under the German Act against Restraints of Competition, see §39 (3) Nr 2 GWG.

[31] For instance, preconditions similar to the HSR 4(c) documents in the US.

ie 15 working days, seems to be appropriate for the acquisition of minority shareholdings. If a case examined appears prima facie problematic, the Commission could request a notification from the parties during this period; in this case the normal procedure would start and the stand-still obligation would apply in order to ensure the effectiveness of a later decision. However, if the Commission did not request a notification within the 15 working days after the receipt of the information notice and no referral request exists, the parties would be free to close the transaction.

As in the case of concentrations, the parties involved would be able to request a derogation[32] from the waiting period/stand-still obligation under paragraph 3 of Article 7 of Regulation 139/2004.[33]

Furthermore, introduction of a waiting period might require adapting the wording of paragraph 2[34] of Article 7 of the Merger Regulation for the acquisition of minority shareholdings. More specifically, in such a case the wording ought to be changed in order to allow acquisitions of shares via a stock exchange without complying with the three-week waiting period. Such an acquisition would not be considered as an early implementation under the precondition that, during the three-week waiting period, the voting rights are not exercised. Such a proposed application of paragraph 2 of Article 7 of the Merger Regulation, if applied, take into account a concern expressed by stakeholders in the public consultation that reforms must not harm the fluidity of stock markets.

Furthermore, in order to create the opportunity for the business community to come forward with complaints, the Commission ought to be free to take up a case within a short period of time after the implementation of the transaction. Such a limited period offers the Commission the opportunity to avoid precautionary investigations during the initial waiting period, in order 'not to be blocked from investigating a transaction in case complainants come forward later on'.[35] A large number of respondents referred to the limitation period of four months under the UK system as an appropriate period; but several other respondents suggested periods of 6–12 and up to 24 months. Having taken into account the content of the responses, the Commission suggested a limitation period of four or six months following the submission of the information notice. If the Commission decides to open an investigation during this period and the transaction has already been (partially) implemented, the Commission suggests reassessing all the steps already taken. Nevertheless,

[32] See P Fotis, M Polemis and N Zevgolis, 'Stock Price Performance as an Argument for Derogation from Suspension of Concentrations: Reality or Myth?' (2009) 30(5) *European Competition Law Review* 216. See also P Fotis, M Polemis and N Zevgolis, 'Robust Event Studies for Derogation from Suspension of Concentrations in Greece during the Period 1995–2008' (2011) 11(1) *Journal of Industry, Competition and Trade* 67.

[33] Art 7, para 3 states: 'The Commission may, on request, grant a derogation from the obligations imposed in paragraphs 1 or 2. The request to grant a derogation must be reasoned. In deciding on the request, the Commission shall take into account inter alia the effects of the suspension on one or more undertakings concerned by the concentration or on a third party and the threat to competition posed by the concentration. Such a derogation may be made subject to conditions and obligations in order to ensure conditions of effective competition. A derogation may be applied for and granted at any time, be it before notification or after the transaction.'

[34] Art 7, para 2 states: 'Paragraph 1 shall not prevent the implementation of a public bid or of a series of transactions in securities including those convertible into other securities admitted to trading on a market such as a stock exchange, by which control within the meaning of Article 3 is acquired from various sellers, provided that: (a) the concentration is notified to the Commission pursuant to Article 4 without delay; and (b) the acquirer does not exercise the voting rights attached to the securities in question or does so only to maintain the full value of its investments based on a derogation granted by the Commission under paragraph 3.'

[35] The variety of responses to the public consultation regarding an appropriate prescription period is emphasized: *it ranged from periods of 10 working days to 5 years.*

the regular stand-still obligation would apply for any further implementing measures taken by the Commission, which would have the power to issue interim measures, such as for example a 'hold separate' order, to ensure the effectiveness of a decision under Articles 6 and 8 of Regulation 139/2004. It is useful to remark that the 'hold separate' obligation would require a fiscal barrier of the exploitation of the assets, the obligation to nominate a hold-separate manager, etc—ie obligations similar to what is standard practice for divestiture commitments during divestiture periods or the conditions and obligations under paragraph 3 of Article 7 of Regulation 139/2004.

K. Partial or 'Staggered' Acquisitions

'Staggered' acquisitions are those transactions where an initial minority stake is acquired and increased in subsequent, independent transactions. In this kind of acquisition the crucial question is 'whether an information notice would have to be submitted every time that a stake is increased and/or the underlying rights change'.[36] One potential is to require submission of an information notice only the first time that a competitively significant link is established, ie when either a 20 per cent minority stake is acquired by the acquirer or a stake of between 5 and 20 per cent with the addition of the further rights specified above. Subsequent increases would not trigger any new information notices unless they result in acquisitions of control, which would trigger notifications under the existing rules provided mainly in the Merger Regulation.

Furthermore, the Commission can conceive of a system in which each increase in a minority stake *combined with* a change in the underlying rights causes a new information notice. As an alternative, in cases where the acquirer has previously informed the Commission of a '5 per cent + rights' acquisition, the Commission could assess the subsequent information in the case that the acquirer passes the 20 per cent threshold: through such an increase, the type or level of influence held over the target could be changed.

In the second and third options a more conservative framework, ie 'safer', is presented: each change would be newly assessed; however, the truth is that these options could also result in significant additional administrative burden on firms involved. Therefore, given that the Commission would only be competent in the case that the minority shareholding represents a competitively significant link anyway, the first option is suggested.

L. Substantive Analysis

The Commission has suggested applying the substantive test for assessing concentrations to acquisitions of minority shareholdings. According to the specific test, determining whether a transaction would lead to a significant impediment of effective competition in the internal market or a substantive part of it (the so-called SIEC test) is required.[37] Under the SIEC test, the theories of harm could be perfectly suited to the specific circumstances of each minority shareholding case.[38]

[36] Commission Staff Working Document (n 1) para 111.

[37] See especially P Fotis, 'Merger Enforcement: Law and Statistical Evidence Worldwide' (2013) 5(3) *International Journal of Economics and Business Research* 272, 273–77.

[38] Note that examples of the possible theories of harm are set out and analysed in chs 4 and 7.

i. Relationship Between Article 101 TFEU and Assessment Under Regulation 139/2004—The Link Between Agreements and Mergers

For the substantive analysis of minority shareholding acquisitions, a clearance decision under the Merger Regulation 139/2004 is necessary to clarify the extent to which any further agreements between the acquirer and the target are covered at the same time the minority stake is acquired, *but which go beyond the acquisition of minority shareholding.* Such agreements could, for instance, concern some additional cooperation between the parties involved.

According to the Commission's suggestion, which is in line with current practice, such agreements are subject to assessment under Articles 101 and 102 TFEU unless they constitute restrictions which are directly related and necessary for the implementation of the transaction or the concentration, ie ancillary restraints.[39] Thus, any merger analysis 'would be limited to competition issues specific to the structural link created by the acquisition of the minority stake and they would not prejudice any future antitrust investigations'.[40] Every additional agreement between the parties, which is not directly related and necessary for the implementation of the concentration,[41] would remain subject to Articles 101 and 102 TFEU. This means in practice that only those agreements which are considered as 'ancillary restraints' are covered by the clearance decision.[42]

Furthermore, in line with the Commission's practice under Regulation 139/2004, the Commission might take these specific agreements into account when assessing the transaction under merger control rules. The Commission should assess the current market conditions and their likely development in the future, ie mainly in terms of market's contestability, potential competition and barriers to entry and, for example, any long-term contracts that form part of this market reality.[43]

As happens with ancillary restraints, the parties ought to assess, with the help of the Commission's notice on restrictions directly related and necessary to concentrations,[44] 'whether any agreement fulfils the relevant criteria, unless they explicitly request that the Commission do so because of novel or unresolved questions giving rise to genuine uncertainty'.[45]

[39] See para 1(b), subpara 2 of Art 6 and para 2, subpara 3 of Art 8 of the Merger Regulation and Commission notice on restrictions directly related and necessary to concentrations [2005] OJ C56/24. About ancillary restraints, see also MB Louis, 'Restraints Ancillary to Joint Ventures and Licensing Agreements: Do Sealey and Topco Logically Survive Sylvania and Broadcast Music?' (1980) 66 *Virginia Law Review* 879–80; P Lugart and L Hancher, 'Honey I Shrunk the Article! A Critical Assessment of the Commission's Notice on Article 81(3) of the EC Treaty' [2004] *European Competition Law Review* 410; JR Modrall, 'Ancillary Restrictions in Commission's Decisions under the Merger Regulation: Non-competition Clauses' [1995] *European Competition Law Review* 40; J Venit, 'Pronuptia: Ancillary Restraints on Unholy Alliances?' (1986) 11 *European Law Review* 213'; N Zevgolis, 'The Non Compete Clause as an Ancillary Restraint' [2007] *Nomiki Bibliothiki* (in Greek).

[40] See also Case IV/M.1168 *Deutsche Post/DH* L, 26 June 1998, para 37.

[41] See, for instance, Case IV/M.1482 *Kingfisher/Grosslabor*, 12 April 1999, paras 24 and 25.

[42] See also Case IV/M.1188 *Kingfisher/Wegert/Promarkt*, 18 June 1998, para 17; Case IV/M.1097 *Wacker/Air Products*, 4 August 1998, para 17; Case IV/M.786 *Birmingham International Airport*, para 28.

[43] See for example COMP/M.6541 *Glencore/Xstrata*, 22 November 2012, para 26.

[44] [2005] OJ C56/24.

[45] See recital 21 of the Merger Regulation, where it is mentioned that:

> This Regulation should also apply where the undertakings concerned accept restrictions directly related to, and necessary for, the implementation of the concentration. Commission decisions declaring concentrations compatible with the common market in application of this Regulation should automatically cover

However, a different approach is observed in paragraph 85 of Case T-251/00 *Lagardère SCA & Canal+SA v Commission*:

> It is true, as the defendant observes, that the question whether particular contractual clauses are directly related and necessary to a concentration has been examined, in Community competition law, in the context of Article 81 EC (see, in particular, the judgment in Case 42/84 Remia and Others v Commission [1985] ECR 2545, and the M6 judgment). Similarly, even if the question is examined in the context of Regulation No 4064/89, *such examination is a 'step in the interpretation of Article 81 EC'* in so far as Regulation No 4064/89 was adopted on the basis of Article 83 EC, which is the legal basis for the adoption of regulations or directives with a view to applying the principles of Article 81 EC in particular.[46]

However, paragraph 7 of the Commission notice on restrictions directly related and necessary to concentrations[47] states that:

> To the extent that restrictions are directly related and necessary to the implementation of the concentration, Article 21(1) of the Merger Regulation provides that this Regulation alone applies, to the exclusion of Council Regulations (EC) No 1/2003.

Furthermore, the Commission Guidelines on the application of Article 81(3) of the Treaty[48] declare that:

> The application of the ancillary restraint concept must be distinguished from the application of the defence under Article 81(3) which relates to certain economic benefits produced by restrictive agreements and which are balanced against the restrictive effects of the agreements. The application of the ancillary restraint concept does not involve any weighing of pro-competitive and anti-competitive effects. Such balancing is reserved for Article 81(3).[49]

M. Acquisition of Non-controlling Minority Shareholdings and Joint Ventures

As has already been suggested by the Consultation Paper, acquisitions of minority shareholdings in joint ventures, *which perform on a lasting basis all the functions of an autonomous economic entity*,[50] must also be covered by the new competence.

Under the revised Merger Regulation, joint ventures which are not jointly controlled but rather have several shareholders with minority stakes who are in reality decision-makers through changing majorities would also fall under the new competence under the precondition that the joint venture is full-function in nature.

such restrictions, without the Commission having to assess such restrictions in individual cases. At the request of the undertakings concerned, however, the Commission should, in cases presenting novel or unresolved questions giving rise to genuine uncertainty, expressly assess whether or not any restriction is directly related to, and necessary for, the implementation of the concentration. A case presents a novel or unresolved question giving rise to genuine uncertainty if the question is not covered by the relevant Commission notice in force or a published Commission decision.

46 Emphasis added.

47 Above n 39.

48 [2004] OJ C101/97.

49 Above n 39. See also Case T-112/1999 *Métropole télévision (M6) and others* [2001] ECR II-2459.

50 A so-called full function joint venture. See especially para 4 of Art 3 of Merger Regulation 139/2004.

In terms of procedure, the acquisitions of minority shareholdings by several firms in a joint ventures would constitute *one single transaction* either in the case that the share purchasing agreements are conditional upon each other or if they are concluded simultaneously. Nevertheless, this would not necessarily mean that the turnover would be calculated in the same way as it is currently calculated for joint ventures. For jurisdictional purposes, *it might be more appropriate to calculate the turnover for each acquirer separately.* If a joint venture is newly created and two of the shareholders acquire joint control (which requires a notification) while a minority stake without control is acquired by a third shareholder (which requires only an information notice), the third shareholder must also join the notification if the operation constitutes one single transaction. Due to this obligation (of the third shareholder to join the notification), 'it is ensured that the transaction assessment is not artificially divided'.[51]

N. Creeping Transactions: Hidden, Step-by-Step Transactions and Relevant Framework of Analysis

The term 'creeping transaction' concerns cases where minority shareholdings are developed slowly, step-by-step; in those cases the relevant framework for assessing the acquisition would use the status quo ante, ie the status before the transaction provoking the notice, as the benchmark. This is also compatible with the current viewpoint of Regulation 139/2004.

O. Concluding Remarks

A targeted transparency system, as described above, appears appropriate to capture potentially problematic transactions and thus prevent consumer harm, which can be the consequence of acquisitions of minority shareholdings and which the Commission is not adequately equipped to deal with under Regulation 139/2004. Furthermore, a system such as that described above would not disproportionately burden business, since only very few cases would require the filing of an information notice to the Commission. Needless to say, the introduction of an information notice instead of a full notification further reduces the burden on businesses in terms of the information gathering that is required.

Although the truth is that the design of such a system for controlling minority shareholdings is not simple, since it poses a number of challenges regarding, on the one hand, the proper procedure and jurisdictional scope, and on the other hand, substantive assessment, none of these challenges seems insurmountable. The implementation of such a system needs to be adjusted precisely in order to ensure a smooth integration into the existing procedures for merger control not only at the EU level, but also at the Member State level.

[51] Commission Staff Working Document (n 1) para 121.

9

Commission's White Paper in Practice

I. The Commission's White Paper and its Practicability

The Commission's White Paper and its accompanying Staff Working Documents set out the proposals for possible amendments of the current functioning of Council Regulation (EC) No 139/2004 on the control of concentrations between undertakings. The White Paper also provides the fundamentals criteria for a balanced control system of non-controlling minority interests taking into account the theories of harm and the main principles analysed in the previous chapter.

In this chapter we provide our view regarding the practicability and applicability of non-controlling minority interests within the existing Merger Regulation system.

A. The Case Law cannot be Ignored

It is important to underline the sense and significance of control as framed by the ECJ:[1]

> That will be true [ie the fact that the acquisition of an equity interest in a competitor does not by itself restrict competition; nevertheless, it might serve as an instrument to this goal] in particular where, by the acquisition of a shareholding or through subsidiary clauses in the agreement, the investing company obtains *legal or de facto control* of the commercial conduct of the other company or where the agreement provides for commercial co-operation between the companies or creates a structure likely to be used for such co-operation. That may also be the case where the agreement give the investing company the possibility of reinforcing its position at a later stage and taking effective control of the other company.[2]

The specific case law created the necessary preconditions for the adoption of Regulation (EEC) No 4064/89 just a few years later.

B. The ECMR Regulations Following the Case Law

It should be recalled here that, according to Regulation (EEC) No 4064/89, the main criterion was the 'creation or strengthening of a dominant position' test. However, in 2004,

[1] The *Philip Morris* case (142 and 156/84 [1987] ECR 4487, [1988] 4 CMLR 24) with the *Continental Can* case (ie 6/72 *Europemballage and Continental Can v Commission*, 6/72, [1973] ECR 215, CMLR 199) are considered the precursors for the adoption of Regulation (EEC) No 4064/89.

[2] Ibid, *Philip Morris* case paras 38 and 39 (emphasis added).

with the implementation of Regulation 139/2004, the 'significant impediment of effective competition' (SIEC) test was introduced (among other things) as the relevant criterion for assessing mergers, replacing the previous 'creation or strengthening of a dominant position' test. Regulation 139/2004 continued, like its 'predecessor', to *apply only to concentrations*, ie those transactions involving acquisitions of control by enterprises over other enterprises or parts of them.[3]

C. The White Paper's Point—First Questions

Nevertheless, the experience gained since 2004 shows that acquisitions of equity stakes which are below the level of control and therefore are not captured by Regulation 139/2004 may in a few cases lead to structural changes in the market. Hence, the discussion that took place in the Commission's Staff Working Document[4] had the intention of examining whether the Merger Regulation should be extended to cover such transactions. But at this point the reasonable question is, do we really need this? To be more specific, is there the intention of ignoring the legal or de facto control demanded for the creation of a merger? Is there the intention of examining through new/future provisions included in Regulation 139/2004 structural changes in a market without the existence of a concentration?

D. In Terms of *De Lege Ferenda* does the Practice of the Commission and the Relevant Case Law Justify this Change?

The conclusion of the White Paper is that greater convergence not only between the Commission and NCAs but also among the NCAs is important for the creation of a truly level playing field and the avoidance of undesirable inconsistencies,[5] even an absence of an initiative of legislative harmonisation. For these serious reasons, the Commission and the Member States should continue to conform their practices by enhancing cooperation and sharing experience, using all available tools and forums (obviously, the Merger Working Group constitutes the main forum). Furthermore, regarding individual cases, NCAs ought to intensify their cooperation.

[3] See also P Fotis, 'Merger Enforcement: Law and Statistical Evidence Worldwide' (2014) 5(3) *International Journal of Economics and Business Research* 272, 273–77.

[4] Commission Staff Working Document accompanying the White Paper 'Towards More Effective EU Merger Control', Brussels 9 July 2014, SWD(2014) 221 final.

[5] See especially recital no 14 of Regulation 139/2004:

> The Commission and the competent authorities of the Member States should together form a network of public authorities, applying their respective competences in close cooperation, using efficient arrangements for information-sharing and consultation, with a view to ensuring that a case is dealt with by the most appropriate authority, in the light of the principle of subsidiarity and with a view to ensuring that multiple notifications of a given concentration are avoided to the greatest extent possible. Referrals of concentrations from the Commission to Member States and from Member States to the Commission should be made in an efficient manner avoiding, to the greatest extent possible, situations where a concentration is subject to a referral both before and after its notification.

For instance, it is observed that the Commission is emphasizing cooperation and deals with referral and competence.

However, the undisputable truth is that since 2004 no Commission decision either approving or prohibiting a merger has been definitively annulled by the EU courts; on the contrary, nearly all decisions in merger cases taken by the Commission during the period, despite the fact they were appealed, have been upheld by the EU courts. To be precise, the only Commission decision in a merger procedure taken after 2004 and annulled by an EU court with an irreversible judgment did not concern the compatibility of the merger with the internal market but with 'the approval of a proposed purchaser of a business that had to be divested according to a conditional clearance decision'.[6]

In addition, the truth is that commitments constitute the most important instruments for merger control, taking into account that the large majority of cases that raise competition concerns are not prohibited, but are cleared with commitments. Indeed, during the last 25 years only 24 transactions have been prohibited. Furthermore, the overall percentage of merger cases where the Commission intervened in order to maintain effective competition in the single market has been stable at around 5–8 per cent of all notified mergers in recent years.

Consequently, *de lege ferenda* speaking, the reasons why the Commission's Staff Working Document[7] decided to examine whether the Merger Regulation ought to be extended to cover transactions that do not constitute concentrations are not clear.

Furthermore, the combination of quantitative evidence with qualitative evidence is considered as a *condicio sine qua non* for the completeness and accuracy of a merger analysis, the existence of which demands de jure or de facto control. More specifically, on the one hand, economic and numerical evidence (ie quantitative) is considered to be important in assessing merger cases. In addition, on the other hand, it is acceptable that this quantitative analysis ought always to be integrated into the context of the more qualitative evidence on file: qualitative evidence constitutes, for example, minutes of interviews with market participants at the horizontal or vertical level (suppliers or distributors, etc), replies by customers and competitors to requests for information, and internal documents of the parties involved. It is crystal clear that these two types of evidence are counterbalancing to, rather than substitutable for, each other. Therefore the main issue, the *desideratum*, is the supplementation and not the substitutability. Consequently, the combination of quantitative evidence with qualitative evidence constitutes the necessary means which leads with (legal) certainty to the ascertainment of existence or non-existence of the control demanded. Furthermore, the Commission's Staff Working Document[8] recognizes that, assessing the consequences of the financial and economic crises,[9] the content of the Merger Regulation is in a position to provide all the necessary tools for applying effective merger control even in times of economic stress.

[6] See COMP/M.2978 *Lagardère/Natexis/VUP*, decision of 30 July 2004, which was annulled in last resort by judgment of the Court of Justice of 6 November 2012 in Joint Cases C-553/10 P and C-554/10 P *Commission and Lagardère v Editions Odile Jacob* (nyr).

[7] Above n 4.

[8] Ibid.

[9] Concerning competition policy for mergers in periods of economic downturn, see especially P Fotis, 'Competition Policy in Periods of Economic Downturn' (2012) 4(5) *International Journal of Economics and Business Research* 560.

E. The Success of the Merger Regulation 139/2004, the Role of the NCAs and the Minimum Legislative Convergence

The success story of the Merger Regulation 139/2004 is undisputable, since it has truly succeeded on the one hand at levelling the playing field, and on the other hand provides a one-stop shop for scrutinizing mergers with an EU dimension.[10] Nevertheless, it is also accepted that Member States play significant roles in merger control enforcement in the EU. More specifically, in the seven years between 2001 and 2007 the NCAs together handled nearly 4,000 merger cases per year on average. The necessity for a truly functional system that will scrutinize mergers throughout the EU demands cooperation, efficient work-sharing and convergence between the Commission and the 27 Member States engaged in merger control.[11]

Although NCAs usually apply Articles 101 and 102 TFEU together with their national laws, the EU Merger Regulation already constitutes a model applied for many national merger control regimes. Therefore, a basic *minimum* legislative convergence across national jurisdictions is observed, particularly regarding the substantive test for assessing transactions.[12] It is remarkable that, according to the present data, most of the NCAs apply the SIEC or a kind of similar test in their substantive analysis.

F. The Commission's Point of View

In cases where the acquisition of a minority shareholding does not lead or is not related to acquisition of control, the Commission is not authorized to investigate or intervene against it. In the context of a notified merger concerning a separate acquisition of control, only a concentration party's pre-existing minority shareholdings in a competitor or a company which is activated in an upstream or downstream market can be taken into account by the Commission. Nevertheless, if the minority shareholding is acquired *after* the examination of the acquisition of control by the Commission, there is no competence under Regulation 139/2004 for the Commission to raise possible competition concerns.

The experience acquired by the Commission, the Member States and third countries has shown that at least in some cases the acquisition of a non-controlling minority shareholding, such as, for example, one firm acquiring a 20 per cent shareholding in a competitor, can harm competition and, consequently, consumers. According to the Commission, this type of minority shareholding 'can lead to a SIEC which cannot be adequately addressed under the Merger Regulation in its current form'.[13]

In addition, there are three EU Member States, namely Austria, Germany and the United Kingdom, that, according to their national merger control rules, have the competence

[10] See especially R Whish, *Competition Law*, 5th edn (Oxford, Oxford University Press, 2005) 816 et seq; BE Hawk and HL Huser, *European Community Merger Control: A Practitioner's Guide* (The Hague, Kluwer Law International, 1996) ch IV; CJ Cook and CS Kerse, *EC Merger Control*, 3rd edn (London, Sweet & Maxwell, 2000) ch 1.9; N Levy, *European Merger Control Law: A Guide to the Merger Regulation* (Newark, NJ, LexisNexis, 2003) ch 1.3.

[11] Luxembourg is exempted.

[12] As a very characteristic example: in 2013 Germany the previous dominance test was replaced with the SIEC test, thereby following the instance of Merger Regulation 139/2004.

[13] Above n 4, para 47.

to review acquisitions of non-controlling minority shareholdings.[14] The NCAs in these Member States have intervened against acquisitions of minority shareholdings that raised competition concerns. Likewise, structural links under merger control rules are examined by many jurisdictions outside the EU, such as Canada, the US and Japan.[15]

G. Assessment of Minority Shareholdings' Effects—Financial Interests and Corporate Rights

The economic effects of minority shareholdings on competition in the market are determined by factors such as the size of the minority shareholding, the resulting financial interests and the corporate rights conferred by these. *Financial interests* refer to the acquiring firm's right to a share of the target firm's profits, whereas *corporate rights* refer to the ability to influence the acquired firm's commercial decisions.

The acquisition of a minority shareholding in a competitor firm can lead to non-coordinated anticompetitive effects by increasing the acquirer's incentive and ability unilaterally to raise prices or restrict output. It has been observed that, by instinct, where undertakings have financial stakes in their competitors' profits, they may decide to incorporate the positive effects of their own output reductions or price increases on their competitors' profits. This may happen when the minority shareholding is passive, eg its holder is unable to influence the target firm's decisions.

A fortiori, the above-mentioned potential anticompetitive effects may also materialize if a minority shareholding is active, eg its holder can influence the target undertaking's decisions. This scenario can occur if the acquirer is able to influence the result of special resolutions at shareholder meetings, which are needed for the approval of certain strategies related to significant investments, eg engaging in mergers and acquisitions, product lines, geographical scope, raising capital and advertising. In this respect, according to the predictions of economic theory, the acquiring enterprise may be able to influence the target undertaking to increase its prices, since the acquiring firm fully benefits from the positive externalities of the competitor's price increase but is liable for only part of the costs, depending on the level of its financial ownership rights. If the target company is finally enforced to stop competing with the acquiring firm, the situation would be similar in reality to a full merger but without any of the cost-saving efficiencies that a merger can create (economies of scale or economies of scope, etc).[16]

According to the Commission and the Member States' findings, competition concerns are more likely to be significant mainly in the case that a minority shareholding grants some degree of influence over the target enterprise's decisions.

[14] As we have already noted in previous chapters, Lithuania is the fourth state which, according to its national merger control rules, has the competence to review acquisitions of non-controlling minority shareholdings. See especially ch 3, section B.

[15] About Japan, see especially E Kameoka, *Competition Law and Policy in Japan and the EU* (Cheltenham, Edward Elgar, 2014) 113–14.

[16] See also B Ignjatovic and D Ridyard, 'Minority Shareholdings, Material Effects?' [2012] January (1) *CPI Antitrust Chronicle* 3–4.

> [If] a minority shareholding does enable the acquirer to influence the decisions of the target firm, that also raises the possibility that such influence could be used to make the target compete less aggressively against the acquirer. Therefore, the substantive analysis must be extended to assess the effect of the transaction on the ability of the acquirer to impose increases in price or reductions in service quality of the target. In this case, the acquirer's incentives to increase prices of the target company may well be higher than is the case in a full-fledged merger.[17]

However, degree of influence in reality means level of control (either joint or sole). Thus, the crucial question is inevitably raised: regarding minority shareholdings, do we really need a modification of the Merger Regulation provisions?

H. The Core of the *Ryanair/Aer Lingus* Case, According to the European Legal Framework

Competition concerns may also arise where the financial interests of the buyer firm in the target firm are limited but the acquirer is in a position to use its minority shareholding to limit the competitive strategies available to the target firm, thereby weakening it (indirectly) as a competitor. Competition concerns of this specific type were at the core of several recent European and UK minority shareholding cases, of which the *Ryanair/Aer Lingus* case constitutes probably the best-known example.

As discussed in chapter 5, section I.A(iii), Ryanair had a priori acquired a significant minority shareholding in the share capital of its competitor, Aer Lingus. Ryanair then notified the Commission in 2006 of its proposal to acquire full control of its competitor. On 20 December 2006 the Commission decided to initiate a detailed examination procedure (Phase II), in accordance with paragraph (1)(c) of Article 6 of the Merger Regulation 139/2004, because it had serious concerns that the transaction would hurt competition by creating or strengthening Ryanair's dominant position on a number of routes. Pursuant to paragraph 3 of Article 8 of the Merger Regulation, the Commission stated that the notified concentration was incompatible with the common market (now the internal market) and therefore Ryanair maintained, at least at that time, its a priori obtained minority shareholding of 29.4 per cent in Aer Lingus.[18]

The Commission blocked a second attempt by Ryanair to acquire control over Aer Lingus in February 2013. However, as was confirmed by the General Court, the Merger Regulation did not give the Commission authorization to order Ryanair to divest the shareholding it already held in Aer Lingus.[19] Nevertheless, Aer Lingus raised the argument that Ryanair's minority shareholding would have significant negative effects on competition between the two air companies, since Ryanair would use the minority shareholding to restrict Aer Lingus's ability to compete. However, on 11 June 2015 the Competition and Markets Authority in the UK (CMA) decided that Ryanair must reduce its shareholding in Aer Lingus to 5 per cent.[20]

[17] Ibid.

[18] See Case COMP/M.4439 *Ryanair/Aer Lingus I*, decision of 27 June 2007 (Decision C(2007) 3104).

[19] Case T-411/07 *Aer Lingus v Commission* [2010] ECR II-3691.

[20] The *Ryanair/Aer Lingus* case is thoroughly analysed in ch 5, section A.iii above.

In our view, the main issue in this notable case is the following: despite the fact that a significant minority shareholding in the share capital of Aer Lingus was acquired by its competitor Ryanair, notification of this first acquisition never took place. Rather, notification took place later, when Ryanair decided to acquire full control of its competitor. That means that in practice research about a possible joint control by Ryanair and Aer Lingus never took place, despite the significant minority shareholding which was acquired by Ryanair. Furthermore, the question of whether there was a creeping transaction at the time when a significant minority shareholding in the share capital of Aer Lingus was acquired by its competitor Ryanair remains unanswered. The authors have no intention of prejudging the result of such research. However, the truth is that at least at the beginning of this interesting story the case for a possible joint control between Ryanair and Aer Lingus was not examined. However, the fact that Aer Lingus did not react at the beginning of this story, eg when Ryanair acquired the significant minority shareholding, lead us to the probably safe conclusion that Aer Lingus considered that it was not about a case of joint control; it was simply about a financial interest. Therefore, it is suggested that the only way to have achieved a different legal result in the *Ryanair/Aer Lingus* case would be to have considered this specific case from a different angle, namely to consider the acquisition of a significant minority shareholding by Ryanair as the first step of a concentration which was planned step by step, and completed through the notification to the Commission by Ryanair of its proposal to acquire full control of its competitor later on.

I. Are Articles 101 and 102 TFEU Appropriate for Dealing Effectively with Anticompetitive Minority Shareholdings?

During the public consultation, a number of stakeholders, such as law firms and business associations, had the opportunity to answer the question whether the limited number of problematic transactions would justify broadly extending the Merger Regulation's scope. Some stakeholders had the opinion that the rules on restrictive agreements and abuse of dominance, set out in Articles 101 and 102 TFEU, respectively, constituted adequate substitutes, since they could capture many of the problematic transactions.

Nevertheless, 'the Commission's ability to use Article 101 and Article 102 TFEU to intervene against anti-competitive minority shareholdings may be limited'.[21] More specifically, as far as it concerns Article 101 TFEU, 'it is not clear whether acquiring a minority shareholding would constitute an "agreement" having the object or effect of restricting competition within the meaning of Article 101 TFEU in all cases'.[22]

More specifically, the following are observed: regarding acquisitions of a series of shares via a stock exchange, the application of Article 101 TFEU might present a number of conceptual difficulties depending on whether or not an agreement existed. In case that there is an agreement, the Commission would still have to define whether such an agreement would have the object or effect of deterring competition and, in the case of a positive answer, whether purchase agreement does actually impede competition. The same questions probably concern the application of the articles of association of a firm, the purpose of which

[21] Above n 13, para 62.
[22] Ibid.

is generally to define and make clear 'the corporate governance of the company and the relationship between it and its shareholders'.[23] However, in the authors' view, the potential anticompetitive effects following a stock exchange investment probably offer a relatively clear sign that it is about an agreement.[24]

Concering the application of Article 102 TFEU, 'its provision requires that the firm acquiring a minority shareholding already hold a dominant position and that the acquisition would constitute an abuse of that dominant position'.[25] Consequently, the necessary circumstances under which the Commission has the authorization to 'intervene against competitive harm arising from acquisitions of minority shareholdings are therefore quite narrow'.[26] According to the Commission's view, the *Ryanair/Aer Lingus* case constitutes an indicative relevant example. Nevertheless, regarding this case, the authors have the opposite opinion for the reasons mentioned in the previous section. Furthermore, the authors consider that potential anticompetitive effects following the acquisition of a minority shareholding under preconditions are probably a clear sign that it is a dominant company abusing its position, under the precondition that the acquisition of a minority shareholding can be combined with specific anticompetitive results occurring.

In the Commission's point of view, the theories relevant to a competition assessment of minority shareholdings are similar to those arising from acquisitions of control (ie horizontal, non-coordinated and vertical effects), since they focus on structural changes in the market. For these reasons, the SIEC test applied in the Merger Regulation seems to be much more appropriate than the tests applied in Articles 101 and/or 102 TFEU. Nevertheless, in the authors' view, Articles 101 and/or 102 TFEU complete the Merger Regulation. The obvious difference is that the merger control constitutes a version of a forward-looking and predictive competition policy, since it is about ex ante control, regarding mainly the structure of the relative market. On the contrary, the application of Articles 101 and/or 102 TFEU constitutes suppressive competition practice applied by the authorized authorities, since it is always about ex post control.

In addition, in the Commission's view, there is a contradiction that should be emphasized: while some respondents to the public consultation claim that Articles 101 and 102 TFEU should be applied, the same respondents also stress the significance of legal certainty for firms making investments. The procedures laid down in Council Regulation (EC) No 1/2003[27] for the appropriate enforcement of Articles 101 and 102 TFEU essentially require undertakings to self-assess whether they comply with the competition rules and offer the Commission and NCAs the legal power to intervene a posteriori against any anticompetitive conduct without any time restrictions. This self-assessment procedure appears to provide less legal certainty for enterprises, and therefore, in comparison with the procedural framework of the Merger Regulation, it is less appropriate for examining the effect of lasting acquisitions of minority shareholdings. Under this angle, the Commission should make a decision within a short, legally binding deadline.

[23] Ibid.

[24] See also the analysis presented in ch 3, section II.B.i above.

[25] Above n 13.

[26] See Case T-411/07 *Aer Lingus v Commission* [2010] ECR II-3691, in particular para 104, and Case 6/72 *Continental Can v Commission* [1973] ECR 216.

[27] Council Regulation (EC) No 1/2003 of 16 December 2002 on the implementation of the rules on competition laid down in Articles 81 and 82 of the treaty [2003] OJ L1/1, as already been amended.

Therefore, according to the above remarks, the Commission seems to support the need to extend Regulation 139/2004 to the acquisition of non-controlling minority shareholdings and that 'it is appropriate to apply the substantive test of the Merger Regulation. While it is expected that only a limited number of cases would be examined, past cases have shown that this initiative would demand a relevant enforcement activity.'[28]

However, in the authors' view, such a change would basically constitute the transformation/modification of the Commission to an element/factor that would co-decide with the interested enterprise about whether or not to make an investment. This evolution, if it happened, would mean in reality that the interested undertaking would be substituted by the Commission and the latter would take on a business role, completely different and irrelevant in comparison with the role of competition watchdog that the Commission ought to play. And the unavoidable question is whether such a modification would be acceptable to the so-called Community *acquis*.

J. Proposed Realistic Approach

As has already been mentioned, a successive system for controlling minority shareholdings at the EU level should strike the right balance between three main principles. First and most importantly, taking into account not only the overall aim of preventing harm to consumers but also the theories of harm analysed above, the system ought to focus on detecting and capturing potentially problematic cases.

Secondly, it must avoid unnecessary and disproportionate administrative burdens, not only for enterprises but also for the Commission and NCAs. It ought to be emphasized that in the public consultation, stakeholders expressed their concerns that the Commission's proposal would constitute a far-reaching system with a high administrative burden on business, even though few transactions would be problematic. Stakeholders often pointed out that most minority shareholdings are perfectly harmless, such as those acquired only for investment purposes or during recapitalization or restructuring of problematic undertakings by financial institutions. Hence, subjecting such shareholdings to mandatory review under merger control rules without any discrimination might go beyond what is necessary in order to prevent effectively anticompetitive transactions.

While the above-mentioned first two principles are significant for a system of controlling minority shareholdings in any jurisdiction, a third principle is important for a system for the control of minority shareholdings at the EU level. More specifically, the system ought to fit with the existing merger control systems at both EU and national level.

The NCAs considered that any system for controlling minority shareholdings at the EU level should be consistent with national systems. The NCAs' point is important given that the Member States that currently control the acquisition of minority shareholdings would lose in such a case the competence to review transactions above the turnover thresholds of the Merger Regulation. More specifically, regarding the outlining of competences between the Member States and the Commission, it would be provided that the turnover thresholds of Regulation 139/2004 would also apply to the acquisitions of minority shareholdings and that, furthermore, the referral system would apply for minority shareholdings in order to

[28] Above n 13, para 65.

allow for a precise adjustment of case allocation to the 'more appropriate authority' where this is not achieved via the turnover thresholds. Several NCAs expressed the opinion that a high level of protection of competition would only be achieved under the precondition that the Commission is at least informed about the fact that a transaction is examined and takes a clear position on whether it will investigate that transaction. In such a case, Member States should be allowed to request a referral if the Commission were to decide not to investigate a case.[29]

A system for controlling minority shareholdings must also fit without problems into the existing legal and procedural framework of Regulation 139/2004 in order to avoid complicating EU merger control in an unnecessary way. It can achieve this goal without necessarily extending the notification system.

There is a direct relation between the scope of the Commission's jurisdiction and the answer to the question of what procedure is considered to be more appropriate and adequate. For instance, if the Commission's competence covers all acquisitions of minority shareholdings above a certain threshold, eg a 'safe harbour', a pre-merger notification system would create a heavy administrative burden (and cost) on businesses since unproblematic mergers would also be covered. In the case of a Commission's jurisdiction over all acquisitions of minority shareholdings above a certain threshold, the existence of a self-assessment system might be more appropriate, since, in this case, the Commission would be free to investigate transactions on its own initiative (ex officio investigation). However, the undisputable administrative burden imposed by a notification or transparency system would be much lower in cases where the Commission's jurisdiction was limited to only potentially problematic transactions. The relationship between the design of the procedural system and the scope of jurisdiction is crystal clear and this is the reason why it was frequently mentioned in responses to the public consultation.

K. The Decentralization Tradition Created by Regulations 1/2003 and 651/2014 and the Paradox of the White Paper's Proposal

The self-assessment system could be the most appropriate potential alternative. Under this system, the parties involved would not be obliged to notify the acquisition of a minority shareholding a priori and could proceed to the acquisition without prior approval by the Commission. This system, if preferred, would oblige the Commission to continue to do what it is currently doing, ie relying on its own market intelligence (ex officio process) or complaints to become aware of transactions that may raise competition concerns; then the Commission would be free to select the potentially problematic cases (acquisitions below a 'safe harbour' would be excepted) and examine them.

The self-assessment system is followed by Regulation 1/2003.[30] It was accepted that:

> [T]he centralised scheme set up by Regulation No 17 no longer secured a balance between the two main objectives, ie the need to ensure effective supervision, on the one hand, and to simplify administration to the greatest possible extent, on the other.[31]

[29] Ibid, para 71.
[30] See [2003] OJ L1/1.
[31] Ibid, recital no 3.

On the contrary, this scheme hampered application of the Community (now EU) competition rules by the courts and competition authorities of the Member States, and the system of notification it involved prevented the Commission from concentrating its resources on curbing the most serious infringements. It also imposed considerable costs on undertakings.[32] Therefore it was considered necessary to replace the Regulation No 17 system by a directly applicable exception system in which the competition authorities and courts of the Member States would have the power to apply not only Article 81(1) EC Treaty (now Article 101(1) TFEU) and Article 82 EC Treaty (now Article 102 TFEU), which would have direct applicability by virtue of the case law of the Court of Justice of the European Communities, but also Article 81(3) EC Treaty (now Article 101(3) TFEU).[33]

Furthermore, according to recital no 38 of the specific Regulation:

> Legal certainty for undertakings operating under the Community competition rules contributes to the promotion of innovation and investment. Where cases give rise to genuine uncertainty because they present novel or unresolved questions for the application of these rules, individual undertakings may wish to seek informal guidance from the Commission.

The same provision could probably be applied in merger issues regarding the acquisition of minority shareholdings.

The self-assessment system is also followed by Regulation 651/2014.[34] More specifically, the following ought to be underlined:

> According to the provisions of the specific Regulation,[35] with its Communication on EU State Aid Modernisation (SAM),[36] the Commission launched a wider review of the State aid rules. The main objectives of this modernisation are considered the following: (a) to achieve sustainable, smart and inclusive growth in a competitive internal market, while contributing to Member State efforts towards a more efficient use of public finances, (b) to focus Commission *ex ante* scrutiny of aid measures on cases with the biggest impact on the internal market, while strengthening Member State cooperation in State aid enforcement, and (c) to make more efficient the rules and provide for faster, better informed and more robust decisions based on a clear economic rationale, a common approach and clear obligations. Under this angle, the review of Regulation (EC) No 800/2008 constitutes a central element of State Aid Modernization.
>
> This Regulation ought to allow for better prioritisation of State aid enforcement activities, greater simplification and should enhance transparency, effective evaluation and the control of compliance with the State aid rules at national and Union levels, while preserving the institutional competences of the Commission and the Member States. In accordance with the principle of proportionality this Regulation does not go beyond what is necessary in order to achieve those objectives.
>
> The Commission's experience in applying Regulation (EC) No 800/2008 has allowed it to better define the conditions under which certain categories of aid can be considered compatible with the internal market and to extend the scope of block exemptions. It also revealed the necessity to strengthen transparency, monitoring and proper evaluation of very large schemes in light of their effect on competition in the internal market.

[32] Ibid.
[33] Ibid, recital no 4.
[34] See [2014] OJ L187/1.
[35] Ibid, recitals no 2–6.
[36] See COM(2012) 209.

> The general conditions for the application of this Regulation should be defined on the basis of a set of common principles that ensure the aid serves a purpose of common interest, has a clear incentive effect, is appropriate and proportionate, is granted in full transparency and subject to a control mechanism and regular evaluation, and does not adversely affect trading conditions to an extent that is contrary to the common interest.
>
> Aid that fulfils all the conditions laid down in this Regulation both general and specific to the relevant categories of aid should be exempted from the notification obligation laid down in para 3 of Article 108 TFEU.

Therefore, according to the above remarks on EU competition policy during the last twelve years, as this policy is constantly expressed and applied through Regulations 1/2003 and 651/2014, respectively, a procedural decentralization is observed; however, this correct decentralization seems to be absolutely contrary to the proposal of the Commission, according to the White Paper. Consequently, there is a paradox: the Commission's propositions, as defined in its White Paper regarding minority shareholdings, are moving in the opposite direction to EU competition policy during the last twelve years. More specifically, while the main purpose of Regulations 1/2003 and 651/2014 is to permit the Commission to focus on the really important competition issues, eg cartels,[37] abuse of dominance or better prioritization of state aid enforcement activities, the Staff Working Document[38] seems to prefer a completely different approach towards a more administrative 'red tape' system, since it ultimately favours unnecessary and disproportionate administrative burdens which, if regulated, would in reality prevent the Commission from focusing on the really problematic acquisition cases. This choice of the Commission, as outlined in its White Paper regarding minority shareholdings, is in the authors' eyes absolutely incomprehensible and completely unreasonable.

The undisputable truth is that the design of a system for controlling minority shareholdings is not that simple, since it poses a number of challenges regarding on the one hand the proper procedure and jurisdictional scope, and on the other hand substantive assessment; in the authors' view, none of these challenges seems capable of being overcome. Theoretically speaking in terms of *de lege ferenda*, the implementation of such a system needs to be adjusted precisely in order to ensure a smooth integration into the existing procedures for merger control not only at the EU level, but also at the Member State level. However, this would create extremely heavy administrative burden and consequently will not be at all practical.

L. The Safe Harbour of Exchanging Confidential Information Between Commission and Member States

Paragraphs 1 and 2 of Article 19 of the Merger Regulation[39] contain a provision for exchanging information about certain cases between NCAs and the Commission. According to the

[37] According to a quite famous American antitrust case [*Verizon Communications v Law Offices of Curtis V Trinko*, 540 US 398, 408 (2004)] Cartels remain 'the supreme evil of antitrust'.

[38] Above n 4.

[39] '1. The Commission shall transmit to the competent authorities of the Member States copies of notifications within three working days and, as soon as possible, copies of the most important documents lodged with or issued by the Commission pursuant to this Regulation. Such documents shall include commitments offered by the

Commission's Staff Working Document,[40] the Commission ought to consider modifying this provision to ensure that in cases where Member States refer cases to the Commission and vice versa, under Article 22 and Article 9 of the Merger Regulation, respectively, 'the authority that continues the investigation can use the information already obtained by the authority that referred the case'.[41]

However, in the authors' view, modification of the above provisions is not necessary: since in reality the NCA has already obtained the necessary information, it can confirm the specific information by asking the appropriate question of the undertaking involved, without any reference to the information exchanged with the Commission. If the undertaking involved takes the risk of applying in an inappropriate way, it may jeopardize its involvement by supplying incorrect or misleading information in response to a request by the NCA. Virtually all national laws regarding merger control contain a provision similar to the provision of Article 14 of the Merger Regulation.

II. Minority Interests from an Economic Point of View

A. Theoretical Insights

Economists have estimated in detail the potential anticompetitive effects of passive minority interests, both in static and dynamic terms. The majority of relevant papers in the literature, which are extensively analyzed in chapters 4 and 6, indicates that passive minority acquisitions decrease the level of competition in the markets by enhancing cooperation among firms or by increasing the probability that a dominant firm will abuse its dominant position. As regards the static effects of minority interests, the relevant literature shows that they decrease consumer welfare by increasing the product price and reducing its quantity.[42]

More precisely, the economic literature has shown that passive minority shareholdings can harm competition either unilaterally or via coordinated effects. The magnitude of these

undertakings concerned vis-à-vis the Commission with a view to rendering the concentration compatible with the common market pursuant to Article 6(2) or Article 8(2), second subparagraph.

2. The Commission shall carry out the procedures set out in this Regulation in close and constant liaison with the competent authorities of the Member States, which may express their views upon those procedures. For the purposes of Article 9 it shall obtain information from the competent authority of the Member State as referred to in paragraph 2 of that Article and give it the opportunity to make known its views at every stage of the procedure up to the adoption of a decision pursuant to paragraph 3 of that Article; to that end it shall give it access to the file.'

40 Ibid, paras 38, 181.

41 Ibid, para 181.

42 Passively acquired interests may also raise arguments in favour of efficiencies. H Ono, T Nakazato, C Davis and W Alley, 'Partial Ownership Arrangements in the Japanese Automobile Industry; 1990–2000' (2004) 7(2) *Journal of Applied Economics* 355 argue that passive minority interests positively influence firms' profits, while ES Amundsen and L Bergman, 'Will Cross-Ownership Re-establish Market Power in the Nordic Power Market?' (2002) 23(2) *Energy Journal* 73 argue that cost reduction enable a firm to acquire minority shareholdings in their rivals. PP Ouimet, 'What Motivates Minority Acquisitions? The Trade-offs between a Partial Equity Stake and Complete Integration' (2012) 26(4) *Review of Financial Studies* 1021 states, inter alia, that minority acquisitions are more common when the target firm owns a large number of patents while, in vertical integration, active rather than passive minority shareholdings eliminate the double marginalization problem. See the analysis presented in ch 4.

effects depends on the share of the target's profits to which the acquiring firm is actually entitled as a result of the acquired minority shareholding, and the ability of the acquiring firm materially to influence the target's strategic behaviour. If passive financial interests are accompanied by corporate rights, then such structural links may alter the competitive behaviour of both acquiring and target firm.

The anticompetitive effects of structural links are higher on the horizontal than on vertical level. On the horizontal level, silent interests alter firms' strategic choices in favour of coordination among them. For instance, the acquiring firm may have an incentive to compete less aggressively with its competitor, and therefore will raise its product price or restrict its output. It earns profit, the magnitude of which depends on the percentage of its minority shareholding in the issue capital of the target firm.

Vertical passive minority interests can harm competition by imposing input (upward) or customer (downstream) exclusion. The acquiring firm may exclude competitors from the markets where the target firm is active, and if they are accompanied by corporate rights, then the acquiring firm may gain the ability to exclude the target's competitors from its input and customer base. The more concentrated the markets, the more the concerns for either type of exclusion. The economic literature has focused on examining whether partial vertical integration raises fewer anticompetitive concerns about either type of exclusion than full vertical integration.

The acquiring firm's incentives to exclude are higher with corporate rights than with solely financial interests. When the acquiring firm has access to commercial data of the target firm, then the gains from exclusion are higher than in the case of a vertical merger. This is due to the fact that the acquiring firm internalizes the whole stream of profits that come from the other levels of supply chain and at the same time incurs only a small portion of the costs caused by the anticompetitive strategy. However, when the minority shareholding includes only a financial interest, then the acquiring firm has no access to appropriate data in order to proceed to a successful exclusion.

Passively acquired interests also enable the firms involved to coordinate their conduct. Coordination between the firms stems from the fact that the acquiring firm internalizes part of the target's profit. Moreover, the level of transparency is enhanced in the presence of corporate rights. In particular, when a unilateral passive interest is under scrutiny the one-way acquisition of information (from the target to the acquiring firm) enables the latter to monitor the commercial policy of the former. However, when a reciprocal minority shareholding is under scrutiny, then the flow of the information exchange is reciprocal between the firms involved and therefore the level of transparency is enhanced.

The level of transparency in a market is enhanced further where indirect minority shareholdings have associated corporate rights. Both of these enlarge the scope of coordination and enable the coordinating players to detect possible deviations from the common target which aims at maximizing the monopoly profits.

The anticompetitive effects of non-horizontal minority shareholdings have also been examined in the economic literature. Conglomerate minority shareholdings raise anticompetitive issues only in the cases where the acquiring firm acquires a minority stake in the target firm which is active in a market related to that of the acquiring firm. In such a case a conglomerate minority shareholding may facilitate firms to make sales of one product contingent on the sales of others via bundling, tying or similar practices such as exclusive dealing or full-line forcing.

Passive minority interests may sometimes deter entry either for potential entrants that are not active or for active firms that are interested in expanding their product range. Moreover, the acquiring firm may hinder another firm from getting an access to the capital stock of the target firm.[43] Therefore, the acquiring firm has an increased incentive to deter entry by credibly committing to the potential entrant. If the financial interest is accompanied by corporate rights that influence the competitive behaviour of the target firm, then this issue further prevents a potential entrant from entering.

B. Is there Enough Empirical Evidence for an Extension to the Merger Regulation?

On 11 December 2001 the Commission of the European Communities published a Green Paper on the review of Council Regulation (EEC) No 4064/89. According to this, the Commission was particularly interested in transactions among competitors that did not entail acquisition of control, ie non-controlling joint or sole minority shareholdings as well as strategic alliances. The Commission's interest was due to the structural impact of such transactions on the markets involved and the difficulty of defining them for the purposes of an ex ante notification.[44]

The Commission, after an examination of the relevant case law, stated that only a limited number of such transactions raised competitive effects that could not be satisfactorily assessed under Articles 81 and 82 EC Treaty. Therefore, the Commission indicated that 'it would appear disproportionate to subject all acquisitions of minority shareholdings to the ex ante control of the Merger Regulation'.[45] In addition, the Commission could not reach an appropriate definition 'capable of identifying those instances where minority shareholdings and interlocking directorships would warrant such treatment'.[46]

In the authors' view the picture remains the same regarding case law of minority interests during the period from 2005 to 2011. As we have already showed in chapter 5, DG Competition carried out an analysis of certain information contained in the Zephyr Database,[47] including information on transactions resulting in changes of ownership in listed undertakings within the EU for the period between 2005 and 2011. The purpose of this analysis was to have at least a first understanding about the frequency of the creation and changes of structural links in the internal market. In addition, it could offer answers about the question whether certain transactions that are currently not subject to merger control would on a preliminary basis have been deemed worthy of competition scrutiny. Of the total number of transactions mentioned in the Zephyr Database only about 5 per cent (91 transactions of varying size and value) of all cases determined by the Commission during the same period 2005–11 under the Merger Regulation, following the normal procedure, as potentially meriting competition scrutiny were identified by DG Competition. It is emphasized that 43 of

[43] See, for instance, the argument of Aer Lingus regarding Ryanair's minority shareholding in its capital stock.
[44] See COM(2001) 745 final, para 101.
[45] Ibid, para 109.
[46] Ibid.
[47] The Zephyr database is an international dataset containing information on transactions that change the ownership of listed companies within the EU.

these 91 transactions fulfilled the additional criterion, according to which they were likely to have an EU dimension and fall under the Merger Regulation.

Therefore, even though the true consequences of anticompetitive effects in both the static and dynamic dimensions of minority interests are well established by economic theory, and despite the fact that the Zephyr Database was designed to underestimate rather than overestimate the real importance of transactions involving structural links, it is clear that over the last two decades there have *not* been significant numbers of cases with a potential EU dimension that would warrant competition scrutiny but currently fall outside the scope of the Merger Regulation because they do not involve a change of control.[48]

C. Concluding Remarks

The analysis in this chapter clearly indicates that on the one hand economists are aware of the effects of passive minority interests on competition, and on the other hand competition law within the EU is well established to deal with cases involving minority interests that fall outside the Merger Regulation system. Furthermore, the same analysis indicates that there have not been significant numbers of cases with a potential EU dimension that would warrant competition scrutiny but currently fall outside the scope of the Merger Regulation because they do not involve a change of control.

The authors believe that the existence of an enforcement gap in EU competition law regarding potential anticompetitive effects from acquisitions of non-controlling minority shareholdings has not been confirmed. EU competition law already has the tools necessary to deal effectively with anticompetitive practices or effects. For the reasons analysed above, it is considered that any potential change to the existing legal framework regarding minority shareholdings would create more problems rather than resolving issues regarding concentrations and minority shareholdings. Unless, that is, as far as it concerns minority shareholdings, the Commission wishes to establish for itself a different role, namely as a decision-maker on business issues that do not create preconditions for control.

[48] This is a rephrase of para 99 in the Annex to the Commission Staff Working Document, 'Towards More Effective EU Merger Control'.

10

Conclusion

I. Legal and Economic Issues

This book provides an up-to-date retrospective view of the legal and economic issues concerning minority interests. It particular, it presents the merger control regime within the EU and worldwide and thoroughly investigates the concept of minority interests under this regime. It also evaluates the European Commission's proposal regarding its intention to reform the current merger control regime in order to incorporate the notion and control of minority interests.

Regulation (EEC) No 4064/89 introduced a comprehensive and systematic approach to ex ante merger control into EU competition law. The main criterion for assessing mergers under this Regulation was the creation or strengthening of a dominant position test. The current Merger Regulation 139/2004 is the result of a reassessment of Council Regulation (EEC) No 4064/89. The implementation of the Merger Regulation introduced inter alia an effective competition test as the relevant criterion for assessing mergers, replacing the creation or strengthening of a dominant position test. The former was designed to identify mergers that allowed firms unilaterally to raise prices; however, these mergers do not create or reinforce either a single or a collective dominant position.

The current Merger Regulation applies, like its 'predecessor', only to concentrations, eg transactions involving acquisitions of control by firms over other firms or parts of them. Nevertheless, the experience gained over the last fifteen years shows that acquisitions of equity stakes which are below the level of control, and therefore not captured by Regulation 139/2004, may in some cases lead to structural changes in the market. Therefore, there is ongoing discussion as to whether the Merger Regulation should be extended to cover such transactions.

With the publication of the Green Paper on the review of Council Regulation (EEC) No 4064/89 the Commission was particularly interested in the structural impact of minority interests on the markets and the difficulty of defining these interests for the purposes of an ex ante notification. Minority shareholdings and interlocking directorships were viewed as vehicles to alter the competitive incentives of the firms involved. However, the Commission decided not to subject all acquisitions of minority interests to the ex ante control of Merger Regulation 139/2004 since only a limited number of such transactions raised competitive effects that could not be satisfactorily assessed under Articles 81 and 82 EC Treaty.

The Commission subsequently launched a tender offer requiring data on the importance of minority shareholdings in the EU. Its aim was to acquire a critical database of minority shareholdings. Furthermore, Commissioner Almunia expressed concern that EU merger control is unable to analyse minority equity stakes as mergers and indicated an enforcement gap regarding them among Member States and between the EU and the Member States.

The Commission recently launched a working document concerning, inter alia, its ability to examine minority interests (or structural links). Its intention is to design a system for the control of minority shareholdings. Such a system should strike the right balance between three main principles: the system ought to detect and capture potentially problematic cases; it must avoid unnecessary and disproportionate administrative burdens; and it ought to fit with the existing merger control systems at both EU and national level. Considering these three principles, the Commission proposed a targeted transparency system for the control of minority interests between competitors or vertically related firms. Under this system, minority shareholdings of around 20 per cent would be subject to control, while minority shareholdings between 5 and 20 per cent would have to be accompanied by specific interlocking directorships in order to be considered competitively significant. Furthermore, minority shareholdings below 5 per cent might be captured by the Member States' merger control regimes or by Articles 101 and 102 TFEU.

Minority interests consist of various types of non-controlling interests in competitors' performance such as minority shareholdings, interlocking directorships, or both. Loans and other financial products among competitors may also play a crucial role in creating mutual motives. Active and pre-existing minority shareholdings are the only forms of minority interests that fall under the scope of the EU Merger Regulation.

Regarding the treatment of minority interests across the EU Member States, Germany, the UK, Austria and Lithuania have already adopted national merger control rules that give them the competence to review non-controlling partial acquisitions. In the US the legal treatment of minority interests involves both minority shareholdings and interlocking directorships. In particular, section 7 of the Clayton Act applies to any percentage of an acquired equity stake, while section 8 of the same Act prohibits a member of a firm from serving as a member of a competitor's board of directors. Around the world passive minority interests are subject to national merger control systems in Ecuador, Brazil, Japan, Korea, Taiwan, Israel, South Africa, Indonesia, Russian Federation, Chinese Taipei, Ukraine, Canada, Republic of Armenia, Hong Kong, Namibia, Nigeria, Swaziland and Zambia.

Articles 101 and/or 102 TFEU may apply to minority interests in situations where there is evidence of an anticompetitive agreement or concerted practice among the investigated firms or the firms engaged in the acquisition of non-controlling stakes and/or one or more firms have a dominant position. During the public consultation by the DG Competition in 2013 some stakeholders argued in favour of the fact that Articles 101 and 102 TFEU could address competitive concerns raised by the acquisitions of minority shareholdings. Others believed that antitrust rules may not cover all the cases regarding minority shareholdings and therefore the current Merger Regulation system must be updated to make the Commission's assessment of competition more effective. The Commission has stated that an acquisition of a minority shareholding may not constitute an agreement which restricts by object or effect competition. As a consequence, it may not be possible to intervene in cases that involve potentially anticompetitive minority shareholdings.

In addition, Regulation 1/2003 equipped the Commission with an enhanced set of enforcement tools, notably the ability to take decisions making commitments offered by parties binding and enforceable under Article 9. In the light of the above the Commission has intervened in one particular sector (transport) to assess profit-sharing joint ventures that may restrict competition.

The economic literature has shown that passive minority shareholdings can harm competition either unilaterally or via coordinated effects. The higher the financial interest, the higher the harmful effects of minority interests on competition, while the existence of corporate rights potentially enables the acquiring firm significantly to influence the competitive policy of the target firm. If financial interests are accompanied by corporate rights, then such structural links may alter the competitive behaviour of both the acquiring and the target firm.

Regarding the unilateral effects of minority interests, the acquiring firm may have an incentive to compete less aggressively with its competitor and therefore raise its product price or restrict its output when the firms engaged in acquisitions of minority interests are direct competitors. Acquisitions of passive minority interests between firms that are active at another level of the supply chain can harm competition by imposing input or customer foreclosure. The acquiring firm's incentives to engage in foreclosure are higher with corporate rights than with solely financial interests.

The coordinated effects of minority interests stem from the fact that the acquiring firm internalizes part of the target's profit. Moreover, the level of transparency is enhanced in the presence of corporate rights. The presence of indirect minority shareholdings with their associated corporate rights enhances the level of transparency in the market under scrutiny. Moreover, non-horizontal minority shareholdings are also prominent in the economic literature. Vertical minority interests may lead more to enhanced competition concerns, while conglomerate minority interests raise anticompetitive issues only in the cases where the firms involved are active in related markets.

Minority interests deter entry either for potential entrants or for active firms which are interested in expanding their product range. The losses of the acquiring firm from blocked entry are limited to the amount of its minority shareholding. Therefore it has an incentive to deter entry by credibly committing it (eg either by expanding its capacity or lowering its price of the product) to the potential entrant.

The fact that the costs of the acquiring firm are limited to the amount of its minority shareholding may constitute an argument in favour of the minority interest. Other arguments in favour of minority interests are the transferring of technology and managerial skills and the creation of cost synergies (cost reduction through sales cooperation and learning), and in vertical acquisitions the elimination of double marginalization and incomplete information.

II. Cases Involving Minority Interests within EU and Worldwide

The Commission used its experience from the *Phillip Morris* and *Gillette* cases in order to deal with certain types of minority interests (active, pre-existing and veto rights) from the outset of the implementation of the Merger Regulation 4064/89 until the application of Regulation 139/2004. However, in recent years the Commission has not sought to apply Articles 101 and 102 TFEU in order to challenge passive minority shareholdings. Moreover, the Commission has applied Council Regulation 1/2003 in two cases regarding profit-sharing joint ventures in the air transport sector (COMP/39.595, COMP/39.596).

The data from the Zephyr Database reveals that from 2005 to 2011 within the EU 91 transactions of varying size and value potentially meriting competition scrutiny were identified by DG Competition, almost 5 per cent of all cases decided by the European Commission during the same period 2005–11 under the Merger Regulation following the normal procedure. The average value of the transactions was €139 million, the average turnover of the buyer was €7.2 billion and of the target €3.2 billion. Minority interests varied from 1 to 44.7 per cent. It is emphasized that 43 of these 91 transactions were likely to have an EU dimension and fall under Merger Regulation 139/2004.

Cases involving minority shareholdings in the UK represent for approximately 5 per cent of all notified mergers. In Germany notified transactions regarding minority shareholdings represented 10 per cent of all notified transactions from 1990 to 2010, while transactions notified under the 'competitively significant influence' criterion accounted for only 0.6 per cent of all notified cases but about 11 per cent of all mergers prohibited.

Between 1 July 2000 and 30 June 2001 11.46 per cent of all the concentrations notified to the Austrian competition authority concerned acquisitions of minority shareholdings (29 cases). Moreover, in 2011 15.04 per cent of total notified concentrations concerned acquisitions of minority shareholdings (34 cases). In the US from 1996 until June 2011 18 cases involving minority acquisitions were detected about which the Department of Justice raised concerns. In cases that were found to violate section 7 of the Clayton Act the minority shareholdings were at least 15 per cent. Following enforcement of section 8 of the Clayton Act the experience so far has shown that the types of commitments that have been enforced in cases that violated it were the resignation of the director in one of the two or more firms involved and the divestiture of part of the firm so that the firms concerned were no longer competitors.

The Greek coastal navigation case (Decision No 427/V/2009 of the Hellenic Competition Commission) constituted the first case regarding minority shareholdings and their role on competition in Greece. It was based on an ex officio investigation by the Directorate-General of Competition into the non-disclosure under the Articles 4-4f of law 703/77 (now law 3959/11), as applicable, of the concentration of Sea Star Capital plc and Anonymous Shipping Company of Crete. The decision, which was issued on 8 January 2009, imposed fines on Sea Star Capital plc, imposed a fine on the owner of Sea Star for his refusal to provide the information requested, and ordered the conduct of an ex officio investigation under the provisions of Article 4c of law 703/77, as applicable. The Administrative Appeal Court of Athens rejected the appeal of Sea Star Capital plc against decision no 427/V/2009 of the HCC.

III. The Commission's Argument Regarding Minority Interests

Recently, the Commission's White Paper and its accompanying Staff Working Documents set out the proposals for possible amendments to the current functioning of Council Regulation (EC) No 139/2004 on the control of concentrations between undertakings and provided the fundamental criteria for a balanced control system of non-controlling minority interests. Indisputably, Council Regulation (EC) No 139/2004 has truly succeeded, on the one hand, at levelling the playing field, and on the other hand, at providing a 'one-stop shop' for scrutiny of mergers with an EU dimension. Member States have also played significant roles in merger control enforcement in the EU.

According to the Commission, the SIEC test applied in the Merger Regulation is much more appropriate than the tests applied in Articles 101 and/or 102 TFEU. Moreover, the European Commission seems to support the need to extend the Regulation 139/2004 to the acquisition of non-controlling minority shareholdings. In the authors' view, such a change would basically constitute the transformation/modification of the European Commission to an entity that would co-decide with the interested enterprise about whether or not to make an investment. Moreover, the design of a system for controlling minority shareholdings is not that simple, since it poses a number of challenges regarding, on the one hand, the proper procedure and jurisdictional scope, and on the other hand, substantive assessment; in the authors' view, it seems unlikely that these challenges can be overcome.

IV. The Authors' Argument Regarding Minority Interests

According to the authors' approach, Articles 101 and/or 102 TFEU complete the Merger Regulation. Merger control constitutes a version of a forward-looking and predictive competition policy, since it is about ex ante control, regarding mainly the structure of the relative market. The application of Articles 101 and/or 102 TFEU constitutes suppressive competition practice applied by the authorized authorities, since it is always about ex post control.

Economically speaking, even though the actual impacts of anticompetitive effects of minority interests, both in static and dynamic terms, are well established by economic theory and despite the fact that the Zephyr Database was designed to underestimate rather than overestimate the real importance of transactions involving structural links, it is clear that over the last two decades there have *not* been significant numbers of cases with a potential EU dimension that would warrant competition scrutiny but currently fall outside the scope of the Merger Regulation because they do not involve a change of control.

The appearance or existence of an enforcement gap in EU competition law regarding potential anticompetitive effects from acquisitions of non-controlling minority shareholdings is not confirmed. EU competition law already has the tools necessary to deal effectively with anticompetitive practices or effects. For the reasons analysed above, it is considered that any potential change to the existing legal framework regarding minority shareholdings would create more issues rather of resolving problems regarding concentrations and minority shareholdings. However, it should never be forgotten that the quest for 'perfection' is the main enemy of achieving the 'good'.

INDEX